W9-BXD-830

A
DICTIONARY OF CHINESE MYTHOLOGY

A

DICTIONARY

OF CHINESE

MYTHOLOGY

E. T. C. Werner

introduction by Professor Hyman Kublin

THE JULIAN PRESS, INC. PUBLISHERS

NEW YORK

1961

Published by The Julian Press, Inc.
80 East 11th Street, New York 3

Library of Congress Catalog Card Number 61–17239
© Copyright 1961 by The Julian Press, Inc.
Manufactured in the United States of America

This edition is a re-issue of the classic work
originally published by Kelly and Walsh, Ltd.,
Shanghai, 1932

PRINTED IN THE U.S.A.   BY NOBLE OFFSET PRINTERS, INC.,   NEW YORK 3, N. Y.

INTRODUCTION

An anonymous wit once defined a classic as a book which is always praised but never read. Though this quip might otherwise be tenable, it is scarcely applicable to E. T. C. Werner's *A Dictionary of Chinese Mythology*. Copies of this celebrated classic of sinology, wherever found, are more than likely to boast the earmarks of constant use.

Werner's compendium of Chinese mythology, inimitably described by the author himself as a "Who's Who of the Chinese Otherworld," has been a choice collector's item for many years. It was originally published in 1932 with the illustrious imprint of Kelly and Walsh of Shanghai. But like many another notable work in the field of Chinese studies brought out by this famous publishing house Werner's volume has long been unavailable to numerous would-be readers and purchasers. A new printing has been urgently needed for some time.

It would not be shameless adulation to assert that few Westerners other than the late E. T. C. Werner could ever have compiled so unique a work as his handbook of the Chinese supernatural. The indisputable fact remains that his breed of scholar has vanished like the old China he loved so dearly. In the fashion of many another giant in Asian studies he was a career officer in the British foreign service. Yet long after he had retired from active duty he uninterruptedly pursued his researches on Chinese history and civilization. Thoroughly conversant with the Chinese language and deeply steeped in Chinese culture, he made the land of the Han his home on and off for almost seventy years.

Doubtless because he always had something to say in writing Edward Theodore Chalmers Werner sought to save time and space by abbreviating his overly long personal names to their primary initials. Born in Dunedin, New Zealand, on November 12, 1864, he was the second son of the fairly wealthy but incorrigibly footloose Joseph Werner. His self-sacrificing mother, who pined after a settled life in "Merrie England," nevertheless put up with her husband's compulsion for foreign travel. Before he had reached his teens Edward's own taste for life abroad had been indelibly fixed.

Werner, like most well-born young men of his times, was educated in the solid classical tradition for which England has been proverbial. After graduating from the respectable Tonbridge School, he successfully passed a highly competitive examination at London University for a student interpretership in His Majesty's foreign service. Then for five years, from 1884 to 1889, he was attached to the chancery of the British Legation in Peking, laying the foundation for a consummate knowledge of the Chinese language. Thereafter he served in various consular posts in China. His last official post before his retirement in 1914 was as Consul at Foochow.

For the greater part of his extremely long life Werner was either a bachelor or a widower. Marrying at about the age of forty-five, he was, not surprisingly, a devoted and doting husband until his wife's unfortunate death from meningitis a decade later. To compound the tragedy of his personal life his adopted daughter was murdered in Peking during the chaotic 'thirties. His restless intellect and his almost slavish enchantment with things Chinese apart, it may well be that he sought a retreat from his personal sorrows in a literally monastic routine of scholarship.

Once he had withdrawn from government service, Werner looked forward exuberantly to the prospect of passing his remaining years in full-time historical inquiry. Both his hopes and work were given tremendous impetus when at the end of World War I he was appointed a member of the Historiographical Bureau of the Chinese Government. The first foreigner to be so honored, he held and cherished the position for many years. Furthermore, in 1922 he was elected President of the Peking Historical Association. For the next quarter of a century and more his doyen of Western scholars in China doggedly carried on his studies of traditional Chinese civilization.

Despite the fact that several of his principal publications are now partly dated, Werner's bibliography is still impressive. He himself was exceedingly proud of his first book, *Descriptive Sociology: Chinese,* which provided the foundation for several of his later studies. The product of many years of research, its staggering erudition evoked sheer awe amongst reviewers. His incomparable *Myths and Legends of China,* first published in 1922 and subsequently reprinted five times, was an auspicious forerunner of his *magnum opus, A Dictionary of Chinese Mythology,* which appeared a decade later. Werner's last great work, *A History of Chinese Civilization* came off the press on the eve of World War II in the Pacific. In addition to these noteworthy studies, several minor volumes, and various contributions to scholarly journals, Werner also lent his extraordinary talents to invaluable translation and editorial functions.

So rugged an individualist as E. T. C. Werner was not easily to be pushed about by the war lords and warmongers who plagued China not so long ago. After the outbreak of the Sino-Japanese Incident in 1937 and, particularly, after the opening of World War II in 1941 he continued to carry on his studies in the British Embassy in Peking. Interned by the Japanese two years later, he hastened to resume his scholarly investigations upon his release in 1945. But the old China to which he was so devoted was then rapidly crumbling. Dismayed by the rise to power of the Chinese Communists under Mao Tse-tung, he saw no alternative but to return to England. There Werner died in early 1954 at the age of eighty-nine.

E. T. C. Werner was not a professionally trained academician but who among the great Orientalists of his day was? But painstakingly precise in his own work and acidly intolerant of shoddy scholarship, he draconically demanded the maintenance of the highest standards. Catholic in his interests and richly imaginative and reflective, he was an omnivorous but discriminating reader as well as an eagle-eyed observer of the dramas of passing life. And though scholars with similar talents may not be overwhelmed by his facility with foreign languages, they cannot but be impressed by the measured beauty of his English phrases. His Introduction to *A Dictionary of Chinese Mythology* is a work of literary art.

The reason for Werner's absorption in the myths of the Chinese is not hard to discover. "If you wish to understand a strange people," he approvingly noted, "first study their gods." Bored by annalistic history, by the lifeless and seemingly repetitive accounts of the rise and fall of dynasties, he was drawn rather to the larger and less overt themes in the evolution of Chinese civilization. But for all his enthusiasm for his subject of study, he had few illusions about the place and function of myths in the life of the people amidst whom he lived for so long.

The true age of Chinese myths, Werner knew, lay in the dim and remote past. The ancestors of the Chinese, he also recognized, had not been particularly creative or original as myth-makers, since the rational and constrictive streams of thought, which ultimately came to a head in this-worldly Confucianism, were fundamentally inimical to free-wheeling imagination. But while he perceived that

Chinese explorations of the supernatural had not blossomed into the delicious flights of fancy of other peoples of antiquity, he took it as axiomatic that the era of myths was a foundational stage in the unfolding of Chinese civilization. Insight into the nature of China necessitated, according to Werner, not only a respectful appreciation of those times when the other world was real but also awareness of the heritage which that vanished age had transmitted to subsequent generations.

In his ventures into the realm of Chinese mythology Werner was swayed neither by nostalgia for a bygone era nor by the romanticism of the litterateur. He was a capable historian, an excellent sociologist, and a forerunner of the cultural anthropologists of the post-World War I years. He refused to look superciliously upon the ingenuous faith of the old-time Chinese in the world beyond this world. He would not view their traditional myths merely as quaint and charming tales worthy only for the entertainment of children. Nor would he agree with many an intolerant missionary that the popular beliefs in spirits, demons, wraiths, and ghosts were nothing more than devilish impediments to true salvation. For such crudities he had little patience.

As a creative scholar with a mind of his own Werner detected in the theanthropomorphism of the Chinese and their ancestors a gallery of the symbols of the unconscious, a mirror of the mind of one-quarter of mankind. In the myriad of denizens of the supernal and infernal worlds, in the fairies, hobgoblins, and phantasmal images and entities, which for a hundred generations and more of Chinese had been no less real because they were not exactly man, the perceptive Werner discovered voluble spokesmen for a dead but not completely forgotten folk. And in the fears, fancies, and elemental ignorance of primitive days, enduring through the centuries in incarnate forms, he pointed to a language and means of communication as eloquent as the written and spoken word.

Werner was well aware that myths, legends, and their anthropomorphic expressions furnished more than a key to unlock the gates of the past. Though the grip of primal mysteries upon the mind of vulnerable men had weakened under the challenge of sophisticated theism and skeptical philosophy, he was alert to the stubbornness of traditions and customs which persisted long after their *raison d'être* had fallen by the wayside of history. The meaning and purport of mythological symbols, glyptically represented in the multitude of figurines adorning temples, households, shops, and portals in his own day were, he knew, not always apparent. And the colorful figures of speech in daily parlance, the tantalizing phraseology of literary allusion, as well as the postures and clichés of the popular theater required, as he knew, a sensitivity to life, thought, and emotions that no longer existed.

Werner knew that sooner or later the unearthly and spectral entities, which had for several millennia been a source of hope and awe, of love and dread, would be washed away in the flow of time. In *A Dictionary of Chinese Mythology* he sought to inter them with appropriate obituaries. To everyone who has yearned to explore the other China of the Chinese this classic is an indispensable guide-book. Its reprinting at this time by the Julian Press cannot be too highly commended.

Hyman Kublin
Professor of History

July 1961
Brooklyn College

PREFACE

This dictionary has been written with the object of furnishing, in a compact form, information concerning the entities, animate and inanimate, constituting the Chinese supernal and infernal hierarchies. It may be regarded as covering the ground between that dealt with in the dictionaries of Chinese Biography and that which would form the subject-matter of a dictionary of Chinese Superstitions, did a dictionary of that kind exist. It is a *Who's Who* of the Chinese Otherworld, compiled from the Chinese and foreign works named in the Bibliography, from personal observations in Chinese temples, houses and streets, and from conversations with Chinese scholars, priests and peasants during forty-eight years' residence in China. The people named in it live, or lived (for gods die also), in that Otherworld and are honoured or worshipped by those in this world. They are usually, though not always, human beings who have died, as we understand death, but in some cases they were deified while still living and continued to lead a theanthropical life on this earth. Chinese literature abounds in allusions to them, and they are not only represented in pictures but form the principal *motif* in embroidery patterns and in the decoration applied to furniture, implements, etc. It has been said: "If you wish to understand a strange people, first study their gods." A knowledge of these is essential to a proper understanding of the Chinese mind, of Chinese history, literature, art and drama, and, moreover, enhances the interest of living in this fascinating country and facilitates intercourse with the people. It adorns our environment in a rather drab, workaday world with many interesting and variegated pictures.

Mythology tells us the why and the wherefore of many things perplexing to the uninitiated. In walking in Chinese streets and roads one comes across, at certain places, stone tablets bearing the characters 石敢當 *shih kan tang,* "the stone dares to oppose." This is generally explained as meaning that the tablet is set up as an antidote to inauspicious influences, and few know that the characters represent the name of a man, and that a legend associated with this name led to the custom of erecting these stones all over China.

Similarly, the cord hanging round a Chinese child's neck— a familiar sight in every thoroughfare—is generally explained as merely an ornament, or a plaything, as "bringing it good luck," as "tying it to life." These are only partial explanations. The mythologist sees in the cord the halter placed round the neck of Mi-lo Fo 彌勒佛, the God of Silversmiths, after he had stolen the palace ingots.

Why Ts'an Nü 蠶女, the silk-weaving maiden, should be shown clothed in a horse's skin is not apparent without mythological interpretation. It is impossible without the clue furnished by mythology, to understand why Chun T'i 準提, the Goddess of Dawn, should be represented in pictures with three heads, one of which is that of a sow. Most foreign residents recognize the figure of T'ieh-kuai Li 鐵拐李, but comparatively few know how he got his lame leg, gold band and iron crutch. Nor, seeing Chang Kuo-lao 張果老 riding on his mule, do they know that the animal was capable of being folded up, like a map, and carried in the pocket when not in use.

Most people, strolling through a Chinese temple and leaving again, after a hasty glance at the many images, even if they recognize the image of Wei T'o 韋陀 make no inquiry as to why it is always placed in the temples dedicated to Ti-tsang Wang 地藏王. The latter is the King of the Earth's womb, the Lord of Hades; the former is a tutelary *deva* borrowed from India to guard Buddhist temples. The legend gives the reason.

Dragons are often depicted in human form, and without the clue furnished by mythology it is, as a rule, impossible to tell which of the two one is looking at. It is also not at first sight apparent why the image of T'u-ti Lao-yeh 土地老爺 should, since the Ming 明 dynasty, have been placed, not on an elevated throne suitable to a deity, but on the ground, however appropriate such a position might seem to be for the local god of the land.

On the other hand, the unpleasantness of a stuffy, incense-laden atmosphere, over hot, or over cold, and sometimes not too clean surroundings, may be to a large extent nullified by the interest and instruction derived from a visit when the names of the gods and the myths connected with them are known, just as a knowledge of the actors and the plot enhances our enjoyment of a play, and we can listen more intelligently to classical music if possessed of some facts about the composer and some clue to his intention.

Seeing the representation of Tsao Chün 竈君, the Kitchen God, few see also the ox associated with the legend and the inscription on a piece of silk found in its stomach, or know how it got there.

There is more interest in being able to tell what dragons are hidden in a cloud, and why, than merely in regarding it as a plain cloud.

As to the gods of China, it was easier for men to become gods there than it is now in Western countries. Examples are the case of the scholar who was deified as the result of a practical joke played on him by his school fellows (see Lei Hai-ch'ing 雷海青), or that of Chên Wu Ta-ti 眞武大帝, whose position of minister to Yü Ti 玉帝, the Pearly Emperor, was due to his having seen a woman grinding down a large iron rod to make a needle.

The universally known God of Happiness had his origin in an emperor's liking for dwarfs.

Dreams have frequently caused the apotheosis, either of the dreamer himself, or of some other person.

The element of accident, also, seems to have entered as largely into mythology as it has into history.*

The mistake of one Chinese character for another caused Liu Mêng Chiang-chün 劉猛將軍, the God of Grasshoppers, to be represented with a bell for a skirt.

And so on.

This facility, combined with the great length of the national life and the persistence of superstition resulting from isolation from the main world-current for so many centuries, caused the gods of China to be extremely varied and extremely numerous. In the country, meeting an old man, Du Bose inquired, "Have you any gods around here?" "Oh, yes," he said. "What gods?" I asked. "The Three Pure Ones." "Any others?" "The gods of the fields." "Any others?" "The Goddess of Mercy." "My old friend, I am afraid your gods are not a few." "Foreign teacher," was his literal reply, "verily, verily, our gods are ten thousand times ten thousand, and thousands of thousands." In production of gods the Oriental mind is extremely prolific—as reference to the body of this work will show, though naturally it has been impossible to include them all. Every one of the million villages has its ch'êng-huang 城隍, every hill, every tree on every hill, almost every part of every organism, its spiritual counterpart. Birds, beasts, insects, plants, inanimate objects, as well as the powers of nature are represented among the gods. There is in China hardly anything animate or inanimate which has not been at some time or other, worshipped or at any rate propitiated. In that larger, other world, densely populated by ex-residents of this one, we find "a polytheism limited only by a polydemonism." The Otherworld, so far from being a remote and almost inaccessible Heaven, is in fact, a duplicate of this world, plus ancestral hierarchies of gods and goddesses growing ever less distinct as we look further back into the misty depths of antiquity.

"This likeness explains why the hierarchy of beings in the Otherworld concerns itself not only with the affairs of the Otherworld, but with those of this world as well. There, as here, the popular cults must be distinguished from the

---

* The subject of History as determined by accident has been fully dealt with in *Autumn Leaves*, pp. 321-82.

ordered worship of the Olympian hierarchy. So faithful is the likeness that we find the gods . . . subjected to many of the rules and conditions existing on this earth. Not only do they . . . differ in rank,* but they hold *levées* and audiences and may be promoted for distinguished services, just as the Chinese officials are. They may rise from humble to the very highest positions. They rotate in office, as Chinese officials do in real life; though the temple remains the same, the spirit dwelling in the idol changes, the idol thus having a different name, birthday, and tenant. So the gods are not always the same to-day as yesterday." † And the distinction between god and man, god and spirit, is not always strictly observed, and it has not always been possible to observe the latter in this book. According to Chinese ideas even man himself, *qua* man, may be a god (see art. *Shên* 神).

And not only deserving people, but also some of the worst criminals have received this highest distinction, a fact re-illustrating the saying that "East is East and West is West"—in past and present mentality at least, whatever the distant future may have in store.

Abundant material was found in the legends and history of early China. To the mind of the Chinese their ancient world was crowded with heroes, fairies, and devils, who played their part in the mixed-up drama, and left a name and fame which have resounded through the ages.

Chinese gods, even those whose names—like that of Kuan Ti 關帝, the God of War—might fail to indicate their true character, are generally protective and helpful, and are appealed to by the people in their distress. This is but natural and logical for, being the creation of their own minds, they would not have imagined them as wholly malevolent. This statement is not discredited by the fact that evil and malignant demons, ghouls, goblins, vampires, and such like, are also the creation of their own minds, for they are sensible enough to recognize that this is a world of good and evil, and these unwelcome ideas are the inevitable outcome of their unpleasant experiences, mistaken though their interpretation of those experiences may be.

To enable them to deal with these disagreeable conditions in their environment, as well as to fulfil more congenial missions, these deified beings, varying greatly both in size and aspect, are endowed with certain powers not usually given to ordinary mortals. They become supernal creatures able to walk the unwalkable way, to name the unnameable name, to annihilate time and space, and transform themselves into any form human or sub-human. The marvellous implements and weapons

---

* That of prince was first bestowed on gods in the T'ang 唐 dynasty.

† *Myths and Legends of China,* p. 99. See also Du Bose, *Dragon, Image, and Demon,* pp. 282, 286, 361, 409, 410.

which they can make, or have bestowed upon them, are the stock "properties" of Chinese tales and will be referred to in detail in the following pages.

Incidentally Chinese mythology furnishes abundant data invaluable in the study of the primitive mind as found in many other parts of the world. For example (to give one only), numerous instances are quoted in the following pages showing clearly that conception was not considered as in any way related to the sexual act. These myth-makers (or builders) did not understand the nexus between sex-activity and procreation.

Chinese thoughts have not been, and are not now, as our thoughts. Consequently, the preparation presently to be named is indispensable to the right interpretation of ideas resulting from an environment and experiences differing from our own. Minds which conceive of persons drowned in a river as still alive, of corpses as capable of resuscitation, of human souls passing into inanimate objects, plants, animals, or other human beings, of stones becoming human beings and talking, are not likely to draw from the same data the conclusions we should draw from them. People who can make a god even out of a grammatical particle, who do not fear the severance of a limb, since they can immediately grow a new one, would almost seem to be subject to different psychological laws.

This divergence of mentality is further shown in their attitude toward their gods. We find both extreme reverence and its opposite. A person who approaches his god, not seated in a comfortable pew among others striving to outdo him or her in display of fashionable attire, but alone, from afar off, in rags and tatters, prostrating himself for days, weeks or even months, in all weathers, on a rough road, cannot rightly be considered as possessed of the same mental constitution as the more dignified and possibly less sincere worshipper in other lands.

Yet in spite of this over-reverent attitude of the Chinese worshipper, he is paradoxical enough to adopt toward his gods an attitude not only of an equal, but of a superior. Though regarded as more powerful than rulers of flesh and blood Chinese gods are not necessarily "above" mortals, though they may be supposed to reside in the upper air, in this or that more or less distant heaven, or to float at a greater or lesser altitude—sometimes only a few feet above the heads of mankind, according to the time of day or night. They are in so far anthromorphic that they exhibit such human traits as fear and anger; they may sin, marry, kidnap pretty women, be bambood, go to the theatre, be sent to prison, or even be murdered. They may also be made to rise from the dead. This oscillation process may continue for an indefinite period; or they may become really and finally immortal. This last word must, however, be read with the qualification that both the lower and the higher types of spiritual being into which man separates at "death" die eventually, though the former becomes extinct much sooner than the latter.*

A change, desirable or not, according to the standard by which it is tested, is now taking place. China has begun to cast down the wood-and-plaster saints she has worshipped for nineteen centuries before and nineteen centuries after Christ. As civilization advances, people begin to throw away their gods, or at least the superfluous ones, and we thus find Western nations becoming quasi-monotheistic (Trinitarians), or monotheistic (Theists, Unitarians, etc.), or discarding all supernatural powers (Atheists), or admitting that while there must be some Ultimate Cause behind phenomena, the human mind is too limited to comprehend It or Its nature (Agnostics). With this deanthropomorphizing process, mythology naturally declines, for want of its objective. China is now either Buddhistic, Agnostic, or Atheistic, other faiths or ideas having but little vogue or influence, and from none of these can it now be expected that any fresh myths will emerge. Superstitions will still be born, but myth-making in China is probably dead for all time.

It may assist the student of Chinese mythology to note briefly a few points of importance regarding mythology in general.† Myth has its roots in ignorance,‡ for it is an incorrect explanation of observed phenomena, or a mere unsubstantiated product of the creator's imagination. It is the outcome of a kind of thought that is almost extinct in civilized races. The story being later than "the thing done" in any cult, myth has often originated in ritual practice misunderstood. Ridicule is as much out of place as it would be in regard to primitive religion. We may laugh at such things as pills of immortality, as scientists of future generations may laugh at some of our ideas, but they at least indicate a healthy desire, on the part of a people not yet scientific, to find a means of attaining to the one thing mankind most hankers after. The object of mythology is not to ascertain why men believe in gods, but why they tell these strange stories about them. The first prerequisite to a satisfactory explanation is a knowledge of biology and psychology sufficient to enable us to understand the type of mind without which the myths would either remain unborn or, if born, have a different character from what we actually find.

---

* The Chinese Idea of the Second Self, p. 20.

† Cf. Myths and Legends of China, Chapter II.

‡ Pope, whose own God was not unassociated with clouds and wind (see especially, Daniel, vii. 13; Luke, xxi. 27; Revelations, i. 7; Proberbs, xxx. 4), in his lines—

> "Lo, the poor Indian! whose untutored mind
> Sees God in clouds, or hears him in the wind,"

was right, in so far,—whether he meant, as the schoolboy thought, one particular Indian, or whether he meant all (myth-making) Indians,—in ascribing the origin of his or their myths to ignorance. He might have said the same of "Lo, the poor Chinaman,"—but a mere highbrow gibe helps nobody. Note also, in the second line the mythological significance of the capital G and the second small h.

The idea so created is itself powerful enough. In fact, an idea may have far-reaching results—for good or for evil. Examples of the former are the vast benefits to humanity arising from scientific inventions. Of the latter, as good an example as any is that of the Crusades, lasting nearly three centuries and carried on at an incalculable expense in money and human lives in a distant land in order to recover possession of an empty grave. The Chinese mother shields her child's eyes that it may not look on the passing foreigner, just as people of other nations still take precautions against the "evil eye."* That her action is not irrational is proved by the case, which occurred in Peking in 1927, of a Chinese child dying of fright at the sight of a foreign toy horse. Similar proof of tragic results is seen in the death, taking place about the same time, of a Chinese man who, on entering a temple stepped on the concealed board attached to wires, causing the wood-and-plaster images to wave spears and swords, open and shut their mouths, and roll their eyes.

It is easy to imagine that the varying shapes of clouds, now resembling a lion, now a dragon, now a man fighting a tiger, would be enough in themselves to originate a myth in the primitive mind, but, in fact, this is not so. Something more is required to originate a genuine myth; otherwise, myths would be produced without ceasing, every day and everywhere. To see these things may add poetry to life, but is not necessarily to create myth.

The ways in which gods originate are many and various, but those who seek for explanations find that all paths converge to the ultimate question of the origin of the idea of god. This fascinating topic does not here concern us, for it falls within the sphere of religion and outside that of mythology. Leaving to religion the problem of explaining the root, mythology seeks to explain the branches and leaves.

We find that some amount of constructive imagination is required; but if this, the highest form of intellectual activity, passes beyond a certain point, it becomes self-critical and destroys its own creations. Myth, as noted above, is the unscientific man's explanation. The philosopher or scientist studies or criticizes myth, he does not make it.

There must also be unwavering belief in the created myth and, further, there must be not only stimulus, but persistent soul expression continuing through periods of time sufficient for the myth to be transmitted to posterity, and elaborated, till it assumes a form sufficiently attractive to appeal to the human mind.

Close study of the facts as found in China points to the conclusion that a historical basis may in practically every case be discovered, if the investigation is carried far enough. Euhemerism

---

* "The ' evil eye ' is not a mere medieval fairy story. A woman's eye [through a form of ultra-violet rays given off by human bodies generally] has killed yeast cells simply by looking at them at Cornell University."—Press Telegram from Syracuse, New York, August 31, 1932.

has its dangers; but, on the other hand it would be as great an error to seek the origin of these mythological tales in some fundamental animistic intuition as to suppose that we can trace the origin of religion to the same source.

Cui bono? Myths being but phantasies of the imagination—"vain repetitions of the heathen" (Matthew, vi. 7)—the student will want to know why they should have been seriously studied and even made the subject of fierce polemics. True it is that we deal here with ideas, and that those ideas relate to another world than our own. But of what use are these ideas to those daily treading the monotonous round of life, to the weary and heavy-laden, who will never taste of the sweets of work transformed into pleasure?

The answer is that, in common with literature in general, poetry, music, and the other aesthetic products, these ideas are for the exaltation of life. They are rungs in the great ladder, without which it were difficult to climb, or even to hold on. Myth binds the ages together, and so deeply have the myths and stories of the dawn of culture impressed themselves on our civilization that they have become part of our daily speech, and may even contribute to life's sustenance. They fulfil a social function in the same way as the bible of a poverty-stricken, aged widow in a city slum, whose faith sustains and comforts her, may make tolerable a dull, monotonous, unrewarded existence. It would be as wrong ethically to deprive her of that comfort and support as it would be to ridicule the aesthetic products of which myth is one. The care-worn Chinese beggar in his rags and dirt, to whom life offers no prospect of happiness, finds his existence less intolerable, believing that, through the eternal law of rhythm, and the alternating *yin* 陰 and *yang* 陽, he will be a *t'u-ti* 土地 in the next world. His belief may not hold out to him the prospect of avoiding death and, like Elijah of Tishbe, ascending to heaven in a chariot of fire, or like Huang Ti 黃帝 of old, on one drawn by six dragons; but at least it encourages him to cling to life with both hands and make the most of it while he has it. The alternative would be despair and, perhaps, suicide.

Evolution will eradicate error in its own slow, but sure way, and leave behind for our edification, instruction and amusement these children of the relatively primitive mind. For, as already repeated, it is the unscientific mind—not necessarily (in spite of Jung and Freud) the sub-conscious or dream mind—that gives rise to myth, and not, as was formerly supposed, even by scientific students, that of the scientist or philosopher. To that mind we must therefore express our gratitude for the colour and interest it has added to life.

Myth-birth takes place also among nations distinguished as civilized, but in ever-diminishing degree as science advances. Thus the functions of myth are gradually taken over (with those who still need them) by the hopes and consolations of religion.

When people cease telling stories about their gods they still continue to fall down and worship them, and, as monotheism gains ground, to do so with increasing sincerity and truth.

With so many gods, so easily created, it would naturally be concluded that China was wealthy in myth. But this we do not find. That is to say, that China has not constructed myths which may be called world-great and immortal. And this was chiefly because sober, materialistic Confucianists and other rationalistic philosophers gradually but surely gained the victory over the more fanciful and poetical myth-creators.

The phases through which myth has passed in China may be briefly summarized. Though the beginnings of Chinese myth are hidden from us, there is good reason to believe that Chinese and Indian myth had a common origin, which was somewhere outside of China. When myth is first discernible, we find "an age of magic" followed by "an heroic age." "Primitive mythology" is said to have been invented or imitated from foreign sources after 820 B.C. Before that date myths are very rare. In the following century myths of an astrological character began to attract attention. In the age of Lao Tzŭ 老 子 (born 604 B.C.) fresh legends appear, and then there is a gap during the long classical period until the time of the Warring States (*Chan Kuo* 戰 國, 500-100 B.C.) when new stimuli and great emotion prompted to mythological creation. After this myth seems to have existed sporadically and (being also differently affected by the various views of this and the other world as found in the Taoist, Buddhist, and Confuciist systems) precariously, until the Sung 宋 philosophers gave it its death-blow, any subsequent signs of life being but the quiverings or throes of the final agony.

It is not true, as someone has said, that "all stories come from India," but a definite line of demarcation between Indian and Chinese mythology is difficult to draw. The two inosculate, and this inosculation has necessitated the inclusion of a small percentage of Hindu gods and Sanskrit, Pali, etc., names and terms, these being referred to when necessary for the understanding of the event described. Thus, with few exceptions there are included here only the names and descriptions of those Indian gods which have become established as gods in China and have their place in the Chinese supernal hierarchy, though they may not be Chinese gods.

In those cases where the myths are too long to be reproduced in detail, abbreviated versions have been given and reference made to the works where they may be found *in extenso*.

The Chinese characters for the names of persons and places have been inserted to enable those readers who do not use the Wade romanization system to identify the persons and places named. Those readers will therefore ignore the romanized forms and merely read their own sounds direct from the Chinese characters. To give the romanization in more than one dialect—

not to say in all the dialects—would of course be impracticable.

Some help on this point may be obtained from the memorandum on the Pronunciation of Chinese Words inserted after the Preface, but owing to the peculiar nature of the Chinese language, directions of this kind can never be a complete guide.

An Index to the myths has also been included, since in many cases they are not readily traceable by the title-words of the sections in which they occur.

A table of the Chinese dynasties has been added after the Index to Myths to facilitate reference to the dates of these, the dates (reign-periods) of the individual sovereigns, when referred to, being given in the text.

A list of the works consulted and quoted in the preparation of this volume is given in the appended Bibliography. Of these, those which will be found of most value for the student are:— *Li-tai shên-hsien t'ung-chien* 歷代神仙通鑑; *Fêng-shên yen-i* 封神演義; *Fêng-shên pang* 封神榜; *Shên-hsien lieh-chuan* 神仙列傳; *Sou-shên chi* 搜神記, Doré, *Recherches sur les Superstitions en Chine;* Kennelly, *Researches into Chinese Superstitions;* Plopper, *Chinese Religion seen through the Proverb;* and the standard works on Indian and Chinese Buddhism. The present writer's *Myths and Legends of China,* first issued in 1922, is both concise and comprehensive, and includes an attempt to treat the subject scientifically.

EDWARD THEODORE CHALMERS WERNER.

PEKING,
1932.

THE PRONUNCIATION OF CHINESE WORDS

During the course of Chinese history the restriction of intercourse due to mountain-chains or other natural obstacles between various tribes or divisions of the Chinese people led to the birth of a number of families of languages, which again became the parents of numerous local dialects. These dialects have in most cases restricted ranges, so that that of one district may be partially or wholly unintelligible to the natives of another situated at a distance of only a hundred miles or less.

The Court or Government language is that spoken in Peking* and the [erstwhile] metropolitan district, and is the language of official communication throughout the country. Though neither the oldest nor the purest Chinese dialect, it seems destined more than any other to come into universal use in China. The natives of each province or district will of course continue to speak to each other in their own particular dialect, and foreign missionaries or merchants, for example, whose special duties or transactions are connected with special districts will naturally learn and use the dialects of those districts; but as a means of intercommunication generally between natives of different provinces, or between natives and foreigners, the Court language seems likely to continue in use and to spread more and more over the whole country. It is to this that the following remarks apply.

The essentials of correct pronunciation of Chinese are accuracy of sound, tone, and rhythm.

SOUND

Vowels and Diphthongs

a as in *father*.
ai as in Italian *amâi*.
ao. Italian *ao* in *Aosta*; sometimes *á-oo*, the *au* in *cauto*.
e in *eh, en*, as in *yet, lens*.

---

* These statements remain unaffected by the recent change of this name to Peip'ing and the transfer of the seat of the central government to Nanking.

ei. Nearly *ey* in *grey*, but more as in Italian *lei, contei.*

ê. The vowel-sound in *lurk.*

êi. The foregoing *ê* followed enclitically by *y*. Money without the *n=mêi.*

êrh. The *urr* in *purr.*

i. As a single or final syllable the vowel-sound in *ease, tree*; in *ih, in, ing*, as in *chick, thing.*

ia generally as in the Italian *Maria.*

iai. The *iai* in the Italian *vecchiaia.*

iao as in *ia* and *ao*, with the terminal peculiarity of the latter.

ie as in the Italian *siesta.*

io. The French *io* in *pioche.*

iu as a final, longer than the English *ew*. In *liu, niu* almost *leyew, neyew.* In *chiung, hsiung, iung*, is *eeyong* (*ō* in *roll*).

o. Between vowel-sound in *awe* and that in *roll.*

ou. Really *êo*; *ou* in *round.*

ü. The vowel-sound in the French *tu, eût.*

üa. Only in *üan*, which in some tones is *üen.* The *ü* as above; the *an* as in *antic.*

üe. The vowel-sounds in the French *tu es.*

üo. A disputed sound, used, if at all, interchangeably with *io* in certain syllables.

u. The *oo* in *too*; in *un* and *ung* as in the Italian *punto.*

ua. Nearly *ooa*, in many instances contracting to *wa.*

uai as in the Italian *guai.*

uei. The vowel-sounds in the French *jouer.*

uê. Only in final *uên=ú-ŭn*; frequently *wên* or *wun.*

ui. The vowel-sounds in *screwy*; in some tones *uei.*

uo. The Italian *uo* in *fuori*; often *wo*, and at times nearly *ŏō.*

ŭ. Between the *i* in *bit* and the *u* in *shut.*

CONSONANTS

ch as in *chair*; but before *ih* softened to *dj.*

ch'. A strong breathing *Much-harm* without the italicized letters=*ch'a.*

f as in *farm.*

h as *ch* in Scotch *loch.*

hs. A slight aspirate preceding and modifying the sibilant, which is, however, the stronger of the two consonants; e.g. *hsing=hissing* without the first *i.*

j. Nearly the French *j* in *jaune*; the English *s* in *fusion.*

k. *c* in *car*, *k* in *king*; but when following other sounds often softened to *g* in *go, gate.*

k'. The aspirate as in *ch'.* *Kick-hard* without the italicized letters=*k'a*; and *kick-her=k'ê.*

l as in English.

m as in English.

n as in English.

ng. The italicized letters in the French mo*n* g*a*lant=*nga*; mo*n* g*ai*llard=*ngai*; so*n* g*o*sier=*ngo*.

p as in English.

p'. The Irish pronunciation of *p*arty, *p*arliament. *Sl*aph*ard* without the italicized letters=*p'a*.

s as in English.

sh as in English.

ss. Only in *ssŭ.* The object of employing *ss* is to fix attention on the peculiar vowel-sound *ŭ* (see above).

t as in English.

t'. The Irish *t* in *t*orment. *Hit*-h*ard* without the italicized letters=*t'a.*

ts as in je*ts*am; after another word softened to *ds* in gla*ds*ome.

ts'. The aspirate intervening, as *ch'*, etc. *Bets*-h*ard* without the italicized letters=*ts'a.*

tz. Employed to mark the peculiarity of the final *ŭ*; hardly of greater power than *ts.*

tz' like *ts'.* This, *tz*, and *ss* used only before *ŭ.*

w as in English; but very faint, or even non-existent, before *ü.*

y as in English; but very faint before *i* or *ü.*

TONE

The correct pronunciation of the sound (*yin*) is not sufficient to make a Chinese spoken word intelligible. Unless the tone (*shêng*), or musical note, is simultaneously correctly given, either the wrong meaning or no meaning at all will be conveyed. The tone is the key in which the voice is pitched. Accent is a 'song added to,' and tone is emphasized accent. The number of these tones differs in the different dialects. In Pekingese there are now four. They are best indicated in transliteration by numbers added to the sound, thus:

pa (1) pa (2) pa (3) pa (4)

To say, for example, pa (3) instead of pa (1) would be as great a mistake as to say 'grasp' instead of 'trumpet'. Correctness of tone cannot be learnt except by oral instruction.

RHYTHM

What tone is to the individual sound rhythm is to the sentence. This also, together with proper appreciation of the mutual modifications of tone and ryhthm, can be correctly acquired only by oral instruction.

ROMANIZATION

The Wade system of romanization of Chinese words has been adopted throughout this dictionary, as being the best yet devised and the one most widely used by foreigners. The pronunciation of the words according to this system is detailed above. Other suggested systems usually omit these indispensable guides.

Contents

DICTIONARY OF CHINESE MYTHOLOGY

A

A HSIANG 阿香.—Hsiang the First (or Elder). Chariot-eeress to the Ministry of THUNDER (see Lei Pu 雷 部) (Yu hsüeh Ku shih ch'iung lin 幼 學 故 事 瓊 林, chüan i, p. 2). Some works specialize her as charioteeress to Tien Mu 電 母, the Mother of Lightning.

ABHINNA.—The six kinds of supernatural wisdom.—See *Dhyana*.

ADI-BUDDHA.—The first Buddha, the primary Buddha, Buddha from the beginning, Buddha unoriginated, existing by himself. The primordial Buddha-god. Has never been seen. Is in Nirvana. Nevertheless is "pure light," he issues from the "void"; and his names are innumerable. Prayers are not addressed to him, yet he is worshipped in his temple. He dwells in the upper region of the world of forms, as if it had been forgotten that in the Buddhist cosmology there are numerous formless heavens. He has, besides, like every divinity, a mystic circle, for conjuratory or mystical purposes.

He was invented to serve as a counterpart to the One Universal Spirit Brahma (*q.v.*), the one eternally existing spiritual essence, from which all existing things are mere emanations. The idealiza-tion of Buddha's personality led to his deification as an omniscient and everlasting god. Traces of this development are to be found even in Southern Buddhism. He soon (*v. infra*) came to be regarded as the omnipotent primordial god, the Universal Essence of a pantheistic nature.

The conception of an Adi-Buddha (at first thought to be of comparatively late origin) existed (as will be seen presently) in very early times. The evolution of monotheism from polytheism is illustrated when the Adi-Buddha is apotheosized and placed, as a

I

monotheistic deity, over the five Dhyani Buddhas (*v. infra*), the mystic counterparts of the earthly Buddhas or of whom the latter are reflections or emanations.

The ancient hymns of the Aryan settlers on the banks of the Indus and in the land of the Five Rivers cover a long period, the length and the era of which can only be conjectured, but fifteen hundred years before Christ is about the mean of the various ages assigned to them. Toward the end of the *Rig-veda Sanhita,* in the hymns of the latest date, the idea of one Supreme Being assumed a more definite shape, and the Hindu mind was perceiving, even if it had not distinctly realized, the great conception. At first a force, it later becomes personified.

To each of the five groups of worlds of the Great Vehicle (Mahayana, or Northern Buddhism) was assigned a Special Buddha, called Dhyani Buddha, or Buddha of abstract contemplation.

As the Buddha himself had reached *parinirvana* (final termination and escape from the bonds of trouble and vexation), had completely passed away, "the pious Buddhist naturally turned with peculiar reverence and longing to those Bodhisattvas (Buddhas Elect, or future Buddhas) supposed to be now living as angels in heaven, who are the present result of the *karma* which will produce the Buddhas of the future.

These hypothetical beings were probably the invention of Buddhists, whose minds were steeped in Brahman philosophy and mythology; and who were so imperfectly converted to Gautama's system of salvation by self-control and moral culture, that their hearts craved after Buddhist gods to fill the place of the dead gods of the Hindu pantheon, or to make them live again in their descendants.

"The idea seems to be that every earthly mortal Buddha has his pure and glorious counterpart in the mystic world, free from the debasing conditions of this material life; or rather that the Buddha under material conditions is only an appearance, the reflection, or emanation, or type of a Dhyani Buddha living in the Ethereal mansions of those worlds of idea and mystic trance. The number of Dhyani Buddhas is accordingly, in theory, infinite, like the number of the Buddhas, but only the five are practically acknowledged."

The first of the series of Dhyani Buddhas seems to have been Amitabha, or "the Boundless Light." This metaphysical creation first appears in works about the beginning of our era, and seems to embody a sun-myth and to show Persian influence. For he was given a paradise in the west, to which all the suns hasten, and his myth seems to have arisen among the northern Buddhists when under the patronage of Indo-Scythian converts belonging to a race of sun-worshippers. Indeed, he is believed by Eitel and others to be a form of the Persian sun-god; and he was made the spiritual father of the historical Buddha.

Afterwards he was quintupled, apparently to adapt him to the theory of the five earthly Buddhas, the coming one and the four of the past, as well as to the other mystical groups of five—the five senses, the five *skandhas* (the five attributes of every human being: form, perception, consciousness, action, and knowledge), the five virtues, the five cardinal points. Each of these five celestial Buddhas was made to preside over a particular direction. Images of this series of Buddhas are found amongst the lithic remains of India about the seventh century A.D., if not earlier.

By the twofold power of knowledge and contemplation, to which they owe their existence, they give birth to "Bodhisattvas of contemplation." These are the actual creators of the universe, but the worlds which they produce are perishable, and three of these creations have already ceased to exist. That of which we form a part is the fourth, *i.e.* it is the work of Avalokitesvara, the fourth Bodhisattva, the "Providence" of the present; and has as its special Buddha, "protector" and "conqueror" Amitabha, who is enthroned in the midst of his elect. For its instructor it has had Sakyamuni, the fourth human Buddha. There are five human Buddhas (seven in Nepal), who correspond to the five Buddhas of contemplation. They are not, however, incarnations of them, but rather "reflexes" or "magical projections."

These Dhyani Buddhas, like their types or antitypes the Buddhas, must have their Bodhisattvas also, and the following three sets of five are thus co-ordinated:—

Dhyani Buddhas.	Their Bodhisattvas.	Emanations. Manushi (human) Buddhas.
1. Vairochana.	Samanta-bhadra.	Kraku-chanda.
2. Akshobya.	Vajrapani.	Kanaka-muni.
3. Ratna-sambhava.	Ratnapani.	Kasyapa.
4. Amitabha.	Padmapani-Avalokitesvara.	Gautama.
5. Amogasiddha.	Vis-vapani.	Maitreya.

To these is sometimes added a sixth, Vajrasattva, who creates (or causes to be created) immaterial substances, while the five others create corporeal forms.

By this theory, each of the five Buddhas has become three, and the fourth of these five sets of three, occupying the highest and most important rank, is the second Buddhist Trinity, the belief in which must have arisen after the seventh century of our era.

In the more developed theory, tending toward monotheism, a First Great Cause, under the title of the primordial or Adi-Buddha, is placed above these five celestial Buddhas as their spiritual father and creator. To this rank was promoted the first and central one of the metaphysical Buddhas, namely Vairocana (*q.v.*) or Vairochana, "The Omni-present," or his reflex Samanta-bhadra (*q.v.*), "The All Good."

"Northern Buddhism did not stop here. There is one step still further removed from Gautama's doctrines—the step from polytheism to monotheism, and this step it also afterwards took. But all this was not enough to satisfy the Tibetan and Nepalese

3

hankering after goods many, and lords many. In the tenth century A.D., a new being—this time infinite, self-existent, and omniscient—was invented, and called Adi-Buddha, the Primordial Buddha. He was held to have evolved out of himself the five Dhyani Buddhas by the exercise of the five meditations; while each of these evolved out of himself by wisdom and contemplation the corresponding Bodhisattvas, and each of them again evolved out of his immaterial essence a cosmos, a material world. Our present world is supposed to be the creation of the fourth of these, that is of Avalokitesvara" (Davids, *Buddhism,* pp. 203-4, 206-7).

The Adi-Buddha system—a new third (or fourth) kind of Buddhism—consists, properly speaking, in superimposing on the five or six Buddhas (Vajrasattva included) a Being who, however invisible and inactive he may be in principle, is nevertheless a god. His body, which is a "body of law," is called *samanta-bhadra,* "universally propitious," or "all-good," a title borrowed from the Bodhisattva of that name. There are attributed to him the thirty-two marks, etc., of the Buddhas and of Great Men, which are the characteristics of the beatific body. (On the other hand, Adi-Buddha resembles Brahma. The *Tantras* issue from his five mouths, as the four *Vedas* from the four mouths of Brahma, etc.). More fortunate than Brahma, he is worshipped. The ordinary Buddhas, etc., are not his "reflections" in an inferior world; he is different from them, for they proceed from him at a fixed moment of his existence. In place, therefore, of the underlying and scarcely veiled identity of the tantric or purely ontological system of the five Buddhas, there is substituted emanation or creation by means of *dhyana.*

Sometimes the Adi-Buddha is identified with Vajrasattva or Samanta-bhadra, although these beings are otherwise classified as Bodhisattva. This appears analogous to the procedure common in Hinduism by which a devotee declares that his special deity is all the gods and the supreme spirit.

An Adi-Buddha is called Vajrasatta (whose essence is thunderbolt) in Sanskrit. He is the Buddha of supreme intelligence. He is worshipped in China as Kan-tzŭ-lo-sa-to 幹資羅薩埵 (in Japanese, Kongosatta).

"He has both a 'mild' and 'ferocious' form. The mild form has usually two arms and is seated on a lotus throne which is often supported by an elephant. The ferocious form has six arms, a third eye, and a fierce expression. Above the forehead is a skull. His colour is red. In this form he is not supported by an elephant." (Getty).

The Adi-Buddha or Svayambhu produces Avalokita by meditation, and Avalokita produces the material world and the gods of Hinduism from his body, Siva from his forehead, Marayana from his heart and so on.

With respect to the modes of manifestations of the universal essence: "As there is no limit to the immensity of reason and measurement to the universe, so all the Buddhas are possessed of infinite wisdom and infinite mercy. There is no place throughout the universe where the essential body of Vairocana (or other supreme Buddha, varying with the different sects) is not present. Far and wide through the fields of space he is present, and perpetually manifested." (Beal, *Catena of Buddhist Scriptures from the Chinese,* p. 123).

"The modes in which this universal essence manifests itself are the three bodies (Tri-kaya), namely—(1) *Dharma-kaya* or Law-body, Essential Bodhi, formless and self-existent, the Dhyani Buddha, usually called Vairocana Buddha or the ' Perfect Justification,' or Adi-Buddha. (2) *Sambhoga-kaya* or Compensation-body, Reflected Bodhi, the Dhyani Bodhisats, usually named Lochana or ' glorious,' and (3) *Nirmana-kaya* or Transformed-body, Practical Bodhi, the human Buddhas, as Sakya Muni." (Waddell, p. 127).

"Now these three bodies of the Buddhas, human and super-human, are all included in one substantial essence. The three are the same as one—not one, yet not different. When regarded as one the three persons are spoken of as Tathagata. But there is no real difference, these manifestations are only different views of the same unchanging substance."—Waddell, *The Buddhism of Tibet,* p. 127; Eitel, *Handbook of Chinese Buddhism,* pp. 179, 180; Beal, *Catena of Buddhist Scriptures,* p. 123; Vassilief, *Le Buddhisme,* p. 127; Csoma Korösi, *Tibetan Grammar;* Köppen, *Die Religion des Buddha;* for the several Adi-Buddha systems, L. de la Vallée Poussin in Hastings, *Encyclopaedia of Religion and Ethics,* art. Adi-Buddha; Kern, *Lotus of the True Law;* Bernouf, *Introduction à l'Histoire du Bouddhisme Indien;* Oldenberg, *Buddha;* Rhys Davids, *Buddhism;* Bastian, *Der Buddha in seiner psychologie;* Benoy Kumar Sarker, *Chinese Religion Through Hindu Eyes;* Kern, *Manual of Buddhism;* Schlaginweit, *Buddhism in Tibet;* Grünwedel, *Buddhistische Kunst in Indien;* Monier Williams, *Buddhism;* Foucher, *L'Art bouddhique.*

AGENTS, THE FIVE NATURAL.—See *Wu Hsing* 五行.

AGNI. (Nom. Agnis—Ignis). Fire. One of the most ancient and sacred objects of Hindu worship. He appears in three places —in heaven in the sun, in mid-air as lightning, on earth as ordinary fire. Agni is one of the chief deities of the *Vedas* and great numbers of the hymns are addressed to him, more indeed than to any other god. He is one of the three great deities—Agni, Vayu (or Indra), and Surya—who respectively preside over earth, air, and sky, and are all equal in dignity. He is considered as the mediator between men and gods, as protector of men and their homes, and as witness to their actions; hence his invocation on all solemn occasions, at important ceremonies, etc. Fire has ceased to be an object of worship, but is held in honour for the part it performs in sacrifices. Agni is represented as having seven tongues, each of which has a distinct name, for licking up the butter used in sacrificing. He is guardian of the south-east quarter, being one of the eight *lokapalas* (supporters or guardians of the world), and his region is called Pura-jyotis.—See *Huo Pu* 火部 and *Garuda*.

AGRICULTURE, THE GODS OF.—See *Hsien Nung* 先農; *Hsien Sê* 先嗇; *Lai Cho* 來啜; *Liu Mêng Chiang-chün* 劉猛將軍; *Mang Shên* 芒神; *Miao Hu* 猫虎; *Pai Chung* 百種; *Shên Nung* 神農; *Shui Fang* 水防; *Shui Yung* 水庸; and *Ssŭ Cho* 司啜.

AJITA.—"Unconquered." A title given to Vishnu, Siva, and many others.—See *Lo-han* 羅漢.

A-LA-HAN 阿羅漢.—See *Lo-han* 羅漢.

ALMSBOWL, THE BUDDHIST.—See *Patra*.

AMIDA, AMITA.—See *Amitabha*.

AMIDIST OR LOTUS SCHOOL.—See *Buddhist Schools,* XVII, 7.

AMITA BUDDHA.—See *Amitabha*.

AMITABHA.—Also Amida, Amita, O-mi-t'o 阿彌陀, etc.—A fabulous personage worshipped assiduously—like Kuan-yin 觀音 —by the Northern Buddhists, but unknown in Siam, Burma, and Ceylon. Abides in Hsi T'ien 西天, the Western Heaven. The Western Paradise promised to the worshippers of Amida Buddha is inconsistent with the doctrine of Nirvana. It promises immortality instead of annihilation.

It was a feeling, much the same as that which prompted Sakyamuni to break away from Brahmanism, which led Amitabha to insert a new doctrine into Buddhism. · His desire was to bring salvation within the reach of all people. The teaching of Sakyamuni made absorption into Nirvana possible for one by meditation, abstemiousness, and good works, through countless periods of years. Amitabha brought the new doctrine of redemption through faith. As this method put deliverance within the reach of all, it quickly gained favour, and soon the worship had spread over all China, and even into Korea and Japan.

At first the term was impersonal, meaning the ideal, and boundless light. It was probably a Persian or Gnostic idea introduced into the Buddhism of Kashmir or Nepal, whence it reached China via Tibet. It is not mentioned by Fa Hsien 法顯 or Hsüan Tsang 玄奘, it is unknown in Southern Buddhism, or in the earliest *sutras* brought to China; and the first *sutra* that alludes to Amita does not give him any importance. He came to the front early in the fifth century A.D. When the poetical notions of the Lotus-school, Lien-hua Tsung 蓮花宗, or Pure-land school, Ching-t'u Tsung 淨土宗 (See *Buddhist Schools*), concerning a Paradise in the West began to influence the common people Amita became the favourite Buddha, and is now the most popular Buddha, in China.

There are various traditions as to his origin. He is an incarnation of the ninth son of the ancient Buddha Mahabhidjna jnana bhibhu (a fabulous Buddha); or the second son of a certain Indian of the lunar race; or he is the celestial reflex of Sakyamuni, etc.

He is strangely obscure in the early art and literature of Indian Buddhism, and is in fact barely mentioned. It is also to be noticed that the Chinese translations of the principal Amidist scriptures—two in the second century and four in the third—are all by natives of Central Asia, while the chief features of the cult are all Persian. (Eitel; Johnston).

Amitabha was supposed to have been a powerful ruler, but because of his compassion for his fellow men, gave up his throne and became a monk, under the name of Fa Tsang 法藏, or Dharmakara. During his seeking he became a pupil of Shih Tzu-tsai Wang 世自在王, or Lokesvararaja, who taught him the method of becoming a Buddha. After a great deal of meditation he made forty-eight vows. They were that he would become a Buddha, on the condition that he would be able to save every living being, and establish a kingdom of blessedness, where all who should wish to go, should have a happy life after this.—See *O-mi-t'o Fu* 阿彌陀佛, *San Pao* 三寶, *Adi-Buddha,* and *Buddhist Schools.*

A-MI-T'O FO 阿彌陀佛.—See *O-mi-t'o Fo* 阿彌陀佛.

AMOGHA.—O-MO[MU]-K'A PO-CHE-LO 阿摩[日]佉跋折羅. Also called AMOGHA VAJRA. Chinese PU K'UNG 不空.—The chief representative of the *Tantra* School in China, which he was successful in spreading widely through the patronage of three emperors (*infra*). Said to have been a monk who came from Ceylon to China about A.D. 719, and eventually succeeded Vajramati in the leadership of the Yogatchara School (A.D. 732) (see *Buddhist Schools*, XIII). He went at first to the Imperial Court at Ch'ang-an 長安, and followed it later to Lo-yang 洛陽. He had proved his skill in magic by taming a herd of wild elephants. As he was travelling, a herd of those animals had rushed toward him. He sat quietly on the way side. The elephants all knelt down before him and retired. He was held in high esteem by three successive emperors, Hsüan Tsung 玄宗 (A.D. 713-56), Su Tsung 肅宗 (A.D. 756-63), and Tai Tsung 代宗 (A.D. 763-80), of the T'ang 唐 dynasty. He was officially deputed by the imperial government to proceed to India and especially to Ceylon (A.D. 741-46), to bring back from there the greatest possible number of *tantras,* for which there was a great demand in China. He made Tantrism the fashionable sect.

He introduced into the country a large number of *dharanis,* or magic formulas, as well as the Hindu ceremony of feeding hungry ghosts, the Chinese *Yü-lan Hui* 盂蘭會 (Sanskrit *Ulamba*), held annually on the fifteenth day of the seventh moon. This was grafted on to the native ancestor-worship. His book *Yü-chia yen-k'ou* 瑜伽炎口 contains directions for calling hungry spirits to be fed, by magical arrangements of the fingers, delineations of Sanskrit characters, etc. From his journey through India and Ceylon he brought back more than 500 *sutras* and *s'astras* previously unknown in China. He introduced a new alphabet for the transliteration of Sanskrit and published 108 works, mostly translations.

When he came to China, he produced, it is said, a great reformation of manners in court and country. If judged by his works, however, consisting of unintelligible charms with many pictures of Bodhisattvas, he brought a grosser superstition than existed before; but it is to be noted that in the numerous collections bearing his signature, there are none of the immodest things with which competent authors reproach Sivait, Indian and Tibetan Tantrism.

It is related that one day Hsüan Tsung 玄宗 begged him to stop the prolonged rain, which was causing much damage throughout the country. Amogha moulded five or six little clay images of dragons—(the dragon in China is "a deity symbolic of fertile rain, rain-sending clouds, thunder and lightning; as a water-god, he soars in the clouds, and pours out his blessings on the parched earth")—placed them in a basin of water, and recited over them a magic formula, with the result that the rain ceased forthwith. Besides this, he had a special method of procuring rain. He erected a platform and adorned it with various stuffs; then taking in his hand a wooden image about six inches in height, he recited over it various magic formulas, till the image opened its mouth, displayed its teeth, and even moved its eyes. Hereupon rain began to fall in great abundance.

Having retired from Court life in the early part of A.D. 773, he died in A.D. 774. Hsüan Tsung 玄宗 (A.D. 713-56) had prohibited his retiring to India, Su Tsung 肅宗 (756-63) gave him the title Tripitaka Bhadanta (Ta-kuang-chih San-tsang 大廣智三藏). and Tai Tsung 代宗 (763-80) granted him the posthumous rank of a Minister of State as well as a posthumous title.

The following saying is attributed to him: "It is easy to procure rain or sunshine, but difficult to rid the country of evil-doers."— See also *Buddhist Schools,* XIII and XV.

ANADA.—See *Adi-Buddha.*

AN-AGAMI.—See *Lo-han* 羅漢.

ANAGAMIN.—AN-NA-HAN 阿那含 = *pu huan* 不還 not returning (*ana,* no, *gamin,* return), or *pu lai* 不來, not coming, *i.e.* not to be reborn into the world of desire.—The third of the four degrees of saintship (grades of discipleship, or "fruits"), the third class of *aryas,* embracing all those who are no longer liable to be reborn as men, though they are to be born once more as *devas,* when they will forthwith become *arhats* and enter Nirvana. —See *Su-da-wan, Si-da-gam,* and *Lo-han* 羅漢 (*A-la-han* 阿羅漢).

ANANDA. — A-NAN-T'O 阿難陀 or A-NAN 阿難. — A son of Dronodana (a prince of Magadha, father of Dêvadatta and Mahanama, uncle of Sakyamuni). Called Ananda (joy), because he was born at the moment when Sakyamuni attained to Buddha-ship. Under the teaching of the latter, Ananda became an Arhat, famed especially for his memory or experience (*to wên* 多聞), The most intimate friend and favourite attendant of his cousin, Gautama. The compilation and editing of the earliest *sutras* is attributed to him. Died 866 or 463 B.C. (the chronology is obscure: see *Sakyamuni*). Images of Kasyapa and Ananda, the first two patriarchs of Indian Buddhism, are found in many Buddhist temples in China.—See *Patriarchs.* For the narrative of his temptation see Edkins, *Chinese Buddhism,* pp. 291-300.

ANANGA.—*Lit.* "The bodiless." A name of Kama, the Hindu god of love.—See *Kama.*

ANAVATAPTA.—A dragon-king.—See *Lung Wang* 龍王.

ANGAJA.—See *Lo-han* 羅漢.

ANGIDA.—See *Lo-han* 羅漢.

ANGILA.—See *Lo-han* 羅漢.

ANIDA BUDDHA.—See *Amitabha.*

AN KUO 安國.—A saintly Buddhist saint. Eighth century A.D. One of those invited to the annual banquet of the gods (see *Hsi Wang-mu* 西王母). The teacher of Yüan Kuei Ch'an-shih 元珪禪師 (*q.v.*).

AO CH'IN 敖欽.—A dragon-king.—See *Lung Wang* 龍王 and *Shui Fu* 水府, IV (1).

AO JUN 敖閏.—A dragon-king.—See *Lung Wang* 龍王 and *Shui Fu* 水府, IV (1).

AO KUANG 敖廣.—A dragon-king.—See *Lung Wang* 龍王 and *Shui Fu* 水府, IV (1).

AO PING 敖丙.—The god of the star Hua-kai 華蓋. The third son of Ao Kuang 敖光, the Dragon-king of the Eastern Sea.

9

Killed by No-cha 哪吒 when he went to demand justice for the murder of his father's messenger.—See *Lung Wang* 龍王.

AO SHUN 敖順.—See *Lung Wang* 龍王 and *Shui Fu* 水府, IV (1).

APOTHECARIES, GODS OF.—See *Shên Nung* 神農, *Huang Ti* 黃帝, *T'ieh-kuai Li* 鐵拐李, and *Yao Pu* 藥部, Ministry of Medicine.

APOTHEOSIZED PHILOSOPHERS.—Though the Chinese philosophers Lieh Tzŭ 列子 (Ma Tan 馬丹), Huai-nan Tzŭ 淮南子 (Nan-hua Chuang-shêng 南華莊生), Chuang Tzŭ 莊子, Mo Tzŭ 墨子, etc., have been apotheosized, nothing very remarkable is related of them in their supernatural state. For the biographies of these sages see Wieger's *Histoire des Croyances Religieuses et des Opinions Philosophiques en Chine,* and his *La Chine à Travers les Ages;* also Giles's *Chinese Biographical Dictionary.* Here are noted only the reasons for their apotheosis and any short legends connected with them. The second (*v. infra*), who was a king, when taken by the Eight Immortals to the genii's Heaven forgot now and then to address them as superiors, and but for their intercession with Yü Ti 玉帝, the Pearly Emperor, would have been reincarnated. In order to humiliate himself, he thereafter called himself Huai-nan Tzŭ 淮南子, the Sage of the South of the Huai. The third, Chuang Tzŭ 莊子, Chuang Shêng 莊生, or Chuang Chou 莊周, was a disciple of Lao Tzŭ 老子. Chuang Tzŭ 莊子 was in the habit of sleeping during the day, and at night would transform himself into a butterfly, which fluttered gaily over the flowers in the garden. On waking, he would still feel the sensation of flying in his shoulders. On asking Lao Tzŭ 老子 the reason for this, he was told: "Formerly you were a white butterfly which, having partaken of the quintessence of flowers and of the *yin* 陰 and the *yang* 陽, should have been immortalized; but one day you stole some peaches and flowers in Wang-mu Niang-niang's 王母娘娘 garden. The guardian of the garden slew you, and that is how you came to be reincarnated." At this time he was fifty years of age.

One of the tales associated with him describes how he saw a young woman in mourning vigorously fanning a newly made grave. On his asking her the reason of this strange conduct, she replied; "I am doing this because my husband begged me to wait until the earth on his tomb was dry before I remarried!" Chuang Tzŭ 莊子 offered to help her, and as soon as he waved the fan once the earth was dry. The young widow thanked him and departed.

On his return home, Chuang Shêng 莊生 related this incident to his wife. She expressed astonishment at such conduct on the part of a wife. "There's nothing to be surprised at," rejoined the husband; "that's how things go in this world." Seeing that he was poking fun at her, she protested angrily. Some little time after this Chuang Shêng 莊生 died. His wife, much grieved, buried him.

A few days later a young man named Ch'u Wang-sun 楚王孫 arrived with the intention, as he said, of placing himself under the instruction of Chuang Shêng 莊生. When he heard that he was dead he went and performed prostrations before his tomb, and afterwards took up his abode in an empty room, saying that he wished to study. After half a month had elapsed, the widow asked an old servant who had accompanied Wang-sun 王孫 if the young man was married. On his replying in the negative, she requested the old servant to propose a match between them. Wang-sun 王孫 made some objections, saying that people would criticize their conduct. "Since my husband is dead, what can they say?" replied the widow. She then put off her mourning garments and prepared for the wedding.

Wang-sun 王孫 took her to the grave of her husband, and said to her: "The gentleman has returned to life!" She looked at Wang-sun and recognized the features of her husband. She was so overwhelmed with shame that she hanged herself. Chuang Shêng 莊生 buried her in an empty tomb, and then began to sing.

He burnt his house, went away to P'u-shui 濮水, in Hupei 湖北, and occupied himself in fishing. From there he went on to Chung-t'iao Shan 中條山, where he met Fêng Hou 風后 and her teacher Hsüan Nü 玄女, the Mother of Heaven, T'ien Mu 天母. In their company he visited the palaces of the stars. One day, when he was attending a banquet at the palace of Hsi Wang-mu 西王母, Shang Ti 上帝 gave him as his kingdom the planet Jupiter, and assigned to him as his palace the ancient abode of Mao Mêng 茅濛, the stellar god reincarnated during the Chou 周 dynasty. He had not yet returned, and had left his palace empty. Shang Ti 上帝 had cautioned him never to absent himself without his permission.

As regards Huai-nan Tzŭ 淮南子, the following legend is related in the *Shên-hsien t'ung-chien* 神仙通鑑: "About this time (second century B.C.) it was noticed that a young man calling himself Wang Chung-kao 王中高 was making frequent visits. An old man related that he had seen him before, and that he reappeared every generation. This was brought by a scholar named Wu Pei 伍被 to the notice of King Liu An 劉安 (of the Ch'ien Han 前漢 dynasty) who received him with honour. A long while afterward Wang Chung-kao 王仲高 confided to the King that he was the brother of Hsüan-yüan Huang-ti 軒轅皇帝 (2698-2598 B.C.), and that he had retired to Pei Shan 北山, Northern Mountain, at Shang-ku 上谷, because the Emperor Ch'in Shih Huang-ti 秦始皇帝 (221-209 B.C.) had called him there to write some characters. He added that he was trying to teach the people the doctrine of immortality. The King asked him what one should do to become immortal. "My friends will come to teach you," he replied. Some months later Wang Chung-kao 王仲高 left the country, and when he had gone, eight old white-haired and white-bearded men came to the palace and requested an audience.

The King's messenger informed them that his Majesty required three things: immortality, a profound knowledge of the Doctrine, and magic power for slaying wild beasts, etc. He added that they, being only three old men, could give him none of these things. The old men, having remarked that they were deceiving themselves and that, according to them, only young men could do anything useful, suddenly transformed themselves into youths in the prime of life. The King, on hearing of this, did not wait even to put on his shoes, but ran barefoot to welcome them at the palace gates. He led them to the Ssŭ-hsien T'ai 思仙臺 palace, and declared himself their disciple. They then resumed the form of old men, and the King requested them to teach him the recipe for immortality, going daily with them to gather medicinal herbs. They prepared the drug of immortality on Pa-kung Shan 八公山, Mount Pa-kung, near the town of Shou-chou 壽州.

In 122 B.C., the son of Liu An 劉安, Prince Liu Ch'ien 劉遷, who believed himself unrivalled in swordsmanship, invited a military officer named Lei Pei 雷被, who was a clever swordsman, to have a bout with him. Having inadvertently wounded the Prince, and greatly fearing the consequences, he consulted his friend Wu Pei 伍被, and they drew up a memorial accusing the King of Huai-nan 淮南 and the King of Lu-chiang 廬江 to the Emperor Wu Ti 武帝 (140-86 B.C.) of the Han 漢 dynasty, saying that the two brothers were plotting a revolt. The Emperor sent Tsung Chêng 宗正 to punish them. Liu Hsi 劉賜, King of Lu-chiang 廬江, on hearing this news, hanged himself.

Before the arrival of the imperial delegate at Huai-nan 淮南, the Eight Immortals came to invite King Liu An 劉安 to follow them. "I wish to bring my brother with us," he answered. He was unaware that he had committed suicide, but on learning the sad news was overwhelmed and wished to slay Lei Pei 雷被 and Wu Pei 伍被, the two calumniators. The old men dissuaded him, asking him how we could kill human beings when we spare even insects. The eight old men and Liu An 劉安, reassembled on Pa-kung Shan 八公山, mounted clouds and disappeared into the heavens. They left behind them on the mountain their herbs and alchemical stove. Fowls and dogs which ate of their composition became immortal. The Eight Immortals guided the King to the mountain beyond the sea, where they found all the genii assembled. The old men then said to them: "You will call them your uncles the Immortals, and serve them with respect, and thus you will be admitted to Yü Ti's 玉帝 palace."

Liu An 劉安 obeyed, but, being a king, accustomed to being served and respected, complied only with difficulty with all the humiliating services, his language remained haughty, and he sometimes so far forgot himself as to refer to himself as king; briefly, seated, standing, or in conversation, he was lacking in humility. The result was that Yü Ti 玉帝 condemned him to be reincarnated. On the petition of the Eight Immortals, however, Yü Ti 玉帝 gave him another chance, and (as stated above) the King, in order to humiliate himself, changed his name to Huai-nan Tzŭ 淮南子, the Sage of Huai-nan 淮南. At his request the Eight Immortals went to the Western Sea to rescue his brother. They made pills from a perfumed tree called *fan-hun shu* 返魂樹, the tree which recalls the soul. These they gave to the corpse, which revived, and the brother thenceforth gave himself up to the practice of virtue and was saved. The Eight Immortals returned to Huai-nan Tzŭ 淮南子, acquainted him with all the mysteries of his origin, and then took him to Tung Wang-kung 東王公, the king of the Immortals, who appointed him to the post vacated by T'ai-chi Chên-jên 太極眞人.

Ma Tan 馬丹, of the Ti 狄 clan, generally known by the name of his work, Lieh Tzŭ 列子, was, after five years' waiting and rejection, admitted as a disciple of Yin Hsi 尹喜 (*q.v.*), who taught him how to attain to longevity and immortality. After being instructed by other masters he reached perfection, and could walk in the heavens on the wings of the wind. Having changed his name to Yü K'ou 禦冦, he went to the Kingdom of Chêng 鄭, where he remained forty years. It was here, at P'u-t'ien 圃田, that he composed the eight sections of his book, the title of which was later changed to *Ch'ung-hsü ching* 冲虛經.

Mo Tzŭ 墨子. Personal name Ti 翟. A high official of the Sung 宋 Kingdom. Reputed author of the work *Mo Tzŭ* 墨子, which, however, was drawn up by others. When the war broke out between the Sung 宋 kingdom and that of Ch'u 楚, the famous Kung Shu-pan 公輸般 (*v. Lu Pan* 魯班) had invented some scaling ladders to attack the enemy's fortresses. Mo Ti 墨翟 travelled for seven days and seven nights to beseech him not to apply the resources of his fertile intellect to a power opposed to his own, and one besides who had undertaken a most unjust war.

At the age of 82 he retired to Chou-ti Shan 周狄山, where he became an Immortal.

APSARAS.—The celebrated nymphs of India's heaven. The name, signifying "moving in the water," has some analogy to that of Aphrodite. It is said that when they came forth from the waters neither the gods nor the *asuras* would have them for wives, so they became common to all. In Indian works sometimes seven, sometimes fourteen classes are named. There are said to be 35,000,000 of them, but only 1,060 are the principal.—See *T'ien Nü* 天女.

ARAHATS.—Those who have entered the Four Paths (see *Four Paths* and *Dhyana*) and are clear from the first five Fetters (see *Ten Fetters*).—See also *Lo-han* 羅漢.

ARCHERY, THE GOD OF.—See *Hsü Ch'ang* 續 長.

ARCHITECTURE, THE GOD OF.—See *Huang Ti* 黃 帝.

ARHAN 阿 漢.—See *Lo-han* 羅 漢.

ARHAT.—See *Lo-han* 羅 漢.

ARHAT WHO SUBDUED THE DRAGON, THE.—See *Lo-han* 羅 漢.

ARHAT WHO TAMED THE TIGER, THE.—See *Lo-han* 羅 漢.

ARM OF THE GOD OF T'AI SHAN 泰 山, THE RIGHT. —See *Wên Yüan-shuai* 温 元 帥.

ARMPITS, THE GODS OF THE.—See *Hun-p'o Chao* 魂 魄 兆.

ART, THE LO-HAN IN CHINESE.—See *Lo-han* 羅 漢.

ARTHAS'IDDHI.—See *Fo* 佛.

ARYA.—A-Lo 阿 暑, *Shêng* 聖, holy, or *Tsun-ch'i* 尊 耆, the Reverend.—See *Lo-han* 羅 漢.

AS'AIKCHA.—See *Lo-han* 羅 漢.

ASAMGHA.—See *Buddhist Schools,* XIII (2) and XV.

ASANGHA.—See *Buddhist Schools,* XIII (2) and XV.

ASEKHAS.—Those who have finished the Fourth Path (see *Four Paths* and *Dhyana*) and are free from *all* the Ten Fetters (*q.v.*).

A-SHIH-TO 阿 氏 多.—See *Lo-han* 羅 漢.

ASITA.—A-ssū-t'o 阿 私 陁 or A-shih-to 阿 氏 多.—A *richi* (*hsien* 仙) who was able to detect the marks of Buddha on a child. Sakyamuni was his slave in a former life.—See *Lo-han* 羅 漢.

ASOKA.—A-shu-chia(ka) 阿 恕 迦, or A-shu-chia(ka) 阿 輸 伽 or A-yü 阿 育 (= Wu-yu 無 憂, sorrowless).—The most distinguished of the lay followers of Gautama; now most often thought of as the philanthropic and righteous Buddhist Emperor. But he loved to call himself, "Asoka, the delight *of the gods*"; and though

14

he was an earnest Buddhist, it would be more exact to call him a Hindu of the Buddhist sect.

The Chinese say that he gained the throne by assassination of his nearest relatives, and that he was converted to Buddhism through an arhat whom he had boiled alive and who proved invulnerable. The name given to him on his conversion was Dharmasoka. He is supposed to be identic with the Piyadasi whose edicts are found inscribed on pillars and rocks throughout India (*v. infra*).

Dowson (*Hindu Dic.*) says: "A celebrated king of the Maurya dynasty of Magadha, and grandson of its founder, Chandra-gupta. 'This king is the most celebrated of any in the annals of the Buddhists. In the commencement of his reign he followed the Brahmanical faith, but became a convert to that of Buddha, and a zealous encourager of it. He is said to have maintained in his palace 64,000 Buddhist priests, and to have erected 84,000 columns (or topes) throughout India. A great convocation of Buddhist priests was held in the eighteenth year of his reign, which was followed by missions to Ceylon and other places.' He reigned thirty-six years, from about 234 to 198 B.C., and exercised authority more or less direct from Afghanistan to Ceylon. This fact is attested by a number of very curious Pali inscriptions found engraven upon rocks and pillars, all of them of the same purport, and some of them almost identical in words, the variations showing little more than dialectic differences . . . These inscriptions show a great tenderness for animal life, and are Buddhist in their character, but they do not enter upon the distinctive peculiarities of that religion."

"Asoka has emerged from the legendary cloudland in which he once reigned. To the Chinese pilgrims in India centuries after his death he was the magician at whose behest genii raised mighty buildings; to us he is the unwearied seeker of all beings' good, whose deeply personal message of remorse and benevolence is graven on the rocks. The decipherment of his records is a moving story. . . . The main facts of Asoka's life are widely known; his remorse after his one great war of conquest known to us, his conversion, his efforts to spread the knowledge of the Excellent Law, his missions to Ceylon, his rock-edicts that were not to boast of his greatness or victories but to exhort his subjects to a life of religion," though many details remain obscure (see Radhakumud Mookerji, *Asoka*) "his name is honoured wherever the teachings of the Buddha have spread, and is reverenced from the Volga to Japan, from Ceylon and Siam to the borders of Mongolia and Siberia . . . He was converted by a miracle, so highly do the Buddhist scribes estimate his adhesion to their cause. And yet it cannot be doubted that it was the first great step on the downward path of Buddhism, the first step to its expulsion from India; not of course, that the conversion itself injured the church. . . . After his conversion, which took place in the tenth year of his reign, he became a very zealous supporter of the new religion. He himself built many monasteries and dagabas, and provided many monks with the necessaries of life; and he encouraged those about his court to do the same. He also established gardens and hospitals for man and beast, and published edicts throughout his empire, enjoining on all his subjects morality and justice." (Davids, pp. 221-2).

ASSESSORS OF THE KING OF REMEDIES, THE TEN.—See *Shih Ming I* 十明醫.

ASURA, ASURAS.—A-hsiu-lo 阿脩羅, A-so-lo 阿素羅, or A-hsü-lun 阿須倫. Meaning *fei-t'ien* 非天, those who are not dêvas (*q.v.*).—Evil demons always at war with the gods. The fourth class of sentient beings, the mightiest of all demons, titanic enemies of the dêvas. They dwell under the foundations of Mount Meru (*q.v.*), or in solitary woods and mountain hollows. Are connected with eclipses (Hardy). Placed in Buddhist works second in the six states of ignorance (*fan* 番). Dragon-kings (see *Lung Wang* 龍王).

ASVAGOSHA. Ma-ming 馬鳴.—A Buddhist patriarch.—See *Lo-han* 羅漢.

ATHLETES OF THE WESTERN COUNTRY.—See *Huang-chin Li-shih* 黃金力士.

ATHLETES OF THE YELLOW TURBAN.—See *Huang-chin Li-shih* 黃金力士.

AVATAR OF A *CHIA* 甲 SPIRIT, THE.—See *Wên Yüan-shuai* 温元帥.

AVATARA.—A-po-to-lo 阿跛多羅.—"A descent." Metamorphosis, *hua-shêng* 化生, birth by transformation. The Brahminical idea of incarnation of a deity, especially of Vishnu. One of the kinds of supernatural birth (from a lotus-flower, etc.), in full maturity, such as is ascribed to Buddhas and Bodhisattvas, the latter coming from Tuchita (*q.v.*), by this birth into the world.

AVATARAS.—See *Vishnu*.

B

BACK, THE GOD OF THE.—See *Nü Chio* 女爵.

BAISHAJYAGURU. The Buddha who instructs in healing. —See *Yao-shih Fo* 藥師佛.

BANQUET OF THE GODS.—See *Hsi Wang-mu* 西王母 and *P'an-t'ao Hui* 蟠桃會.

BARBERS, BEGGARS, AND CORN-CUTTERS, THE GOD OF.—See *Lo-tsu Ta-hsien* 羅祖大仙.

BAREFOOTED IMMORTAL, THE.—See *Ch'ih-chiao Hsien* 赤脚仙.

BASKET-MAKERS, THE GOD OF.—See *Liu Pei* 劉備.

BATTLE-AXE, THE GOD OF THE.—The name of this god is Wang Chang 王章.—*Lung yü ho t'u* 龍魚河圖.

BEAN-CURD SELLERS, THE GODS OF.—See *Kuan Yü* 關羽, *Huai-nan Tzŭ* 淮南子, and *Chiao Kuan* 膠管.

BED, THE DUKE OR GENTLEMAN OF THE.—See *Ch'uang Kung, Ch'uang P'o (or Mu)* 牀公牀婆 (母).

BED, THE MALE AND FEMALE SPIRITS OF THE.— See *Ch'uang Kung, Ch'uang P'o (or Mu)* 牀公牀婆 (母).

BED, THE MOTHER OF THE.—See *Ch'uang Kung, Ch'uang P'o (or Mu)* 牀公牀婆 (母).

BEDS OF RIVERS, THE SPIRIT OF FORMER.—See *Shui Fu* 水府, D (2) (f).

BEGGARS, THE GOD OF.—See *Lo-tsu Ta-hsien* 羅祖大仙.

BHADRA.—See *Lo-han* 羅漢.

BHARADVAJA.—See *Lo-han* 羅漢.

BHIKSHU.—A mendicant. The Brahman in the fourth and last stage of his religious life. See *Brahman* and *Lo-han* 羅漢.

BLACK, MR.—See *Ch'êng Huang* 城隍.

BLACK PAVILIONS, THE LORD OF THE.—See *Hsüan-t'ien Shang-ti* 玄天上帝.

BLACK RULER, THE.—See *Mercury.*

BLACKSMITHS, THE GOD OF.—See *Lao Tzŭ* 老子.

BLOWER, THE.—See *Hêng Ha êrh chiang* 哼哈二將.

BLUE BIRD.—See *Shên-nung Huang-ti* 神農黃帝.

BLUE DRAGON.—See *Ch'ing Lung, Pai Hu* 青龍白虎.

BLUE GOWN, THE GOD OF THE.—See *Ch'ing-i Shên* 青衣神.

BODHI.—See *P'u-t'i* 菩提 and *Fo* 佛.

BODHIDHARMA.—A saintly Buddhist monk and Buddhist patriarch. Sixth century A.D. One of those invited to the annual banquet of the gods.—See *Patriarchs* and *Hsi Wang-mu* 西王母.

BODHISATTVA.—See P'u-t'i-sa-to 菩提薩埵.

BODY, THE GODS OF THE.—See the various parts of the body (Heart, Lungs, etc.).

BOWELS, THE GOD OF THE.—See *Chao T'êng-k'ang* 兆滕康.

BRAHMA (Masculine).—Fan-t'ien Wang 樊天王.—*Lit.* the father of all living beings (*i-ch'ieh chung-shêng chih fu* 一切衆生之父). The first person of the Brahminical Trimurti (the Hindu triad) "adopted by Buddhism, but placed in an inferior position, being looked upon, not as creator, but as a transitory *dêvata* whom every saint, on obtaining *bodhi,* surpasses." The supreme spirit manifested as the active creator of the universe. He sprang from the mundane egg deposited by the supreme first cause, and is the Brajapati, or lord and father of all creatures, and in the first place of the Rishis or Prajapatis.

When Brahma has created the world it remains unaltered for one of his days, a period of 2,160,000,000 years. The world and all that is therein is then consumed by fire, but the sages, gods, and elements survive. When he awakes he again restores creation, and this process is repeated until his existence of a hundred years is brought to a close, a period which it requires fifteen figures to express. When this period is ended he himself expires, and he and all the gods and sages, and the whole universe are resolved into their constituent elements. His name is invoked in religious services, but he is worshipped in India at only a few places.

He is said to be of a red colour. He has four heads; originally he had five, but one was burnt off by the fire of Siva's central eye because he had spoken disrespectfully. He has four arms; and in his hands he hold his sceptre, or a string of beads, or his bow Parivita, or a water-jug, and the *Veda*. His consort is Saraswati, goddess of learning, also called Brahmi. His vehicle is a swan or goose, from which he is called Hansa-vahana. His residence is called Brahma-vrinda.

Two points connected with Brahma are remarkable. As the father of men he performs the work of procreation by incestuous intercourse with his own daughter, variously named Vach or Saraswati (speech), Sandhya (twilight), Satarupa (the hundred-formed), etc. Secondly, that his powers as creator have been arrogated to the other gods Vishnu and Siva, while Brahma has been thrown into the shade. In the *Aitareya Brahmana* it is said that Prajapati was in the form of a buck and his daughter was Rohit, a deer. According to the *Satapatha Brahama* and *Manu,* the supreme soul, the self-existent lord, created the waters and deposited in them a seed, which seed became a golden egg, in which he himself was born as Brahma, the progenitor of all the worlds. As the waters (*nara*) were "the place of his movement, he (Brahma) was called Narayana." Here the name Narayana is referred distinctly to Brahma, but it afterwards became the name of Vishnu. The account of the *Ramayana* is that "all was water only, in which the earth was formed. Thence arose Brahma, the self-existent, with the deities. He then, becoming a boar, raised up the earth and created the whole world with the saints, his sons. Brahma, eternal and perpetually undecaying, sprang from the ether; from him was descended Marichi; the son of Marichi was Kasyapa. From Kasyapa sprang Vivaswat, and Manu is declared to have been Vivaswat's son." A later recension of this poem alters this passage so as to make Brahma a mere manifestation of Vishnu. Instead of "Brahma, the self-existent, with the deities," it subsititutes for the last three words, "the imperishable Vishnu." The Vishnu Purana says that the "divine Brahma called Narayana created all beings," that Prajapati "had formerly, at the commencement of the (previous) *kalpas,* taken the shape of a fish, a tortoise, etc. (so now), entering the body of a boar, the lord of creatures entered the water." But this "lord of creatures" is clearly shown to be Vishnu, and these three forms, the fish, the tortoise, and the boar, are now counted among the Avataras of Vishnu (see *Avatara*). This attribution of the form of a boar to Brahma (Prajapati) had been before made by the *Satapatha Brahmana,* which also says, "Having assumed the form of a tortoise, Prajapati created offspring." The *Linga Purana* is quite exceptional among the later works in ascribing the boar form to Brahma. The *Mahabharata* represents Brahma as springing from the navel of Vishnu or from a lotus which grew thereout; hence he is called Nabhi-ja, "navel-born"; Kania, "the lotus"; Sarojin, "having a lotus"; Abja-ia, Abja-yoni, and Kanja-ja, "lotus-born." This is, of course, the view taken by the *Vaishnavas*. The same statement appears in the *Ramayana,* although this poem gives Brahma a more prominent place than usual. It represents Brahma as informing Rama of his divinity, and of his calling him to heaven in "the glory of Vishnu." He bestowed boons on Rama while that hero was on earth, and he extended his favours also to Ravana and other Rakshasas who were descendants of his son Pulastya. In the *Puranas* also he appears as a patron of the enemies of the gods, and it was by his favour that the Daitya King Bali obtained that almost universal dominion which required the incarnation of Vishnu as the dwarf to repress. He is further represented in the *Ramayana* as the creator of the beautiful Ahalya, whom he gave as wife to the sage Gautama. Brahma, being thus inferior to Vishnu, is represented as giving homage and praise to Vishnu himself and to his form Krishna, but the *Vaishnava* authorities make him superior to Rudra, who, they say, sprang from his forehead. The *Saiva* authorities make Maha-deva or Rudra to be the creator of Brahma, and represent Brahma as worshipping the Linga and as acting as the charioteer of Rudra.

Brahma was the father of Daksha, who is said to have sprung from his thumb, and he was present at the sacrifice of that patriarch, which was rudely disturbed by Rudra. Then he had humbly to submit and appease the offended god. The four Kumaras, the chief of whom was called Sanat-kumara or by the patronymic Vaidhatra, were later creations or sons of Brahma.

Brahma is also called Vidhi, Vedhas, Druhina, and Srashtri, "creator"; Dhatri and Vidhatri, "sustainer"; Pitamaha, "the great father"; Lokesa, "lord of the world"; Parameshta, "supreme in heaven"; Sanat, "the ancient"; Adikavi, "the first poet"; and Dru-ghana, "the axe or mallet."—See also *Fan Wang* 梵王.

BRAHMA, BRAHMAN (Neuter).—The supreme soul of the universe, self-existent, absolute, and eternal, from which all things emanate, and to which all return. This divine essence is incorporeal, immaterial, invisible, unborn, uncreated, without beginning and without end, illimitable, and inappreciable by the sense until the film of mortal blindness is removed. It is all-pervading and infinite in its manifestations, in all nature animate and inanimate, in the highest good and in the meanest creature. This supreme soul receives no worship, but it is the object of that abstract meditation which Hindu sages practise in order to obtain absorption into it. It is sometimes called Kala-hansa, and has also been represented as the active creator. The Veda (*q.v.*) is sometimes called Brahma or Brahman Veda, "because it claims to be the *Veda* for the chief sacrificial priest, the Brahman."

BRAHMALOKA.—Fan T'ien 梵天, *lit.* the heavens of Brahma, or Shih-chu T'ien 世主天, *lit.* the heavens of the ruler of the world.—Eighteen heavenly mansions constituting the world of form and divided into four regions of contemplation (see *Dhyana*). Southern Buddhism knows only sixteen.—See also *Loka.*

BRAHMAN.—The first of the four Hindu castes; the sacerdotal class, the members of which may be, but are not necessarily, priests. A Brahman is the chief of all created beings; his person is inviolate; he is entitled to all honour, and enjoys many rights and privileges. The chief duty of a Brahman is the study and teaching of the *Vedas,* and the performance of sacrifices and other religious ceremonies; but in modern times many Brahmans entirely neglect these duties, and they engage in more of the occupations of secular life.

When the light-skinned ancestors of the present Hindus first came to India, they found there a darker, thicker-featured native race, the Dravidians, builders of the great temples of the south. And the priests of the newcomers desired that the blood of their people be not mixed with the native stock, but be kept of one strain. So they declared Dravidians to be unclean, "untouchable."

Then the old lawmakers, gradually devising the caste system, placed themselves at the head thereof, under the title of "earthly gods"—Brahmans. Next beneath them they put the Kshattryas, or fighting men; after the fighters, the Vaisyas, or cultivators, upon whom the two above look down; and finally, the fourth division, or Sudra caste, born solely to be servants to the other three.

Of these four divisions, themselves to-day much subdivided, was built the frame of Hindu society. Outside and below all caste, in a limbo of scorn earned by their sins of former existences, must for ever grovel the Untouchables.

BRAIN, THE GOD OF THE.—See *Chio Yüan-tzǔ* 覺元子.

BREAST, THE GOD OF THE.—See *Hu Pên* 虎賁.

BRIDGE OF SORROWS.—See *K'u-ch'u Ch'iao* 苦楚橋 and *Mêng P'o* 孟婆.

BRIDGES, THE GODS OF—When a funeral procession crosses a bridge, the chief mourner kneels and worships the god of the bridge. These gods are not represented by images. They rule the spirits of the drowned.

BRIGANDS, THE GODS OF.—See *Wu Tao Chiang-chün* 五盜將軍, *Liu Chih* 柳跖, *Sung Chiang* 宋江, and *Shih Ch'ien* 時遷.

BROOM, THE GODDESS OF THE.—See *Sao-ch'ing Niang*
掃 晴 娘.

BROTHELS, THE GODDESS OF.—See *P'an Chin-lien*
潘 金 蓮.

BROTHERS, THE THREE SWORN.—See *San I Ko* 三 義 閣.

BUDDHA.—See *Fo* 佛; *Adi-Buddha; Ananda; San Shêng*
三 聖; *San Pao* 三 寶. For the twenty-four mythical Buddhas who
appeared before Sakyamuni, see Monier Williams, *Buddhism*,
p. 136, note; Waddell, *Buddhism of Tibet*, p. 345, note 5; Hardy,
Manual of Buddhism, p. 94; Doré, *Recherches*, vi. 74, and
Kennelly, vi. 99-100. For the Seven Tathagatas, *Ch'i Ju-lai*
七 如 來, see Doré, vi. 75.

BUDDHA FROM THE BEGINNING.—See *Adi-Buddha*.

BUDDHA UNORIGINATED.—See *Adi-Buddha*.

BUDDHABHADRA.—See *Fo-t'o-po-to-lo Ch'an-shih* 佛 陀 跋
多 羅 禪 師 and *Fa Hsien* 法 顯.

BUDDHAJANGA.—See *Fo-t'u-ch'êng* 佛 圖 澄.

BUDDHI.—See *Fo* 佛.

BUDDHIST SCHOOLS.—In addition to the Mythical Buddhas who appeared during the *kalpas* preceding Sakyamuni, the
most important Bodhisattvas, and the Six Patriarchs of Chinese
Buddhism,[1] references are made in Chinese and at times also in
foreign literature to the founders of the various Buddhist Schools
and their disciples, who are venerated and worshipped in the
principal monasteries.

Detailed information regarding the biographies of the founders
of the chief of these Schools and of the deified monks belonging
to them is the result of long and laborious investigation by Doré
(VIII, 389-462). Besides personal research, the source of his
information is a work by Shou I 守 一 entitled *Ch'ung-k'o Fo-tsu-
chêng-tsung-tao-ying* 重 亥 佛 祖 正 宗 道 影, *New Illustrated Edition,
setting forth the list of Buddhist Patriarchs and Founders of
Schools*, published at Soochow 蘇 州, reprinted in 1880. The
work is characterized by monotony, the author giving but little

---

[1] The sixth Chinese patriarch did not appoint a successor (see *Patriarchs*).
The monastic habit and rice-bowl that had descended to him were, in accordance
with what Bodhidharma had said, not communicated to a new patriarch. In
the five petals the flower, as he had expressed it, would be complete, he himself,
the first of the six, being the stem on which the others grew.

information regarding the doctrine of these Schools, and what discriminates them from each other. He dwells especially on biographical details—the family name of the monk, where he was born, the name of his teacher, and where he lived and died.

Doré states: "In large establishments, a special hall is set apart for the founders and eminent teachers, who lived and taught there; incense is burnt before their images or tablets, and people come to beg their intercession in various public calamities. It is thus that the ten former abbots of the T'ai-hsing 泰 興 monasteries are placed round the image of Maitreya, Mi-lo Fo 彌 勒 佛, and worshipped on several occasions. . . . These famous Worthies, honoured by the votaries of each sect, are held to be the principal protectors of the monasteries where they taught. Here, their biographies and images are conserved with the greatest care, as the heirlooms of the family." These images, and those in the temples, were moulded according to these documents, which constitute the most authentic record procurable at the present day. The pictures number two hundred and fifty, and are accompanied by a short biographical notice. In the light of the information thus furnished, visitors to Buddhist monasteries will have at their command particulars regarding the principal founders and the eminent teachers who flourished and taught within their precincts.

Besides many doctrinal differences in these Buddhist Schools, there is also much variety in the canonical books selected by each sect, the extracts recited by the monks, traditions, methods of contemplation, details of worship, interior monastic administration, and discipline.

Buddhism undoubtedly suffered severely in the last stages of its career in India from the iconoclastic fury of the Mohammedans. Its decay was also largely due to the influence of the Yogacharya, or Tantric Buddhists, who from about the sixth century A.D. began to admit Saivite deities into what now may be called the Buddhist pantheon. This helped to obliterate the characteristic features of Buddhism, which thus gradually ceased to maintain itself as a separate religion (see Johnston, *Buddhist China,* p. 24, note 2). The Hinayana was so called because, according to its opponents, it was capable of conveying to the "other shore" of Nirvana only those rare individuals who by their own strenuous exertions had earned for themselves the prize of salvation; whereas the Great Vehicle (Mahayana) offered salvation to all beings in all the worlds. The more correct name for Hinayana would be Theravada—the School of the Elders or Presbyters. The Theravadins were also known as the Haimavantas, or (to use the Chinese term) Hsüeh-shan Pu 雪 山 部, the School of the Snowy Mountains (*ibid*).

Ta-mo's [Bodhidharma's] teachings are partly responsible for the decay of learning in the Chinese monasteries. His advice was taken too literally. Books were neglected, and monkish energy concentrated itself on ecstatic meditation. In many cases religious zeal died away for want of substantial nourishment, and there is reason to suspect that some of the monks who believed themselves to have attained the exalted state of mystical union were apt to confuse that state with the less honourable condition of physical somnolence. On the other hand, the influence of Ta-mo and his successors undoubtedly tended to save Chinese Buddhism from the evils of priestcraft and "clericalism" and from a slavish worship of images and relics, dogmas, and sacred books. The images, etc., in Buddhist temples are not regarded as ultimate objects of religious reverence except by those to whom spiritual religion is an unattainable experience.

The subdivision into sects which took place after the time of the sixth patriarch (see *Patriarchs*) was not a consequence of any disruptive forces set in motion by Confuciism, but was due rather to the growth of what may be described as a sort of religious individualism within the pale of Buddhism itself, and to the fact that after the death of Hui-nêng 慧能 the leading Ch'an 禪 Buddhists separated into two branches—the Northern and the Southern. The rivalry between the Wu Tsung 五宗—The Five Sects that regarded Hui-nêng 慧能 and his predecessors as their common patriarchs—was as a rule healthy and friendly, and it was not till comparatively recent times that a tendency toward reunion was brought about by the gradual decay of learning and of religious fervour in the monasteries.

"It is in the discussions of these (Mahayana) Schools, orthodox and unorthodox, that we must look for the ultimate sources of the principal streams that flow into the ocean of Mahayanist belief."

It is necessary to note that, as Doré points out, "the names of famous monks are generally associated with the names of the mountain or place where the monastery stood, and they are indiscriminately designated either by their religious appellation, or that of the mountain beside which they lived and taught."

A list of the principal Schools and their founders is appended.

To avoid complication of cross-references, the Principal and Secondary Schools have been numbered consecutively without sub-division.

	SCHOOL.	FOUNDER.	DIED A.D.
I.	Niu-t'ou Chih 牛頭支.	Tao-hsin 道信, through his disciple Fa-jung 法融	651
II.	Ch'ih-su Chiao 喫素敎. *Principal branch.*	Hui-nêng 慧能.	712
III.	Nan-yo Chêng-tsung 南嶽正宗. *Secondary branches.*	Huai-jan 懷讓.	744
IV.	Wei-yang Tsung 潙仰宗.	Wei-shan Ling-yu 潙山靈佑	840
V.	Lin-chi Tsung 臨濟宗.	I-hsüan 義玄.	867

SCHOOL.	FOUNDER.	DIED A.D.
Principal branch.		
VI. Ch'ing-yüan Chêng-tsung 青原正宗.	Hsing-ssǔ 行思 and disciples of Hui-nêng 慧能.	730
Secondary branches.		
VII. Ts'ao-tung Mo 曹洞脈.	Ts'ao-shan Pên-chi 曹山本寂.	901
VIII. Yün-mên Mo 雲門脈.	Yün-mên Wên-yen 雲門文偃.	954
IX. Fa-yen Mo 法眼脈.	Fa-yen Wên-i 法眼文益.	958
X. Fa-hua Tsung 法華宗 (T'ien-t'ai Chiao 天台教).	Hui-wên 慧文.	550
XI. Hua-yen Tsung 華嚴宗 (Hua-yen Hsien-shou Chiao 華嚴賢首教).	Tu-shun 杜順.	640
XII. Ch'an Tsung 禪宗.	Ta-mo 達磨.	535
XIII. Chü-shê Tsung 俱舍宗.	Shih-ch'in 世親.	170
XIV. Fa-hsiang Tsung 法相宗 (Tz'ǔ-ên Chiao 慈恩教).	Ta'u-chih Ju-lai 大乘如來 (fictitious). Hsüan-tsang 玄奘 (T'ang-sêng 唐僧), Chinese founder.	664
XV. Chên-yen Tsung 眞言宗 (Yü-chia Chiao 瑜伽教).	P'u-hsien-wu-chê 普賢無著. Pu-k'ung 不空, propagator.	160 774
XVI. Nan-shan Lü Tsung 南山律宗.	Tao-hsüan 道宣.	667
XVII. Lien-shê Tsung 連社宗 (Ching-t'u Chiao 淨土教).	Hui-yüan 慧遠.	454

I. Niu-t'ou Chih 牛頭攴.— The Buffalo-head School. Founded by Tao-hsin 道信, through his disciple Fa-jung 法融. With Hui-nêng 慧能, the sixth and last patriarch of Chinese Buddhism (see *Patriarchs*), the record is brought down to the thirty-third generation after Sakyamuni.

II. Ch'ih-su Chiao 喫素教.—The Vegetarian School. Founded by the Sixth Chinese Patriarch, Hui-nêng 慧能 (see *Patriarchs*).

III. Nan-yo Chêng-tsung 南嶽正宗.—Chief School of the Southern [Sacred] Mountain. Founded by Hui-nêng's 慧能 disciples, Li-hui Ch'an-shih 李惠禪師 and others. The Nan-yo 南嶽, also known as Hêng Shan 衡山, is situated on the west side of the Hsiang Chiang 湘江, Hsiang River, in Hunan 湖南, and is about 4,000 feet high. In this, as well as in the Ch'ing-yüan 青原 School, there was no real difference in sentiment from the doctrine of the parent stem. According to the *San-chiao i-shu* 三 教 一 束, the chief influence in the formation of these two Schools was that of the Sixth Patriarch upon the minds of Tu Huai-jang 杜 懷 讓 and Liu Hsing-ssŭ 劉 興 嗣.

BRANCHES OF THE NAN-YO TSUNG 南 嶽 宗,

SCHOOL OF THE SOUTHERN [SACRED] MOUNTAN.

IV. **Wei-Yang Tsung** 潙 仰 宗.—The Wei-yang School. This School was founded by Ling-yu Ch'an-shih 靈 祐 禪 師 (*q.v.*), a disciple of Huai-hai Ch'an-shih 懷 海 禪 師 (*q.v.*), and flourished at Wei Shan 潙 山.

V. **Lin-chi Tsung** 臨 濟 宗.—The Lin-chi School. Founded by I-hsüan Ch'an-shih 義 玄 禪 師 (*q.v.*), who studied under Hsi-yün Ch'an-shih 希 運 禪 師 (*q.v.*). The branch developed rapidly at Lin-chi 臨 濟, in Shantung 山 東, and acquired great influence in North China. I-hsüan 義 玄 died in A.D. 867.

VI. **Ch'ing-yüan Chêng-tsung** 青 原 正 宗.—The Ch'ing-yüan (Pure Spring) Orthodox School. Situated near Ch'üan-chou Fu 泉 州 府, Fukien 福 建. Founded by the disciples of Hui-nêng 慧 能 (see *Patriarchs*).

THREE BRANCHES OF THE CH'ING-YÜAN TSUNG 青 原 宗,

CH'ING-YÜAN SCHOOL.

First branch.

VII. **Ts'ao-tung Mo** 曹 洞 脈.—The Cave of the Gods Sect. The Ts'ao and Tung Branches. Founded at Ts'ao Shan 曹 山, Kiangsi 江 西, by [Ts'ao-shan] Pên-chi Ch'an-shih [曹 山] 本 寂 禪 師 (*q.v.*), a disciple of [Tung-shan] Liang-chieh Ch'an-shih [洞 山] 良 价 禪 師 (*q.v.*). He died A.D. 901.

Second branch.

VIII. **Yün-mên Mo** 雲 門 脈.—Cloud-gate Branch. Founded at Yün-mên 雲 門 by [Yün-mên] Wên-yen Ch'an-shih [雲 門] 文 偃 禪 師 (*q.v.*), a disciple of [Mu-chou] Tao-ming Ch'an-shih [睦 州] 道 明 禪 師 (*q.v.*) and [Hsüeh-fêng] I-ts'un Ch'an-shih [雪 峰] 義 存 禪 師 (*q.v.*). Died A.D. 954.

Third branch.

IX. **Fa-yen Mo** 法 眼 脈.—Eye-of-the-Law Branch. Founded by [Fa-yen] Wên-i Ch'an-shih [法 眼] 文 益 禪 師 (*q.v.*). Died A.D. 958.

X. **T'ien-t'ai Chiao** 天 台 教.—T'ien-t'ai School; also called T'ien-t'ai Tsung 天 台 宗, and Fa-hua Tsung 法 華 宗. The chief characteristic of the T'ien-t'ai Tsung 天 台 宗, T'ien-t'ai School, is that it struck a middle course between the rejection of books, and empty contemplation; between the credulous acceptance of the sacred books as literally true, and their entire rejection by extreme idealism. The fundamental subdivision of the system, into three modes of contemplation, the empty, the inventive, and the medial, originated with Nagarjuna (Lung Shu 龍樹) (*q.v.*). It selected the *Fa-hua ching* 法華經 (*Saddharma-pundarika*), or *Lotus of the Good Law,* one of the Canonical books of the Nepalese, the standard classic of the Lotus School, as its favourite book, and interpreted it in its own symbolical manner. It also admitted image worship, developed ceremonial and elaborate chanting of prayers. "It is strongly saturated with Tantra (*q.v.*) ideas. Chap. 24 treats on Kuan Yin 觀音, and is published separately for the devotees of the goddess."

As to its doctrine, the following principles are gleaned from the works of Chih-k'ai 智顗 (*q.v.*). 1. There is no living personal Buddha, but a moral one within us. 2. The aim of the school is to restore man's moral nature, and improve the heart. 3. This is to be obtained through "Perfected Observation," or the "Inner Look." 4. Knowledge is vacancy of mind, shutting out the external world, and the activity of the senses, all of which delude (Edkins, *Chinese Buddhism,* pp. 180-1).

The centre of this school was at T'ien-t'ai 天台, Chêkiang 浙江. T'ien-t'ai 天台 lies about 50 miles S. of Ning-po 寧波, and 180 miles S.E. of Hang-chou 杭州. It is the earliest, largest, and richest seat of Buddhism in China. It dates from the 4th century (rather from the close of the 5th century, while P'u-t'o 普陀 dates only from the 10th), and abounds in antiquities.

XI. **Hua-yen Hsien-shou Chiao** 華嚴賢首教.—The Hua-yen School. Also called Hua-yen Tsung 華嚴宗. The name arose from the adoption of the *Hua-yen ching* 華嚴經 as the School's chief canonical text-book. The characters Hsien-shou 賢首 were added, because its third patriarch, Fa-tsang Fa-shih 法藏法師 (*q.v.*), received the honorary title of Hsien-shou 賢首, Excellent Leader. The *Hua-yen ching* 華嚴經 (*cf. supra,* X.), attributed to Nagarjuna (*q.v.*), is a work of the early Mahayana School. "It is full of legendary embellishments, and fantastic glorifications of Buddha; how he appeared in various heavens accompanied by all sorts of extraordinary miracles before he appeared on earth. After the [*Fa-hua ching* 法華經] *Lotus of the Good Law,* it is the book most highly prized by Chinese Buddhists. Much of the Mahayana philosophy is derived from it, its legends giving full scope to the imagination about supernatural beings (Hackmann, *Buddhism as a Religion,* pp. 240-1; Edkins, *Chinese Buddhism,* pp. 230, 237).

Other branches.

XII. **Ch'an Tsung** 禪宗.—The Contemplative School. Founded by Ta-mo Ta-shih 達摩大師 (Bodhidharma) (*q.v.*). There is a fundamental difference between this and the other

27

schools. In the latter, study of books and outward ritual are discarded. Disciples are instructed only by word of mouth. Contemplation and the "inward look" are the most important things.

XIII. **Chü-shê Tsung** 俱舍宗.—The Yogachara School. Introduced into China by Vasubandu (*q.v.*) in the sixth century A.D. The teaching of the Yogachara School is an amalgamation of Brahmanism and Sivaitic idéas, combined with the philosophy of the Mahayana School. Its proper business is the repeating of unintelligible magic formulas for all purposes: rain, protection from storms, etc. (see further, in Eitel, *Sanskrit-Chinese Dic.,* art. Yogatcharya). Eitel also says: "This Yoga (or Tantra or Mantra) system was made known in China (A.D. 647) by Hiuen-[Hsüan-]tsang's [玄奘] translation of the *Yogatcharya bhumi s'astra,* on which basis Amoghavadjra (A.D. 720) (see *Amogha*) established the Chinese branch of the Yoga School which was popularized chiefly by the labours of Vadjrabodhi (A.D. 732)."

XIV. **Tz'ŭ-ên Chiao** 慈恩敎.—The School of Kindness and Compassion; also called Fa-hsiang Tsung 法相宗, The Law's Nature School. The original (mythical) founder was Tz'ŭ-shih Ju-lai 慈氏如來, a fictitious Buddha. The Chinese founder was T'ang Sêng 唐僧 (see *Sun Hou-tzŭ* 孫猴子), better known as Hsüan Tsang 玄奘. This school selected as its canonical work the *Wei-shih lun* 唯識論, attributed to Vasubandu (See *Shih-ch'in P'u-sa* 世親菩薩) and translated by Yüan Tsang 元奘 (*i.e.* Hsüan Tsang 玄奘). According to its doctrine, all things are unreal, and proceed from man's mind. A special kind of contemplation is built on this opinion. Much value is attached to kindness toward all beings, hence the name of the school.

XV. **Yü-chia Chiao** 瑜伽敎.—The Tantra School; also called Chên-yen Tsung 眞言宗, The School of True Words. Said to owe its origin to P'u-hsien 普賢 (Samanta-bhadra) (see *P'u-hsien Hsin-li* 普監心離), and Wu-chê 無著 (Asangha) (*q.v.*). The four great propagators of this system in China were: Chin-kang Chih 金㓇智 (Vajrabodhi) (see *Chin-kang Chih* 金剛智); Wu-wei Ch'an-shih 無畏禪師 (Subhakara) (*q.v.*); Pu K'ung 不空 (Amogha, *q.v.*); and I-hsing Ch'an-shih 一行禪師 (*q.v.*).

XVI. **Nan-shan Lü Tsung** 南山律宗.—The Vinaya School (Vinaya: one of the three great divisions of the Buddhist Canon, embracing all rules and discipline of monasteries). Founded by Tao-hsüan Lü-shih 道宣律師 (*q.v.*), who taught at Nan Shan 南山, the Southern (sacred) Mountain. The school sets the greatest value on discipline and the strict observance of old monastic regulations. The monks dress in black. They have a large monastery at Pao-kai Shan 寶蓋山, E. of Nanking 南京. They take only two meals a day, in accordance with the ancient Hindu regulations, and are only allowed to drink tea. They observe their devotional ceremonies with great strictness.

XVII. Lien-shê Tsung 蓮社宗.—The Amidist School; also known as Ching-t'u Chiao 淨土教, The School of the Pure Land. This school arose with the belief in Amitabha and Kuan Yin 觀音, hence its name. It selected for its canonical books the *O-mi-t'o ching* 阿彌陀經, *Sutra of Amitabha,* and the *Wu-liang-shou ching* 無量壽經, *Sutra of Boundless Years.* It developed and popularized the idea of a Hsi T'ien 西天, Western Paradise, inconsistent with the doctrine of Nirvana, originally held by Buddhism; in other words, it promises immortality instead of annihilation.

The Ching-t'u 淨土 ("Pure Land") or Amidist School occupies a position of great prominence in the religious systems of both China and Japan, and inculcates the form of Buddhism which appeals most strongly to the Buddhist layman. It teaches salvation through faith in the god-Buddha Amitabha, and holds out the promise of a future life of unalloyed happiness in the Pure Land or Western Paradise, where Amitabha reigns in unending glory. (The convenient terms *Amidism* and *Amidist* are taken from the Japanese form—Amida—of the name Amitabha.)

Strictly speaking, this school is quite separate from—not to say antagonistic to—the other great schools of Buddhist thought. A Chinese writer justly observes that believers in the Pure Land doctrines do not belong either to the Ch'an 禪 school or to the Lü 律. But as a matter of fact we find nowadays that nearly every Ch'an 禪 monk is more or less of an Amidist; and most of the Ch'an 禪 monasteries—that is to say, a large proportion of the great monasteries now existing in China—are perfectly tolerant of the Pure Land teachings. Many enlightened Chinese Buddhists will declare that the Ch'an 禪 and Ching-t'u 淨土 teachings are not really inconsistent with one another, but that the Ch'an 禪 doctrines are to the educated Buddhist what the Amidist doctrines are to the ignorant. At the same time the fact must be admitted that the religion of the average Chinese layman has little in common with the religion of a highly-trained and perhaps mystically-minded Buddhist monk. The layman's creed—in China as in other countries—is a nebulous one. His religious conceptions are often crude, irrational, and superstitious; he is liable to mistake symbol for objective truth; and he is apt to assume that faith is a sufficient guarantee of historic fact.

The Pure Land, or Amidist, teachings have given rise to one phrase which may be said to sum up the hopes and beliefs of a very large part of Buddhist China—a phrase which is constantly on the lips of monks and laymen alike, is inscribed on the tablets and walls of countless temples, and is carved on the rocks and cliffs of a hundred caverned mountains. This is *Namo Omito-Fo* or simply O-mi-t'o Fo 阿彌陀佛, "Infinite-Buddha."

These words are nothing more than an invocation of the name of Amitabha, the most revered of the so-called Dhyani or "Meditation" Buddhas. L. de la V. Poussin doubts whether the terms Dhyanibuddha and Dhyanibodhisattva are actually used in the Sanskrit text, and whether Amitabha and the rest should not rather be described as "the five Buddhas" or "the five Jinas" (see Hastings, I, 94).—Johnston, *Buddhist China,* pp. 92-4.

The name of the school was changed, between A.D. 990-5, to Ching-hsing Shê 淨行社, by Hsing-ch'ang Lü-shih 省常律師 (*q.v.*).

Note.—An epitomized biography of each of the 197 deified monks belonging to the above seventeen Schools has been entered under his name (religious appellation) in the body of the dictionary, with a cross-reference showing his place in the School.

BUDDHOCHINGA or BUDDOJANG.—See *Fo-t'u-ch'êng* 佛圖澄.

BUDDOJANG.—See *Fo-t'u-ch'êng* 佛圖澄.

BUFFALO-HEAD SCHOOL.—See *Buddhist Schools,* I.

BUTCHERS, THE GOD OF.—See *Fan K'uei* 樊噲 and *Chang Fei* 張飛.

C

CAKRAVARTI.—See *Chakravarti*.

CALICO BAG, THE MONK WITH THE.—See *Pu-tai Ch'an-shih* 布袋禪師.

CANDLE MERCHANTS, THE PATRON DEITY OF.— See *Po Ssŭ* 波斯.

CARDINAL POINTS, THE SPIRIT OF THE FIVE.—See *Wu-fang Shên* 五方神 and *Shui Fu* 水府, C (2) (b) and C (2) (e).

CARPENTERS, THE GOD OF.—See *Lu Pan* 魯班.

CAVE OF THE GODS SECT, THE.—See *Buddhist Schools*, VII.

CAVE-HEAVENS.—See *Shih ta Tung-t'ien* 十大洞天.

CAVERNS, THE GODS OF.—"Every cave, whether on the mountain side or in the depths of the sea, has its presiding divinity" (Du Bose, p. 75).

CELESTIAL IMMORTAL WHO BRINGS CHILDREN, THE. See *Pi-hsia Yüan-chün* 碧霞元君.

CELESTIAL SPIRIT OF THE YEAR, THE.—See *T'ai Sui* 太歲.

CENTIPEDE SPIRIT, THE.—See *Wu-kung Ching* 蜈蚣精.

CHAKRAVARTI. *Shê-wei-ti-t'o* 舍衞抵陀.—*Lit.* a holy king, who turns the wheel. A military monarch and conqueror who governs part or the whole of a universe. A universal ruler.

CHAN HSIU. 詹秀 —The god of the star T'ien-ku 天孤. —See *T'ien-kang* 天罡.

CHAN-JAN TSUN-CHÊ 湛然尊者.—A deified Buddhist monk. Ranked eighth in Buddhist School, X (*q.v.*). A member of a literary family named Chi 戚. At the age of 17, he began his studies under Fang Yen 方巖, in Chêkiang 浙江. Trained in the traditional principles of Chih-kuan 止觀, Perfected Observation, a system invented by Chih-k'ai 智顗 (*q.v.*), and "purporting to free the mind from ignorance, the dust of the world, and the deceptive activity of the senses." Three years later, he became a disciple of Hsüan-lang Tsun-chê 玄郎尊者 (*q.v.*). "On the day of his arrival, this second teacher beheld him in a dream wearing the garb of a monk, and surrounded by two fiery wheels revolving in a large river. This vision inspired him with the idea of teaching him Perfected Observation, *Chih-kuan* 止觀, for the salvation of the living and the dead." At 38, when fully trained, he preached the doctrine unceasingly. Though thrice summoned to Court—by the Emperors Hsüan Tsung 玄宗 (A.D. 713-56) and Tai Tsung 代宗 (A.D. 763-80) of the T'ang 唐 dynasty —he yet remained in his monastery. At the close of his life he returned to Fu-lung 佛隴, where he died. Posthumous title: Yüan-t'ung Tsun-chê 圓通尊者, Accomplished and Perspicuous Monk.

CHAN TZŬ-CHIANG 展子江.—See *Hsüan-t'ien Shang-ti* 玄天上帝 and *Shih-êrh ting-chia Shên* 十二丁甲神.

CH'AN 禪 (formerly pronounced *Shan*).—The Meditative, or Contemplative School of Buddhism.—See *Ch'an-shih* 禪師 and *Buddhist Schools,* XII: *Ch'an Tsung* 禪宗.

CH'AN-SHIH 禪師. Sanskrit Jaina (now a special Hindu sect).—One of the three orders of Buddhist monks. *Ch'an* 禪, to sit abstractedly in contemplation as required by *dhyana; shih* 師, a master, a teacher. Hence the expression has become a term for Buddhist monks of the Contemplative School, or teachers of the Law.

"The other two orders of Buddhist monks are (1) *Lü-shih* 律師, or 'Disciplinists,' who go barefoot and follow rigidly the rules enjoined in the early ages of Buddhism, for the observance of all who entered on the ascetic life; (2) *Fa-shih* 法師, or those who perform the common duties of priests, engage in popular teaching, and study the literature of their religion. The word *ch'an* 禪 (in old Chinese, *jan* and *dan*), originally signifying 'resign,' had not the meaning to 'contemplate' (now its commonest sense), before the Buddhists adopted it to represent the Sanscrit term *dhyana*. The word in Chinese books is spelt in full *jan-na* 禪那, and is explained, 'to reform one's self by contemplation or quiet thought.' Perhaps an Eastern extension of the Jaina, or some lost sect, still existing in India, took place thus early. The marked difference between the Buddhism of Bodhidharma, and that already existing in China, requires some such supposition. These three orders still exist. The common priests met with in temples are not considered to deserve either denomination, but on the supposition that they fulfil their duties, they are *fa-shih* 法師. Distinguished priests are called *ch'an-shih* 禪師. The emperors till very recently have always been accustomed to give names to distinguished priests. The early translators were honoured with the title *San-tsang fa-shih* 三藏法師. In common cases the title *ch'an-shih* 禪師 is all that is appended to the new name given by the imperial favour to those who, from their learning and character, are supposed to deserve it" (Edkins, p. 129, n. 1).

"In the Monastery of Vast Felicity, Kuang-fu Ssŭ 廣福寺, at T'ai-hsing 泰興, Kiangsi 江西, there is a temple dedicated to a contemplative Buddhist monk, Ch'an-shih 禪師, who is widely honoured throughout the country. It was here that he became illumined. About the same time, a tiger devoured travellers and inhabitants of the country, situated at the foot of Ku-shan 孤山, Orphan Hill. The monk proceeded to his haunt, and ordered him to cease ravaging the place. The monster obeyed, and followed him like a little dog.

This monk is represented in monasteries clothed in flowing Buddhist cope, a vermillion mark on the forehead, and a tiger crouching at his feet.

The T'ai-hsing 泰興 and Ku-shan 孤山 monks erected a temple in memory of his marvellous feats.

Country-folks greatly frequent this temple, and beg the monk to grant rain in seasons of drought.

The ten monks that surround the image of Maitreya, Mi-lo Fo 彌勒佛, in the same temple, were former inmates of the Monastery.

Before the erection of the large and splendid monastery, which is still admired at the present day, the monks of the place were divided into ten groups, each under the control of its own abbot. When the new monastery was completed, they all joined to form a single community. The ten abbots who ruled the former small monasteries were canonized as saints, and their images surround that of Maitreya, Mi-lo Fo 彌勒佛. Incense is burnt daily in their honour.

This is an example of how these monks raise their various members to the honours of the altar, make them Buddhas, and present them to the people as divine beings. This case, but one of many, may be verified at the present day by anyone who visits the above temple" (Doré, VIII, 606-7).

CH'AN TSUNG 禪宗. —See *Buddhist Schools*, XII.

CHANG 張, THE GOD OF THE CONSTELLATION.— See *Wan Hsiu* 萬修 and *Hsieh Ting* 薛定.

CHANG 張, THE SPIRIT OF THE STAR.—See *Chang Hsien* 張仙.

CHANG-CHI 張機.—See *Shih Ming-i* 十明醫, i.

CHANG CH'I 張奇.—The god of the star Ti-yu 地佑.—See *Ti-sha* 地煞.

CHANG CHIH-HO 張志和.—See *Hsüan Chên-tzŭ* 玄眞子.

CHANG CHIH HSIUNG 張智雄.—The god of the star T'ien-hui 天慧.—See *T'ien-kang* 天罡.

CHANG FEI 張飛.—One of the Gods of Butchers. An assessor of Kuan Kung 關公. Born near Cho Chou 涿州, Chihli 直隸. A.D. 191-223. Was butcher to Liu Pei 劉備 (A.D. 162-223) and Kuan Kung 關公 (Kuan Yü 關羽, died A.D. 219), and later became an itinerant pork-seller. Described as being eight feet in height, with a panther's head, round sparkling eyes, a voice like thunder, and a swallow's chin (*San Kuo: Han* 三國漢.)—See also *Kuan Ti* 關帝, *Composite Deities,* and *Fan K'uei* 樊噲.

CHANG-FÊNG 張鳳.—The god of the star Tsuan-ku 鑽骨. One of Chou Wang's 紂王 officers at Lin-t'ung Kuan 臨潼關. Killed by his subaltern Hsiao Yin 蕭銀.

CHANG HSIEN 張仙.—The Purveyor of Children. The patron deity of child-bearing women. In the family sleeping-apartments in Chinese houses hang pictures of Chang Hsien 張仙, a white-faced, long-bearded man with a little boy by his side, and holding in his hand a bow and arrow, with which he is shooting the Heavenly Dog. The dog is the Dog-star, and if the "fate" of this family is under this star there will be no son, or the child will be short-lived. Chang Hsien 張仙 was worshipped under the Sung 宋 dynasty by women desirous of offspring. The introduction of this name into the Chinese pantheon is due to an incident in the history of Hua-jui Fu-jên 花蕊夫人, a name given to Lady Fei 費, concubine of Mêng Ch'ang 孟昶, the last ruler of the Later Shu 蜀 State, A.D. 935-65. When she was brought from Shu 蜀 to grace the harem of the founder of the Sung 宋 dynasty, in A.D. 960, she is said to have preserved secretly the portrait of her former lord, the prince of Shu 蜀, whose memory she passionately cherished. Jealously questioned by her new consort respecting her devotion to this picture, she declared it to be the representation of Chang Hsien 張仙, the divine being worshipped by women desirous of offspring.

No less than ten different opinions are recorded as to the origin of this god: He is (1) The "God of the Dream," *i.e.* the Spirit, seen in a dream by the Emperor Jên Tsung 仁宗 (A.D. 1023-64) of the Sung 宋 dynasty, of a handsome young man with an unusually white skin and black hair, carrying a bow in his hand. He said to the Emperor: "The star T'ien-kou 天狗, Heavenly Dog, in the heavens is hiding the sun and the moon, and on earth devouring small children. It is only my presence which keeps them at bay." On waking, the Emperor at once ordered the young man's portrait to be painted and exhibited, and from that time childless families would write the name Chang Hsien 張仙 on tablets and worship them. (2) The Spirit of the star Chang 張, supposed to preside over the kitchen of Heaven and to arrange the banquets given by the gods. (3) The portrait of Mêng Ch'ang 孟昶, King of Shu 蜀, who submitted to the Emperor T'ai Tsu 太祖 (A.D. 960-76) in A.D. 965 (*v. supra*). (4) The portrait of T'ai Tsung 太宗 (A.D. 627-50) of the T'ang 唐 dynasty—a variation of (2) *supra*. (5) The Spirit of Ssŭch'uan 四川, Chang Hsien 張仙, purveyor of children—another variation of (2) *supra*. (6) Chang Hsien 張仙 is Chang Yüan-hsiao 張遠霄 of Ssŭch'uan 四川, who one day met an old man, each of whose eyes had two eyeballs, carrying a bamboo cross-bow and three iron shot, which he offered to sell for three hundred strings of cash. Chang Yüan-hsiao 張遠霄 agreed without bargaining. The old man said to him: "My cross-bow has the virtue of driving away epidemics, and is a marvellous and precious weapon." The old man afterwards returned and bestowed on him the gift of immortality. (7) Chang Hsien 張仙 became a purveyor of children through a play on the words *Chang Kung chia-tan* 張弓挾彈; Chang, the archer, drawing the bow, "and *Chang Kung chia-tan* 張公加誕, Chang Kung increases the number of births": the one set of characters being gradually substituted for the other, and sacrifices offered to the bow-drawer as the propagator of childbirth. (8) A person, or representation, of the ancient ceremony in honour of Kao Mei 高謀, a Spirit prayed to by those desiring offspring. (9) Sha Mo-han 沙漠汗, son of Wei Shih-tsu 魏始祖. Posthumous name Wên Ti 文帝. Was a skilled hunter. (10) Yüan Jung-tsu 垣榮祖, a famous hunter of Pi-chou 邳州, Kiangsu 江蘇.

As it is considered undignified in China for persons of rank to exert themselves in any way, the duty of conveying the desired offspring to its destination devolves, in the case of male children, on Chang Hsien's 張仙 son, Chien-t'an 堅壇, and in the case of female children, on Sung-tzŭ Niang-niang 送子娘娘 (see *Pi-hsia Yüan-chun* 碧霞元君).

Erh Lang 二郎 (*q.v.*), also called by his own name Yang Chien 楊戩, is always represented with the celestial dog, because that transcendent animal obeys all his wishes. This is the same animal represented in the pictures of Chang Hsien 張仙. The god is armed with a bow and shoots an arrow at the monster, in order to prevent him from devouring newly-born children. See also *Kou Ching* 狗耕.

CHANG-HSIUNG TAO-JÊN 張雄道人.—The god of the constellation Lou 婁. Alternatively with Liu Lung 劉隆.

CHANG HUAN 張煥.—The god of the star Ti-ch'a 地察. —See *Ti-sha* 地煞.

CHANG KUEI-FANG 張桂芳.—The god of the star Sang-mên 喪門. A general in command of the troops at Ch'ing-lung Kuan 青龍關, who committed suicide during the siege of Hsi-ch'i 西岐.

CHANG K'UEI 張奎.—The god of the star Ch'i-sha 七殺. A superior general, commander-in-chief of Chou Wang's 紂王 armies at Min-ch'ih Hsien 澠池縣. When defeated, fled to the borders of the Yellow River, where he was slain by Wei T'o 韋馱.

CHANG KUNG-I 張公藝—The Model of the Heads of Families. A native of Tung-p'ing 東平, Shantung 山東, in whose very numerous family such complete harmony prevailed that the Emperor Kao Tsung 高宗 (A.D. 650-84) of the T'ang 唐 dynasty enquired of him his secret. To which he replied by writing the character *jên* 忍, patience, or forbearance, on a piece of paper and handing it to the Emperor, who understood and heartily congratulated him.

His qualities in maintaining domestic harmony caused him to be worshipped by later generations as the model of family chiefs. His image is seen in temples, as well as in private houses, and on them is written the character *jên* 忍 (or 刃) and Chang kung-i's 張公藝 portrait is drawn surrounded by eight others representing the eight generations of those who lived with him in such complete harmony.

CHANG-KUO LAO 張果老.—See *Pa Hsien* 八仙.

CHANG LAO 張老.—An Immortal of Liu-ho Hsien 六合縣, in Yang-chou 揚州.

CHANG LIANG 張良.—Honoured in many Taoist temples for his numerous martial feats. A historical personage, who died in 189 or 187 B.C. Famous for his part in assisting the Han 漢 dynasty against the Ch'in 秦. Became one of the Taoist Im-mortals.

CHANG LUNG 張龍.—See *Lung Wang* 龍王.

CHANG SAN-FÊNG 張三豐.—A Taoist who possessed a *Chü-pao p'ên* 聚寶盆, or cornucopia, and was deified as the Protecting Spirit of Riches. Name, Chang Chün-shih 張君實, or Chang Ch'üan-i 張全一. Nick names, Chang La-t'a 張邋遢,

Chang the filthy. A native of Kuang-ning Hsien 廣寧縣, Chin-chou 金州, Fêng-t'ien Fu 奉天府, Shêng-ching 盛京 (Liao-tung 遼東). He was sometimes called Yüan Yüan-tzŭ 元元子. Lived in the reign of the Emperor Hung Wu 洪武 (A.D. 1368-99) of the Ming 明 dynasty, and resided in the Ying-hsiang Kuan 迎祥觀 temple to the north-east of Ying-chou Fu 潁州府, Anhui 安徽. Temples in his honour are to be found in most of the provinces.

CHANG SHAN 張山.—The god of the star T'êng-shê 螣蛇. One of Chou Wang's 紂王 generals killed by Têng Chiu-kung 鄧九公 when besieging Hsi-ch'i 西岐.

CHANG SUI 張遂.—See *I-hsing Ch'an-shih* 一行禪師.

CHANG TA-TI 張大帝.—See *Tzŭ-shan Chang Ta-ti* 祠山 張大帝.

CHANG-TAN 張單 (Tzŭ-kuo 子郭).—See *Tsao Chün* 灶(竈)君.

CHANG TAO-LING 張道陵.—Also called Chang T'ien-shih 張天師. A descendant of Chang Liang 張良 in the eighth generation. Born at T'ien-mu Shan 天目山, Chêkiang 浙江, A.D. 35, in the reign of the Emperor Kuang Wu-ti 光武帝 (A.D. 25-58) of the Han 漢 dynasty. The *Shang yu lu* 尙友錄 gives his name as Fu Han 輔漢, and states that at the age of 7 years he understood the *Tao-tê ching* 道德西 geomancy, the mystery of the waters, and astronomy. "He was spiritual and temporal head of what constituted, for a time, a state within a state, in the hill country of western China. This organization was broken down and absorbed in the civil state in A.D. 215, when the enfeebled Han dynasty was on the verge of ruin" (Willoughly-Meade). He was the real founder of modern Taoism. He it was who gave it its present orientation and obtained for it its means of subsistence, first through his new mysterious alchemical and magic recipes for the preparation of the pills of immortality, and then especially by his invention of talismans for the cure of all sorts of sicknesses. The origin of the hereditary title of T'ien-shih 天師, Master of Heaven, is variously ascribed to the time of the Emperor T'ai-wu Ti 太武帝 (Shih Tsu 世祖) (A.D. 424-52) of the Pei Wei 北魏 dynasty, and to that of the Emperor Hsuan Tsung 玄宗 (A.D. 713-56) of the T'ang 唐 dynasty; but it was later changed more than once. The Yüan 元 dynasty called his descendants Chên-jên 眞人, Perfect Men (or Heroes), though the original title persisted among the people, and was used in that and after times in spite of the action of the Emperor T'ai Tsu 太祖 (A.D. 1368-99) of the Ming dynasty in abolishing it on the ground that "Heaven, the noblest of all beings, could have no teacher." In modern times, the festival of Chang Tao-ling 張 道 陵, or anniversary of his birth, is celebrated on the fifteenth day of the first moon. The title of Pope, usually given to him in books and conversation, is, in its Western sense, not rightly applicable to him or his descendants. The *Sou-shên chi* 搜 神 記 gives his birthplace as T'ien-mu Shan 天 目 山, Heaven's Eye Mountain, in Lin-an Hsien 臨 安 縣, Hang-chou Fu 杭 州 府, Chêkiang 浙 江, but the *Shên-hsien chuan* 神 仙 傳 states that he was a native of P'ei 沛, a small kingdom situated to the N.W. of Nan-hsiu Chou 南 秀 州, Fêng-yang Fu 鳳 陽 府, Anhui 安 徽. A noted scholar, he one day exclaimed: "What can literature do to prolong life?" and thereafter devoted his studies to alchemy and the preparation of the drug of immortality, having taken up his abode on Pei-mang Shan 北 邙 山, Mount Pei-mang 北 邙, to the N. of Ho-nan Fu 河 南 府, the capital of Honan 河 南. He refused the invitations of the Emperors Chang Ti 章 帝 (A.D. 76-89) and Ho Ti 和 帝 (A.D. 89-106) to the Court, and after visiting the various famous mountains, reached those around Hsing-an Hsien 興 安 縣, Kiangsi 江 西, and descended thence to the Yün-chin Tung 雲 錦 洞, a cave of the Immortals. He there continued his studies of alchemy for three years, and at length succeeded in effecting the alliance between the blue dragon and the white tiger (the Taoist alchemical formula), wherefrom he was able to make the pill of immortality. Having eaten this, though then 60 years of age, his face assumed the appearance of youth. Besides this, he received as a divine gift a mysterious book, containing recipes for spiritualization, changing form and appearance at will, and casting out devils and goblins. Afterwards he left Kiangsi 江 西 for Ssŭch'uan 四 川, and settled on the high Yün T'ai 雲 臺, Cloud Plateau, in Ts'ang-ch'i Hsien 蒼 溪 縣, Pao-ning Fu 保 寧 府. From this elevated place he ascended to Heaven, leaving as a legacy to his children a mysterious book, a collection of talismans, his seal, and his magic sword. This is said to have taken place in A.D. 157, which would make him 123 years old.

His own son was named Chang Hêng 張 衡, his grandson Chang Lu 張 魯, and his great-grandson Chang Shêng 張 盛. The latter took up his abode on Lung-hu Shan 龍 虎 山, in Kuei-ch'i Hsien 貴 溪 縣, Kuang-hsin Fu 廣 信 府, Kiangsi 江 西. The heir of the family in direct line has from generation to generation retained the title of Chên-jên 眞 人, Perfect Man.

The account in the *Shên-hsien chuan* 神 仙 傳 varies some of the details (besides that concerning his birthplace) as follows: His parents being poor agriculturists, he could not obtain the funds necessary to carry on his experiments. Having heard that the Ssŭch'uanese were simple and credulous, he proceeded thither and took up his abode on Ho-ming Shan 鶴 鳴 山, Mount Ho-ming, in Ta-i Hsien 大 邑 縣, a dependency of Chiung-chou 邛 州. He there composed a book of recipes in twenty-four chapters. A celestial messenger, with a large retinue, appeared to him, seated in a golden chariot and his followers mounted on tigers and dragons. He announced himself as Chu Hsia-shih 桂 下 史 or Lao-tzŭ 老 子 or Tung-hai Hsiao-t'ung 東 海 小 童, the "Youth of the Eastern Sea." He disclosed to Chang Tao-ling 張 道 陵 the secrets for healing all sicknesses. Thereby he almost immediately gained great influence over the people, who named him Master, his disciples numbering tens of thousands. These being too many for the control of one man, he established a hierarchy of inferior chiefs, who carried out his instructions to requisition rice, fuel, utensils, etc., from the people, and set them to repair roads, build bridges, etc., the penalty for refusal being the infliction of sickness of one kind or another. Thus he acquired great power, the simple country-folk believing that he had been sent by Heaven to carry out these works.

One of his methods was to order anyone afflicted with a malady to write down all the faults he had committed during his life and plunge into a river or lake holding the paper in his hands, and swear in the presence of the Spirits not to err again in the future. The people were thus persuaded that sicknesses were caused by sin, and were ashamed to commit the same faults again. The whole district thus became regenerated.

From these practices Chang Tao-ling 張 道 陵 derived vast profits. For treating a case of sickness he demanded five bushels of rice. Thence the nickname Mi-tsei 米 賊, Rice-thief, given him by the inhabitants of the province.

Having thus obtained the means of purchasing the required materials, he set about his alchemical task of making the pill of immortality. This accomplished, he ate only one-half, not wishing to ascend to Heaven all at once, and preferring to divide himself into one or more beings. One of these took recreation in a boat on the lake in front of his dwelling. His other personality entertained his visitors in the house. He told them that though they could not, like him, renounce the world, they could nevertheless, by following his example in regulating his life and his family, obtain the privilege of eating enough of the medicine to prolong their lives for several centuries. As to the crucible in which Huang-ti 黃 帝 had prepared the drink of immortality, he said he had given it to his disciple Wang Ch'ang 王 長. Later, another man would arrive from Eastern lands on the seventh day of the first moon who would bring it for his use, and he drew his portrait and showed it to them. On the day indicated Chao Shêng 趙 昇 arrived from the East, and Chang Tao-ling 張 道 陵 led all his three hundred disciples to the highest peak of the Yün T'ai 雲 臺. Below them they saw a peach-tree growing near a pointed rock, stretching out its branches like arms above a fathomless abyss. It was a large tree, covered with ripe fruit. Chang said to his disciples: "I will communicate a spiritual formula to the one among you who will dare to gather the fruit of that tree." They all leaned over to look, but each declared the feat to be impossible. Chao Shêng 趙昇 alone had the courage to rush out to the point of the rock and up the tree stretching out into space. With firm foot he stood and gathered the peaches, placing them in the folds of his cloak, as many as it would hold, but when he wished to climb back up the precipitous slope, his hands slipped on the smooth rock, and all his attempts were in vain. Accordingly, he threw the peaches, three hundred and two in all, one by one up to Chang Tao-ling 張道陵, who distributed them. Each disciple ate one, as also did Chang 張, who reserved the remaining one for Chao Shêng 趙昇, whom he helped to climb up again. To do this Chang 張 extended his arm to a length of thirty feet, all present marvelling at the miracle. After Chao 趙 had eaten his peach, Chang 張 stood on the edge of the precipice, and said with a laugh: "Chao Shêng 趙昇 was brave enough to climb out to that tree and his foot never tripped. I too will make the attempt. If I succeed I will have a big peach as a reward." Having spoken thus, he leapt into space, and alighted in the branches of the peach-tree. Wang Ch'ang 王長 and Chao Shêng 趙昇 also jumped into the tree and stood one on each side of him. There Chang 張 communicated to them the mysterious formula. Three days later they returned to their homes; then, having made final arrangements, they repaired once more to the mountain peak, whence, in the presence of the other disciples, who followed them with their eyes until they had completely disappeared from view, all three ascended to Heaven in broad daylight (Doré, IX).

Edkins (pp. 389-91) gives the popular version of the legend as follows: "In the latter part of the second century, this Pope of the Tauists, if he may be so called, was engaged in the province now called Si-ch'wen [Ssŭch'uan 四川] in the Ho-ming Shan [鶴鳴山] Mountain, . . . in manipulating the 'elixir of the dragon and tiger,' *lung-hu-tan* [龍虎丹]. He met a spirit who said, 'In the Pe-sung [Pei Sung 北嵩] mountain is a stone house where may be found writings of the three emperors and a liturgical book. By getting these you may ascend to heaven, if you pass through the course of discipline which they enjoin.' He dug and found them. By means of them he was able to fly, to hear distant sounds, and to leave his body. Lau-kiün [Lao Chün 老君] then came down to him on the night of the feast of lanterns, and ordered him to subdue the demons of the 'Shu country' Si-ch'wen [Ssŭch'uan 四川], in order to confer blessings on humanity. Lau-kiün gave him a powerful and secret 'charm' (*lu*) [籙], a 'liturgy' (*king*) [*ching* 經], a 'composition in verse or measured prose' (*kiue*) [*chüeh* 絕], a 'sword' (*kien*) [*chien* 劍], and a 'seal' (*yin*) [印]. After going through a thousand days of discipline, and receiving instructions from a certain goddess called Yü-nü [玉女], who taught him to walk about among the stars, he proceeded to fight with the king of the demons, to divide mountains and seas, and to command the wind and thunder to come and go. All the demons fled before him, leaving not a trace behind of their retreating footsteps. On account of the prodigious slaughter of demons by this hero, the wind and thunder were reduced to subjection, and various divinities came with eager haste to acknowledge their faults. In nine years he gained the power to ascend to heaven and prostrate himself before the first in rank of the Three Pure Ones. A temple in Ch'êng-tu [成 都] is said to have been the place where Lau-kiün discoursed to Chang Tau-ling. He afterwards went eastward, and settled his residence on the mountain Lung-hu Shan [龍 虎 山], where his descendants have ever since resided in possession of great honour and emolument, as his hereditary representatives. The present [1893] occupant of the patriarchate had to fly at the time of the T'ai-p'ing [太 平] rebellion, and the temple where he resides was partially destroyed," but repaired in that year.

Since the Han 漢 dynasty, "the Taoist fraternity have held their headquarters in the province of Kiangsi 江 西, and a succession of high priests or chief devil-quellers have exercised some sort of authority over the Taoist 'clergy' down to modern times." Pictures of Chang Tao-ling 張 道 陵 are "issued under their rules for practising magic, showing him as an old bearded man of forbidding aspect, riding on a tiger. His functions were very similar to those of the equally or even more popular Chung K'uei 鍾 馗" (Willoughby-Meade).

The name of Chang Tao-ling 張 道 陵, the Heavenly Teacher, is a household word in China. He is on earth the Vice-regent of Yü Ti 玉 帝, the Pearly Emperor, in Heaven, and the Commander-in-Chief of the hosts of Taoism. He, the chief of the wizards, the "true [i.e. ideal] man," as he is called, wields an immense spiritual influence throughout the land. The present (1932) pope boasts of an unbroken line for sixty-three generations. His family obtained possession of Lung-hu Shan 龍 虎 山, the Dragon-tiger Mountain, in Kiangsi 江 西, about A.D. 1000. "This personage," says a pre-Republican writer, "assumes a state which mimics the imperial. He confers buttons like an emperor. Priests come to him from various cities and temples to receive promotion, whom he invests with titles and presents with seals of office" (Du Bose).

His estates were confiscated by the Republican government on the ground that he was spreading superstition among the people.

For variations of details regarding the career of Chang Tao-ling 張 道 陵, see Doré, IX, 531-4; for a resumé of the Taoist legends according to the Chinese historical books, *ibid.* pp. 534-6; and for the accounts in the *San-kuo chih* 三 國 志, *ibid.* pp. 536-40.

CHANG T'IEN-SHIH 張 天 師. — See *Chang Tao-ling* 張 道 陵.

The Chang T'ien-shih 張 天 師 myth can be traced back to the Sung 宋 dynasty, when a Taoist priest by the name of Chang 張 claimed to be able to perform miracles with his amulets. His long finger nails are handed down from generation to generation, and used by his descendants to write amulets. The amulets, written with red ink on yellow paper, can heal all kinds of malady when taken by the patients. According to popular belief the present Chang T'ien-shih 張 天 師 has lost his power of divination, because the finger nails of the Great Taoist Priest somehow or other have been missed by the Chang 張 family at Lung-hu Shan 龍 虎 山.

CHANG WÊN-T'UNG 張 文 通.—See *Hsüan-t'ien Shang-ti* 玄 天 上 帝, and *Shih-êrh ting-cha Shên* 十 二 丁 甲 神.

CHANG YA-TZǓ 張 亞 子.—See *Wên Ch'ang* 文 昌.

CHANG YÜAN-HSIAO 張 遠 霄.—See *Chang Hsien* 張 仙.

CHANG YÜAN-SHUAI 張 元 帥.—Generalissimo Chang 張. Son of Chang Kuei 張 珪 and Huang Shih 黄 氏. Born in A.D. 703 at Ning-hai 寧 海, Shantung 山 東. Before giving him birth his mother dreamt she saw the Spirit Chin-chia 金 甲 (*q.v.*), and so gave him the name T'u 徒, Disciple or Follower. In physical beauty and his fine beard he resembles Wang Ling-kuan 王 靈 官 (*q.v.*). Of keen intellect, he became an honoured and just administrator, and an epidemic of smallpox spared his district. Consequently the people built a temple in his honour, and Yü Ti 玉 帝 bestowed on him the title of Prompt Revenger of Injustice, with the Superintendency of Epidemics and Protection of Children from Smallpox. He is one of the male protectors against that disease—one of the Gods of smallpox—and his image is to be seen in numerous temples.—See *Tou Shên* 痘 神.

CH'ANG-CHUNG CH'AN-SHIH 嘗 忠 禪 師 (62nd generation).—A deified Buddhist monk. Ranked fifty-first in Buddhist School, VI (*q.v.*). Studied at Hsiao Shan 小 山, Small Hill, and spent three years at the Shao-lin Ssǔ 少 林 寺, Few Forests Monastery, where he taught for twenty years without once leaving the monastery. Died A.D. 1588, aged 75.

CH'ANG-ÊRH HO-SHANG 長 耳 和 尚.—The Long-eared Monk. Family name Ch'ên 陳. Monastic name Hsing-hsiu 行 修. His mother, who lived at Ch'üan-nan 泉 南, dreamed that she swallowed the sun, and on waking was trembling with fear, and forthwith gave birth to the child. He had long ears reaching down to his shoulders. Until 7 years of age he could not speak. Later, having improved, he entered the Wa-kuan Ssǔ 瓦 棺 寺, Earthenware-coffin Monastery, at Chin-ling 金 陵 (modern Nanking

南 京). He was gifted, like so many of these apotheosized monks, with great power over animals, and throughout his life performed extraordinary feats. The King of Wu-yüeh 吳越 (comprising. modern Chêkiang 浙江, Kiangsu 江蘇, and territory extending to the P'o-yang 鄱陽 Lake), A.D. 250, to whom he had been sent as an adviser, treated him as an incarnation of Jan-têng Fo 燃燈佛, Dipamkara. The Sung dynasty (A.D. 960-1280) conferred on him the posthumous title of Tsung-hui Ta-shih 宗慧大師, Revered and Intelligent Preceptor.

CH'ANG-ÊRH TING-KUANG HSIEN 長耳定光仙.—The Long-eared Fix-light Immortal. Deserted his master T'ung-t'ien Chiao-chu 通天敎主, when the latter was conquered by Amida, and took the side of Wu Wang 武王 (1121-1114 B.C.). Buddhas having long ears, his name became a synonym for fugitive.

CH'ANG HAO 常昊.—The god of the star Tao-chên 刀砧. The transcendent serpent, a genie of Mei Shan 梅山. Commanded Chou Wang's 紂王 troops at Mêng-ching 孟津. Was slain by Yang Chien 楊戩 who, transformed into a huge centipede, bit through his neck.—See also Shê Wang 蛇王.

CH'ANG-JUN CH'AN-SHIH 嘗潤禪師 (62nd generation).— A deified Buddhist monk. Ranked fiftieth in Buddhist School, VI (q.v.). Family name Wang 王. A native of Chin-hsien 進賢, in Nan-ch'ang Fu 南昌府, Kiangsi 江西. Studied first under Ta-fang Lien-kung 大方蓮公, and later at Hsiao Shan 小山, Small Hill. Died A.D. 1585.

CH'ANG-MEI SÊNG 長眉僧.—See Lo-han 羅漢.

CH'ANG Ô 嫦娥.—She stole from her husband, Hou I 后羿, the drug of immortality given him by Hsi Wang-mu 西王母, and fled to the moon. She dwells there in a beautiful palace, and has become the Goddess of the Moon. She is the same as Hêng Ô 姮娥, the name being changed because it was the tabooed personal name of the Emperors Mu Tsung 穆宗 of the T'ang 唐 dynasty and Chên Tsung 眞宗 of the Sung 宋 dynasty.—See Hou I 后羿 and Shên I 神羿.

CH'ANG TSAI 嘗宰.—See Spleen, The Gods of the.

CH'ANG YANG 菖陽.—A saintly Buddhist monk. Fifth century A.D. Reborn in the Hsiao 蕭 family by order of Sakya-muni. One of those invited to the annual banquet of the gods.— See Hsi Wang-mu 西王母.

CH'ANG YÜ-CH'UN 常遇春.—An assessor of Kuan Kung 關公.—See Kuan Ti 關帝.

CH'ANG YÜAN 長源.—See *Shui Fu* 水府, D (1).

CHAO CH'I 趙啟.—The God of the star T'ien-shê 天敝. A royal censor. Died a devoted victim to the salvation of the kingdom, in the reign of the Emperor Jên Tsung 仁宗 (A.D. 1023-64) of the Sung 宋 dynasty.

CHAO FA-SHIH 黎法師.—A saintly Buddhist monk. One of those invited to the annual banquet of the gods.—See *Hsi Wang-mu* 西王母.

CHAO FÊNG 朝風.—See *Lung Wang* 龍王.

CHAO HUNG 晁悶.—See *Shui Fu* 水府, C (1) (d).

CHAO KUNG-MING 趙公明.—Worshipped by merchants in general.—See *Ministries: Finance,* and *Ts'ai Shên* 財神.

CHAO KUNG-MING HSÜAN-T'AN CHÊN-CHÜN 趙公明玄壇眞君.—See *Ts'ai Shên* 財神.

CHAO LEI 趙累.—A commissariat officer in Kuan Kung's 關公 army.—See *Kuan Yü* 關羽.

CHAO PAI-KAO 趙白高.—The god of the constellation Kuei 鬼. Alternatively with Wang Pa 王霸.

CHAO PING 趙丙.—See *Wu Tou* 五斗.

CHAO SAN-NIANG 趙三娘.—The Goddess of Wig-sellers. Her husband Ts'ai Pai-chieh 蔡伯喈, a scholar who had married an imperial princess, being kept from home by many pressing duties, his parents and wife lived in poverty. The wife by working procured fair nourishment for the parents, she herself living on husks. When they discovered this, they insisted on subsisting on the same fare, but died in consequence.

Having no money wherewith to buy coffins, she cut off her long hair and sold it. But when the news of this reached her husband, she was in a dilemma, as she could not appear before him with a shaven head. She, however, managed to procure some hair which she made into a wig, and so was able to preserve her dignity on her husband's arrival.

She is worshipped by sellers of false hair and by wig-makers.

CHAO SHÊNG 趙昇.—The god of the star Yang-jên 羊刃. One of Têng Chiu-kung's 鄧九公 officers, who joined him in siding with Chiang Tzǔ-ya 姜子牙.

CHAO T'ÊNG-K'ANG 托滕康.—The God of the Bowels. His designation is Tao Huan 道邅. His body is two and four-tenths inches high, and of a yellowish-red colour.—*Yün chi ch'i ch'ien* 雲笈七籤.

CHAO-TSUNG-JÊN CH'AN-SHIH 朝宗忍禪師 (68th generation).—A deified Buddhist monk. Ranked fifty-third in Buddhist School, III (*q.v.*). A native of Ch'ang-chou 常州, Kiangsu 江蘇. Studied under Yüan-wu Ch'an-shih 圓悟禪師 (*q.v.*) at Ching-shan 徑山. Later, he started his own school at Pao-hua Ssǔ 寶華寺, Precious Flower Mountain, Kiangsi 江西.

CHAO TZǓ-JÊN 趙子任.—See *Hsüan-t'ien Shang-ti* 玄天上帝 and *Shih-êrh ting-chia Shên* 十二丁甲神.

CHAO YÜN 趙雲.—An assessor of Kuan Kung 關公.—See *Kuan Ti* 關帝.

CH'AO FU 巢父.—See *Lo-han* 羅漢.

CH'AO LEI 晁雷.—See *Wu Tou* 五斗.

CH'AO-PAO CH'AN-SHIH 超寶禪師 (70th generation).—A deified Buddhist monk. Ranked sixty-fifth in Buddhist School, III (*q.v.*). Family name Liu 劉. A native of Lü-ling 廬陵, in Yü-chang 豫章, Kiangsi 江西. Taught from A.D. 1697-9 at T'ien-mu Shan 天目山, Heavenly-eye Mountain. Later, he lived in seclusion at Huo-mai An 活埋庵, Huo-mai Convent, and died there in A.D. 1709, aged 75. His tomb is on T'ien-mu Shan 天目山.

CH'AO T'IEN 晁天.—The god of the star Sui-p'o 歲破. Deserted from Chou Wang's 紂王 to Wu Wang's 武王 side in the Yin-Chou 殷周 wars.

CH'Ê K'UN 車坤.—The god of the star Ti-hui 地慧.—See *Ti-sha* 地煞.

CH'Ê-TI FU-JÊN 微地夫人.—The goddess of the star Yüeh-k'uei 月魁. Wife of general Tou Jung 寶榮. Killed at Yu-hun Kuan 遊魂關 by the genie Mu T'o 木吒.

CHÊN 軫, THE GOD OF THE CONSTELLATION.—See *Liu Chih* 劉直 and *Hu Tao-yüan* 胡道元.

CHÊN CHI 眞寂.—A saintly Buddhist monk. Seventh century. One of those invited to the annual banquet of the gods (see *Hsi Wang-mu* 西王母). Sometimes called the seventh patriarch of the South, his first teacher, Chih Ch'êng 至誠, being called the seventh patriarch of the North (see *Patriarchs*).

CHÊN JÊN 眞人.—Perfect or Ideal Beings. The second class of deified mortals. They dwell in the second, or Upper Azure,

45

CHÊN JÊN

(Shang Ch'ing 上清) Heaven of Ling-pao T'ien-tsun 靈寶天尊 (*q.v.*). They are "ideal men" who have disciplined themselves in Taoist mysticism, and attained perfect rule over themselves and over nature. On entering the priesthood, a Taoist relinquishes his given name and is called Chên Jên 眞人, in the same way that a Buddhist is called Sêng 僧, and a nun, Ni 尼. Chên Jên 眞人 or Tsu Shih 祖師 is the title given to Taoist gods, that given to Buddhist gods being P'u-sa 菩薩, and to Confucianist gods, Shên Ling 神靈. See also *Shêng Jên* and *Hsien Jên*.

CHÊN KUO-JÊN 陳[陣]果仁.—See *Chung-yu Wu-lieh Ta-ti* 忠佑武烈大帝.

CHÊN SHÊN 疹神.—The Spirit of Measles. A specialist attached to the celestial Ministry of Medicine. An Assistant to his mother, Tou-shên Niang-niang 痘神娘娘 (*q.v.*). *Chên* 疹 is the more serious of two kinds of measles distinguished by the Chinese, which attacks adults as well as children.—See *Sha Shên* 痧神 and *T'ien I-yüan* 天醫院.

CHÊN-SHÊN CH'AN-SHIH 振深禪師 (47th generation). —A deified Buddhist monk. Ranked thirty-fourth in Buddhist School, VI (*q.v.*). Family name Hsia 夏. A native of Shou-ch'un Fu 壽春府, Anhui 安徽. At 14 years of age, he entered the Ling-yen Ssŭ 靈巖寺, Spiritual Cliff Monastery, at Su-chou (Soochow) 蘇州, Kiangsu 江蘇, and studied under Ching-chao Ch'an-shih 淨照禪師. He afterwards withdrew to the Pao-shan Ssŭ 包山寺, Precious-hill Monastery, where he died. His tomb is to the rear of the monastery.

CHÊN WU 眞武.—See *Hsüan-t'ien Shang-ti* 玄天上帝.

CHÊN-YEN TSUNG 眞言宗.—See *Buddhist Schools*, XV.

CHÊN YÜ-NÜ 眞玉女.—See *Shui Fu* 水府, D (2) (h).

CHÊN-YÜAN HSIEN 鎭元仙.—An Immortal who lived as a hermit on Wan-shou Shan 萬壽山, Longevity Mountain, at Hsi-t'u 西土. His elder brother was T'ai-i Huang-jên 泰壹皇人 (*q.v.*). Having been taught magic by the master Yü-ch'ên Ta-fa-shih 玉晨大法師, he went to his brother at O-mei Shan 峩嵋山, and listened to the lectures he delivered in the Pai-yü Lou 白玉樓, White-jade Tower (Temple). The two were among the guests invited to the P'an-t'ao Hui 蟠桃會 (*q.v.*), Flat-Peach Gathering, which implies that they were Immortals.

CH'ÊN 陳 OF KU-T'IEN 古田, THE LADY.—See *Pi-hsia Yüan-chün* 碧霞元君.

CH'ÊN CHI-CHÊNG 陳季貞.—The god of the star Ssŭ-ch'i 死炁. A commander in the army of the feudatory prince Su Hu 蘇護, Governor of Chi Chou 冀州, Chihli 直隸.

CH'ÊN CHI-CHÊNG 陳繼貞.—The god of the star Mieh-mo 滅沒. Slain during the Yin-Chou 殷周 wars. Also the god of the star Ti-k'uei 地魁.—See *Ti-sha* 地煞.

CH'ÊN CHI-TS'UNG 辰祭從.—See *Tou Mu* 斗母.

CH'ÊN CH'I 陳奇.—See *Hêng Ha êrh chiang* 哼哈二將.

CH'ÊN CHIU-KUNG 陳九公.—See *Ministries: Finance.*

CH'ÊN CHÜN 陳俊.—The god of the constellation Pi 畢. Alternatively with Chin Shêng-yang 金繩陽.

CH'ÊN FU-JÊN 陳夫人.—See *Pi-hsia Yüan-chün* 碧霞元君.

CH'ÊN HSÜN 陳奢 —See *Shui Fu* 水府, D (1) (b).

CH'ÊN K'AN 陳坎.—The god of the star T'ien-kuei 天貴. —See *T'ien-kang* 天罡.

CH'ÊN KÊNG 陳庚.—The god of the star Sui-sha 歲殺. An officer of the advance-guard in Chou Wang's 紂王 armies at San-shan Kuan 三山關. Slain at Hsi-ch'i 西岐 by Huang T'ien-hua 黃天化.—See also *Wên Pu* 瘟部.

CH'ÊN MÊNG-KÊNG 陳夢庚.—The god of the star Ti-kou 地狗.—See *Ti-sha* 地煞.

CH'ÊN Ô 晨莩.—See *Pi-hsia Yüan-chün* 碧霞元君.

CH'ÊN T'IEN-CHÜN 陳天君.—See *Chu T'ien-chün* 朱天君.

CH'ÊN T'UNG 陳桐.—The god of the star T'ien-lo 天羅. An officer of the royal army in the Yin-Chou 殷周 wars. Slain by Huang T'ien-hua 黃天化.

CH'ÊN-WU 陳梧.—The god of the star Yüeh-hsing 月刑. Slain by general Huang Fei-hu 黃飛虎 during the latter's successful assault on Ch'uan-yün Kuan 穿雲關.

CH'ÊN YÜAN 陳元.—The god of the star Ti-wei 地微.—See *Ti-sha* 地煞.

CHÊNG-CH'UAN CH'AN-SHIH 正傳禪師 (66th generation).—A deified Buddhist monk. Ranked forty-fourth in Buddhist School, III (*q.v.*). Family name Lü 呂. A native of Li-yang 溧陽, Kiangsu 江蘇. His teacher was Tê-pao Ch'an-shih 德寶禪師 (*q.v.*), and he spent his whole life at the Lung-ch'ih Ssŭ 龍池寺 Dragon-pool Monastery.

CHÊNG CH'UN 鄭椿.—The god of the star Fou-ch'ên 浮沉. Fought on the side of the Chou 周 under general Chang Kuei 張奎. Was slain by Huang Fei-hu 黃飛虎 at the battle of Min-ch'ih Hsien 澠池縣.

CHÊNG LUN 鄭倫.—See *Hêng Ha êrh chiang* 哼哈二將.

CHÊNG SAN-KUNG 鄭三公.—A patron deity of fishermen. A fisherman of Kiangsu 江蘇 who with Hou Erh-kung 侯二公 and Kêng Ch'i-kung 耿七公 formed a sworn fraternity and fished together in a branch of the Chiang 江. One day they saw a yellow rock protruding above the water. A spirit appeared and informed them that it was made of gold. Finding it in spite of all their efforts too heavy to remove, they prayed to Buddha, promising to build him a temple in exchange for his assistance, whereupon the rock immediately became light and was easily transported to their house. The temple was built near Su-chou (Soochow) 蘇州, and called Hsüan-miao Kuan 玄妙觀, The Temple of the Prodigy. The images of the three fishermen, placed therein, are worshipped as patron deities of fishermen.

CHÊNG T'IEN-CHÜN 鄭天君.—See *Chu T'ien-chün* 朱天君.

CHÊNG YÜAN-HO 鄭元和.—The God of Strolling Singers. A poor scholar who sang in the streets for a living and later became a *chuang-yüan* 狀元, Palace Graduate (*optimus*).

CHÊNG-YÜAN TAO-JÊN 鄭元道人.—The god of the constellation Nü 女. Alternatively with Ching Tan 景丹.

CH'ÊNG HUANG 城隍.—The God of Ramparts and Ditches. The City God. The Celestial Mandarin. Every fortified city or town in China is surrounded by a wall, *ch'êng* 城, composed usually of two battlemented walls, the space between which is filled with earth. This earth is dug from the ground outside, making a ditch, or *huang* 隍 running parallel with the *ch'êng* 城. The Ch'êng Huang 城隍 is the spiritual official of the city or town. Each of the sixteen hundred cities has its city god; also the one hundred great market towns each claim a local god, and not a few of the million villages have their village gods. All the numerous Ch'êng Huang 城隍 constitute a celestial Ministry of Justice, presided over by a Ch'êng Huang 城隍 -in-chief.

The origin of the worship of the Ch'êng Huang 城隍 dates back to the time of the Emperor Yao 堯 (2357-2255 B.C.), who instituted a sacrifice called Pa Cha 八 蜡 (*q.v.*), in honour of eight Spirits, of whom the seventh, Shui Yung 水 庸 (*lit.* City-water), had the meaning of, or corresponded to, the dyke and rampart known later as Ch'êng Huang 城隍. The city moat and wall protected the people and so were given this spirit or god, whom they thought lived in them. The later worship was a development of this ancient one. Afterwards human defenders of the people were deified to represent this spirit, and thus was produced the City God. Just as the magistrate protects the city from visible dangers, the god guards it from spiritual enemies and influences. His duties are multifarious; he acts as governor, judge, magistrate, tax-collector, and coroner, and has a retinue of secretaries and attendants. He controls the demons of his district, and can compel them to release his territory from drought and plagues. The magistrate is the *yang* 陽 official, the Ch'êng Huang 城 隍 is the *yin* 陰 official. They are of equal rank. The magistrate offers incense as a matter of courtesy. They are jointly responsible for the welfare of the city. In case the magistrate has a case he cannot manage, he goes to the Ch'êng Huang 城隍, who is able to see what he cannot, for help and council. In case the city needs rain the Ch'êng Huang's 城 隍 image is carried out, that he may see the need and help. Since the Sung 宋 dynasty, sacrifices have been offered to the Ch'êng Huang 城 隍 all over the country, though now and then some towns have adopted another or special god as their Ch'êng Huang 城 隍, such as Chou Hsin 周 新, adopted as the Ch'êng Huang 城 隍 of Hang-chou 杭 州, the capital of the Chêkiang 浙 江 Province. Concerning Chou Hsin 周 新, who had a "face of ice and iron," and was so much dreaded for his severity that old and young fled at his approach, it is related that once when he was trying a case a storm blew some leaves on to his table. In spite of diligent search the tree to which this kind of leaf belonged could not be found anywhere in the neighbourhood, but was eventually discovered in a Buddhist temple a long way off. The judge declared that the priests of this temple must be guilty of murder. By his order the tree was felled, and in its trunk was found the body of a woman who had been assassinated, and the priests were convicted of the murder.

Different opinions, however, exist as to the origin of the worship. Some regard it as unknown. Besides those who ascribe it to the time of the Emperor Yao 堯 (as above stated), others affirm that in ancient times there were only the gods of the soil and grains (see *Shê Chi* 社 稷), and that the worship of the Ch'êng Huang 城隍 began much later, namely, in the time of Ta Ti 大 帝 (A.D. 222-52) of the Wu 吳 Kingdom. On the other hand, mention is made of a temple to him existing in 240 B.C. But it is certain that the worship increased greatly under the T'ang 唐 dynasty and was general under the Sung 宋 dynasty.

The choice of a Ch'êng Huang 城 隍 is usually made by the people of some meritorious local warrior or civil official, but less meritorious ones, or even some guilty of criminal action or negligence, have sometimes been adopted.

They were prayed to for rain, victory over enemies, peace, cessation of epidemics, etc., and in case of all public or private misfortunes. Appointment to the office or change of incumbent had to be sanctioned by the head of the Taost religion, Chang Tao-ling 張道陵 (q.v.) or his successor.

Several Ch'êng Huang 城隍 have been honoured by various emperors with the title of Wang 王, King, Kung 公, Duke, Hou 侯, Marquis, or Po 伯, Count. Their status and the sacrifices offered have also varied from time to time.

The festival of the Ch'êng Huang 城隍 takes place annually on the twenty-first day of the fifth moon as well as on his birthday anniversary, the twenty-fifth day of the ninth moon. It is accompanied by processions of various types and representations (for detailed description see *Doré*, XI, pp. 884-9; and *Harlez,* p. 463, for description of the official sacrifices). He is also specially worshipped at New Year, and on the first and fifteenth days of each month, when sheep and pigs are sacrificed to him. Processions in his honour take place three times a year on the occasion of the great annual festivals.

The Ch'êng Huang 城隍 is represented in pictures and temple-images attended by two secretaries, two constables, Niu T'ou 牛頭, Ox-head, and Ma Mien 馬面, Horse-face, and also Pai lao-yeh 白老爺, Mr. (or Sir) White, and Hei lao-yeh 黑老爺, Mr. (or Sir) Black (q.q.v.), as well as a bevy of attendants of lower rank (see also *Ch'ien-li Yen* 千里眼, *Shun-fêng Êrh* 順風耳, and P'an Kuan 判官). It is their duty to keep him informed of what is happening in his domain. P'an Kuan 判官 assists him in judging the souls of those in his district. Representations in miniature of the punishments inflicted in the ten Hells (see *Hades*) are also placed in his temple.

In the temples an image of Madame Ch'êng Huang 城隍 is placed in a suite of rooms set apart for her and her attendants. These are behind the main hall containing the image of Ch'êng Huang 城隍 himself.—See also *Shê Chi* 社稷.

CH'ÊNG-KUAN KUO-SHIH 澄觀國師.—A deified Buddhist monk. Ranked fourth in Buddhist School, XI (q.v.). Secular name Hsia-hou Ta-hsiu 夏候大休. A native of Shan-yin 山陰, Shansi 山西. He was 9 feet 4 inches in height, and his hands descended below his knees. He had forty teeth in each jaw, and at night his eyes were luminous. In a single day, he could memorize 10,000 characters, grasp the meaning of seven lines at a time, and learn by heart a whole book during half a day's journey. At 7 years of age, he entered a Buddhist monastery. Expounded the *Hua-yen ching* 華嚴經 at Wu-t'ai Shan 五臺山. In A.D. 780, the Emperor Tê Tsung 德宗 (A.D. 780-805) of the T'ang 唐 dynasty conferred on him the honorary title of Ch'ing-liang Kuo-shih 清涼國師, Pure and Fresh State-Preceptor. He lived during the reigns of nine emperors, expounding the doctrine to seven of them. Died A.D. 838, aged 120. Buried at Chung-nan Shan 終南山. A tower erected over his remains bears the inscription Miao-chio 妙覺, Wonderful Intelligence.

A monk informed the Emperor that a golden-clad genie appeared to him at Ts'ung-ling 葱嶺, and brought two teeth of the deceased teacher, begging that they be publicly venerated. "This," says Kennelly, "is hero-worship, which in China differs little from that due to the divinity." The Emperor ordered the coffin to be opened; the features were fresh and undecayed, but two of the teeth were missing.

CH'ÊNG SAN-I 程三益.—The god of the star T'ien-ch'iao 天巧.—See *T'ien-kang* 天罡.

CH'ÊNG-TSAI 程宰.—See *Shui Fu* 水府, C (1) (c).

CH'ÊNG-YÜAN CH'AN-SHIH 澄遠禪師 (11st generation).—A deified Buddhist monk. Ranked seventeenth in Buddhist School, VI (*q.v.*). Generally called Shang-kuan 上官. A native of Mien-chu 綿竹, in Han-chou 漢州, Ssŭch'uan 四川. Studied under Wên-yen Ch'an-shih 文偃禪師 (*q.v.*). Taught in the Hsiang-lin Yüan 香林院, Fragrant Forest Monastery, at Ch'ing-ch'êng 青城, Shantung 山東. His tomb is on the mountain, near the same place.

CH'ÊNG-YÜAN TA-SHIH 承遠大師.—A deified Buddhist monk. Ranked third in Buddhist School, XVII (*q.v.*). The third ancestor. Nothing recorded as to name and birth-place. Studied under Chên-kung 真公 at Yü-ch'üan 玉泉, Kansu 甘肅, and afterwards taught at Hêng Shan 衡山, his school being attended by more than 10,000 disciples. Of unattractive mien, he lived at the foot of a rock, and cut firewood in a forest, carrying it back on his shoulders, exhorting the while all folk to invoke Buddha and repeat the name of O-mi-t'o Fo 阿彌陀佛, Amitabha. Throughout the country, the people engraved his prayer-formulas on stone, and built for him the Mi-t'o Ssŭ 彌陀寺, Mi-t'o Monastery. As the result of a vision, the monk Fa-chao Kuo-shih 法照國師 (*q.v.*) declared himself his disciple, and afterwards founded his own school, whence issued the propagators of Amidism, during the reign of the Emperor Tai Tsung 代宗 (A.D. 763-80) of the T'ang 唐 dynasty. It was Fa-chao Kuo-shih 法照國師 who brought his virtues to the notice of the Emperor, who erected for him the Pan-chou Tao-ch'ang 般舟道塲, Pan-chou Tao-ch'ang Monastery, the title Pan-chou 般舟 being therefore added to Ch'êng-yüan's 承遠 name. Died A.D. 802.

CHI 齊.—See *Tsao Chün* 灶(竈)君.

CHI 箕, THE GOD OF THE CONSTELLATION.—See *Fêng I* 馮異 and *Yang Chên* 楊眞.

CHI CH'ANG 紀昌.—The god of the star T'ien-chien 天間. —See *T'ien-kang* 天罡.

CHI HSIANG 奇相.—See *Shui Fu* 水府, D (1) (e).

CHI HSIN 紀信.—A celebrated *ch'êng-huang* 城隍, or city god (of Lan-chou 蘭州, Kansu 甘肅). Han 漢 dynasty, time of the Emperor Kao Tsu 高祖 (206-194 B.C.).

CHI K'ANG 季康.—The god of the star T'ien-kou 天狗. An officer of the advance-guard at San-shan Kuan 三山關 in the Yin-Chou 殷周 wars. Went over to Wu Wang 武王 together with his chief Hung Chin 洪錦.

CHI KUANG 姬光.—See *Patriarchs: Shên Kuang* 神光.

CHI-KUNG LAO-FO P'U-SA 蹩公老佛菩薩.—An incarnation of Ch'ang-mei Ch'an-shih 長眉禪師, the monk with the long eyebrows (Maha Kasyapa, first patriarch of Indian Buddhism) who is reckoned among the Eighteen Arhats. His family name was Chi 蹩, and his personal name Ts'un-chên 存眞. His incarnation took place at Shui-chi 水吉, a village of Ou-ning 甌寧, in Fukien 福建. From his early years, he practised Buddhist abstinence, and devoted himself especially to Kuan Yin 觀音, who one night appeared to him in a dream, touched his head, and made him a Buddha. Thenceforth a cloud appeared suspended above his head, and followed him wherever he went.

He lived for several years in the house of Ts'êng Kung-chin 曾公瑾, working and living in his own way, unmindful of popular opinion. As he laboured in the fields, everybody was astonished at the cloud floating above his head. When his outdoor work was over, he would make straw sandals, which he hung on a tree for the poor to take. These good deeds obtained for him the affection of the people, who addressed him as Chi-kung 蹩公, Mr. Chi 蹩, instead of using his personal name. He was treated with respect by Ts'êng Kung-chin 曾公瑾, but a jealous maid-servant tried to make him break his vows by mixing fish and shrimps with his food. Chi-kung 蹩公, however, threw these into the water, when they immediately came to life again, and swam away.

He showed his transcendent power by ridding the inhabitants of the district around Lien-yüan Shan 蓮源山, Lien-yüan Hill, of a dangerous snake, which had devoured so many people that their bones formed quite a large mound. Two genii of the hill, P'an-t'u Wang 槃荼王 and Chu Pang-shih 朱邦式, declared themselves his disciples, and came with 500 heavenly warriors to help him to defeat the snake. The latter was assisted by other redoubtable superhuman monsters, and the two genii were very hard pressed in the battle. Chi-kung 蟄公, however, tossed into the air a paper fan he held in his hand, and forthwith it was changed into an enormous centipede, which fell upon the snake and bit it in the abdomen. The vanquished monster begged Chi-kung 蟄公 to spare its life, and its request was granted, but he gave the centipede to the Genie of the hill, telling him to hang it on his armour as a protection from his enemy the snake. He then commanded the serpent to keep itself hidden in a hole in the ground, and cease from molesting the people. From that time snakes have lived in holes in the ground.

Chi-kung 蟄公 also showed his skill by indicating places where water could be found, when he was living with Ts'êng Kung-chin 曾公蓳 in a large temple erected by the latter at the foot of the mountain.

When the time came for Chi-kung 蟄公 to enter Nirvana, he took a bath and said to the maid-servant: "When your master returns, tell him to wash in the same water which I have used." She, however, out of spite allowed the water to run out on to the floor.

When Ts'êng 曾 returned, hearing what had happened, he quickly rolled in what water still remained on the floor, and the same day set out for Hsi T'ien 西天, the Western Paradise, accompanied by the monk.

This took place on the tenth day of the sixth month, A.D. 1152. Chi-kung 蟄公 had thus lived 365 years. This number corresponding to the number of days in the year, he was called Lao Fo 老佛, the Old Buddha.

He has been worshipped from the Sung 宋 dynasty to the present time, and though in 1188 the S. Sung 宋 Emperor Hsiao Tsung 孝宗 (A.D. 1163-90) bestowed upon him the posthumous title of Ting-ying Tung-hsüeh Ta-shih 定應通學大師, Steady and Intelligent Master, and the Mongol emperors gave him further titles, he is generally known as Chi-kung Lao-Fo P'u-sa 蟄公老佛菩薩, Old Buddha Chi-kung.

CHI SHIH 姬氏.—See *Patriarchs: Shên Kuang* 神光.

CHI SHU-CHI 姬叔吉.—The god of the star Ti-kang 地鋼. Brother of Chou Wang 紂王.

CHI SHU-CH'IEN 姬叔乾.—The god of the star T'ien-kuei 天貴. Twelfth son of Wên Wang 文王. Killed by Fêng-lin 風林, when defending Hsi-ch'i 西岐.

CHI SHU-I 姬叔義.—The god of the star Tu-huo 獨火.

CHI SHU K'UN 姬叔坤.— The god of the star Fei-lien 飛廉. Apotheosized after dying on the field of battle. No further details recorded regarding him.

CHI SHU-LI 姬叔禮.—The god of the star T'ai-shên 胎神. Slain during the Yin-Chou 殷周 wars.

CHI SHU-MING 姬叔明.—See *Wu Tou* 五斗.

CHI SHU-SHÊNG 姬叔昇.—See *Wu Tou* 五斗.

CHI SHU-TÊ 姬叔德.—The god of the star Tsê-lung 宅龍. An officer of Wu Wang's 武王 clan. Canonized after the successful close of the war.

CHI-TIEN TSU-SHIH 濟顛祖師.—The Dissolute Preceptor —a name given him from the dissolute life he led when, as a fully-qualified monk, he retired to Ching-tz'ŭ 淨慈. Family name Li 李, his father being Li Mao-ch'un 李茂春, a relative of one of the Sung 宋 emperors of the South. The son's personal name was Tao-chi 道濟. His mother bore him after dreaming that the sun had entered her womb. At the age of 18 he entered the Ling-yin Ssŭ 靈隱寺, Monastery of Mystic Retirement. He died when a little more than 60 years of age, and is said to have reappeared at the foot of the Lu-ho 魯和 Tower soon after his burial. In spite of his irregular life, he is honoured in several monasteries.

CHI TSUN 祭遵.—The god of the constellation Niu 牛. Alternatively with Li Hung 李弘.

CHI-TU 計都, THE GOD OF THE STAR.—See *Wang Pao* 王豹.

CHI-YEN CH'AN-SHIH 濟嵒禪師 (70th generation).—A deified Buddhist monk. Ranked sixty-sixth in Buddhist School, III (*q.v.*). Family name Kuo 郭. A native of Jên-ho 仁和, in Hang-chou (Hang-chow) 杭州 Prefecture. Studied under Fatsang Ch'an-shih 法藏禪師 (*q.v.*). Died in the Ling-yin Ssŭ 靈隱寺, Monastery of Mystic Retirement, A.D. 1670, and is buried near it.

CH'I 棄.—See *Shê Chi* 社稷.

CH'I CH'ÊNG 成成.—The god of the star T'ien-shou 天壽. —See *T'ien-kang* 天罡.

CH'I CHI-KUANG 戚繼光.—An assessor of Kuang Kung 關公.—See *Kuan Yü* 關羽.   CH'I-PAO

CH'I KU-TZŬ 七姑子.—The Seven Young Ladies. Supposed to be either seven *shan-kuei* 山鬼, mountain spirits, or seven terrestrial spirits, or the seven ladies Hsin 莘. Their origin is unknown. In temples to the Seven Ladies at T'ingchou Fu 汀州府, Fukien 福建, they are represented as seven women described as *shan-kuei* 山鬼, mountain demons. Mention is made of an old temple to the Seven Ladies, regarded as terrestrial spirits, in the same district (then called Hsing-chiang 鄞江). Temples to them are very numerous throughout the prefecture.

The Seven Ladies Hsin 莘, whose tomb exists in the village of Ming-ch'i 明溪, Kuei-hua Hsien 歸化縣, Fukien 福建, lived in the time of the Wu Tai 五代, Five Dynasties (A.D. 907-60). They are prayed to in times of droughts, floods, epidemics, etc. A temple was erected to them by the villagers. The identity of these Seven with the Ch'i Ku-tzŭ 七姑子 has, however, been questioned. See also *Composite Deities*.

CH'I KUNG 齋公.—The god of the star Ti-ch'ang 地猖. —See *Ti-sha* 地煞.

CH'I-KUNG TZŬ 戚公子.—The son of Duke Ch'i 戚. A divinity of the Ming 明 dynasty. Period A.D. 1522-67. Worshipped in numerous temples. His apotheosis was due to his disobeying, when he was in command of the advance guard of the troops, his father Ch'i Chi-kuang's 戚繼光 order that no one, under pain of death, was to look back. His father had him put to death on the spot. The people, after his father's victory, mourned the death of his son, and erected a temple to his memory, honouring him with the title of Son of Duke Ch'i (as above).— See also *Composite Deities*.

CH'I LIEN-SHAN 祁連山.—See *T'ien Shan* 天山.

CH'I PAI 歧伯.—The Chinese Aesculapius. The legendary minister of Huang Ti 黃帝.

CH'I-PAO 七寶.—The Seven Precious Things (*Saptaratna*). (1). *Chin-lun* 金輪, the golden wheel or disc. (2). *Yü-nü* 玉女, lovely (gemmous), female consorts. (3). *Ma* 馬, horses. (4). *Hsiang* 象, elephants. (5). *Chu-tsang shên* 主藏神, divine guardians of the treasury. (6). *Chu-ping ch'ên* 主兵臣, ministers in command of armies. (7). *Ju-i chu* 如意珠, the wonder-working pearl.

The latter, *Ju-i* 如意, *lit.* "as you wish," a fabulous pearl, in China, is a symbol of Buddhism, and gods bear it in their hands. It is also found in the hands of Taoist deities, and seems to have been borrowed from Buddhism.—See also Eitel, p. 122; Laufer, *A Study in Chinese Archaeology and Religion*, p. 339. Eitel explains *Sapta Ratna* (Sa-pu-ta lo-ti-na 薩不荅羅的捺 or Ch'i Pao 七寶) as follows: (1) The insignia of a Tchakravartti, *viz.* a *tchakra* (lit. a wheel; symbol) of gold, concubines, horses, elephants, guardian spirits, soldiers and servants, the mani. (2) Another series of seven treasures, not necessarily belonging to a Tchakravartti . . . *Suvarna* (gold), *Rŭpya* (silver), *Vaidurya* (lapis lazuli), *Sphatika* (white pearl), *Rohitamukti* (ruby or red pearl), *As'magarbha* (amber, coral, diamond, or emerald), and *Musâragalva* (amethyst, agate, or coral). For the Seven Gems of Lamaism, see Waddell, pp. 389-90.

CH'I-PIN CH'AN-SHIH 契斌禪師 (58th generation).—A deified Buddhist monk. Ranked forty-sixth in Buddhist School, VI (*q.v.*). Family name Wang 王. A native of Po-yi 亳邑, Honan 河南. Died A.D. 1452. Buried at Shao-li 少林.

CH'I PO 岐伯.—A demi-god. Born at Pei-ti 北地. A descendant of I Ch'i-shih 伊祁氏, the ancient king. Taught by Chiu Tai-chi 僦貸季. A member of the commission appointed by Huang Ti 黄帝 (*q.v.*) to continue and complete the labours of Shên Nung 神農 on natural history and the medicinal properties of plants. Huang Ti 黄帝 gave him the title of T'ien-shih 天師, Celestial Master. Ch'i Po 岐伯 and Kuei-ku Tzŭ 鬼谷子 were close friends of Huang Ti 黄帝, who was fond of conversing with them on astronomy and geology. These two men drew up a memorandum of eighty-one answers to difficult questions in anatomy, which was deposited in the palace archives with the medical treatises of Fu Hsi 伏羲 and Shên Nung 神農.—See *T'ien I-yüan* 天醫院.

CH'I 溪 RIVERS, THE SPIRIT OF THE TWELVE.—See *Shui Fu* 水府, D (2) (h).

CH'I-SHA 七殺, THE GOD OF THE STAR.—See *Chang Kuei* 張奎.

CH'I-T'IEN TA-SHÊNG 齊天大聖.—See *Sun Hou-tzŭ* 猻猴子.

CHIA CH'ÊN SHÊN 甲辰神.—See *Shih-êrh ting-chia Shên* 十二丁甲神.

CHIA CH'ÊNG 買成.—The god of the star Ti-yung 地勇. —See *Ti-sha* 地煞.

CHIA CH'ING 戞清.—The god of the star Ti-yu 地㓇. —See *Ti-sha* 地煞.

CHIA FU 賈 復.—The god of the constellation Shih 氏.   CHIA-LAN
Alternatively with Kao-ping Tao-jên 高 丙 道 人.

CHIA-HSÜ SHÊN 甲 戌 神.—See *Shih-êrh ting-chia Shên* 十二丁甲 神.

CHIA-LAN 伽 藍.—*Chia (ch'ieh)=Ka.* A generic name= *Ga-lam,* (derived from a Sanscrit term meaning park of the priesthood or dwelling of priests) for tutelary gods or protectors of monasteries (*Sangarama*). "They comprise some of the higher Chinese divinities, such as the God of War, the Four Maharajas, or Heavenly Kings, Veda, and even others who are not genuinely Buddhistic, as Confucius, Wên Ch'ang 文 昌, and the Kitchen God (of Taoist origin) who is found in every Buddhist monastery" (Edkins).

They are generally placed in the outer hall or near the front entrance of the temple. They discharge the duties of gatekeepers and menials. Whilst their main duty is that of protecting the temple or monastery, that of Wei T'o 韋 馱 (*q.v.*), placed just behind them but in front of the main outer hall, is the protection of the religion.

Chia-lan 伽 藍 was one of Buddha's disciples. Sakyamuni, the Buddha of the present *kalpa,* sometimes sends Chia-lan 伽 藍 to invite the gods and goddesses to a banquet in the celestial temple of Thunder, Lei-yin Ssǔ 雷 音 寺.

The Chia-lan 伽 藍 are represented sitting or standing, and with three eyes, the third being in the middle of the forehead.

The following legend (from the seventh century A.D.) shows how Shên Hsiu 神 秀, the Divine Graduate, became a *chia-lan* 伽 藍. He was the sixth patriarch of Buddhism, and a contemporary of Hui Nêng 慧 能 (*q.v.*). After obtaining his *hsiu-ts'ai* 秀 才, or B.A., degree he became a Buddhist monk.

Having been initiated into the Buddhist ritual by his teacher Hung Jên 弘 忍, he was at Tang-yang 當 陽, near Yü-ch'üan Shan 玉 泉 山, on his way to Huang-mei Shan 黄 梅 山, when a large snake, coming out of the brushwood, advanced toward him. But as he showed no fear, the snake did not attack him. On the following day, he discovered a large quantity of gold on the spot, and with it built a large monastery. To do this, he had to demolish the shrine of Kuan Kung 關 公, the Duke of War. This enraged the inhabitants of the locality, and Kuan Kung 關 公 appeared out of a dark cloud, mounted on his war-horse. Brandishing his sword, he demanded of Shên Hsiu 神 秀 the reason for the demolition of his shrine. Shên Hsiu 神 秀, overawed by these threats, restored the shrine, but as a punishment for his crime was condemned by Kuan Kung 關 公 to be the gate-keeper and guardian (*chia-lan* 伽 藍) for the rest of his life. On his appointment, the word *shên* 神 was added to his literary degree, and he thus became *Shên Hsiu* 神 秀, "the divine graduate." Owing to this legend, Shên Hsiu 神秀 came to be regarded as a *chia-lan* 伽藍, and guardian of Buddhist temples.

CHIA-LI-CHIA 迦理迦 .—See *Lo-han* 羅漢.

CHIA-LOU-LO 迦樓羅.—A dragon-king.—See *Lung Wang* 龍王.

CHIA-SHÊN SHÊN 甲申神.—See *Shih-êrh ting-chia Shên* 十二丁甲神.

CHIA SHIH 賈氏.—The goddess of the star Mao-tuan 貌端. Wife of Huang Fei-hu 黃飛虎. Died in escaping from the evil designs of the tyrant Chou 紂.

CHIA 甲 SPIRIT, THE AVATAR OF A.—See *Wên Yüan-shuai* 溫元帥.

CHIA-TZŬ SHÊN 甲子神.—See *Shih-êrh ting-chia Shên* 十二丁甲神.

CHIA-WU SHÊN 甲午神.—See *Shih-êrh ting-chia Shên* 十二丁甲神.

CHIA-YEH MO-T'ÊNG 迦葉摩滕.—Kasyapa Matanga. A saintly Hindu Buddhist monk. Arrived in China during the reign of the Emperor Ming Ti 明帝 (A.D. 58-76) of the Hou Han 後漢, After Han, dynasty. One of those invited to the annual banquet of the gods (see *Hsi Wang-mu* 西王母).

CHIA-YIN SHÊN 甲寅神.—See *Shih-êrh ting-chia Shên* 十二丁甲神.

CHIANG CHUNG 姜忠.—The god of the star Ti-chên 地鎮. —See *Ti-sha* 地煞.

CHIANG 姜, THE EMPRESS.—The goddess of the star T'ai-yin 太陰 (the moon). The first wife of the tyrant Chou 紂, who put her to a cruel death for refusing to implicate her father in a palace plot.

CHIANG HSIANG-KUNG 蔣相公.—Chiang 蔣, a native of Hang-chou 杭州, Chêkiang 浙江, in the time of the Emperor Kao Tsung 高宗 (A.D. 1127-63) of the Sung 宋 dynasty. Was apotheosized for his charity to the poor.—See *Composite Deities*.

CHIANG-HSIUNG 蔣雄.—See *Wu Yo* 五嶽.

CHIANG HUAN-CH'U 姜桓楚.—The god of the star Ti-ch'ê 帝車. A feudatory grand prince of Shantung 山東. Cut into mincemeat by the tyrant Chou Wang 紂王.

CHIANG NAN PO 江南伯.—See *Shui Fu* 水府, D (1) (e).

CHIANG T'AI-KUNG 姜太公.—See *Chiang Tzŭ-ya* 姜子牙.

CHIANG TZŬ-WÊN 蔣子文.—A celebrated T'u Ti 土地 (*q.v.*).

CHIANG TZŬ-YA 姜子牙.—In the wars which resulted in the overthrow of the tyrant Chou Wang 紂王 and his dynasty and the establishment of the great Chou 周 dynasty, the most influential generalissimo was Chiang Tzŭ-ya 姜子牙. His family name was Chiang 姜, and his own name Shang 尚, but owing to his descent from one of the ministers of the ancient King Yao 堯, whose heirs owned the fief of Lü 呂, the family came to be called by that name, and he himself was known as Lü-shang 呂尚. His honorific title was T'ai-kung Wang 太公望, Hope of T'ai-kung, given him (1129 B.C.) by Wên Wang 文王, who recognized in the person of Chiang Tzŭ-ya 姜子牙 the wise minister whom his father T'ai-kung 太公 had caused him to expect before his death. He is said to have been born 1210 B.C. and died 1120 B.C. He is the most celebrated character in the "Book of Appointing Gods"; a distinguished warrior, and a counsellor to the chief of the West, "he wielded a valiant sword and slaughtered his enemies; he was, however, as magnanimous as he was brave, for he immediately made the foe weltering in his blood a god. In this way he is the god of Chinese gods. The account of his early exploits and heavenly deeds is perhaps the greatest book of marvels ever printed. His picture is pasted on the walls of houses, so that if an inauspicious word is spoken it will be powerless to injure the occupants. He is the pivot of Chinese mythology, and around him the celestial hosts revolve" (Du Bose, pp. 343-4).

Chiang Tzŭ-ya 姜子牙 was originally in the service of the tyrant Chou Wang 紂王, but transferred his services to the Chou 周 cause, and by his wonderful skill enabled that family finally to gain the victory. The decisive battle took place at Mu-yeh 牧野, situated to the south of Wei-hui Fu 衞輝府, in 1122 B.C. The soldiers of Yin 殷, 700,000 in number, were defeated, and Chou 紂, the tyrant, shut himself up in his magnificent palace, set it alight, and was burned alive with all his possessions. For this achievement Chiang Tzŭ-ya 姜子牙 was granted by Wu Wang 武王 the title of Father and Counsellor, and was appointed Prince of Ch'i 齊, with perpetual succession to his descendants.

The following legends (typical of those relating to the earlier periods of Chinese history) in which he was concerned are abridged from some of the numerous ones to be found in the *Fêng-shên yen-i* 封神演義.

After No-cha 哪吒 (*q.v.*), by means of his Heaven-and-earth Bracelet, had vanquished Fêng-lin 風林 (*q.v.*), a star-god and subordinate officer of Chang Kuei-fang 張桂芳 (*q.v.*), in spite of the black smoke-clouds which he blew out of his nostrils, the defeated warrior fled and sought the aid of his chief, who fought No-cha 哪吒 in some thirty to forty encounters without succeeding in dislodging him from his Wind-fire Wheel, which enabled him to move about rapidly and to perform prodigious feats, such as causing hosts of silver flying dragons like clouds of snow to descend upon his enemy. During one of these fights No-cha 哪吒 heard his name called three times, but paid no heed. Finally, with his Heaven-and-earth Bracelet he broke Chang Kuei-fang's 張桂芳 left arm, following this up by shooting out some dazzling rays of light which knocked him off his horse.

When he returned to the city to report his victory to Tzŭ-ya 子牙, the latter asked him if during the battle Kuei-fang 桂芳 had called his name. "Yes," replied No-cha 哪吒, "he called, but I took no heed of him." "When Kuei-fang 桂芳 calls," said Tzŭ-ya 子牙, "the *hun* 魂 and *p'o* 魄 (*anima* and *umbra*) become separated, and so the body falls apart." "But," replied No-cha 哪吒, "I had changed myself into a lotus-flower, which has neither *hun* 魂 nor *p'o* 魄, so he could not succeed in getting me off my magic wheel."

Tzŭ-ya 子牙, however, still uncertain in mind about the finality of No-cha's 哪吒 victories, went to consult Wu Wang 武王 (whose death had not yet taken place at this time). After the interview, Tzŭ-ya 子牙 informed Wu Wang 武王 of his wish to visit K'un-lun 昆崙 Mountain. Wu Wang 武王 warned him of the danger of leaving the kingdom with the enemy so near the the capital; but Tzŭ-ya 子牙 obtained his consent by saying he would only be absent three days at most. So he gave instructions regarding the defence to No-cha 哪吒, and went off in his spirit chariot to K'un-lun 昆崙. On his arrival at the Unicorn Precipice he was much enraptured with the beautiful scenery, the colours, flowers, trees, bridges, birds, deer, apes, blue lions, white elephants, etc., all of which seemed to make earth surpass heaven in loveliness.

From the Unicorn Precipice he went on to the Jade Palace of Abstraction. Here he was presented by Pai-hao T'ung-tzŭ 白鶴童子, White Crane Youth, at the Pa-kua T'ai 八卦台, Eight Diagrams Terrace, to Yüan-shih 元始. From him he received the List of Promotions to Immortals, which Nan-chi Hsien-wêng 南極仙翁, Immortal of the South Pole, had brought, and was told to go and erect a Fêng-shên T'ai 封神台, Spirits' Promotion Terrace, on which to exhibit it. Yüan-shih 元始 also warned him that if anyone called him while he was on the way he was to be most careful not to answer. On reaching the Unicorn Precipice on his way back, he had just begun to quicken his pace when he heard someone call "Chiang Tzŭ-ya 姜子牙!" This happened three times without his paying any heed. Then the voice was heard to say: "Now that you are Prime Minister how devoid of feeling and forgetful of bygone benefits you must be not to remember one who studied with you in the Jade Palace of Abstraction!" Tzŭ-ya 子牙 could not but turn his head and look. He then saw that it was Shên Kung-pao 申公豹. He said: "Brother, I did not know it was you who were calling me, and I did not heed you as Shih Tsun 始尊 told me on no account to reply." Shên Kung-pao 申公豹 said: "What is that you hold in your hand?" He told him it was the List of Promotions to Immortals, and that he was going to exhibit it on the Fêng-shên T'ai 封神台. Shên Kung-pao 申公豹 then tried to entice Tzŭ-ya 子牙 from his allegiance to Chou 周. Amongst Shên's 申 tactics was that of convincing Tzŭ-ya 子牙 of the superiority of the magical arts at the disposal of the supporters of Chou 紂. "You" he said, "can drain the sea, change the hills, and suchlike things, but what are those compared with my powers, who can take off my head, make it mount into space, travel 10,000,000 *li,* and return to my neck just as complete as before and able to speak? Burn your List of Promotions to Immortals and come with me." Tzŭ-ya 子牙, thinking that a head which could travel 10,000,000 *li* and be the same as before was exceedingly rare, said: "Brother, you take your head off, and if in reality it can do as you say, rise into space and return and be as before, I will be willing to burn the List of Promotions to Immortals and return with you to Chao-ko 朝歌, your capital." Shên Kung-pao 申公豹 said: "You will not go back on your word?" Tzŭ-ya 子牙 said: "When your elder brother has spoken, his word is as unchangeable as Mount T'ai 泰. How can there be any going back on my word?"

Shên Kung-pao 申公豹 then doffed his Taoist cap, seized his sword, with his left hand firmly grasped the blue thread binding his hair, and with his right cut off his head. His body did not fall down. He then took his head and threw it up into space. The head floated about, continuing to rise all the time. Tzŭ-ya 子牙 gazed with upturned face as it continued to rise, and was sorely puzzled. But the Ancient Immortal of the South Pole had kept a watch on the proceedings, seen Shên Kung-pao 申公豹 mount a tiger and follow Tzŭ-ya 子牙 to the Unicorn Precipice, and then the head floating in space. He said: "Tzŭ-ya 子牙 is a loyal and honest man; it looks as if he had been deceived by this charletan." So he ordered White Crane Youth to assume quickly the form of a crane, fetch Shên Kung-pao's 申公豹 head, and bring it to the Southern Seas. White Crane Youth acted accordingly and brought the head back to the Ancient Immortal.

Tzŭ-ya 子牙 was still gazing upwards when he felt a slap on his back and, turning round, saw that it was the Ancient Immortal of the South Pole. Tzŭ-ya 子牙 quickly asked: "My elder brother, why have you returned?" Hsien Wêng 仙翁 said: "You are a fool. Shên Kung-pao 申公豹 is a man of unholy practices. These few small tricks of his you take as realities. But if the head does not return to the neck within an hour and three-quarters the blood will coagulate and he will die. Shih Tsun 始尊 ordered you not to reply to anyone; why did you not hearken to his words? Even now there are armies coming to slay you. From the Jade Palace of Abstraction I saw you speaking together, and knew you had promised to burn the List of Promotions to Immortals. If you had done so, what would have been the result? So I ordered White Crane Youth to bring the head to the South Seas. After an hour and three-quarters Shên Kung-pao 申公豹 will be recompensed."

Tzŭ-ya 子牙 said: "My elder brother, since you know all you can pardon him. In the Taoist heart there is no place where mercy cannot be exercised. Remember the many years during which he has faithfully followed the Path." Eventually the Ancient Immortal was persuaded. But in the meantime Shên Kung-pao 申公豹, finding that his head did not return, became very much troubled in mind. In one hour and three-quarters the blood would stop flowing and he would die. But when Tzŭ-ya 子牙 implored the Ancient Immortal to save his life, the latter beckoned to White Crane Youth, who was flying about in space with the head in his beak, to let it drop. He did so, but when it reached the neck it was facing backward. Shên Kung-pao 申公豹 quickly put up his hand, took hold of his ear, and turned his head the right way round. He was then able to open his eyes, when he saw the Ancient Immortal of the South Pole. The latter arraigned him in a loud voice saying: "You as-good-as-dead charlatan, who by means of corrupt tricks try to deceive Tzŭ-ya 子牙 and make him burn the List of Immortals and help Chou 紂 against Chou 周—what do you mean by all this? You should be taken to the Jade Palace of Abstraction to be punished!"

Shên Kung-pao 申公豹, ashamed, could not reply; mounting his tiger, he made off; but as he left he hurled back a threat that the Chou 周 would yet have their white bones piled mountains high at Hsi-ch'i 西岐. However, Tzŭ-ya 子牙, carefully preserving the List of Promotions to Immortals, after many adventures succeeded in building the Fêng-shên T'ai 封神台 and posted the List on it. Having accomplished his mission, he returned in time to resist the capture of Hsi-ch'i 西岐 by Chang Kuei-fang 張桂芳, whose troops were defeated with great slaughter.

In another of the many conflicts between the two rival States Lao Tzŭ 老子 entered the battle, whereupon Ch'iung Hsiao 瓊霄, a goddess who fought for the House of Yin 殷, hurled into the air her gold scaly-dragon scissors. These floated about in empty space, opening and closing in a most ominous manner; but as they descended toward him, Lao Tzŭ 老子 merely waved the sleeve of his jacket and they fell into the sea and became absolutely motionless. Many similar tricks were used by the various contestants. The Gold Bushel of Chaotic Origin would be defeated by the Wind-Fire Sphere, and so on. Ch'iung Hsiao 瓊霄 resumed the attack with some magic two-edged swords, but was killed by a blow on the skull from White Crane Youth's Three-Precious Jade Sceptre, thrown at her by Lao Tzǔ's 老子 orders. Pi Hsiao 碧霄, her sister, attempted to avenge her death, but Yüan Shih 元始, producing from his sleeve a magical box, threw it up into the air and caught Pi Hsiao 碧霄 in it. When it was opened it was found that she had melted into blood and water.

After this Lao Tzǔ 老子 rallied many of the skilful spirits to help Chiang Tzǔ-ya 姜子牙 in his battle with Wên Chung 聞仲, providing them with the Ancient Immortal of the South Pole's Sand-blaster and an earth-conquering light which enabled them to travel a thousand *li* 里 in a day. From the hot sand used the contest became known as the Red Sand Battle. Jan Têng 燃燈, on P'êng-lai 蓬萊 Mountain, in consultation with Tzǔ-ya 子牙 also arranged the plan of battle.

The fight began with a challenge from the Ancient Immortal of the South Pole to Chang Shao 張紹. The latter, riding his deer, dashed into the fray, and aimed a terrific blow with his sword at Hsien Wêng's 仙翁 head, but White Crane Youth warded it off with his Three-Precious Sceptre. Chang 張 then produced a two-edged sword and renewed the attack, but, being disarmed, dismounted from his deer and, going on to the terrace, took up several handfuls of hot sand and threw them at Hsien Wêng 仙翁. The latter, however, easily fanned them away with his Five-fire Seven-feathers Fan, rendering them harmless. Chang 張 then fetched a whole bushel of the hot sand and scattered it over the enemy, but Hsien Wêng 仙翁 counteracted the menace by merely waving his fan. White Crane Youth struck Chang Shao 張紹 in the middle of the back with his jade sceptre, knocking him off his horse, and then despatched him with his two-edged sword.

After this battle Wu Wang 武王 was found to be already dead. Jan Têng 燃燈 on learning this ordered Lei Chên-tzǔ 雷震子 to take the corpse to Mount P'êng 蓬 and wash it. He then dissolved a pill in water and poured the solution into Wu Wang's 武王 mouth, whereupon he revived and was escorted back to his palace.

Preparations were then made for resuming the attack on Wên Chung 聞仲. While the latter was consulting with Ts'ai-yün Hsien-tzǔ 彩雲仙子 and Han Chih-hsien 菡芝仙, he all of a sudden heard the sound of the Chou 周 guns and the thunder of their troops. Wên Chung 聞仲, mounting his black unicorn, galloped like a whiff of smoke to meet Tzǔ-ya 子牙, but was stopped by blows from two silver hammers wielded by Huang T'ien-hua 黃天化. Han Chih-hsien 菡芝仙 came to Wên's 聞 aid, but was opposed by Pi Hsiang-yang 壁廂楊. Ts'ai-yün Hsien-tzǔ 彩雲仙子 dashed into the fray, but No-cha 哪吒 stepped on to his Wind-fire Wheel and opposed him. From all sides other Immortals joined in the terrific battle, which was a turmoil of rolling drums, flags brandished like flying clouds, long bows and cross-bows, iron armour and brass mail, striking whips and falling hammers, spears and swords, weapons cleaving mail and mail resisting weapons, lances piercing helmets, helmets diverting lances. In this fierce contest, while Tzŭ-ya 子牙 was fighting Wên Chung 閗仲, Han Chih-hsien 菡芝仙 released a black wind from his magic wind-bag, but he did not know that the Taoist Barge of Mercy (which transports departed souls to the Land of Bliss), sent by Kuan Yin 觀音, the Goddess of Mercy, had on board the Stop-wind Pearl, by which the black storm was immediately quelled. Thereupon Tzŭ-ya 子牙 quickly seized his Vanquish-spirits Whip and struck Han Chih-hsien 菡芝仙 right in the middle of the skull, so that the brain-fluid gushed forth and he died. No-cha 哪吒 then slew Ts'ai-yün Hsien-tzŭ 彩雲仙子 with a spear-thrust.

Thus the fierce fight went on, until finally Tzŭ-ya 子牙, under cover of night, attacked Wên Chung's 閗仲 troops simultaneously on all four sides. The noise of slaughter filled the air. Generals and rank and file, lanterns, torches, swords, spears, guns, and daggers were one confused melée; guns roared like thunder, heaven could scarcely be distinguished from earth, dragon flags and tiger banners waved like flashes of lightning, blood flowed like rivers, and corpses were piled mountains high.

Tzŭ-ya 子牙, having broken through seven lines of the enemy's ranks, forced his way into Wên Chung's 閗仲 camp. The latter mounted his unicorn, and brandishing his magic whip dashed to meet him. Tzŭ-ya 子牙 drew his sword and stopped his onrush, being aided by Lung Hsü-hu 龍鬚虎 casting a rain of hot stones on to the troops. In the midst of the fight Tzŭ-ya 子牙 brought out his great magic whip, and in spite of Wên Chung's 閗仲 efforts to avoid it succeeded in wounding him in the left arm. The enemy's troops were further assailed with more showers of hot stones thrown by Lung Hsü-hu 龍鬚虎. All was confusion, the Chou 周 troops fighting like dragons lashing their tails and pythons curling their bodies. To add to their disasters, the Chou 村 now saw flames rising behind the camp and knew that their provisions were being burned by Yang Chien 楊戩.

The Chou 村 armies, with gongs beating and drums rolling, advanced for a final effort, the slaughter being so great that even the devils wept and the spirits wailed. Wên Chung 閗仲 was eventually driven back seventy *li* 里 to Ch'i Shan 岐山, Ch'i Hill. His troops were on the point of death, and could do nothing but sigh and stumble along. He made for Peach-blossom Range, but as he approached it he saw a yellow banner hoisted and under it was Kuang Ch'êng-tzŭ 廣成子. Being prevented by him from escaping in that direction he again joined battle, but by use of red-hot sand, his two-edged sword and his Turn-heaven Seal Kuang Ch'êng-tzŭ 廣成子 put him to flight. He then made off toward the west, followed by Têng Chung 鄧仲. His only course was to try and make for Swallow Hill, which he reached after several days of weary marching. Here he saw another yellow banner flying, and Ch'ih Chung-tzŭ 池中子, who was standing under it, informed him that Jan Têng 然燈 had forbidden him to stop at Swallow Hill or to go through the Five Passes. This led to another pitched battle, Wên Chung 聞仲 using his magic whip and Ch'ih 池 his spiritual two-edged sword. After several bouts Ch'ih 池 brought out his *yin-yang* 陰陽 mirror, by use of which irresistible weapon Wên 聞 was finally driven to Yellow Flower Hill and Blue Dragon Pass, and so on from battle to battle, until he was drawn up to heaven from the top of Dead-dragon Mountain.

Chiang 姜 is worshipped as the God of Fishermen. Is said to have angled with a "straight hook and a grain of rice for bait" till he was eighty years of age, when he become the premier.

CHIAO-CH'ÊN-JU 憍陳如.—A saintly Hindu Buddhist monk. The Chinese characters are a translation from Sanskrit as given by Eitel. He was one of those invited to the annual banquet of the gods (see *Hsi Wang-mu* 西王母). A prince of Magadha, and maternal uncle of Sakyamuni, whose first disciple he became, together with four other companions.

CHIAO KO 膠鬲.—The god of the star Tsou-shu 奏書. A censor. Committed suicide after reproving the tyrant Chou Wang 紂王.

CHIAO KUAN 膠管.—One of the Gods of Bean-curd (*tou-fu* 荳腐) Sellers.—See also *Kuan Kung* 關公 and *Huai-nan Tzŭ* 淮南子.

CHIAO LUNG 焦龍.—The god of the star Ti-yin 地陰.—See *Ti-sha* 地煞.

CHIAO NÜ 嬌女.—The God of the Ear (*Chên-kao* 眞誥).—See also *K'ung Hsien* 空閒.

CHIEH HUO T'IEN-CHÜN 接火天君.—See *Huo Pu* 火部.

CHIEH-K'UNG 解空.—A saintly Buddhist monk who renounced the attainment of Nirvana for the happiness of becoming a Taoist Immortal. One of those invited to the annual banquet of the gods (see *Hsi Wang-mu* 西王母). Received Huai-nan Tzŭ 淮南子 and Yang Tê-tsu 楊德祖 in the Yün Kung 雲宮, Cloud Palace, and twice tried to poison Yang 楊 with golden pills. The latter thereupon told him he was not destined to become an Immortal and advised him to return to earth, which he did the next morning before sunrise.

65

CHIEH LIEN-CH'IAO 結連翹.—See *Shui Fu* 水府, C (2) (c).

CHIEH YEN 節菴.—See *Shih Ming-i* 十明醫, 5.

CH'IEH-CHO-NO CH'AN-SHIH 且搐訥禪師 (66th generation).—A deified Buddhist monk. Ranked sixty-ninth in Buddhist School, VI (*q.v.*). Family name Wang 王. A native of Hu-kuang 湖廣. Trained by [Jui-pai] Ming-hsüeh Ch'an-shih [瑞白] 明雪禪師 (*q.v.*). Settled at I-shan 義山, in Hu-kuang 湖廣, where he taught for several years. Died A.D. 1673. Buried on I Shan 義山.

CHIEN T'AN 堅譚.—The god of the constellation Wei 危. Alternatively with Hou T'ai-i 侯太乙.

CHIEN T'AN 堅壋.—See *Chang Hsien* 張仙.

CHIEN T'O 建馱.—See *Wei T'o* 韋它.

CHIEN-YÜAN CH'AN-SHIH 鑑源禪師.—A Buddhist monk whose birthplace is unknown. He is reputed to have been highly virtuous and to have occupied himself incessantly in explaining the *Hua-yen ching* 華嚴經 (see *T'ung-hsüan Ch'an-shih* 通玄禪師), which he called *The Monk's Manual*. After his death, the monks of the Po-li Shan 玻璃山, Vitreous Hill, Monastery, where he had spent his life, found that, owing to his influence, their annual supply of rice never diminished.

In connection with this monk, the *Sou-shên chi* 搜神記 relates that during the twenty-nine years from A.D. 713-42 a certain influential person named Chi Ning 冀寧, being convinced that the monks were deceiving the people, ordered that no lamps should be lit by the latter within ten miles. He then secretly ascended a hill, and kept watch throughout the night. On the third and many succeeding nights, hundreds of lanterns, projecting rays of light, precious pearls ten feet in diameter, luminous arcs, divine beings bathed in light, etc., appeared, and caused him to fall on his knees and repent of his incredulity.

Indian as well as Chinese monks were seen passing over a luminous bridge, and following them Chi Ning 冀寧 was led to the San-hsüeh 三學, Three Schools, Monastery. It was here that two fervent followers of Buddha, Wei Liang 韋爾 and K'ang Kao 康臯 used to come every three months to celebrate the anniversary, known as *San-pai p'u-sa ta-chai* 三百菩薩大齋, on which three hundred divinities had been seen by the "lantern-gazing monk."

CH'IEN I 錢乙.—See *Shih Ming-i* 十明醫, 3.

CH'IEN-LI YEN, SHUN-FÊNG ÊRH 千里眼順風耳.—Thousand-*li* 里 Eye (Lynx-eye) and Following-wind Ear (Sharp-ear). The Transcendent Peach-tree and the Transcendent Pomegranate-tree. Two brothers named Kao Ming 高 明, Piercing Sight, and Kao Chio 高 覺, Keen Perception. When they arrived at Chao-ko 朝 歌, Fei Lien 蜚 廉 (*q.v.*) presented them to King Chou, Chou Wang 紂 王 (1154-1121 B.C.). On account of their martial bearing they found favour with this tyrant emperor, who appointed them generals, and sent them to serve with Generalissimo Yüan Hung 袁 洪 (who was a monkey which had taken human form) at Mêng-ching 孟 津.

Kao Ming 高 明 was very tall, with a blue face, flaming eyes, a large mouth, and prominent teeth like those of a rhinoceros.

Kao Chio 高 覺 had a greenish face and skin, two horns on his head, a red beard, and a large mouth with teeth shaped like swords.

One of their first encounters was with No-cha 哪 吒 (*q.v.*), who hurled at them his magic bracelet, which struck Kao Chio 高 覺 on the head, but did not leave even a scratch. When, however, he seized his fire-globe, the brothers thought it wiser to retreat.

Finding no means of conquering them, Yang Chien 楊 戩, Chiang Tzŭ-ya 姜 子 牙 and Li Ching 李 靖 took counsel together and decided to have recourse to Fu Hsi's 伏 羲 trigrams, and by smearing them with the blood of a fowl and a dog to destroy their spiritual power. This, however, failed, and, after further fruitless consultations, Yü-ting Chên-jên 玉 鼎 眞 人, Hero Jade-tripod, showed Yang Chien 楊 戩 how his object might have been accomplished. He informed them that one was a spiritual peach-tree, the other a spiritual pomegranate-tree, which had become spiritual beings and taken up their abode in the clay images of Lynx-eye and Sharp-ear in a temple dedicated to Huang Ti 皇 帝. He was to tell Chiang Tzŭ-ya 姜 子 牙 to have the roots of those trees torn up and burned, and the images destroyed. The soldiers were simultaneously to wave flags and beat tom-toms and drums to prevent Lynx-eye and Sharp-ear from seeing or hearing what was being done. While these operations were being carried out Lei Chên-tzŭ 雷 震 子 also attacked them with his troops.

Lynx-eye and Sharp-ear could neither see nor hear: the flags effectually screened the horizon and the infernal noise of the drums and tom-toms deadened all other sound. They did not know how to stop them.

The following night Yüan Hung 袁 洪 decided to take the camp of Chiang Tzŭ-ya 姜 子 牙 by assault, and sent the brothers in advance. They were, however, themselves surprised by Wu Wang's 武 王 officers, who surrounded them. Chiang Tzŭ-ya 姜 子 牙 then threw into the air his "devil-chaser" whip, which fell on the two scouts and cleft their skulls in twain.

CH'IEN PAO 錢保.—The god of the star T'ien-i 天醫. Killed by Têng Chiu-kung 鄧九公 at the siege of Hsi-ch'i 西岐.

CH'IEN WU-SU 錢武肅.—See *Wu Tou* 五斗.

CHIH CH'AN-SHIH 志禪師 (41st generation).—A deified Buddhist monk. Ranked sixteenth in Buddhist School, VI (*q.v.*). Nothing recorded concerning him, except that he taught at Hung-chou 洪州, Kueichou 貴州, in the T'ung-an Ssŭ 同安寺, United Peace Monastery.

CHIH-CHÊ KUO-SHIH 智者國師.—State Preceptor Chih-chê 智者. Family name Lou 婁. Personal name Tê-su 德素. A native of Wu-shang 烏傷, in Tung-yang Hsien 東陽縣, Chêkiang 浙江. An eccentric monk. At 17 years of age entered the Tung-shan Ssŭ 東山寺, East Hill Monastery, where he lived on pine-cone grains.

He performed many marvellous feats. Magpies and peacocks came to hear him expounding the Law, and at his funeral two cranes hovered in the air, uttering plaintive cries. The Emperor Wu Ti 武帝 (A.D. 502-50) of the Liang 梁 dynasty, conferred on him the honorary title of Chih-chê 智者, Enlightened.

CHIH-CHÊ TA-SHIH 智者大師.—A deified Buddhist monk. Ranked third in Buddhist School, X (*q.v.*). Family name Ch'ên Chih-k'ai 陳智顗. A native of Ching-chou 荆州, Hupei 湖北. At 18, studied in the Kuo-yüan Ssŭ 果願寺, Kuo-yüan Monastery; afterwards he removed to the monastery of Ta-su Shan 大蘇山, where Hui-Ssŭ Tsun-chê 慧思尊者 (*q.v.*) was teaching. "On seeing him arrive, the master exclaimed: 'Already in a previous existence, we studied together the *Fa-hua ching* 法華經 (*Lotus of the Good Law*) at Ling Shan 靈山 (Mystic Hill), and now behold we meet again!'" Both of these Buddhist teachers admit the doctrine of metempsychosis, holding that the soul must travel through creation, until it is sufficiently purified to enter the Impersonal Absolute. Pantheism and metempsychosis are the basis of all Buddhistic philosophy and life (Monier Williams, *Buddhism*, p. 124).

Chih-k'ai 智顗 resided first at Nanking 南京, Kiangsu 江蘇, and afterwards, when advanced in years, removed to T'ien-t'ai 天台, Chêkiang 浙江, and settled there. He is called the Sage of T'ien-t'ai 天台, and held (but erroneously) to be the founder of the school. He used the *Prajna-paramita* and the *Saddharma-pundarika* in constructing his system. The Emperor Yang Ti 煬帝 (A.D. 605-17) of the Sui 隋 dynasty conferred on him the honorary title of Chih-chê 智者, Learned Monk, and thenceforth he was generally called Chih-chê Ta-shih 智者大師, the Learned Master. He was a copious and learned writer, twenty-two of his works having been included in the Canon. He died pronouncing the names of the San-tsun Ta-fo 三尊大佛, Three Great Buddhas. His posthumous title is Fa-k'ung Pao-chio Ling-hui Tsun-chê 法空寶覺靈慧尊者, Venerable Monk, who knew the Law and the Unreality of Things, of Superior Intelligence and Mystic Wisdom.

CHIH CH'ÊNG 至誠.—See *Chên Chi* 眞寂.

CHIH CH'IEN 支謙.—A saintly Buddhist monk. Third century A.D. A *upasaka,* or lay member of the Buddhist Brotherhood, who, without entering upon monastic life, observed the five chief rules of conduct. A native of Yüeh-shih Kuo 月氏國, the Yüeh-shih Kingdom, or country of the White Huns. Family name Yüeh 越. Surname Kung-ming 恭明. A linguist and voluminous translator. One of those invited to the annual banquet of the gods (see *Hsi Wang-mu* 西王母).

CHIH-HSÜAN CH'AN-SHIH 智玄禪師.—No details are recorded of the birth and early life of this monk. He arrived at Ch'ang-an 長安, the then capital of China, during the T'ang 唐 dynasty, at the beginning of the reign of I Tsung 懿宗 (A.D. 860-74).

The venerable monk Kanaka, Chia-no-chia Tsun-chê 迦諾迦尊者 was then in the city. He suffered from a terrible disease called *chia-mo-lo* 迦摩羅 (attributed to Mara, the Buddhist god of evil). Though everyone held aloof from him, Chih-hsüan 智玄 went to see him. Out of gratitude, the Kanaka said: "If any misfortune befall you, come to me at Ch'a-lung Shan 茶隴山 in P'êng Chou 彭州, Ssŭch'uan 四川. Two pine trees near the place will serve to guide you." He then left. Chih-hsüan 智玄 proceeded to An-kuo Ssŭ 安國寺, Peaceful Realm Monastery, where, in A.D. 861, he was visited by the Emperor, a fervent Buddhist, who bestowed upon him a valuable stool of fragrant wood and the honorary title of Wu-ta Kuo-shih 悟達國師, Intelligent and Shrewd Teacher of the Kingdom.

Soon after this, a curious ulcer resembling a human head and face broke out on his knee. Several doctors having failed to afford relief, he set out for Ssŭch'uan 四川. Having identified the place by the two pine trees, he proceeded in the direction of a vast temple, where he found Kanaka awaiting him. The next morning he informed the monk of his affliction, and was told by him to wash his knee every morning in a limpid stream which flowed at the foot of the hill. As he proceeded to do so, however, a human voice was heard saying: "Wait a moment. You have read in the history of the Western Han, Hsi Han 西漢 dynasty that Yüan Ang 袁盎 caused the death of Ch'ao Ts'o 鼂錯. Well, you are Yüan Ang 袁盎, and I am Ch'ao Ts'o 鼂錯. I am here to avenge myself on you. Your virtuous life prevented me doing so before, but since the Emperor has honoured you, you have fallen from grace. Now, however, Kanaka having advised you to wash your sore in the stream of the Saṇ-mei fa-shui 三昧法水, Samadi Law (the highest pitch of abstract ecstatic meditation, a sort of terrestrial Nirvana), this prevents me from taking vengeance on you."

On hearing these words, Chih-hsüan 智玄 trembled from head to foot. As soon as he washed his sore in the stream, he felt an excruciating pain in his bones, and fell senseless. When he revived, the pain had disappeared, and the ulcer was healed.

As a sign of gratitude for his restoration to health, he laid the foundation of a large temple on the bank of the stream. The Emperor T'ai Tsung 太宗 (A.D. 976-98) of the Sung 宋 dynasty, bestowed on it the title of Chih-tê Ch'an-ssŭ 智德禪寺, Buddhist Monastery of Highest Virtue. Chih-hsüan 智玄, being unable to find his benefactor, composed a work in three volumes entitled *Shui-ch'an* 水懺, Water Repentance, or Water Rituals (or Dirges). He recited these praises of the transcendent virtues of the stream in his monastery till the day of his death.

CHIH JIH 值日.—The God of the Day.—See also *Tung Chün* 東君.

CHIH-KUNG 誌公.—Also known as Pao-chih 寳誌. A.D. 425-514. The monk Chih-Kung 誌公. The priests habitually call him the third patriarch of Chinese Buddhism, but this dignity is more generally ascribed to Sêng-ts'an 僧粲 (see *Patriarchs*). A native of Nanking 南京. Surname Chu 朱.

The legend of his birth, as given in the *Shên-hsien t'ung-chien* 神仙通鑑, is that in A.D. 424, during the reign of Wên Ti 文帝 (A.D. 424-54) of the Liu Sung 劉宋 dynasty, P'i-chia-na 毘伽那, a former disciple of Sakyamuni, was seized with the desire to return to earth to work for the salvation of mankind. Not wishing to be reborn in a woman's womb, he transformed himself into a small infant at Tung-yang Chên 東陽鎭, Chêkiang 浙江, and then entered the nest of a hawk, built in one of the old trees of a forest.

An old woman named Chu 朱, having gone to the forest to cut firewood, heard the child's cries, rescued it, and took it to her house.

At seven years of age he entered the Tao-lin Ssŭ 道林寺 Buddhist Monastery of Tao-lin 道林, at Chung Shan 鍾山, Kuangsi 廣西. Here he was initiated into the life and duties of the contemplative monks, and received the religious name Pao-chih 寳誌. He belonged to the school of Bodhidharma, and wrote and preached in its defence.

In A.D. 465, under the reign of Ming Ti 明帝 (A.D. 465-73) of the Liu Sung 劉宋 dynasty, when Pao-chih 寳誌 was 40 years of age, he adopted a roving life. Letting his hair fall loose to his shoulders, he went from place to place, barefooted, and leaning on a pilgrim's staff, to which were attached a mirror, a pair of scissors, and two silk tassels. He could speak several languages, and is credited with being able to appear in three different places at the same time.

The *Shên-hsien t'ung-chien* 神仙通鑑, XIII, i, pp. 4-5; ii, 1-2, gives a series of short legendary notices of the powers of the monk.

It states that, on the accession (A.D. 479), of Kao Ti 高帝 (A.D. 479-83) of the Ch'i 齊 dynasty, Pao-chih 寶誌, then 54 years of age, developed extraordinary magical powers. He could remain several days without food, and predict future events, being held in high esteem both by the common people and the Scholars (Literati).

In A.D. 483, being suspected by the Emperor Wu 武 (A.D. 483-94), Kao's 高 successor, of using his powers to deceive the people, the ruler cast him into prison at Chien-k'ang 建康 (modern Nanking). Though he had been put in chains, he was seen on the following morning walking in the streets of the city, whilst at the same time the gaoler found him securely chained in the prison, and was told by him that somebody had brought him food in a golden dish, and asked him to go to the gate and bring it in to him.

The prince imperial, Wên Hui 文惠, and a prince of the blood royal, son of King Ching Ling 竟陵, provided him with the necessaries of life during his imprisonment.

Lü Wên-hsien 呂文顯, the Governor of Chien-k'ang 建康 having reported these extraordinary events to the Emperor, the monk was transferred to a secluded place at the back of the palace, and kept under strict surveillance.

One day, the Emperor having summoned him to his private garden, Hua-lin Yüan 華林園, he appeared wearing three cloth hats, one on the top of the other, though it was in the hottest part of the summer. (Only sick people wear caps or hats in the summer, and wearing one has become synonymous with being unwell.) Shortly afterwards, the Emperor, the heir-apparent, and a high official named Yü Chang-wang 豫章王 died. It was then understood why the monk had presented himself wearing three hats.

On another occasion, as he was entering his room, he lifted up his gown, saying: "Here there will soon be blood which might soil one's garments." Soon afterwards, the corpse of Yü Lin 鬱林, a man who had just been murdered, was carried in, and blood flowing from wounds in his neck fell on the spot indicated by Chih-kung 誌公. This was another proof of his ability to forsee future events.

In A.D. 502, the Emperor Wu-ti 武帝 (A.D. 502-50), founder of the Liang 梁 dynasty, one of the greatest patrons and students of Buddhism, who became his devout disciple, proclaimed by edict that Chih-kung 誌公 (a title of honour, composed of the second character of his name *kung* 公, duke) was not an ordinary mortal and should not be confined in a secluded part of the palace. He was accordingly permitted to go out when he pleased, and was moreover granted the title of *Kuo-shih* 國 師, State Preceptor.

One day, during an imperial banquet, some Chinese white-bait (*kuei-yü* 鱠 魚, *Leucosoma Argentea,* also known in Shanghai as *yin-yü* 銀魚, silver-fish, or *wu-wang yü* 吳 王 魚, King of Wu fish, which ascends the Yang-tzǔ 揚 子 River at a fixed time every year) was served. The Emperor said to Chih-Kung 誌 公: "I, your disciple, have not eaten of this fish for ten years; when did you last eat it?" The monk replied by vomiting a large number of small live *kuei-yü* 鱠 魚. From that day on, says the legend, this fish has been found in great abundance in the neighbouring waters.

Shu-chou 舒 州 was an old tribe and feudal State on the Huai Ho 淮 河, Huai River, the name being still retained in the district of Huai-ch'êng 淮 城, near Lu-chou Fu 盧 州 府, Anhui 安 徽. On the foothills of Ch'ien Shan 濳 山 was a charming landscape, and Chih-kung 誌 公 and a Taoist priest known as Pai-ho Tao-jên 白 鶴 道 人, White Crane Taoist Monk, were contending for its possession. The Emperor Wu 武 said to them, that as they were both magicians, the first to reach the hill should be the owner of the site. Thereupon, White Crane started off at full speed, but just as the bird was on the point of alighting, Chih-kung's 誌 公 wand came whizzing through the air. This so frightened the crane that it flew away to a more distant hill. Chih-kung 誌 公 was accordingly declared to be the lawful owner, and erected a temple on the spot.

A few months after the death of the Empress Hsi 郗, the Emperor was awakened by an extraordinary noise. On rising he saw an enormous snake coiling round one of the rafters of his bedroom. Whilst he was trembling with fear, the snake said to him: "I am the Empress Hsi 郗, now transformed into a snake as a punishment for my jealousy and harsh treatment of the imperial concubines. I am wandering about without food or shelter. Under the scales covering my body, worms devour my flesh, and torture me terribly. I pray you to be gracious and deliver me from my sufferings by offering some good deed as expiation to the Ruler of Hades" (*Yama,* or *Yen-lo wang* 閻 羅 王, *q.v.*).

The next day, the Emperor asked Chih-kung 誌 公 what good deed would suffice to deliver the Empress from her sufferings. The monk replied that nothing but the all-powerfulness of Buddha could procure that favour. Accordingly Wu-ti 武 帝, in collaboration with Chih-kung 誌 公, composed a work of Buddhist prayers in nineteen volumes, to which they gave the title: *Hui-tsui wên* 悔 罪 文, *Penitential Litanies.* A large number of priests were summoned to the palace to recite them. This work subsequently was known as *Liang-huang pao-ch'an* 梁 皇 寶 懺, *Precious Rituals of the Liang Emperor.*

A few days later, the Emperor felt himself imbued with a balmy fragrance, and beheld a lady of great beauty, who said to him: "Your generosity has saved me; I am the transformation of the serpent who caused you such great alarm, and am now about to ascend to heaven." She then disappeared.

In A.D. 514, in the twelfth moon, Chih-kung 誌 公 ordered the monks to place the Ssŭ ta Chin-kang 四 大 金 剛, Four Great Diamond Kings (see *Ssŭ ta T'ien-wang* 四 大 天 王), outside the temple door, because the *p'u-sa* 菩 薩 would take his departure within ten days. Before this period had elasped, Chih-kung 誌 公 died peacefully while seated cross-legged in his chair. He was in his ninety-first year.

Wu-ti 武 帝 purchased the Ting-lin Ssŭ 定 林 寺, Ting-lin Monastery, at the cost of 200,000 taels, and had the monk buried on the Tu-lung Fou 獨 龍 阜, Solitary Dragon Mound, in front of the temple.

Wu-ti's 武 帝 daughter, Princess Yung Ting 永 定, used her allowance to build a seven-storied pagoda near to the monk's tomb. The emperor on his part ordered the engraver Lu Ch'ui 䂖 磓 to engrave the principal events of his life on a memorial monument, and donated some crystal pendants for the adornment of the tower erected over his tomb.—See also *Patriarchs: Sêng Ts'an* 僧 粲.

CHIH NÜ 織 女.—The Weaver-girl. The Goddess of Weavers. In the myths and legends which have clustered about the observations of the stars by the Chinese they are subjects for pictorial illustration without number. One of these stories is the fable of Aquila and Vega, known in Chinese mythology as the Herdsman and the Weaver-girl. The latter, the daughter of the Sun-god, was so constantly busied with her loom that her father became worried at her close habits and thought that by marrying her to a neighbour, who herded cattle on the banks of the Silver Stream of Heaven (the Milky Way), she might awake to a brighter manner of living.

No sooner did the maiden become wife than her habits and character utterly changed for the worse. She became not only very merry and lively, but quite forsook loom and needle, giving up her nights and days to play and idleness; no silly lover could have been more foolish than she. The Sun-king, in great wrath at all this, concluded that the husband was the cause of it, and determined to separate the couple. So he ordered him to remove to the other side of the river of stars, and told him that hereafter they should meet only once a year, on the seventh night of the seventh moon. To make a bridge over the flood of stars, the Sun-king called myriads of magpies, who thereupon flew together, and, making a bridge, supported the poor lover on their wings and backs as if on a roadway of solid land. So, bidding his weeping wife farewell, the lover-husband sorrowfully crossed the

River of Heaven, and all the magpies instantly flew away. But the two were separated, the one to lead his ox, the other to ply her shuttle during the long hours of the day with diligent toil, and the Sun-king again rejoiced in his daughter's industry.

At last the time for their reunion drew near, and only one fear possessed the loving wife. What if it should rain? For the River of Heaven is always full to the brim, and an extra drop causes a flood which sweeps away even the bird-bridge. But not a drop fell; all the heavens were clear. The magpies flew joyfully in myriads, making a way for the tiny feet of the little lady. Trembling with joy, and with heart fluttering more than the bridge of wings, she crossed the River of Heaven and was in the arms of her husband. This she did every year. The husband stayed on his side of the river, and the wife came to him on the magpie bridge, save on the sad occasions when it rained. So every year the people hope for clear weather, and the happy festival is celebrated alike by old and young.

These two constellations are worshipped principally by women, that they may gain cunning in the arts of needlework and making of fancy flowers. Water-melons, fruits, vegetables, cakes, etc., are placed with incense in the reception-room, and before these offerings are performed the kneeling and the knocking of the head on the ground in the usual way.

The *Shên-hsien t'ung-chien* 神仙通鑑, VII, ix, 7, gives the name of the youth as Tung Yung 董永, a poor farmer of Kan-ch'êng 干乘, Hupei 湖北. In order to obtain the necessary funds for his father's funeral expenses he entered the employ of a Mr. Fei 裴 of An-lu 安垄, who lent him 10,000 pieces of money. On his way back from the burial he met a young lady who asked him to marry her, and they went together to his creditor to arrange about the debt. The latter having stipulated for 300 pieces of silk, the young lady set to work and wove them all within a month. She then informed Tung Yung 董永 that she was Chih Nü 織女, the Spinning Damsel (the goddess of the star Lyræ), one of the 30,000 Celestial Weavers, and that she had been deputed by the Lord of Heaven to help him as a reward for his filial piety. She then ascended to heaven, promising to send him two sons within a year. This promise she kept, and Tung Yung 董永 and his two sons (who were named Po-ch'i 伯齊 and Chung-shu 仲舒, respectively) were offered official posts in the Emperor's palace. These, however, they refused, and went to live in Kuang-ch'uan 廣川, the territory of a petty king named P'êng Tsu 彭祖. Soon after this, the elder son, saying their mother was calling them, took his father on his back and flew up to heaven. These incidents are assigned to the second century B.C., in the second year of the reign of the Emperor Ching Ti 景帝 (156-140 B.C.). The Emperor had a temple erected in Tung Yung's 董永 honour, and he later became one of the twenty-four Examples of Filial Piety.

CHIH-TSAO CH'AN-SHIH 智璪禪師.—A monk of the
Chang 張 family. A native of Ch'ing-ho 清河. Left an orphan
at the age of twenty-two, he was healed of a long and tedious
illness by dreaming that a genie approached his bed and breathed
on his body.

He entered the Pao-lin Ssŭ 寶林寺, Monastery of the Precious
Forest, in A.D. 586. Having attained to complete monkhood, he
devoted himself to the ecstatic meditation *Fa-hua san-wei* 法華
三昧, *San-wei (Samadi)*, Flower of the Law, *Sadharma Pundarika
Samadi,* explained as a degree of ecstatic meditation, culminating
in absolute indifference to all external influences. The ceremony
included the lighting of several lamps, and extinguishing them
one by one, until complete abstraction and cessation of all mental
activity was reached.

After he had suffered the molestations and distractions of
demons for twenty-one nights, a spirit, clothed in blue, appeared
and congratulated him, informing him that all would thenceforth
be well with him.

He died in A.D. 638.

CHIH TUN 支遁.—A saintly Buddhist monk. Fourth
century. A native of Ch'ên-liu 陳留. Family name Kuan 關.
Personal name Tao-lin 道林. One of those invited to the annual
banquet of the gods (see *Hsi Wang-mu* 西王母).

CHIH-WEI CH'AN-SHIH 智威禪師 (36th generation).—
A deified Buddhist monk. Ranked fifth in Buddhist School, I
(*q.v.*).

CHIH-WEI TSUN-CHÊ 智威尊者.—A deified Buddhist
monk. Ranked fifth in Buddhist School, X (*q.v.*). The legend
concerning this monk is as follows: An official of the name of
Hsü Ling 徐陵 who lived in the time of the Ch'ên 陳 dynasty (A.D.
557-89), listening to the exhortations of Chih-chê Ta-shih 智者大
師 (*q.v.*), resolved to take the Buddhist vows, and after his death
was reincarnated in the Chu 朱 family, at Chin-yün 縉雲, Chêkiang 浙江. Having reached the age of 18, he was about to
marry, but was reminded by a Hindu monk of his promises made
in a previous existence. He forthwith entered the Kuo-ch'ing Ssŭ
國清寺, at Chang-an 章安, in the same province, and was
admitted as a disciple of Kuan-ting Fa-shih 灌頂法師 (*q.v.*),
who explained to him the *Fa-hua ching* 法華經, *Lotus of the
Good Law*. When his training was finished, he was undecided
as to where to preach the doctrine, and in his perplexity tossed his
staff into the air, and saw it move off in the direction of Lien-tan
Shan 鍊丹山, the former seat of Hsüan Yüan 軒轅 (*q.v.*). Having
settled there, he changed its name to Fa-hua Shan 法華山. He
spent his days in preaching, and his nights in prayer. His disciples
numbered several hundreds. He was quite 7 feet in height, and

when he preached his head appeared to be surrounded with a halo of purple clouds.

As he took his daily meals at Hsien-chü 仙 居, twenty-six miles away, he was considered eccentric. Died A.D. 680. During his lifetime, his title was Ssŭ Ta-shih 四 大 師, Master of the Four Branches. Posthumous title (conferred under the Sung 宋 dynasty): Hsüan-ta Tsun-chê 玄 達 尊 者, Profound and Intelligent Venerable.

CHIH-YEN CH'AN-SHIH 智 嚴 禪 師 (33rd generation).— A deified Buddhist monk. Ranked second in Buddhist School, I (*q.v.*).

CHIH-YEN FA-SHIH 智 儼 法 師.—A deified Buddhist monk. Ranked second in Buddhist School, XI (*q.v.*). Secular name Chao Chih-hsiang 趙 至 相. Born A.D. 609. After praying to Buddha, he ascertained by casting lots in Tsang-ching Lou 藏 經 樓, the monastic library, that the *Hua-yen ching* 華 嚴 經 (*q.v.*) would be the best book to commit to memory. Having accomplished this task, he was admitted as one of Tu-shun Ho-shang's 杜 順 和 尚 (*q.v.*) disciples. He made rapid progress, and preached the doctrine of the *Hua-yen ching* 華 嚴 經 unceasingly, his school becoming one of the most flourishing of the time. Died A.D. 668.

CHIH-YÜAN CH'AN-SHIH 智 遠 禪 師.—A saintly Buddhist monk. One of those invited to the annual banquet of the gods (see *Hsi Wang-mu* 西 王 母).

CH'IH CHIANG TZŬ YÜ 赤 將 子 輿.—See *Shen I* 神 羿.

CH'IH-CHIAO HSIEN 赤 脚 仙.—The Barefooted Immortal. In A.D. 1009, during the reign of the Emperor Chên Tsung 眞 宗 (A.D. 998-1023) of the Sung 宋 dynasty, a high Court official was deputed by the Emperor to go to Mao Shan 茅 山, the mountain where Mao Chün 茅 君 (Mao Ying 茅 盈) was worshipped, to beg him to grant him an heir to the throne. Mao Chün 茅 君, whose wife was Pi-hsia Yüan-chün 碧 霞 元 君, was then staying at T'ai Shan 泰 山, the sacred mountain of the East. He referred the matter to the god of that mountain, who passed it on to Yü Ti 玉 帝. The latter, then in his palace T'ung-ming Tien 通 明 殿, with the dozen barefooted Immortals around him, saw that the third one was laughing, and ordered him to go and be reincarnated on earth and rule mankind. To overcome his reluctance Yü Ti 玉 帝 gave him two *ch'ü* 曲 Spirits, one civil and one military, to assist him. Ch'ih-chiao Hsien 赤 脚 仙 accordingly departed and was reincarnated, but felt great remorse at the laugh which had been the cause of his being obliged to return to earth.

On the tenth day of the fifth moon in the year A.D. 1010 a hereditary prince was born to Chên Tsung 眞 宗, and was named

Shou I 受益, Benefit Received, but soon after birth the child began to cry, and was quite inconsolable. The Emperor, by edict, called for a remedy, and one Lou Tao-chê 婁道者 came to the palace, placed his hand on the infant prince's head and said: "Cry no more! cry no more! It would have been better not to have laughed when you were in Yü Ti's 玉帝 palace. Console yourself. Wên Ch'ü 文曲 and Wu Ch'ü 武曲 will help you." The child then stopped crying. A month after its birth, a branch of the *ch'ing-ling chih* 青靈芝, the herb of the Immortals, sprouted under his cradle. The young prince, from his earliest days, always loved to go barefooted.

CH'IH-KUO 持國.—See *Ssǔ ta T'ien-wang* 四大天王.

CH'IH-LAN SHU 赤爁怒.—See *Mars*.

CH'IH-SU CHIAO 喫素教.—See *Buddhist Schools*, II.

CH'IH SUNG-TZǓ 赤松子.—See *Huang Ch'u-p'ing* (皇) 黃初平.

CH'IH TI 赤帝.—See *Mars*.

CH'IH-WÊN 蚩吻.—See *Lung Wang* 龍王.

CHILD-BIRTH, THE MATRON WHO HASTENS.—See *Ts'ui-shêng Niang-niang* 催生娘娘.

CHILDREN, THE PURVEYOR OF.—See *Chang Hsien* 張仙.

CHIN 金.—See *Feet, The Gods of the*.

CHIN, THE GODS OF THE.—See *T'ai-yin Shên* 太陰神.

CHIN-CHA 金吒.—See *Li No-cha* 李哪吒.

CHIN CH'AN TZǓ 金蟬子.—A Taoist hermit who was tutor to Sakyamuni in China for thirteen days. He is also known by the names of Jan-têng Fo 燃燈佛, Wang Tan 王丹, and Hsi-ch'êng Wang-chün 西城王君. Hsi ch'êng 西城 is the mountain resort where he spent his life in meditation and prayer, and thereby attained immortality.—See *Jan-têng Fo* 燃燈佛 and (for details) Doré, vi, 69-73.

CHIN CH'ÊNG 金成.—The god of the star Yin-ts'o 陰錯. An officer of the feudatory Ch'ung Hou-hu 崇侯虎. Died while defending his prince against Wên Wang's 文王 armies, being slain by Hsin Chia 辛甲 during the assault on the capital Ch'ung-ch'êng 崇城.

CHIN-CHIA 金甲.—Golden Armour Bearers. Confucian genii.—See *Wên Ch'ang* 文昌.

CHIN-CH'IAO CHIO 金喬覺.—See *Ti-tsang Wang* 地藏王.

CHIN-CH'ÜEH SHANG-TI 金闕上帝. YU-CH'ÜEH SHANG-TI 玉闕上帝. Sovereign Emperor of the Golden Palace. Sovereign Emperor of the Jade Palace. During the period of the Five Dynasties (A.D. 907-60), Chih-chêng 知證 and Chih-ê 知諤, sons of Hsü Wên 徐溫, at the head of their armies, restored peace at Fu-chou (Foochow) 福州, in Fukien 福建. For this they were worshipped, and statues were erected to them.

A Sung 宋 dynasty emperor canonized them as Chên Jên 眞人, Heroes or Perfect Men, the rank next below that of Shêng Jên 聖人, Saint. The Emperor Ch'êng Tsu 成祖 (A.D. 1403-25) of the Ming 明 dynasty, having effectively prayed to them during an illness, bestowed on them the title of Ti Chün 帝君, Sovereign Emperor. The Emperors Ying Tsung 英宗 (A.D. 1436-50) and Hsien Tsung 憲宗 (A.D. 1465-88) gave them the title of Shang Ti 上帝, Supreme Sovereign. In A.D. 1488, in the reign of Hsiao Tsung 孝宗 (A.D. 1488-1506), the Minister of Rites cancelled this title as improper, and curtailed the sacrifices offered to them.

CHIN-FU 金府, THE GOD OF THE STAR.—See *Hsiao Chên* 蕭臻.

CHIN HSIA T'UNG-ÊRH 金霞童兒.—A disciple of T'ai-i 太乙.

CHIN HSING 金星.—See *Venus*.

CHIN HUNG 金虹.—See *Pi-hsia Yüan-chün* 碧霞元君.

CHIN KANG 金剛.—The Four Diamond Kings of Heaven; governors of the four continents surrounding Mount Sumêru (Hsü-mi Shan 須彌山 or Hsü-mi Lou 須彌樓).—See *Ssǔ ta T'ien-wang* 四大天王.

CHIN-KANG CHIH 金剛智, or CHIN-KANG SAN-TSANG 金剛三藏, Vajramati or Vajrabodhi: Wisdom of the Vajra (the sceptre of Indra, as god of thunder and lightning, with which he slays the enemies of Buddhism).—An Indian monk of royal descent. The sacred Hindu monk Vajramati. Eighth century A.D. One of those invited to the annual banquet of the gods (see Hsi Wang-mu 西王母). Born in the Kingdom of Mo-lai-chi 摩賴卽, in India, he arrived at Canton about A.D. 720 with the monk Wu-wei 無畏 (*q.v.*) during the reign of Hsüan Tsung 玄宗 (A.D. 713-56) of the T'ang 唐 dynasty, and proceeded to Lo-yang 洛陽, Honan 河南. He was the first to introduce the Yogatcharya (or *Yogachara*) system, but he was surpassed in influence and activity by Amogha. Eitel (*Sanskrit-Chinese Dic.*) says: "This Yoga (or Tantra or Mantra) system wa. made known in China (A.D. 647) by Hiuen Tsung's [Hsüan-tsang's] 玄奘 translation of the *Yogacharya bhumi s'astra* [the text book of that School], on which Amogha-vadjra (A.D. 720) established the Chinese branch of the Yoga School which was popularized chiefly by the labours of Vadjrabodhi (A.D. 732)." Hsüan Tsung 玄奘 was extremely superstitious. He set up Chiang T'ai-kung 姜太公 as tutelary god of the dynasty, and in A.D. 740 raised Confucius to the rank of prince. His Court was frequented by countless Buddhist monks, endowed with magic powers. Vajramati was one of the most famous and favoured among them. He gained the favour of the imperial concubine Hui-fei 惠妃, and during his stay at and visits to the Court performed numerous miracles, such as producing a perfect *ju-i* 如意 from his sleeve; enclosing Yeh Fa-shan 葉法善 in a bottle (a trick, however, which failed when he was asked to get him out again); restoring a torn-up cope to a perfect state of preservation; causing a cope placed in a heavily-guarded coffer to vanish, procuring rain in time of drought; etc.

He is said to have ended his days in silent meditation.—See also *Buddhist Schools*, XV.

CHIN-KANG-TSANG CH'I HSI 金剛藏起息.—One of the twelve divine Buddhist teachers. Name Ch'i Hsi 起息.

CHIN KU 進姑.—See *Pi-hsia Yüan-chün* 碧霞元君.

CHIN-KU HSIEN 金箍仙.—The Golden-crowned Genie. A disciple of T'ung-t'ien Chiao-chu 通天敎主. Was present at the rout at Chieh-p'ai Kuan 界牌關, and had to flee before the victorious gods.

CHIN-KUANG HSIEN 金光仙.—The Shining-gold Immortal. The origin of the *chin-mao hou* 金毛犼, the monkey-wolf with golden-coloured hair, placed under Kuan Yin's 觀音 feet, and serving as her steed. This genie was the disciple of T'ung-t'ien Chiao-chu 通天敎主, the first patriarch of modern Taoism. He was called Chin kuang 金光, Shining-gold, because in his real state he was a monkey-wolf with golden-coloured hair. He was captured by Kuan Yin 觀音 (Tz'ŭ-hang Tao-jên 慈航道人) during the historical battle of the Ten Thousand Genii at T'ung-kuan 潼關, during the Yin-Chou 殷周 wars. When struck, at Lao Tzŭ's 老子 command, on the neck by Shou Shên 壽神, the God of Longevity, he immediately resumed his primitive form. Yüan-shih T'ien-tsun 元始天尊 then gave him to Kuan Yin 觀音 to use as a mount, and she tied a label on his neck explaining his origin.

CHIN KUEI 金夅.—See *Wu Tou* 五斗.

CHIN-LUNG SSŬ TA WANG 金龍四大王.—See *Lung Wang* 龍王.

CHIN-MAO HOU 金毛犼.—See *Chin-kuang Hsien* 金光仙.

CHIN MÊN 金門.—The Golden Gate. The entrance to Yü Ch'ing's 玉清 palace.—See *San Ch'ing* 三清.

CHIN MU 金母.—See *Wu Lao* 五老 and *Hsi Wang-mu* 西王母.

CHIN-NA-LO 緊那羅.—A dragon-king.—See *Lung Wang* 龍王.

CHIN NAN-TAO 金南道.—The god of the star Ti-shou 地獸.—See *Ti-sha* 地煞.

CHIN NIU 金牛.—See *Niu Wang* 牛王 and *Hun Shou-lo* 渾壽羅.

CHIN SHAN 金蟬.—See *Pi-hsia Yüan-chün* 碧霞元君.

CHIN SHÊN 金神, MU SHÊN 木神.—The Gods of the Upper Parts of the Feet.—*Yün chi ch'i ch'ien* 雲笈七籤.

CHIN SHÊNG-YANG 金繩陽.—The god of the constellation Pi 畢. Alternatively with Ch'ên Chün 陳俊.

CHIN TA-SHÊNG 金大升.—The god of the star T'ien-wên 天瘟. The transcendent buffalo, a genie of Mei Shan 梅山, Mount Mei. Fought under Yüan Hung 袁洪 at Mêng-ching 孟津. Captured by Nü Wa 女媧 (*q.v.*) and delivered to Yang Chien 楊戩. Slain, by command of Chiang Tzǔ-ya 姜子牙, by general Nan Kung-kua 南宮适.—See *Niu Wang* 牛王 and *Ch'ing-yün Nü-t'ung* 青雲女童.

CHIN TI-TSANG 金地藏.—See *Ti-tsang Wang* 地藏王.

CHIN-YA HSIEN 金牙仙.—The Gold-tooth Immortal. A disciple of T'ung-t'ien Chiao-chu 通天敎主, one of the celestial defenders of Chou Wang 紂王.

CH'IN HSIANG 秦祥.—The god of the star Ti-hsing 地刑.—See *Ti-sha* 地煞.

CH'IN-KUANG WANG 秦廣王.—The President of the First Court of Hades (*q.v.*). He keeps the register of the living and the dead, and measures the length of men's lives.

On the arrival of the soul in Hades, it is taken to the steelyard, a hook is fastened in its back, and its sins are weighed. If its merits outweigh its sins, it is ordered by the President to be sent to the Tenth Court, where transmigration takes place. If its sins outweigh its merits, it is placed on the Mirror Tower, Yeh-ching T'ai 孽鏡台, to behold its fate in the next life for the sins of the past—a cow, an ass, a dog, or a reptile. After this the soul is sent to the Second Court, where its tortures begin.

CH'IN SU-PAO 秦叔寶.—See *Shên Shu Yü Lü* 神荼鬱壘.

CH'IN YÜ-PO 秦裕伯.—A celebrated *ch'êng-huang* 城隍, or city-god (of Shanghai 上海). End of Yüan 元 and beginning of Ming 明 dynasties.

CHINESE ART, THE LO-HAN IN.—See *Lo-han* 羅漢.

CHING 脛.—See *Feet, The Gods of the.*

CHING 井, THE GOD OF THE CONSTELLATION.—See *Yao Ch'i* 姚期 and *Shên Kêng* 沈庚.

CHING-HSING SHÊ 淨行社.—See *Buddhist Schools,* XVII.

CHING-HSING TI-TZǓ 淨行弟子.—See *Hsing-ch'ang Lü-shih* 省常律師.

CHING-HSÜAN CH'AN-SHIH 鷟玄禪師 (43rd generation).—A deified Buddhist monk. Ranked twenty-second in Buddhist School, VI (*q.v.*). Family name Chang 張. A native of Chiang-hsia 江夏, Hupei 湖北. At the age of 19, was already regarded as an eminent teacher. Studied under Yüan-kuan Ch'an-shih 緣觀禪師 (*q.v.*), and taught for fifty years in the T'ai-yang Ssŭ 太陽寺, Sun Monastery. Died A.D. 1027, aged 85. His tomb is on T'ai-yang Shan 太陽山, Sun Mountain.

CHING-KUANG TSUN-CHÊ 淨光尊者.—A deified Buddhist monk. Ranked fourteenth in Buddhist School, X (*q.v.*). Secular name Hu Ch'ang-chao 胡常昭. A native of Yung-chia 永嘉, Chêkiang 浙江. He entered the Ch'ing-sung 剛竦 Monastery at an early age. "One day," says the legend, "as he reached the cell of his teacher at Kuo-ch'ing 國清, he beheld a majestic throne upon which were written the words: Wên-shu T'ai 文殊臺, 'Chair of Manjusri' (the Buddha of Transcendent Wisdom: a fanciful and mystic creation of the Mahayana and Yoga Schools). All around was a barrier, which hindered the young monk from advancing according to his desires. Hereupon Kuan Yin 觀音 (*q.v.*), the Goddess of Mercy, appeared in the air, drew him towards her, and forthwith transformed him into the same substance as herself. From that day forth he delighted in preaching the *Wu-chin shih-luan ching* 無盡世亂經, *Classic of the World's Unceasing Trouble.*" It was during the lifetime of this monk that the king of Wu-yüeh 吳越 sent messengers to Japan to fetch the Buddhist canon, *Chiao-tien* 敎典. The king erected for Ching-kuang 淨光 the monastery of Ting-hui 定慧, Fixed Intelligence, and conferred on him the honorary title of Ching-kuang Tsun-chê 淨光尊者, Pure and Brilliant Teacher.

CHING TAN 景丹.—The god of the constellation Nü 女. Alternatively with Chêng-yüan Tao-jên 鄭元道人.

CHING-TS'AN CH'AN-SHIH 淨瘁禪師 (66th generation). —A deified Buddhist monk. Ranked sixty-fifth in Buddhist School, VI (*q.v.*). Family name Chu 朱. A native of Chin-ling 金陵 (modern Nanking 南京, Kiangsu 江蘇). Studied under [Jui-pai] Ming-hsüeh Ch'an-shih [瑞白] 明雪禪師 (*q.v.*) at Pien Shan 弁山, Chêkiang 浙江. In 1646, he became Superior of the same monastery. Died at Ku-su Chou 姑蘇州 A.D. 1658, aged 59. His tomb is on Pien Shan 弁山.

CHING T'U 淨土.—"Pure Land" School. See *Hsi T'ien* 西天, *Buddhist Schools*, XVII, and Plopper, pp. 361-2.

CHING-T'U CHIAO 淨土敎.—See *Buddhist Schools*, XVII.

CHING WAN 靜琬.—A saintly Buddhist monk. Seventh century A.D. One of those invited to the banquet of the gods (see *Hsi Wang-mu* 西王母). He lived during the reign of the Emperor Yang Ti 煬帝 (A.D. 605-18) of the Sui 隋 dynasty, inhabiting the Shih-ching Tung 石經洞, Stone-classic Cave, on Fang Shan 房山, Mount Fang. On the walls of the cave he engraved a whole book of prayers. A close friend of Sêng Ts'an 僧瘁, the third patriarch of Chinese Buddhism. Both died in A.D. 606.

CHING-YEH CH'U-WO 淨業除我.—One of the twelve divine Buddhist teachers.

CH'ING CHI 卿忌.—See *Tsao Chün* 灶(竈)君.

CH'ING-CHI 慶忌.—See *Shui Fu* 水府, D (3) (c).

CH'ING-CHING-HUI SHUO-FA 淸靜慧說法.—One of the twelve divine Buddhist teachers.

CH'ING-CHING-SÊ 淸淨色.—A dragon-king.—See *Lung Wang* 龍王.

CH'ING-HSÜ TAO-TÊ CHÊN-CHÜN 清虛道德眞君.
—A denizen of the Tzŭ-yang Tung 紫陽洞 on Ch'ing-fêng Shan
清峰山. Fought for Wu Wang 武王 and killed Wang I 王奕,
in spite of the latter's powerful charm consisting of three gourds
full of red water, a drop of which changed anybody into a pool
of blood. Ch'ing-hsü Tao-tê Chên-chün's 清虛道德眞君 counter-
charm was his "five-fire fan," by a single movement of which he
could reduce his adversary to ashes. Worshipped as a demi-god.

CH'ING I-SHÊN 青衣神.—The God of the Blue Gown.
One of the Gods of Silkworms. Ts'an Ts'ung 蠶叢, Duke and
then King of the Shu 蜀 State (modern Ssŭch'uan 四川). From
his custom of wearing blue clothes when travelling in the country
of the barbarian tribes, to whom he taught the rearing of silkworms, he was nicknamed "Blue Gown." In gratitude for this
service, the peasants apotheosized him.—See *Composite Deities*.

CH'ING LIEN 青蓮.—A saintly Buddhist monk. One of
those invited to the annual banquet of the gods (see *Hsi Wang-mu*
西王母).

CH'ING LUNG 青龍.—The God of the Lungs. His
designation is Yen lung tzŭ fang 燕龍子方 (*Yün chi ch'i ch'ien*
雲笈七籤).—See also *Hao Hua* 皓華 and *Su Ling-shêng* 素靈生.

CH'ING-LUNG 青龍, THE GOD OF THE STAR.—See
Têng Chiu-kung 鄧九公.

CH'ING LUNG, PAI-HU 青龍白虎.—Blue Dragon and
White Tiger. The functions discharged by Hêng 哼 and Ha 哈
(*q.v.*) at the gates of Buddhist temples are in Taoist temples
discharged by Ch'ing Lung 青龍 and Pai Hu 白虎.

The former, the Spirit of the Blue Dragon Star, was Têng
Chiu-kung 鄧九公, one of the chief generals of the last emperor
of the Yin 殷 dynasty. He had a son named Têng Hsiu 鄧秀,
and a daughter named Ch'an-yü 嬋玉.

The army of Têng Chiu-kung 鄧九公 was camped at San-
shan Kuan 三山關, when he received orders to proceed to the
battle then taking place at Hsi-ch'i 西岐. There, in standing up
to Nocha 哪吒 and Huang Fei-hu 黃飛虎, he had his left arm
broken by the former's magic bracelet, but, fortunately for him,
his subordinate, T'u Hsing-sun 土行孫, a renowned magician,
gave him a remedy which quickly healed the fracture.

His daughter then came on the scene to avenge her father.
She had a magic weapon, the Five-fire Stone, which she hurled
full in the face of Yang Chien 楊戩. But the Immortal was not
wounded; on the other hand, his celestial dog jumped at Ch'an-yü
嬋玉 and bit her neck, so that she was obliged to flee. T'u
Hsing-sun 土行孫, however, healed the wound.

After a banquet, Têng Chiu-kung 鄧九公 promised his daughter in marriage to T'u Hsing-sun 土行孫 if he would gain him the victory at Hsi-ch'i 西岐. Chiang Tzŭ-ya 姜子牙 then persuaded T'u's 土 magic-master, Chü Liu-sun 懼留孫, to call his disciple over to his camp, where he asked him why he was fighting against the new dynasty. "Because," he replied, "Chiu-kung 九公 has promised me his daughter in marriage as a reward of success." Chiang Tzŭ-ya 姜子牙 thereupon promised to obtain the bride, and sent a force to seize her. As a result of the fighting that ensued, Chiu-kung 九公 was beaten, and retreated in confusion, leaving Ch'an-yü 嬋玉 in the hands of the victors. During the next few days the marriage was celebrated with great ceremony in the victor's camp. According to custom, the bride returned for some days to her father's house, and while there she earnestly exhorted Chiu-kung 九公 to submit. Following her advice, he went over to Chiang Tzŭ-ya's 姜子牙 party.

In the ensuing battles he fought valiantly on the side of his former enemy, and killed many famous warriors, but he was eventually attacked by the Blower, from whose mouth a column of yellow smoke struck him, throwing him from his steed. He was made prisoner, and executed by order of General Ch'iu Yin 邱引. Chiang Tzŭ-ya 姜子牙 conferred on him the kingdom of the Blue Dragon Star.

The Spirit of the White Star is Yin Ch'êng-hsiu 殷成秀. His father, Yin P'o-pai 殷破敗, a high courtier of the tyrant Chou Wang 紂王, was sent to negotiate peace with Chiang Tzŭ-ya 姜子牙, but was seized and put to death by Marquis Chiang Wên-huan 姜文煥. His son, attempting to avenge his father's murder, was pierced by a spear, his head was cut off and carried in triumph to Chiang Tzŭ-ya 姜子牙.

As compensation he was, though somewhat tardily, canonized as the Spirit of the White Tiger Star.—See also *Hêng Ha êrh chiang* 哼哈二將.

CH'ING-MIAO HUI 青苗會.—See *Pa Cha* 叭咋.

CH'ING-SUNG TSUN-CHÊ 清竦尊者.—A deified Buddhist monk. Ranked thirteenth in Buddhist School, X (*q.v.*). A native of T'ien-t'ai 天台, Chêkiang 浙江. Trained by Yüan-hsiu Tsun-chê 元琇尊者 (*q.v.*). Summoned all the monks to pray for the continuance of the peace enjoyed under the rule of Ch'ien-liu 錢鏐, founder of the kingdom of Wu-yüeh 吳越, A.D. 907.

CH'ING TI 青帝.—See *Jupiter*.

CH'ING-WA SHÊN 青蛙神.—The Frog-spirit. Frog-spirits are worshipped for commercial prosperity and prevention and healing of sickness at Chin-chi Hsien 金谿縣, Fu-chou Fu 撫州

府, Kiangsi 江西, and at Hang-chou 杭州, Chêkiang 浙江 (where there are temples dedicated to it). In the latter city, near the Yung-chin 湧金 temple is the temple of the Marshal of Chin Hua 金華, where formerly Ts'ao Kao 曹杲, a high officer of the Wu-Yüeh 吳越 State, was worshipped. He is now regarded by the people as the Frog-spirit, this being due to his having, in A.D. 978, constructed a watercourse near to the city which was known as Yung-chin 湧金 and to the people gradually in error mistaking Ts'ao Kuo 曹杲 for the Frog-spirit.

Another Frog-spirit is a military officer whose temple is at Yenp'ing Fu 延平府, Fukien 福建, and who died fighting bravely against the rebel chief Huang Ch'ao 黄巢 in the reign of the Emperor Hsi Tsung 僖宗 (A.D. 874-89) of the T'ang 唐 dynasty.

A female Frog-spirit is Shih Niang 十娘 who, in the time of the Ch'u 楚 State, married Pi K'un-shêng 薜昆生. Just after their wedding, large numbers of frogs appeared in the courtyard, and his wife reproved Pi K'un-shêng 薜昆生 for crushing them with his feet. This caused their temporary separation, the wife returning when the husband had repented of his cruel conduct. Before long, she gave birth to twins, and eventually they had such numerous progeny that the people described them as the frog-family.

Moulders and sculptors of images of this god place in its stomach a live tortoise, a snake, a large and a small bird, the idea being that these living creatures will communicate life to the wood or clay, etc., of which the images are made.

A similar case to the creation of the Frog-spirit occurred in the reign of the Emperor Shên Tsung 神宗 (A.D. 1068-86) of the Sung 宋 dynasty, when a Tortoise-spirit was created through Yang Shih (Chung-li) 楊時 (中立), who lived some years at the foot of Wu-kuei Shan 烏龜山, Black Tortoise Mountain (South of Ch'ang-chou Fu 常州府, Kiangsu 江蘇), being commonly styled Kuei-shan Hsien-shêng 龜山先生, the Master of Tortoise Mountain.

CH'ING-WEI T'IEN 清爲天.—Yü Ch'ing 玉清, The Pearly Azure. A heaven. One of the three divisions into which the primordial cosmic ether separated.—See *San Ch'ing* 三清 and *Yü Ch'ing* 玉清.

CH'ING-YÜAN 清源.—See *Shui Fu* 水府, D. (1).

CH'ING-YÜAN CHÊNG-TSUNG 青原正宗.—See *Buddhist Schools*, VI.

CH'ING-YÜN NÜ-T'UNG 青雲女童.—Another name for Ch'ing-yün T'ung-êrh 青雲童兒, the serving maid of Nü Wa 女媧. Yang Chien 楊戩 was in pursuit of Chin Ta-shêng 金大升, the Transcendent Buffalo, with whom he had just engaged in a terrific battle, when Nü Wa 女媧, riding her phoenix, foretold to him the final triumph of the new Chou 周 dynasty, and then ordered Ch'ing-yün Nü-t'ung 青雲女童 to bring Chin Ta-shêng 金大升 to her.

By means of her magic lasso she caught him by his nose and took him captive. Having made him change into a buffalo, she sent him back to Yang Chien 楊戩 and Chiang Tzŭ-ya 姜子牙 ordered him to be decapitated.

CH'ING-YÜN T'UNG-ÊRH 青雲童兒.—See *Ch'ing-yün Nü-t'ung* 青雲女童.

CHIO 角, THE GOD OF THE CONSTELLATION.—See *Têng Yü* 鄧禹 and *Po-lin Tao-jên* 柏林道人.

CHIO HSIEN 覺賢.—See *Fo-t'o-po-to-lo Ch'an-shih* 佛陀跋多羅禪師.

CHIO YÜAN-TZŬ 覺元子.—The God of the Brain. His designation is Tao Tu 道都. His body is one inch and one-tenth in height, and his colour completely white. There are also three other brain-gods, Ni 泥, Wan 丸, and Chün 君. *Yün chi ch'i ch'ien* 雲笈七籤.

CHIU-CH'OU 九醜, THE GOD OF THE STAR.—See *Lung Hsü-hu* 龍鬚虎.

CHIU-CHUNG PA HSIEN 酒中八仙.—See *Pa Hsien* 八仙.

CHIU-HUA SHAN 九華山.—First called Chiu-tzŭ Shan 九子山, Hill of the Nine Philosophers.—See *Ti-tsang Wang* 地藏王.

CHIU-LI-HU HSIEN 九鯉湖仙.—The Immortals of the Nine-Carp Lake. Ho T'ung-p'an 何通判 'and his wife Lin 林 had nine sons, the eldest of whom was lame, and the rest blind. They lived in Hsien-yu Hsien 仙遊縣, Hsing-hua Fu 興化府, Fukien 福建. The father having decided to slay all his sons, their mother got a man to take them away to the mountain to the north-east, known as the Mount of the Nine Immortals. Near by was a lake, on the borders of which the nine hermits succeeded in composing their potion of immortality. This done, each of them mounted a red carp and disappeared. Hence the name of the lake. A temple built on its banks is frequented by pilgrims, who burn incense to these gods.

The poet Huang Mêng-liang 黃孟良, after describing the beautiful scenery of this spot, adds to the legend that the nine carp were transformed into nine dragons which bore the Immortals to Heaven.

The *Shên-hsien t'ung-chien* 神仙通鑑 (VII, 7, 8, 8, i.), which places these events in the time of the Emperor Wu Ti 武帝 (A.D. 140-86 B.C.) of the Han 漢 dynasty, when Wu Chê 無諸, King of Fu-chien 福建, had built a magnificent palace on Niao-shih Shan 鳥石山, Mount Niao-shih, describes the miracles performed by the nine brothers Ho 何 at a royal banquet on the ninth day of the ninth moon, 125 B.C.

In answer to the Emperor's query, they informed His Majesty that after a banquet on Hsü-mi Shan 須彌山, Mount Sumeru, they had become disciples of T'ai-chi Chên-jên 太極眞人, and that each was in possession of a different magical art.

The first brother, merely by waving his hand, caused a gold cup on the banquet-table to fly up in the air and drop into the lake. The second, by merely pointing at a mountain, caused its side to open and lotus flowers appear. The third flew into the air, wrote some characters on the face of a cliff, and then returned safely to the palace. The fourth, by merely blowing with his mouth, caused a violent wind to raise rocks into the air like a swarm of flies, and then return to their former places on the mountain. The fifth caused a fir-tree to be uprooted and changed into a dragon, which flew into the sky and was recalled at will by the Immortal fishing for it with a bamboo twig, and changing it back again into a fir-tree. The sixth, by waving his hand, caused a mountain to move toward the east, and to be replaced by the mountain on the north. This being done, the seventh said: "We have completed the mixture which confers immortality, and must depart." Turning toward the lake he called to the fish, and nine carp came out. The nine brothers mounted on their backs and were carried away into the heavens. Thenceforth the lake was called the Nine-Carp Lake, and the mountain the Mount of the Nine Immortals. King Wu Chê 無諸 and all his suite fell on their knees at seeing them disappear from sight. The fifth let fall the bamboo rod he had used to catch the dragon, and the King had the Ling-hsiao T'ai 凌霄臺, Ling-hsiao Terrace, built opposite Niao-shih Shan 鳥石山, Mount Niao-shih, in which to preserve it as a memorial of these miracles, and also a temple on the border of the lake for sacrifices to be performed annually to the Nine Immortals.

CHIU-MO-LO-SHIH CH'AN-SHIH 鳩摩羅什禪師, or **CHIU-MO-LO-CH'I-P'O** 鳩摩羅耆婆.—The saintly Buddhist monk Kumarajiva. A.D. 360-415. One of those invited to the annual banquet of the gods (see *Hsi Wang-mu* 西王母). An Indian monk who lived in Hsi-yü 西域 (Tangut) during the reign of Fu Chien 符堅 (A.D. 337-84), the petty independent prince who ruled at Ch'ang-an 長安 over parts of what are now Kansu 甘肅, Shensi 陝西, and Ssŭch'uan 四川. His father, Kumarayana, Chiu-mo-lo-yen 鳩摩羅炎, was invited by King Po Shun 帛純 of Kuei-tzŭ Kuo 龜茲國, the Kingdom of Kuei-tzŭ (in central Asia), to Kharachar (or Karasha, a town S. W. of Turfan, and a short distance N. W. of Lake Bagrach), where he became his favourite and one of his State Preceptors, and married his younger daughter, who became the mother of Kumarajiva. He was only seven years of age when his father died, and both he and his mother then entered a monastery. His memory was so good that he could repeat daily with understanding a thousand *gathas,* or religious chants of thirty-two verses each. At the age of 12 he migrated to Sha-lo 沙疌 and remained there a year, studying the Mahayana system, as well as astrology and kindred subjects, becoming proficient in all. At 20 he returned to Kharachar, and expounded the *sutras* in public, as well as to high officials who came asking him to explain to them their mystic meaning.

In A.D. 382-3, after the war in which Lü Kuang 呂光, Fu Chien's 符堅 General, defeated the prince of Turfan and forced Kumarajiva by a trick to marry the daughter of the deposed king's brother, Prince Chên 震, whom he had enthroned in his stead, Lü Kuang 呂光 was returning with Kumarajiva, when, through a cloud-burst, several thousands of his men were drowned in their tents, and he in his dismay resolved to go back to Tangut and govern it as ruler. Being dissuaded by the monk, and hearing of Fu Chien's 符堅 downfall, he established himself at Liang-chou Fu 梁州府 in N. W. Kansu, where Kumarajiva lived in honour at Ku-tsang 姑臧, the new capital, and was allowed full liberty to preach his doctrine. Lü-kuang 呂光, on establishing himself at Liang-chou Fu 梁州府 styled himself first Viceroy, and then King. He was treated with equal kindness by Lü Tsuan 呂纂, who, on the death of his father Lü Kuang 呂光 usurped the throne and assassinated the rightful heir Lü Ch'ao 呂超. At this time a series of strange events occurred. Two dragons came out of a well to the east of the royal apartments, and a third appeared at the palace door. In the royal park there suddenly appeared wolves, horses, pheasants, peacocks, and turtle-doves, all of a white colour. A sow was said to have given birth to a child with three heads. Though the ruler saw in these phenomena nothing but propitious omens, the monk was inclined to view them less favourably. He said the dragon was a creature that lived in hiding, and his making himself too conspicuous was a bad sign. The king, however, paid no further heed, though he ordered the monk to say prayers on his behalf.

One day, when the king and Kumarajiva were playing chess, the former, every time he took a piece, said to his companion: "I have killed a barbarian monk" (lit. Hunnish slave, *hu-nu* 胡奴). "The barbarian monk will also cut off the head of a king," replied Kumarajiva (himself known as *Vibasha,* the "Great Barbarian"). The king's cousin, who was surnamed Hu-nu 胡奴, eventually murdered the king, thus fulfilling Kumarajiva's prophecy.

Kumarajiva had a good knowledge of Sanskrit and Chinese, and when, in A.D. 401, he went to the Court of Yao Hsing 姚興, Emperor of the Hou Ch'in 後秦, who was an ardent Buddhist, he was promoted (A.D. 405) to be a *Kuo-shih* 國師, State Preceptor, allowed to reside in the Hsi-ming Ko 西明閣, Palace of Western Brightness, and ordered to translate the *sutras*. This king (he had reduced his rank to that of a *wang* 王 in 399) "reverenced him as a god" (Giles, *Bio. Dic.*, p. 390), and it was for him that Kumarajiva wrote the *Shih-hsiang lun* 實相論 *shastra* on Reality and Appearance. He was an industrious and judicious translator, his knowledge enabling him to correct the errors of previous translators, though most of his treatises are abridgements of the original Sanskrit works. By comparing the liturgies used by the 800 monks of the capital and its environs with the Indian text in his possession and one in that of the king, he was enabled to make an exact translation, afterwards adding commentaries and dissertations, the whole forming more than 300 volumes. (See also Edkins, *Chinese Buddhism*, pp. 89-90.) He translated some fifty works, the principal one being the *Prajna-paramita*, or *Transcendental Wisdom* (intelligence as a means to reach Nirvana), which he abridged from its original 120 volumes (this work, of a vague pantheistic nature, admits an Impersonal Absolute, but denies the reality of all worldly phenomena, and the validity of knowledge derived through the senses); the *Amitabha Sutra;* the *Saddharma-pundarika,* or *Lotus of the Good Law (Miao-fa lien-hua ching* 妙法蓮華經), the *Shih-sung lü* 十誦律, *Discipline of the Ten Chants;* and the *Mahalamkara Sutra,* a series of sixty-six sermons, written by Asvaghosa. He also wrote a life of the latter, and introduced a new alphabet.

As regards the translation of the *Vinaya Pitaka, Lü-tsang* 律藏, the second division (consisting of works on ascetic morality and monastic discipline) of the *Tripitaka,* or Buddhist canon, Kumarajiva, hearing that the priest Fo-yeh to-lo 佛葉多羅 was well versed in these regulations, got him called to the palace, and collaborated with him in translating this work. Fo-yeh to-lo 佛葉多羅 died before its completion, and it was finished by Buddhadjiva Fo-t'o-shih 佛陀什 (a native of Kabul; arrived in China A.D. 423). Doré, however, says that in A.D. 405 the monk Liu-chih 流支 of Tan-mo 曇摩 , "arrived in China; it was with his help that the translation of the Lü-tsang 律藏 could be brought to an end." Edkins mentions that Dharmakakala had already translated the *Vinaya* or *Chieh-lü* 戒律 *(Discipline)* at Lo-yang 洛陽 and adds: Kumarajiva "found that in the corrections he proposed to make in the sacred books, he had been completely anticipated by his Chinese fellow-religionist" Tao-an 道安, a remarkably intelligent Buddhist priest of Ch'ang Shan 常山, Chê-kiang 浙江, who, however, died in 385, before he could meet Kumarajiva. The two had the highest regard for each other. Kumarajiva with his assistants made clear the sense of many profound and extensive *sutras* (*ching* 經) and *shastras* (*lun* 論), twelve works in all. Under the influence of the Chinese Scholars, to whom the ponderous verbosity and extensive repetitions of the originals were intolerable, he made a practice of omitting repetitions and superfluities. "The divisions into sections and sentences were formed with care. The finishing touch to the Chinese translation of these compositions was given by Seng-chau" (Edkins, p. 108-9). Kumarajiva was the most distinguished for ability among the "several tens of priests at Ch'ang-an 長安." His name is third in the Biographical Notices of the principal translators of the *sutras*. His translations of the *Vimakita, Wei-mo* 維摩, *Fa-hua* 法華 and *Ch'êng-shih* 成識 (complete) *sutras,* with the three by Dharmaraksha (the *Nirvana sutra,* the *Chin-kuang ching* 金光經, *Golden-light sutra,* and the *Ming-ching* 明經, *Bright Sutra*), and some others, together form the *Great Development* course of instruction. (For those forming the *Smaller Development* course, see Edkins, *Chinese Buddhism,* p. 110).

The king, besides granting him many other favours, conferred on him the title of *San-tsang Fa-shih* 三藏法師, Doctor of the Three Pitakas. The high officials also held him in great esteem.

In response to a hint that, after seeing some children playing in the royal park, he longed for posterity, the king sent him two wives from his harem, later adding ten concubines. Thenceforth he never set foot in the monastery, but lived at home with his wife and children.

The other monks expressing a wish to follow his example, he swallowed a handful of needles in their presence, saying that those who survived the ordeal might imitate him; but none dared to make the experiment.

Soon after this he fell ill, and in spite of recitations by himself and his disciples of the *San-fan shên-chu* 三番神咒 prayers, died on the twenty-second day of the eighth moon in A.D. 415 (409 and 412, according to other writers). Before his death he said to the Buddhist monks at his bedside: "If all the translations I have made are exact, may my tongue remain whole when my body is cremated." After his cremation in the Hsiao-yao Yüan 逍遙園, his tongue was found to have been untouched by the flames. He is known as one of the Four Suns of Buddhism.

The lion and the bird seen on images of the monk are allusions to prodigies observed in the royal park before the assassination of Lü Tsuan 呂纂.—See also *Lo-han* 羅漢.

CHIU-MO-LO-TO TSUN CHÊ 鳩摩羅多尊者.—See *Lo-han* 羅漢.

CHIU-MO-LO-YEN 鳩摩羅炎.—Kumarayana, the father of Kumarajiva. A saintly Hindu Buddhist monk. His forefathers were successively ministers in the country. He migrated, while still a youth, to Karashar, where he married Jiva, younger sister of the local ruler. He was one of those invited to the annual banquet of the gods (see *Hsi Wang-mu* 西王母).

CHIU-T'IEN LEI KUNG 九天雷公.—The Thunder-god of the Nine Heavens. A duplicate of Wên Chung 聞仲, the President of the Ministry of Thunder (see *Lei Tsu* 雷祖). Canonized as First Principle of the Nine Orbs of Heaven. As a talisman against disaster from thunder (see *Lei Kung* 雷公 and *Tien Mu* 電母) the following inscription is pasted on the lintels of doors: *Chiu-t'ien ying-yüan lei-shêng p'u-hua T'ien-tsun* 九天應元雷聲普化天尊 (written with each character surmounted by 雨), First Principle of the Nine Heavens, Transforming Voice of Thunder, Honoured of Heaven. Chiu-t'ien Lei Kung 九天雷公 is nothing but a personification of this title. —See also *Wu-fang Lei Kung* 五方雷公 and *Lei Pu* 雷部.

CHIU-T'OU SHIH 九頭氏.—See *Tou Mu* 斗母.

CHIU-TZŬ SHAN 九子山.—See *Chiu-hua Shan* 九華山.

CHIU YAO 九曜.—Nine constellations, each of which is presided over by a deified warrior who died in the *Wan-hsien Chên* 萬仙陣, The Battle of the Ten Thousand Genii, at T'ung-kuang 潼關, in the wars between the Yin 殷 and the Chou 周. Their names are:—Ch'ung Ying-piao 崇應彪, Kao Hsi-p'ing 高系平, Han P'êng 韓鵬, Li Chi 李濟, Wang Fêng 王封, Liu Chin 劉禁, Wang Ch'u 王儲, P'êng Chiu-yüan 彭九元, Li San-i 李三益.

CH'IU-NIU 囚牛.—See *Lung Wang* 龍王.

CH'IU-SHOU HSIEN 虬首仙.—A transcendent lion which changed into a human being. A disciple of T'ung-t'ien Chiao-chu 通天敎主. Fought in the Yin-Chou 殷周 wars. Was captured by Wên Shu 文殊, who pinioned him with his "Spirit-capturing" handcuffs. After Yüan-shih T'ien-tsun 元始天尊 had ordered him to resume his original state of a grey-haired lion, he was thenceforth employed as a mount by the Buddha Wên Shu 文殊.

CH'IU YIN 邱引.—The god of the star Kuan-so 貫索. Escaped seizure by Chiang Tzŭ-ya 姜子牙 at Ch'ing-lung Kuan 青龍關, but was slain by the flying sword of Lu-ya Tao-jên 陸壓道人 at the Battle of the Ten Thousand Genii.

CH'IUNG HSIAO 瓊霄.—See *K'êng San Ku-niang* 坑三姑娘.

CHO KUNG 卓公.—The god of the star Ti-man 地溺.—See *Ti-sha* 地煞.

CH'O CH'AN-SHIH 綽禪師.—See *Shan-tao Ho-shang* 善導和伺.

CHOTA (CUDA) PANTHAKA.—See *Lo-han* 羅漢.

CHOU CHI 周紀.—See *Wu Tou* 五斗.

CHOU HSIN 周信.—The god of the star Shih-ô 十惡. An officer under command of K'ung Hsüan 孔宣 at San-shan Kuan 三山關 in the Yin-Chou 殷周 wars. Slain under the walls of Hsi-ch'i 西岐 by Lei Chên-tzŭ 雷震子.—See *Wên Pu* 瘟部.

CHOU-HSIN 周新.—A celebrated *ch'êng-huang* 城隍, or city-god (of Hang-chou 杭州). Ming 明 dynasty.

CHOU KÊNG 周庚.—The god of the star Ti-mo 地獸. —See *Ti-sha* 地煞.

CHOU-LI PAN-T'O-CHIA 周利半託迦.—See *Lo-han* 羅漢.

CHOU PAO 周寶.—The god of the constellation Hsü 虛. Alternatively with Kai Yen 蕃延.

CHOU TA T'IEN-CHÜN 周大天君.—See *Ch'ü-hsieh Yüan* 驅邪院.

CHOU TS'ANG 周倉.—The standard-bearer of the God of War.—See *Kuan Yü* 關羽.

CHOU WANG 紂王.—The God of Sodomy. The tyrant Chou 紂 (1154-1121 B.C.), the last Emperor of the Yin 殷 dynasty, barbarously lustful, cruel, and extravagant. There is a temple dedicated to him at Chi Hsien 汲縣, in Wei-hui Fu 衞輝府, Honan 河南. The god of the star T'ien-hsi 天喜.

CHOU WU 周武.—See *San Kuan* 三官.

CHOU YÜ-CHI 周遇吉.—An assessor of Kuan Kung 關公. —See *Kuan Yü* 關羽.

CHU 柱.—See *Shê Chi* 社稷.

CHU-CH'A (T'A) PAN-T'O-CHIA 注茶半託迦.—See *Lo-han* 羅漢.

CHU CHAO 朱昭.—The god of the constellation Wei 尾. Alternatively with Ts'ên P'êng 岑彭.—See *Huo Pu* 火部.

CHU CHÊN-HÊNG 朱震亨.—See *Shih Ming-i* 十明醫, 4.

CHU CH'IAO 朱雀 (Red Bird), The god of the star.—See *Ma Fang* 馬方.

CHU-CHÜAN SHÊN 猪櫊 [圊] 神.—The God of Pigsties. Chu Tzŭ-chên 朱子眞 of Mei Shan 梅山, Mount Mei, is the transcendental pig. "He had a black face, short beard, long lips, and large ears. He wore a silk waist-belt to tie his black garments, and armed with a sword always fought on foot. His body was formed of coagulated air." He was canonized as the Spirit of the Star Fu-tuan 伏斷, and is extensively worshipped in pork-dealing districts.

When an officer under Yüan Hung 袁洪 at Mêng-ching 孟津, in his battle with Yü Chung 余忠, he changed himself into a gigantic pig, and swallowed Yang Chien 楊戩 who, however, at the victory banquet, threatened to tear out his heart and liver unless he reassumed his primitive form and submitted to Chiang Tzŭ-ya 姜子牙. He consented, and carried Yang Chien 楊戩 in his stomach to Chiang Tzŭ-ya's 姜子牙 tent. Yang Chien 楊戩 called out that he was in the pig's stomach, and begged him to kill the monster quickly and deliver him. So Nan Kung-kua 南宮适, at Chiang Tzŭ-ya's 姜子牙 command, cut off his head, and freed Yang Chien 楊戩, whereupon Chu Tzŭ-chên 朱子眞 re-appeared in his human form.

CHU FA-LAN 竺法蘭.—Dharmananda.—A saintly Hindu Buddhist monk. Came from Matanga to China during the reign of the Emperor Wu Ti 武帝 (140-86 B.C.) of the Ch'ien-Han 前漢, Former Han, dynasty. Translated several works, including a life of Buddha. One of those invited to the annual banquet of the gods (see *Hsi Wang-mu* 西王母).

CHU I 朱衣.—See *Wên Ch'ang* 文昌.

CHU I 朱義.—The god of the star T'ien-ying 天英.—See *T'ien-kang* 天罡.

CHU JUNG 祝融.—See *Huo Pu* 火部.

CHU [CHOU]-LI PAN-T'O CHIA 朱 [祝] 利半託迦.—See *Lo-han* 羅漢.

CHU-LIANG 祝良.—See *Shui Fu* 水府, C (2) (b).

CHU NIAO 朱鳥.—The God of the Heart. His "channel" is through the tongue (*Tsŭ hua tsŭ* 千華千).—See also *Hao Ch'iu* 豪邱; *Huan Yang-ch'ang* 煥陽昌; and *Tan Yüan* 丹元.

CHU PA-CHIEH 猪八戒.—See *Sun Hou-tzŭ* 猻猴子.

CHU SHÊNG 朱昇.—The god of the star Kua-hsü 寡宿. Major-domo of Chou Wang's 紂王 palace. Committed suicide when the capital fell into the enemy's hands.

CHU-SHÊNG NIANG-NIANG 注生娘娘.—See *Pi-hsia Yüan-chün* 碧霞元君.

CHU TAN 朱丹.—See *Wu Yo* 五嶽.

CHU TAO-SHÊNG 竺道生.—A saintly Hindu Buddhist monk. Fifth century. Lived at Lu Shan 廬山. A contemporary of Hui-yüan 慧遠 (*q.v.*) (A.D. 371-454). Later took up his abode at Hu-ch'iu Shan 虎邱山, Tiger-mound Hill, where he preached so successfully to a row of stones that they rose up, bowed to him, and expressed their agreement with his doctrine. One of those invited to the annual banquet of the gods (see *Hsi Wang-mu* 西王母).

CHU T'IEN-CHÜN 朱天君, CH'ÊN T'IEN-CHÜN 陳天君, CHÊNG T'IEN-CHÜN 鄭天君.—Three figures of Celestial Princes (T'ien-chün 天君) of terrifying aspect, invented by the Taoists with the object of inspiring dread and representing the formidable power of the gods of storms and hurricanes. Yü Shih 雨師 (*q.v.*), the Master of Rain, is often called Ch'ên T'ien-chün 陳天君.—See also *Lei Pu* 雷部.

CHU T'IEN LI SHIH 柱天力士.—See *Feet, The Gods of the*.

CHU T'IEN-LIN 朱天麟.—See *Wên Pu* 瘟部.

CHU TZǓ-CHÊN 朱子眞.—See *Chu-chüan Shên* 猪欄(闌)神.

CHU YIN-Ê 朱隱娥.—See *Shui Fu* 水府, C (2) (c).

CHU YING 朱映.—A God of the Eyes (*Yün chi ch'i ch'ien* 雲笈七籤).—See also *Hsüan Kuang* 玄光; *Ming Shang* 明上; and *Ying Ming* 英明.

CHU YU 朱祐.—The god of the constellation Tou 斗. Alternatively with Yang Hsin 楊信.

CH'U-CHIANG WANG 楚江王.—The President of the Second Court of Hades (*q.v.*).

CH'U-CH'IEN FA-SHIH 處謙法師.—Teacher of Yüan-chao Lü-shih 元昭律師 (*q.v.*).

CH'U-SHA 除殺, THE GOD OF THE STAR.—See *Yü Chung* 余忠.

CH'U TSAI 廚宰.—One of the Gods of the Sides of the Mouth (*Yün chi ch'i ch'ien* 雲笈七籤).—See also *Shou Shên* 守神 and *T'ai-i Chün* 太一君.

CH'U-YÜAN CH'AN-SHIH 楚圓禪師 (44th generation).—

A deified Buddhist monk. Ranked seventeenth in Buddhist School, III (*q.v.*). A native of Ch'ing-hsiang 清 湘, Ch'üan-chou 全 州 Department. Having been repulsed for two years, and even beaten, by Shan-chao Ch'an-shih 善 昭 禪 師 (*q.v.*), who at length silenced him, he was eventually illumined by Buddha himself. During seven years he followed the school of Shan-chao Ch'an-shih 善 昭 禪 師, who then sent him to the Southern provinces to expound the Doctrine there. Died A.D. 1041, aged 54.

CHUAN-LUN WANG 轉 輪 王.—King of the Revolving Wheel [of Metempsychosis]. The President of the Tenth Court of Hades (*q.v.*).

CH'UAN-SUI CH'AN-SHIH 傳 遂 禪 師 (67th generation). —A deified Buddhist monk. Ranked eighty-first in Buddhist School, VI (*q.v.*). Family name Wu 武. A native of Huai-an 淮 安, Kiangsu 江 蘇. Taught by [Sung-ju] Tao-mi Ch'an-shih [嵩 乳] 道 密 禪 師 (*q.v.*) at P'u-t'i 菩 㟁. Expounded the doctrine in the monasteries of Pao-ên 報 恩, Kuan-yin 觀 音, and T'an-tu 檀 庭. He was held to be a splendid orator, and monks flocked from all sides to listen to him." Died at the age of 29. His tomb is on Po-ch'ih Shan 鉢 池 山, Alms-bowl Lake Hill.

CHUANG-CHOU 莊 周.—See *Apotheosized Philosophers* and *Mao Mêng* 茅 濛.

CHUANG TSUNG 莊 宗.—See *Lao Lang* 老 浪.

CHUANG TZǓ 莊 子.—See *Apotheosized Philosophers* and *Mao Mêng* 茅 濛. For an account of the historical Chuang Tzǔ 莊 子 and his work see Finn, pp. 150-3.

CH'UANG KUNG. CH'UANG MU (P'O) 牀 公 牀 母 (婆). —The Duke of the Bed. The Mother of the Bed. The Male and Female Spirits of the Bed. Two Spirits whose duty is to protect the bedroom and especially the bed, but are particularly worshipped to procure childbirth. Offerings of tea, wine, fruit, and cakes are made to them in the bedroom; the wine being offered to the "Mother" and the tea to the "Duke" or "Gentleman." Sometimes an image of them is worshipped. Sometimes obeisance is made (and this usually by newly-married couples on entering the nuptial chamber) toward the bed alone, the invisible spirits being supposed to be present.

CHUN T'I 准 提.—Maritchi.—The Goddess of the Dawn, or the Goddess of Light. The Personification of Light. Represented as a female with eight arms, two of which hold aloft the sun and the moon. The protectress against war. Also styled Queen of Heaven, *T'ien Hou* 天 后, and Mother of the Southern

Dipper, *Tou Mu* 斗 母. With the Hindus, Taoists, and Japanese Buddhists, she is a stellar divinity, residing in the Great Bear. Sometimes her chariot is depicted as drawn by seven pigs, which may represent the seven chief stars of that constellation, or the seven horses that draw the chariot of the sun. When the goddess is represented with three heads, the one on the right is that of a sow (in China and Japan, on the right, in India, on the left). The reason for this is to be found in the legend which relates that one of the abbesses of the monastery of Semding, in Tibet, in whom the goddess is believed to be successively incarnated, had an excrescence resembling a sow's ear at the back of her head. In Taoist mythology, she has a husband, known as the "Worthy Deva, Father of the Southern Dipper," *Tou-fu T'ien-tsun* 斗 父 天 尊, and nine children. The Taoist legend, taken from its Tantra Buddhist forerunner at a time when Tantrism had given Maritchi a warlike character, accordingly represents her as a male warrior and a purely Taoist deity. Having thus appropriated her from Buddhism, the Taoists set her up in their own pantheon, in the seventh and eighth centuries A.D. She thus, in their mythology, is no longer the Goddess of the Dawn, but an Immortal with warlike attributes. These she displayed to the full in taking a leading part in the Yin-Chou 殷 周 wars, which led to the establishment of the Chou 周 dynasty, and performing innumerable marvellous feats described in detail in the *Fêng-shên yen-i* 封 神 演 義, *Hui* 回 70-82. Tantra Buddhism had represented her as a warlike being with sixteen or eighteen arms, bearing in her hands a sword, hatchet, bow, arrow, and thunder-bolt. She also carried a rosary, lotus, vase, etc., and is described as using magic formulas (*dharanis*).

The birthday of this goddess is celebrated on the sixteenth day of the third moon. Nowadays, she is worshipped both in Buddhist and Taoist temples. "The original idea is almost entirely ignored, except in pictorial art, where she, or he, is represented with eight arms and three heads, one of which is that of a sow (Kennelly, vii, 311).

CHUN-T'I P'U-SA 準 提 菩 薩.—The Buddhist *Chun T'i* 準 提 (*q.v.*).

CHUN-T'I TAO-JÊN 準 提 道 人.—The Taoist *Chun-t'i* 準 提 (*q.v.*).

CH'UN SHÊN-CHÜN 春 申 君.—A celebrated *ch'êng-huang* 城 隍, or city-god (of Su-chou 蘇 州). Third century B.C. Also a *t'u-ti* 土 地 (*q.v.*).

CH'UN YÜAN-CHÊN 春 元 眞.—See *Kidneys, The Gods of the.*

CHUNG-HSIEN CH'AN-SHIH 重顯禪師 (43rd generation).—A deified Buddhist monk. Ranked twenty-third in Buddhist School, VI (*q.v.*). Family name Li 李. A native of Sui-ning Fu 遂寧府, Ssŭch'uan 四川. Attended the school of Kuang-tsu Ch'an-shih 光祚禪師 (*q.v.*), who illumined him by forbidding him to speak and striking him with his fly-whisk (*fu-tzŭ* 拂子) (*cf. I-hsüan Ch'an-shih* 義玄禪師). He lived first at the Ts'ui-fêng Ssŭ 翠峰寺, Kingfisher Peak Monastery, and later at Hsüeh Tou 雪竇, Snow Cave, where he died. His tomb is at Hsi-wu 西塢, Chêkiang 浙江. Posthumous title: Ming-chio Ta-shih 明覺大師, Brilliant and Intelligent Teacher.

CHUNG K'UEI 終葵.—See *Ch'ü-hsieh Yüan* 驅邪院.

CHUNG K'UEI 鍾馗.—The slayer of devils. A deified hero. A domestic god. Depicted as an aged man, clad in ragged apparal and attended by a bat (the symbol of *fu* 福, happiness).—See *Ch'ü-hsieh Yüan* 驅邪院.

CHUNG K'UEI PI-HSIEH 鍾馗辟邪,—See *Ch'ü-hsieh Yüan* 驅邪院.

CHUNG-LI 重黎.—See *Tsao Chün* 灶 (竈) 君 and *Huo Po* 火部.

CHUNG-LI CH'ÜAN 鍾離權.—See *Pa Hsien* 八仙.

CHUNG-SHU 仲舒.—See *Chih Nü* 織女.

CHUNG-YU WU-LIEH TA-TI 忠佑武烈大帝.—The Great Emperor, Illustrious Militarist, Faithful and Protecting. Name Ch'ên Kuo-jên 陳果仁, personal name Shih-wei 世威. Born in A.D. 549 in the reign of the Emperor Wu-ti 武帝 (A.D. 502-50) of the Liang 梁 dynasty, at Chin-ling 晉陵 (in modern Wu-chin Hsien 武進縣), Ch'ang-chou Fu 常州府, Kiangsu 江蘇. A brave militarist, not only during his terrestrial, but also in his celestial life, who, in spite of having revolted against his sovereign, was honoured by a temple being erected to him and by numerous other titles, including those of King and Emperor, besides the one above-mentioned conferred on him by his fellow-countrymen.— See *Composite Deities*.

CHUNG-YÜAN TI-KUAN 中元地官.—The Earthly Ruler controlling the Middle Period.—See *San Kuan* 三官.

CH'UNG HOU-HU 崇侯虎.—The god of the star Ta-hao 大耗. A powerful feudatory prince, with his capital in the North named Ch'ung Ch'êng 崇城. Incurred the enmity of, and was put to death, together with his son, by Wên Wang 文王.

97

CH'UNG-HSIN CH'AN-SHIH 崇信禪師 (37th generation).
—A deified Buddhist monk. Ranked sixth in Buddhist School,
VI (q.v.). A native of Chu-kung 渚宮, Hupei 湖北. As a boy,
sold cakes at the monastery gate, and gave ten to the monk Tao-
wu Ch'an-shih 道悟禪師 (q.v.), who returned one to him,
saying: "For the benefit of the family." He finally became a
Buddhist monk, and taught at T'ien-huang 天皇, a temple in
Ching-chou 荊州, in the same province.

CH'UNG-HSIN CH'AN-SHIH 崇信禪師 (46th generation).
—A deified Buddhist monk. Ranked thirty-second in Buddhist
School, VI (q.v.). A disciple of Tsung-pên Ch'an-shih 宗本
禪師 (q.v.). Taught at Ch'ang-lu 長盧, Chihli 直隸, where he
died.

CH'UNG LING-YÜ 冲靈玉.—The God of the Nose. His
designation is Tao Wei 道微 (Ssŭ Ming 四命).—See also Yung
Lu 勇盧 and Yü Lung 玉龍.

CH'UNG-T'AN 崇覃.—See Pi-hsia Yüan-chün 碧霞元君.

CH'UNG YING-PIAO 崇應彪.—See Chiu Yao 九曜.

CHÜ CH'ÊNG 巨乘.—See Shui Fu 水府, C (2) (b).

CHÜ-LIU SUN 拘留孫—Lived in the Fei-yün Tung 飛雲洞,
on Chia-lung Shan 夾龍山. Captured by Chao Chiang 趙江.
Later a member of the Ministry of Thunder, bound and taken to
Chiang Tzŭ-ya 姜子牙, who had him put to death. The first
Buddha of the present kalpa (Krakuchanda).

CHÜ-SHÊ TSUNG 俱舍宗.—See Buddhist Schools, XIII.

CHÜ-TI HO-SHANG 俱胝和尚.—See Lo-han 羅漢.

CH'Ü-HSIEH YÜAN 驅邪院.—The Ministry of Exorcism.
This Ministry is a Taoist invention and is composed of seven chief
ministers, whose duty is to expel evil spirits from dwellings and
generally to counteract the annoyances of infernal demons. It is
composed of the following members: Yang 楊, Shih 施, Chou 周,
Sung 宋, Ning 寧, Li 李, and Ho 賀, the title appended to each
of these names being Ta T'ien-chün 大天君, Great Heavenly
Prince. The two gods usually referred to in the popular legends
are P'an Kuan 判官 and Chung K'uei 鍾馗. The first is really
the Guardian of the Living and the Dead in the Otherworld,
Fêng-tu P'an Kuan 酆都判官 (Fêng-tu 酆都, or Fêng-tu Ch'êng
酆都城, being the region beyond the tomb). He was originally
a scholar named Ts'ui Chio 崔珏, who became Magistrate of
Tz'ŭ Chou 磁州, and later Minister of Ceremonies. After his

death he was appointed to the spiritual post above mentioned. His best-known achievement was his prolongation of the life of the Emperor T'ai Tsung 太宗 (A.D. 627-50) of the T'ang 唐 dynasty by twenty years by changing *i* 一, "one," into *san* 三, "three," in the life register kept by the gods. The term P'an Kuan 判官 is, however, more generally used as the designation of an officer or civil or military attendant upon a god than of any special individual, and the original P'an Kuan 判官, "the Decider of Life in Hades," has been gradually supplanted in popular favour by Chung K'uei 鍾馗, "the Protector against Evil Spirits."

Chung K'uei 鍾馗 is described as dressed in a green robe, one eye half closed, a buckled belt, and one foot shod. He wears a cap over his dishevelled hair. With his left hand he is shown stabbing a demon, whose eye he is tearing out with his right hand.

The Emperor Ming Huang 明皇 (A.D. 713-56) of the T'ang 唐 dynasty having been attacked by fever whilst on a military expedition to Mount Li 驪 in Shensi 陝西, dreamt that he saw a small demon fantastically dressed in red trousers, with a shoe on one foot but none on the other, and a shoe hanging from his girdle. Having broken through a bamboo gate, he took possession of an embroidered box and a jade flute, and then began to make a tour of the palace, sporting and gambolling. The Emperor grew angry and questioned him. "Your humble servant," replied the little demon, "is named Hsü Hao 虛耗, 'Emptiness and Devastation.'" "I have never heard of such a person," said the Emperor. The demon rejoined, "Hsü 虛 means to desire Emptiness, because in Emptiness one can fly as one wishes; Hao 耗 'Devastation,' changes people's joy to sadness." The Emperor, irritated by this flippancy, was about to call his guard, when suddenly a great devil appeared, wearing a tattered headcovering and a blue robe, a horn clasp on his belt, and official boots on his feet. He went up to the sprite, tore out one of his eyes, crushed it up, and ate it. The Emperor asked the newcomer who he was. "Your humble servant," he replied, "is Chung K'uei 鍾馗, Physician of Chung-nan Shan 終南山 in Shensi 陝西. In the reign of the Emperor Kao Tsu 高祖 (A.D. 618-27) of the T'ang 唐 dynasty I was ignominiously rejected and unjustly defrauded of a first class in the public examinations. Overwhelmed with shame, I committed suicide on the steps of the imperial palace. The Emperor ordered me to be buried in a green robe [reserved for members of the imperial clan], and out of gratitude for that favour I swore to protect the sovereign in any part of the Empire against the evil machinations of the demon Hsü Hao 虛耗." At these words the Emperor awoke and found that the fever had left him. His Majesty called for Wu Tao-tzŭ 吳道子 (one of the most celebrated Chinese artists) to paint the portrait of the person he had seen in his dream. The work was so well done that the Emperor recognized it as the actual demon he had seen in his sleep, and rewarded the artist with a hundred taels of gold. The portrait is said to have been still in the imperial palace during the Sung 宋 dynasty.

Another version says that Chung K'uei's 鍾馗 essay was recognized by the examiners as equal to the work of the best authors of antiquity, but that the Emperor rejected him on account of his extremely ugly features, whereupon he committed suicide in his presence, was honoured by the Emperor and accorded a funeral as if he had been the successful first candidate, and canonized with the title of Great Spiritual Chaser of Demons for the Whole Empire.

The worship of Chung K'uei 鍾馗 rests on the above legends, which date from the T'ang 唐 dynasty (see *infra*), and is a private cult, there being no temples erected in his honour. As time went on, the people began to put representations of him over their doors to keep off evil spirits. Even likenesses of a female Chung K'uei 鍾馗 were used, because Tsung Ch'io's 宗懿 younger sister's name was Chung K'uei 鍾葵, the sound of the two characters being the same (the latter being also the name of a leaf to which magic virtues were attributed). Doubt as to whether the legends do not antedate the dream of the Emperor Ming Huang 明皇 (A.D. 713-56) of the T'ang 唐 dynasty has been based on the facts that the name Chung K'uei 鍾馗 occurs as early as the Han 漢 dynasty; and on the custom in ancient times of attributing the power of destroying demons to a large tablet called Chung K'uei 終葵 used by the Grand Exorcist to frighten away evil spirits. This name was afterwards given protectively to children, the characters *chung k'uei* 終葵 having the same sound as 鍾馗, to crush devils. The power attributed to the instrument was transferred to the bearers of the name. The latter occurs quite often in the times of the Pei Wei 北魏, Northern Wei dynasty, etc., in pre-T'ang 唐 times.

Later on, the meaning of the expression was made clearer by the second character *k'uei* 葵 being altered to *k'uei* 馗, *i.e. chiu* 九, nine, *shou* 首, heads, a devil with nine heads, the combination Chung K'uei 鍾馗 thus making more obvious to the popular eye the meaning of the characters as a devil-dispeller.

The attribution to human beings of the power ascribed to the instrument was confirmed in the popular mind through the knowledge that in the time of the Emperor T'ai Wu 太武 (A.D. 424-52) of the Wei 魏 dynasty there lived an officer called Yao Hsüan 堯瞳, whose name was Chung K'uei 鍾葵, and his first name Pi Hsieh 辟邪. The last two characters form the ordinary phrase for the exorcizing virtue of talismans; and naturally it was thought that Chung K'uei 鍾葵 had the same power. In this way, the magic power ascribed to the tablet came to be ascribed to the human being.

The above data furnish the ground for the belief held by many Chinese writers that the legends relating to Chung K'uei 鍾馗 date from a time earlier than that of the T'ang 唐 dynasty.

CH'Ü T'AN 瞿曇.—A saintly Buddist monk. Sixth century. One of those invited to the annual banquet of the gods (see *Hsi Wang-mu* 西王母). A native of Shên-tu Kuo 身毒國, Sind, in N. W. India. Generally called Ku Fo 古佛, the Old Buddha, on account of his prodigious knowledge of the Law. His personal name was Hsiao Shih-chia 小釋迦 (*q.v.*), Little Sakyamuni. He lived during the reign of the Emperor Wu Ti 武帝 (A.D. 502-50) of the Liang 梁 dynasty.

CHÜAN-SHÊ 卷舌, THE GOD OF THE STAR.—See *Yu Hun* 尤渾.

CH'ÜAN-HSÜ CH'AN-SHIH 全豁禪師 (39th generation). —A deified Buddhist monk. Ranked tenth in Buddhist School, VI (*q.v.*). Family name K'o 柯. A native of Ch'üan-chou 泉州, Fukien 福建. Entered the Pao-shou Ssŭ 寶壽寺, Precious Longevity Monastery, at Ch'ang-an 長安, Shensi 陝西. A friend of Hsüeh-fêng Ch'in-shan 雪峰欽山 (*q.v.*), he followed the teaching of the Yen-t'ou 巖頭 school, in the O-chou 鄂州 department, Hupei 湖北. "During the period of persecution, he became a ferryman, and navigated his own punt in order to gain a livelihood. One day, a band of rebels arrived and asked him for some food, but as he could supply none, they killed him with their swords. When his disciples cremated his body, forty-nine precious stones fell from the heavens. A tower was erected over his remains." Posthumous title: Ch'ing-yen Ch'an-shih 清嚴禪師, Pure and Dignified Monk.

CHÜN 君.—A brain-god.—See *Chio Yüan-tzŭ* 覺元子.

CHÜN-MING 君明.—See *Tung Wang-kung* 東王公.

CITY, THE GOD OF THE.—See *Ch'êng Huang* 城隍.

CITY WALL, THE GOD OF THE.—"Called 'The Eighth Minister.' He rules the city wall, and directs the military operations in case of a siege; he is worshipped by the Board of Public Works" (Du Bose, p. 141).

CLASSICS, THE GOD OF THE.—Name Chêng K'ang-ch'êng 鄭康成 Han 漢 dynasty. Was able to expound the most intricate passages of the Classics. Punished the misdemeanours of his handmaids by requiring them to memorize the words of Confucius, so his amahs became classical scholars.

CLOUDS SECT, GATE OF THE.—See *Buddhist Schools*, VIII.

COBBERS AND HARNESS-MAKERS, THE GOD OF.— See *Sun Pin* 孫臏 (賓).

COMB-SELLERS, THE GOD OF.—See *Hei-lien Tsu-shih* 黑連祖師.

COMMISSIONER, THE GRABBING.—See *Liang-shua Shih* 掠刷使.

COMPASS, THE GODS OF THE.—See *Wu-fang Shên* 五方神 and *Shui Fu* 水府, C (2) (b) and (e).

COMPOSITE DEITIES.—Combinations of Human and Animal Forms.—Yin Yüan-shuai 殷元帥. Marshal Yin, a personification of T'ai Sui 太歲, the Year-spirit, was a son of Chou 紂, the last king of the Yin 殷 dynasty (1154-1122 B.C.). His mother was the Queen Chiang 姜. His name in infancy was Yin Chiao 殷郊. He is represented as a man with a leopard's head, three eyes, a lion's nose, a tiger's mouth, a bear's tongue, a boar's tusks, and three pairs of arms. Above his ears are tufts of hair known as *ya-êrh mao* 壓耳毛, lit., "ear-pressing hair," and on the top of his otherwise bald skull is a head-dress known as *k'uei-ying* 盔纓.

The above representation is regarded as a "bad picture," or likeness of an evil being. Another, regarded as a "good picture," shows Yin Yüan-shuai 殷元帥 with a man's head and body, two eyes, "ear-pressing hair," three pairs of arms, and hair standing erect on the back of his head.

Sun Hou-tzǔ 猻猴子 (*q.v.*), the hero of the popular romance *Hsi-yu chi* 西遊記, is known by a variety of names, such as Sun Wu-k'ung 孫悟空, Mei Hou-wang 美猴王, etc. He originated from a stone monkey born from an egg which formed on the summit of Hua-kuo Shan 花果山, in Ao-lai Kuo 傲來國, a kingdom in the Eastern continent beyond the seas known as Shêng-shên Chou 勝神洲. Though of stone, he seems to have been almost from the first imbued with life, the stone being one of the spiritualized fragments left over by Nü-wa Shih 女媧氏 when she repaired the heavens.

He is represented with a monkey's body, head, face, two eyes, arms, hands, legs, and feet. His body, hands, and feet were later on changed to those of a male human being. When he had acquired sufficient age and skill he could change into any form he pleased. He wears a priest's hat surmounted by a topknot (*ko ta'rh* 疙疸兒).

Ma T'ou 馬頭, Horse-head. One of the attendants on Ch'êng Huang 城隍, the God of Ramparts and Ditches, or the City God. He is represented with a human body and a horse's head.

Kou Ching 狗精, the Dog-spirit. His name was Tai Li 戴禮, and he was an officer sent by King Chou 紂 of the Yin 殷 dynasty to help Yüan Hung 袁洪, the general in command of the troops at Mêng-ching 孟津. He is represented with a man's body, a dog's head, long snout, large hanging ears, and shines with a strange light. He is shown mounted on a horse and armed with two swords. From his mouth he projects a large red pearl, which wounds or kills his enemies. He usually accompanies Yang Chien 楊戩 (Êrh Lang 二郎), nephew of Yü Huang 玉皇, the Jade Emperor (the Chinese Jupiter). He often kills warriors otherwise invincible. He appears also in pictures of Chang Hsien 張仙, the God of Dreams, who shoots arrows from a bow to prevent Kou Ching 狗精 from devouring newly-born infants (v. infra).

Chu Pa-chieh 猪八戒. An invention of the author of the Hsi-yu chi 西遊記 (cf. Sun Hou-tzŭ 孫猴子, supra). When occupying the post of Overseer-General of the Navigation of the Milky Way he was exiled to earth for re-incarnation as a punishment for assaulting the daughter of Yü Huang 玉皇, but entering by mistake the womb of a sow he was born half-man, half-pig. He was ordained a priest by Kuan Yin 觀音 under the religious name of Wu Nêng 悟能, "Seeker after Strength." The pictures show him with a human body and the head, eyes, ears, mouth, snout, and bristly skin of a pig.

The attendant of Yang Yüan-shuai 楊元帥, Marshal Yang, is represented with a human body and a pig's head. He belongs to the time of the Shang 商 dynasty, and is the Pig God Chu Tzŭ-chên 朱子貞, originally a pig, who now can change himself back into the form of a large pig at will. He is usually depicted as a man with a black face, short beard, large ears, long lips and riding a white horse.

The god or spirit of each of the twenty-eight constellations, êrh-shih pa su 二十八宿, was originally a sub-human creature, usually an animal. These were the crocodile, dragon, badger, fox, dog, wolf, hare, porcupine, rat, leopard, griffon, bat, pheasant, gibbon, cock, crow, horse, dew-worm, deer, monkey, snake, stag, goat, tapir, swallow, ox, tiger, and pig. Thus, of the twenty-eight, twenty-six belong or belonged to the vertebrata (nineteen mammalia, four aves, and three reptilia), one to the chiroptera, and one to the annelida. They are sometimes represented as human beings, at other times with composite bodies partly human, partly animal (or other creature concerned). Frequently, the latter is represented only by the head, as, for example, the head of a sheep on a human body.

Combinations of Human and Bird Forms.—Lei Kung 雷公, the Duke of Thunder, is represented as of natural stature, with a human bust, monkey's head, two eyes, two cow's horns (these are sometimes omitted), a falcon's beak, "ear-pressing tufts," two falcon's wings, two human arms, two hands with long claws, and two falcon's feet. In one hand he holds a mallet, in the other a steel awl. Across his shoulders is a necklet of drums. His statues are made with eyes which move in their sockets. Sometimes he is depicted with a cock's head and claws. Originally, Chinese works represented him as a strong man (not as a bird), with a cluster of drums in one hand, and a hammer in the other.

As regards the wings, these used to be drawn as those of a bat, but in later pictures they resemble those of the Indian divine bird Garuda.

Lei Chên Tzǔ 雷震子. A Son of Thunder. His name when a child was Wên Yü 文玉. "He was hatched from an egg after a clap of thunder and found by the soldiers of Wên Wang 文王, in some brushwood near an old tomb. The infant's chief characteristic was its brilliant eyes. Wên Wang 文王, who already had ninety-nine children, adopted it as his hundredth, but gave it to a hermit named Yün Chung-tzǔ 雲中子 to rear as his disciple. The hermit showed him the way to rescue his adopted father from the tyrant who held him prisoner. In seeking for some powerful weapon the child found on the hillside two apricots, and ate them both. He then noticed that wings had grown on his shoulders and was too much ashamed to return home.

"But the hermit, who knew intuitively what had taken place, sent a servant to seek him. When they met the servant said: 'Do you know that your face is completely altered?' The mysterious fruit had not only caused Lei Chên Tzǔ 雷震子 to grow wings, known as Wings of the Wind and Thunder, but his face had grown green, his nose long and pointed, and two tusks protruded horizontally from each side of his mouth, while his eyes shone like mirrors" (*Myths and Legends of China,* pp. 202-3).

The pictures show him with a monkey's head, three eyes, two human arms, "ear-pressing tufts," a falcon's nose, back, feet, and wings, two tusks, and a head-dress (*kuan* 冠).

Wu-fang Lei Kung 五方雷公, Lei Kung of the Five Cardinal Points. A purely mythical Taoist invention intended to correspond with Chiu-t'ien Lei Kung 九天雷公, the Duke of Thunder of the Nine Heavens (a duplicate of Wên Chung 聞仲). Is depicted with a monkey's head, three eyes, a falcon's beak, wings and feet, two human arms, and a head-dress (*kuan* 冠).

T'ao-t'ien Chün 陶天君. Was one of the subaltern officers of Lei Tsu 雷祖 (*v. infra*). Is shown with a monkey's head, a falcon's beak, nose, wings, and feet, "ear-pressing tuffs," and two human arms.

Pa Cha 叭咤, The God of Grasshoppers. This deity, who destroys grasshoppers, locusts, and noxious insects, is said to have originated in the province of Hsin-chiang 新疆 (*Kashgaria*), where a farmer whose crops were never attacked by insect pests was prayed to by the others as their protecting deity against those destructive agencies. He is worshipped in the trans-frontier districts of China Proper (the former "Eighteen Provinces"), but in the latter is said to be the same as Liu Mêng Chiang-chün 劉猛將軍, Marshal Liu Mêng, represented as the protector against destructive insects, or as his lieutenant.

He is portrayed with the head, two eyes, nose, beak, feet, claws (also on hands), of a falcon or bird of prey which feeds on insects of this kind, "ear-pressing tufts," a coiffure (*tao kuan'rh* 道冠兒), pendulous breasts, two human arms, and a bell as a skirt. The latter curious garment had its origin in the confusion of the words *chung* 鐘, bell, and *ch'ung* 蟲, insect. On the skirt the four characters *Kuo t'ai min an* 國泰民安, "When the kingdom is at peace, the people are tranquil," are often written or engraved.

Combinations of Human and Other Forms.—This class comprises numerous deities composed partly of the human form and partly of lower non-human forms other than animal, such as snakes, centipedes, frogs, etc. Two of these have been referred to in connection with the Twenty-eight Constellations. In the pictures the deity is usually represented in the human form, perhaps because of the difficulty of combining satisfactorily the two forms or parts of them, and in those cases the creature in question is shown as if it were a spirit issuing from the crown of the head, or is shown in the same picture, in its natural form, placed in proximity to the human form. In some, however, the combination is made, as, for example, in that of Nü-wa Shih 女媧氏, shown with a human female head on a snake's body. P'an Ku 盤古, also, is (though not invariably) represented with a dragon's head on a man's body.

Variations on the Human Form.—Lei Tsu 雷祖, the Ancestor of Thunder and President of the Ministry of Thunder, known generally as Wên Chung T'ai-shih 聞仲太師; colloquially as Wên T'ai-shih 聞太師, His form is wholly human, except for an additional eye in the centre of his forehead (*v. infra*).

Ma Yüan-shuai 馬元帥, Marshal Ma. Known also as "The Divine (or Marvellous) Officer Marshal Ma," Ling-kuan Ma Yüan-shuai 靈官馬元帥. Is an avatar of the god Chih Miao-chi 至妙吉, whom Ju-lai 如來 Buddha condemned to reincarnation for shewing too much severity in the repression of evil spirits. In the shape of five globes of fire he entered the womb of Ma Chin-mu 馬金母, where he re-clothed himself with the human form. He was born with three eyes, and so was also called San-yen Ling-kuan 三眼靈官, "The Divine (or Marvellous) Officer with Three Eyes." He is portrayed with three pairs of arms, but is said originally to have had but one pair (*v. infra*). He is not known to have had any but a mythological history.

Huo-te Hsing Chün 火德星君, or Lo Hüan 羅宣, The Prince of the Virtue of Fire. The stellar god of the planet Mars. Is placed in temples on the right of Chu-jung Ta-ti 祝融大帝, the Sovereign God of Fire. He has three heads and three faces, the front one with three eyes, the other two with two each; and three pairs of arms. He has no fourth head facing backwards, otherwise he could see in that direction also, and so could not be killed!

Tou Mu 斗母, the Mother of the North Pole. A Taoist stellar

divinity. Having married Ch'ên Chi-tsung 辰祭從, king of Chou Yü 周御, a kingdom situated in the northern regions, she became the mother of the nine human sovereigns, Jên Huang 人皇. Was called Mo Li-chih 摩利支; also known as Wan T'ai-yang 萬泰陽. Was born in the Western kingdom of T'ien-chu Kuo 天竺國 (India), thus being the Maritchi of Brahmanic mythology. She is represented with a human female body, three eyes, and nine pairs of arms.

Wang Ling-kuan 王靈官, the Divine (or Wonderful) Officer Wang, the Taoist equivalent of the Buddhist divinity Ch'ieh [chia] Lan 伽藍 (Ga-lam, originally one of Buddha's disciples, see *Chia-lan*), a name given to a class of gods of Chinese origin who act as servants and gatekeepers at monasteries and are their tutelary gods or protectors (*Sangharama*). Like a good many others, such as Ch'ih Ching Tzǔ 赤糈子, the God of Fire, he has a human form, with an additional eye in the centre of his forehead.

Kuan Yin 觀音, Goddess of Mercy, for her supreme self-sacrifice, has at times as many as a thousand arms and hands (though not limited to any definite number).

Other human forms differ only from the ordinary human body in being completely covered with hair, or in having a cleft in the middle of the skull, causing it to look like two hillocks instead of a round globe. These might indicate vestigial horns (but this explanation is open to question).

For gods represented by two or more separate individuals or by animals, etc., into which they were transformed, see: *Ch'ing-i Shên* 青衣神; *Ma-t'ou Niang* 馬頭娘; *T'ien Ssǔ-fang* 天駟房; *Wu Shêng* 五聖; *Tz'ǔ-shan Chang Ta-ti* 祠山張大帝; *Wu Ti* 五帝; *Liu Pei* 劉備; *Kuan Ti* 關帝; *Chang Fei* 張飛; *Ma Ku* 麻姑; *Yo Fei* 岳飛 and his assessors; *Shê Chiang-chün* 佘將軍; *Tu T'ien* 莟天; *Yang Chou Wu Ssǔ t'u* 揚州五司徒; *Chiang Hsiang-kung* 蔣相公; *Ts'ui Fu-chün* 崔府君; *Ch'i Kung-tzǔ* 威公子; *Chung-yu Wu-lieh Ta-ti* 忠佑武烈大帝; *Pai-chi* 柏姬 or 白雞; *Ch'i Ku-tzǔ* 七姑子; *Tsung Kuan* 總管; *Hsiao Ho* 蕭何; *Shêng Ku* 聖 (昇) 姑; *Wei-chi Hou* 威齊侯; *Sung-li Hsiang-kung* 萬里相公; *Ling-ku Hou* 靈派侯; *Yüan Ch'ien-li* 真千里; *Kuan Kung* 關公 and his assessors.

CONCUBINE OF HEAVEN, THE.—See *T'ien Fei* 天妃.

CONFUCIUS.—See *K'ung-fu Tzǔ* 孔夫子.

CONSTABLE-GODS, THE.—See *T'u-ti* 土地.

CONSTELLATIONS, SPIRITS OF THE.—See *Huo Pu* 火部 and *Erh-shih-pa Hsü* 二十八宿.

CONTEMPLATIVE SCHOOL, THE.—See *Buddhist Schools*, XII.

CORN-CHANDLERS, THE GOD OF.—See *Lei Tsu* 雷祖.

CORN-CUTTERS, THE GOD OF.—See *Lo-tsu Ta-hsien* 羅祖大仙.

CORNER, THE GODDESS OF THE.—"It is customary for young ladies to apply to this deity to have their fortunes told. After burning incense they take a peck measure turned upside down, with a flower on it; this is for a sedan; then one enquires, 'Is Miss Corner at home?' Answer, 'No.' 'Is the second Miss Corner here?' 'No.' 'Is little Miss Corner present?' 'Yes.' She takes her seat in the peck measure and is carried to the table, on which rice is spread as an offering. One bows and asks of the oracle what her fortune is to be. The peck basket is held over the rice, and the answer is written by a needle attached to it" (Du Bose, p. 340), similarly to the system of the Western *planchette*.

CORPSE, THE GODDESSES OF THE.—There are three of these (known as dead ghosts). They are P'ang Chu 彭朱, P'ang Ch'ê 彭車, and P'ang Chiao 彭蹻. They are nuns, dressed in green, white, and red garments respectively. They reside in the body. To prevent them leaving it, it is necessary to observe a night-watch (according to the almanac); otherwise, on that night. if one sleeps, the goddesses go to heaven and inform the gods of his sins.

COUNT OF WATERS, THE.—See *Shui Fu* 水府, D (3) (d).

COW, THE.—That which distinguishes Hinduism from all other religions is the worship of the cow. "But for the most striking words on spiritual cow-herding we must go to China. Zen [Ch'an 禪] Buddhism was founded in China by Bodhi-Dharma in the sixth century. Zen is perhaps the most mystical sect of the Buddhist faith. It differs in several respects from other Buddhist sects, but chiefly in the fact that it ignores the necessity of climbing slowly to the heights of Buddhahood. . . . The stages in the mystic life which is the result of Zen discipline are illustrated by means of pictures of a cow and a cowherd. The religious life is spiritual cow-herding.

"During the Sung 宋 dynasty a Zen teacher called Seikyo illustrated the stages of spiritual progress by a gradual purification or whitening of the cow until she herself disappears. These pictures, six in number, are now lost, but a popular series of the ten Cow-herding Pictures illustrating the end of Zen discipline in a more thorough and consistent manner were painted by Kakuan, a monk of the Rinzai school. Each of the ten pictures has a short introduction in prose followed by a summing-up in verse. In the last four pictures the cow does not appear, and the words accompanying these pictures are in the nature of a commentary on what has gone before. They tell of the results of the spiritual cow-herding which ends with the sixth picture.

"The followers of Zen are, of course, familiar with the many references to the cow in their own literature. . . . The Cow-herding Pictures show the upward steps of spiritual training. . . . It seems evident that the Buddha himself might have written the notes on the Cow-herding Pictures. These notes are also good Taoism. They sum up the message of Lao Tse [Tzŭ] and Chuang Tzŭ. . . . When we read that Lao Tse went towards the western hills, on the back of a cow, and, further, that he has since preached his gospel in other parts of the world, we can see, behind the human incidents of the story, a parable of the Oneness of all Life.

"Spiritual cow-herding leads to the calm assurance that *'Things are one.'* And then comes the duty of carrying this bliss-bestowing thought into the world of men. All our problems await solution in the light of the doctrine of the Motherhood of God. Strife will cease, hatreds will vanish and war will end when all men have caught the Cow" (Hayes, *The Book of the Cow*, pp. 67-76). The Cow-god is Mang Shên 芒 神 (*q.v.*).

Du Bose (p. 324) says that the God of Horses and Cows is much worshipped in North China, and pays special attention to the domestic animals. "Theatricals are paid for by the owners of stock. The temples are under official patronage. In the temple in honour of these gods the grooms attached to the yamêns worship in order to secure health and mettle to their horses."— See also *Po Yao (Lo)* 伯 樂 and *T'ien Ssŭ* 天 駟.

CRANE-SPIRIT, THE.—See *Pai-ho T'ung-tzŭ* 白 鶴 童 子.

CRUELTY, THE GOD OF.—Du Bose (p. 339) says: "He was called 'Two Worlds.' After death he was a monster of cruelty. The Chinese sometimes go before the city god, and tell him of any difficulty they have had with another, and ask him to adjudicate it after death."

CYCLE, THE GODS OF THE.—The cycle-gods are also star-gods. There are sixty years in a Chinese cycle, and over each of these presides a special star-deity. The one worshipped is the one which gave light on the birthday of the worshipper, and therefore the latter burns candles before that particular image on each suceeding anniversary. These cycle-gods are represented by most grotesque images.—See also *Star-gods* and *T'ai Sui* 太 歲.

D

DAITYAS.—Titans. Descendants from Diti by Kasyapa. They are a race of demons and giants in India, who warred against the gods and interfered with sacrifices. They were in turn victorious and vanquished. They and the Danavas are generally associated, and are hardly distinguishable. As enemies of sacrifices they are called Kratus-devishas.—*Cf. Danava.*

DAME CH'ÊN 陳.—See *Pi-hsia Yüan-chün* 碧霞元君.

DANAVA.—Descendants from Danu by the sage Kasyapa. They were giants who warred against the gods.—*Cf. Daityas.*

DAWN, THE GODDESS OF THE.—See *Chun T'i* 準提.

DAY, THE GOD OF THE.—The name of this god is Tung Chün 東君, the Eastern Emperor, or Emperor of the East. —*Han shu chu* 漢書注. *Cf. Chih Jih* 值日.

DAY AND NIGHT RECORDERS.—One of these gods records the good and bad deeds done during the day, and the other takes account of those done during the night.

"DEAF CELESTIAL," THE. T'ien Lung 天聾 — See *Wên Ch'ang* 文昌.

DEATH HAS ITS PART.—See *Ssŭ yu fên* 死有分.

DEFENDER OF THE LAW.—See *Wei T'o* 韋馱.

DELICATE PERCEPTOR, THE.—See *Ch'ien-li Yen* 千里 眼. *Cf. Shun-fêng Erh* 順風耳.—These two names conjointly are synonymous for those who see things which are not apparent, and hear things they are not supposed to hear.

DEMON-KINGS.—See *Shih-tien Yen-wang* 十殿閻王.

DEMON RAVISHERS.—See *Pretas.*

DESERT SAVAGE, THE.—See *Yeh Jên* 野人.

DEVA (Nom. Devas=Deus, from the root *Div,* to shine).—God. A deity. The gods of Brahmanism. The Hindu gods are spoken of as thirty-three in number, eleven for each of the three worlds. In Chinese *T'i-p'o* 提婆 meaning *T'ien-shên* 天神, spirits of heaven, or *Fan-t'ien jên* 梵天人, inhabitants of the Brahmalokas (heavens of Brahma). (1) General designation of the gods of Brahmanism, and of all inhabitants of the Devalokas (*q.v.*) who are subject to metempsychosis. (2) Name of the fifteenth patriarch (*infra*).

In Chinese Buddhist works Devas, including all the Hindu gods that are mentioned, whether great or small, are called T'ien 天, Heaven. Beings inferior to the Devas are designated collectively the Eight Classes (*Pa pu* 八部). They are called Nats by the Burmese. All these beings—Apsaras, Asuras, Devas, Gandharas, Garudas, Kinnaras, Nagas—including the most venerated and powerful of the gods, are introduced as disciples of Buddha.

The combination of ascetic eminence and profound philosophy in Sakyamuni raises him to a position higher than any of them. Beings of every rank in earth or heaven confess their inferiority to the human Buddha by becoming his humble and attentive auditors.

The Hindus, having become acute metaphysicians, thought themselves superior to every being in the universe.

Deva is also the name of the fifteenth Patriarch, a native of Southern India, a disciple of Nagardjuna, also called Desabodhisattva, T'i-p'o P'u-sa 提婆菩薩, and Arya Deva, Shêng T'ien 聖天, author of nine works, a famous antagonist of Brahminism.

DEVA OF DEVAS.—God of gods.—See *Fo* 佛.

DEVADATTA.—T'i-p'o-ta-to 提婆達多, or Tiao-ta 調達. Lit. *T'ien-shou* 天授, gift of devas.—The rival and enemy of Sakyamuni, an incarnation of Asita, swallowed up by hell, worshipped as Buddha by a sect, up to A.D. 400, supposed to reappear as Buddha Devaradja (*T'ien Wang,* 天王) in a universe called Devasoppana (*T'ien Tao* 天道) (Eitel).

DEVALOKA.—T'ien-kung 天宮, the heavenly mansions of devas.—The six celestial worlds, situated above Mount Meru, between the earth and the Brahmalokas (q.v.).—See *Tuchita.*

DEVA-NAGAS.—Dragon-kings—See *Lung wang* 龍王.

DEVATA.—A term for members of the highest class of Hindu gods.

DEVATIDEVA.—T'ien-chung-t'ien 天中天, the deva among devas.—See *Fo* 佛.

DEVI.—T'i-p'i 提鞞. T'ien-nü 天女.—A female deva. The same as *apsaras* (*q.v.*). "The goddess," or Maha-devi, "the great goddess," wife of the god Siva, and daughter of Himavat, *i.e.*, the Himalaya mountains. As the Sakti or female energy of Siva she has two characters, one mild, the other fierce; and it is under the latter that she is especially worshipped. She has a great variety of names, referable to her various forms, attributes, and actions, but these names are not always used accurately and distinctively. In her milder form she is Uma, "light," and a type of beauty; Gauri, "the yellow or brilliant"; Parvati, "the mountaineer"; and Haimavati, from her parentage; Jagan-mata, "the mother of the world"; and Bhavani. In her terrible form she is Durga, "the inaccessible"; Kali and Syama, "the black"; Chandi and Chandika, "the fierce"; and Bhairavi, "the terrible." It is in this character that bloody sacrifices are offered to her, that the barbarities of the Durga-puja and Charak-puja are perpetrated in her honour, and that the indecent orgies of the Tantrikas are held to propitiate her favours and celebrate her powers. She has ten arms, and in most of her hands there are weapons. As Durga she is a beautiful yellow woman, riding on a tiger in a fierce and menacing attitude. As Kali or Kalika, "the black," "she is represented with a black skin, a hideous and terrible countenance, dripping with blood, encircled with snakes, hung round with skulls and human heads, and in all respects resembling a fury rather than a goddess." As Vindhya-vasini, "the dweller in the Vindhyas," she is worshipped at a place of that name where the Vindhyas approach the Ganges, near Mirzapur, and it is said that there the blood before her image is never allowed to get dry. As Maha-maya she is the great illusion.

DHARMA.—An ancient sage, sometimes classed among the Prajapatis. He married thirteen (or ten) of the daughters of Daksha, and had a numerous progeny; but all his children "are manifestly allegorical, being personifications of intelligences and virtues and religious rites" (Buddhist Law personified), and being therefore appropriately wedded to the probable authors of the Hindu code of religion and morals, or the equally allegorical representation of that code, *Dharma,* moral and religious duty.—See *O-mi-t'o Fo* 阿彌陀佛, *San Po* 三寶, and *Fa Pao* 法寶.

DHARMA-KAYA.—See *Adi-Buddha.*

DHARMANANDA.—See *Chu Fa-lan* 竺法蘭.

DHARMA-SASTRA.—A law-book or code of laws. This term includes the whole body of Hindu law, but it is more especially applicable to the laws of Manu, Yajnawalkya, and other inspired sages who first recorded the *Smriti* or "recollections" of what they had received from a divine source. These works are generally in three parts: (1) *Achara,* rules of conduct and practice; (2) *Vyavahara,* judicature; (3) *Prayaschitta,* penance.

DHARMASOKA.—See *Asoka.*

DHARMATALA.—See *Lo-han* 羅漢.

DHARMATARA.—See *Lo-han* 羅漢.

DHARMATRATA.—See *Lo-han* 羅漢.

DHRITARASHTRA.—See *Ssŭ ta T'ien-wang* 四大天王.

DHYANA.—Mystic meditation. Abstract meditation intended to destroy all attachment to existence. Buddhism taught that it was possible by intense self-absorption and mystic meditation to attain to a mental state by which six kinds of supernatural wisdom (*abhinna*) and ten supernatural powers (*iddhi*) were acquired. A Buddha always possessed them; whether Arahats (*q.v.*), *as such,* could work the particular miracles in question, and whether, of mendicants, only Arahats, or only Asekhas (*q.v.*), could do so is at present not clear. They adhere, however, to the *karma,* so that a person who has practised mystic ecstacy, or been very wise or very virtuous in one birth, may have extraordinary (supernatural) good fortune or powers in the next. This throws, perhaps, some light on the origin of the belief. Ordinary *karma* was held sufficient to produce ordinary continuous states; but when some quite unexpected and extraordinary piece of good luck happened to some one who had evidently done nothing to deserve it, some quite extraordinary religious exaltation in the last birth was postulated to explain it.

The mental condition by which these powers were apparently acquired is called in Pali *jhana,* in Sanskrit *dhyana,* of which there are four stages. It is only by the completion of the fourth *jhana* that *abhinna* is acquired. The first *jhana* is a state of joy and gladness born of seclusion, full of reflection and investigation, the mendicant having separated himself from all sensuality and all sin. The second is a similar state born of deep tranquillity, without reflection or investigation, these being suppressed; it is the tranquillization of thought, the predominance of intuition. In the third the mendicant is patient by gladness and the destruction of passion, joyful and conscious, aware in his body of that delight which the Arahats announce, patient, recollecting, glad. The fourth is purity of equanimity and recollection, without sorrow and without joy, by the destruction of previous gladness and grief, by the rejection of joy, and the rejection of sorrow. The *Great Vehicle* teaches five instead of the four stages found in the *Pitaḳas* and the *Lalita Vistara*. The earlier Buddhism teaches that above the worlds of the gods are "sixteen worlds of Brahma" (Brahmalokas), one above another; those who attain on earth to the first, second, or third Dhyana, are reborn in the lower of these worlds, three worlds being assigned to each Dhyana. Those who attain the fourth Dhyana enter the tenth or eleventh Brahmaloka; the remaining five being occupied by those who attain to the third path here on earth, and who will reach Nirvana in this new existence. To each of these five groups of worlds the *Great Vehicle* assigns a special Buddha, called Dhyani Buddha. —See also *Adi-Buddha*.

DIAMOND, THE.—Hindu mythology is full of mystic tales about the diamond. In the *Puranas,* the city of Dwaraka where Krishna took up his abode is described as a high and square city, measuring a hundred *voyanas,* and furnished with cupolas of diamonds, pillars of emeralds, and courtyards of rubies. The Tree of Hindu religion, a symbolical offering to the gods, is also described as a glowing mass of precious stones with diamonds for its base, sapphire for its roots, and pearls and rubies for its leaves and fruit.

The celebrated Chinese traveller, Hsüan Tsang 玄 奘, also tells us of a "Diamond Throne" which, according to the legend, once stood near the Tree of Knowledge beneath whose spreading branches Gautama Buddha received his Supreme Enlightenment. The construction of this throne out of a single diamond was believed to have taken place at the very dawn of creation, and it measured one hundred feet in circumference, and "upon it the thousand Buddhas of the Kalpa had reposed and fallen into ecstasy of the diamond." But since the Kaliyuga began, earth and sand have covered it so completely that it can no longer be seen by the fleshly eye.

DIAMOND KINGS, THE FOUR GREAT.—See *Ssŭ ta T'ien-wang* 四 大 天 王.

DIAPHRAGM, THE GOD OF THE.—The name of this god is Tao Kung 氜 公 — *Ko chih ching yüan* 格 致 镜 原.

DIPAMKARA.—The Buddha of fixed light. The twenty-fourth predecessor of Sakyamuni (who foretold the coming of the latter), a disciple of Varaprabha. He was "eighty cubits high."— See *Jan-têng Fo* 然 燈 佛.

DIPPER, THE GOD OF THE.—See *Pei Tou* 北 斗.

DIVINE ARCHER, THE.—See *Shên I* 神 羿.

DIVINE HUSBANDMAN, THE.—See *Shên Nung* 神農.

DJATAKAS or DJATAKAMALA.—Shê-to-[ka] Chia 闍多伽, Chih yeh 祗夜, or Pên shêng shih 本生事. "Adventures of original (former) births." Books detailing previous incarnations of saints.

DOMESTIC SACRIFICES, THE FIVE.—See *Ts'ai Shên* 財神.

DOOR, THE FAMILY GODS OF THE.—See *Shên Shu Yü Lü* 神荼鬱壘.

DOOR, THE OFFICIAL GODS OF THE.—See *Mên Shên* 門神.

DOOR-GODS, THE.—See *Shên Shu Yü Lü* 神荼鬱壘 and *Mên Shên* 門神.

DOORS, PROTECTORS OF.—See *Shên Shu Yü Lü* 神荼鬱壘 and *Mên Shên* 門神.

DOOR-SPIRITS, THE.—See *Shên Shu Yü Lü* 神荼鬱壘 and *Mên Shên* 門神.

DRAGONS.—See *Lung* 龍 and *Lung Wang* 龍王.

DRAGON-BOAT, THE.—See *Féng-huo Yüan T'ien Yüan-shuai* 風火院田元帥.

DRAGON-HORSE, THE.—See *K'ang Yüan-shuai* 康元帥.

DRAGON-KINGS.—See *Shui Fu* 水府.

DREAM, THE GOD OF THE.—See *Chang Hsien* 張仙.

DRIED-UP LAKES, THE SPIRITS OF THE.—See *Shui Fu* 水府, D (2) (e).

DRISANA.—See *Virochana*.

DUKE OF THE BED, THE.—See *Ch'uang Kung Ch'uang Mu* 牀公牀母.

DUKE OF THUNDER, THE.—See *Lei Kung* 雷公.

DYERS, THE GODS OF.—See *Ko Hsien-wêng* 葛仙翁.

E

F, KUEI 餓鬼.—See *Prêtas*.

EAR, THE GOD OF THE.—The name of this god is given in the *Chên kao* 眞誥 as Chiao Nü 嬌女. The *Huang-t'ing ching* 黃庭經 states the name as K'ung Hsien 空閑, with Yu T'ien 幽田 as his style (*tzŭ* 字).

EARTH, THE.—Ti 地.—"Mother Earth" was worshipped by the Emperor at Peking (Peiching 北京) on the Altar of Earth, sacrifices being at the same time offered to the seas, the mountains, and the rivers. Written prayers and rolls of silk were buried (instead of being burned, as in the worship of Heaven). In South China, the peasants set up a clod of earth, and lit incense in front of it, in token of thanksgiving for an abundant harvest.—See also *Wên Ch'ang* 文昌 and *Granet*, p. 172.

EARTH, THE ELEMENT.—See *Wu Hsing* 五行.

EARTH, THE SPIRIT OF THE.—See *Hou T'u* 后土 and *Wu Lao* 五老 (*Huang Lao* 黃老).

"EARTH-DUMB" (TI-YA 地啞),—See *Wên Ch'ang* 文昌.

"EARTH MOTHER" (TI-MU 地母).—See *Wên Ch'ang* 文昌.

EASTERN AIR, THE SOVEREIGN OF THE.—See *Tung Wang-kung* 東王公.

EASTERN PEAK, THE GOD OF THE.—See *T'ai Shan* 泰山.

EAVES, THE GOD OF THE.—The ancient God of the Eaves, Chung Liu 中霤, is now embodied in the worship of the Earth Gods of the home (*Li chi* 禮記, III, 5).

EIGHT GODS, THE.—The Eight Gods worshipped by the Emperor in ancient times were those of Heaven, Earth, War, Male Principle of Nature, Female Principle of Nature, Sun, Moon, and Four Seasons.

EIGHT IMMORTALS, THE.—See *Pa Hsien* 八仙.

EIGHTEEN LOHAN 羅漢, **THE.**—See *Lo-han* 羅漢.

EIGHTH GREAT KING, THE.—This was the counterpart in the Otherworld of the special official who attended to the legal affairs of the Manchus. He was the Eighth Prince, an uncle of the last of the Ming 明 Emperors, and gave his allegiance to the new Manchu Dynasty. He was, however, stoned to death by the inhabitants of Soochow 蘇州, Kiangsu 江蘇, and subsequently apotheosized.

ELEMENT OF WATER, THE SUBTILE SPIRIT OF THE.—See *Shui Fu* 水府, D (3) (c).

ELEMENTS, THE FIVE.—See *Wu Hsing* 五行.

ELEPHANT, THE WHITE.—See *Kuan Yin* 觀音.

EMBROIDERY, THE GODDESS OF.—The third concubine of Hsüan Yüan 軒轅. Being skilled in needlework, was appointed goddess of the needle and of embroidery. Worshipped by girls learning this handicraft.

EMPEROR ON HIGH, THE PURE AUGUST.—See *Yü Huang* 玉皇.

EMPEROR, THE JADE.—See *Yü Huang* 玉皇.

EMPRESS OF HEAVEN, THE.—See *T'ien Fei* 天妃.

"EMPTINESS AND DEVASTATION."—See *Wên Pu* 瘟部

EPIDEMICS, THE MINISTRY OF.—See *Ch'ü-hsüeh Yüan* 驅邪院.

ÊRH LANG 二郎.—Son of Li Ping 李冰 (*q.v.*). Family name Chao 趙; personal name Ching 景. A disciple of the Taoist Li Chio 李珏. Having been appointed Prefect of Kuanchou 灌州, in Ssŭch'uan 四川, by the Emperor Yang Ti 煬帝 (A.D. 605-17) of the Sui 隋 dynasty, he found that the peasants' fields were annually inundated by the Lêng 泠 and Yüan 源 Rivers, whose waters were caused to swell by a dragon which, under the guise of an ox, lived therein.

Accordingly, when, in the fifth moon, the floods returned, Chao Ching 趙景, with a flotilla of seven hundred ships, a thousand officers and soldiers, together with ten thousand men standing on the banks, shouted and beat drums, making a deafening noise, and then, armed with a sword, threw himself into the water and joined battle with the dragon.

The spectators saw the water redden, stones projected from it as by an explosion, and heard a terrifying noise like that of thunder. Then the victorious Chao Ching 趙景 reappeared, holding his sword in one hand and the monster's head in the other. At this time he was twenty-six years of age. During the succeeding period of political unrest he resigned and disappeared.

In a subsequent flood at Kuan-chou 灌口, the inhabitants, during some stormy weather, perceived him mounted on a white horse, walking on the water, accompanied by the celestial dog, generally known as Ying Ch'üan 鷹犬, the Eagle Dog.

To commemorate the benefits resulting from his slaying of the dragon, the people of the district built a temple to him at Kuan-chiang K'ou 灌江口, and he is now generally known as Kuan-chiang K'ou Êrh Lang 灌江口二郎, Êrh Lang of Kuan-chiang K'ou. His posthumous title is given in the *Sou-shên chi* 搜神記 as Great Marshal, Divine Nephew.

The universally-accepted identification of Êrh Lang 二郎 with Yang Chien 楊戩, the nephew of Yü Huang 玉皇, is probably based on an incident related in the *Hsi-yu chi* 西遊記, where Êrh Lang 二郎 is deputed by Yü Huang 玉皇 to fight Sun Hou-tzŭ 孫猴子 (*q.v.* and Werner, *Myths and Legends*, p. 331). When they met, Êrh Lang 二郎 said: "How is it you do not recognize me? Do you not know I am Yü Ti's 玉帝 nephew? My posthumous name is Hui-ling Hsien-wang Êrh Lang 惠靈顯王二郎. I have come to fight you by orders from Yü Ti 玉帝."

Sun Hou-tzŭ 孫猴子 replied: "I remember that Yü Ti's 玉帝 younger sister came down to earth and married Yang Chün 楊君, and had a son. That is you! If you value your life, flee at once, or I will be obliged to kill you."

It follows from this that Yang Chün 楊君, the father of Yang Chien 楊戩, was the brother-in-law of Yü Ti 玉帝, and that Êrh Lang 二郎 or Yang Chien 楊戩, his son, was the nephew of Yü Ti 玉帝.

He is represented with his celestial dog and also with his famous *chao-yao ching* 照妖鏡, devil-revealing mirror.

Among the chief of his numerous posthumous titles are: Ch'ing-yüan Miao-tao Chên-chün 清源妙道眞君 and Ch'ih-ch'êng Wang 赤城王, given him by the Emperor Chên Tsung 眞宗 (A.D. 998-1023) of the Sung 宋 dynasty and by the Emperor Ming Huang 明皇 (A.D. 713-56) of the T'ang 唐 dynasty, respec-

tively; and Êrh Lang Shên-shêng Chên-chün 二郎神聖眞君.—
Cf. the legend of Li Ping 李冰 (see *Kuan-k'ou Shên* 灌口神).

ÊRH-SHIH-PA HSÜ 二十八宿.—The Twenty-eight Constellations. These were all originally animals or other sub-
human creatures, afterwards changed into men, and then into
star-gods. The gods of these constellations were all disciples of
the Taoist patriarch T'ung-t'ien Chiao-chu 通天教主, who
became immortals through practising his teaching. Having taken
the part of Chou Wang 紂王 against the Chou 周, he and all his
disciples were slain in the battle of the Ten Thousand Immortals.
Chiang Tzǔ-ya 姜子牙 conferred on them the apanage of the
Twenty-eight Constellations. The Chinese works *Tsêng-kuang
yü-hsia chi* 增廣玉匣記 and *Fêng-shên yen-i* 封神演義 give
different names for the star gods. The alternative names are
given in the separate entries of the gods. See *Têng Yü* 鄧禹,
Wu Han 吳漢, *Chia Fu* 賈復, *K'ou Hsin* 寇恂, *Liu Lung* 劉隆,
Ma Wu 馬武, *Kêng Yen* 耿弇, *Tsang Kuan* 臧官, *Kai Yen*
蓋延, *Fêng I* 馮異, *Chu Yu* 朱祐, *Ching Tan* 景丹, *Wu Ch'êng*
烏成, *Tu Mao* 杜茂, *Wang Liang* 王良, *Ch'ên Chün* 陳俊,
Li Chung 李忠, *Liu Chih* 劉直, *Jên Kuang* 任光, *Fu Chün* 傅俊,
P'ei T'ung 邳仝, *Wan Hsiu* 萬修, *Wang Pa* 王覇, *Yao Ch'i*
姚期, *Chien Tan* 堅譚, *Chi Tsun* 祭遵, *Ts'ên P'êng* 岑彭,
Kêng Shun 耿純, and *Zottoli, Cursus Litteraturæ Sinicæ*, II, p. 51.

EVERLASTING, THE.—See *Yüan-shih T'ien-tsun* 元始天尊.

EXORCISM, THE MINISTRY OF.—See *Ch'ü-hsieh Yüan*
驅邪院.

EYE, THE GODDESS OF THE LIGHT OF THE.—See
Yen-kuang P'u-sa 眼光菩薩.

EYE, THE GODS OF THE.—The God of the Eye is Ming
Shang 明上, his *tzǔ* 字 being Ying Hsüan 英玄 (*Huang-t'ing
ching* 黃庭經). The *Yün chi ch'i ch'ien* 雲笈七籤 says that
there are six spirits of the two eyes, namely, the spirits of the sun
and the moon (*jih yüeh ching* 日月精). The *tzǔ* 字 of the left
eye is Ying Ming 英明, of the right eye Hsüan Kuang 玄光. It
further gives the name of the God of the Eye as Chu Ying 朱眽
and as Hsü Chien-shêng 虛監生, with the *tzǔ* 字 as Tao T'ung
道童. It is three and six-tenths inches in height, and wears
garments of five colours (or, a five-coloured garment).

EYE OF THE LAW SECT, THE.—See *Buddhist Schools,* IX.

EYEBROWS, THE GODS OF THE.—The names of these
gods, three in number, are Nan-chi Lao-jên 南極老人, Yüan
Kuang 元光, and T'ien-lung Chün 天龍君.—*Yün chi ch'i ch'ien*
雲笈七籤.

F

FA-CHAO KUO-SHIH 法照國師,—A deified Buddhist
monk. Ranked fourth in Buddhist School, XVII (q.v.).
The fourth ancestor. Lived in the Yün-fêng Ssŭ 雲封寺,
Yün-fêng Monastery, at Hêng-chou 衡州, Hunan 湖南. "One
day, looking into his alms-bowl, he saw in the midst of a
radiant cloud a scene representing a rock with a stream flowing
at its foot; a narrow passage between the boulders led to a
monastery, on the front of which was the inscription: Ta-
shêng Chu-lin Ssŭ 大聖竹林寺, Great Sacred Monastery of the
Bamboo Forest. He was told that this represented a place at Wu-
t'ai Shan 五臺山. The following night, a fiery pillar led him to
the foot of the rock which he had seen in his vision; two guardians
introduced him into this enchanting place, and led him to a hall,
where two venerable doctors were explaining the doctrine. One
of these was Wên-chu 文殊 (Manjusri, the Buddha of Transcendent
Wisdom; a fanciful and mystic creation of the Mahayana and Yoga
Schools [see *Buddhist Schools*]), who said to him: 'Nothing is
more profitable for a monk than to invoke the name of O-mi-t'o
Fo 阿彌陀佛, Amitabha, which is all-powerful, and confers on
all who pronounce it eternal bliss.' The doctors then placed their
hands on Fa-chao's 法照 head." The legend of this prodigy was
engraved on stone, and the monk erected the Chu-lin Ssŭ 竹林寺,
Monastery of the Bamboo Forest, on the spot indicated in the
vision. When the building was completed, he said: "My task is
accomplished," and expired.

FA-CHIH TSUN-CHÊ 法智尊者.—A deified Buddhist monk.
Ranked sixteenth in Buddhist School, X (q.v.). Secular name Chin
Chih-li 金知禮. A native of Ssŭ-ming 四明. The legend says: His
mother beheld in a dream a heaven-sent monk, who presented her
with a child, saying: "He is the Buddha Lo-hou-lo" 羅睺羅, Rahula

FA-CHIH TSUN-CHÊ (the eldest son of Sakyamuni. After his father's death, he founded a philosophical, realistic school. He is nowadays revered as the patron saint of all Buddhist novices). On waking, she found she was with child, and in due time gave birth to a handsome babe, who became a Buddhist monk, and was trained by I-t'ung Tsun-chê 義 通 尊 者 (*q.v.*). His father also had a dream, in which he clearly saw the teacher of Chin Chih-li 金 知 禮 pouring into his mouth the contents of a phial, which being completely absorbed, his intelligence was illumined. Finally, after the death of his teacher, the monk himself dreamt that he was carrying on his shoulder the head of his teacher. On waking, he said: "It is a sign that I must propagate the doctrine," a determination which he carried out to the end of his life. Died A.D. 1028, uttering the name of Buddha with his last breath. His disciples did not bury him for twenty-four days, at the close of which time his corpse was as fresh as when living. His tongue remained uncorrupted, and five-coloured relics, *shê-li* 舍 利, fell in abundance from the sky.

FA-CH'IH CH'AN-SHIH 法 持 禪 師 (35th generation).— A deified Buddhist monk. Ranked fourth in Buddhist School, I (*q.v.*).

FA-CHIU 法 救.—See *Lo-han* 羅 漢.

FA-HSIANG TSUNG 法 相 宗.—See *Buddhist Schools*, XIV.

FA-HSIEN 法 顯.—A saintly Buddhist monk. A.D. 374-460. A native of Wu-yang Hsien 武 陽 縣, a dependency of P'ing-yang Fu 平 陽 府, Shansi 山 西. Family name Kung 龔. Visited India, where he showed his power of quieting lions. Returned to China in A.D. 414. Settled at Nanking 南 京. The incidents of his journey abroad were related to Buddhabhadra, a Hindu fellow labourer, who committed them to writing, thus forming the work known as *Fo-kuo chi* 佛 國 記, *Records of Buddhistic Kingdoms,* published about A.D. 420. He died at the age of 86 (or 88), being, it is said, borne away to the Hsi T'ien 西 天, Western Paradise, by Buddhajanga, Fo-t'u-ch'êng 佛 圖 澄 (*q.v.*). Fa Hsien 法 顯 was one of those invited to the annual banquet of the gods (see *Hsi Wang-mu* 西 王 母).

FA-HUA CHING 法 華 經.—See *Buddhist Schools*, X.

FA-HUA TSUNG 法 華 宗.—See *Buddhist Schools*, X.

FA-JUNG 法 融.—A saintly Buddhist monk. Seventh century. One of those invited to the annual banquet of the gods (see next entry and *Hsi Wang-mu* 西 王 母). A disciple of Tao-hsin 道 信 (*q.v.*).

FA-JUNG CH'AN-SHIH 法融禪師 (32nd generation) [The name of the mountain or place where the School is situated is often prefixed to the religious name, *e.g.* Niu-t'ou Shan Fa-jung Ch'an-shih 牛頭山法融禪師.].—A deified Buddhist monk. Ranked first in Buddhist School, I (*q.v.*). Born at Jun-chou 潤州 (modern Chên-chiang 鎮江, Chinkiang, Kiangsu 江蘇). A member of the Wei 韋 family. At the age of 19 he went to Mao Shan 茅山, near Chü-jung Hsien 句容縣 S. of Nanking 南京, and afterwards withdrew to a cave to the N. of Niu-t'ou Shan 牛頭山, Buffalo-head Mountain, and gave himself up to contemplation. Here he met Tao-hsin 道信, the fourth Buddhist patriarch (see *Patriarchs*), and became his disciple. This was between A.D. 627 and 650. Tao-hsin 道信 transmitted to him the doctrine of the third Buddhist patriarch, Sêng-ts'an 僧粲 (see *Patriarchs*).

Fa-jung 法融 then proceeded to Sung Shan 嵩山, Mount Sung, where he opened a school which became famous. He had three hundred disciples. In times of scarcity, he went to beg food for them at Tan-yang 丹陽, about 26 miles away. He died about A.D. 659.

During the last year of his life, he transmitted the doctrine to Chih-yen 智巖, the most intelligent of his disciples.

FA-LIU 法柳.—A saintly Buddhist monk. Fourth century. One of those invited to the annual banquet of the gods (see *Hsi Wang-mu* 西王母).

FA-NA-P'O-SSŬ 伐那婆斯.—See *Lo-han* 羅漢.

FA PAO 法寶.—The Precious Law (*Dharma*).—See *O-mi-t'o Fo* 阿彌陀佛; *San Pao* 三寶.

FA-SHÊ-LO-FU-TO-LO 伐闍羅弗多羅.—See *Lo-han* 羅漢.

FA-SOU P'AN-T'OU 法藪盤頭.—Vasubandu, *q.v.* and *Buddhist Schools*, XIII.

FA-TSANG CH'AN-SHIH 法藏禪師 (68th generation).—A deified Buddhist monk. Ranked forty-ninth in Buddhist School, III (*q.v.*). Family name Su 蘇. A native of Hsi-shan 錫山. His teacher was Yüan-wu Ch'an-shih 圓悟禪師 (*q.v.*). Later he had a school of his own at San Fêng 三峰, Three Peaks. His tomb is on the same mountain.

FA-TSANG FA-SHIH 法藏法師.—A deified Buddhist monk. Ranked third in Buddhist School, XI (*q.v.*). Family name K'ang 康. A native of K'ang-chü Kuo 康居國, Sogdiana (the biographies state that he was a Hindu, but Wieger regards him as Chinese). Having reached Ch'ang-an 長安, Shensi 陝西, he followed the teaching of Chih-yen Fa-shih 智儼法師 (*q.v.*). The Empress Wu-hou 武后 (A.D. 684-705), an ex-Buddhist nun, conferred on him the honorary title of Hsien-shou 賢首, Excellent Leader, whence the name Hsien-shou Chiao 賢首教, Excellent Leader School.

The Empress further ordered him to assist Shih-ch'a-nan-t'o 實叉難陀, Sikchananda (meaning "pleasure of study," a native of Kustana, who, in A.D. 605, introduced an alphabet for the translation of Sanskrit) in translating the *Hua-yen ching* 華嚴經 into Chinese, and when it was finished, requested him to add some notes on the new prayers. Whilst he was engaged in this task, a severe earthquake shook the imperial palace. Fa-tsang Fa-shih 法藏法師 was also admitted to Court during the reign of the Emperor Jui Tsung 睿宗 (A.D. 710-13), and explained there thirty chapters of the *Hua-yen ching* 華嚴經. Died A.D. 712, in the Ta-chien-fu Ssǔ 大薦福寺, Ta-chien-fu Monastery. Posthumous title: Hung-lu Ch'ing 鴻臚卿, Swan-like Minister.

FA-TSU 法祚.—A saintly Buddhist monk. Fourth century A.D. A contemporary of Buddhajanga (see *Fo-t'u-ch'êng* 佛圖澄). One of those invited to the annual banquet of the gods (see *Hsi Wang-mu* 西王母).

FA-YEN CH'AN-SHIH 法演禪師 (47th generation).—A deified Buddhist monk. Ranked twenty-second in Buddhist School, III (*q.v.*). Family name Têng 鄧. A native of Mien-chou 棉州. His teacher was Shou-tuan Ch'an-shih 守端禪師 (*q.v.*), of Pai-yün Shan 白雲山, White Cloud Mountain. Died A.D. 1104.

FA-YEN MO 法眼脈.—See *Buddhist Schools*, IX.

[FA-YEN] WÊN-I CH'AN-SHIH [法眼] 文益禪師.—See *Buddhist Schools*, IX.

FACE-CREAM AND PERFUME SELLERS, THE GODDESS OF.—See *Hsi Shih* 西施.

FALSE-HAIR SELLERS, THE GODDESS OF.—See *Chao San-niang* 趙三娘.

FAN CH'ANG-SHOU 范長壽.—An Immortal. Nothing further is recorded concerning him.

FAN HUAN 樊煥.—The god of the star Ti-t'ui 地退.—See *Ti-sha* 地煞.

FAN K'UEI 樊噲.—One of the Gods of Butchers. A native of P'ei Hsien 沛縣, Kiangsu 江蘇. At first gained his livelihood by killing dogs and selling their flesh. Then joined Liu Pang 劉邦 (247-195 B.C.) in his campaigns, and protected his master at the peril of his own life. For this he was rewarded with the title of Marquis of Wu-yang 舞陽, Honan 河南. He is sacrificially worshipped by butchers.—See also *Chang Fei* 張飛.

FAN PIN 范斌.—The god of the star Ti-lieh 地劣.—See Ti-sha 地煞.

FAN-T'IEN 梵天.—The Brahma heaven, Brahmaloka. The Brahmas (*Fan*; formerly *Bam* or *Vum*) are the inhabitants of the heaven (eighteen heavenly mansions) called Brahmaloka, over which Fan-t'ien Wang 梵天王 (Mahabrahma or the chief Brahma) presides. They live through twenty small *kalpas,* and he through sixty.

The heaven of Brahma is said to have been formed by wind blowing on water, in which grew up of itself a vast mass of moist matter. On this again the wind blew, and out of it formed the palace of Brahma, which exhibited in abundance the most beautiful combinations of the precious metals and stones of every kind known to man.

FAN-T'IEN WANG 梵天王.—Fan-wang 梵王 (*q.v.*) or Fan-t'ien Wang 梵天王 is the name given by Chinese Buddhists to Brahma. Brahmaloka (*q.v.*), the eighteen heavenly mansions, of which Brahma is the over-lord.—See *Fan-t'ien* 梵天.

FAN-WANG 梵王.—The father of all living beings. The one who evolved, or hatched (as a hen setting) the universe from eternal cosmic matter (Monier Williams). The first person of the Brahminical Trimurti adopted by Buddhism, called by Buddhists Fan-wang 梵王 or Ta Fan-wang 大梵王, but placed in an inferior position, being looked upon, not as a creator, but as a transitory *devata* whom every saint, on obtaining *bodhi,* surpasses.

"He is eternal and quiescent matter, the diffused essence of the world. In a later phase of philosophical evolution, he is held to be the 'soul of the Universe,' an impersonal, Pantheistic being, awaking after endless ages of apathy, and brooding over the 'cosmic egg,' whence the present world was finally evolved."

Brahma and Indra were most popular divinities in the early stage of the Hinayana. Later on, they were relegated to a more subordinate position, and became finally the attendants and servants of Buddha (Hackmann enumerates both among the tutelary gods).

They are in fact vassals at the court of Buddha, and the position assigned them is meant to proclaim the supremacy of Buddhism over Brahmanism and Taoism.—See also *Fan-t'ien* 梵天.

FAN-YIN 反吟, THE GOD OF THE STAR.—See *Yang Hsien* 楊顯.

FANG 房, THE GOD OF THE CONSTELLATION.—See *Kêng Yen* 耿弇 and *Yao Kung-po* 姚公伯.

FANG CH'ANG-I 方長宜.—See *Liver, The Gods of the*.

FANG CHÊNG-HSÜEH 方正學.—See *Shê Wang* 蛇王.

FANG CHI 方吉.—The god of the star Ti-ming 地明.—See *Ti-sha* 地煞.

FANG CHI-CH'ING 方吉清.—The god of the constellation Pi 壁. Alternatively with Tsang Kuan 臧官.

FANG-HUI CH'AN-SHIH 方會禪師 (45th generation).—A deified Buddhist monk. Ranked nineteenth in Buddhist School, III (*q.v.*). Family name Lêng 冷. A native of I-ch'un 宜春, a dependent district of Yüan-chou 袁州. His teacher was Tz'ŭ-ming Ch'ang-shih 慈明禪師. Lived most of his life in the Buddhist monastery at Yang-ch'i 楊岐. Died A.D. 1049.

FANG I-CHÊN 方義眞.—The god of the star Kuan-fu 官符. After the fall of the fortress of Ch'uan-yün Kuan 穿雲關 was annihilated on his way to the capital, Ch'ao-ko 朝歌, by Yang Jên 楊任 waving his "five-fires" magic fan.

FANG KUEI 方貴.—The god of the constellation Tsui 觜. Alternatively with Fu Chün 傅俊.—See *Huo Pu* 火部.

FANG-NIEN CH'AN-SHIH 方念禪師 (63rd generation).—A deified Buddhist monk. Ranked fifty-second in Buddhist School, VI (*q.v.*). Family name Yang 楊. A native of Ku-t'ang 古唐, Hupei 湖北. Studied under Ch'ang-jun Ch'an-shih 嘗潤禪師 (*q.v.*). Later, started his own school at Hui-chi 會稽 Chêkiang 浙江. At the request of the Scholars (Literati), he opened another school at Chih-fêng T'u 止風壺. His tomb is on Nan Shan 南山, Southern Mountain.

FANG PAO 方保.—The god of the star T'ien-man 天滿.—See *T'ien-kang* 天罡.

FAN-SELLERS, THE GODS OF.—See *Ho Ho* 和合.

FARRIERS, THE GOD OF.—See *Li Lao-chün* 李老君.

FAVOURABLE-WIND EAR.—See *Chien-li yen* 千里眼.

FEAST OF PEACHES, P'AN-T'AO HUI 蟠桃會.—See *Hsi Wang-mu* 西王母.

FEET, THE GODS OF THE.—There are two gods, one for the upper part (*ching* 脛) of each foot. Their names are Chin 金 and Mu 木, respectively; the *tzŭ* 字 being Sui K'ung-tzŭ 隨孔子. Besides these, the gods of the feet themselves are two T'ai Yin 太陰 spirits whose *tzŭ* 字 is Chu T'ien-li Shih 柱天力士.—*Yün chi ch'i ch'ien* 雲笈七籤.

FEI CHUNG 費仲.—The god of the star Kou-chiao 勾絞. A favourite of the tyrant Chou Wang 紂王. Put to death by Chiang Tzŭ-ya 姜子牙 after having been sent to seize Wu Wang's 武王 capital.

FEI-JÊN 非人.—See *Kinnara*.

FEI-LIEN 飛廉, THE GOD OF THE STAR.—See *Chi Shou-k'un* 姬叔坤.

FEI LIEN 飛廉.—A spiritual bird (the Garuda: see *Garuda*). Described in the *Yu hsüêh* 幼學 as the Wind-god. The god of the constellation Chi 箕, and therefore called Chi Po 箕伯 (*q.v.*). As a member of the Ministry of Thunder he is called Fêng Po 風伯. Popularly known as Fêng lao p'o-p'o 風老婆婆.

FEI-P'O 斐虣.—See *Liang-shua Shih* 掠刷使.

FEI T'OU-T'O 斐頭陀.—A saintly Buddhist monk. A native of Honan 河南. Founded the famous monastery Chin-shan Ssŭ 金山寺, Golden Hill Monastery, on Golden Island, near Chên-chiang (Chinkiang) 鎮江, Kiangsu 江蘇. One of those invited to the annual banquet of the gods (see *Hsi Wang-mu* 西王母).

FEI YÜEH 裴悅.—See *Shui Fu* 水府, D (1) (c).

FEMALE ARHATS.—See *Lo-han* 羅漢.

FEMALE IMMORTAL OF THE WATERS, THE.—See *Shui Fu* 水府, D (4).

FÊNG HSIU-CH'ING 馮修清.—See *Shui Fu* 水府, C (2)(c).

FÊNG-HUO YÜAN T'IEN YÜAN-SHUAI 風火院田元帥.—Three sons were born to T'ien Chien 田鐕 and Tiao Ch'un-hsi 刁春喜 of the T'ai-p'ing Kuo 太平國, T'ai-p'ing Kingdom. The eldest was T'ien Hsün-liu 田荀留, the second T'ien Hung-i 田洪義, and the youngest T'ien Chih-piao 田智彪. During his reign-period K'ai-yüan 開元 (A.D. 713-42), the Emperor Hsüan Tsung 玄宗 (A.D. 713-56) of the T'ang 唐 dynasty engaged them as his music masters. They were such skilled players that even clouds stopped to listen to them, and the *la-mei hua* 臘梅花 (very fragrant flowers which open only in the coldest part of the winter) blossomed. The Emperor having fallen ill, saw them in a dream playing the mandolin and violin, and was promptly restored to health. As a reward he bestowed on them the title of Marquis.

A ravaging epidemic having broken out, the Grand Master of the Taoists sought the musicians' aid. T'ien Yüan-shuai 田元帥 had a large *shên-chou* 神舟, spirit-boat, built, and called together a million spirits, whom he instructed to beat drums placed on it, whereupon all the demons came out of the city to listen to the music, and were seized and expelled by the musician and the Taoist Grand Master. This is said to be the origin of the dragon-boats to be seen everywhere in China on the fifteenth day of the first moon.

Chang Ta-shih 張大師 having recognized his great ability and power, memorialized the Emperor, who canonized the three brothers as Marquises, and all the members of their family and near relatives were given posthumous titles.

FÊNG I 馮夷.—A God of Waters. Attaché to the God of the Huang Ho 黃河, Yellow River. A native of Hua-yin 華陰, Shensi 陝西. Also called Wu I 無夷, and Ping I 冰夷 but, according to some writers, these are separate spirits. When on earth was a water official. Became a god after drinking a magic potion. After death, deified as Shui Shên 水神, the Water-god. Is represented as riding upon a pair of dragons.—See *Shui Fu* 水府, D (1) (e), and *Chuang Tzŭ*, Chap. VI.

FÊNG I 馮異.—The god of the Constellation Chi 箕. Alternatively with Yang Chên 楊眞.

FÊNG-KAN CH'AN-SHIH 豐干禪師.—See *Lo-han* 羅漢.

FÊNG-LIN 風林.—The god of the star Tiao-k'o 弔客. An officer under Chang Kuei-fang 張桂芳. Was killed at the siege of Hsi-ch'i 西岐 by Huang T'ien-hsiang 黃天祥, son of Huang Fei-hu 黃飛虎.

FÊNG PO 風伯.—The Earl of Wind. Represented as an old man with a white beard, yellow cloak, and blue and red cap. He holds a large sack, and directs the wind which comes from its mouth in any direction he pleases.

He is regarded as a stellar divinity under the control of the star Ch'i 箕 (in Sagittarius, or the Sieve; Chinese constellation of the Leopard), because the wind blows at the time when the moon leaves that celestial mansion. He is also said to be a dragon called Fei Lien 飛 廉, at first one of the supporters of the rebel Ch'ih Yu 蚩 尤, who was defeated by Huang Ti 黃 帝 (*v. infra*). Having been transformed into a spiritual monster, he stirred up tremendous winds in the southern regions. The Emperor Yao 堯 sent Shên I 神 羿 with three hundred soldiers to quiet the storms and appease Ch'ih Yu's 蚩 尤 relatives, who were wreaking their vengeance on the people. Shên I 神 羿 ordered the people to spread a long cloth in front of their houses, fixing it with stones. The wind, blowing against this, had to change its direction. Shên I 神 羿 then flew on the wind to the top of a high mountain, whence he saw a monster at the base. It had the shape of a huge yellow and white sack, and kept inhaling and exhaling in great gusts. Shên I 神 羿, concluding that this was the cause of all these storms, shot an arrow and hit the monster, whereupon it took refuge in a deep cave. Here it turned on Shên I 神 羿 and, drawing a sword, dared him to attack the Mother of the Winds. Shên I 神 羿, however, bravely faced the monster and discharged another arrow, this time hitting it in the knee. The monster immediately threw down its sword and begged that its life might be spared.

This dragon, originally one of the wicked ministers of the tyrant Chou 紂, could walk with unheard-of swiftness. Both he and his son O-lai 惡 來, who was so strong that he could tear a tiger or rhinoceros to pieces with his hands, were killed when in the service of Chou Wang 紂 王. Fei Lien 飛 廉 is also said to have the body of a stag, about the size of a leopard, with a bird's head, horns, and a serpent's tail, and to be able to make the wind blow whenever he wishes.—See also *Lei Pu* 雷 部.

FÊNG-SHÊN T'AI 封 神 臺.—Spirits' Promotion Terrace.—See *Chiang Tzŭ-ya* 姜 子 牙.

FÊNG SHÊNG 馮 勝.—An assessor of Kuan Kung 關 公.—See *Kuan Yü* 關 羽.

FÊNG-TU TA TI 豐 都 大 帝.—A rebel, named Ch'u Pa-wang 楚 霸 王, in the time of the Ch'in 秦 dynasty. On his death he was made the Emperor Fêng-tu 豐 都. Fêng-tu 豐 都 of the Shades is his spiritual home. Through him all the Kings of Hell report the doings of the Underworld to Heaven. All souls entering these regions are interviewed by him, and their names registered, before being sent into the First Section. Each month the Ten Kings make a record of what has happened within their districts, and forward it to Ch'in Kuang-wang 秦 廣 王, the King of the First Section, who submits it to the Emperor Fêng-tu 豐 都. These monthly statements he forwards to the God of the Eastern Peak and the Pearly Emperor. Through him all the affairs of Hades are managed.

FÊNG WÊN-I 馮文懿.—See *Wu Tou* 五斗.

FETTERS, THE TEN.—See *Ten Fetters*.

FIELD-ANCESTOR, THE.—Shên Nung 神農 was originally God of the Field, but as he became the God of Medicine, his son, Hsü Chün 許君, is considered as the Field-ancestor God (see *Du Bose*, p. 328).

FINANCE, THE MINISTRY OF.—See *Ts'ai Shên* 財神.

FINE WEATHER, THE GODDESS OF.—See *Sao-ch'ing Niang* 掃晴娘.

FIRE, THE GOD OF.—See *Agni* and *Huo Pu* 火部.

FIRE, THE MINISTRY OF.—See *Huo Pu* 火部.

FIRE, THE SPIRIT OF, CH'IH CHING TZǓ 赤精子. —See *Wu Lao* 五老.

FIRE-CRACKERS, THE GOD OF.—Name Li T'ien 李畋. "In the mountains in the west there is a giant devil over ten feet high, at the sight of whom men grow faint. Li T'ien 李畋 found that the popping of fire-crackers would frighten him away, hence they are considered a protection from evil spirits, and are not so much intended for boys to use in sport as for an article of heathen worship" (*Du Bose*, p. 339).—See also *Plopper*, p. 94.

FIRE-RULER, THE.—See *God of the Summer*.

FIRST BUDDHA, THE.—See *Adi-Buddha*.

FIRST CAUSE, THE.—See *T'ai Chi* 太極.

FIRST HEAVEN, THE RULER OF THE.—See *Yüan-shih T'ien-tsun* 元始天尊.

FIRST PRINCIPLE, THE.—See *Yüan-shih T'ien-tsun* 元始天尊.

FISHERMEN, PATRON DEITIES OF.—See *Chêng San-kung* 鄭三公, and *Chiang Tzǔ-ya* 姜子牙.

FIVE ANIMALS, THE.—The fox, weasel, hedgehog, snake, and rat. "These animals are much dreaded and worshipped under the name of the Five Great Families (*Wu ta chia* 五大家). They have the objectionable habit of lying down in the road. If anyone steps on their claws at such times, he is promptly bewitched" (*Arthur Smith*, p. 321).

FIVE CARDINAL POINTS, THE SPIRIT OF THE.—See *Wu-fang Shên* 五方神, and *Shui Fu* 水府, C (2) (b) and (e).

FIVE CELESTIAL SOVEREIGNS, THE RULER OF THE. —See *T'ai I* 太一.

FIVE DIRECTORS OF YANGCHOU, THE.—See *Yang Chou wu Ssŭ-t'u* 揚州五司徒.

FIVE DOMESTIC SACRIFICES, THE.—See *Ts'ai Shên* 財神.

FIVE ELEMENTS, THE.—See *Wu Hsing* 五行.

FIVE EMPERORS OF HEAVEN, THE.—See *Wu Ti* 五帝.

FIVE GODS OF THE HOME, THE.—The original five gods of the home were those of the door (*mên* 門), the well (*ching* 井), the windows (*hu* 戶), the stove (*tsao* 竈), and the eaves (*chung liu* 中霤).

FIVE GRADUATES, THE.—See *Wên Pu* 瘟部.

FIVE NATURAL AGENTS, THE SPIRITS OF THE.—See *Wu Lao* 五老.

FIVE NATURAL FORCES, THE.—See *Wu Hsing* 五行.

FIVE OLD MEN, THE.—See *Wu Lao* 五老.

FIVE PEAKS, THE.—See *Wu Yo* 五嶽.

FIVE PLANETS, THE GODS OF.—See *T'ai-po Chin-hsing* 太白金星, *Mao Mêng* 茅濛, (Mercury), *Hsieh T'ien-chün* 謝天君, (and Saturn).

FIVE SACRED MOUNTAINS, THE MINISTRY OF THE. —See *Wu Yo* 五嶽.

FIVE SAINTS, THE.—See *Wu Shêng* 五聖.

FIVE SOVEREIGNS OF HEAVEN, THE.—See *Wu Ti* 五帝.

FIVE VISCERA, THE GODS OF THE.—Wu Tsang 五臟. —See *Heart, Liver, Stomach, Lungs,* and *Kidneys.*

FIVE SPIRITS OF ROADS, THE.—See *Ts'ai Shên* 財神.

FIX-LIGHT BUDDHA, THE.—See *Jan-têng Fo* 燃燈佛.

FLOWERS, THE GODS AND GODDESSES OF.—There
are twelve of these deities, one for each month. They are worshipped by florists on the twelfth day of the second moon, with
music, refreshments, and floral decorations.

FO 佛.—Buddha. Also Fo-t'o 佛陀, Fou-t'u 浮圖, P'o t'a
勃塔, Mu-t'o 毋馱, or Mei-t'a 沒塔. The one who is awake or
has understanding (*chio* 覺). (1) The first person of the Triratna
(*q.v.*). (2) The highest degree of saintship, Buddhaship. (3)
Every intelligent person who has broken through the bondage of
sense, perception and self, knows the unreality of all phenomena,
and is ready to enter Nirvana.

"In China, Adi Buddha, or Amitabha, is called '*Omito Fo,*
and his mother, the Sanskrit '*Maya,*' is called '*Moyo,*' the 'o' in
both cases being substituted for the 'a.' It should also be noted
that in Boutan and Tibet, Buddha is called ,'*But,*' '*Put,*' '*Pot,*' '*Pout,*'
and '*Poto';* in Cochin, '*But,*' and in Siam, '*Pout,*' while in the
vernacular of Siam, '*Pout,*' or '*Pot,*' is pronounced '*Po,*' the 't'
being quiescent as in the French. In China the 'p' is aspirated
and becomes '*Pho*' or '*Fo.*' In the Tamulic dialect the name is
pronounced '*Poden,*' or '*Pooden.*' Mr. Edkins gives some of the
curious changes of pronunciation, as follows: '*Fuh,*' old sound
'*But*'; in Amoy, '*Put*'; in Nanking, '*Fuh*'; in Peking '*Fo.*' In
Japan, Buddha is called '*Budso,*' '*Amita Fo,*' '*Toka Daibod,*' or
'*Deva Bod*' (the Divine Bod), and '*Ab buto,*' or 'Father Buto.'

"Buddha is also known as '*Heri Maha,*' 'The Great Lord'; as
'*Datta,*' '*Deva Tat,*' and '*Deva Twashta*'; as '*Mahi-man,*' in '*Menu,*'
or '*Men Nuh.*' 'Mahi-man would thus mean 'the great Mind,'
which is exactly the character given to Buddha. He is also known
as '*Ma Hesa*' and '*Har Esa,*' 'The Great Hesa,' and 'Lord Hesa.' "
—Garnier, *The Worship of the Dead,* p. 103, quoting *Asiatic Res.,*
Faber, and Edkins.

It is a mistake always to render Fo 佛 by "Buddha," meaning
the historical Buddha. The latter "withdraws very decidedly into
the background in real Mahayana, and, when he is mentioned,
it is often as a new metaphysical figure, clad in the garb of
spiritual glory" (Reichelt).

The true history of the Buddhist religion begins with Sakyamuni. In all Buddhistic countries Sakyamuni (Shih-chia-mou-ni
釋迦牟尼) is considered the principal Buddha, the real Ju-lai Fo
如來佛, and the source of this religion. Shih-chia-mou-ni 釋迦
牟尼 is the name used by Chinese Buddhists for the founder of
Buddhism in preference to the name Gautama (Kao-ta-mo
喬荅摩) meaning "the most Victorious on Earth" (ti-tsui-shêng
地最勝), which is the priestly name of the S'akya family. Other

names for Sakyamuni are Shih-chia-wên 釋迦文, meaning "Mighty in charity, seclusion and silence" (Nêng jên [s'akya] chi mo [muni] 能仁寂默, and Siddharta (Sarvarttasiddha) or Arthas' iddhi—rendered by Sa-p'o-hsi-to 薩婆悉多, and explained by i-ch'ieh i-ch'êng 一切義成, "the realization of all auguries," the name given to the new-born Sakyamuni (with reference to the miracles which happened at his birth).

The Ju-lai Fo 如來佛, "Thus-come Buddha," is one whose arrival and departure is in proper relation to other Buddhas. [The Chinese equivalent for the Sanskrit Tathagata.] The principal day celebrated in his worship is his birthday on the eighth day of the fourth month. "He is usually represented as a gilded image, sitting cross-legged on a lotus blossom. His eyes are half closed as though in contemplation. There is a nimbus of fire back of his head and shoulders, which is supposed to be light emanating from his body. He is thought to be all-powerful and wise, ever looking with compassion upon the sincere heart, and happy that he has made a way of escape possible for such a one" (*Plopper*).

The events of the life of Sakyamuni the Buddha are related in many well-known works (*e.g.* Edkins, *Chinese Buddhism; Doré, Recherches,* Vol. XV; Eitel, *Sanscrit-Chinese Dictionary,* etc.).

The tradition is, that Buddha was both king and priest in a country of the west, with a queen whom he made a divinity: that he was obliged to abdicate his power and seek a secluded retreat for twelve years, after which he taught the dogma of the metempsychosis, or transmigration of souls, making that the vehicle of a system of rewards and punishments hereafter. He is said ultimately to have regained his power, and to have departed this life at an advanced age, being transformed at once into the god Fo, or Buddha. It is a common saying of his disciples, that "Fo is one person, but has three forms," which are represented by three distinct gilded images, called the "Three precious, or pure Buddhas." The mother of the god is said to have dreamed that she had swallowed an elephant, whence the veneration for elephants in Siam and Pegu. Buddha's character as a reformer is indicated by the Chinese legend, that he aimed at instructing men "to amend their conduct and practise virtue."

He is supposed to have five eyes; the eye of the body (*jou-yen* 肉眼), the eye of the heavens (*t'ien-yen* 天眼), the eye of wisdom (*hui-yen* 慧眼), the eye of the Law (*fa-yen* 法眼), and the eye of Buddha (*fo-yen* 佛眼) (*Plopper*). His plan of salvation and how he arrived at it are well stated by Plopper: "When Sakyamuni, having searched in many places and in many ways for the truth, at last seated himself at the foot of the bo tree [the bo, or bodhi, flower, the symbol of Buddha] with the determination not to arise until he had obtained enlightenment, all the world rejoiced. Mara (Ma-lo 魔羅) (*q.v.*) alone was worried, and moved to opposition. He tried, by various methods, to shake the holy one's resolution, and lead him back to the old life, but without avail. Finally when he and his demons, baffled and defeated, had taken to flight, the awakening came, and Sakyamuni was able to see and understand the entire universe. He saw that the passions and desires of men were empty and vain. He came to believe in the non-existence of the objective world, and therefore, of suffering and death. He was moved with a great compassion for his fellow men, and determined to use his new-found benefit in letting others also receive the truth he had obtained. Through it, they might also win salvation from delusion and sorrow. Thus did he, through the merit of previous lives, added to his untiring search in this, together with his sacrificing spirit and unselfishness, gain the light. Not alone did he aid himself, but he also opened the way to limitless opportunities to others.

"The plan of Sakyamuni for his followers was that of abstemiousness, purity, and merit. With his enlightenment, came the recognition of four fundamental truths, which were necessary for complete salvation. He looked about him and saw sickness, old age, and death on every hand. This led him to the first truth, namely, that to all life there is more of suffering and pain than of joy, and that all which man loves and most appreciates is transient and perishes. His second truth was that this sorrow was caused through the cravings of the individual. So his disciples were to throw aside the world and its vanities. They were to rid themselves of earthly longings, as nearly as possible, while they with a whole heart sought the road to freedom. Then in the priesthood they were to find, through fasting and contemplation, a way of escape. Thus the third truth was that they were to learn the emptiness of carnal things, and abandon all desires, even to that for continued life. Sakyamuni taught that release was to come through this inner experience; and through the realization of the non-existence of everything. In addition to this, man was to follow the eightfold path. This was the fourth and final truth, by which man was to gain his complete deliverance. This path men must follow with pure and sincere hearts, holding a rigid control over self, and seeking, through helping others, to lay up sufficient merit to eventually, after having passed through several lives, gain enlightenment and liberty. Thus they were to forsake the frivolities and conventions of society, and through austerity and good works, win the inner light, lose the wish for earthly existence, and in this way gain an entrance into Nirvana.

"It was a feeling, much the same as that which prompted Sakyamuni to break away from Brahmanism, which led Amitabha to insert a new doctrine into Buddhism. His desire was to bring salvation within the reach of all people. The teaching of Sakyamuni made absorption into Nirvana possible for one by meditation, abstemiousness, and good works, through countless periods of years. Amitabha brought the new doctrine of redemption through faith. As this method put deliverance within the reach of all, it quickly gained favour, and soon the worship had spread over all China, and even into Korea and Japan."

Sakyamuni is the fourth Buddha of the present *kalpa*. He will be followed by the fifth Buddha, Maitreya, Mi-lo-fo 彌勒佛, who will appear on earth after a lapse of three thousand years.

"Following the life of Sakyamuni, there were to be three periods in the world's history. First, a five hundred year period, in which Dharma's Wheel, or the Wheel of the Law, would be constantly turned, and many lives saved. Then there was to be a period of a thousand years when commentators would explain the Law, and images would be set up to hold its idea before men. This will be followed by a three thousand year period in which the world will go away into sin, until even Buddhism is not remembered.

"At the close of this third period Mi-lo-fo (彌勒佛), or Maitreya, is to come and again explain the Law, and recall men to its observance. The image of this Buddha, who is yet to come, is to be found in nearly all temples, in a little shrine, in the centre of the passage, facing the front door to the temple. He is easily recognized by his laughing and hope-inspiring face. Although he is yet But a Lohan 佛 光 (the Cloth-bag Lohan) he is thought of as already watching over, and protecting Buddhism."

The excellent summary of the myth and life (which is an "indispensable key to the understanding of Buddhist doctrines") of Sakyamuni, given by Eitel (*Dictionary*, pp. 135-9) follows:

"The last of the Sapta Buddha, one of Sapta Tathagata, the fourth of the 1,000 Buddhas of the Bhadra *kalpa*. The name by which Chinese books refer to Gautama Buddha. The *Lalita-vistara* [translation of biography of Sakyamuni] and the popular aphorisms of Wang P'u 王溥 (*Shih-chia ju-lai Ch'êng-tao-chi* 釋迦如來成道記) tell the story of his life. . . . Some 5,000 Djatakas (*q.v.*) are on record, in the course of which he worked his way up through as many different stages of trans-migration, from the lowest spheres of life to the highest, practising all kinds of asceticism and exhibiting in every form (Maitribala-radja, Kapindjala radja, Mayura radja, etc. [former reincarnations of Sakyamuni] the utmost unselfishness and charity. Having attained to the state of Bodhisattva as Prabhapala, he was reborn in Tuchita and there considered where he ought to be reborn on earth to become Buddha. The S'akya (*q.v.*) family of Kapilavastu was selected and in it Maya, the young wife of S'uddhodhana, as the purest on earth. In the form of a white elephant (*v. P'u-t'i-sa-t'o* 菩提薩埵) he descended and entered through Maya's right side into her womb (eighth day of the fourth moon, 1028 or 622 B.C.), where he was visited thrice a day by all the Buddhas of the universe. On the eighth day of the second (or fourth) moon, 1024 or 621 B.C.,[*] Maya, standing in Lumbini under an As'oka

---

[*] Or 1027 and 687. The former is commonly given in Chinese books. Doré xv, 30-33, shows that 557 is the most probable date.

(or Sala) tree, painlessly gave birth to a son who stepped out of her right side, being received by Indra (the representative of popular religion) and forthwith baptized by Naga kings. Thereupon the newborn babe walked seven steps towards each of the four points of the compass and, pointing with one hand to heaven and with the other to earth, said, with a lion's voice, 'I have received the body of my final birth; of all beings in heaven above and beneath the heavens, there is none but myself to be honoured.' At the moment of his birth an Udambara flower sprouted up, and a series of forty-two miraculous events (earthquakes, flashes of five-coloured light, lotus flowers, etc.) announced to the universe the birth of Buddha. His skin exhibited thirty-two fanciful tracings; on the soles of his feet there were sixty-five mystic figures, and his body possessed eighty forms of beauty, which were interpreted by Asita as the characteristic marks of Buddhaship. He was named Sarvarthasiddha. Maya having died seven days after his birth, Maha Pradjapati nursed him. When three years old, he was presented in a Shiva temple, when all the statues of Shivaitic deities did obeisance to the infant Buddha, who was then named Devatideva. When he was seven years old, Arata Kalama and Rudrakarama taught him the Pantcha Vidya S'astras, and Kchanti deva (*Ch'ün-t'i-t'i p'o* 羼提 提婆) taught him gymnastics. When ten years old, he was peerless in strength, hurled an elephant to some distance, and opened an artesian well by the discharge of an arrow. He was married to Yas'odhara and took several concubines. When nineteen years old, he was converted through S'uddhavasa deva who presented himself successively in the form of an old man, a sick man, a corpse, a religious mendicant, and excited in him disgust regarding domestic life. His father sought to divert his mind, by sensual excitements and by proposing to him the career of a Tchakravartti as a military conqueror of the world, but, strengthened by S'uddhavasa deva, he overcame the temptations of lust and ambition and fled from home . in the night of the eighth day of the second moon, 1003 or 597 B.C. Yakchas, Devas, Brahma, Indra and the Tchatur Maharadjas assisted him to escape. He cut off his locks and swore to save humanity from the misery of life, death and transmigration. After a brief attempt to resume study under Arata, he spent six years as a hermit on the Himalaya, testing the efficacy of Brahmanic and Shivaitic meditation. Dissatisfied with the result, he visited Arata and Rudraka and then repaired to Gaya, where he practised ascetic self-torture. [About that time his son Rahula was born.] Having spent six years at Gaya, on a daily allowance of one grain of hemp (opium?) and one grain of wheat, and seeing the uselessness of such fasting, he determines to strike out a new path henceforth. Devas minister to the needs of his body, which threatens to break up, by bathing him with perfumes, and induce Nanda and Bala to nurse him with rice boiled in milk. Resting on a couch prepared by Indra under the Bodhidruma, he now gives himself up to Samadhi, whilst Mara and his armies endeavour, in vain, to tempt him in various disguises and finally through Mara's four beautiful daughters. Unmoved he continues in Samadhi, until he reaches at last the state of Bodhi, and becomes a Buddha, in the night of the eighth day of the twelfth moon, 998 or 592 B.C. The spirits of the earth forthwith announce the glad tidings to the spirits of the atmosphere and those again report it to the spirits in the various heavens. Heaven and earth rejoice. Seven days afterwards two merchants, Trapus'a (T'i Wei 提謂) and Bhallika (P'o Li 波利), passing by, present him with offerings of barley and honey. Soon he gathers round himself five disciples, Kaundinya, Bhadrika, Vachpa, As'vadjit and Mahanama. With them he starts from the Bodhidruma (997 or 592 B.C.) and preaches his new gospel at Mrigadava, where his five disciples attain to the state of Arhat and 1,000 persons are converted. In the course of the following year, he preached chiefly to Naga kings (i.e. against popular worship of snakes). The year 995 or 589 B.C. is marked by the conversion of S'ariputtra and Maudgalyayana with 250 others. In the course of the following year Anathapindika presented Buddha with the Djêtavana. In the year 991 or 585 B.C., a victory having been gained over Shivaism by the conversion of Angulimaliya and his followers, Buddha ascended to Trayast-rims'as in order to convert his mother, and stayed there ninety days. Meanwhile Presênadjit, frightened by his prolonged absence, ordered Maudgalyayana and the deva Vis'vakarman, transformed as artists, to ascend to Traiyastrims'as and to take a likeness of S'akyamuni. They did so and carved, in sandal wood, a statue which thenceforth became an object of worship. Here we have the origin of Buddhist idolatry. On S'akyamuni's return, the statue lifted itself into mid-air and saluted him, where-upon he uttered a prophecy which was fulfilled when Kas'yapa Matanga took that statue to China. In 990 (or 584) B.C. S'akyamuni visited Magadha and converted Vatsa. In the following year he predicted the future of Maitreya, and in the next year he revisited Kapilavastu, when he preached to his putative father. From the year 983 (or 577) B.C. to the time of his death, he gave particular attention to doctrinal exposition, delivering the Samyuktasantchaya in 983 (or 577) B.C., the Pradjnaparamita in 982 (or 576), the Suvarnaprabhasa and Saddharmapundarika in 905 (or 544), and the Parinirvana sutra in 949 (or 543). Ananda was converted in 977 (or 571) B.C. and Pradjapati admitted to rights of priesthood together with other women. When S'akyamuni, in the year 949 or 543 B.C., felt his end drawing near, he went to Kus'inagara. Heaven and earth began to tremble and loud voices were heard, all living beings groaning together and bewailing his departure. On passing through Kus'inagara, he took his last meal from the hands of one of the poorest ('Tchunda), after refusing the offerings of the richest. Declaring that he was dying, he went to a spot where eight Sala trees stood in groups of two. Resting on his right side, he gave his last instructions to his disciples, reminding them of the immortality of the Dharma kaya, and then engaged in contemplation. Passing mentally through the four degrees of Dhyana, and thence into Samadhi, he lost himself into Nirvana and thus his earthly career was ended. His disciples put his remains into a coffin which forthwith became so heavy that no power on earth could move it. But his mother, Maya, suddenly appeared in the air, bewailing her son, when the coffin rose up, the lid sprang open and S'akyamuni stepped forth for a moment with folded hands to salute his mother. On attempting cremation, his disciples found that his body, being that of a Tchakravartti, could not be consumed by common fire, when suddenly a jet of flame burst out of the Svastica on his breast and reduced his body to ashes. If the above semi-legendary account is at all trustworthy, it indicates that S'akyamuni's mind is supposed to have gradually developed, departing step by step from the popular religions of his time, Brahminism and Shivaism, until, without premeditation, he came to found a new religion, being even pushed to laying a sort of preliminary foundation of an ecclesiastical system. As a teacher, he appears to have been liberal and tolerant, countenancing, rather inconsistently, the worship of those deities which were too popular to be discarded, though he assigned to them a signally inferior position in his own system. Immoral sects, however, whether Brahmanic or Shivaitic, he fought resolutely, conquering generally through magic power rather than by disputations. He remodelled almost every Brahmanic dogma, substituting atheism for pantheism, and ethics for metaphysics. His teachings were in later years further developed by the Mahayana, Madhyimayana, Yogatcharya and other Schools. The chronology of Buddhism is not yet sufficiently cleared up. The year when S'akyamuni entered Nirvana is, according to Chinese accounts, the fifty--third year of King Mu [穆] of the Chou [周] dynasty, that is to say, 949 or about 749 B.C., whilst Southern Buddhist tradition fixed upon the year 543 B.C., but modern excavations, inscriptions and coins indicate the year 275 B.C. as the year of Buddha's Nirvana."

From this it will be seen that the apotheosis of Sakyamuni may be regarded as having taken place either when, at the age of three years, on his presentation in the temple of Mahes'vara (S'wa) (T'ien Wang 天 王, King of Devas, or Ta Tzŭ-tsai大 自 在 Great Sovereign), the statues of all the Shivaitic gods prostrated themselves before him, and he was named Devatideva (T'ien-chung tien 天 中 天), Deva of Devas, 'God of Gods,' or when (in 998 or 591 B.C.) he reached the state of Boddi (*p'u-t'i* 菩 提, or *chêng-chio* 正 覺), "truly awake," in contradistinction to Buddhi, the faculty of intelligence. Bodhi, or Sambodhi is the intelligence or knowledge by which one becomes a Buddha (or believer in Buddhism).

Though Buddhism was known in China some two centuries earlier, its official introduction into China took place during the reign of the Emperor Ming Ti 明帝 (A.D. 58-76) of the Han 漢 dynasty, when the Indian monks Mo Têng 摩騰 and Chu Fa-lan 竺法蘭 brought to China the Buddhist doctrine and books (Hinayana, the Lesser Vehicle).

The disciples of Sakyamuni are called *Lo-han* 羅漢 (*q.v.*). This term, in places, includes the entire one thousand two hundred, in others the five hundred, but in most places only the eighteen prominent disciples are meant. It is in the latter sense that the term is commonly used in China.

For the various grades of Buddhist disciples, see *Lo-han* 羅漢.

"Despite its countless errors and illusions, its imaginary gods, its use of magic and charms, Buddhism is a great human effort to rise above the passions and entanglements of the world, seek religious experience, and do good to others, with the object of reaching Nirvana, the happiness of the Hsi-t'ien 西天, Western Heaven" (Saunders).

The outstanding characteristics of the doctrine are (1) Mercy, not fierceness, (2) Quick transmigration, (3) Every soul (living being) must ultimately be saved (reach Nirvana).

Primitive Buddhism, the doctrine preached by Sakyamuni, ceased to exist several centuries ago.

The earliest, largest and richest seat of Buddhism in China is on T'ien-t'ai Shan 天台山, about fifty miles to the south of Ningpo, Chêkiang 浙江. It dates from the fourth century, and abounds in antiquities (Edkins, p. 171).

FO PAO 佛寶.—The Precious Buddha (*Gautama*).—See *San Pao* 三寶.

FO-T'O 佛陀.—See *Fo* 佛.

FO-T'O-PO-T'O-LO CH'AN-SHIH 佛馱跋陀羅禪師.— Buddhabhadra. In Chinese, Chio-hsien 覺賢, Enlightened Sage. A native of Kapilavastu. His family name was Sakya, Shih 釋, and he traced his origin to Amritodana, uncle of Sakyamuni. His parents having died, he was placed at a very early age in a Buddhist monastery by his grandfather Chiu-p'o-li 鳩婆利. Here he showed extraordinary aptitude, his teacher saying that he did the work of thirty persons.

Having become a fully-trained monk, he was seized with a desire to preach the Law in distant countries. After three years he reached the foot of the Ts'ung Ling 葱嶺, Karakorum Mountains. Having tarried at Chiao-chih 交趾, Cochin-China, he set sail thence for China. On reaching Tung-lai Chün 東萊郡 (Ch'ing-chou 青州, Shantung 山東) about A.D. 406, he heard that Kumerajiva (*q.v.*) was at Ch'ang-an 長安, Shensi 陝西, and went there to visit him. They conversed on abstract subjects. Buddhabhadra, however, held aloof from the Court, where Yao-hsing 姚興 had assumed the title of Emperor (A.D. 394-9) of the Hou-Chin 後晉, Later Chin, dynasty, reducing himself to the rank of Wang 王, King, in 399. He was a fervent Buddhist, and showed special favour to the thousands of monks who lived in the capital. He was expelled from the monastery as a visionary, refusing to return when recalled by the emperor. Proceeding toward the South, he continued his wanderings, and eventually, being recommended to the Sung 宋 generalissimo during the reign of Wu Ti 武帝 (A.D. 420-3), he was given the Tao-ch'ang Ssŭ 道場寺, Tao-ch'ang Monastery, the Monastery of Intelligent Halls, as his residence. He died in A.D. 429 at the age of 71 years. He was recognized and venerated as a seer.

FO-T'O-YEH-SHÊ CH'AN-SHIH 佛陀耶舍禪師.—A monk born in Chi-pin 罽賓, modern Kashmir (formerly Kubha or Cophene). His father, having maltreated a mendicant friar, became paralyzed, his feet and hands being bent backwards. Magicians summoned to effect a cure informed him that this affliction was a punishment for having ill-treated a virtuous man. Having apologized to the latter, he was restored to health, and sent his son, aged 13, to be trained by the same monk in a Buddhist monastery.

Yeh-shê 耶舍, or Yasha, whose full name was Buddhayasha, was called the Red-haired Vibasha (Barbarian). He was famous for his marvellous memory and for his numerous translations and writings. At the age of 15 he was able to learn 20,000 to 30,000 characters a day from his prayer-books, and at 19 knew by heart "several millions [?tens of thousands] of characters" from the *Ta-hsiao shêng-ching* 大小乘經. At the age of 27 he had been received as a fully-trained monk, and travelled in the Sha-ch'in Kuo 沙勤國, Kingdom of Sha-ch'in 沙勤, where he restored the ruler to health. After this, he joined the translator Chiu-mo-lo-shih 鳩摩羅什, Kumarajiva, then residing at Kuei-tzŭ Kuo 龜茲國, Karashar (or Harashar). When the latter had settled at the Court of Lü Kuang 呂光 (died A.D. 399), founder of the Hou-Liang 後涼 dynasty, he resolved to join him at Ku-tsang 姑臧, Kansu 甘肅. When he and his disciples reached that place, Chiu-mo-lo-shih 鳩摩羅什 had left for Ch'ang-an 長安 (modern Hsi-an Fu 西安府, Shensi 陝西), and was living in the palace of Yao Hsing 姚興 (who, in A.D. 394, had assumed the title of Hou-Ch'in 後秦, but in 399 became a petty prince, or *wang* 王). Chiu-mo-lo-shih 鳩摩羅什 begged the emperor to call Yeh-shê 耶舍 to the capital, but it was only when he was informed of his profound knowledge of Buddhism that he consented and summoned him to the Court. He allowed him to reside in the Hsiao-yao Yüan 逍遙園, Garden of Leisurely Rambles. When he gave him the *Ch'iang-ch'ieh yao-fang* 羌藉藥方 as a test, he read the whole fifty thousand characters in one day, and was able to recite them from memory without a single mistake. He refused a present of ten thousand pieces of silk offered him by the emperor.

In A.D. 411, he translated forty-one books of the *Ssŭ-fang lü* 四方律, *Discipline of the Four Regions,* and wrote the *Ch'ang-o shih* 長阿詩 and other works, which were translated into Chinese at Liang-chou 涼州, Kansu 甘肅, by the Indian monk Fo-nien 佛念. All these translations are said to have been done in two years; but, according to Beal (*Lectures,* p. 19), between A.D. 402 and 412 he translated altogether four works in sixty-nine chapters. Edkins (*Chinese Buddhism,* p. 110) attributes to him the translation of the *Ch'ang o-han ching* 長阿含經, *Longer Agama Sutra,* and of the *Ssŭ-fên lü* 四分律, *Discipline of the Four Divisions.*

He possessed transcendental power over animals and remarkable skill in healing the sick. He had as many as five hundred disciples. Eventually he returned to his native country, Kashmir, where he secured the work *Hsü-k'ung ts'ang-ching* 虛空藏經.

FO-T'U-CH'ÊNG 佛圖澄.—Buddhajanga, Buddhochinga, or Buddhojang. Also styled Buddhasimha. Original name P'u 普. A saintly Hindu Buddhist monk. Fourth century A.D. Arrived at Lo-yang 洛陽, Honan 河南, in A.D. 310. Obtained for Buddhism liberty of propaganda. Foretold future events by the wind. One of those invited to the annual banquet of the gods (see *Hsi Wang-mu* 西王母). Better known as a wonder worker and founder of monasteries than as a translator. Died A.D. 348.

FOOT, THE GOD OF THE.—See *Feet.*

FORCES, THE FIVE NATURAL.—See *Wu Hsing* 五行.

FORMER BEDS OF RIVERS, THE SPIRITS OF—See *Shui Fu* 水府, D (2) (f).

FORNICATION, THE GODDESS OF.—See *P'an Chin-lien* 潘金蓮.

FORTUNE-TELLERS, THE GOD OF—See *Kuei-ku Tzŭ* 鬼谷丁.

FORTY MASTERS, THE.—"There are seventy-two masters or teachers, who are grouped in one small temple, the devotee worshipping the one he wishes to propitiate; of these thirty-two are physicians and belong to the medical Chapter. The others are of varied callings, such as Warding-off-Evil Master, etc. For the full lists see Du Bose, pp. 329, 404, where however, forty-three are given as Masters and twenty-eight as Teachers (See *Thirty-Teachers, The*).

FOU-CH'ÊN 浮沉, THE GOD OF THE STAR.—See *Chêng Ch'un* 鄭椿.

FOU-SHIH-HSIEN CH'AN-SHIH 浮石賢禪師 (68th generation).—A deified Buddhist monk. Ranked fifty-eighth in Buddhsit School, III (*q.v.*). Family name Chao 趙. A native of Tang-hu 當湖. Studied under Yüan-wu Ch'an-shih 圓悟禪師 (*q.v.*), and afterwards started his own school at Shih-fo Ssŭ 石佛寺, Stone Buddha Monastery, near Sung-lin Tun 松林遁, Pine-forest Solitude. He was buried on the slope of Ching Shan 徑山.

FOU-T'U 浮圖.—See *Fo* 佛.

FOU-YU WÊN YÜAN-SHUAI 孚祐温元帥.—See *Wên Yüan-shuai* 温元帥.

FOUR GREAT DIAMOND KINGS, THE—See *Ssŭ ta T'ien-wang* 四大天王.

FOUR GREAT HEAVENLY KINGS, THE—See *Ssŭ ta T'ien-wang* 四大天王.

FOUR OLD MEN, THE—See *Wu Lao* 五老.

FOUR PATHS, THE—Buddhism is convinced that if a man reaps sorrow, disappointment, pain, he himself, and no other, must at some time have sown folly, error, sin; and if not in this life, then in some former birth. Where then in the latter case, is the identity between him who sows and him who reaps? In that which alone remains when a man dies, and the constituent parts of the sentient being are dissolved; in the result, namely, of his action, speech, and thought, in his good or evil *karma* (literally his "doing"), which does not die. It counsels, therefore, the shaking off of delusions, and the entering resolutely on the "Path" which leads from this restless life to the Joy and Rest of the Nirvana of Wisdom and Goodness and Peace.

Gautama laid down the "four Noble Truths" concerning Sorrow, its Cause, its Suppression, and the Path leading to its extinction (see *Four Truths*). The four Paths or Stages of the Path are:

1. The "entering upon the stream," Conversion; which follows on, (i) companionship with the good, (ii) hearing of the law, (iii) enlightened reflection, or (iv) the practice of virtue. The unconverted man is unwise, under the influence of sin, enmity, and impurity; but if by one or more of the means just mentioned he has arrived at a perception of the "four Noble Truths," he has become converted, and has entered the first Path. While in this path he becomes free successively, (i) from the delusion of self, (ii) from doubt as to the Buddha and his doctrines, and (iii) from

the belief in the efficacy of rites and ceremonies. "Better than universal empire in this world, better than going to heaven, better than lordship over all worlds is (this three-fold) fruit of the first Path."

2. The path of those who will only return once to this world. —The converted man free from doubt and the delusions of self and ritualism, succeeds in this path in reducing to a minimum lust, hatred and delusion.

3. The path of those who will never return to this world: in which the last remnants of (iv) sensuality and (v) malevolence, being destroyed, not the least low desire for oneself, or wrong feeling toward others can arise in the heart.

4. The path of the Arahats, the men set free by insight, in which the saint becomes free from (vi, vii) desire for material, or immaterial, existence; from (viii, ix, x) pride, self-righteousness, and ignorance.

He is now free from all error; he sees and values all things in this life at their true value; evil desires of all kinds being rooted up from his mind, he only experiences right desires for himself, and tender pity and regard and exalted spiritual love for others. "As a mother, even at the risk of her own life, protects her son, her only son: so let him cultivate goodwill without measure among all beings. Let him cultivate goodwill without measure toward the whole world, above, below, around, unstinted, unmixed with any feeling of differing or opposing interests. Let a man remain steadfastly in this state of mind all the while he is awake, whether he be standing, walking, sitting, or lying down. This state of heart is the best in the world."—*Cf. Four Truths.*

FOUR SEAS, THE GODS OF THE.—See *Shui Fu* 水府.

FOUR SEASONS, THE GODS OF THE.—The Green Ruler (Jupiter), Fire Ruler (Summer), White Ruler (Venus), and Black Ruler (Mercury).

FOUR TRUTHS, THE—The Four Truths laid down by Gautama concerning Sorrow, its Cause, its Suppression, may be briefly explained as follows:

1. That (those events which are distinctive of individual existence, such as) birth, the five *Skandhas,* decay, disease, death and (those which bring forcibly into mind the sense of separate existence, such as) contact with disagreeable objects, separation from pleasant ones, unfulfilled desire of possession, are precisely those states which are full of suffering or sorrow.

2. The kind of craving excitement, which follows on sensation, and causes the delusion of self and the lust of life—creating either delight in the objects that present themselves, or an eager desire to supply a felt want—his eager yearning thirst (*Trishna,*

Pali, tanha), growing into sensuality, desire of future life, or love of the present world, is the origin of all suffering.

3. Sorrow and suffering will be overcome, extinguished, if this "thirst" be quenched, this lust of life destroyed. "He who overcomes this contemptible thirst (difficult to be conquered in this world), sufferings fall off from him, like water drops from a lotus leaf."

4. To accomplish this end there is only one way,—the "Noble Path" of a virtuous and thoughtful life; "Enter on this Path and make an end of sorrow: verily the Path has been preached by me, who have found out how to quench the darts of grief. You yourselves must make the effort: the Buddhas are only preachers: the thoughtful who enter the Path are freed from the bondage of the deceiver, Mara." And this means of salvation is not a mere vague admonition to "be good"; it is worked out into detail, expressed in the Eight Divisions and Four Stages (see Rhys Davids, p. 108).

FOX, THE.—"Certain animals can at will appear under the human form, behave as men, and have intercourse with men. That is especially the case with foxes. They transform themselves into boys or girls, and play the part of incubi and succubi of mediaeval legends. Dogs, wolves, asses, pigs, and other animals sometimes do the same. All animals which burrow in the ground, which live in holes, are somewhat transcendent. Because, during the silence of the night, they hear something of what takes place in the lower world, says the theory. Foxes are amenable to a special jurisdiction, the centre of which is at the sacred mountain T'ai Shan 泰 山" (Wieger, pp. 618-9). The belief in the transformation of foxes, especially of foxes transformed into women, is universal.

FROG SPIRITS, THE.—See *Ch'ing-wa Shên* 青 蛙 神 and Shên I 神 翼.

FROST, THE GODDESS OF.—The Green Maiden, who sends frost on the third day of the ninth moon, and was worshipped by military officials. Spring rules birth, and autumn death.

FU 佛.—The literary sound of 佛 Fo (*q.v.*).

FU 傅, THE VENERABLE.—See *Fu Ta-shih* 傅 大 士.

FU CHÜN 傅 俊.—The god of the constellation Tsui 觜. Alternatively with Fang Kuei 方 貴.

FU HAI 福 海.—See *Shou Hsing* 壽 星.

FU HSI 傅翁.—See *Fu Ta-shih* 傅大士.

FU HSI 伏羲.—See *Shui Fu* 水府, D (2) (a), and *Huo Pu* 火部.

FU LO-PU 傅羅卜.—See *Ti-tsang Wang* 地藏王 and *Mu Lien* 目連.

FU-LUNG 伏龍, THE GOD OF THE STAR.—See *Huang Ming* 黃明.

FU SHÊN 福神.—The Spirit or God of Happiness. His name was Yang Ch'êng 陽城 or Yang Hsi-ch'i 陽昔溪. He was Criminal Judge of Tao Chou 道州, Yung-chou Fu 永州府, Hunan 湖南. He owes his origin to the predilection of the Emperor Wu Ti 武帝 (A.D. 502-50) of the Liang 梁 dynasty for dwarfs as servants and comedians in his palace. The number levied from the Tao Chou 道州 district became greater and greater, until it seriously prejudiced the ties of family relations. When Yang Ch'êng 陽城 was Criminal Judge of Tao Chou 道州, he represented to the Emperor that, according to law, the dwarfs were his subjects but not his slaves. Being touched by this remark, the Emperor ordered the levy to be stopped.

Overjoyed at their liberation from this hardship, the people of that district set up images of Yang 陽 and offered sacrifices to him. Everywhere he was venerated as the Spirit of Happiness. It was in this simple way that there came into being a god whose portraits and images abound everywhere throughout the country, and who is worshipped almost as universally as the God of Riches himself.

Another person who attained to the dignity of God of Happiness (known as Tsêng-fu Hsiang-kung 增福相公, "the Young Gentleman who Increases Happiness") was Li Kuei-tsu 李詭祖, the minister of the Emperor Wên Ti 文帝 (A.D. 535-52) of the Wei 魏 dynasty, the son of the famous Ts'ao Ts'ao 曹操, but in modern times the honour seems to have passed to Kuo Tzŭ-i 郭子儀 (*q.v.*). He was the saviour of the T'ang 唐 dynasty from the depredations of the Turfans in the reign of the Emperor Hsüan Tsung 玄宗 (A.D. 713-56). He lived A.D. 697-781, was a native of Hua-chou 華州, in Shensi 陝西, and one of the most illustrious of Chinese generals. He is very often represented in Chinese pictures clothed in blue official robes, leading his small son Kuo-ai 郭曖 to Court.—See also *Kuo Tzŭ-i* 郭子儀.

FU TA-SHIH 傅大士.—The Venerable Fu. A Buddhist monk. Name Fu-hsi 傅翁. A native of I-wu 義烏, Chêkiang 浙江. Through his knowledge at an early age of Confucianism, Buddhism and Taoism, he acquired the title of Shan-hui Ta-shih 善慧大士, Virtuous and Clever Scholar.

In A.D. 520, as the result of his meeting Sung-t'ou-t'o 嵩頭陀, an Indian monk, who assured him that he was an incarnation of Maitreya, Mi-lo Fo 彌勒佛, the Future Buddha, and showed him his reflection in a brook, wearing the religious cap surrounded by a nimbus, he joined the priesthood. Whilst living on Yün-hung Shan 雲橫山, eight miles south of I-wu 義烏, he succeeded in taming the dangerous wild animals which infested it by giving them a special kind of food, thus bringing long-wished-for security to the inhabitants of the district. He was universally honoured throughout the country, and became known as Fu Ta-shih 傅大士, the Scholarly Fu.

He was greatly esteemed by Wu Ti 武帝 (A.D. 502-50), founder of the Liang 梁 dynasty, who bestowed upon him various articles of use in his calling. After his death, King Chung Hsien 忠獻 repaired to Wu Chou 婺州 in Chêkiang 浙江, the modern Chin-hua Fu 金華府, and had a tower erected there to his memory. The *Sou-shên chi* 搜神記 adds that he also took one of his bones, and placed it at the foot of Pu-lung Shan 不龍山, Dragonless Hill, whereupon the rock retired, leaving sufficient room for the construction of the Lung-ch'ê Ssŭ 龍車寺, Dragon-chariot Monastery. Out of the bone they carved a miniature figure of Fu Ta-shih 傅大士, and placed it in the temple reliquary.

FU-TSANG LUNG 伏藏龍.—The Dragon of the Hidden Treasures.—See *Lung Wang* 龍王.

FU-TUAN 伏斷, THE GOD OF THE STAR.—See *Chu Tzŭ-chên* 朱子眞 and *Chu-chüan Shên* 猪橺 (閣) 神.

FU-YIN 伏吟, THE GOD OF THE STAR.—See *Yao Shu-liang* 姚庶良.

FU-YING YÜAN-SHUAI 副應元帥.—Son of Fu Ho-kung 副賀公 and Ou-yang Shih 歐陽氏. They lived at the foot of T'ai Shan 泰山, Shantung 山東. He was born in A.D. 882, and named T'ai-yü 泰宇.

He was of a lively and irascible nature. Having failed to pass the government examinations, he devoted himself assiduously to private study. One night, whilst he was studying, a transcendent fox with nine tails, taking the form of a man, opened the door and wished to enter into conversation with him. However, he took no notice. On the morrow, the fox knocked at the window, but with the same result. The fox then transformed itself into a monstrous giant, with eyes the size of bells, the cheeks of a dragon, and the jaws of a tiger. Entering the room, he seated himself at the tea-table, and with a firebrand burnt his eyes and nose. The hermit, without taking his eyes from his book, said to him: "You knocked at my door yesterday to frighten me, but that is quite useless, for I fear you not." So saying, he threw his writing-brush in the monster's face, when it suddenly changed into a woman, who thanked him and said: "You are a great official, and before long Yü Ti 玉 帝 will make you Overseer of all the spirits and goblins of the land. I hope that then you will pardon my faults." "Henceforth," said the student to her, "you must reform and practise virtue."

Shortly afterwards Yü Ti 玉 帝 summoned Fu-ying Yüan-shuai 副 應 元 帥 by edict and conferred on him the high office of Regent and Principal of the whole region.

FU-YÜ CH'AN-SHIH 福 裕 禪 師 (52nd generation).—A deified Buddhist monk. Ranked fortieth in Buddhist School, VI (q.v.). Family name Chang 張. A native of Wên-shui 文 水 in T'ai-yüan Fu 太 原 府, Shansi 山 西. Trained first by Hsing-hsiu Ch'an-shih 行 秀 禪 師 (q.v.). Later, when residing in the Shao-lin Ssŭ 少 林 寺, Shao-lin Monastery, he was summoned to Court by the emperor, and made governor of the Hsing-kuo Ssŭ 興 國 寺, Hsing-kuo Monastery, at Ho-lin 和 林, Karakorum. In A.D. 1260, the Emperor Shih Tsu 世 祖 (A.D. 1260-95) of the Yüan 元 dynasty, appointed him President of all the Buddhist monks in China, and conferred on him the title of Kuang-tsung Chêng-pien 光 宗 正 辯, Brilliant Ancestor and Orthodox Critic. Died A.D. 1275.

FU-YÜ CH'AN-SHIH 弗 遇 禪 師 (54th generation).—A saintly Buddhist monk. Ranked forty-second in Buddhist School, VI (q.v.). Family name Wang 王. A native of Ling-shih 靈 石, in the department of Ho-chou 霍 州, Shansi 山 西. In A.D. 1286, he entered the Buddhist monastery of Yung-ch'ing 永 慶, and later on taught there. In 1295, the emperor appointed him President over the Shao-lin Ssŭ 少 林 寺, Few Forests Monastery, a well-known monastery in the Têng-fêng 登 封 district, Honan 河 南, the inmates of which were famous for their skill in boxing. Died A.D. 1313, aged 69.

FU YÜN-SOU 拂 雲 叟.—See *Wu Lao* 五 老.

FURNACE, THE PRINCE OF THE.—See *Tsao Chün* 竈 君.

G

GALL, THE GOD OF THE.—The *Huang-t'ing ching* 黃 庭
經 gives the name of this god as Lung Yao 龍 曜, with Wei Ming
威 明 as his style. In the *Yün chi ch'i ch'ien* 雲 笈 七 籤 his name
is given as Lung Tê-chü 龍 德 拘, and his style as Tao Fang 道 放,
his height being three and six-tenths inches and his colour blue,
yellow and green.

GAMBLERS, THE GOD OF.—Du Bose (pp. 340-1) says:
"His name is 'Wang 王, the Pure.' He was a celebrated gambler,
and lost £200,000 at the Faro Bank. After that he did not
gamble, but when he saw a friend reduced to beggary by gaming,
he took him to his home and taught him the science. Wang, the
Pure, is the gambler's god. Unfortunately many trust in him and
pray to him." He is represented holding dice in his hand.

GANDHARA.—Kan-t'o-lo 乾 陀 羅.—A country and city on
the west bank of the Indus about Attock. An ancient kingdom
in the North of the Punjab, famous as a centre of Buddhism.
Mohammedan geographers call it Kandahar, but it must not
be confounded with the modern town of that name. It is the
Gandaritis of the ancients, and its people are the Gandarii of
Herodotus. The *Vayu Purana* says it was famous for its breed
of horses. Sakyamuni, in a former life, lived there and tore out
his eyes to benefit others.

GANDHARVA.—The "heavenly Gandharva" of the *Veda*
was a deity who knew and revealed the secrets of heaven and
divine truths in general. He is thought by Goldstücker to have
been a personification of the fire of the sun. The Gandharvas
generally had their dwelling in the sky or atmosphere, and one
of their offices was to prepare the heavenly soma juice for the gods.

GANDHARVAS.—Kan-t'a-p'o 乾闥婆.—Demons (superior to men), living on Ganda Madana or Hsiang Shan 香山, Incense Mountain, one of the ten fabulous mountains known to Chinese Buddhism; the musicians of Indra; musicians who play and sing for amusement of the devas; the retinue of Dhritarachtra and others.—See also *Lung Wang* 龍王.

GARGYA, GARGYA BALAKI.—Son of Balaki. He was a Brahman, renowned as a teacher and as a grammarian, who dealt especially with etymology, and was well read in the *Veda,* but still submitted to receive instruction from the *Kshatriya Ajata-satru.*

GARUDAS.—Chin-ch'ih Niao 金翅鳥.—A bird-like race. Golden-winged birds, large enough to devour the Nagas (*q.v.*), whose deadly enemies they are. The winged steeds of the gods. The *garuda* is described as a mythical bird or vulture, half-man, half-bird, on which Vishnu rides. He is the king of birds, and descended from Kasyapa and Vinata, one of the daughters of Daksha. He is the great enemy of serpents, having inherited his hatred from his mother, who had quarrelled with her co-wife and superior, Kadru, the mother of serpents. His lustre was so brilliant that soon after his birth the gods mistook him for Agni and worshipped him. He is represented as having the head, wings, talons, and beak of an eagle, and the body and limbs of a man. His face is white, his wings red, and his body golden. He had a son named Sampati, and his wife was Unnati, or Vinayaka. According to the *Maha-bharata,* his parents gave him liberty to devour bad men, but he was not to touch Brahmans. Once, however, he swallowed a Brahman and his wife, but the Brahman so burnt his throat that he was glad to disgorge them both.

Garuda is said to have stolen the *amrita* [the ambrosian food of the gods] from the gods in order to purchase with it the freedom of his mother from Kadru. Indra discovered the theft and fought a fierce battle with Garuda. The *amrita* was recovered, but Indra was worsted in the fight, and his thunderbolt was smashed.—See also *Lun Wang* 龍王, *Fei Lien* 蜚(飛)廉, and *Lei Kung* 雷公.

GATE OF THE CLOUDS SECT, THE See *Buddhist Schools,* VIII.

GATI.—*Liu Tao* 六道 or *Liu Ch'u* 六趣. *Lit.* Six Paths or Places.—Six conditions of sentient existence, viz., devas, men, asuras, beings in hell, prêtas, and animals. The latter three are distinguished as the Three Lower Paths (*Hsia san t'u* 下三途).

GAUTAMA.—See *Fo* 佛 and *San Pao* 三寶.

GENERATION, THE MATRON OF—See *Pi-hsia Yüan-chün* 碧霞元君.

GENIE OF THE POLE STAR, THE—See *T'ai I* 太一.

GENII.—See *Immortals*.

GENII, THE TEN T'AI I 太一.—See *T'ai I* 太一.

GENTLEMAN OF THE BED, THE.—See *Ch'uang Kung, Ch'uang P'o* 牀公牀婆.

GOAT SPIRIT, THE—See *Yang Ching* 羊精.

GO-BETWEENS, THE GODDESS OF.—See *Nü Wa* 女媧.

GOD OF THE IMMORTALS, THE—See *Wu Lao* 五老.

GOD OF LITERATURE, THE.—See *Wên Ch'ang* 文昌.

GOD OF LONGEVITY, THE.—See *Nan-chi Hsien-wêng* 南極仙翁.

GOD OF T'AI-SHAN 泰山, THE RIGHT ARM OF THE.
—See *Wên Yüan-shuai* 温元帥.

GODDESS OF THE LIGHT OF THE EYE, THE—See *Yen-kuang P'u-sa* 眼光菩薩.

GODDESS OF MERCY, THE—See *Kuan Yin* 觀音.

GODS OF THE SACRED MOUNTAINS.—See *Pi-hsia Yüan-chün* 碧霞元君 and *Wu Yo* 五嶽.

GODS SECT, THE CAVE OF THE—See *Buddhist Schools*, VII.

GOLD, THE GOD OF.—See *Mi-lo Fo* 彌勒佛, *Tung-fang Shuo* 東方朔, and *Wu Hsing* 五行.

GOLDEN-BEARDED TURTLE, THE.—See *Chun T'i* 準提.

GOLDEN BIG PINT.—See *Chin Ta-shêng* 金大升.

GOLDEN BUSHEL OF TROUBLED ORIGINS, THE—See *K'êng San Ku-niang* 坑三姑娘.

GOLDEN-CROWNED GENIE, THE.—See *Chin-ku Hsien* 金箍仙.

"GOLDEN CUIRASS, MR."—See *Wên Ch'ang* 文昌.

GOLDEN PALACE, THE SOVEREIGN EMPEROR OF THE—See *Chin-ch'üeh Shang-ti* 金闕上帝.

GOLDEN-WINGED RUKH, THE GREAT.— See *Yü-i Hsien* 羽翼仙.

GOLDSMITHS AND SILVERSMITHS, THE GOD OF.— See *Mi-lo Fo* 彌勒佛, *Tung-fang Shuo* 東方朔, and *Hua-kuang Fo* 華光佛.

GOLD-TOOTH IMMORTAL, THE.—See *Chin-ya Hsien* 金牙仙.

GOPAKA.—See *Lo-han* 羅漢.

GOVERNORS.—See *Tsung Kuan* 總管.

GRABBING COMMISSIONER, THE. See *Liang-shua Shih* 掠刷使.

GRANARY, THE GOD OF THE.—"His image is a large one, and he has three eyes. He is worshipped by the landed gentry about the time they collect their 'rent rice.' Every granary, or storehouse, has a tablet of this deity" (*Du Bose,* pp. 141-2).

GRASSHOPPERS, THE GOD OF.—See *Pa Cha* 叭咋.

GRASSHOPPERS, THE GODDESS OF.—See *Pa Cha* 叭咋.

GRASSHOPPERS, THE GREAT KING OF.—See *Pa Cha* 叭咋.

GRASSHOPPERS, THE PROTECTING SPIRIT AGAINST. —See *Liu-mêng Chiang-chün* 劉猛將軍.

GREAT BEAR, THE GOD OF THE.—See *Wên Ch'ang* 文昌. *Ursa Major,* the Great Bear, having been deified by the Taoists, no indecency may be committed by anyone when turned toward the north.

GREAT (BUDDHIST) SAINT, THE.—See *Ta Shêng* 大聖.

GREAT FOUR KINGS OF HEAVEN, THE—See *Ssŭ ta T'ien-wang* 四大天王.

GREAT GOLDEN-WINGED RUKH, THE—See *Yü-i Hsien* 羽翼仙.

GREAT KING OF LOCUSTS OR GRASSHOPPERS, THE.
—See *Pa Cha* 叭 咋.

GREAT ONE, THE—See *T'ai I* 太 一 .

GREAT UNITY, THE—See *T'ai I* 太 一 .

GREATLY HONOURED DAME, THE—See *Ta-nai Fu-jên*
大 奶 夫 人.

GREEN LION, THE.—See *Kuan Yin* 觀 音.

GREEN MAIDEN, THE.—See *Frost, The Goddess of*.

GREEN RULER, THE—See *Jupiter*.

GUARDIAN OF THE GATE OF HEAVEN, THE.—See
Li Ching 李 靖.

H

HA 哈. See *Hêng Ha êrh chiang* 哼哈二將.

HADES.—The Sanskrit *Naraka,* the abode of demons; in Chinese *Ti Yü* 地獄, the earth prison. (See also *Shih-tien Yen-wang* 十殿閻王). "The invisible," a phase of metempsychosis, rather than a place of final retribution (see *Buddhism* and *Nirvana*). It is visited by compassionate Buddhas to rescue souls from its torments.

The Buddhist Hades is situated 20,000 *yoganas* (280,000 miles) below the Great Sea at the foot of *Wu-chiao Shih* 沃燋石 (*lit.* the "Rock of Purification," *i.e.* Mount Meru, also called Wu-chiao Shan 山, identified by some with the Himalayas, but *v. infra*). Around Hades there are mountains, a wide sea, and a circular mass of iron. Each hell or court measures from 5,000 to 8,000 feet on each side. The situation of the courts in respect of Mount Meru and the names of their Presidents are as follows:

		Situation.	*President.*	
First	Court	W.	Ch'in-kuang Wang	秦廣王
Second	„	S.	Ch'u-chiang „	楚江王
Third	„	S.E.	Sung-ti „	宋帝王
Fourth	„	E.	Wu-kuan „	五官王
Fifth	„	N.E.	Yen-lo „	閻羅王
Sixth	„	N.	Pien-ch'êng „	卞城王
Seventh	„	N.W.	T'ai-shan „	泰山王
Eighth	„	W.	Tu-ti „	都帝王
Ninth	„	S.W.	P'ing-têng „	平等王
Tenth	„	(direction not given)	Chuan-lun „	轉輪王

Being inconveniently distant from China, this Hindu Hades was transferred by the Taoists to the Province of Ssŭch'uan 四川,

under a high mountain near the city of Fêng-tu Hsien 酆 都 縣.

"During the reign of the Emperor Wan Li 萬 歷 (A.D. 1573-1620) of the Ming 明 dynasty the governor of the province, named Kuo 郭, had the above entrance forcibly opened. He then provided himself with a powerful torch, and boldly penetrated into the interior of the mountain. Proceeding for some time, he discovered an opening leading down into the earth. Nothing undaunted, he prepared a strong box, and sitting within it, had it lowered by means of ropes into the yawning chasm below. After descending about 200 feet, he found solid ground, and coming out from his box, lighted his torch, and set to explore the unknown land. In reality, he had reached the border-land of Hades, and looking round, beheld a vast landscape covered with luxuriant vegetation. Further on, arose a majestic portal closed with a strong iron gate, studded with countless nails. It was the entrance to the First Court of the Infernal regions.

"The governor knocked at the great gate, and much to his surprise, was received by Kuan Yü 關 羽, the Chinese God of War. The deified warrior showed him over his palace, and ended by leading him to the Second Court of Hades, then to the Third Court and Fourth, all of which he visited in detail.

"Upon reaching the Fifth, Yama, the President of this Court, begged him sit down and partake of some tea. The conversation turned on the administration of the Underworld. 'We, judges of Hades,' said the President, 'have to punish all the souls of the dead, without distinction of position or rank while they lived in the world above. These souls, after death, wander throughout the world, but are seized by our lictors, and brought to this dismal region.' The conversation being ended, Yama led his visitor back to the great gate of Hades, and there bade him farewell. Hereupon, the governor resumed his position in the strong box, and was soon hauled up into the vital air. Having returned to the world of mortals, he related in detail all that he had seen and heard in the infernal regions, and a slab embodying the story was erected at Ku'ei-chou Fu 夔 州 府, a city in the North-East of Ssŭch'uan 四 川, not far from the Northern bank of the Yangtzŭ 揚 子 River."

Originally divided into eight hells, its departments were increased through the addition by the Northern (*Mahayana*) School of eight others, making eight cold and eight hot hells. According to other accounts, the divisions number 128, *i.e.* eight large hells each divided into sixteen small hells, to which are added a "Hell of Females" (on the right of the Ninth Court) and a "City of Suicides," making 130 in all. Another work increases the number to 180. Under the Sung 宋 dynasty there originated a division into ten Courts or Departments, each presided over by a judge or demon-king. Of these ten Departments, the first and last are not places of torture, but an ante-chamber where an entrance examination is held and an outer court where the destiny

of beings (or "souls") after they have expiated their sins, is   HADES
determined respectively.

The hells are places in which souls are purged, or punished
for evil-doing and violating the laws of the Buddha, to fit them
for re-birth in one or other of the six states of existence (gods or
devas, men, *asuras* or demons living underground, animals, *prêtas*
or hungry ghosts, and beings undergoing torments in hell).
They are not, as already noted, places of eternal punishment.
After a longer or shorter period (with a minimum of 500 years)
every being must leave the hells and pass through other states
until it reaches *Nirvana*, the final extinction of personal existence.
In Buddhism, there are only the six forms of existence above-
mentioned. On death, rebirth is into one of these six classes.
The being or "soul" cannot pass, as in the Brahminical system, into
a plant, a stone, or other inorganic form. The "soul" is not the
form of existence usually connoted by that term (for the Buddhist
holds that man has no soul), but rather the "second-self" yet with
visible bodily shape, human feelings, etc. This so-called shade,
on reaching the tenth court or department, is reborn as a man, a
brute, a fish, a bird, a reptile, or an insect, according to its merits
or demerits in a previous existence. Those which are still unre-
generate are "clubbed to death" with peach cudgels by the most
savage lictors, but presumably even these emerge eventually on
the road to *Nirvana*.*

As regards the constitution and functions of the Ten Courts:
Each hell was situated under the Great Sea at one or other of the
points of the compass around the foot of Wu-chiao Shan 沃 焦 山
(Mt. Meru, or Sumeru, the fabulous centre of the Buddhist world);
was presided over by a President or Governor; and administered
a special kind of punishment for special kinds of sins. In the
First Court the President keeps the register of the living and the
dead, and measures the length of men's lives. Good people may
immediately be despatched to the Tenth Court, where transmigration takes place. In the Tenth Court it is determined in what
class of beings and in what place, all beings ("discarnate souls"),
whether they have passed through, or been exempted from, the
nine previous hells, are to be reborn. For details of the Ten
Courts see Doré, *Recherches sur les Superstitions en Chine*, vi,
173-95.

Before passing out of Hades into a new form of existence, all
"souls" are obliged to visit the "Hall of Oblivion," where Mêng P'o

---

* "The ultimate goal of Buddhism is neither heaven nor hell, but Nirvana,
or the being blown out, and extinction of all personal existence."—Kennelly, vii,
250. "At death, all elements of the previous being are dissolved, like a flame
that is put out. There is, therefore, no continuous existence, no personality
which passes from one body to another; there is but succession, metamorphosis,
or rather, palingenesis. What passes is *karma*, or act-force, but this being a
moral cause is quite inadequate to produce a physical being"—Monier Williams,
Buddhism, p. 110.

孟婆 makes them drink of the broth of Lethe, which causes them to forget all that happened up to that time.—See *Mêng P'o* 孟婆 and *Ti Yü* 地獄.

HADES, COURTS OF.—The Courts are numbered One to Ten, in order, and named after their Presidents.—See list under *Hades*.

HAI LUNG-WANG 海龍王.—See *Lung Wang* 龍王.

HAIL, THE PROTECTOR AGAINST.—See *Hu Shên* 胡神.

HAIR, THE GOD OF THE.—The name of this god is stated in the *Yün chi ch'i ch'ien* 雲笈七籤 to be Hsüan Wên-hua 玄文華, and his style Tao Hêng 道衡. His height is one inch and one-tenth, and his colour black. The same work also gives the name as *Shou Ch'ang* 壽長, the gods of the hair of the head being seven star-spirits.

HALF-MEN.—See *Composite Deities*.

HALL OF OBLIVION, THE.—See *Mêng P'o* 孟婆 and *Hades*.

HAN CH'IN-HU 韓擒虎.—An assessor of Kuan Kung 關公.—See Kuan Ti 關帝 and *Yen-lo Wang.* 閻羅王.

HAN CHUNG-LI 漢鍾離.—See *Pa Hsien* 八仙.

HAN HSIANG-TZŬ 韓湘子.—See *Pa Hsien* 八仙.

HAN JUNG 韓榮.—The god of the star Lang-chi 狼籍. Colonel of Fan-shui Kuan 氾水關. Committed suicide during the Yin-Chou 殷周 wars when he saw that his two sons had been slain.

HAN P'ÊNG 韓朋.—See *Chiu Yao* 九曜.

HAN PIEN 韓變.—See *Wu Tou* 五斗.

HAN 漢 RIVER, THE SPIRIT OF THE.—See *Shui Fu* 水府, D (2) (b).

HAN SHAN 寒山.—See *Ho Ho êrh-hsien* 和合二仙.

HAN-SHAN TA-SHIH 寒山大士 or HAN-SHAN TZŬ 寒山子.—Eighth century. The Monk of the Cold Cave (*lit.* Hill): a name derived from his living a solitary life in a cold cave at K'ang-hsing Hsien 康興縣, Kiangsi 江西. Subsisting on charity, he wandered along the roads leading to the monasteries, and occasionally wrote scraps of poetry on rocks and stone walls. His features were most repulsive, and he dressed in rags, wearing a cap made of bark.

Lü Ch'iu-yin 閭邱胤, the chief magistrate of T'ai-chou 台州, Chêkiang 浙江, at the instance of Fêng Kan 豐干, who had cured him of a violent headache, went to the Kuo-ch'ing Ssŭ 國清寺, Kuo-ch'ing Monastery, and worshipped him and his colleague Shih Tê 拾得, but was exhorted rather to worship O-mi-t'o Fo 阿彌陀佛, Amitabha.

Later, when the same official went to visit Han-shan 寒山 in his cold cave, the monk, by his magical powers, reduced his body to the size of an atom, and disappeared in the hollow of the rock, saying: "Be of good courage, and persevere in doing good." He is said to have been an incarnation of Wên Shu 文殊, Manjusri (*q.v.*).—See also *Lo-han* 羅漢.

HAN-SHAN TZŬ 寒山子.—See *Han-shan Ta-shih* 寒山大士 and *Lo-han* 羅漢.

HAN SHÊNG 韓昇.—See *Wu Tou* 五斗.

HAN SHIH-CHUNG 韓世忠.—An assessor of Kuan Kung 關公.—See *Kuan Yü* 關羽.

HAN SHU NIU 含樞紐.—See *Saturn*.

HAND, THE GODS OF THE.—These are two sun spirits, their style being Hun Yin 魂陰.—*Yün chi ch'i ch'ien* 雲笈七籤.

HAO CH'IU 豪邱.—See *Heart, The Gods of the.*

HAO HUA 皓華.—See *Lungs, The God of the,* and *Teeth, The Gods of the.*

HAO YÜ-SHOU 浩鬱狩.—See *Wu Yo* 五嶽.

HAPPINESS, THE GOD OF.—See *Fu Shên* 福神 and *Kuo Tzŭ-i* 郭子儀.

HARE IN THE MOON, THE.—See *Shên I* 神翼.

HARVESTS, THE GOD OF THE SOIL AND.—See *Shê Chi* 社稷.

HEAD, THE GODS OF THE.—There are three gods of the head, their name being Tung Wang-fu 東王父.—*Yün chi ch'i ch'ien* 雲笈七籤.

HEAD OF FAMILIES, THE MODEL.—See *Chang Kung-i* 張公藝.

HEART, THE GODS OF THE.—The gods of the heart are Chu Niao 朱鳥 (*Tzŭ hua tzŭ* 子華子), Hao Ch'iu 豪邱 (*Yün chi ch'i ch'ien* 雲笈七籤), and Huan Yang-ch'ang 煥陽昌, style Tao Ming 道明, height nine inches, colour red (*ibid.*), Tan Yüan 丹元, style Shou Ling 守靈 (*Huang t'ing nei ching* 黃庭內經).

HEARTH, THE GOD OF THE.—See *Tsao Chün* 灶(竈)君.

HEAVEN.—See *T'ien* 天.

HEAVEN and EARTH.—See *T'ien* 天 and *Ti* 地.

HEAVEN, THE EMPRESS OF.—See *T'ien Fei* 天妃.

HEAVEN, THE HIGHEST IN.—See *Yüan-shih T'ien-tsun* 元始天尊.

HEAVEN, THE RULER OF THE FIRST.—See *Yüan-shih T'ien-tsun* 元始天尊.

HEAVEN, THE TREASURE OF.—See *Yüan-shih T'ien-tsun* 元始天尊.

HEAVEN-DEAF.—T'ien-lung 天聾.—See *Wên Ch'ang* 文昌.

HEAVENLY DOG, THE.—See *Chang Hsien* 張仙.

HEAVENLY KINGS, THE FOUR GREAT.—See *Ssŭ ta T'ien-wang* 四大天王.

HEAVENLY TEACHER, THE.—See *Chang Tao-ling* 張道陵.

HEI LAO-YEH 黑老爺.—See *Ch'êng Huang* 城隍.

HEI-LIEN TSU-SHIH 黑連祖師.—The God of Comb-sellers.

HEI-SHA 黑殺, **THE GOD OF THE STAR.**—See *Kao Chi-nêng* 高繼能.

HEI TI 黑帝.—See *Mercury*.

HELL.—See *Hades*.

HEN, THE WHITE.—See *Pai Chi* 柏姬 or 白雞.

HÊNG HA ÊRH CHIANG 哼哈二將.—The two Marshals Hêng and Ha. At the time of the overthrow of the Yin 殷 and

establishment of the Chou 周 dynasty in 1121 B.C. there lived
two marshals, Chêng Lun 鄭倫 and Ch'ên Ch'i 陳奇. These
were Hêng 哼 and Ha 哈, the Snorter and Blower respectively.

The former was the chief superintendent of supplies for the
armies of the tyrant Chou 紂, the Nero of China. The latter was
in charge of the victualling department of the same army.

From his master, Tu O 度厄, the celebrated Taoist magician
of the K'un-lun 崑崙 Mountains, Hêng 哼 acquired a marvellous
power. When he snorted, his nostrils, with a sound like that of
a bell, emitted two white columns of light, which destroyed his
enemies, body and soul. Thus, through him, Chou 紂 gained
numerous victories. But one day he was captured, bound, and
taken to the General of Chou 周. His life was spared, and he
was made general superintendent of army stores as well as
generalissimo of five army corps. Later on he found himself face
to face with the Blower. The latter had learnt from the magician
how to store in his chest a supply of yellow gas which, when he
blew it out, annihilated anyone whom it struck. By this means
he caused large gaps to be made in the ranks of the enemy.

Being opposed to each other, the one spurting out great streaks
of white light, the other blowing streams of yellow gas, the combat
continued until the Blower was wounded in the shoulder by
No-cha 哪吒, of the army of Chou 周, and pierced in the stomach
with a spear by Huang Fei-hu 黃飛虎, Yellow Flying Tiger.

The Snorter in turn was slain in this fight by the Marshal
Chin Ta-shêng 金大升, Golden Big Pint, who was an ox-spirit
and endowed with the mysterious power of producing in his
entrails the celebrated *niu-huang* 牛黃, ox-yellow, or bezoar.
Facing the Snorter, he spat in his face, with a noise like thunder,
a piece of bezoar as large as a rice-bowl. It struck him on the
nose and split his nostrils. He fell to the earth, and was immediately cut in two by a blow from his victor's sword.

After the Chou 周 dynasty had been definitely established
Chiang Tzŭ-ya 姜子牙 canonized the two marshals Hêng 哼
and Ha 哈, and conferred on them the offices of guardians of
the Buddhist temple gates, where their gigantic images may be
seen.—See also *Ch'ing-lung Pai-hu* 青龍白虎.

HÊNG SHAN 恒山, THE GOD OF.—See *Pi-hsia Yüan-chün*
碧霞元君 and *Wu Yo* 五嶽.

HÊNG SHAN 衡山, THE GOD OF.—See *Pi-hsia Yüan-chün*
碧霞元君 and *Wu Yo* 五嶽.

HERDSMAN AND THE WEAVER-GIRL, THE.—See
Chih Nü 織女.

HIGHEST IN HEAVEN, THE.—See *Yüan-shih T'ien-tsun*
元始天尊.

HO 何.—See *Ta Shêng* 大聖.

HO CHIH-YÜAN 霍之元.—The god of the star Ti-k'uang 地狂.—See *Ti-sha* 地煞.

HO HO ÊRH HSIEN 和合二仙.—The Two Immortals Ho Ho 和合. The patron deities of merchants. Worshipped by these in general, and especially by potters, lime-burners, and fan-sellers. Opinions differ as to whether Ho Ho 和合 represents one person or two. The generally accepted version is the latter, and in pictures, etc., they are represented as two, with the title Ho Ho êrh hsien 和合二仙. They are prayed to by merchants for prosperity in their business, and are often associated with the pictures and images of the God of Wealth.

Those who state that Ho-ho 和合 was one person give the name of this Spirit as Wan-hui 萬回, *lit.* 'ten thousand return,' a name arising from his having performed the journey from Ho-nan 河南 to An-hsi 安西 (Hsi-an Fu 西安府, Shensi 陝西) and back, a distance of 10,000 *li* 里, in one day, when sent there by his parents to bring news of his brother, who was enrolled in the army at that place. He was a native of Wên-hsiang Hsien 閿鄉縣, Honan 河南, and born in A.D. 632, in the reign of T'ai Tsung 太宗 (A.D. 627-50) of the T'ang 唐 dynasty, his father's name being Chang 張.

The version according to which Ho 和 and Ho 合 are two distinct persons describes them as two priests named respectively Han Shan 寒山 (Ho 和) and Shih-Tê 拾得 (Ho 合).

In A.D. 627, in the reign of T'ai Tsung 太宗 (*supra*), Han Shan 寒山 retired to the retreat of Han-yen 寒巖, to the West of T'ien-t'ai Hsien 天台縣, Chêkiang 浙江, whence he paid period-ical visits to the monastery Kuo-ch'ing Ssŭ 國清寺, situated to the west of that city. He was in the habit of crying aloud and swearing, at the same time looking up into the sky, and when driven away by the priests merely broke into ribald laughter. Later on, he concealed himself in a cave excavated in Han-yen 寒巖 Mountain, and was not seen or heard any more.

The other priest, Shih Tê 拾得, was a foundling (hence his name) rescued by Fêng-kan 豐干, the chief priest of Kuo-ch'ing Ssŭ 國清寺 (*supra*), where, when grown up, he worked in the kitchen and scullery. He carefully preserved what was left of the meals and gave it to Han Shan 寒山 each time he visited the monastery.—See also *Ministries: Finance.*

HO HSIEN-KU 何仙姑.—See *Pa Hsien* 八仙.

HO HSIU-CHI 和修吉.—A dragon-king.—See *Lung Wang* 龍王.

HO JO-PI 賀若弼.—An assessor of Kuan Kung 關公.—See *Kuan Yü* 關羽.

HO KU 河 姑.—See *Shui Fu* 水府, D (2) (b).

HO KU 郝 姑.—See *Shui Fu* 水府, D (3) (e).

HO-K'UEI 河魁, THE GOD OF THE STAR.—See *Huang Fei-piao* 黃飛彪.

HO PO 河伯.—The Spirit, or Earl, of the Waters.—See *Shui Fu* 水府.

HO TA T'IEN-GHÜN 賀大天君.—See *Ch'ü-hsieh Yüan* 驅邪院.

HOME, THE.—See *Five Gods of the Home*.

HORSE, THE WHITE.—See *Sun Hou-tzŭ* 孫猴子.

HORSE-FACE, MR.—See *Ch'êng Huang* 城隍.

HORSE'S HEAD, THE LADY WITH THE.—See *T'an Nü* 蠶女.

HORSE-KING, THE.—See *Ma Wang* 馬王.

HORSES, THE GOD OF.—See *Cow, The,* and *Po Yao* 伯樂.

HOU CHI 后稷.—See *Shê Chi* 社稷.

HOU ÊRH-KUNG 侯二公.—See *Chêng San-kung* 鄭三公.

HOU I 后羿.—The Archer Lord. Said to have been a chieftain in the service of the Emperor K'u 嚳 (2436-2366 B.C.), and, alternatively, his descendant, who performed wonderful feats of archery in the service of the Emperor Yao 堯 (2357-2255 B.C.). The descendant is said to have shot arrows into the sky to deliver the moon during an eclipse. Another legend states that in the time of Yao 堯 there were ten suns, which burnt up the grass and trees, causing confusion and death upon earth. The life of each sun was bound up in a large crow. Yao 堯 commanded Hou I 后羿 to shoot arrows at the false luminaries. With his bow and arrows he killed nine of the crows, whereupon their respective suns disappeared, leaving only the present one to give light and warmth to the earth.

A myth, dating from the time of Yao 堯, states that Hou I 后羿, when searching for his wife Ch'ang O 嫦娥 (*q.v.*), who had fled from him to the moon, was blown out of his course, and found himself at the palace of Tung Wang-kung 東王公. The latter appointed him the sun as his palace, and he became the Sun God. Later he went to the moon, found his wife, and made peace with her.—See *Shên I* 神羿.

HOUR (OR TWO-HOUR PERIOD), THE GOD OF THE.
—Name Liu Hung 劉 洪.—See *T'ai Sui* 太 歲.

HOU T'AI-I 侯 太 乙.—The god of the constellation Wei 危.
Alternatively with Chien Tan 堅 鐔.

HOU T'U 厚 土.—See *Hou T'u* 后 土.

HOU T'U 后 土.—The Sovereign Earth. Various meanings
have been assigned by different writers to the expression Hou-T'u
后 土: the earth *t'u* 土, simply; the Spirit of the earth, T'u Shên
土 神; the patron deity of the soil, Shê 社; the Spirit of Humanity,
Jên Shên 仁 神; the son of Kung Kung 共 工, *Kung Kung chih
tzŭ* 共 工 之 子, because he was Minister of Agriculture (Kung
Kung 共 工, his name being K'ang Hui 康 回); the patron deity
of the whole Earth, *i.e.* the whole Kingdom, as distinguished
from local patrons; the Emperors (of various dynasties) coadjuter
to that patron deity, their ancestors, or favoured empresses; the
whole Earth, *hou* 后, in the expression *hou-t'u* 后 土, having
originally been written *hou* 厚, thick; and also, locally, the Mother
of the Earth, Hou-t'u Niang-niang 后 土 娘娘. Thus, sacrifices
have been offered to the Earth itself, to the Spirit of the Earth, to
the Patron Deities of the Soil, to the Emperors and certain
Empresses, and to the earth in the form of a deified female.
Sacrifices to the Earth originated in 113 B.C., when the
Emperor Wu Ti 武 帝 (140-86 B.C.) of the Han 漢 dynasty
officially sacrificed to Hou T'u 后 土, *i.e.* the Earth in its totality,
or the Sovereign Earth. This ceremony was performed on the
hill Hui-ch'iu 睢 丘 to the south of the River Fên 汾; hence the
name given to it: Fên-yin tzŭ 汾 陰 祠, the sacrifice on the south
of the Fên 汾. The Emperor prostrated himself before the five
mounds which he venerated with the same ceremonies he performed before the Kings of Heaven. This sacrifice was alternately
suppressed and re-instituted by succeeding emperors. The
emperor sacrificed an ox, *ta-lao* 大 牢, the tributary chiefs, a sheep,
hsiao-lao 小 牢. For an account of the sacrifice as performed
under the Republic at Ju-kao 如 皋 see *Doré*, XI. 872-4.

HOU-T'U NIANG-NIANG 后 土 娘娘.—See *Hou T'u* 后 土.

HOUSEHOLD, THE GODS OF THE.—"In every house,
except the hovels of the poor, just within the gateway or first
entrance-room, and opposite the front door, high up are three
pigeon-holes, where reside the family gods. In the middle one,
on the tablet, are the words, 'Heaven, Earth, Ruler, Parent, and
Teacher; on the left, inscribed on the tablet, 'We burn incense to
the holy multitude of family gods'; on the right are the ancestral
tablets, placed in order of rank, the oldest in the rear" (Du Bose,
pp. 130-1).—*cf. Shê chi* 社 稷.

HSI 熙.—See *Shui Fu* 水府, D (3) (b).

HSI-CH'IEN 希遷.—See *Patriarchs: Hui Nêng* 慧能.

HSI-CH'IEN CH'AN-SHIH 希遷禪師 (35th generation).—A deified Buddhist monk. Ranked second in Buddhist School, VI (*q.v.*). Family name Ch'ên 陳. A native of Kao-an 高安, in the department of Jui-chou 瑞州. Became a Buddhist novice at the age of 16. Taught by Hui-nêng 慧能 (see *Patriarchs*), at Ts'ao-ch'i 曹谿, and afterwards by Hsing-ssŭ Ch'an-shih 行思禪師 (*q.v.*). Founded a famous school in the Tou-shuai Ssŭ 兜率寺, Tou-shuai Monastery, from which came all the prominent teachers of this branch. Died at Liang-tuan 梁端, A.D. 790. Posthumous title: Wu-chi Ta-shih 無際大師, Unlimited Master.

HSI-PIEN CH'AN-SHIH 希辯禪師 (47th generation).—A deified Buddhist monk. Ranked thirty-third in Buddhist School, VI (*q.v.*).—Family name Huang 黃. A native of Hung-chou 洪州, Kueichou 貴州. Entered a Buddhist monastery at the age of 11, soon after his father's death. Was ordained at the age of 18. Successively at the schools of Tzŭ-chio Ch'an-shih 自覺禪師 (*q.v.*) at Hsiang-chou 襄州, Shensi 陝西,, and of Tao-k'ai Ch'an-shih 道楷禪師 (*q.v.*) at Tan-hsia 丹霞, Fukien 福建. About A.D. 1119-20, he lived in the Ta-kuan Ssŭ 大觀寺, Ta-kuan Monastery, at T'ien-ning 天寧, Chêkiang 浙江, and afterwards in the Wan-shou Ssŭ 萬壽寺, Endless Longevity Monastery, at Yang Shan 仰山, Kiangsi 江西, where he died in A.D. 1149, aged 60.

HSI-SHÊN 喜神.—The God of Joy. No person is known to whom this title is given. He is represented carrying a basket, or oftener a sieve, on which are planted three arrows made of peachwood. This picture or image is almost always placed in front of a bride's wedding-chair when she is taken to her future husband's home. It is an exorcizing talisman.

Another representation is that of the God of Joy born on the shoulders of the God of Wealth, holding in his hand the character *hsi* 喜, joy,—riches and joy being inseparable according to Chinese ideas.

A third representation is that of a Joy-god dressed in green, carrying the same character in his hand or smilingly heaping up gold and silver ingots in a large basket.

HSI-SHIH 西施.—[The young lady] Shih [from the village to the] West [of the mountain.] The goddess of face-cream sellers and perfume sellers. A lady of great beauty, the daughter of a poor wood-cutter, chosen out of two thousand others, who was educated, clothed luxuriously, and adorned with face-cream and perfume to be sent by Kou Chien 勾踐, king of Yüeh 越 (494-464 B.C.) to Fu Ch'ai 夫差, King of Wu 吳.

She is worshipped by face-cream and perfume sellers because, they say, on her way to the king of Wu 吳 the perfume from her dress embalmed the air for ten *li* 里 around.

HSI T'IEN 西天.—The Western Paradise (*Sukhavati*).— Unknown to primitive Buddhism (which knew only the heaven of Maitreya, Mi-lo Fo 彌勒佛), the Western Paradise was invented when the worship of Amitabha (*q.v.*) spread among the Northern Buddhists. It was substituted for the Hindu Nirvana, which the Chinese could not comprehend. The invention is ascribed principally to the *Ching-t'u* 淨土 or "Pure Land" School, founded by Hui Yüan 慧元, in the 4th century A.D. (See *Buddhist Schools,* XVII).

This wonderful paradise is located in distant space far to the West. Those who reach it will henceforth escape all subsequent births. There is no fear of becoming a hungry ghost (*prêta*), or an animal by transmigration, for such modes of life are unknown there. It is composed of gold, silver, lapis-lazuli, beryl, ruby and cornelian. There are all kinds of beautiful flowers, which the inhabitants pluck, and offer to the thousands of Buddhas who visit them from other worlds. Birds of gay plumage sing night and day the praises of Buddha, the Law and the Brotherhood. Fountains bubble up on all sides. In the middle of the lakes are lotus flowers, large as a chariot wheel, blue, yellow, red and white, each reflecting brilliant hues of its own colour, and possessed of the most perfect and delightful fragrance. In fine, it is a place of splendour, beauty and pleasure, a blissful land, whence sorrow, grief and pain are banished for ever.

The ruler of this paradise is Amitabha, O-mi-t'o Fo 阿彌陀佛, (*q.v.*), who is attended by the two Bodhisattvas Avalokitesvara, the Chinese Kuan Yin 觀音, Goddess of Mercy, and Mahastama, the emblem of might and power. These act as guides and protectors of men, in their perilous journey over the ocean of life and death. The ruler admits to this paradise those who faithfully repeat his holy name and trust in his abounding power and pity. Those who have left their families and devoted their lives to religion enter immediately into the joys of this paradise; others must first pass through a transitory stage of longer or shorter duration similar to the Roman Catholic purgatory. "During this period of expiation, they lie imprisoned within the closed calix of a lotus flower."

Though this paradise is still regarded by some as a stepping-stone to Nirvana, it is but a matter of time before it will completely supplant the latter as the final goal of genuine Buddhism.

HSI T'IEN CHIAO-CHU 西天教主.—Sovereign Teacher of the Western Paradise. One of the names given to Amitabha (see *O-mi-t'o Fo* 阿彌陀佛), *Adi--Buddha,* and *P'i-lu Fo* 毗盧佛.

HSI-TSU 西祖.—See *Patriarchs*.

HSI WANG-MU 西王母.—The Western Royal Mother. Chin Mu 金母, the Golden Mother. This deity was formed of the pure quintessence of the Western Air, in the legendary continent of Shên Chou 神州. She is often called the Golden Mother of the Tortoise. Her family name is variously given as Hou 侯, Yang 楊, and Ho 何. Her personal name was Hui 回, and first name Wan-chin 婉妗.

She had nine sons and twenty-four daughters.

As Mu Kung 木公, formed of the Eastern Air, is the active (*yang* 陽) principle of the male air and sovereign of the Eastern Air, so Hsi Wang-mu 西王母, born of the Western Air, is the passive or female principle (*yin* 陰) and sovereign of the Western Air. These two principles, co-operating, engender Heaven and earth and all the beings of the universe, and thus become the two principles of life and of the subsistence of all that exists. She is the head of the troop of genii dwelling on the K'un-lun 崑崙 Mountains (the Taoist equivalent of the Buddhist Sumeru), and from time to time holds intercourse with favoured imperial votaries.

King Mu, Mu Wang 穆王 (1001-946 B.C.) of the Chou 周 dynasty is said in the *Hsien-fo chi-tsung* 仙佛集踪 and the *Mu-t'ien-tzŭ-chuan* 穆天子傳 to have visited a Western Queen named Hsi Wang-mu 西王母 who lived on K'un-lun Shan 崑崙山, the K'un-lun Mountains, and to have had an interview with her on the bank of the Yao Ch'ih 瑤池, Jasper Lake (*v. infra*).

She is sometimes represented as having a human form, panther's tail, tiger's teeth, and dishevelled hair. On the *chih-ma* 紙馬, paper horses, burnt to convey spirits to the Otherworld, she is represented with Tung Wang-kung 東王公, and the names printed on them are Mu Kung 木公 and Chin Mu 金母.

About 400 B.C., during the Chou 周 dynasty, Kou Chien 句踐 of the Yüeh 越 Kingdom (modern Chêkiang 浙江), and the conqueror of the Wu 吳 Kingdom, at the request of his minister Wên-chung 閘仲, erected an altar to Hsi Wang-mu 西王母 in the Western suburb of the capital. Kou Chien 句踐 had sacrifices offered to her there, praying for long life and happiness. This became a custom in subsequent ages, she being represented under the form of a noble matron.

The legend relates that in 110 B.C. Hsi Wang-mu 西王母 descended in person to the palace of the Emperor Wu Ti 武帝 (140-86 B.C.) of the Han 漢 dynasty on his birthday and presented him with seven peaches of immortality (*v. infra*).

Hsi Wang-mu's 西王母 palace is situated in the high mountains of the snowy K'un-lun 崑崙. It is 1000 *li* (about 333 miles) in circuit; a rampart of massive gold surrounds its battlements of precious stones. Its right wing rises on the edge of Ts'ui Ho 翠河, the Jasper River. It is the usual abode of the Immortals, who are divided into seven special categories according to the colour of their garments—red, blue, black, violet, yellow, green, and 'nature-colour.' There is a marvellous fountain built of precious stones, where the periodical banquet of the Immortals is held. This feast is called P'an-t'ao Hui 蟠桃會, 'the Feast of Peaches' (*lit*. peaches from the curling peach tree).

It takes place on the borders of the Yao Ch'ih 瑤池, Jasper Lake, and is attended by both male and female Immortals. Besides several superfine meats, they are served with bears' paws, monkeys' lips, dragons' liver, phœnix marrow, and peaches gathered in the orchard, endowed with the mystic virtue of conferring longevity on all who have the good luck to taste them. It was by these peaches that the date of the banquet was fixed. The tree put forth leaves once every three thousand years, and it required three thousand years after that for the fruit to ripen. These were Hsi Wang-mu's 西王母 birthdays, when all the Immortals assembled for the great feast, "the occasion being more festive than solemn, for there was music on invisible instruments, and songs not from mortal tongues."

From this legend arose the custom of presenting women of fifty years of age with an image of Hsi Wang-mu 西王母. To it they offer incense, bow down and pray for length of days. Offerings are also made to this goddess in times of drought.

For notes on some of her daughters, see Doré, IX. 491-2.

HSI-YÜ SÊNG CH'AN-SHIH 西域僧禪師.—The Meditative Monk from Hsi-yü 西域. A Buddhist monk who came from Hsi-yü 西域 (probably Kotan, Kashmir, or Tangut), reaching Ch'ang-an 長安, Shensi 陝西, in A.D. 639. No other name is given him in the histories. He was known for his unprepossessing features and his habit of wearing sandals.

Having called at the house of a Mr. Wei 韋 just when the latter had invited a party to celebrate the birth of his son, he was placed at a separate table in the inner courtyard, and later, when he was called upon to forecast its future, told the father that it was an incarnation of Chu-ko Liang 諸葛亮, the famous general and politician (A.D. 181-234), and that he had come purposely to greet him. The child eventually became a Chung-shu-ling 中書令, Imperial Secretary.

In A.D. 639, the State Historiographer Fu I 傅奕, a stern enemy of Buddhism, having fallen ill, the monk's boasted incantations failed to have any effect, the monk collapsing at his feet; and about the same time a Hindu bonze named P'o-lo-mên 婆羅門, Brahmana, "he who walks in purity," stated to the same official that a tooth of Buddha he possessed could not be destroyed by the hardest metal. Fu I 傅奕, however, had it shattered by a blow with an antelope's horn, "the people being thus undeceived."

Doré states that "despite the above failures to prove their transcendent powers, these two monks are held to be holy personages, and are venerated in several Buddhist temples." Parker assigns important results to these incidents: "It appears that the supreme test which decided the Emperor [T'ai Tsung 太宗 (A.D. 627-50)], to make a clean sweep of all the bonzes, nuns, and Taoist priests in the empire, was the failure of a Western bonze to 'strike the Confucianist dead,' as he boasted he could do, by holy incantations; he himself collapsed. Another test was the alleged indestructibility of Buddha's tooth" (*China and Religion*, p. 129).

HSI-YÜN CH'AN-SHIH 希運禪師 (37th generation).—A deified Buddhist monk. Ranked sixth in Buddhist School, III (*q.v.*). A native of Fu-chou Fu 福州府, Fukien 福建. Studied in the school of Huai-hai Ch'an-shih 懷海禪師 (*q.v.*). Died A.D. 849. Posthumous title: Tuan-chi Ch'an-shih 斷際禪師, Fair and Balanced Monk.

HSIA CHAO 夏招.—The god of the star Yüeh-tê 月德. A censor of Chou Wang 紂王. Committed suicide on failing to assassinate him,

HSIA HSIANG 夏祥.—The god of the star Ti-ch'iang 地强. —See *Ti-sha* 地煞.

HSIA-LA CH'AN-SHIH 夏臘禪師.—A saintly Buddhist monk. One of those invited to the annual banquet of the gods (see *Hsi Wang-mu* 西王母). A disciple of Hua-yen Ho-shang 華嚴和尚 (*q.v.*).

HSIA YÜAN T'IEN-KUAN 下元天官.—See *San Kuan* 三官.

HSIANG SHAN 香山.—See *Gandharvas*.

HSIANG SHÊN 香神 and HUA SHÊN 花神.—The Incense and Lotus-bearing genii attendants of the Buddha. Placed as ornaments on Buddhist altars.
Hsiang Shên 香神 carries a plate on which is a stick of incense and offers it as an act of worship to Vairocana, the Buddha Supreme and Eternal (see P'i-lu Fo 毗羅佛).
Hua Shên 花神 holds a lotus-flower, whence emerges a child. The lotus is a sacred plant and Hua Shên 花神 also offers it to Vairocana.

HSIANG TI-WU 象地無.—See *Kidneys, The Gods of the*.

HSIAO CHÊN 蕭臻.—The god of the star Chin-fu 金府. A disciple of Yüan-shih T'ien-tsun 元始天尊. Died at the siege of Hsi-ch'i 西岐, while fighting on behalf of Chiang Tzŭ-ya 姜子牙.

HSIAO-HAO 小 耗, THE GOD OF THE STAR.—See *Yin P'o-pai* 殷 破 敗.

HSIAO-HO 蕭 何.—Originally a writer of petitions in the Governor's office at P'ei Hsien 沛縣, Hsü-chou Fu 徐州府, Kiangsu 江 蘇, he eventually became the right-hand man of Liu Pang 劉邦, to whom he was of great assistance in conquering the Empire and becoming first Emperor of the Han 漢 dynasty, 202 B.C. His temple is near the Lo Bridge, Lo-ch'iao 樂橋, in Suchou (Soochow) 蘇 州, in the same province.—See also *Composite Deities.*

HSIAO KUNG 蕭公.—The Protecting Deity of Rivers. Family name Hsiao 蕭; personal name Po-hsüan 伯軒. Described as having arched eyebrows, a full head of curled hair, a plain face, but fine beard. Was known for his firmness, uprightness and self-possession, speaking and laughing but rarely. He died in A.D. 1275, the last year of the reign of the Emperor Tu Tsung 度宗 (A.D. 1265-75) of the Sung 宋 dynasty, and, having become a Spirit, passed into the body of his son. So certain were his predictions of good fortune, that he seemed to be its "sovereign arbiter," and a temple was erected to him on the island of T'ai-yang Chou 太洋州, Kiangsi 江 西.

His son Hsiao Hsiang-shu 蕭祥叔, and grandson Hsiao T'ien-jên 蕭天任, each on his death having exercised the transcendental powers of Hsiao Kung 蕭公 had their images placed by the people in the latter's temple, where, by the Emperor's order, offerings were made to them.

In A.D. 1419, the Emperor Yung Lo 永樂 (A.D. 1403-25) of the Ming 明 dynasty canonized Hsiao Kung 蕭公 as Illustrious and Helpful Marquis of the Palace of the Waters, who answers prayers by benefits and prodigies, and exercises his miraculous power over the Nine Rivers, the Eight Streams, the Five Lakes, and the Four Seas.

The remarkable fact is, that a man who had done nothing extraordinary during his life should have been so greatly honoured after his death.

HSIAO LU 小 路.—See *Lo-han* 羅 漢.

HSIAO SHÊNG 蕭 昇.—See *Ministries: Finance.*

HSIAO SHIH-CHIA 小 釋迦.—The Little Sakyamuni. A saintly Buddhist monk. Eighth century A.D. One of those invited to the annual banquet of the gods (see *Hsi Wang-mu* 西 王 母). Family name Li 黎. Called the Little Sakyamuni from his profound knowledge of the Law. Lived first at Kuei Shan 桂 山, Cassia Hill, and later in the Yün-fêng Ssŭ 雲 封 寺, Cloud-capped Monastery, at the foot of Mei Ling 梅 嶺, Plum-tree Range, which separates Kuangtung 廣 東 from Kuangsi 廣 西.

His mother having served him a dish of meat, he, when the meal was over, repaired to the brink of a stream, cut open his stomach, washed out the prohibited food (Buddhists being vegetarians), returned to his monastery and expired.

HSIAO TIEN 蕭 電.—The god of the star Ti-k'ung 地 空.—See *Ti-sha* 地 煞.

HSIEH HSÜAN 謝 玄.—An assessor of Kuan Kung 關 公.—See *Kuan Yü* 關 羽.

HSIEH-KUANG 血 光, THE GOD OF THE STAR.—See *Ma Chung* 馬 忠 and *Sun Yen-hung* 孫 焰 紅.

HSIEH-KUANG CHÜ 叶 光 矩.—See *Mercury*.

HSIEH T'IEN-CHÜN 謝 天 君.—The god of the planet Mars, Huo Hsing 火 星. Son of Hsieh Ên 謝 恩. Born amid unusual celestial omens during the reign of the emperor T'ai Tsung 太 宗 (A.D. 627-50) of the T'ang 唐 dynasty. He was called Hsieh Shih-jung 謝 仕 榮, his personal name being Lei-hsing 雷 行. Though irascible and fearless he was always correct in his conduct. Having become Sub-prefect of Shan-yin 山 陰, Shansi 山 西, and exposed the Prefect's malpractices, the latter tried unsuccessfully to destroy him, and he was canonized by Yü Ti 玉 帝 as Huo-tê T'ien-chün 火 德 天 君, Celestial Sovereign of the beneficent planet Mars. He regulates the summer season, wears the Taoist headgear, has two fire-wheels under his feet, and holds in his hand a golden sword or stick. Otherwise he is represented with three heads and six arms, his feet mounted on firewheels.

HSIEH TING 薛 定.—The god of the constellation Chang 張. Alternatively with Wan Hsiu 萬 修.

HSIEN 仙.—An Immortal (*Ch'ang shêng pu ssŭ* 長 生 不 死). The immortal Taoists. They live on the mountains, hence the modern character *hsien* 仙, man and mountain. A man, *jên* 亻, who rose *hsien* 罨 (*chien* 僊) by the Taoist practices, above mortals, or above the human state or condition. Also said to have been formerly written 仚, *i.e.* one who *ju* 入, entered, or lived on, *shan* 山, a hill or mountain.

Instead of the Hsi T'ien 西 天, Western Paradise, of the Buddhists, Taoism offers immortality to its followers. "They call it *nei-tan* 內 丹, or internal elixir, and in its formation use the 'three precious things,' in the body of a man—the fecundating fluid, the breath, and the saliva; the first to be drawn upward, the second to be inhaled more than exhaled, and the third to be swallowed. The first unites with the breath, the breath unites with the saliva, and these three form an invisible boy in the body of a man. This immaterial child grows larger and larger, and may go out of the body and return again to its home, but it needs to be protected, as it is liable to be devoured by devils and hobgoblins. When the young spiritual China man becomes as large as the man's body, it can tarry on the earth or depart to the better land at pleasure; if the latter, it goes like the cicada, leaving its shell, and is a heavenly immortal; if it wishes to remain in the world, it becomes one of the earth genii and lives for ever" (Du Bose, p. 356).

Immortals appear to die, but do not really do so. A corpse is merely a metamorphosis. The bones are transformed. After death, Immortals retain all the properties of living beings: their feet do not become livid, their skin remains fresh, their eyes do not become dim: though apparently dead, they are more alive than ever. Some throw off the "mortal coil" even before burial; others are already able to fly in the air when their hair begins to fall off. In every case, the corpse form is only a transition, the sheath of the transformation. The metamorphosis of a *hsien jên* 仙人 takes place in daylight, of a *chên jên* 眞人 at midnight, and of a *shêng jên* 聖人 in the morning or the evening.—See also *Chên Jên* 眞人 and *Shêng Jên* 聖人.

HSIEN CHÊNG 顯正.—See *Ts'ai Shên* 財神.

HSIEH CHI 薛巳.—See *Shih Ming-i* 十明醫, 10.

HSIEN-CHIEH CH'AN-SHIH 咸傑禪師 (51st generation). —A deified Buddhist monk. Ranked twenty-seventh in Buddhist School, III (*q.v.*). Family name Chêng 鄭. A native of Fukien 福建. He studied under T'an-hua Ch'an-shih 曇華禪師 (*q.v.*). Lived at Wu-chü 烏巨, then at the Ling-yin Ssŭ 靈隱寺, Monastery of Mystic Retirement, on Ching Shan 徑山, and toward the close of his life on T'ai-pai Fêng 太白峰 (*q.v.*), where his tomb still exists.

HSIEN CHIH 顯直.—See *Ts'ai Shên* 財神.

HSIEN-CH'IH 咸池, THE GOD OF THE STAR.—See *Hsü Chung* 徐忠.

HSIEN JÊN 仙人.—Immortals or Genii. The third class of deified mortals. They dwell in the third, or lowest, Supreme Azure (T'ai Ch'ing 太清) Heaven of Lao Tzŭ 老子 (*q.v.*). They are human souls endowed with divine powers. They form the most numerous class. Among them are philosophers, alchemists, mystics, old recluses, and countless magicians. Taoist ascetics, who through the practice of virtue and the taking of certain drugs, render themselves independent of the material body.

After death, which for them is rather a metamorphosis, they rove through the universe, enjoying perfect health and happiness. In Taoism, there are two grades higher than the Hsien Jên 仙 人: the Chên Jên 真 人, Hero, and the Shêng Jên 聖 人, Saint (*q.q.v.*). —See also *Hsien* 仙.

HSIEN MING 顯 明.—See *Ts'ai Shên* 財 神.

HSIEN MU 先 牧.—See *Ma Wang* 馬 王.

HSIEN NUNG 先 農.—See *Shên Nung* 神 農.

HSIEN SÊ 先 嗇.—See *Shên Nung* 神 農.

HSIEN TÊ 顯 德.—See *Ts'ai Shên* 財 神.

HSIEN TS'UNG 顯 聰.—See *Ts'ai Shên* 財 神.

HSIN 心, THE GOD OF THE CONSTELLATION.—See *K'ou Hsün* 仙 帥 and *Nu pông Tao jên* 糈 元 道 人

HSIN-HSING KOU YÜAN-SHUAI 辛 興 苟 元 帥.—A poor woodcutter of Yung Chou 雍 州, Shensi 陝 西, when seeking for fuel on Shên-lei Shan 神 雷 山, Spiritual Thunder Mountain, in Ku-yung Chou 古 雍 州, to give to his mother, found five hens at the bottom of a deep crevasse. Taking them home, he presented them to his mother, who put four of them under a crate and covered them with a garment, keeping the fifth out to kill and eat. But the fowl spoke and said to her: "I am the Spirit of Thunder. You cannot eat me. Take good care not to injure me." (The Spirit of Thunder came out of the mountain in the tenth moon; during the summer and autumn it hid there in the form of a fowl).

The old lady refused to heed this warning; at that moment there was a clap of thunder, and she fell backwards on the ground. When Hsin-hsing 辛 興 returned with some fuel and wine, he found his mother lying dead on the floor. "Alas," said he, "my mother was good; she could not be killed by an evil spirit. What has caused her death?" No sooner had he said this than the wind blew, the thunder crashed, and the Spirit of Thunder came from the clouds of Heaven to kill him also. However, in consideration of his filial piety, the image of a Taoist came, saluted him, and said: "If I killed your mother, it was because she was about to kill me; bear me no resentment; I am the Spirit of Thunder and ask your pardon." He then gave him twelve fire-pills, and as soon as he had eaten them he was completely transfigured; his mouth became elongated to a point; he grew wings; in one hand he held a hammer, in the other a spike, and five drums supported his feet. Having rescued his mother he disappeared.

Out of regard for his filial piety, the Lord of Heaven canonized him as Generalissimo of the star Kou 荀 of the Ministry of Thunder. He shares with Pi Yüan-shuai 畢元帥 (*q.v.*) the control of the devils of the five directions.

He is a Taoist invention, an imitation of Lei Kung 雷公 (*q.v.*). His image, together with that of Pi Yüan-shuai 畢元帥, is often seen in temples dedicated to *Chên Wu* 眞武 (See *Hsüant'ien Shan-ti* 玄天上帝).

HSIN-LO 新羅.—See *Sinlo*.

HSIN T'IEN-CHÜN 辛天君. T'AO T'IEN-CHÜN 陶天君. —Two subalterns of Lei Tsu 雷祖 (*q.v.*). Hsin T'ien-chün's 辛天君 name was Hsin Huan 辛環. Having opposed and been vanquished by Wên Chung 聞仲 (Lei Tsu 雷祖) in the mountain defiles of Huang-hua Shan 黃花山, Mount Huang-hua, he and his companion T'ao Jung 陶榮 (T'ao T'ien-chün 陶天君) submitted and, having been incorporated in the victor's army, were taken to Hsi-ch'i 西岐 to fight against the armies of Wu Wang 武王. Being utterly defeated, they fell back on Huang-hua Shan 黃花山. T'ao Jung 陶榮 was killed in the battle when trying to stab Huang T'ien-hsiang 黃天祥, brother of Huang T'ien-hua 黃天花. Chiang Tzǔ-ya 姜子牙 canonized him as T'ao T'ien-chün 陶天君, and appointed him a member of the Ministry of Thunder.

Hsin Huan 辛環 managed to escape, but, on his reaching Huang-hua Shan 黃花山, Huang T'ien-hua 黃天花 fell upon him and pierced his ribs with his "heart-piercing nail." Fleeing from the victors, he was severely bitten in the leg by Yang Chien's 楊戩 (*i.e.* Erh Lang's 二郎) celestial hound, fell to earth, and was killed by a blow from Lei Chên-tzǔ's 雷震子 (*q.v.*) staff.

HSING 星, THE GOD OF THE CONSTELLATION.— See *Li Chung* 李忠 and *Lü Nêng* 呂能.

HSING-AN FA-SHIH 省庵法師.—A deified Buddhist monk. Ranked ninth in Buddhist School, XVII (*q.v.*). Ninth ancestor. Secular name Shih Shih-hsien 時實賢. A native of Ch'ang-shu 常熟, a dependency of Su-chou (Soochow) 蘇州, Kiangsu 江蘇. Surnames Ssǔ-ch'i 思齊, and Hsiang-an 省庵, but generally known by the latter. He was very learned and an eloquent speaker. Spent his days studying the *Tsangching* 藏經, *Tripitaka,* and his nights in prayer. "He made a pilgrimage to O-yü-wang Shan 阿育王山 and at the feet of Buddha's statue, he burnt his fingers (as an act of penance, manifesting zeal for Buddha and the Law), and pronounced forty-eight vows. A shower of precious stones fell from the heavens. His disciples could not refrain from weeping" when reading his work *P'u-t'i hsin-wên* 菩提心文, *Intelligence of the Heart.* Died A.D. 1734.

"Before expiring, he turned his eyes towards the West and forthwith gave up the ghost. While his corpse was being taken to the grave, he opened his eyes and said to those who accompanied the coffin: 'I am departing, but I shall return [metempsychosis]; recite always with fervour the name of Buddha, for life and death are of the utmost importance.' Hereupon he joined his hands and closed his eyes in death, invoking the name of Buddha" (Doré, viii, 462).

HSI MÊN PAO 西門豹.—Prefect of the Wei 魏 country, circ. 410 B.C. His name is associated with his noble action in putting an end to offerings of girls made to the God of the Yellow River. The events resulting in his apotheosis are related in Chapter 126 of the *Shih-chi ts'ê-i* 史記測議 as follows:

In the former town of Yeh 鄴, in the modern Lin-chang Hsien 臨漳縣, Chang-tê Fu 彰德府, Honan 河南, there was a witch and some officials attendants who collected money from the people yearly for the marriage of the River-god.

The witch would select a pretty girl of low birth, and say that she should be the Queen of the River-god. The girl was bathed, and clothed in a beautiful dress of gay and costly silk. She was then taken to the bank of the river, to a monastery which was beautifully decorated with scrolls and banners. A feast was held, and the girl was placed on a bed which was floated out upon the tide till it disappeared under the waters.

Many families having beautiful daughters moved to distant places, and gradually the city became deserted. The common belief in Yeh 鄴 was that if no queen was offered to the River-god a flood would come and drown the people.

One day Hsi-mên Pao 西門豹, Magistrate of Yeh Hsien 鄴縣, said to his attendants: "When the marriage of the River-god takes place I wish to say farewell to the chosen girl."

Accordingly Hsi-mên Pao 西門豹 was present to witness the ceremony. About three thousand people had come together. Standing beside the old witch were ten of her female disciples. "Call the girl out," said Hsi-mên Pao 西門豹. After seeing her, Hsi-mên Pao 西門豹 said to the witch: "She is not fair. Go you to the River-god and tell him that we will find a fairer maid and present her to him later on." His attendants then seized the witch and threw her into the water.

After a little while Hsi-mên Pao 西門豹 said: "Why does she stay so long? Send a disciple to call her back." One of the disciples was thrown into the river. Another and yet another followed. The magistrate then said: "The witches are females and therefore cannot bring me a reply." So one of the official attendants of the witch was thrown into the river.

Hsi-mên Pao 西門豹 stood on the bank for a long time, apparently awaiting a reply. The spectators were alarmed. Hsi-mên Pao 西門豹 then bade his attendants send the remaining disciples of the witch and the other official attendants to recall their mistress. The wretches threw themselves on their knees and knocked their heads on the ground, which was stained with the blood from their foreheads, and with tears confessed their sin.

"The River-god detains his guest too long," said Hsi-mên Pao 西門豹 at length. "Let us adjourn."

Thereafter none dared to celebrate the marriage of the River-god.

This took place in the reign of Wên Hou 文侯, the first sovereign of the Wei 魏 (425-387 B.C.).

HSING-CH'ANG LÜ-SHIH 省常律師.—A deified Buddhist monk. Ranked seventh in Buddhist School, XVII (q.v.). Seventh ancestor. Secular name Yen Tsao-wei 顏造微. A native of Ch'ien-t'ang Hsien 錢塘縣, Chêkiang 浙江. Donned the Buddhist robe at the age of 7, and was a fully-trained monk by the time he was 17. Lived at Chao-ch'ing 昭慶 from A.D. 990-5. Made a statue of O-mi-t'o Fo 阿彌陀佛, Amitabha, and wrote out with his blood the *Hua-yen ching-hsing-p'in* 華嚴淨行品. From that time, he changed the name Lien-shê Tsung 蓮社宗, Lotus or Amidist School, until then given to the sect, to Ching-hsing Shê 淨行社, Sect of the Pure Doctrine. One hundred and twenty Scholars (Literati) gave their names to the new sect, Wang Wên-chêng 王文正 being their president. When the membership had grown to more than a thousand associates, they took the name Ching-hsing Ti-tzŭ 淨行弟子, Disciples of the Ching-hsing School.

In A.D. 1020, when he was 62 years old, Hsing-ch'ang 省常 suddenly exclaimed: "Behold Buddha!" and expired. "All the objects surrounding his corpse assumed a golden hue." His tomb was placed next to that of Wu-k'o Ch'an-shih 烏窠禪師 (see *Lo-han* 羅漢).

HSING-HSIEN 杏仙.—See *Wu Lao* 五老.

HSING-HSIU CH'AN-SHIH 行秀禪師 (51st generation).— A deified Buddhist monk. Ranked thirty-ninth in Buddhist School, VI (q.v.). Family name Ts'ai 蔡. A native of Ho-nei 河內 Honan 河南. Studied under Hui-man Ch'an-shih 慧滿禪師 (q.v.), and lived in the monasteries at Ching-t'u 淨土 and Wan-shou 萬壽.

In A.D. 1193, the emperor Chang Tsung 章宗 (A.D. 1190-1209) of the Kin 金 dynasty summoned him to Court, presented him with a gold-cloth cope, and assigned him the Yang-shan Ssŭ 仰山寺, Yang-shan Monastery, as a residence. Died A.D. 1246, during the reign of Li Tsung 理宗 (A.D. 1225-65) of the Nan-Sung Chi 南宋紀, Southern Sung dynasty. ˋ

HSING-NIEN CH'AN-SHIH 省念禪師.—See *Shêng-nien Ch'an-shih* 省念禪師.

HSING SAN-LUAN 邢三鸞.—The god of the star Ti-su 地速.—See *Ti-sha* 地煞.

HSING-SÊN CH'AN-SHIH 行森禪師 (69th generation).—A deified Buddhist monk. Ranked sixty-third in Buddhist School, III (*q.v.*). Family name Li 黎. A native of Po-lo 博羅. Studied under Yüan-hsin Ch'an-shih 圓信禪師 (*q.v.*) and T'ung-hsiu Ch'an-shih 通琇禪師 (*q.v.*). In 1660 he refused an honorary title offered him by the Emperor Shun Chih 順治 (A.D. 1664-62), whereupon the Emperor styled him Tz'ŭ Wêng 慈翁, Merciful Greybeard. Having returned to Chê-chiang (Chekiang) 浙江, he lived in the Lung-ch'i Ssŭ 龍溪寺, Dragon-brook Monastery. Its name was changed by the Emperor to Yüan-chao Ssŭ 圓照寺, Wholly-illumined Monastery. Hsing-sên 行森 died in the Hua-yen Ssŭ 華嚴寺, Hua-yen Monastery, at Wu Shan 吳山, A.D. 1677, aged 64. His ashes were brought to the Yüan-chao Ssŭ 圓照寺, where a tower was erected in his honour. In A.D. 1733, the Emperor Yung Chêng 雍正 (A.D. 1723-36) of the Ch'ing 清 dynasty bestowed on him the posthumous title of Ming-tao Chêng-chio 明照正知, Monk of Bright Intelligence and Orthodox Knowledge.

HSING-SSŬ 行思.—See *Patriarchs: Hui Neng* 慧能.

HSING-SSŬ CH'AN-SHIH 行思禪師 (34th generation).—A deified Buddhist monk. Ranked first in Buddhist School, VI (*q.v.*). Family name Liu 劉. A native of An-ch'êng 安成, in Chi-chou 吉州. Originally apathetic, on hearing of the reputation of Hui-nêng 慧能 (see Patriarchs), who was teaching at Ts'ao-ch'i 曹谿, he set out for his school, and became his disciple. When he had become proficient in the Doctrine, Hui-nêng 慧能 sent him forth to preach, and returning to his native country, he built the Ching-chü Ssŭ 靜居寺 Ching-chü Monastery, at Ch'ing-yüan 青原, Pure Spring, where he taught for more than thirty years. This was the origin of the Ch'ing-yüan Chêng-tsung 青原正宗.
Hsing-ssŭ 行思 died in A.D. 730. The Emperor Hsi Tsung 僖宗 (A.D. 874-9) of the T'ang 唐 dynasty conferred on him the honorary title of Hung-chi Ch'an-shih 弘濟師禪.

HSIU 修.—See *Shui Fu* 水府, D (3) (b).

HSÜ 虛, THE GOD OF THE CONSTELLATION.—See *Kai Yen* 蓋延 and *Chou Pao* 周寶.

HSÜ CH'ANG 續長.—See *I Mei* 義梅.

HSÜ CHÊN-CHÜN 許眞君.—The Dragon-slayer. Family name Hsü 許. First name Ching-chih 敬之. Ordinary name Sun 遜. A native either of Ju-ning Fu 汝寧府, Honan 河南, or, according to the *Kuang-yü chi* 廣輿記, of Nan-ch'ang Fu 南昌府, Kiangsi 江西. Father's name Hsü Su 許肅; grandfather's Hsü T'an 許酘. His mother became pregnant after dreaming that a golden-plumaged phœnix let a pearl drop from its beak into her womb, the child being born in A.D. 239. In his youth he studied the magical practices of the Taoists; when grown up he was especially filial and temperate.

At forty-one years of age, when he was Magistrate of Ching-yang 旌陽, near the modern Chih-chiang Hsien 枝江縣, Hupei 湖北, during times of drought he had only to touch a piece of tile to turn it into gold, and thus relieve the people of their distress. He also saved many lives by curing sickness through the use of talismans and magic formulæ.

During the dynastic troubles in the period of San Kuo 三國, the Three Kingdoms, and Chin 晉 dynasties, he resigned and joined the famous magician Kuo P'o 郭璞. Together they proceeded to the minister Wang Tun 王敦, who had risen against the Tung Chin 東晉, Eastern Chin, dynasty. Kuo P'o's 郭璞 remonstrances only irritated the minister, who cut off his head.

Hsü Sun 許遜 then threw his chalice on the ridgepole of the room, causing it to be whirled into the air. As Wang Tun 王敦 was watching the career of the chalice, Hsü 許 disappeared and escaped. When he reached Lu-chiang K'ou 盧江口, in Anhui 安徽, he boarded a boat, which two dragons towed into the offing and then raised into the air. In an instant they had borne it to the Lu Shan 盧山 Mountains, to the south of Chiu-chiang (Kiu-kiang) 九江, Kiangsi 江西. The perplexed boatman opened the window of his boat and took a furtive look out. Thereupon the dragons, finding themselves discovered by an infidel, set the boat down on the top of the mountain and fled.

In this country was a dragon, or spiritual alligator, which transformed itself into a young man named Shên Lang 慎郎 and married Chia-yü 賈玉, daughter of the Chief Judge of T'an Chou 潭州 (Ch'ang-sha Fu 長沙府, capital of Hunan 湖南). The young people lived in rooms below the official apartments. During spring and summer Shên Lang 慎郎, as dragons are wont to do, roamed in the rivers and lakes. One day Hsü Chên-chün 許眞君 met him, recognized him as a dragon, and knew that he was the cause of the numerous floods which were devastating Kiangsi 江西 Province. He determined to find a means of getting rid of him.

Shên Lang 慎郎, aware of the steps being taken against him, changed himself into a yellow ox and fled. Hsü Chên-chün 許眞君 at once transformed himself into a black ox and started in pursuit. The yellow ox jumped down a well to hide, but the black ox followed suit. The yellow ox then jumped out again, and escaped to Ch'ang-sha 長沙, where he reassumed a human form and lived with his wife in the home of his father-in-law. Hsü Sun 許遜, returning to the town, hastened to the *yamên*

衙 門, and called to Shên Lang 慎 郎 to come out and show himself, addressing him in a severe tone of voice as follows: "Dragon, how dare you hide yourself there under a borrowed form?" Shên Lang 慎 郎 then reassumed the form of a spiritual alligator, and Hsü Sun 許 遜 ordered the spiritual soldiers to kill him. He then commanded his two sons to come out of their abode. By merely spurting a mouthful of water on them he transformed them into young dragons. Chia-yü 賈 玉 was told to vacate the rooms with all speed, and in the twinkling of an eye the whole *yamên* 衙 門 sank beneath the earth, and there remained nothing but a lake where it had been.

Shü Chên-chün 許 眞 君, after his victory over the dragon, assembled the members of his family, to the number of forty-two, on Hsi Shan 西 山, outside the city of Nan-ch'ang Fu 南 昌 府, and all ascended to Heaven in full daylight, taking with them even the dogs and chickens. He was then 113 years old. This took place on the first day of the eighth moon of the second year (A.D. 374) of the reign-period Ning-k'ang 寧 康 of the reign of the Emperor Hsiao-wu Ti 孝 武 帝 (AD. 373-97) of the Tung Chin 東 晉, Eastern Chin, dynasty.

Subsequently a temple was erected to him, and in A.D. 1111 he was canonized as Just Prince, Admirable and Beneficent.

HSÜ CHÊNG-TAO 徐 正 道.—The god of the star T'ien-yu 天 佑.—See *T'ien-kang* 天 罡.

HSÜ CH'ÊNG 須 成.—The god of the star Ti-wei 地 威.—See *Ti-sha* 地 煞.

HSÜ CHI 徐 吉.—The god of the star Ti-chin 地 進.—See *Ti-sha* 地 煞.

HSÜ CHIEN-SHÊNG 虛 監 生.—See *Eye, The Gods of the*.

HSÜ CHÜN 許 君.—See *Field-ancestor God, The*.

HSÜ CHUNG 徐 忠.—The god of the star Hsien-ch'ih 咸 池. One of Chou Wang's 紂 王 officers, killed in the Yin-Chou 殷 周 wars.

HSÜ FANG 徐 芳.—The god of the star Sui-hsing 歲 刑. Brother of Hsü Kai 徐 蓋. One of Chou Wang's 紂 王 generals. Captured by the enemy at Ch'uan-yün Kuan 穿 雲 關 and put to death.

HSÜ HAO 虛 耗.—Emptiness and Devastation.—See *Ch'ü-hsieh Yüan* 罷 邪 院.

HSÜ KAI 徐 蓋.—The god of the star T'ai-yang 太 陽 (the

sun). A regimental commander under Chou Wang 紂王. Was made prisoner and submitted to the victor.

HSÜ K'UN 徐坤.—The god of the star Hsüan-wu 玄武. One of Chou Wang's 紂王 chief officers, put to death by Chi K'ang 季康, one of Chiang Tzǔ-ya's 姜子牙 officers.

HSÜ LIEH-FU 旭烈兀.—An assessor of Kuan Kung 關公.— See *Kuan Yü* 關羽.

HSÜ-MI SHAN 須 (or 蘇) 彌山.—See *Sumeru*.

HSÜ SHAN 徐山.—The god of the star Ti-ch'ou 地醜. —See *Ti-sha* 地煞.

HSÜ TA 徐達.—An assessor of Kuan Kung 關公.—See *Kuan Yü* 關羽.

HSÜAN CHÊN-TZǓ 玄眞子.—A hermit named Chang Chih-ho 張志和, who lived on Kuei-chi Shan 會稽山, Mount Kuei-chi, in the time of the Emperor Su Tsung 肅宗 (A.D. 756-63) of the T'ang 唐 dynasty. Renounced official life for solitude. A hard drinker, without getting drunk (even after three bushels of wine). Owing to his system of diet could roll in snow without feeling cold, and keep under water without drowning. Spread his mat to cross lakes or rivers, drinking and singing during the passage. A crane carried him up to Heaven.

HSÜAN-CHIEN CH'AN-SHIH 宣鑑禪師 (38th generation). —A deified Buddhist monk. Ranked eighth in Buddhist School, VI (*q.v.*). Family name Chou 周. A native of Chien-chou 簡州, Ssǔch'uan 四川. Studied under Ch'ung-hsin Ch'an-shih 崇信 禪師 (*q.v.*). Died A.D. 865. Posthumous title: Chien-hsing Ch'an-shih 見性禪師, Monk who Understood the Nature of Things.

HSÜAN KUAN 玄光.—See *Eye, The Gods of the.*

HSÜAN-LANG TSUN-CHÊ 玄朗尊者.—A deified Buddhist monk. Ranked seventh in Buddhist School, X (*q.v.*). Secular name Hui-ming 慧明, a descendant in the sixth generation from the family of Fu Ta-shih 傅大士 (*q.v.*). A native of Tung-yang 東陽, a dependency of Wu-chou 婺州, Chêkiang 浙江. Became a monk at T'ien-t'ai 天台 at the age of 50, but quickly grasped the doctrine, and settled at P'ing-yen Hsüeh 憑嚴穴, where he adopted the name of Tso-ch'i 左溪. Whenever he was about to wash his alms-bowl, a band of monkeys came forward and handed it to him, and birds hovered around him while he prayed. One day, a blind dog having besought his compassion, he prayed for it, and its sight was restored within ten days. He also replenished the monastery cistern merely by striking the ground with his staff. Died A.D. 754. Posthumous title: Ming-chio Tsun-chê 明覺尊者, Brilliant and Intelligent Teacher.

HSÜAN MING 玄冥.—See *Shui Fu* 水府, C (2) (b) and (e), D (3) (b), and *Kidneys, The Gods of the*.

HSÜAN NÜ 玄女.—See *Apotheosized Philosophers*.

HSÜAN-SU CH'AN-SHIH 玄素禪師 (37th generation).— A deified Buddhist monk. Ranked sixth in Buddhist School, I (*q.v.*).

HSUAN-T'AN P'U-SA 玄壇菩薩.—Worshipped by merchants in general.—See *Ts'ai Shén* 財神.

HSÜAN-T'IEN SHANG-TI 玄天上帝.—The Lord of the Black [Pavilions of] Heaven. Also called Chên Wu 眞武, and Pei-chi Yu-shêng Chên-chün 北極佑聖眞君. A reincarnation of Yüan ... T'ai ... (...), ... born on a ray of light, entered the womb of Shan Shêng 善勝, Queen of the Kingdom of Ching-lo 淨樂. At fifteen years of age, he left his parents and went to T'ai-ho Shan 太和山, Mount T'ai-ho, in Hupei 湖北, where the patriarch Tzŭ-hsü 紫虛 descended from Yü-ch'ing 玉淸, Third Heaven, to teach him the wonderful doctrine, and bestowed on him a magic sword. On an elevated peak of this mountain he practised for forty-two years the exercises which brought him the ability to float in the air, etc.

When Yüan-shih T'ien-tsun 元始天尊 heard of this he deputed five leading chiefs of the Heroes of Shang Ch'ing 上淸, the Second Heaven, and a troop of Immortals of the First Heaven, to invite him to ascend to the celestial regions. On receipt of this invitation Hsüan-t'ien 玄天 ascended in his golden palace to Heaven.

This was in the time of the Emperor Chou 紂 (1154-1121 B.C.), the last ruler of the Yin 殷 dynasty, when the *kuei-wang* 鬼王, demon-kings, at the head of their infernal legions, were ravishing the universe. Yüan-shih T'ien-tsun 元始天尊 ordered Yü Huang 玉皇 to place Hsüan-t'ien 玄天 at the head of the twelve great chiefs of the celestial legions and send him to earth, with dishevelled hair, bare-footed, girdled with a gold cuirass, clothed in a black gown, and hoisting his black sacred banner in the midst of the black flags of his troops.

The names of these twelve celestial officers were:—Ssŭ-ma Ch'ing 司馬卿, Chang Wên-t'ung 張文通, Shih Shu-t'ung 石叔通, Wang Wên-ch'ing 王文卿, Hu Wên-chang 扈文長, Mêng Fei-ch'ing 孟非卿, Chao Tzŭ-jên 趙子任, Tsang Wên-kung 臧文公, Ts'ui Shih-ch'ing 崔石卿, Chan Tzŭ-chiang 展子江, Wei Shang-ch'ing 衞上卿, and Ming Wên-chang 明文章.

He joined battle with the king of the demons at Tung-yin 洞陰, Dark Grotto. Mo Wang 魔王 (*q.v.*) made out of the surrounding air a grey tortoise and an enormous serpent (according to the *Hsi-yu chi* 西遊記 these are two marshals under this divinity's orders) which fought on his side, but in spite of all Hsüan Wang 玄王 and his celestial troops were victorious, trampled him down, and captured all the demons, whom they cast into the Fêng-tu 酆都 abyss (the entrance to the infernal regions) in Ssǔch'uan 四川.

The conqueror returned in his golden palace to Heaven, where Yüan-shih T'ien-tsun 元始天尊 rewarded him for his victory by conferring on him the title Hsüan-t'ien Shang-ti 玄天上帝, First Lord of the Highest Heaven. (His name Hsüan Wu 玄武 is said, in the *Hsü Wên-hsien t'ung-k'ao* 續文獻通考, to be the name of the North Star.) The name Hsüan Wu 玄武 was changed to Chên Wu 眞武 by the Emperor Chên Tsung 眞宗 (A.D. 998-1023) of the Sung 宋 dynasty, because the character *hsüan* 玄 was part of his own name. The Emperor Ch'êng Tsung 成宗 (A.D. 1294-1307) of the Yüan 元 dynasty granted him the honorary title of Leading Good and Majestic Saint, First Lord of the Highest Heaven.

[For the appearance of Hsüan-t'ien Shang-ti 玄天上帝 in a vision to the Emperor Hui Tsung 徽宗 (A.D. 1101-26) of the Sung 宋 dynasty, see Doré, IX, 481-2, and *Sung-shih* 宋史, bk. 463, p. 9.]

Mention is made in the *Ming-shih* 明史 (bk. 50, pp. 16, 18) of a temple built in A.D. 1416 for sacrificing to Hsüan Wu 玄武 under the title of Veritable Saintly and Helpful Master of the Pole Star. Later generations called him Chên Chün 眞君, True Master, placing at the feet of his image a tortoise and a serpent.

In temples dedicated to Chên Wu 眞武 there are to be seen fourteen images arranged in two lines, seven on each side of the altar behind which he is enthroned. Eight of these are the Pa-p'an Shan-tao 八盤山盜, brigands met by him on his way to worship Buddha at that mountain, and who became his disciples; the other six being demon-kings whom he conquered in the above-related battle. Some Taoists state that these are merely four of his military and two of his civil officers.

HSÜAN TSANG 玄奘 or YÜAN TSANG 元奘.—A saintly Buddhist monk. A.D. 602-64. One of those invited to the annual banquet of the gods (see *Hsi Wang-mu* 西王母). The great Chinese Master of Law, who, having studied Hindu culture in T'ien chu 天竺 (*i.e.* India) for sixteen years (A.D. 629-45) during one of the most brilliant epochs of Indian imperialism under Harshavardhana and Pulakesin II, propagated it extensively in his native land under the patronage of the T'ang 唐 Emperor T'ai Tsung 太宗 (A.D. 627-50) and thus laid the foundations of a re-interpreted Confucianism.—See also *Sun Hou-tzǔ* 孫猴子.

HSÜAN-TSANG FA-SHIH 玄奘法師.—A deified Buddhist monk. Ranked first in Buddhist School, XIV (*q.v.* and *Sun Hou-tzŭ* 猻猴子).

HSÜAN T'UNG-TZŬ 玄童子.—See *Wên Ch'ang* 文昌.

HSÜAN WÊN-HUA 玄文華.—See *Hair, The Gods of the*.

HSÜAN-WU 玄武, THE GOD OF THE STAR.—See *Hsü K'un* 徐坤.

HSÜAN-YÜAN HUANG-TI 軒轅黄帝.—A God of Spectacle-merchants. Also worshipped as the God of Tailors. The legendary Emperor Huang Ti 黄帝 (2698-2598 B.C.) is said to have been the inventor of spectacles. (These, however, only came from Arabia in the thirteenth century).—See also *Kuei Ku-tzŭ* 鬼谷子 and *Yen-kuang P'u-sa* 眼光菩薩.

HSÜAN (YÜAN)-T'AN P'U-SA 玄(元)壇菩薩.— See *Hsüan-t'an P'u-sa* 玄壇菩薩 and *Ts'ai Shên* 財神.

[HSÜEH-FÊNG] I-TS'UN CH'AN-SHIH [雪峰]義存禪師. —See *Buddhist Schools*, VIII.

[HSÜEH-KUAN] TAO-YIN CH'AN-SHIH [雪關]道閒 禪師.—See *Tao-yin Ch'an-shih* 道閒禪師 and *Wei-chung-fu Ch'an-shih* 位中符禪師.

HU LEI 胡雷.—See *Wu Tou* 五斗.

HU PAI-YEN 呼百顏.—The god of the star Ti-chieh 地傑. —See *Ti-sha* 地煞.

HU PÊN 虎賁.—See *Breast, The God of the*.

HU SHÊN 胡神.—The protector against Hail. A man named Hu T'u 狐突, who was put to death for disobeying King Huai Kung 懷公 (639 B.C.). The characters *Hu-t'u* 狐突 gradually became changed into *Hu-t'u* 糊塗, which is the name of a temple (origin unknown) at Wan-ch'üan Hsien 萬全縣, Hsüan-hua Fu 宣化府, Chihli 直隸, the inscription over the gate of which is now Hu Shên 胡神, the Spirit Hu. He is worshipped with great ceremony on the first day of the seventh moon, the anniversary of his birthday, and for three or four days afterwards, the object of the worship being the protection of the crops from hail, the control of which is said to be vested in him. He is depicted as having an ugly countenance of Persian type, with a bristly beard resembling the spikes of a hedgehog.

HU SHÊNG 胡升.—See *Wu Tou* 五斗.

HU TAO-YÜAN 胡道元.—The god of the constellation Chên 軫. Alternatively with Liu Chih 劉直.

HU T'U 狐突.—See *Hu Shên* 胡神.

HU T'U 糊鹻.—See *Hu Shên* 胡神.

HU WÊN-CHANG 扈文長.—See *Hsüan-t'ien Shang-ti* 玄天 上帝 and *Shih-êrh ting-chia Shên* 十二丁甲神.

HU YÜN-P'ÊNG 胡雲鵬.—See *Wu Tou* 五斗.

HUA FU 華(化)敷.—See *Hua T'o* 華陀.

HUA-HU TIAO 花狐貂.—The White Rat of Mo-li Shou 魔禮壽.—See *Ssŭ ta T'ien-wang* 四大天王.

HUA-KAI 華蓋, THE GOD OF THE STAR.—See *Ao Ping* 敖丙.

HUA-KUANG FO 華光佛.—The Hua-kuang Buddha. One of the gods of goldsmiths and silversmiths. Also a protecting deity of temples. Represented sitting with his feet resting on two gold ingots. One of the principal disciples of Shih-chia Fo 釋迦佛 (Sakyamuni), surnamed Chih Hui 智慧. He died with Sakyamuni, but is said to be destined to return under the name of Hua-kuang Fo 華光佛, the name by which he is usually designated, though the priests also refer to him as Shê-li Fo 舍利佛 (Padmaprabha＝S'ariputtra). His festival is celebrated on the twenty-eighth day of the ninth moon. See also *Mi-lo Fo* 彌勒佛 and *Tung-fang Shuo* 東方朔.

HUA-LIN CH'IH 華林池.—See *Shui Fu* 水府, D (2) (g).

HUA SHAN 華山, THE GOD OF.—See *Pi-hsia Yüan-chün* 碧霞元君 and *Wu Yo* 五嶽.

HUA SHÊN 花神.—See *Hsiang Shên* 香神.

HUA T'O 華陀.—Next to Sun Ssŭ-miao 孫思邈 (see *Yao Wang* 藥王) the most celebrated member of the Chinese apotheosized medical profession. The Chinese surgeon specialist *par excellence*, and the patron deity of surgeons. One of the specialists attached to the celestial Ministry of Medicine. A native of Ch'iao-chün 譙郡, a city in the P'ei 沛 State. His *tzŭ* 字 was Yüan-hua 元化. Sometimes referred to as Hua Fu 化敷. Lived toward the close of the second century A.D. (Hou-Han 後漢 and San Kuo Wei 三國魏), and died A.D. 220. Studied medicine and surgery under the famous Yang Li-kung 陽勵公 (*q.v.*). Hua

T'o's 華陀 method is described in his own words as follows: "If the complaint is internal, I administer a potion, then open the stomach and take out the intestines, removing the injurious tumours; that done, I apply a poultice to the injured part, sew up the skin, and healing quickly follows. If the complaint is external, the remedy is still easier." Numerous instances of his marvellous skill are given in the *Shên-hsien t'ung-chien* 神仙通鑑. He was skilled as a diagnostician and in the use of acupuncture and cauterization, and only operated when these failed, giving hashish as a soporific. He is said to have been able to foretell the sex of children. On one occasion he cured Kuan Kung's 關公 arm, poisoned by an arrow-wound, by opening the flesh and scraping the bone, whilst the latter was playing a game of chess with Ma Liang 馬良. However, a suggestion to trepan Ts'ao Ts'ao's 曹操 skull under an anaesthetic caused the latter's wrath, and he was thrown into prison. Out of gratitude to the gaoler for kind treatment he gave him his precious book of recipes, which, however, was burnt by the gaoler's wife, only two or three pages being saved. Seeing death inevitable, Hua T'o 華陀 put an end to his life by taking a narcotic beverage. For more than a year after his death a column of smoke rose from his tomb.— See also *T'ien I-yüan* 天醫院.

HUA YEN HO-SHANG 華嚴和伺.—A monk, a former disciple of Sakyamuni, Shih-chia Fo 釋迦佛, named O-hsiu-lo 阿修羅, who had been sent into the world during the reign of the Emperor Wu Ti 武帝 (A.D 502-50) of the Liang 梁 dynasty to preach the Buddhist doctrine to mortals. He derived his name of Hua Yen 華嚴 monk from his habit of reciting the *Hua-yen ching* 華嚴經, *Hua-yen sutra* (a work of the Mahayana School, attributed to Nagarjuna) when on his journey from the Wei 魏 Kingdom to the T'ien-kung Ssŭ 天宮寺, Monastery of the Heavenly Palace, at Lo-yang 洛陽, Honan 河南. This journey was the result of his dislike to be born as a child from a woman's womb, and he had accordingly assumed the appearance of an old monk who lived in the Wei 魏 Kingdom. He was a contemporary of Chih-kung 誌公 (A.D. 425-514) and, having more than 300 disciples, was called the Patriarch of the North. He attained to a high degree of virtue, and displayed much zeal in expounding the doctrine of the *Hua-yen ching* 華嚴經.

The following interesting account of the main incidents of Hua Yen Ho-shang's 華嚴和伺 career, is related by Doré (viii, 319-21):—"Among his disciples, one Hsia La 夏臘, who was the most fervent of all, happened to be ailing, and was obliged to remain in his cell. The monk Sha Mi 沙彌, not finding his rice-bowl on the table in the dining-hall, took the one belonging to Hsia La 夏臘; but before he had finished eating, the sick monk requested that his rice-bowl be brought to him. Sha Mi 沙彌 quickly emptied the contents and delivered the bowl, but as he was passing through the door-way of the dining-room, a brick fell down and shattered the vessel to pieces. Upset by this untoward mishap, the monk made every possible excuse to Hsia La 夏臘. The latter, however, flew into a towering rage (one of the 'ten fetters' of Buddhism), and said that they wanted him to starve to death. In fact, his fit of anger was so severe that it caused his death.

More than a hundred disciples, including Hsia La 夏臘, were listening to Hua Yen 華嚴 explaining the law, when all of a sudden a blast of wind swept over the valley. "Hide behind me," said the teacher to Sha Mi 沙彌. Soon afterwards, a large snake appeared in the courtyard, and approaching the lecture-hall, seemed to be seeking for somebody. Hua Yen 華嚴 seized a stick and bade the monster remain still. The snake bowed its head, closed its eyes, and obeyed. The teacher then struck it gently on the head, and said: 'Since you already know all the duties of a monk, you should faithfully serve Buddha.' Hua Yen 華嚴 requested all the monks to pray to this purpose, and imposed on the snake the duty of observing the five Buddhist prohibitions, after which the monster disappeared. Later on, Hua Yen 華嚴 explained the mystery to his disciples. 'Hsia La 夏臘,' said he, 'was a monk of great virtue, and could attain to the state of a Buddha, but because he gave way to anger, on seeing his rice-bowl shattered to pieces, he was changed into a snake immediately on expiring. His object in coming here was to avenge himself on Sha Mi 沙彌; had he succeeded in devouring him, his sin could not be remitted, and he would suffer the torments of Hades for ever' (a contradiction of the Buddhist idea that every soul must ultimately be saved). 'I imposed on him the five prohibitions of the Buddhist Law, but on leaving the hall he will die forthwith; go and see if this takes place.' Hereupon all the monks went out and followed him for a long distance, as he crept through the brushwood and long grass. At last, reaching a deep glen, he struck his head against a rock, and expired. The monks returned and informed their teacher of the sad end of the monster. Hua Yen 華嚴 then disclosed to them that he was reborn in the family of Fei K'uan 斐寬, an official of the Ministry of War, and would appear again in the world as a female child, but was to die on reaching the age of 18. In a subsequent rebirth, he would again be changed into a man. When coming into the world as a girl, his mother would suffer greatly during the pangs of childbirth, and they should pray for her speedy delivery. Thereupon the monks proceeded to Fei K'uan's 斐寬 house, and found the family in a state of great distress.

'For five or six days,' said the good man, 'my wife has been in the pangs of childbirth, and her life is in jeopardy.' The monks told him to place a bed and a mat at the door of the patient's room. They then offered incense, crying out thrice: 'Monk, monk, monk!' [The unborn babe was the ex-monk

Hsia La 夏 臘, condemned for his uncontrolled anger to be reborn as a female in a new phase of existence.] Forthwith the woman in travail gave birth to a female child, who died on reaching the age of 18.

Twenty years after the damsel's demise, a young man came to the monastery, and begged Hua Yen 華 嚴 to receive him into the monkhood. The abbot shaved his head with his own hands [part of the admission ceremony of a Buddhist novice], and gave him the name of Shih Chio 始 覺, 'First Illuminated.' He then said to his disciples; 'This monk is Hsia La 夏 臘, formerly born as a female child in the family of Fei-k'uan 斐 寬, and who to-day again becomes a member of the Brotherhood.' Hsia La 夏 臘 later on reached the rank of a Buddha.

Hua Yen 華 嚴 had no sooner learnt of the arrival of Chih-kung 誌 公 at Lo-yang 洛 陽, than he bade farewell to his disciples, and said to them: 'I am proceeding to Hsi T'ien 西 天, the Western Paradise, together with him'; whereupon he expired."

HUA-YEN HSIEN-SHOU CHIAO 華 嚴 賢 首 敎.— See *Buddhist Schools*, XI.

HUA-YEN SÊNG 華 嚴 僧. A saintly Buddhist monk. Sixth century. One of those invited to the annual banquet of the gods (see *Hsi Wang-mu* 西 王 母 and *Hua Yen Ho-shang* 華 嚴 和 伺).

HUA-YEN TSUNG 華 嚴 宗.—See *Buddhist Schools*, XI.

HÜAI-HAI CH'AN-SHIH 懷 海 禪 師 (36th generation).—A deified Buddhist monk. Ranked fourth in Buddhist School, III (*q.v.*). Secular name Wang 王. A native of Ch'ang-lo 長 樂, Fu-chou Fu 福 州 府, Fukien 福 建. Trained by Ma Tsu 馬 祖 (*q.v.*). Later, lived at Ta-hsiung Shan 大 雄 山, Big Cock Mountain, in the Hung-chou 洪 州 Department. Died A.D. 814. Posthumous title: Ta-chih Ch'an-shih 大 智 禪 師, Monk of Vast Intelligence.

HUAI-JANG CH'AN-SHIH 懷 讓 禪 師 (34th generation).— A deified Buddhist monk. Ranked first in Buddhist School, III (*q.v.*). Family name Tu 杜. He lived at Chin-chou 金 州. and for eight years studied at Ts'ao-ch'i 曹 谿, a place in the mountainous country between Kuangtung 廣 東 and Kiangsi 江 西 (see *Hui-nêng* 慧 能). Having finished his training, he went to Hêng Shan 衡 山, and died there in A.D. 744. The Emperor Hsüan Tsung 玄 宗 (A.D. 713-56) of the T'ang 唐 dynasty, conferred on him the title of Ta-hui Ch'an-shih 大 慧 禪 師, Monk of Vast Intelligence. He was one of the most famous of the disciples of the Sixth Chinese Patriarch.

HUAI-NAN TZǓ 淮 南 子.—The authentic God of Beancurd (*tou-fu* 荳 腐) Sellers, he having invented that commodity. See also *Kuan Yü* 關羽, *Chiao Kuan* 膠管, and *Apotheosized Philosophers*.

HUAN YANG-CH'ANG 煥陽昌.—See *Heart, the Gods of the*.

HUANG 黃.—The goddess of the star Ti-hou 地后. Second wife of the tyrant Chou Wang 紂王. Younger sister of Huang Fei-hu 黃飛虎. Put to death by the tyrant Chou Wang 紂王 for expressing her horror at his treatment of her sister-in-law.

HUANG CH'I-KUNG 黃七公.— See *Huang Hsien-shih* 黃仙師.

HUANG-CHIN LI-SHIH 黃巾力士.— See *Huang-chin Li-shih* 黃金力士.

HUANG-CHIN LI-SHIH 黃金力士.—A generic name for the Liu-ting 六丁 spirits, descendants of the Wu-ting Li-shih 五丁力士, living in Ssŭch'uan 四川. Gold is the elemental force of the West, hence these genii are called "The Athletes of the Western Country," or Region of Gold. Otherwise known as Huang-chin Li-shih 黃巾力士, "Athletes of the Yellow Turban," which expresses the same idea.

HUANG CHING-YÜAN 黃景元.—The god of the star Ti-sha 地煞.—See *Ti-sha* 地煞.

HUANG CH'U-P'ING (皇)黃初平.—Born at Tan-chi 丹溪 in the Kingdom of Chin 晉. Taken, when tending his sheep, by a Taoist to Chin-hua Shan 金華山, Mount Chin-hua 金華, he lived there in a cave for forty years. Eventually, he was found by his brother, who asked him what had become of his sheep. Pointing to some white stones, Ch'u-p'ing 初平 said: "There they are," and the stones were immediately changed into thousands of sheep. Seeing that he had become a Spirit, his brother asked him to instruct him, and was told that he had only to wish for the power and it would be his. So he also left his parents' family and with his brother's aid attained immortality.

Ch'u-p'ing 初平 changed his name to Ch'ih Sung-tzŭ 赤松子, and his elder brother Ch'u-ch'i 初起 took the name of Lu Pan 魯班.

HUANG-ÊN 皇恩, THE GOD OF THE STAR.—See *Li Chin* 李錦.

HUANG-FAN 黃旛, THE GOD OF THE STAR.— See *Wei Pi* 魏賁.

HUANG FEI-HU 黃飛虎.—See *Yen-lo Wang* 閻羅王 and *Wu Yo* 五嶽.

HUANG FEI-PAO 黃飛豹.—The god of the star T'ien-ssŭ 天嗣. Third brother of Huang Fei-hu 黃飛虎. With his brothers deserted the cause of Chou Wang 紂王 for that of Wu Wang 武王.

HUANG FEI-PIAO 黃飛彪.—The god of the star Ho-k'uei 河魁. Second brother of Huang Fei-hu 黃飛虎. Both joined Wu Wang's 武王 party.

HUANG HSIEN-SHIH 黃仙師.—Family name Huang 黃. Generally known as Huang Ch'i-kung 黃七公, Huang the Seventh, he having been the seventh brother. A native of Shang-hang Hsien 上杭縣, Chiang-chou 江州, Fukien 福建.

By profession a magician and drawer of talismans, he drove away evil spirits with a whip. When a mountain goblin and a transcendent rock were causing trouble in the neighbourhood, Huang Ch'i-kung 黃七公 quieted them with his charms and himself disappeared into the rock and was not seen again. The contour of the rock is said to resemble him. A memorial temple was built to him on the rock Shih-chi 石岐 at Chung-liao Ch'ang 鍾寮場, but was eventually moved to the South of Shang-hang Hsien 上杭縣.

HUANG K'UN 黃昆.—The God of Incense-makers and Incense-sellers. In the time of Yao 堯 (2357-2255 B.C.), lightning having struck one of the trees in Hsi T'ien 西天, the Western Paradise, one of the branches fell into the Blue River. When cast on the bank, it gave forth so sweet a perfume that it was taken and presented to the Emperor. No one but Huang K'un 黃昆 was able to explain its origin. Yao 堯 had incense-sticks made from it and ordered them to be burnt in honour of the gods. From that time Huang K'un 黃昆 was regarded as the first promoter of this nation-wide industry, and was worshipped as the patron deity of incense-makers and incense-sellers.

HUANG LAO 皇老.—A genie.—See *Yüan-shih T'ien-tsun* 元始天尊.

HUANG-LUNG CHÊN-JÊN 黃龍眞人.—Lived in Ma-ku Tung 麻姑洞, on Êrh-hsien Shan 二仙山. At the siege of Hsi-ch'i 西岐, Wu Wang's 武王 capital, he was captured by Chao Kung-ming 趙公明, who hung him up on a high pole, with a charm tied to his head. Yang Chien 楊戩, sent by Yü-ting Chên-jên 玉鼎眞人, transformed him into an ant, which crept up the pole, and by removing the charm freed Huang-lung Chên-jên 黃龍眞人, who then returned to the camp of his master Chiang Tzŭ-ya 姜子牙. Honoured as a demi-god.

HUANG MING 黃明.—The god of the star *Fu-lung* 伏龍.

Sworn brother of Huang Fei-lu 黃飛虎. Joined the party of Chiang Tzŭ-ya 姜子牙.

HUANG PING-CH'ING 黃丙慶.—The god of the star Ti-tso 地佐.—See *Ti-sha* 地煞.

HUANG PU 皇甫.—See *Shih Ming-i* 十明醫, 2.

HUANG SHIH 黃始.—See *Huang Tao-p'o* 黃道婆.

HUANG TAO-P'O 黃道婆.—The Lady who introduced the cotton-plant into Chiang-nan (Kiangnan) 江南. Family name Huang 黃. A native of Wu-ni-ching 烏泥涇, South West of Shanghai 上海, Kiangsu 江蘇. In the reign of Ch'êng Tsung 成宗 (A.D. 1295-1308) of the Yüan 元 dynasty she brought the cotton plant from Yai-chou 崖州 in Hainan 海南, Kwangtung 廣東, to Kiangsu 江蘇. For this valuable service a temple was erected to her in her native place, and sacrifices were made to her annually.

The cotton-plant was imported from abroad to China by Huang Shih 黃始 and a temple erected by the Cantonese in his honour. It gradually spread from Kwangtung 廣東 to Fukien 福建 and Chiangnan 江南.

HUANG TI 黃帝.—The Yellow Emperor (2698-2598 B.C.). Worshipped as the God of Architecture. One of the legendary sovereigns who succeeded P'an Ku 盤古 (*q.v.*). Reputed founder of the Chinese Empire after his victory over the aboriginal Miao tribes under their chief Ch'ih Yu 蚩尤. Before this he was called Hsüan Yüan 軒轅. Said to have had, as an infant, a full command of language. May have been head of a nomad tribe. Said to have invented wheeled vehicles, armour, ships, pottery, etc., regulated the sacrificial and religious ceremonies of his people, and improved upon Shên Nung's 神農 agricultural work by determining the time when cereals were to be sown and trees planted. Devoted his attention to the animal kingdom with the same object. Studied astronomy, waves of the sea, rocks, metals, and jade. Cut passages through the hills and built roads. Persecuted the refractory, but did not disturb the peaceful. Became emperor by virtue of his superior energy. Extended his Empire in the East to the sea coast of Shantung 山東, in the West far beyond Kansu 甘肅, and in the South to the Yang-tzŭ 揚子 River, while in the North he drove away the Hun-[Hsüan]-yü 薰育 (probably the Hsiung-nu 匈奴, the ancestors of King Attila's Huns).

The phoenix and the *ch'i-lin* 麒麟 appeared at the end of his reign in approval of his wise and beneficent rule.—See also *Tsao Chün* 灶(竈)君 and *Saturn*.

HUANG T'IEN-HSIANG 黃天祥.—See *Wu Tou* 五斗.

HUANG T'IEN-HUA 黄天化.— Son of Huang Fei-hu 黄飛虎.

HUANG T'IEN-LU 黄天祿.—See *Wu Tou* 五斗.

HUANG T'ING 黄庭.—See *Spleen, The Gods of the.*

HUANG TS'ANG 黄倉.—The god of the constellation Mao 昴. Alternatively with Wang Liang 王良.

HUANG WU 黄烏.—The god of the star Ti-sun 地損.—See *Ti-sha* 地煞.

HUANG-WU 荒燕, THE GOD OF THE STAR.—See *Tai Li* 戴禮.

HUANG YÜAN-CHI 黄元濟.—The god of the star Ts'an-ch'u 蠶畜. Second in command under Ch'ung Hou-hu 崇虎侯 in the Yin-Chou 殷周 wars. Slain in a combat with Nan Kung-kua 南宮适, one of Wen Wang's 文王 officers.

HUI-CHAO CH'AN-SHIH 慧照禪師 (60th generation).— A deified Buddhist monk. Ranked thirty-eighth in Buddhist School, III (q.v.). Family name Wang 王. A native of Hu-kuang 湖廣 (modern Hupei 湖北 and Hunan 湖南). Studied under P'u-ch'ih Ch'an-shih 普持禪師 (*q.v.*). Afterwards withdrew to the Tung-ming Ssŭ 東明寺, Monastery of Eastern Brightness, where he died in A.D. 1441.

HUI-CHI CH'AN-SHIH 慧寂禪師 (38th generation).—A deified Buddhist monk. Ranked eleventh in Buddhist School, III (*q.v.*). Family name Yeh 葉. A native of Shao-chou 韶州. Cut off one of his fingers (some say two: *v.* Johnston, *Buddhist China,* p. 89) as a protest to his parents that instead of marrying he wished to become a monk. Trained by Ling-yu Ch'an-shih 靈祐禪師 (*q.v.*). Taught at Yang Shan 仰山.

HUI-CHING CH'AN-SHIH 慧經禪師 (63rd generation).— A deified Buddhist monk. Ranked fifty-third in Buddhist School, VI (*q.v.*). Family name P'ei 裴. A native of Ch'ung-jên 崇仁 in Fu-chou Fu 撫州府, Kiangsi 江西. His teacher was a monk of Lin Shan 廩山, Granary Hill. He erected a monastery at O Fêng 峨峰, High Peak. Died A.D. 1618. Buried at Fang-chang 方丈.

HUI-FANG CH'AN-SHIH 慧方禪師 (34th generation).— A deified Buddhist monk. Ranked third in Buddhist School, I (*q.v.*).

HUI FEI 惠妃.—See *Chin-kang Chih* 金剛智.

HUI-HAI CH'AN-SHIH 慧海禪師 (36th generation).—A deified Buddhist monk. Ranked fifth in Buddhist School, III (q.v.). A disciple of Ma-tsu 馬祖 (q.v.). Family name Chu 朱. A native of Chien-chou 建州. Trained in the Doctrine by Huai-hai Ch'an-shih 懷海禪師 (q.v.) in the Ta-yün Ssŭ 大雲寺, Great Cloud Monastery, at Yüeh-chou 越州, where he was received as a fully-trained monk. Toward the close of his life, he returned to his native place, and composed the *Ju-Tao yao-mên* 入道要門, *The Master-key to Entering the Path* (understanding the Doctrine), which he dedicated to Ma Tsu 馬祖. Styled by his numerous disciples Ta-chu Ho-shang 大珠和尙, Great Gem Priest.

HUI K'O 慧可.—See *Patriarchs*.

HUI KUNG 慧恭.—A.D. 371-454. A saintly Buddhist monk. One of those invited to the annual banquet of the gods.—See *Hsi Wang-mu* 西王母 and *Lo-han* 羅漢.

HUI LI 慧理.—A saintly Buddhist monk. One of those invited to the annual banquet of the gods.—See *Hsi Wang-mu* 西王母, *Niu Wang* 牛王, and *Chin Mu* 金母.

HUI LU 回祿.—See *Huo Pu* 火部.

HUI-MAN CH'AN-SHIH 慧滿禪師 (50th generation).—A deified Buddhist monk. Ranked thirty-eighth in Buddhist School, VI (q.v.). A disciple of Pao-kung Ch'an-shih 寶公禪師, but abandoned him to follow the school of Shih-t'i Ch'an-shih 師體禪師 (q.v.).

HUI-NAN CH'AN-SHIH 慧南禪師 (45th generation).—A deified Buddhist monk. Ranked eighteenth in Buddhist School, III (q.v.). Family name Chang 章. A native of Hsin-chou 信州. He had two teachers of the Doctrine: Lo T'an-chêng 泐潭澄 and T'zŭ-ming Ch'an-shih 慈明禪師. He lived in the Huang-lung Shan 黃龍山, Yellow-dragon Hill, Monastery. Died A.D. 1068, and was buried on the same hill. Posthumous title: P'u-chio Ch'an-shih 普覺禪師, Universally Intelligent Monk.

HUI NÊNG 慧能.—A.D. 637-712. A saintly Buddhist monk. One of those invited to the annual banquet of the gods (see *Hsi Wang-mu* 西王母). The sixth patriarch of Chinese Buddhism.

HUI-SSŬ TSUN-CHÊ 慧思尊者.—Family name Li 李. A deified Buddhist monk. Ranked second, in Buddhist School, X (q.v.). A native of Wu-ching 武津, Honan 河南. He was specially aided in forming the T'ien-t'ai Tsung 天台宗, Tien-t'ai School, by enthusiastic study of the *Chung-lun*

中 論, *Central Shastra,* and of the *Fa-hua ching* 法華經, *Lotus of the God Law,* and is always represented holding the latter in his hand. While he was still young, P'u-hsien 普賢 (Samanta-bhadra) (see *Buddhist Schools,* XV) appeared to him in a dream, placed his hand on the top of his head, and so illumined his intelligence that he could already read Chinese characters without difficulty. Becoming a monk at 15 years of age, he had for his teacher Hui-wên Tsun-chê 慧文尊者 (*q.v.*), who taught him the new method of contemplation. He afterwards built a monastery at Ta-su Shan 大蘇山 but the political unrest (A.D. 500) compelled him to withdraw to Nan Yo 南嶽, South Peak, hence he is generally known as Nan-yo Hui-ssŭ 南嶽慧思. A heavenly genius, says the legend, accompanied him constantly, in order to protect him from danger.[1] Feeling his end approaching, he summoned all his disciples before him, and addressed them as follows:

"If among you there are eighteen resolute monks, ready to suffer in defence of the *Fa-hua ching* 法華經 (*Lotus of the Good Law*), I am willing to help them; if not, I will pass to another world." As all maintained a respectful silence, he sat down cross-legged, said: "Buddha comes to seek me," and expired.

HUI T'Ê 慧特.—A saintly Buddhist monk. The younger brother of Hui Kung 慧公 (*q.v.*). One of those invited to the annual banquet of the gods (see *Hsi Wang-mu* 西王母).

HUI-TSANG CH'AN-SHIH 惠 [慧] 藏禪師.—See *Lo-han* 羅漢.

HUI-WEI TSUN-CHÊ 慧威尊者.—A deified Buddhist monk. Ranked sixth in Buddhist School, X (*q.v.*). Family name Liu 劉. A native of Tung-yang 東陽, a dependency of Wu-chou 婺州, Chêkiang 浙江. Became a disciple of Chih-wei Tsun-chê 智威尊者 (*q.v.*), at T'ien-t'ai 天台, in the same province, and was known as Hsiao-wei 小威, the Little Wei. Returning later on to his native place, he led the life of a hermit in the Tung-yang Shan 東陽山, Tung-yang Mountain, gorges. After the death of Chih-wei Tsun-chê 智威尊者, he refused the monks' request to return, consenting to teach one, Tso-ch'i 左溪 (*q.v.*), only.

Honorary title (conferred by the T'ang 唐 dynasty): Chao-san Ta-fu Ssŭ Ta-shih 朝散大夫四大師. Posthumous title (conferred by the Sung 宋 dynasty): Ch'üan-chên Tsun-chê 全眞尊者, All-perfect Venerable.

---

1 "This enthusiasm for error is a psychological fact that runs through all human history, and may only be explained on the ground that certain opinions are subjectively believed to be true, while objectively and intrinsically they are false, but have not been sufficiently examined by the individual."—Kennelly, VIII, 687, note 3.

HUI-WÊN TSUN-CHÊ 慧文尊者.—The Venerable Hui-wên 慧文. A deified Buddhist monk. Ranked first in Buddhist School, X (*q.v.*). The first ancestor of the T'ien-t'ai Chiao 天台教, T'ien-t'ai School. Authors generally admit that Chih-chê Ta-shih 智者大師 (*q.v.*) was its founder, but "before him there were two eminent monks who taught him the Law, and whom it is important to know, and the more as in the annals of the sect, they are held to be the two first ancestors of this Buddhist School, which is distinctively of Chinese origin, and has evolved on lines peculiarly Chinese."

Hui-wên 慧文 belonged to the Kao 高 family. He studied the *Ta-chih tu-lun* 大智度論, especially the second part, called *Chung-lun* 中論, the Central, or Medial, Shastra. This is "a work in 500 stanzas, based on the principles of *Prajna-paramita* (Transcendent Wisdom, denying the reality of all world phenomena, and the validity of knowledge derived through the senses), and translated into Chinese early in the fifth century. It originated with Nagarjuna [Lung-shu 龍樹]. Hui-wên 慧文 erected his system on it, and Chih-k'ai 智頫, following him, moulded it to its present form as the doctrine of the T'ien-t'ai Tsung 天台宗, T'ien-t'ai School" (Edkins, *Chinese Buddhism*, p. 184). It was this work that inspired the whole plan of the new system, called Hsin-kuan 心觀, Observation of the Heart.

Hui-wên 慧文 taught this doctrine to his disciple Hui-ssŭ 慧思 (*q.v.*) of the Nan-yo Tsung 南嶽宗, Nan-yo School, who is held to be the second ancestor of the school.

The date of his death is unknown. He was a priest of the North, and lived in the time of the Pei Ch'i 北齊, Northern Ch'i, dynasty (A.D. 550-57).

HUI-YÜAN CH'AN-SHIH 慧遠禪師.—A.D. 371-454. A saintly Chinese Buddhist monk, one of two brothers (the younger being named Hui-t'ê 惠特 of the Chia 賈 family, natives of Lou-fan 樓煩, near Yen-mên Kuan 雁門關, in N. Shansi 山西. He was the founder of the Lotus School (see *Buddhist Schools*), which teaches the doctrine of a Western Paradise, promised to faithful worshippers of Amitabha.

A studious youth, when only 13 he studied at Hsü-ch'ang 許昌 and Lo-yang 洛陽 in Honan 河南 and became proficient in the Classics and Taoist works. The teaching of Tao-an 道安, a Buddhist priest of Ch'ang Shan 常山, and disciple of Buddhojanga (died A.D. 385?), whom he one day heard expounding the Prajna-paramita, *Pan-jo ching* 般若經, at the foot of T'ai-hêng Shan 太恒山, Mount T'ai-hêng, caused him to pull out the bamboo pin which fastened up his hair and have his head shaved as a Buddhist monk. His brother, who had accompanied him, did likewise. He afterwards opened his own school at Lu Shan 盧山, which was attended by thousands of students. Tao-an 道安, whose disciple he became (420) changed the first character of his name from 惠 to 慧. The two brothers led an austere life of poverty and assiduous study, local scholars coming in large numbers to converse with them.

As the result of a dream the purport of which he communicated to Huan I 桓 伊, Prefect of Yü-chang 豫 章, he became the owner of a monastery at Lu-shan K'ou 廬 山 口, in Hupei 湖 北. The site lacking a well, he struck the rock with his staff in the presence of his disciple Hui-yung 慧 永 and immediately water gushed forth and formed a rivulet flowing down to the valley.

Other marvellous feats performed by him were the successful invocation of Lung Wang 龍 王 (see *Lung*) during a drought at Hsün-yang 潯 陽, near Kiukiang 九 江, on the Yang-tzǔ 揚 子 River, causing the name of the temple to be changed to Lung-ch'üan Ssǔ 龍 泉 寺, Dragon's-spring Monastery; and the rescuing of a statue of king Asoka, A-yü Wang 阿 育 王 (king of Magadha, Bahar, one of the first princely converts to Buddhism) which had been fished up out of the river near Wu-ch'ang 武 昌, Hupei 湖 北, and placed in the Han-ch'i Ssǔ 寒 溪 寺, Han-ch'i Monastery, survived the destruction of the monastery by fire, and after again falling into the water proved too heavy for ten boatmen to lift. When Hui-yüan 慧 遠 arrived at the spot, it became so light that it was easily raised, and was afterwards placed in a new shrine.

Whilst still at the Lung-ch'üan Ssǔ 龍 泉 寺, he received a visit from Hui Kung 慧 恭. Hui-yüan 慧 遠 enquired of him what prayers he was in the habit of reciting. On being told that he recited those of Kuan-shih-yin 觀 世 音, Hui-yüan 慧 遠 expressed surprise, whereupon his visitor, mounting a small platform, recited his prayers so effectually that the room was filled with a delicious fragrance, celestial melodies were heard, and flowers fell from the sky and covered the ground. Hui-yüan 慧 遠 wept on seeing how far he still had to go to attain the degree of perfection thus proved to have been reached by this holy monk, and, renouncing all relations with the outer world, gave himself up entirely to solitude and the acquirement of perfection.

Hui-yüan 慧 遠 stayed at the Lu-Shan Ssǔ 廬 山 寺 for more than thirty years, receiving none but eighteen famous scholars. During the last eleven years of his life Amitabha appeared to him three times; the last time, the god warned him that at the close of seven days, he would receive him in the Hsi T'ien 西 天, Western Paradise. When he was on the point of expiring, Amitabha came to receive him. He died, according to some writers, in A.D. 453 or 454, aged 83. Other writers place his death earlier, in A.D. 420, or A.D. 417, fifteen years after the famous translation given to the world by Kumerajiva. A.D. 454 as the date of his death is most likely correct. Another date given (in the *Sou-shên chi* 搜 神 記) for his career is A.D. 333-416, but this is regarded as erroneous.—See also *Lo-han* 羅 漢.

HUI-YÜAN FA-SHIH 慧 遠 法 師.—A deified Buddhist monk.

Ranked first in Buddhist School, XVII (*q.v.*). The first ancestor of the Amidist School in China. He is regarded as their first patriarch, although the Amidist doctrine was well known before his time, owing to the translation of the *Wu-liang-shou ching* 無量壽經, *Sutra · of Boundless Years,* by K'ang-sêng-k'ai 康僧鎧 (Sanghavarma), about A.D. 253. But it was especially Kumarajiva who contributed to make it generally known, through his translation of the *O-mi-t'o ching* 阿彌陀經, *Amitabha Sutra,* and thus paved the way for its later extension by Hui-yüan 慧遠.

HUI-YUNG CH'AN-SHIH 慧顒禪師 (40th generation).— A deified Buddhist monk. Ranked thirteenth in Buddhist School, III (*q.v.*). A native of Ho-pei 河北, Honan 河南. Died A.D. 952.

HUN-CH'I-P'ANG YÜAN-SHUAI 混炁龎元帥.—Generalissimo P'ang 龎. A Taoist genie. Name P'ang-ch'iao 龎喬; personal name Chang-ch'ing 長清. Born A.D. 193. His ancestors had been boatmen, and his parents carried on the same trade at Tu-k'ou 渡口, Han-chiang 漢江, Hunan 湖南.

The legend states that having returned to a lady passenger a hundred pounds of gold she had left in his boat and refused to accept any reward, he was recompensed in the following manner. On the evening of the twenty-eighth day of the twelfth moon a young lady arrived and wished to cross the river. It was snowing and no one dared to put off. Pang-ch'iao 龎喬 gave her shelter for the night, dried her clothes and two days later his father set out to take her in his boat to her destination. A violent storm having capsized the boat, P'ang-ch'iao 龎喬 dived in to save his father, and although he brought him near to the bank was cast back thrice by the tumultuous waves. However, by dint of great exertion they at length succeeded in getting on to the bank. The young lady had disappeared, but it turned out that she was none other than Kuan-yin P'u-sa 觀音菩薩, and she it was who had rescued them. When the father and son had reached the bank they perceived some dozens of *kuei* 鬼 (*q.v.*), who were wailing at being deprived of their prey. These *kuei* 鬼 come from the hills, etc., on the thirtieth day of the seventh moon and on the same day of the twelfth moon to try and drown all who venture on the waters. Anyone of them who succeeds can be reincarnated in place of the drowned person.

HUN-P'O CHAO 魂魄兆.—The name of two gods of the armpits.—*Yün chi ch'i ch'ien* 雲笈七籤.

HUN SHOU-LO 渾壽羅.—A saintly Buddhist monk. Fourth century A.D. Associated with the transportation by a monkey of Ling-chiu Shan 靈鷲山, a peak in India called Gridkrakuta, Vulture's Peak, back from China to its original site.

One of those invited to the annual banquet of the gods (see *Hsi Wang-mu* 西王母).—See also *Niu Wang* 牛王.

HUN-YÜAN CHIN-TOU 混元金斗.—See *K'êng san Ku-niang* 坑三姑娘.

HUNG-CH'ÊNG CH'AN-SHIH 宏成禪師 (69th generation). —A deified Buddhist monk. Ranked sixty-fourth in Buddhist School, III (*q.v.*). Family name Wang 王. A native of Ch'ien-t'ang Hsien 錢塘縣, Chê-chiang (Chekiang) 浙江. Studied under Fa-tsang Ch'an-shih 法藏禪師 (*q.v.*). Died A.D. 1641. His tomb is at Hsi-wu 西塢, in Su-chou (Soochow) 蘇州, Kiangsu 江蘇.

HUNG-CHIH CH'AN-SHIH 宏智禪師 (47th generation). —A deified Buddhist monk. Ranked thirty-fifth in Buddhist School, VI (*q.v.*). Family name Li 李. A native of Hsi-chou 隰州, Shansi 山西. At the age of 14, entered the Ching-ming Ssŭ 淨明寺, Monastery of Pure Brightness. At the age of 18, he began to travel from one monastery to another. After visiting Hsiang-shan Ssŭ 香山寺, Fragrant Hill Monastery, he went to Tan-hsia 丹霞, Shensi 陝西, where Tao-k'ai Ch'an-shih 道楷禪師 (*q.v.*) was teaching. The latter illumined him by striking him with his fly-whisk (*cf. I-hsüan Ch'an-shih* 義玄禪師). He then visited the monasteries of Ch'ang-lu 長蘆, T'ien-t'ung 天童, etc. His disciples were "as numerous as the clouds of heaven." Died A.D. 1157. Buried at Tung-ku 東谷 East Valley, Kansu 甘肅.

HUNG CHIN 洪錦.—The god of the star Lung-tê 龍德. One of Chou Wang's 紂王 superior officers who helped in the siege of Hsi-ch'i 西岐. Killed whilst fighting at T'ung-kuan 潼關.—See *Lung-chi kung-chu* 龍吉公主.

HUNG-CHÜN LAO-TSU 洪鈞老祖.— See *Hung-chün Tao-jên* 洪鈞道人.

HUNG-CHÜN TAO-JÊN 洪鈞道人.—Also called Hung-chün Lao-tsu 洪鈞老祖. A mythical person. He is supposed to reside in the Tzŭ-hsiao Kung 紫霄宮, Purple-sky Palace. The *Fêng-shên yen-i* 封神演義 describes him as the first ancestor of Taoism, who through his lessons trained the founder himself, the first patriarch, and the most powerful of the genii. Hence he is more generally called Hung-chün Lao-tsu 洪鈞老祖, the First Ancestor Hung-chün 洪鈞.

The Taoists regard him as the common master of Yüan-shih T'ien-tsun 元始天尊, of Lao-tsŭ 老子 (*q.v.*), and of T'ung-t'ien Chiao-tsu 通天教祖 (see *T'ung-t'ien Chiao-chu* 通天教主). Neither genealogy nor history is assigned him. He is represented holding a long bamboo staff, the top of which resembles a crozier.

HUNG JÊN 弘 忍.—A.D. 602-75. A saintly Buddhist monk. One of those invited to the annual banquet of the gods (see *Hsi* 西王母). The fifth patriarch of Chinese Buddhism.

HUNG-LUAN 紅 鸞, THE GODDESS OF THE STAR.— See *Lung-chi Kung-chu* 龍吉公主.

HUNG-NÊNG CH'AN-SHIH 弘能禪師 (66th generation).— A deified Buddhist monk. Ranked seventy-eighth in Buddhist School, VI (*q.v.*). Family name P'an 潘. A native of Yü-yao 餘姚, Chêkiang 浙江. Entered a monastery at the age of 33, and was taught by [Sung-ju] Tao-mi Ch'an-shih [嵩乳] 道密禪師 (*q.v.*). His training finished, he expounded the doctrine in the monasteries of Ching-hui Ssŭ 景會寺, Nan-mai 南邁, and Chiang-p'u 江浦. "Monks and lay folks became attached to him as the shadow follows the body. All begged him to come and live at Tu Fêng 獨峰." Died in the Yang-ku An 陽谷菴, Yang-ku Monastery, at the age of 67. Buried on the right of the monastery.

HUNG-T'AN CH'AN-SHIH 弘曇禪師 (66th generation).— A deified Buddhist monk. Ranked seventy-seventh in Buddhist School, VI (*q.v.*). Family name Su 蘇. A native of Chu-ch'êng 諸城, a dependency of Ch'ing-chou 青州, Shantung 山東. Entered the school of [Sung-ju] Tao-mi Ch'an-shih [嵩乳] 道密禪師 (*q.v.*) at Wu-chou 沃州, Chihli 直隸. Was trained in the monastery there, and then proceeded South, and followed the teacher Wu Ho-shang 悟和尚, Priest Wu, who taught at T'ien-t'ung Shan 天童山, Heavenly Lad Hill. He afterwards taught in the monasteries of Pao-ên 報恩, P'u-t'i 菩提, and Cho-hsi 卓錫. Died A.D. 1671. Buried at Pao-ên 報恩.

HUNG-YEN 紅艷, THE GODDESS OF THE STAR.—See *Yang Shih* 楊氏.

HUO-FU 火府, THE GODDESS OF THE STAR.—See *Huo-ling Shêng-mu* 火靈聖母.

HUO HSING 火星.—See *Mars*.

HUO-LI TA-TI 火力大帝.—See *Huo Pu* 火部.

HUO-LING SHÊNG-MU 火靈聖母.—The goddess of the star Huo-fu 火府. Lived at Ch'iu-ming Shan 邱鳴山, and studied with the genie To-pao Tao-jên 多寶道人. Slain by Kuang Ch'êng-tzŭ 廣成子 while defending the ancient capital of the Yin 殷 dynasty.

HUO PU 火部.—The Ministry of Fire. The celestial organization of Fire is the fifth Ministry, and is presided over by a

President, Lo Hsüan 羅宣, whose titular designation is Huo-tê Hsing-chün 火德星君, Stellar Sovereign of the Fire-virtue, with five subordinate ministers, four of whom are star-gods, and the fifth a "celestial prince who receives fire": Chieh-huo T'ien-chün 接火天君. Like so many other Chinese deities, the five were all ministers of the tyrant emperor Chou 紂 (1154-1121 B.C.). Their names are: (1) Chu Chao 朱昭, the Spirit of the constellation Wei 尾, the Tail, or the constellation of the Tiger (nine stars of Scorpio). (2) Kao Chên 高震, the Spirit of the constellation Shih 室, House, or the constellation of the Pig (two stars of Pegasus). (3) Fang Kuei 方貴, the Spirit of the constellation Tsui 觜, the constellation of the Monkey (three stars of Orion). (4) Wang Chiao 王蛟, the Spirit of the constellation I 翼, the Wing, the constellation of the Serpent (twenty-two stars in Crater and Hydra). (5) Liu Huan 劉環, who is Chieh-huo T'ien-chün 接火天君 (supra).

It is related that Lo Hsüan 羅宣 was originally a Taoist priest known as Yen-chung Hsien 焰中仙, of the island Huo-lung 火龍, "Fire-dragon." His face was the colour of ripe fruit of the jujube-tree, his hair and beard red, the former done up in the shape of a fish-tail, and he had three eyes. He wore a red cloak ornamented with the pa kua 八卦; his horse snorted flames from its nostrils and fire darted from its hoofs.

While fighting in the service of the son of the tyrant emperor, Lo Hsüan 羅宣 suddenly changed himself into a giant with three heads and six arms. In each of his hands he held a magic weapon. These were a seal which reflected the heavens and the earth, a wheel of five fire-dragons, a gourd containing ten thousand fire-crows, and, in the other hands, two swords which floated like smoke, and a column of smoke several thousands of li 里 long enclosing swords of fire.

Having arrived at the city of Hsi-ch'i 西岐, Lo Hsüan 羅宣 sent forth his smoke-column, the air was filled with swords of fire, the ten thousand fire-crows, emerging from the gourd, spread themselves over the town, and a terrible conflagration broke out, the whole place being ablaze in a few minutes.

At this juncture there appeared in the sky the Princess Lung Chi 龍吉, daughter of Wang-mu Niang-niang 王母娘娘; forthwith she spread over the city her shroud of mist and dew, and the fire was extinguished by a heavy downpour of rain. All the mysterious mechanisms of Lo-Hsüan 羅宣 lost their efficacy, and the magician took to his heels down the side of the mountain. There he was met by Li 李 (see Li Ching 李靖), the Pagoda-bearer, who threw his golden pagoda into the air. The pagoda fell on Lo Hsüan's 羅宣 head and broke his skull.

Liu Huan 劉環 was also a Taoist magician, with a yellow face, curly beard, and black dress. He assisted Lo Hsüan 羅宣 to burn the city of Hsi-ch'i 西岐, and hurled himself sword in hand at the Princess Lung Chi 龍吉 just when she was tackling

Lo Hsüan 羅宣. She, however, threw up into the air two magic swords, which fell and pierced Liu Huan 劉環, enveloped in a whirlwind of flame.

Of the various fire-gods, Ch'ih Ching-tzŭ 赤精子, the principle of spiritual fire, is one of the five spirits representing the Five Natural Forces. He is Fire personified, which has its birth in the south, on Mount Shih-t'ang 石唐. He himself and everything connected with him—his skin, hair, beard, trousers, cloak of leaves, etc.—are all of the colour of fire, though he is sometimes represented with a blue cap resembling the blue tip of a flame. He appeared in the presence of Huang Lao 黃老 in a fire-cloud. He it was who obtained fire from the wood of the mulberry-tree, and the heat of this fire, joined with the moisture of water, developed the germs of terrestrial creatures.

Chu Jung 祝融, though also otherwise personified, is generally regarded as having been a legendary emperor who made his first appearance in the time of Hsüan Yüan 軒轅 (2698-2598 B.C.). In his youth he asked Kuang-shou Lao-jên 廣壽老人, Old Longevity, to grant him immortality. "The time has not yet come," replied Old Longevity; "before it does you have to become an emperor. I will give you the means of reaching the end you desire. Give orders that after you are dead you are to be buried on the southern slope of the sacred mountain Hêng Shan 衡山; there you will learn the doctrine of Ch'ih Ching-tzŭ 赤精子 and will become immortal."

The Emperor Hsüan Yüan 軒轅, having abdicated the throne, sent for Chu Jung 祝融, and bestowed upon him the crown. Chu-Jung 祝融, having become emperor, taught the people the use of fire and the advantages to be derived therefrom. In those early times the forests were filled with venomous reptiles and savage animals; he ordered the peasants to set fire to the brushwood to drive away these dangerous neighbours and keep them at a distance. He also taught his subjects the art of purifying, forging, and welding metals by the action of fire. He was nicknamed Ch'ih Ti 赤帝, "the Red Emperor." He reigned for more than two hundred years, and became an Immortal. His capital was the ancient city of Kuei 劊, thirty *li* 里 north-east of Hsin-chêng Hsien 新鄭縣, K'ai-fêng Fu 開封府, Honan 河南. His tomb is on the southern slope of Hêng Shan 衡山. The peak is known as Chu Jung 祝融 Peak. His descendants, who went to live in the south, were the ancestors of the Directors of Fire.

Other personifications represent Chu Jung 祝融 as the Spirit of the Southern Sea who went to see Wu Wang 武王 (1121-1114 B.C.), King Wu 武 of Chou 周. It was in the midst of winter, and Chiang Tzŭ-ya 姜子牙 offered him some soup to warm him. Having partaken of it, he offered his services to the king.

Chu Jung 祝融 is also personified as one of the Three Emperors of antiquity, the other two being Fu Hsi 伏羲 and Shên Nung 神農.

Chun Jung 祝 融 as an official title was the official designation of the Prefect or Director of Fire, of antiquity. In those days there were five magistrates of the Five Natural Forces (see *Wu Hsing* 五 行). These were real officials, collectively known as Wu Kuan 五官, the Five Officials, posthumously called Shang Kung 上公 and worshipped as Spirits.

The Director of Fire's official title, Chu Jung 祝融, signifies a great burst of light, and was for that reason adopted to designate the office of the Director of Fire.

Prefects of Fire, Chu Jung 祝 融, worshipped as Spirits of Fire, are (1) Li 黎 (Chung-li 重黎), variously said to have been the son of Lao T'ung 老童 and a descendant of Kao Yang 高陽. He was Prefect of Fire under Ti K'u 帝 嚳 (Kao-hsin Shih 高辛氏) (2436-2366 B.C.). (2) Wu-hui 吳回, son of Chüan Chang 卷章 and great-grandson of Chuan Hsü 顓頊 (2514-2436 B.C.). He was Prefect of Fire under the same Emperor (Ti K'u 帝 嚳). After his death he was worshipped as a Spirit, and his image placed on stoves and sacrificed to.

The most popular Spirit of Fire, however, is Hui Lu 回祿, a celebrated musician who, according to the *Shên hsien t'ung chien* 神仙通鑑, lived some time before the reign of Ti K'u 帝 嚳 (2436-2366 B.C.), the father of Yao 堯 the Great, and had a mysterious bird named Pi-fang 比方 and a hundred other fire-birds shut up in a gourd. He had only to let them out to set up a conflagration which would extend over the whole country. The name is said to be derived from a combination of the sounds attributed to the names of the descendants of Ch'ung Li 重黎 (*q.v.*)

In the principality of Chêng 鄭 Hui Lu 回祿 was the Spirit of Fire (*Tso Chuan* 左傳). This was maintained by the former scholars, but sacrifices were offered indiscriminately to him and Wu Hui 吳回 considered as identical. In this case Hui Lu 回祿 would be Chung-li's 重黎 brother (*v. infra*).

Chung-li 重黎, Prefect of Fire under Ti K'u 帝 嚳, though a capable official who discharged his duties to perfection, was defeated and condemned to death for failing to suppress a revolt stirred up by Kung-kung Shih 共工氏 (see *Nü Wa* 女媧). His post was given to his brother Wu Hui 吳回 (or Hui Lu 回祿). The name Hui Lu 回祿 has become the most popular term to designate the Spirit of Fire, and is a synonym for a conflagration.

Huang Ti 黃帝 ordered Chu Jung 祝 融 to fight Hui Lu 回祿 and also to subdue the rebel Ch'ih Yu 蚩尤. Chu Jung 祝融 had a large bracelet of pure gold—a most wonderful and effective weapon. He hurled it into the air, and it fell on Hui Lu's 回祿 neck, throwing him to the ground and rendering him incapable of moving. Finding resistance impossible, he asked mercy from his victor and promised to be his follower in the spiritual contests. Subsequently he always called himself Huo-shih chih t'u 火師 之徒, "the Disciple of the Master of Fire."

197

Various apparitions of the Spirit of Fire are recorded in Chinese literature, as *e.g.* at Ts'ao-hsien 曹 縣, in Shantung 山 東, in A.D. 1547.

San Lang 三 良 was the third son of the God of T'ai Shan 泰 山, and brother of Pi-hsia Yüan-chün 碧 霞 元 君 (*q.v.*). The latter informed Wên Wang 文 王 (1231-1135 B.C.), King Wên, that she always went about accompanied by wind and rain. The Taoists accordingly reasoned that, fire being the enemy of water, the latter should be summoned in cases of disaster from the former. Thus, if the sister was always accompanied by rain, the brother might well be associated with fire. Consequently he was proclaimed Huo Shên 火 神, the Spirit of Fire.

The Emperor T'ai Tsung 太 宗 (A.D. 627-50) of the T'ang 唐 dynasty bestowed on him the posthumous title of Marshal. The Emperor T'ai Tsung 太 宗 (A.D. 976-98) of the Sung 宋 dynasty made him a Marquis, and the Emperor Chên Tsung 眞 宗 (A.D. 998-1023) of the Sung 宋 dynasty, in A.D. 1008 canonized him and his sister, giving him the title of Chih-shêng Ping-ling Wang 至 聖 炳 靈 王, Most Saintly King Ping-ling 炳 靈, the title by which he is still known in modern times.

Shên Nung 神 農, the God of Agriculture, also adds to his other functions those appertaining to the God of Fire, the reason being that when he succeeded the Emperor Fu Hsi 伏 羲 on the throne he adopted fire as the emblem of his government, just as Huang Ti 黄 帝 adopted the symbol of Earth. Thus he came to be called Huo Ti 火 帝, "the Fire-emperor." He taught his subjects the use of fire for smelting metals and making implements and weapons, and the use of oil in lamps, etc. All the divisions of his official hierarchy were connected in some way with this element; thus there were the Ministers of Fire generally, the officers of Fire of the North, South, etc. Becoming thus doubly the patron of fire, a second fire symbol (*huo* 火) was added to his name, changing it from Huo Ti 火 帝, "Fire-emperor," to Yen Ti 炎 帝, "Blazing Emperor."

The following interesting particulars are stated by Du Bose (pp. 389-90): "The god of fire, called Huo-li Ta-ti 火 力 大 帝, has three eyes and a red beard, and is worshipped on the third, thirteenth, and twenty-third of each month. Some two or three centuries ago there was a great conflagration in Soochow 蘇 州, Kiangsu 江 蘇, which lasted two or three days. After every method to extinguish the devouring element had been exhausted, the Governor threw his hat, shoes, and clothing in the fire, but without effect; at last he jumped in and was burned to death, and was made the god of fire for this city.

"He has eight ministers. The first holds the *fire bow and arrows,* and wherever an arrow flies there is a conflagration. The second minister holds the *fire-crow,* and on the house where this bird of ill omen alights the insurance companies suffer. The third holds the *fire-rat* in his hand, and walls, garrets, and roofs are not safe from his intrusion. The fourth has the *foot measure and fire-spade*; the one to measure the extent of the conflagration, and the other to shovel up sparks. The fifth is the Captain of the 'Black Flags.' The sixth commands the 'fire-engine,' from whose hose fire spouts out. The seventh minister holds the red-hot *fire balls,* and the eighth flashes fire from the *fire-mirror.* These are supplicated in the 'great fire service' of the eighth month."

HUO-PU-CH'ANG 活不長.—See *Mêng P'o* 孟婆.

HUO SHÊN 火神.—See *Huo Pu* 火部.

HUO-TÊ HSING CHÜN 火德星君.—See *Huo Pu* 火部.

HUO TI 火帝.—See *Shên Nung* 神農.

HUO-WU-CH'ANG 活無常.—The Colleague of *Ssŭ-yu-fên* 死有分 (*q.v.*).

I

I 倪.—See *Tung Wang-kung* 東 王 公.

I 奕, THE GOD OF THE CONSTELLATION.—See *Pei T'ung* 邶 仝 and *Wang Chiao* 王 蛟.

I-CHING 義 淨.—A monk who returned from India to China, A.D. 695, bringing with him four hundred *sutras,* an image of Indra and three hundred relics.

I-CH'ING CH'AN-SHIH 義 青 禪 師 (44th generation).—A deified Buddhist monk. Ranked twenty-fifth in Buddhist School, VI (*q.v.*). Family name Li 李. A native of Ch'ing-shê 青 社, Chihli 直 隸. His teacher for six years was Shih-yüan Chien 時 圓 鑑, of Fou Shan 浮 山, Shansi 山 西, who dreamt that he had received an eagle, and should bring him up carefully. His training completed, I Ch'ing 義 青 settled at T'ou-tzŭ 投 子, and later at Hai-hui 海 會, (a temple outside the Yung-ting 永 定 Gate, Peking 北 京, Chihli 直 隸), living as a beggar. Died A.D. 1083. His grave is on San-fêng Shan 三 峰 山, Three-peak Mountain.

IDA.—In the *Rig-veda* Ida is primarily food, refreshment, or a libation of milk; thence a stream of praise, personified as the goddess of speech. She is called the instructress of Manu, and frequent passages ascribe to her the first institution of the rules of performing sacrifices. According to Sayana, she is the goddess presiding over the earth. A legend in the *Satapatha Brahamana* represents her as springing from a sacrifice which Manu performed for the purpose of obtaining offspring. She was claimed by Mitra-Varuna, but remained faithful to him who had produced her. Manu lived with her, and praying and fasting to obtain offspring, he begat from her the race of Manu. In the

Puranas she is the daughter of the Manu Vaivaswata, wife of Buddha (Mercury), and mother of Pururavas. The Manu Vaivaswata, before he had sons, instituted a sacrifice to Mitra and Varuna for the purpose of obtaining one; but the officiating priest mismanaged the performance, and the result was the birth of a daughter, Ida or Ila. Through the favour of the two deities her sex was changed, and she became a man, Su-dyumna. Under the malediction of Siva, Su-dyumna was again turned into a woman, and, as Ila, married Buddha or Mercury. After she had given birth to Pururavas, she, under the favour of Vishnu, once more became Su-dyumna, and was the father of three sons. According to another version of the legend, the Manu's eldest son was named Ila. He having trespassed on a grove sacred to Paravti, was changed into a female, Ila. Upon the supplications and prayers of Ila's friends, Siva and his consort conceded that the offender should be a male one month and a female another. There are other variations in the story which is apparently ancient.

I-HSING CH'AN-SHIH 一行禪師.—A.D. 672-717. I-hsing is the ecclesiastical title of the Buddhist Tantrist monk, astronomer, and mathematician whose secular name was Chang-sui 張遂. A grandson of the ancient feudal prince of the small State T'an Kuo 郯國, in the south of Shantung 山東, he was born at Chü-lu 鉅鹿, or, according to other chroniclers, at Nei-huang 內黃. He translated numerous Indian Tantrist works, and constructed a uranorama, chart of the heavens, tables of the gnomon, etc.

He was gifted with a marvellous memory, being able to recite word for word long documents after having read them over only once. This talent of his so impressed the emperor Hsüan Tsung 玄宗 (A.D. 713-56) of the T'ang 唐 dynasty, to whom he recited the register of all his State officials from beginning to end without a single mistake, that, descending from his throne, he addressed him as Shêng 聖, Holy Man or Prophet—not quite "Saint" in the Western sense. His reformed calendar, which bore the title *"Great Reformed Calendar of the K'ai-yüan Period," K'ai-yüan ta-yen-li* 開元大衍歷, was adopted in A.D. 721. This period lasted from 713 to 740. He is also said, by means of his magical powers, to have foretold the rebellion of An Lu-shan 安祿山. Besides his mathematical and astronomical treaties, he was the author of a large work on ritual.

He is also credited with a sense of justice so keen that, as Giles (*Bio. Dic.,* p. 349-50) says, he refused to interfere with a sentence on the son of an old woman who had been most kind to him as a boy. Doré and Kennelly, however, give the following detailed version: "Although Yi-hsing 一行 was of princely descent, still he was devoid of all worldly goods, and a neighbouring widow named Wang-mu 王姥 lent him a small amount of money in order to help him through his studies during his early years. When Yi-hsing 一行 had acquired influence at

Court, it happened that the son of the above woman was cast into prison for manslaughter, and was soon to pay the last penalty for his crime. The widow hastened to implore the assistance of Yi-hsing 一 行, begging him to save her son. 'I am quite willing,' said the monk, 'to repay tenfold what you have expended on my behalf; but as to obtaining the pardon of your son from the Emperor, that is not an easy matter.' Hereupon, the widow, blinded by maternal love, burst out into bitter invectives. 'Do not get excited,' said the monk, 'I will save your son.' In a neighbouring temple known as that of the Hun-t'ien Ssŭ 渾 天 寺, 'Confused Heavens,' dwelt a large number of workmen. Having summoned them into his presence, the monk begged them let him have the use of a private room. Here, he placed a large earthen jar, and calling a menial of the temple, addressed him in the following words:

"In such a place, there is an uncultivated garden; you shall proceed there at noon on such a day, and await the arrival of seven brutes, that will cross the place at that hour. Here is a bag, into which you shall put the whole gang. Be most careful, and see that not a single one of them escapes; otherwise you will compel me to punish you.' The menial did as he was ordered, and awaited till nightfall, when all of a sudden seven little porkers [i.e. the Great Bear] entered the garden. They were all seized, bagged and taken to Yi-hsing 一 行. The latter congratulated the menial on his thorough obedience, and ordered him to shut up the animals in the large jar, which he would find in the temple. The monk closed the opening with a strong wooden cover, which he sealed, writing thereon some Hindu characters in red ink [imitating the colour of the imperial 'carnation pencil']. All this was done with the utmost secrecy, and nobody grasped the purpose of the monk.

"Next morning, an official of the Board of Astronomy informed the emperor that the seven stars in the constellation of the Great Bear had disappeared from the heavens. The event being ominous in the extreme, Hsüan Tsung 玄 宗 summoned Yi-hsing 一 行 into his presence, and inquired whether he could not bring back the missing stars. 'To avert the misfortunes foreshadowed by such an unwonted prodigy, it will be necessary,' said the monk, 'to grant a general amnesty throughout the empire.' The Emperor granted the request [though the amnesty of A.D. 637 was really to obtain from Heaven prolongation of the Empress's life], and thus the son of the widow, his benefactress, was set at liberty. Nobody suspected the device adopted by the cunning monk.

"During the seven days which ensued, the monk released one of the piggies from the jar, and forthwith one of the stars in the Great Bear re-appeared in the heavens. At the close of the week, the whole constellation was completely restored."

The same authors describe his passing as follows:—"In the closing years of the K'ai-yüan 開 元 period (A.D. 713-40), an official from Honan 河南, named Fei K'uan 斐寬, a zealous Buddhist, came and placed himself under the direction of P'u-tsih [chi] 普寂. One day, as they chatted together, P'u-tsih [chi] 普寂 said to his pupil that an urgent affair called him away for a short time. He proceeded forthwith to the large hall of the temple, lighted incense on the altar, and began praying. Scarcely had a few moments elapsed when a knocking was heard at the door, and a voice said: 'The Great Master Yi-hsing 一行 has arrived.' In fact, the monk advanced forthwith, saluted his teacher, and spoke a few words in secret. P'u-tsih [chi] 普寂 bowed his head, and granted what was demanded. Yi-hsing 一行 saluted anew three times, and proceeding to the Southern Hall, closed the door. P'u-tsih [chi] 普寂 summoned all his disciples, and bade them toll the bells of the monastery as Yi-hsing 一行 was leaving for the Western Paradise. When the monks entered the hall, they found him dead. He was aged 45 years. Fei K'uan 斐寬 mourned for him as a pupil for a renowned teacher.

On the day of his burial, the monks accompanied his remains beyond the city walls. The Emperor lamented him deeply, and to manifest his sorrow, suspended all audiences during three days. His corpse remained exposed for twenty-one days, and seemed as fresh as if he was still living. Hsüan Tsung 玄宗 had an inscription placed over his tomb, and granted 500,000 cash to erect a tower and a brass statue in his honour. Yi-hsing 一行 was canonized under the title of Highly Intelligent Monk, Ta-hwei [hui] shên-shih [ch'an-shih] 大慧禪師."—See also *Buddhist Schools*, XV.

I-HSÜAN CH'AN-SHIH 義玄禪師 (38th generation).—A deified Buddhist monk. Ranked tenth in Buddhist School, III (*q.v.*). The founder of the Lin-chi Tsung 臨濟宗, Lin-chi School (see *Buddhist Schools*, V). Lin Chi 臨濟 is the name of a river in Shantung 山東. I-hsüan's 義玄 home was near by, at Nan-hua Hsien 南華縣, a district dependent on Ts'ao-chou 曹州. His secular name was Hsing 邢.

The Lin-chi 臨濟 School successfully pushed out the other sects, and spread over Northern and Southern China to an enormous extent. Beginning in Shantung 山東, it was accepted throughout the Eighteen Provinces, and in Japan, as the most popular exponent of the teaching of the contemplative school.

Having failed to be admitted as a disciple of Hsi-yün Ch'an-shih 希運禪師 (*q.v.*)—being thrice repulsed, and beaten as well, to test the sincerity of his desire to become a monk, and his ability to endure the austerities of the monastic life—he returned to his parents' home. On Huang-pi's 黃檗 recommendation he studied the Doctrine under Ta-i 大愚. Later, he founded the Lin-chi 臨濟 School at Chên-chou 鎮州, and taught there with great success. He died in A.D. 866. A dagoba was erected over his ashes near Ta-ming Fu 大明府, S. Chihli 直隸. His posthumous title is

Hui-chao Ch'an-shih 慧 昭 禪 師, Intelligent and Brilliant Monk.

I-HUAI CH'AN-SHIH 義 懷 禪 師 (44th generation).—A deified Buddhist monk. Ranked twenty-sixth in Buddhist School, VI (*q.v.*). Family name Ch'ên 陳. A native of Lo-ch'ing 樂 清 in the Wên-chou 溫 州 department, Chêkiang 浙 江. After being repulsed four times (*cf. I-hsüan Ch'an-shih* 義 玄 禪 師), he was received and trained by Chung-hsien Ch'an-shih 重 顯 禪 師 (q.v.). "He became one of the most eminent monks, presided seven times over the solemn prayer meetings of the Brotherhood, and preached the Law throughout the whole empire." Died A.D. 1102. Posthumous title: Chên-tsung Ch'an-shih 振 宗 禪 師, Diligent and Revered Teacher.

I I-LIAO 醫 逸 寮.—See *Shui Fu* 水 府, C (2) (c).

I-MA 驛 馬, THE GOD OF THE STAR.—See *Lei K'ai* 雷 開.

I MEI 義 梅.—The name of the first great archer. Now called Hsü Ch'ang 續 長.

I SHÊN 疑 神.—See *Kinnara*.

I TI 儀 狄.—A god of wine. A native of Chêkiang 浙 江. Was apotheosized after offering the first wine to Yü 禹 the Great (2205-2197 B.C.).— See *Tu K'ang* 杜 康 and *Ti-tsang Wang* 地 藏 王.

I-TS'UN CH'AN-SHIH 義 存 禪 師 (39th generation).—A deified Buddhist monk. Ranked twelfth in Buddhist School, VI (*q.v.*). Family name Tsêng 曾. A native of Nan-an 南 安, in the Ch'üan-chou 泉 州 department. On presenting himself at the school of Hsüan-chien Ch'an-shih宣 鑑 禪 師 (*supra*, VI, 8), he was repelled with violence (*cf. I-hsüan Ch'an-shih* 義 玄 禪 師), and went to Liang-chieh Ch'an-shih 良 价 禪 師 (*q.v.*), who advised him to return to Hsüan-chien 宣 鑑, who eventually admitted him. He became an eminent teacher, and founded a famous school at Hsüeh Fêng 雪 峰 Snowy Peak, in Fukien 福 建. The Emperor I Tsung 懿 宗 (A.D. 860-74) of the T'ang 唐 dynasty presented him with a richly embroidered cope, and conferred on him the title of Chên-chio Ta-shih 真 覺 大 師 Truly Intelligent Master. Died A.D. 908.

I-T'UNG TSUN-CHÊ 義 通 尊 者.—A deified Buddhist monk. Ranked fifteenth in Buddhist School, X (*q.v.*). Family name Yin Wei-yüan 尹 惟 遠. A native of Korea. "Odd-looking in the extreme, his head was crowned with a kind of fleshy excrescence, while his eyebrows and lashes were bushy, and about six inches long." Entering the Kuei-shan Yüan 龜 山 院, Turtle-hill Monastery, in Korea, at an early age, he assiduously studied the *Hua-yen ching* 華嚴經, a work of the Mahayana School, attributed to Nagarjuna. It indulges in fanciful and mythological abstractions, which are deemed to lead to salvation. After reaching China, he lived first at Yün-chü 雲居, in the T'ien-t'ai Shan 天台山, T'ien-t'ai Mountains, and later on at Lo-ch'i 螺溪, where he was taught by Ching-kuang Tsung-chê 淨光尊者 (*q.v.*). He transformed a house given him by a local official into a convent, and preached the doctrine there for twenty years. In A.D. 982, the emperor conferred the title of Pao-yün 寶雲, Precious Cloud, on his temple. Died A.D. 988. Buried to the N.W. of the O-yü-wang Ssŭ 阿育王寺, O-yü-wang Monastery. "Later on, when his coffin was opened, his bones appeared surrounded with light, and five-coloured relics, *shê-li* 舍利 (*cf. Kuang-hsiu Tsun-chê* 廣修尊者), were mingled with them."

I-WU LU SHAN 醫無盧山, THE GOD OF.—See *Pi-hsia Yüan-chün* 碧霞元君.

I-YÜN-CH'Ê CH'AN-SHIH 義雲徹禪師 (67th generation). —A deified Buddhist monk. Ranked eighty-second in Buddhist School, VI (*q.v.*). Family name Wei 魏. A native of Chung-chêng 崇禎, Chi-nan Fu 濟南府, Shantung 山東. Born A.D. 1635. Taught by [Sung-ju] Tao-mi Ch'an-shih [嵩乳] 道密禪師 (*q.v.*) in the Pao-ên Ssŭ 報恩寺, Thanksgiving Monastery, at Huai-an 淮安 Expounded the doctrine in the monasteries of Chin-fêng 金峰 Shih-t'ou 石頭, and T'an-tu 檀度.

ILA.—See *Ida*.

IMMORTAL, THE SHINING-GOLD.— See *Chin-kuang Hsien* 金光仙.

IMMORTAL, THE STRANGE-WINGS.— See *Yü-i Hsien* 羽翼仙.

IMMORTAL OF HEAVEN, THE.—See *Pi-hsia Yüan-chün* 碧霞元君.

IMMORTAL JADE MATRON OF T'AI-P'ING HSIANG 太平項 OF THE SACRED MOUNTAIN T'AI-SHAN 泰山, THE.—See *Pi-hsia Yüan-chün* 碧霞元君.

IMMORTAL OF THE WATERS, THE.—See *Shui Fu* 水府, D (3) (a).

IMMORTAL OF THE WATERS, THE FEMALE.—See *Shui Fu* 水府, D (3) (e).

IMMORTALS.—See *Hsien Jên* 仙 人.

IMMORTALS, THE EIGHT.—See *Po Hsien* 八 仙.

IMMORTALS, THE GOD OF THE.—See *Wu Lao* 五 老.

IMMORTALS, THE GOD AND GODDESS OF THE.—See *Tung Wang-kung* 東 王 公 and *Hsi Wang-mu* 西 王 母.

IMMORTALS OF THE NINE CARP LAKE, THE.—See *Chiu-li-hu Hsien* 九 鯉 湖 仙.

INCENSE-MAKERS OR SELLERS, THE GOD OF.—See *Huang K'un* 黃 昆.

INDRA. —Yin-t'o-lo 因 陀 羅.—*Lit.* Supreme Ruler. A popular god of Brahmanism, adopted by Buddhism as representative of the secular power, protector of the church, but as inferior to any Buddhist saint.—See *Yü Ti* 玉 帝.

INGIDA.—See *Lo-han* 羅 漢.

INNKEEPERS, THE GOD OF.—See *Lei Tsu* 雷 祖.

IRON-HEAD.—See *T'ieh Yüan-shuai* 鐵 元 帥.

IRONMONGERS, THE GOD OF.—See *Lao Tzŭ* 老 子.

J

JADE EMPEROR.—See *Yü Huang* 玉 皇.

JADE MAIDEN, THE.—See *Pi-hsia Yüan-chün* 碧 霞 元 君.

JADE MAID'S LAKE, THE.—See *Pi-hsia Yüan-chün* 碧 霞 元 君.

JADE PALACE, THE SOVEREIGN EMPEROR OF THE. —See *Chin-ch'üeh Shang-ti* 金 闕 上 帝.

JAN-TÊNG FO 然 燈 佛.—The "Lamp-bearing Buddha," the "Light-lamp Buddha," or the "Buddha who illuminates." Also known as Ting-kuang Fo 定 光 佛, "Buddha of Fixed Light," or "Fix-light Buddha." The Sanskrit *Dipamkara* (24th predecessor of Sakyamuni).

There are three theories as to his origin. (1). The first relates that a mendicant woman of Sravasti (Shê-wei 舍 衞), observing the rich offerings placed by wealthy devotees on Buddha's altar, resolved to lay aside a few coins daily to purchase some oil to replenish the lamps burnt before the image of the god. The caretaker of the temple, whose duty it was to extinguish the lamps at night-time, found it impossible to extinguish the one replenished by her, which, in spite of his most strenuous efforts, only continued to burn the more brightly. When the mendicant woman returned to worship Sakyamuni, he prophesied that she would become a Buddha in a future *kalpa*. Subsequently, she became a Buddhist nun, and was finally born as a Buddha. (2). The second theory finds the origin in *Dipamkara,* the teacher of Sakyamuni in a previous *kalpa*. The latter, having met him in the *Tushita* (都 史 多) heaven, where all Bodhisattvas are reborn before finally appearing on earth as Buddha, received from him the true

207

doctrine, and the assurance that he was destined for Buddhahood. He was born on an island, and a large number of bright lights appeared round his cradle; hence the name. (3). The Taoists, frequent plagiarists of Buddhist mythology, maintain that the Taoist hermit Chin Shan-tzǔ 金 蟬 子, also called Jan-têng 燃 燈, who lived on Sung Shan 嵩 山, the highest of the Five Mountains of China, known as the Sacred Mountain of the Centre of the Universe, was the teacher of Sakyamuni. This account is as follows:

Sakyamuni, having failed, though then nineteen years old, to become enlightened by the teaching of his preceptors, set out for China to receive instruction from a hermit called Chin Shan-tzǔ 金 蟬 子, whose honorary name was Jan-têng 燃 燈. Not finding him on Sung Shan 嵩 山, he proceeded to Liang Shan 梁 山, to the east of the T'ai-tai Shan 泰 岱 山, and becoming his disciple, in thirteen days grasped the whole doctrine of Taoist perfection. Returning to India, he preached the new religion, and was known by the name of Sakyamuni. In a subsequent phase of existence he became Ti-tsang Wang 地藏王 (q.v.).

Jan-têng 燃 燈 became a Buddha in the following manner. Living in the Himalaya Mountains as a *rishi,* or Hindu hermit (the Taoist *hsien-jên* 仙 人, *q.v.*), under the name of the Brahman Lao-tu-po-t'i 牢 度 跋 提, he succeeded in converting a thousand kings. He and they then lived in the mountains as hermits. One day, a *yaksha* (*yeh-ch'a* 夜 叉)—a class of good genii, ruled over by the Hindu God of Riches, Kuvera—asked permission to eat their hearts and drink their blood. They refused, but Lao-tu-po-t'i 牢 度 跋 提 gave not only his blood, but his heart also. He subsequently became the Buddha known as Jan-têng 燃 燈, but the thousand kings had to expiate their fault for a whole *kalpa* (the "*kalpa* of stability," *Badhrakalpa*) before becoming the "Thousand Buddhas," *Ch'ien Fo* 千 佛, of the present age. Jan-têng 燃 燈 is popularly believed to have offered to Li Ching 李 靖 (*q.v.*) the pagoda he is represented as carrying on his left hand. This gave to Li 李 the name of "Pagoda-bearer."—See also *Pi-hsia Yüan-chün* 碧 霞 元 君.

JAN-TÊNG TAO-JÊN 燃 燈 道 人.—Lived in the Yüan-chio Tung 圓 覺 洞, on Ling-chiu Shan 靈 鷲 山. In the historical battle of the Ten Thousand Genii in the Yin-Chou 殷周 wars, he killed the goddess Tou Mu 斗 母, Mother of the Pole, by striking her with his steadfast-tide Pearl.

JANG TZǓ 壤 子.—See *Tsao Chün* 灶(竈)君.

JÊN-FEI-JÊN-TÊNG 人 非 人 等.—A dragon-king.—See *Lung Wang* 龍 王.

JÊN HSIEN 人 仙.—Genii of human kind—those who have

succeeded in freeing themselves from perturbation of spirit and the infirmities of flesh.

JÊN HUANG 人皇.—See *Tou Mu* 斗母.

JÊN KUANG 任光.—The god of the constellation Liu 柳. Alternatively with Wu K'un 吳坤.

JÊN LAI-P'IN 任來聘.—The god of the star T'ien-sha 天殺. —See *T'ien-kang* 天罡.

JÊN-SHA 刃殺, THE GOD OF THE STAR.—See *Kung-sun To* 公孫鐸.

JÊN SHÊN 人神.—See *Hou T'u* 后土.

JÊN TSU 仁祖.—See *Shê Chi* 社稷.

JEWELLERS, THE GOD OF.—See *Pien Ho* 卞和.

JHANA.—See *Dhyana*.

JIH-KUANG PIEN-CHAO 日光遍照. — See *Yao-shih Fo* 師藥佛.

JIH YÜEH CHING 日月精.—The Gods of the Eye.—See *Eye, The Gods of the*.

JOY, THE GOD OF.—See *Hsi Shên* 喜神.

JU-I 如意.—"As you wish." A symbol of Buddhism, borne by gods in their hands. One of the *Ch'i Pao* 七寶, Seven Precious Things (Saptaratna); a fabulous pearl.

JU-LAI, CH'I 如來七.—The Seven Tathagatas.—See *Tathagatas*.

JU-LAI FO 如來佛.—Sêng Pao 僧寶, the Precious Monkhood (*Sangha*). The "Thus-come Buddha." The Sanskrit Tathagata (*q.v.*), a title of Buddha. The words mean literally "the Buddha who came thus." One who exhibits perfect human nature, one whose coming and going accords with that of his predecessors. The highest appellation given to every Buddha. The Sanskrit might equally well mean "who went thus," but the Chinese long ago, rightly or wrongly, adopted "came" and not "went."—See also *Fo* 佛, *Buddha, San Pao* 三寶, and *Sakyamuni*.

JU SHOU 蓐收.—See *Shui Fu* 水府, C (2) (b) and (e).

[JUI-PAI] MING-HSÜEH CH'AN-SHIH [瑞白] 明雪禪師.
(65th generation).—A deified Buddhist monk. Ranked fifty-
eighth in Buddhist School, VI (q.v.). Family name Yang 楊.
A native of T'ung-ch'êng 桐城, Anhui 安徽. Having studied at
the Buddhist monastery at Yün-mên 雲門, Cloud Gate, he settled
at Lung-hua 龍華, in Hu-chou 湖州, Chêkiang 浙江, where he
preached the doctrine until his death in A.D. 1641. His tomb is at
Pien-hua 弁華, beside the Lung-hua Ssŭ 龍華寺, Lung-hua
Monastery.

JUGGLERS, THE GOD OF.—Name Ko Hsien-Wêng 葛
仙翁. "He could blow a grain of rice out of his mouth and it
would turn into thousands of bees. He would call them back
and eat them as rice" (Du Bose, p. 336).

JUNG CH'ÊNG 容成.—Said to have been the teacher of the
Emperor Huang Ti 黄帝 (2698-2598 B.C.) and a high official in
his Court. The tradition, as related in the *Hsü Wên-hsien-
t'ung-k'ao* 續文獻通考, states that he returned to the earth about
1010 B.C. He had acquired the power of rejuvenating human
beings, restoring the natural colour to old people's hair, and
re-inserting fallen teeth. Later, he became the instructor of Lao
Tzŭ 老子.

JUPITER, THE GOD OF THE PLANET.—Mu Hsing
木星.—Known as Ch'ing Ti 青帝, the Green Ruler, and Ling
Wei-yang 靈威仰. The God of the Spring. Corresponds to the
Western Zeus, the conqueror of earthly or inferior powers.—See
also *Mao Mêng* 茅濛 and *T'ai Sui* 太歲.

K

KA.—The Sanskrit interrogative pronoun "Who?" This word has been raised to the position of a deity. In the words of Max Müller, "The authors of the *Brahmanas* had so completely broken with the past, that, forgetful of the poetical character of the hymns (of the *Veda*) and the yearning of the poets after the unknown god, they exalted the interrogative pronoun itself into a deity, and acknowledged a god Ka or Who? In the *Taittiriya Brahmana,* in the *Kaushitaki Brahmana,* in the *Tandya Brahmana,* and in the *Satapatha Brahmana,* wherever interrogative verses occur, the author states that Ka is Prajapati, or the lord of creatures. Nor did they stop here. Some of the hymns in which the interrogative pronoun occurred were called *Kadvat, i.e.* having *kad* or *quid.* But soon a new adjective was formed, and not only the hymns but the sacrifice also offered to the god were called *Kaya* or Who-ish . . . . At the time of Panini, this word had acquired such legitimacy as to call for a separate rule explaining its formation. The commentator here explains Ka by Brahman. After this we can hardly wonder that in the later Sanskrit literature of the *Puranas* Ka appears as a recognized god, as a supreme god, with a genealogy of his own, perhaps even with a wife; and that in the laws of Manu one of the recognised forms of marriage, generally known by the name of the Prajapati marriage, occurs under the monstrous title of Kaya." The *Maha-bharata* identifies Ka with Daksha, and the *Bhagavata Purana* applies the term to Kasyapa (*q.v*), no doubt in consequence of their great generative powers and similarity to *Prajapati.*

KA [CHIA] NO-KA [CHIA] FA-TS'O 迦諾迦伐蹉.—See *Lo-han* 羅漢.

KA [CHIA] NO-KA [CHIA] PO-LI-TO-SHÊ 迦諾迦跋釐惰闍.—See *Lo-han* 羅漢.

KAI YEN 蓋延.— The god of the constellation Hsü 虛. Alternatively with Chou Pao 周賓.

K'AI-CHÜN T'UNG 開君童.—See *Liver, The Gods of the*.

K'AI-LU SHÊN 開路神.—The Spirit that Clears the Way. The exorcist.

"The first functioning of the first exorcist is unlikely to be recorded in any history. There must have been many in China who practised this art long before history began to be written. Legge says: 'They were ancient superstitions, not established by the former kings'; but, though they did not originate with the former kings, they were not superstitions, but living beings; and we seem to be very near the beginning of things when we read in Chinese literature of an exorcist who was originally an ordinary military man who carried weapons, and who, perhaps, went mad. This was, apparently, the origin of the *fang-hsiang shih* 方相氏, or inspector of localities, mentioned in the *Chou li* 周禮 and the *Li chi* 禮記; for he was originally, as well as in later times, known as a *k'uang-fu* 狂夫, or maniac, and *k'uang-ch'iang* 壙搶, or grave-hopper. Other names by which he was called were *mo chiang-chün* 陌將軍, general of the roads, and *hsien-tao shên* 嶮神道, spirit of the dangerous roads. Afterwards, and more colloquially, he was also called *k'ai-lu shên* 開路神, the spirit that clears the way, or *k'ai-lu shên-chün* 君, Sir *K'ai-lu shên* 開路神 or spiritual prince who clears the way. The duties of clearing the way and of scouring out the house or grave to rid it of any demons or evil influences lurking therein, were at first performed by one possessed person; but they gradually became differentiated, the *k'ai-lu shên* 開路神 clearing the way up to the house or grave, and the remaining exorcism being carried on by the *k'uang-ch'iang* 壙搶. This is clearly shown in Chinese funeral processions, and exorcism of the grave-pit before the coffin is lowered into it" (Werner).

KALA.—"Time," Chinese *shih* 時, a season.—A name of Yama, the judge of the dead. In the *Atharva-veda* Time is addressed as the source and ruler of all things. "It is he who drew forth the worlds and encompassed them. Being their father, he became their son. There is no other power superior to him." The *Vishnu, Bhagavata,* and *Padma Puranas* state that Brahman existed in the form of Time, "but the *Puranas* do not generally recognize Time as an element of the first cause."—See also *Lo-han* 羅漢.

KALAKA.—A wife of Kasyapa. According to the *Ramayana* and *Maha-bharata* she was a daughter of Daksha, but the *Vishnu Purana* states that she and her sister Puloma were daughters of the Danava Vasiwanara, "who were both married to Kasyapa, and bore him 60,000 distinguished Danavas, called Paulomas and Kalakanjas, who were powerful, ferocious, and cruel." The *Maha-bharata* states that she obtained from the deity, in reward for her severe devotion and penance, the privilege of bringing forth children without pain. The giants or Danavas were called after her Kalakeyas.

KALIKA.—See *Lo-han* 羅漢.

KALPA. — Chinese *chieh-po* 劫波. — A day and night of Brahma, 4,320,000,000 years. A period (*ta shih-fên* 大時分) during which a physical universe is formed and destroyed. There are great *kalpas* (*ta chieh* 大劫) and small *kalpas* (*hsiao chieh* 小劫). Eight small *kalpas* make one large *kalpa*. A great *kalpa* is the period elapsing from the moment when a universe is formed to the moment when another is put in its place. A small *kalpa* is divided into a period of increase (*tsêng chieh* 增劫), four ages of iron, copper, silver, and gold, during which human life gradually increases to 84,000 years and the height of the human body to 84,000 feet; and a period of decrease (*chien chieh* 減劫), divided into three periods (*san tsai* 三災) of distress (pestilence, war, and famine), during which human life is reduced to ten years and the height of the human body to one foot. There are also other distinctions and divisions of *kalpas* (Eitel, pp. 68-9).

KAMA, KAMA-DEVA.—The Hindu God of Love. Eros, Cupid. In the *Rig-veda* (x. 129) desire is said to have been the first movement that arose in the One after it had come into life through the power of fervour or abstraction. "Desire first arose in It, which was the primal germ of mind; (and which) sages, searching with their intellect, have discovered in their heart to be the bond which connects entity with non-entity." "It is well known," observes Dr. Muir, "that Greek mythology connected Eros, the god of love, with the creation of the universe somewhat in the same way." "This Kama or desire, not of sexual enjoyment, but of good in general, is celebrated in a curious hymn of the *Atharva-veda*," which exalts Kama into a supreme God and Creator: "Kama was born the first. Him neither gods, nor fathers, nor men have equalled. Thou art superior to these and for ever great." In another part of the same *Veda* Kama appears to be first desire, then the power which gratifies the desire. Kama is also in the same *Veda* often identified with Agni, and when "distinguished from each other, Kama may be looked upon as a superior form of the other deity." According to the *Taittiriya Brahmana,* he is the son of Dharma, the god of justice, by Sraddha, the goddess of faith; but according to the *Hari-vansa* he is son of Lakshmi. Another account represents him as springing from water, wherefore he is called Ira-ja, "the water-born"; a fifth is that he is Atma-bhu, "self-existent," and therefore he is called, like other of the gods, A-ja, "unborn," or An-anya-ja, "born of no other." In the *Puranas* his wife is Rati or Reva, the goddess of desire. He inspired Siva with amorous thoughts of Parvati while he was engaged in penetential devotion, and for this offence the angry god reduced him to ashes by fire from his central eye, Siva afterwards relented and allowed Kama to be born again as Pradyumna, son of Krishna and Rukmini or Maya, "delusion." He has a son named Aniruddha, and a daughter, Trisha. He is lord of the *apsaras* or heavenly nymphs. He is armed with a bow and arrows: the bow is of sugar-cane, the bowstring a line of bees, and each arrow is tipped with a distinct flower. He is usually represented as a handsome youth riding on a parrot and attended by nymphs, one of whom bears his banner displaying the Makara, or a fish on a red ground. His mysterious origin and the universal operation of the passion he inspires have accumulated upon him a great variety of names and epithets, such as "the beautiful," "the inflamer," "destroyer," "deluder," etc.

KANAKA-BHARADJAVA.—See *Lo-han* 羅 漢.

KANAKA-VATSA.—See *Lo-han* 羅 漢.

KAN-TA-P'O 乾 闥 婆.—A dragon-king.—See *Lung Wang* 龍 王.

K'ANG 亢, THE GOD OF THE CONSTELLATION.—See *Wu Han* 吳 漢 and *Li Tao-t'ung* 李 道 通.

K'ANG-SÊNG HUI 康 僧 會.—The Sogdiana monk Hui 會. A saintly Buddhist monk. A native of K'ang-chü Kuo 康 居 國, Sogdiana (Beal says he was a man of Samarcand). Died A.D. 280. Arrived at Chien-yeh 建 業 (modern Nanking 南 京) in A.D. 247. Said to have saved his life by procuring a relic of Sakyamuni for the ruler of the Wu Kuo 吳 國, Wu Kingdom, which, however, when placed on a brazen platter shattered it to pieces. Being unable to destroy the relic, the emperor built his first monastery, Chien-ch'u Ssŭ 建 初 寺, First-established Monastery, for the monk. He also erected a tower, on the summit of which was placed the precious relic, ever beaming with constant brilliancy. He translated several volumes of prayers. One of those invited to the annual banquet of the gods (see *Hsi Wang-mu* 西 王 母).

K'ANG YÜAN-SHUAI 康 元 帥.—An incarnation of the dragon-horse. Selected as his father Kuang Yu 廣 猶 and his mother, a woman of the Chin 金 family, who lived on the banks of the Huang Ho 黃 河, Yellow River. The incarnation took place in the period Yen-tê 炎 德 of the ninth year of the reign of Jên Huang 人 皇, one of the mythical Sovereigns of Mankind.

He was noted for his merciful nature, never hurting a living being, even worms or ants. He was fond of drinking wine. One day he saw a bird of prey carry off a young heron. The latter fell to the earth with a broken wing. K'ang Yüan-shuai 康元帥 took it home, healed and fed it. When it had grown up it brought a branch of the herb of immortality to him as a sign of gratitude. Locally he was known as "the benefactor," on account of his ability to cure all sicknesses.

The Lord of Heaven granted him the title of Beneficent Saint and Generalissimo, and appointed him Superintendent of the Four Cardinal Points. He is represented holding a club in his right hand and a golden axe in his left.

KAO CHÊN 高震.—The god of the constellation Shih 室. Alternatively with Kêng Shun 耿純.—See *Huo Pu* 火部.

KAO CHI-NÊNG 高繼能.—The god of the star Hei-sha 黑殺. One of K'ung Hsüan's 孔宣 subordinate officers at San-shan Kuan 三山關. Slain by general Huang Fei-hu 黃飛虎.

KAO CHIO 高覺.—See *Ch'ien-li Yen* 千里眼.

KAO HSI-P'ING 高系平.—See *Chiu Yao* 九曜.

KAO K'O 高可.—The god of the star T'ien-t'ui 天退.—See *T'ien-kang* 天罡.

KAO KUEI 高貴.—See *Wu Tou* 五斗.

KAO LAN-YING 高蘭英.—The goddess of the star T'ao-hua 桃花. The wife of general Chang Kuei 張奎, commander of Chou Wang's 紂王 armies at Min-ch'ih Hsien 澠池縣. Slain by a blow from No-cha's 哪吒 magic bracelet.

KAO MEI 高禖.—See *Chang Hsien* 張仙.

KAO MEI 皋禖.—See *Nü Wa* 女媧.

KAO MING 高明.—See *Ch'ien-li Yen* 千里眼.

KAO-PING TAO-JÊN 高丙道人.—The god of the constellation Shih 氐. Alternatively with Chia Fu 賈復.

KAO PO-KUNG 高伯恭.—See *Wu Tou* 五斗.

KAO-TA-MO 喬苔摩.—See *Fo* 佛.

KAO WANG 高王.—See *Kuan Yin* 觀音.

KAO YEN 高衍.—The god of the star T'ien-k'uei 天魁.
—See *T'ien-kang* 天罡.

KAO YÜAN-SHUAI 高元帥.—Generalissimo Kao 高. His
birth is indefinitely said to have taken place on the *chia-tzŭ* 甲子
day of the eleventh moon of the *chia-tzŭ* 甲子 year. He is stated
to have been a reincarnation of T'ai-i Chên-jên 太乙眞人 (*q.v.*)
in the womb of Mei-shih 梅氏, wife of Kao Ch'ung-kung 高春公.
At birth his body shone like fire. Considering him to be an evil
spirit, his parents threw him into the Chiang 江. He was saved
by Yao-shih T'ien-tsung 藥師天尊 (*q.v.*), who adopted him as
his disciple, named him Yüan 員, and taught him all kinds of
mystic recipes. By means of these he cured monkeys, tigers,
snakes, deer, etc. But his marvellous skill was not confined to
sub-human creatures, for he cured an Immortal of a running sore
by cicatrizing it and applying the sap of the *ch'iung-hua* 瓊花,
flower of the Immortals.

In order to entrap him, a Spirit asked him if he could reju-
venate an old dry and dead cypress-tree. This he accomplished by
sprinkling it with lustral Kuang Yin 觀音 water. He also
affirmed his ability to enable very old people to give birth to
children. Thereupon the Spirit asserted that physicians only
cured one evil by causing another, as, for example, injuring plants
to cure men. To this Kao Yüan 高員 agreed, saying that both
could not be saved. He thanked him for that observation, and
gave him a recipe for resuscitating human beings. Kao 高 travelled
widely and saved innumerable people. As a reward, Yü Ti 玉帝
bestowed on him the title of Generalissimo Kao 高, the incarnated
descendant of the Nine Heavens. His image is to be seen in
temples containing that of Yao-shih Fo 藥師佛, the Buddhist
God of Remedies.—See also *Wang Kao êrh Yüan-shuai* 王高二
元帥.

K'AO KO 考鬲.—The god of the star Ti-chêng 地正.—See
Ti-sha 地煞.

KARTTIKEYA.—The Hindu God of War and the planet
Mars, also called Skanda. He is said in the *Maha-bharata* and
Ramayana to be the son of Siva or Rudra, and to have been
produced without the intervention of a woman. Siva cast his
seed into fire, and it was afterwards received by the Ganges:
Karttikeya was the result; hence he is called Agnibhu and
Ganga-ja. He was fostered by the Pleiades (Krittika), and hence
he has six heads and the name Karttikeya. His paternity is sometimes assigned to Agni (fire); Ganga (the Ganges) and Parvati
are variously represented to be his mother. He was born for the
purpose of destroying Taraka, a Daitya whose austerities had
made him formidable to the gods. He is represented riding on
a peacock called Paravani, holding a bow in one hand and an

arrow in the other. His wife is Kaumari or Sena. He has many
titles.

KASANGALA.—See *Lo-han* 羅漢.

KASHAYA.—Sanskrit for a coloured garment. In modern times a cope or outer garment worn by Buddhist priests when officiating.

KASHIAPA.—See *Lo-han* 羅漢.

KASIKA-SUNDARI.—See *Lo-han* 羅漢.

KASYAPA.—A Vedic sage to whom some hymns are attributed. All authorities agree in assigning to him a large part in the work of creation. According to the *Maha-bharata,* the *Ramayana,* and the *Puranas,* he was the son of Marichi, the son of Brahma, and he was father of Vivaswat, the father of Manu, the progenitor of mankind. The *Satapatha Brahmana* gives a different and not very intelligible account of his origin than "Having assumed the form of a tortoise, Prajapati created offspring. That which he created he made (*akarot*); hence the word *kurma* (tortoise). Kasyapa means tortoise; hence men say, 'All creatures are descendants of Kasyapa.' This tortoise is the same as Aditya." The *Atharva-veda* says, "The self-born *Kasyapa* sprang from Time," and Time is often identical with Vishnu. The *Maha-bharata* and later authorities agree in representing that Kasyapa married Aditi and twelve other daughters of Daksha. From Aditi he begat the Adityas, headed by Indra, and also Vivaswat, and "to Vivaswat was born the wise and mighty Manu." The *Ramayana* and *Vishnu Parana* also state that "Vishnu was born as a dwarf, the son of Aditi and Kasyapa." By his other twelve wives he had a numerous and very diversified offspring: demons, *nagas,* reptiles, birds, and all kinds of living things. He was thus the father of all, and as such is sometimes called Prajapati. He is one of the seven great Rishis, and he appears as the priest of Parasu-rama and Rama-chandra.—See also *Ka,* *Lo-han* 羅漢, and *Mahakasyapa.*

KASYAPA MATANGA.—See *Chia-yeh Mo-t'êng* 迦葉摩騰.

KCHINAS'RAVA.—See *Lo-han* 羅漢.

KÊNG CH'I-KUNG 耿七公.—See *Chêng San-kung* 鄭三公.

KÊNG SHUN 耿純.—The god of the constellation Shih 室. Alternatively with Kao Chên 高震.

KÊNG YEN 耿弇.—The god of the constellation Fang 房. Alternatively with Yao Kung-po 姚公伯.

KÊNG YEN 耿顏.—The god of the star Ti-chieh 地捷.—See *Ti-sha* 地煞.

K'ÊNG SAN KU-NIANG 坑三姑娘.—The three Ladies of the Latrine. The *k'êng* 坑 in this phrase, meaning literally a pit, is used for the usually red-coloured, small round tub used by the Chinese as a water-closet. It often is included among wedding-presents (in this case being termed *ching-t'ung* 淨桶, "spotless bucket," or vessel), and it is into it that pregnant women deliver their offspring. Hence the vulgar retort—used to "take down a peg" any unusually conceited person—"Did you not, like everyone else, fall into your mother's latrine?"

The more dignified name of the vessel is *hun-yüan chin-tou* 混元金斗, "Golden bushel of troubled origins." The San Ku 三姑 are the three ladies appointed as goddesses to watch over it.

Who were these persons? They are stated in the *Fêng shên yen i* 封神演義 to have been three sisters, Immortals of the isle of the *San Hsien* 三仙, Three Immortals. Their names were Yün-hsiao 雲霄, Ch'iung-hsiao 瓊霄, and Pi-hsiao 碧霄. Yün-hsiao's 雲霄 brother was Chao Kung-ming 趙公明 (*q.v.*), the the God of Riches, who emerged from his retreat on Mei Shan 峨山, Mount Mei 峨, to fight for the Yin 殷 against the Chou 周. In one of the battles he was killed by an arrow. When his sisters heard of his death, they came to avenge him by fighting in his stead. At first they were successful by means of their magic charms, the "Golden Bushel of Troubled Origins" and the "Golden Dragon-scissors," but these were carried off by Yüan-shih T'ien-tsun 元始天尊 and Lao Tzǔ 老子. The latter ordered Huang-chin Li-shih 黃巾力士 to destroy Yün-hsiao 雲霄, and the former commanded Pai-ho T'ung-tzǔ 白鶴童子 to kill Ch'iung-hsiao 瓊霄 with the "three precious stones of his desires." Finally, Yüan-shih T'ien-tsun 元始天尊 drew from his sleeve a magic bottle in which he imprisoned Pi-hsiao 碧霄, who was changed into water and blood.

After the Chou 周 had proved victorious, Chiang Tzǔ-ya 姜子牙 canonized Yün-hsiao 雲霄, Ch'iung-hsiao 瓊霄, and Pi-hsiao 碧霄 as The Three Ladies, Spirits of Latrines, appointed to watch over the "Golden Bushel of Troubled Origins."—See also *Tzǔ-ku Shên* 紫姑神.

KHATWANGA (also called Dilipa).—1. A Prince of the Solar race. In a battle between the gods and the demons he rendered great assistance to the former, who desired him to ask a boon. He begged that he might know the duration of his life, and the answer was, "Only an hour." He hastened to the world of mortals, and by earnest prayer he became united with the supreme being, Vishnu. "Like unto Khatwanga will there be no one upon earth, who, having come from heaven and dwelt an hour amongst men, became united with the three worlds by his liberality and knowledge of truth."—2.   A club; the club of Siva; it is also called *Khinkhira* and *Pansula*.

KHEMA.—See *Lo-han* 羅漢.

KIDNEYS, THE GOD OF THE.—The God of the Kidneys is stated in the *Huang t'ing nei ching* 黃經庭內 to be Hsüan Ming 玄冥, his designation being Yü Ying 育嬰.   The *Yün chi ch'i ch'ien* 雲笈七籤 gives Shuang I 雙以 as the name of the god, with the designation Lin Tzŭ 林子.   The God of the Left Kidney is Ch'un Yüan-chên 春元眞, with the designation Tao Ch'ing 道卿, his body being three and seven-tenths inches in height, and his colour varying between white, red, green, or any of the five colours.   The God of the Right Kidney is Hsiang Ti-wu 象地無, his designation Tao Shêng 道生, his body three-and-a-half inches in height, and his colour white or black.

KINDNESS AND COMPASSION, THE SCHOOL OF.— See *Buddhist Schools*, XIV.

KING OF MEDICINAL HERBS, THE.—See *Yao shih Fo* 藥師佛.

KINNARAS.—Chin-na-lo 緊那羅 or Fei-jên 非人, not men, or I-shên 疑神, doubtful (horned) spirits.—Demons (dangerous to men), with human bodies and equine heads; the musicians (represented with horses' heads) of Kuvera or celestial choristers looking like horses with horned heads.   A fabulous race of celestial beings.   The Buddhists, to excuse themselves for adopting a Taoist superstition, say that the Kitchen-god they worship is not the Tsao Chün 竈君 venerated commonly by the people, but a king of the Kinnaras, who became a Chinese priest in the T''ang 唐 dynasty, and was appointed at death to preside over the Vegetarian diet of the monks.   The word means "What men?"   Dowson describes them as "mythical beings with the form of a man and the head of a horse.   They are celestial choristers and musicians, dwelling in the paradise of Kuvera on Kailasa.   They sprang from the toe of Brahma with the Yakshas, but according to others, they are sons of Kasyapa.   They are also called Aswa-mukhas Turanga-vaktras, 'horse-faced,' and Mayus."—See also *Lung Wang* 龍王.

KITCHEN, THE GOD OF THE.—See *Tsao Chün* 灶(竈)君.

KNEES, THE GODS OF THE.—The designation of these gods is given in the *Yün chi ch'i ch'ien* 雲笈七籤 as Shu Kung 樞公.

KNIFE GRINDERS, THE GOD OF.—See *Li Lao-chün* 李老君.

KO FANG 葛方.—The god of the star Ti-shu 地數.—See *Ti-sha* 地煞.

KO HSIEN-WÊNG 葛仙翁.—The God of Dyers. He and Mei Hsien-wêng 梅仙翁 were two teachers who became Immortals. Always worshipped together, on the ninth day of the ninth month, their names being both placed on the same tablet. Images are not used.—See *Ko Yung-kuei* 葛永瓊.

KO KAO 革高.—The god of the star Ti-wên 地文.—See *Ti-sha* 地煞.

KO KU 葛姑.—The midwife and bringer of children. One of the specialists attached to the celestial Ministry of Medicine. Known as the Wise Lady Ko 荀. Born at Ko-wu Ts'un 葛烏村, near Ho Chou 和州, Anhui 安徽, she became famous for her skill at confinements, was eventually regarded as a divinity, and after her death, a temple was erected to her in Liu-kuo Hsiang 劉國庠 Village.

Her daughter also became a divinity, and her image is placed beside that of her mother. She had successfully delivered a woman of a child when her mother could not be found, and, being scolded by the latter, had committed suicide.

This worship is of recent origin and became general in the district during the reign of the Emperor Kuang Hsü 光緒 (A.D. 1875-1909). In some country temples Ko Ku's 葛姑 image is placed beside that of Kuan Yin 觀音. A tablet bearing her title is taken to and worshipped in the room of a woman undergoing difficult delivery.—See also *T'ien I-yüan* 天醫院.

KO YUNG 葛雍.—See *San Kuan* 三官.

KO YUNG-KUEI 葛永瓊.—Lived under the Chin 晉 dynasty. Also known as Ko Hsien-wêng 葛仙翁 (*q.v.*). Ko Yung-kuei Shan 葛永瓊山, Mount Ko Yung-kuei, in Ch'êng-tu Fu 成都府, Ssŭch'uan 四川, was named after him in remembrance of his attaining immortality during his residence there.

K'O-CH'IN CH'AN-SHIH 克勤禪師 (48th generation).— A deified Buddhist monk. Ranked twenty-third in Buddhist School, III (*q.v.*). Family name Lo 駱. A native of P'êng-chou 彭州. Studied under Fa-yen Ch'an-shih 法演禪師 (*q.v.*). Died A.D. 1135.

K'O-TS'UNG CH'AN-SHIH 可從禪師 (59th generation).— A deified Buddhist monk. Ranked forty-seventh in Buddhist School, VI (*q.v.*). Family name Hsü 許. A native of Lo-yang 洛陽, Honan 河南. Studied under Ch'i-pin Ch'an-shih 契斌 禪師 (*q.v.*). After staying in the Ting-kuo Ssŭ 定國寺, Nationpacifying Monastery, at Chia-ju 郟鄏, in A.D. 1482 he was head of the monastery at Shao-shih 少室. Died A.D. 1482. Buried at Shao-lin 少林.

KOLITA.—See *Maudgalyayana.*

KOU-CH'ÊN 勾陳, THE GOD OF THE STAR.—See *Lei P'êng* 雷鵬.

KOU-CHIAO 勾絞, THE GOD OF THE STAR.—See *Fei Chung* 費仲.

KOU CHING 狗精.—The Dog Spirit. The Spirit of the Star Huang-wu 荒蕪. Yüan Hung 袁洪, commander of the armies at Mêng-ching 孟津, during the wars at the end of the Yin 殷 dynasty, one day was notified by imperial messenger that an officer named Tai Li 戴禮 had received orders to place himself at his service. The new arrival turned out to be a person with a pointed mouth and large ears, and a strange light shone from his body. When battle was joined, he mounted his horse and fought bravely, using his transcendent weapons and power of transformation, etc., but was eventually slain by No-cha 哪吒 aided by Yang Chien 楊戩 and his faithful celestial hound.—See also *Chang Hsien* 張仙 and *Tai li* 戴禮.

KOU LUNG 勾龍.—See *Shê Chi* 社稷.

KOU MANG 勾芒.—See *Shui Fu* 水府, C (2) (b) and (e).

KOU-TA CH'IU-PO 勾大邱白.—See *Shui Fu* 水府, C (2) (c).

KOU YÜAN-SHUAI 苟元帥.—See *Hsin-hsing Kou Yüan-shuai* 辛興苟元帥.

K'OU CH'IEN CHIH 寇謙之.—A Taoist politician, regarded as an impostor. Fifth century A.D. A native of Ch'ang-p'ing 昌平, Chihli 直隸. Obtained the elixir of life from a Taoist Immortal named Ch'êng Kung-hsing 成功興. "His body emitted a heavenly radiance; and he was appointed (A.D. 424), under the patronage of Ts'ui Hao 崔浩, the counsellor and favourite of King T'o-pa Tao 拓跋燾 of the Pei Wei 北魏 Tonguses, to be the T'ien-shih 天師, Divine Teacher or 'Pope' of the Taoists, in succession to Chang Tao-ling 張道陵" (*q.v.*).

One night he dreamt that Ch'êng Kung-hsing 成功興 beckoned him to the Palace of Immortality, and dissolution immediately set in. A blue vapour issued from his lips and vanished in mid-air, "after which his body gradually sank to nothing."

K'OU CHUN 寇準.—See *Yen-lo Wang* 閻羅王.

K'OU HSÜN 寇恂.—The god of the constellation Hsin 心. Alternatively with Su-yüan Tao-jên 蘇元道人.

KRISHNA.—"Black." This name occurs in the *Rig-veda,* but without any relation to the great deity of later times. The earliest mention of Krishna, the son of Devaki, is in the *Chhandogya Upanishad,* where he appears as a scholar. There was a Rishi of the name who was a son of Viswaka. There was also a great Asura so named, who with 10,000 followers committed fearful devastation, until he was defeated and skinned by Indra. In another Vedic hymn, 50,000 Krishnas are said to have been slain, and it is added in another that his pregnant wives were slain with him that he might leave no posterity. This is supposed to have reference to the Rakshasas (*q.v.*) or to the dark-coloured aborigines of India.

The modern deity Krishna is the most celebrated hero of Indian mythology, and the most popular of all the deities. He is said to be the eighth Avatara or incarnation of Vishnu, or rather a direct manifestation of Vishnu himself. This hero, around whom a vast mass of legend and fable has been gathered, probably lived in the Epic age, when the Hindus had not advanced far beyond their early settlements in the north-west. He appears prominently in the *Maha-bharata,* where his character is invested with a certain degree of mysticism. Additions and interpolations have raised him to divinity, and it is in the character of the "Divine One" that he delivered the celebrated song, *Bhagavad-gita,* a production of comparatively late date, now held to be part of the great epic. In this work he distinctly declares himself to be the Supreme Being. For his birth, exploits, etc., see Dowson, *Class. Dic.,* pp. 161-8.

KSHITIGARBHA.—See *Ti-tsang Wang* 地藏王.

KU-CH'ÊN 孤辰, THE GOD OF THE STAR.—See *Yü Hua* 余化.

KU CHIH-KUNG 孤直公.—See *Wu Lao* 五老.

KU HSI-FÊNG 顧希馮.—See *Ts'ai Shên* 財神.

KU TSUNG 顧宗.—The god of the star Ti-tsou 地走.—See *Ti-sha* 地煞.

KU-YAI TS'UNG CH'AN-SHIH 孤崖聰禪師 (66th generation).—A deified Buddhist monk. Ranked Sixty-seventh in Buddhist School, VI (*q.v.*). A native of Tê-an Fu 德安府, Hu-kuang 湖廣 (modern Hupei 湖北 and Hunan 湖南). Studied in the Chieh-chu Ssǔ 戒珠寺, Chieh-chu Monastery, at Shao-hsing 紹興, under [Jui-pai] Ming-hsüeh Ch'an-shih [瑞白]明雪禪師

(*q.v.*). When trained, he lived at Tung Shan 洞 山, and was highly appreciated for his learning. The people of Kiangsi 江 西 called him Tung Shan Ku Fo 洞 山 古 佛, the Old Buddha of Tung Shan. Died during the reign of Shun Chih 順 治 (A.D. 1644-62) of the Ch'ing 清 dynasty. His tomb is on Chin-niu Fêng 金 牛 峰, Golden Ox Peak.

KU-YEN-KUAN CH'AN-SHIH 古 巖 莞 禪 師 (67th generation).—A deified Buddhist monk. Ranked eighty-third in Buddhist School, VI (*q.v.*). Family name Yüan 寰. Born at Huai-an 淮 安, Kiangsu 江 蘇, in A.D. 1634. Studied under [Sung-ju] Tao-mi Ch'an-shih [嵩 乳] 道 密 禪 師 (*q.v.*) at the P'u-t'i 菩 提 Monastery, and afterwards followed the school of Nan-an-i Ch'an-shih 南 菴 依 禪 師 (*q.v.*). Expounded the doctrine in the Wên-shu Ssŭ 文 殊 寺, Wên-shu Monastery, and died in the Hu-hsin Ssŭ 湖 心 寺, Lake's Heart Monastery.

K'U-CH'U CH'IAO 苦 楚 橋.—See *Mêng P'o* 孟 婆.

KUA-HSÜ 寡 宿, THE GOD OF THE STAR.—See *Chu Shêng* 朱 昇.

KUAN CHUNG 管 仲.—The God of Brothels.

KUAN-FU 官 符, THE GOD OF THE STAR.—See *Fang I-chên* 方 義 眞.

KUAN-K'OU SHÊN 灌 口 神.—The Drain-god. The words *kuan-k'ou* 灌 口 mean an opening through which water is drained off. In the province of Ssŭch'uan 四 川, to the N.W. of Kuan-hsien 灌 縣, in the sub-prefecture of Ch'êng-tu 成 都, is Mount Kuan-k'ou 灌 口. It derives its name from a prefect named Wên Wêng 文 翁, a native of Anhui 安 徽 nominated to Ssŭch'uan 四 川, having, toward the end of the reign of the Emperor Ching Ti 景 帝 (A.D. 156-140 B.C.) of the Han 漢 dynasty, made a breach in it to form a new bed for the Chien Chiang 湔 江, River Chien, to flow in and irrigate the land.

The person venerated as the Spirit of Kuan-k'ou 灌 口, however, is Li Ping 李 冰, who was appointed Prefect of Ch'êng-tu 成 都 by Chao Hsiang-wang 昭 襄 王 (255-250 B.C.) of the Ch'in 秦 dynasty. He breached Li-tui Shan 離 堆 山, Mount Li-tui, situated to the S.W. of the town of Kuan-hsien 灌 縣, thus opening a passage for the waters of the Mo Shui 沫 水, River Mo, and putting an end to the devastating inundations which laid waste that marshy land. He also dug two wide irrigation canals through the city of Ch'êng-tu 成 都, as well as putting a stop to the barbarous custom of immolating human victims to the Spirit of the river. His son was Erh-lang 二 郎 (*q.v.*).

The legend which has gradually grown out of these historical facts relates that Li Ping 李 冰 captured and chained up at the foot of Li-tui Shan 離 堆 山 a dangerous dragon which had been laying waste the country around.

His next exploit was connected with the irrigation canals he had caused to be made. In their waters resided a Spirit to whom two young girls were sacrificed annually. This was known as the marriage of the River Spirit, and huge sums were expended on it.

Li Ping 李 冰 married his own daughter to this Spirit, and on the wedding day, having dressed her in richly-ornamented apparel, when the moment came for her to be flung into the river, went to the temple dedicated to the Spirit and made an offering of wine, but without receiving any response.

At this he indignantly exclaimed: "Lord of the water, you are slighting me; we will have it out between us!" Drawing his sword, he disappeared. It was then seen that two green oxen were at grips with each other in the stream. The struggle lasted a long while, and then Li Ping 李 冰 returned and said to his followers: "The fierce fight has fatigued me; I cannot carry it on any longer. Will you not come to my aid? See to the South, the ox with the white covering of my seal over its flanks, that is I." One of his attendants then stabbed the ox standing on the North, and the Spirit of the stream died. It was never afterwards heard of again.

The Spirit of Kuan-k'ou 灌 口 was widely worshipped in Ssǔch'uan 四 川, given the title of king, and large numbers of sheep sacrificed to him, as many as 40,000 being offered in one year. The tax on these animals at the customs barriers provided a large revenue for the local authorities. His birthday was ceremoniously observed by the officials and people, and honorific titles bestowed on him and his son Erh-lang 二 郎, by the Emperor Wên Ti 文 帝 (A.D. 1330-3) of the Yüan 元 dynasty; the former being styled Saintly King, Virtuous, Universally Beloved, Magnificent and Benevolent; the latter, Magnificent King of Limitless Fame, Eminent in Benevolence and Wisdom, Good and Generous.

In modern times, Erh-lang 二 郎 is more generally worshipped than his father—probably because of the achievements and divine origin ascribed to him in the popular work *Hsi-yu chi* 西 遊 記.

KUAN KUNG 關 公 AND HIS ASSESSORS.—See *Kuan Yü* 關 羽, *Ts'ai Shên* 財 神, and *Composite Deities.*

KUAN PIN 關 斌.—The god of the star Ti-ts'ang 地 藏.—See *Ti-sha* 地 煞.

KUAN P'ING 關 平.—See *Kuan Yü* 關 羽.

KUAN SHIH TZǓ-TSAI 觀 世 自 在.—See *Kuan Yin* 觀 音.

KUAN SHIH YIN 觀 世 音.—See *Kuan Yin* 觀 音.

KUAN SHIH YIN TZŬ-TSAI 觀世音自在.—See *Kuan Yin* 觀音.

KUAN-SO 貫索, THE GOD OF THE STAR--See *Ch'iu Yin* 邱引.

KUAN TI 關帝.—See *Kuan Yü* 關羽, and *Ts'ai Shên* 財神.

KUAN-TING FA-SHIH 灌頂法師.—A deified Buddhist monk. Ranked fourth in Buddhist School, X (*q.v.*). Family name Wu Fa-yün 吳法雲. A native of Chang-an 章安, in the Lin-hai 臨海 district, Chêkiang 浙江. Precocious from the age of 3, he was sur- named Kuan-ting 灌頂, Contemplating the Summits. At 7 years of age, he entered the Shê-ching Ssŭ 攝靜寺 Shê-ching Monastery, and subsequently was taught by Chih-chê Ta-shih 智者大師 (*q.v.*), with whom he remained for several years. A prolific writer, he produced more than a hundred volumes, including the *Nieh-p'an hsüan-i* 涅槃玄義, *Mysterious Principles of Nirvana.* His works contributed greatly to the propagation of the T'ien-t'ai 天台 School doctrine. When he had addressed his parting words to his disciples, the latter joined their hands, and invoked O-mi-t'o Fo 阿彌陀佛 (Amitabha) (*q.v.*), whereupon he died, A.D. 632.

KUAN YIN 觀尹.—See *Kuan Yin* 觀音.

KUAN YIN 觀音 or KUAN SHIH YIN TZŬ TSAI 觀世音自在 (Avalokitesvara), KUAN YIN P'U-SA 觀音菩薩, the Bodhisattva Kuan Yin 觀音.—The Goddess of Mercy. A Chinese female deity, probably an ancient local goddess of mercy (and progeny), worshipped in China, before the advent of Buddhism, under the name of Kuan Yin 觀音 and adopted by Buddhists as an incarnation of Avalokitesvara (or Padmapani). The name Kuan Yin 觀音, *lit.* "looking on, or heeding, the sound" or cry, of the world, is said to be derived from the legend which relates that as she was about to enter heaven she paused on the threshold to listen to the cry of the world, but the real origin is to be found in the identification of Kuan Yin 觀音 as an incarnation of Avalokitesvara, Kuan Yin 觀音, according to this explanation, meaning *avalokita* (*kuan* 觀, looking on) *svara* (*yin* 音, sound, *i.e.* of prayers). The longer name, Kuan shih yin tzŭ tsai 觀世音自在, means the sovereign who looks on the sounds or prayers (sometimes abbreviated to the sovereign who looks on the world— Kuan shih tzŭ tsai 觀世自在). The latter name, often further abbreviated to Kuan tzŭ tsai 觀自在, was introduced by Hsüan Tsang 玄奘, the traveller, from the Sanskrit Avalokitesvara, in place of the older one translated by Kumarajiva (*q.v.*) from the shorter Hindu name Avalokites. The names Kuang shih yin 光世音, sound of the world of light, and Kuan yin 觀尹,

onlooking controller, are also used. Another style is Kao Wang 高王, the august monarch, and Pai-i Ta-shih 白衣大士, white-robed great scholar. Under the latter designation she is represented with a baby on her arm and is worshipped by people desiring progeny. She is also styled Bodhisattva and Abhayam-dada. It is incorrect to say that there was a Chinese divinity of the name Kuan Yin 觀音 (Avalokitesvara) before the intro-duction of the Mahayana into China. But this is disputed by Edkins (pp. 414-5).

Kuan Yin 觀音 is the captain of the Bark of Salvation, Tz'ŭ-hang 慈航, the boat which ferries the soul of man across the sea of life and death to its final rest in the Pure Land, Ching-t'u 淨土, or Lo-t'u 樂土.

According to the Chinese legend, Kuan Yin 觀音 was the third daughter of Miao Chuang Wang 妙莊王 (v. S'ubhav-yuha), a ruler of a northern kingdom identified with Chuang Wang 莊王 (696-681 B.C.) of the Chou 周 dynasty. Determined to devote herself to the religious life, she absolutely refused to be married, in spite of the commands of her parents and the entreaties of her sisters, friends, attendants, etc. At length, she obtained her father's permission to enter the Nunnery of the White Bird in Lung-shu Hsien 龍舒縣. Here, by her father's orders she was put to degrading duties, but without the effect of turning her from her purpose. Her father ordered her to be executed with the sword, but the sword was broken into 1,000 pieces without hurting her. He then ordered her to be stifled, when her soul left the body and went down to hell, but hell forthwith changed into paradise. To save his hell, Yama sent her back to life, whereupon she was miraculously transported, on a lotus flower, to the island of P'ootoo (P'u-t'o 普陀, Potala, or P'u-t'o-lo-ka 普陀洛伽), near Ningpo, where she lived for nine years healing disease and saving mariners from shipwreck. Her father having fallen ill, she cut the flesh off her arms and made it into a medicine which saved his life. To show his gratitude, he ordered a statue to be erected in her honour, saying Ch'üan shou ch'üan yen 全手全眼 "with completely formed (ch'üan 全), arms and eyes, but the sculptor misunderstood the order for Ch'ien shou ch'ien yen 千手千眼, "with a thousand (ch'ien 千) arms and eyes," whence it happened that a statue with a thousand eyes and a thousand arms perpetuated her memory, and she was thenceforth known and revered as Ch'ien shou ch'ien yen ta tz'ŭ ta pei Kuan Yin P'u-sa 千手千眼大慈大悲觀音菩薩 "the Bodhisattva Kwan-yin 觀音 who has a thousand arms and a thousand eyes, great in mercy and great in compassion." (For details of the myth, see Werner, Myths and Legends, pp. 251-87).

Kuan Yin 觀音 is one of the deities worshipped by merchants in general.

Kuan Yin 觀音 (Avalokitesvara) is also "(1) An Indian male divinity, unknown to Southern Buddhism, perhaps an ancient local deity of Southern India, adopted by the followers of the Mahayana School in India (especially in Magadha) and highly revered, from the third to the seventh centuries, in conjunction with Mandjusri, as a Bodhisattva who, from of old, appeared on earth in a variety of places (but especially at Potala) and under numerous forms (but always as male), saving for instance Simhala from shipwreck and generally acting as a sort of Saviour of the faithful, and bearing some similarities to Vishnu. (2) The first male ancestor (Brasrinpo) of the Tibetan nation, the principal tutelary deity of Tibet, adopted by Tibetan Buddhism under the name Padmapani (*i.e.* lotus bearer or lotus-born) as an incarnation of Avalokitesvara, and highly revered, in conjunction with Mandjusri (the representative of creative wisdom, corresponding with Brahma) and Vadjrapani (the representative of divine power, corresponding with Indra), as the representative of compassionate Providence (corresponding partly with Shiva), the controller of metempsychosis and special head of the present Buddhist church. The six mystic syllables *om mani padme hum* are specially used to invoke this male deity, who is often represented with eleven heads (in three tiers) and eight hands, and with the Shivaitic necklace of skulls. He is supposed to have appeared on earth in various incarnations as the spiritual mentor of all believers, and especially to have been incarnate in the King of Tibet called Srong-tsan-gam-bo and in every successive Dalai Lama. The Tantra School of Tibet declared this Tibetan deity to be the Dhyani Bodhisattva (spiritual reflex in the world of forms, produced by contemplation) of Amitabha Buddha. His special sanctuary is on Mount Potala in Lhassa" (Eitel, pp. 23-24).— See also *Lo-han* 羅漢 and *P'u-t'o* 普陀.

KUAN-YIN P'U-SA 觀音菩薩.—See *Kuan Yin* 觀音.

KUAN YING 灌嬰.—A celebrated *ch'êng-huang* 城隍, or city-god (of Sui-yang 睢陽, modern Shang-ch'iu Hsien 商邱縣, Anhui 安徽). Han 漢 dynasty.

KUAN YÜ 關羽.—Also called Kuan Kung 關公, Kuan Ti 關帝, and Wu Ti 武帝. The Chinese God of War. Born in modern Shansi 山西 in A.D. 162, at Chieh-liang 解梁 (afterwards Chieh Chou 解州, now Chieh Hsien 解縣). His personal name Chang Shêng 長生 he later on changed to Shou Chang 壽長 and assumed also that of Yün Chang 雲長. Is also known as Kuan 關 of the Yü 羽 family, as well as by some seven other appellations. Period of the San Kuo 三國: Han 漢.

At first, a seller of bean-curd. Later devoted himself to study. When a youth, after breaking out of a room in which he had been shut up as a punishment by his parents, he killed a magistrate who wished forcibly to make a concubine of the daughter of an aged couple, and fleeing through T'ung Kuan 潼關, the pass to Shensi

陝 西, saw from his reflexion in a brook, that his face had become so changed that he was absolutely unrecognizable. For this reason, and by informing the barrier officials that his name was Kuan 關 (the name by which he was thereafter known), he made good his escape.

One day, after arriving at Cho Chou 涿 州, in Chihli 直 隸, he had a fight with a butcher Chang Fei 張 飛 (othewise known as Chang I-tê 張 翼 德), after lifting a heavy stone the latter had placed over a well, in which he had deposited his meat, and challenged anyone to remove. They were separated by a seller of straw shoes named Liu Pei 劉 備 (otherwise known as Liu Yüan-tê 劉 玄 德), and the three soon became firm friends (A.D. 191).

Either in this way, or as a result (according to another account) of the three meeting in a village inn to drink wine, the famous "Oath in the Peach-orchard" was taken by them, binding them to protect each other and live and die together. (For details of the exploits of these three "Brothers of the Peach Orchard" see *San Kuo chih yen i* 三 國 志 演 義, "The Story of the Three Kingdoms.")

Kuan Yü 關 羽 remained faithful to his oath, even though tempted with a marquisate by Ts'ao Ts'ao 曹 操 (*q.v.*), but he was at length (A.D. 220) captured by Sun Ch'üan 孫 權, a general who rebelled against Ts'ao Ts'ao 曹 操, and put to death.

"Long celebrated as the most renowned of China's military heroes, he was ennobled in A.D. 1120 as Faithful and Loyal Duke. Eight years later he had conferred on him by letters patent the still more glorious title of Magnificent Prince and Pacificator. The Emperor Wên 文 (A.D. 1330-3) of the Yüan 元 dynasty added the appellation Warrior Prince and Civilizer, and, finally, the Emperor Shên Tsung 神 宗 (Wan Li 萬 歷) (A.D. 1573-1620) of the Ming 明 dynasty, in 1594, conferred on him the title of Faithful and Loyal Great *Ti* 帝, Supporter of Heaven and Protector of the Kingdom. He thus became a god, and has ever since received worship as Kuan Ti 關 帝, or Wu Ti 武 帝, the God of War. Temples (1600 State temples and thousands of smaller ones) erected in his honour are to be seen in all parts of the country. He is one of the most popular gods of China. During the last half century of the Manchu Period his fame greatly increased. In 1856 he is said to have appeared in the heavens and successfully turned the tide of battle in favour of the Imperialists, for which service the Emperor Hsien Fêng 咸 豐 (A.D. 1851-62) raised him to the same rank as that accorded to Confucius. His portrait used to hang in every tent, and is still largely used by soldiers as a talisman, but his worship is not confined to the officials and the army, for many trades and professions including the bean-curd (*tou-fu* 荳 腐) sellers have elected him as a patron saint.

"The sword of the public executioner used to be kept within the precincts of his temple, and after an execution the presiding magistrate would stop there to worship for fear the ghost of the criminal might follow him home. He knew that the spirit would not dare to enter Kuan Ti's 關 帝 presence" (Werner, *Myths and Legends of China*, pp. 117-8).

Kuan Yü's 關 羽 family was exterminated by the son, P'ang Hui 龐 惠, of P'ang Tê 龐 德 (whom Kuan Yü 關 羽 had put to death) when he invaded and completed the conquest of Ssŭch'uan 四 川.

The Emperor Hou Ti 後 帝 (A.D. 223-63) bestowed on Kuan Yü 關 羽 the title of Brave and Faithful Marquis, Chuang-miu Hou 壯 繆 侯 (A.D. 260). After this he received various other titles, until he became a *ti* 帝, as noted above (see also Mayers, pp. 92-3).

The God of War is also patron deity of literature, being worshipped by the literati because he was traditionally credited with the ability to repeat the *Ch'un ch'iu Tso chuan* 春 秋 左 傳, "Tso's Commentary on the Annals," from beginning to end. In the images worshipped by the literati he holds this work in his right hand, and is attended by his adopted son, Kuan-p'ing 關 平, who stands on his right and holds an academic head-dress to would-be candidates. But, according to Johnston, if his "reputation as a patron of literature" rests on a "rather slender foundation," his "claims to be regarded as a good Buddhist" are still slighter. Generally, he is worshipped as a god of War, of Literature, or of Riches according to the locality and special needs of the worshipper. Sacrifices are offered to him on the fifteenth day of the second moon and the thirteenth day of the fifth moon. His temple is named Wu-shêng Miao 武 聖 廟.

In 1916, during the Presidency of Yüan Shih-k'ai 袁 世 凱, it was decreed that official worship should be rendered to Kuan Kung 關 公 and Yo Fei 岳 飛. Accordingly the civil and military authorities of T'ai-hsing Hsien 泰 興 縣, Kiangsu 江 蘇, in consultation with the Board of Education, changed the arrangement of the temple of Kuan Kung 關 公 as follows:

The image of Kuan Ti 關 帝 remained on the principal altar, and in front of it was placed a tablet inscribed: *Kuan Chuang-mu Hou Shên-wei* 關 壯 穆 侯 神 位, Spirit Tablet of the imposingly strong Marquis Kuan. Next to it is either the image or (in its absence) the tablet of Yo Fei 岳 飛. The latter is inscribed: *Yo-chung Wu-wang Shên-wei* 岳 忠 武 王 神 位, Spirit Tablet of the Loyal Military King Yo.

On the central altar are seated Kuan Kung 關 公 and his associate Yo Fei 岳 飛. On each side of the hall, on two glazed stands, are placed the tablets of twenty-four Chinese officers who had rendered signal service to their country. Their names are:

The twelve assessors on the East: 1. Ch'i Chi-kuang 戚 繼 光. 2. Hsü Ta 徐 達. 3. Han Shih-chung 韓 世 忠. 4. Kuo Tzŭ-i 郭 子 儀. 5. Li Ching 李 靖. 6. Wang Chün 王 濬. 7. Chang Fei 張 飛. 8. Han Ch'in-hu 韓 擒 虎. 9. Su Ting-fang 蘇 定 方.

10. Ts'ao Pin 曹彬. 11. Hsü Lieh-wu 旭烈兀. 12. Fêng Shêng 馮勝.

The twelve assessors on the West: 1. Lan Yü 藍玉. 2. Kuo K'an 郭侃. 3. Ti Ch'ing 狄青. 4. Li Kuang-pi 李光弼. 5. Ho Jo-pi 賀若弼. 6. Chao Yün 趙雲. 7. Hsieh Hsüan 謝玄. 8. Wei-ch'ih Ching-tê 尉遲敬德. 9. Wang Yen-chang 王彥章. 10. Liu I 劉錡. 11. Ch'ang Yü-ch'un 常遇春. 12. Chou Yü-chi 周遇吉.

For biographies of these twenty-four assessors, see *Doré*, XII, 1168-78.—See also *Huai-nan Tzǔ* 淮南子 and *Chiao Kuan* 廖管.

KUANG CH'ÊNG-TZǓ 廣成子.—One of the first to appear on the Register of Immortals. He lived in a cave on K'ung-t'ung Shan 崆峒山; Mount K'ung-t'ung 崆峒, in Kansu 甘肅. Taught the Emperor Huang Ti 黃帝 (2698-2598 B.C.) the secret of immortality. Said to have been an incarnation of Lao Tzǔ 老子.— See *Chiang Tzǔ-ya* 姜子牙.

KUANG-HSIU TSUN-CHÊ 廣修尊者.—A deified Buddhist monk. Ranked tenth in Buddhist School, X (*q.v.*). Family name Liu 留. A native of Hsia-p'i 下邳, in Tung-yang 東陽, Chêkiang 浙江. An enthusiastic student of the *Fa-hua ching* 法華經. Ably explained the meaning of the *Chih-kuan* 止觀, Perfected Observation (see *Chan-jan Tsun-chê* 湛然尊者), to Wei Hêng 韋珩, an official of T'ien-t'ai 天台. Died A.D. 843. Buried in the Chin-ti Tao-ch'ang 金地道場 Monastery. Later on, when his corpse was cremated by his disciple Liang-hsü 良諝, a thousand precious relics, *shê-li* 舍利 (Sanskrit, *sariras*), fell from the heavens. A tower was erected over his tomb, and the relics placed within it.

KUANG JUN LUNG-WANG TA-TI 廣潤龍王大帝.—See *Shui Fu* 水府, B (3) and C (2) (a).

KUANG LI LUNG-WANG TA-TI· 廣利龍王大帝.—See *Shui Fu* 水府, B (2) and C (2) (a).

KUANG MU 廣目.—"Bright Eyes." An incarnation of Ti-tsang Wang 地藏王 (*q.v.*).—See also *Ssǔ ta T'ien-wang* 四大天王.

KUANG SHIH YIN 光世音.—See *Kuan Yin* 觀音.

KUANG-SHOU LAO-JEN 廣壽老人.—See *Huo Pu* 火部.

KUANG-TÊ LUNG-WANG TA TI 廣德龍王大帝.—See *Shui Fu* 水府, B (1) and C (2) (a).

KUANG TSÊ LUNG-WANG TA TI 廣澤龍王大帝.—See *Shui Fu* 水府, B (4) and C (2) (a).

KUANG-TSU CH'AN-SHIH 光祚禪師 (42nd generation). —A deified Buddhist monk. Ranked twentieth in Buddhist School, VI (q.v.). After having lived at Pei-ta 北塔, North Tower, he started a school, and taught at Chih-mên 智門, Kuangsi 廣西.

KUANG YÜAN 廣源.—See *Shui Fu* 水府, D (1).

K'UANG-FOU HSIEN-SHÊNG 匡阜先生.—See [*Lu-shan*] *K'uang fou Hsien-shêng* [盧山] 匡阜先生.

K'UANG YÜ 匡玉.—The god of the star Ti-ch'üan 地全. —See *Ti-sha* 地煞.

KUEI 隗.—See *Tsao Chün* 灶(竈)君.

KUEI 鬼.—The *kuei* 鬼, as Wieger has shown, are the "dependants" on the living. An idea derived from that of the original second self. The deceased The deceased depend on their former relatives for the maintenance, by offerings and libations, of their after-life existence. The deceased who are not *shên* 神 (q.v.), genii. Spirits, ghosts, devils, goblins, thieves if not fed. Popularly depicted as skeletons in all but the features, which are hideous and repulsive. They were not at first regarded as evil, though they came to be so regarded later on. Are either clothed or unclothed. Are *yin* 陰 and lurk in dark corners. Their bodies throw no shadows. They have no resting places in the abodes either of mankind or of the happier immortals, being denied alike metempsychosis and eternal bliss. Eventually, they die; they are liable to quicker death than the *shên* 神 (q.v.). A dead *kuei* 鬼 becomes a *chi* 鷺, a dead devil. Though *kuei* 鬼 are bad, they are in some cases of a good disposition. But practically all are malicious demons, constantly seeking to deceive and harm. They have nothing to fear from man (though, as compared with man, they are regarded as only three-tenths brave), and are the authors of plague, famine, and pestilence. They enter into human bodies, causing sickness, insanity and death. They are the instruments of the gods in governing the universe and punishing the evil doer. The *kuei* 鬼 of those who have been killed and are seeking revenge are called *yüan-kuei* 冤鬼, and also *ch'ang* 倀. Special methods of counteracting the *kuei's* 鬼 evil actions are adopted, such as building screens behind doors, and high walls in front of the main entrance or around the home (since *kuei* 鬼 can only travel in a straight line), or by placing *shih kan-tang* 石敢當 (q.v.) at inauspicious places. Study of the old Classics also has a countervailing effect. The rich are less liable than the poor to be injured by them.—See also *Prêtas, Yama* and *Werner, The Chinese Idea of the Second Self.*

KUEI 魁, THE GOD OF THE CONSTELLATION.—See
Wang Pa 王霸 and *Chao Pai-kao* 趙白高.

KUEI-CH'ÊN CH'AN-SHIH 桂琛禪師 (41st generation).—
A deified Buddhist monk. Ranked eighteenth in Buddhist School,
VI (*q.v.*). Family name Li 李. A native of Ch'ang Shan 常山,
Chêkiang 浙江. Taught by Shih-k'ou Ch'an-shih 師備禪師 (*q.v.*).
Opened his own school in the Ti-tsang Yüan 地藏院, Ti-tsang
Monastery, where he died A.D. 928. Posthumous title: Chên-ying
Ch'an-shih 眞應禪師, True and Right Monk.

KUEI-CHI FA-SHIH 窺基法師.—A deified Buddhist monk.
Ranked second in Buddhist School, XIV (*q.v.*). The third
founder of the school. Family name Wei-ch'ih 尉遲. A native
of Tai-chün 代郡, Honan 河南. Father's name Ching Tsung
敬宗. His uncle, Ching Tê 敬德, was President of the Board
of Rites. Studied under, and translated Hindu books with T'ang
Sêng 唐僧 (see *Buddhist School,* XIV and *Sun Hou-tzǔ* 猻猴子).
Rendered 100 volumes into Chinese. Ostentatious and proud.
When travelling, transported his books and utensils in three
waggons; hence his nickname, San-ch'ê Fa-shih 三車法師,
Three-waggon Teacher. Heavenly genii brought him his food.
Died A.D. 682.

KUEI HSIEN 鬼仙.—Disembodied Spirits, having no resting
place in the abodes either of mankind or of the happier immortals,
denied alike metempsychosis and eternal bliss (Mayers).—See
Kuei 鬼 and *Shên* 神.

KUEI-KU TZǓ 鬼谷子—A demi-god. Studied under T'ai-i
Huang-jên 泰壹皇人 at O-mei Shan 峨眉山, Mount O-mei 峨眉.
A member of the commission appointed by Huang-ti 黃帝 (*q.v.*)
to continue and complete the labours of Shên Nung 神農 on
natural history and the medicinal properties of plants. The
Emperor appointed him Second Preceptor of the Empire. His
work was to study the transformations of the *yin* 陰 and the *yang*
陽. He wrote some works on the sources of life, the viscera, etc.
He was reincarnated several times (*cf.* next entry).—See *T'ien
I-yüan* 天醫院.

KUEI-KU TZǓ 鬼谷子.—A God of Fortune-tellers. The name
(meaning the "Sage of Devils' Valley" or "Master of the Valley
of the Dead") given to Wang-hsü 王栩 from Kuei-ku Shan
鬼谷山, where he lived. This was in the time of Prince P'ing
平, duke of Chin 晉 (557-531 B.C.), though he is said to have had
several incarnations at different periods. His career is usually
assigned to the fourth century B.C.

He is also a God of Spectacle-sellers. Most fortune-tellers in
China being blind or half-blind, they are in need of spectacles.

It is said that this is why Kuei Ku-tzŭ 鬼谷子 was chosen as the patron deity. Others say that he invented spectacles because he had defective eyes. (The instrument, however, came from Arabia in the thirteenth century A.D.).

A man of many parts, he excelled especially in divination, always correctly foretelling the future. Kuei-ku Tzŭ 鬼谷子 has in modern times become a synonym for skill in divination. He had many disciples. When they left him he passed to the "Kingdom of the Immortals beyond the sea."

The Taoist claim him as one of their patriarchs, and he is even said to have received his principles direct from Lao Tzŭ 老子. Wieger describes him as a "faithless and shameless Taoist politician, who taught the most brazen-faced opportunism," and as being "the master of all the legists for hire, who ruined the feudal princes and prepared the way for the one and absolute empire of the Ch'in 秦"—See also *Hsüan Yüan Huang-ti* 軒轅黄帝.

KUEI-LING SHÊNG-MU 龜靈聖母.—The Transcendent Saintly Mother Tortoise Studied the perfect life with T'ung-t'ien Chiao-chu 通天教主, whom she regarded as her master, and followed during his military adventures.—See *Amida* (*Chieh-yin* 接引).

KUEI T'IEN-LU 桂天祿.—See *Ou-yang T'ien-lu* 歐陽天祿.

K'UEI 奎, THE GOD OF THE CONSTELLATION.—See *Ma Wu* 馬武 and *Li Hsiung* 李雄.

K'UEI HSING 魁星.—See *Wên Ch'ang* 文昌.

KUMARAJIVA.—*c.* A.D. 405. "Carried as a prisoner to China (A.D. 383), where he was styled 'one of the four suns of Buddhism,' introduced a new alphabet, and translated some fifty works" (Eitel, p. 79). A foremost Indian educator of the age of Vikramadityan Renaissance, who "carried forward the missionizing activity of Emperor Asoka the Great (begun with Western Asia and beyond) by bearing the torch of Hindu Thought to the Far Eastern Cathay and thus became instrumental in the establishment of Indian hegemony throughout the Orient." —See *Lo-han* 羅漢 and *Chiu-mo-lo-shih Ch'an-shih* 鳩摩羅什 禪師 and Edkins, pp. 89-90.

KUMARAS.—Mind-born sons of Brahma, who, declining to create progeny, remained ever boys and ever pure and innocent.

KUMARAYANA.—See *Chiu-mo-lo-yen* 鳩摩羅炎.

KUNDADHANA.—See *Lo-han* 羅漢.

K'UN LUN 崑崙.—The two chief Taoist paradises are P'êng-lai Shan 蓬萊山 (q.v.) and K'un-lun Shan 崑崙山. The former is placed off the east coast of Shantung 山東, the latter in the extreme west of China. The Tortoise Mountain, Kuei Shan 龜山, on which is situated Hsi Na 西那, the capital, is ten thousand *li* 里 in circumference and eleven thousand *li* 里 in height. It is thought by the Chinese to be the source of the Yellow River. At the foot of this mountain is the famous Lake of Gems, on whose shores grows the tree of the Old Age Peach, or Peach giving Immortality, the Tree of Pearls, and the Jadestone Tree. To eat the fruits of these trees is said to ensure immortal life. In the K'un-lun 崑崙 country there is perpetual leisure and happiness. Its ruler is Hsi Wang-mu 西王母 (q.v.), the Royal Mother of the West. She alone has the right to bestow the immortality-giving peach. Once in every six thousand years the peaches ripen, and to celebrate the event she has a festival, to which she invites those privileged to attend, both gods and mortals. The land is peopled only by immortals, who with perfected bodies continually live the life of ease and pleasure.

Hsi Wang-mu 西王母 is also called "the Gold Mother of the Nine Spirit Wonderful Tortoise Mountain, Chiu-ling T'ai-miao Kuei Shan Chin Mu 九靈太妙龜山金母, or simply Chin Mu 金母, the Gold Mother, because the west belongs to gold. The Paradise in the East is ruled by her husband, Tung Wang-kung 東王公 (q.v.) who, belonging to the east is called Mu Kung 木公, King of Wood. This land is famous for its mulberries, whose fruit gives immortality.

The property of the peaches bestowed by Hsi Wang-mu 西王母 led to the apotheosis of Hou I's 后羿 wife (see *Ch'ang O* 嫦娥). The Peach Blossom Festival is on Hsi Wang-mu's 西王母 birthday, which thus comes once in six thousand years (the time it takes for the peaches to mature). Consequently peaches are presented as birthday gifts. It was at one of these festivals that Sun Wu-k'ung 孫悟空 stole and ate several of the peaches (see *Sun Hou-tzŭ* 孫猴子).

KUNG CH'IEN 龔倩.—The god of the star Ti-yao 地妖. —See *Ti-sha* 地煞.

KUNG CH'ING 龔清.—The god of the star T'ien-wei 天微. —See *T'ien-kang* 天罡.

KUNG KUNG 共工.—"The first rebel." Toward the end of Nü Wa's 女媧 reign there was among the feudatory princes Kung Kung 共工, whose functions were the administration of punishment. Violent and ambitious, he became a rebel, and sought by the influence of water to overcome that of wood (under which Nü Wa 女媧 reigned). He did battle with Chu Jung 帆融 (see *Huo Pu* 火部), but was not victorious; whereupon he struck his head against the Imperfect Mountain, Pu-chou Shan 不周山, and brought it down. The pillars of Heaven were broken and corners of the earth gave way. Hereupon Nü Wa 女媧 melted stones of the five colours to repair the heavens, and cut off the feet of the tortoise to set upright the four extremities of the earth. Gathering the ashes of reeds she stopped the flooding waters, and thus rescued the land of Chi 冀, Chi Chou 冀州, the early seat of the Chinese sovereignty.

KUNG-KUNG CHIH TZŬ 共工之子.—See *Hou T'u* 后土.

KUNG SHU-TZŬ 公輸子.—See *Lu Pan* 魯班.

KUNG-SUN TO 公孫鐸.—The god of the star Jên-sha 刃殺. A subaltern of Ou-yang Shun 歐陽淳, at Lin-t'ung Kuan 臨潼關, during the Yin-Chou 殷周 wars.

K'UNG CH'ÊNG 孔成.—The god of the star Ti-sui 地邃. —See *Ti-shu* 地朮.

K'UNG-FU TZŬ 孔夫子.—Confucius. Though Confucius is not a Chinese god (Werner, *Autumn Leaves,* p. 247-8), he occupied a quasi-divine position in various periods of Chinese history. His exaltation and degradation in the minds of the Chinese people coincided with the attitude adopted by successive Emperors with regard to his politico-ethical philosophy and to the religions of Buddhism and Taoism. Of these barometrical changes, those having a religious or mythological bearing may be studied in the numerous standard works on Confucius and his doctrines. Noting merely that the name and fame of Confucius owe their immortality to the Burning of the Books in 213 B.C., we find the Emperor Kao Tsu 高祖 (206-194 B.C.) of the Han 漢 dynasty, who had previously insulted the Scholar class (*ju* 儒), offering the *t'ai-lao* 太牢 sacrifice (an ox, a pig, and a goat) to Confucius at Ch'ü-fou Hsien 曲阜縣, Shantung 山東, in 195 B.C. After this titles (of Duke, Emperor, Saint), with the honour of proscription of name in writing, sacrifices, and temples, were conferred on, offered, or erected to him—or taken away from him, or abolished—periodically (the honouring being more frequent than the degrading); images of him were replaced by tablets in A.D. 1382; until, in 1917, the citizens of the Chinese Republic were granted the liberty of honouring Confucius or of following any other religious belief.

The events of the birth and life of Confucius are too well known to need repetition in this work. Students are referred for them to the standard treatises.—See also *San Shêng* 三聖.

K'UNG HSIEN 空閒.—See *Ear, The Gods of the.*

K'UNG HSÜAN 孔玄.—The One-eyed Peacock. During the Yin-Chou 殷周 wars, Chun T'i 準提, a Taoist of the Western Paradise, appeared on the scene when the armies of the rival dynasties were facing each other. K'ung Hsuan 孔玄 was gallantly holding the Chin-chi Ling 金鷄嶺 Pass; Chiang Tzǔ-ya 姜子牙 was trying to take it by assault—so far without success.

Chun T'i's 準提 mission was to take K'ung Hsüan 孔玄 to the abode of the blest, with the object of breaking down the invincible resistance of this powerful enemy and at the same time of rewarding his brilliant talents.

But K'ung Hsüan 孔玄 did not approve of this plan, and a fight took place between the two champions. At one moment Chun T'i 準提 was seized by a luminous bow and carried into the air, but while enveloped in a cloud of fire he appeared with eighteen arms and twenty-four heads, holding in each hand a powerful talisman.

He put a silk cord round K'ung Hsüan's 孔玄 neck, touched him with his wand, and forced him to reassume his original form of a red one-eyed peacock. Chun T'i 準提 seated himself on the peacock's back, and it flew across the sky, bearing its saviour and master to the Western Paradise. Brilliantly variegated clouds marked its track through space.

K'UNG TAO-LING 孔道靈.—The god of the star Ti-nu 地奴.—See *Ti-sha* 地煞.

K'UNG T'IEN-CHAO 孔天兆.—The god of the star Ti-chi 地羇.—See *Ti-sha* 地煞.

KUO CH'ÊN 郭宸.—See *Wu Tou* 五斗.

KUO CHI 郭己.—The god of the star Ti-ling 地靈.—See *Ti-sha* 地煞.

KUO K'AN 郭侃.—An assessor of Kuan Kung 關公.—See *Kuan Yü* 關羽.

KUO-PA-KA.—See *Lo-han* 羅漢.

KUO TZǓ-I 郭子儀.—Worshipped in modern times as the Spirit or God of Happiness (see *Fu Shên* 福神). Born A.D. 697, in the reign of the usurping Empress Wu Hou 武后 (A.D. 684-705) of the T'ang 唐 dynasty, at Hua-chou 華州, in Shensi 陝西. One of the greatest figures of Chinese history, being the saviour of the T'ang 唐 dynasty from the depredations of the Turfans in the reign of the Emperor Hsüan Tsung 玄宗 (A.D. 713-56). Died A.D. 781. He is frequently represented in Chinese pictures clothed in blue official robes leading his small son (the eldest of eight) Kuo-ai 郭曖 to Court (*Kuo Tzǔ-i shang ch'ao* 郭子儀上朝).

In recognition of his father's services, the Emperor Tai Tsung 代宗 (A.D. 763-80) gave to the son one of his daughters in marriage and decreed that after his (the Emperor's) death Kuo-tzŭ-i 郭子儀 (who was distinguished for his great uprightness and unswerving devotion) should become Governor of the Empire. He is praised in the famous Nestorian monument inscription at Hsi-an Fu 西安府, but the conclusion that he had become a Christian is without foundation in fact.

The common saying, seen on pictures, etc., *Kuo tzŭ-i tso-shou* 郭子儀做壽, "Kuo Tzŭ-i celebrates the anniversary of his birth," had its origin in the following legend:—On the night of the seventh moon Kuo Tzŭ-i 郭子儀 was awakened by a bright light and found a very beautiful lady sitting on his bed. He saluted her respectfully and said: "To-day is the seventh day of the seventh moon—you must be the goddess Chih Nü 織女 [*q.v.*]; I beg you to grant me happiness and riches." The goddess replied: "You are the Spirit of Heaven, long life and all kinds of riches and dignities await you."

The Emperor Tai Tsung 代宗 (A.D. 763-80) in A.D. 762 granted him the honorary title of Fen jung Wang 汾陽王, and the Emperor Tê Tsung 德宗 (A.D. 780-805) that of Shang Fu 尚父, Father of the Realm. His posthumous title is Chung-Wu 忠武, Loyal Militarist. He is an assessor of Kuan Ti 關帝 (see *Kuan Yü* 關羽).—See also *Wu Tou* 五斗.

KUVERA.—The Buddhist God of Wealth. Represented as a stout personage, bearing an ingot in his hand. A treasure-box is shown at his feet.

In the *Vedas,* a chief of the evil beings or spirits living in the shades: a sort of Pluto, and called by his patronymic Vaisravana. Later he is Pluto in another sense, as god of wealth and chief of the Yakshas and Guhyakas.—See *Vaisramana.*

KUVALAYA.—See *Lo-han* 羅漢.

L

LADY EMPRESS OF HEAVEN, THE.—See *T'ien Fei* 天妃.

LADY WITH THE HORSE'S HEAD, THE.—See *Ts'an Nü* 蠶女.

LADY (OR MISS) OF THE LATRINE, THE THIRD.—See *Tzŭ-ku Shên* 紫姑神.

LADIES, THE SEVEN YOUNG.—See *Ch'i Ku-tzŭ* 七姑子.

LAI CHO 來啜.—A Guardian of Harvests. The *Li chi* 禮記 mentions *Yu piao cho* 郵表啜, Guardians of Harvests.—See *Pa cha* 八蜡.

LAKES, THE SPIRIT OF THE DRIED-UP.—See *Shui Fu* 水府, D (2) (e).

LAKES, THE SPIRIT OF THE TSÊ 澤.—See *Shui Fu* 水府, D (2) (d).

LAMP, THE GOD OF THE. — Name Ma Chün 馬君. Chiang T'ai-kung 姜太公 "tried to kill him, but three strokes of the executioner's axe did no harm. He tried to burn him, but Ma Chün 馬君 fled on the wings of the flame. He borrowed a mirror from the hobgoblins, and it was seen that he was made of fire. The lamp for one thousand years did not go out, so he became a man (Du Bose, pp. 328-9). Têng-kuan P'u-sa 燈官菩薩 is also a lamp-god.

LAN HU 藍虎.—The god of the star Ti-chio 地角.—See *Ti-sha* 地煞.

238

LAN-KAN 欄杆, THE GOD OF THE STAR.—See *Lung An-chi* 龍安吉.

LAN TS'AI-HO 藍采和.—See *Pa Hsien* 八仙.

LAN-TS'AN CH'AN-SHIH 懶殘禪師.—The Lazy Gluttonous Monk. Lived toward the end of the reign of Hsüan Tsung 玄宗 (A.D. 713-56) of the T'ang 唐 dynasty. The same as Shên-tsan Ch'an-shih 神讚禪師, the fourteenth Arhat (*q.v.*). His real name in religion was Ming-tsan 明瓚, "Bright Libation-cup." He was at first a menial in the Hêng-yo Ssŭ 衡嶽寺, Hêng-yo Monastery, dedicated to the God of the Southern Peak, in Hunan 湖南. (He was nicknamed Lan-ts'an 懶殘, "Lazy Glutton," because he devoured what the monks left from their meals. The second character of his name, *tsan* 瓚, a libation-cup, was changed to ts'an 殘, leavings, and *lan* 懶, lazy prefixed.)

During twenty years, he slept by night in the monastery cattle-pen. At midnight, he was in the habit of chanting his prayers, and after a while his sonorous voice, echoing in the mountain gorges, attracted the attention of the scholar Li Pi 李泌 (A.D. 722-89), who went to see him. The monk at first suspected him and received him rudely, but soon changed his manner, offered him half of a sweet potato he was eating, and told him as a secret that he, Li-pi 李泌, would be Prime Minister of the State for ten years. This prophecy was subsequently fulfilled to the letter.

Lan-ts'an's 懶殘 transcendental powers were manifested on several occasions, *e.g.* when, by merely touching it with his foot, he moved a huge rock which obstructed the road leading to the monastery, and which hundreds of workmen and ten oxen had failed to dislodge; and later, when he had decided to leave the monastery, the forest immediately became infested with numerous tigers, leopards, and other wild animals, and he jumped on the back of a tiger, and disappeared. (Riding on a tiger is one of the privileges of the Taoist immortals, genii, and Buddhist saints.) After that, no more wild beasts appeared on the mountain.

LAN YÜ 藍玉.—An assessor of Kuan Kung 關公.—See *Kuan Yü* 關羽.

LAND AND GRAIN, THE GOD OF THE.—See *Shê chi* 社稷.

LANG-CHI 狼籍, THE GOD OF THE STAR.—See *Han Jung* 韓榮.

LAO CHÜN 老君.—See *Lao Tzŭ* 老子.

LAO LANG 老郎.—The God of Actors. Said to be Chuang

Tsung 莊宗, of the Later T'ang (Hou T'ang 後唐) dynasty. Always represented wearing a dragon crown, and clothed in imperial robes. Actors, before dressing for a play, worship him, failure to do so being regarded as an insult. This would cause him to withdraw his patronage, and permit the demon of the one impersonated to possess the actor, and thus produce insanity. He is served in order to gain the power of appearing like the being who is imitated. No actor can succeed in his profession if he fails to worship him.

LAO TAN 老聃.—See *Lao Tzŭ* 老子.

LAO T'IEN YEH 老天爺.—The Old Master of Heaven. His personality is never defined. He knows everything and cannot be deceived. He takes particular care of human lives. Wronging a man always ruins him who has wronged him (Wieger).

LAO TZŬ 老子, LAO CHÜN 老君, LAO TAN 老聃, LI ÊRH 李耳.—"The Old Master" or "The Old Boy." Style Po Yang 伯陽. The term has also been rendered as "Ancient Philosopher." The God of Blacksmiths and Ironmongers. Born 604 B.C. Date and place of death unknown. Must have lived between 570-490 B.C. Is variously said to have lived 160 and 200 years, as the result of practising his doctrine of the Tao 道. Imperial archivist and first Chinese Taoist writer. He is generally said to have founded the Taoist system of philosophy, but was not its inventor, he having found it in the archives of the third ministry (the depository of the official archives), as is stated in the literary index of the Han 漢 dynasty. He was, however, the editor of the first Taoist work. Taoism itself appears to be, in its main features, a Chinese adaptation of the doctrine of the *Upanishads*.

"To account for the name of 'Old Boy,' a fantastic legend says that his mother bore him from her left side after a gestation of eighty years, and that at birth he had snowy hair and beard, and all the usual marks of advanced age. This account further says he was an incarnation of the supreme celestial being of the Taoist worship (hence the name Lao Chün 老君); and that his birth took place in 1321 B.C. Legends of many kinds have been woven round his name, though no countenance of the supernatural is found in the *Tao tê ching* 道德經 attributed to him; and the fabulous stories seem to have arisen after the arrival of Buddhism, to compete with the marvels told of Buddhist objects of worship. All that is really known about him is found in Ssŭ-ma Ch'ien's 司馬遷 *Historical Memoirs,* where we learn that he was born in 604 B.C. and was therefore an older contemporary of Confucius. His surname is said to have been Li 李, and his name was Erh 耳, ears. His native place was in the modern Honan 河南, and he was keeper of the archives at Lo Yang 洛陽, the capital of the Chou 周 dynasty, where he is said to have been visited by Confucius. The interview was not very successful, Lao Tzŭ 老子 delivering himself of certain caustic and critical remarks, and of various transcendental opinions which made the orthodox sage compare him to 'a dragon soaring above the clouds.' This story rests upon the authority of Chuang Tzŭ 莊子, and though not improbable in itself, is supposed to have been invented by the latter to turn Confucius into ridicule.

Lao Tzŭ 老子 is said to have foreseen that the Chou 周 dynasty was near its fall, and to have retired into a State beyond the western frontier, about 500 B.C. The official, Kuan Yin Tzŭ 關尹子, in charge of the Pass begged the sage for a book of his teachings, and the Tao-tê ching 道德經 was prepared and handed to him, after which Lao Tzŭ 老子 went westward and was seen no more; but in later ages, various traditions arose, such as that he went and converted the Tartars, etc.

He was canonized by Kao Tsung 高宗 (A.D. 650-84) of the T'ang 唐 dynasty, circa 666 A.D., as T'ai-shang Yüan-hsüan Huang-ti 太上元玄皇帝, The Great Supreme Emperor of the Dark First Cause. In A.D. 713, the Emperor Hsüan Tsung 玄宗 (A.D. 713-56) added T'ai-shang Lao-chün 太上老君, The Venerable Prince of the Great Supreme. By Taoists he is worshipped as the first of their Trinity. P'an Ku 盤古 and Yü-huang Shang-ti 玉皇上帝 being the others" (*Ency. Sin.*, art. *Lao Tzŭ*).—See also Wieger, *Histoire*, p. 145, *Apotheosized Philosophers*, *San Ch'ing* 三清, *T'ai Ch'ing* 太清, *Shên Pao* 神寶, *Ling-pao T'ien-tsun* 靈寶天尊, *Hsien Jên* 仙人 and *Li Lao-chün* 李老君.

LASCIVIOUSNESS, THE GOD OF.—See *P'an Chin-lien* 潘金蓮 and *Kuan Chung* 管仲.

LATRINE, THE GODDESS OF THE.—See *Tzŭ-ku Shên* 紫姑神.

LATRINE, THE THIRD LADY (OR MISS) OF THE.—See *Tzŭ-ku Shên* 紫姑神.

LATRINE, THE THREE LADIES OF THE.—See *K'êng San Ku-niang* 坑三姑娘.

LAW SECT, EYE OF THE.—See *Buddhist Schools*, IX.

LAW'S NATURE SCHOOL.—See *Buddhist Schools*, XIV.

LEATHER-WORKERS, THE GOD OF.—See *Li Lao-chün* 李老君.

LEFT KIDNEY, THE GOD OF THE.—See *Kidneys, The Gods of the.*

LEI CHÊN-TZŬ 雷震子.—One of the Sons of Thunder (see *Lei Pu* 雷部 and *Lei Kung* 雷公). Hatched from an egg after a clap of thunder and found by the soldiers of Wên Wang 文王 (1231-1135 B.C.) in some brushwood near an old tomb. Named Wên-yü 文玉. The infant's chief characteristic was its brilliant eyes. Wên Wang 文王, who already had ninety-nine children, adopted it as his hundredth, but gave it to a hermit named Yün Chung-tzŭ 雲中子 to rear as his disciple. The hermit showed him the way to rescue his adopted father from the tyrant who held him prisoner. In seeking for some powerful weapon the child found on the hillside two apricots, and ate them both. He then noticed that wings had grown on his shoulders, and was too much ashamed to return home.

But the hermit, who knew intuitively what had taken place, sent a servant to seek him. When they met the servant said: "Do you know that your face is completely altered?" The mysterious fruit had not only caused Lei Chên-tzŭ 雷震子 to grow wings, known as Wings of the Wind and Thunder, but his face had become green, his nose long and pointed, and two tusks protruded horizontally from each side of his mouth, while his eyes shone like mirrors.

Lei Chên-tzŭ 雷震子 now went and rescued Wên Wang 文王, dispersing his enemies by means of his mystical power and bringing the old man back on his shoulders. Having placed him in safety he returned to the hermit.

LEI HAI-CH'ING 雷海青.— See *Wu-tai Yüan-shuai* 五代 元帥.

LEI K'AI 雷開.—The god of the star I-ma 驛馬. A captain of the royal troops of Chou Wang 紂王. Killed in battle.

LEI K'UN 雷昆.—See *Wu Tou* 五斗.

LEI KUNG 雷公.—The Duke of Thunder. Represented as an ugly, black, bat-winged demon, with clawed feet, monkey's head, and eagle's beak, who holds in one hand a steel chisel, and in the other a spiritual hammer, with which he beats numerous drums strung about him, thus producing the terrific noise of thunder. According to Chinese reasoning it is the sound of these drums, and not the lightning, which causes death.

As regards the suggested identification of this god with the Indian divine bird Garuda, it is known that Lei Kung 雷公 already existed in China when the latter country received her first knowledge of India. Yet his modern image may well owe its wings to the Indian rain-god Vajrapani, who in one form appears with Garuda wings.

The worship of Lei Kung 雷公 seems to have been carried on regularly from about the time of the Christian era. Of the numerous legends concerning him, one relates that a certain Yeh Ch'ien-chao 葉遷韶 of Hsin-chou 信州, Ssŭch'uan 四川, when a youth, used to climb Chien-ch'ang Shan 建昌山, Mount Chien-ch'ang 建昌, for the purpose of cutting firewood and collecting medicinal herbs. One day when he had taken refuge under a tree during a rain-storm there was a loud clap of thunder, and he saw a winged being, with a blue face, large mouth, and bird's claws, caught in a cleft of the tree. This being addressed Yeh 葉 saying: "I am Lei Kung 雷公. In splitting this tree I got caught in it; if you will free me I will reward you handsomely." The woodcutter opened the cleft wider by driving in some stones as wedges, and liberated the prisoner. "Return to this spot to-morrow," said the latter, "and I will reward you." The next day the woodcutter kept the appointment, and received from Lei Kung 雷公 a book. "If you consult this work," he explained, "you will be able at will to bring thunder or rain, cure sickness, or assuage sorrow. We are five brothers, of whom I am the youngest. When you want to bring rain call one or other of my brothers; but call me only in case of pressing necessity, because I have a bad character; but I will come if it is really necessary." Having said these words, he disappeared.

Yeh Ch'ien-chao 葉遷韶, by means of the prescriptions contained in the mysterious book, could cure illnesses as easily as the sun dissipates the morning mist. One day, when he was intoxicated and had gone to bed in the temple of Chi-chou Ssŭ 吉州寺, the magistrate wished to arrest and punish him. But when he reached the steps of the *yamên* 衙門, Ch'ien-chao 遷韶 called Lei Kung 雷公 to his aid. A terrible clap of thunder immediately resounded throughout the district. The magistrate, nearly dead with fright, at once dismissed the case without punishing the culprit. The four brothers never failed to come to his aid.

By the use of his power Ch'ien-chao 遷韶 saved many regions from famine by bringing timely rain.

Another legend relates that an old woman living in Kiangsi 江西 had her arm broken through being struck by lightning, when a voice from above was heard saying: "I have made a mistake." A bottle fell out of space, and the voice again said: "Apply the contents and you will be healed at once." This being done, the old woman's arm was promptly mended. The villagers regarding the contents of the bottle as divine medicine, wished to take it away and hide it for future use, but several of them together could not lift it from the ground. Suddenly, however, it rose up and disappeared into space. Other persons in Kiangsi 江西 were also struck, and the same voice was heard to say: "Apply some grubs to the throat and they will recover." After this had been done the victims returned to consciousness, none the worse for their experience.—See also *Lei Pu* 雷部.

LEI KUNG 雷公.—A demi-god. A legendary physician.

243

Colleague of Ch'i Pai 歧 伯 (*q.v.*). A native of Nan-hao 南 好.
A member of the commission appointed by Huang Ti 黄 帝
(*q.v.*) to continue and complete the labours of Shên Nung 神 農
on natural history and the medicinal properties of plants. Diag-
nozed sicknesses by feeling the pulse. Determined the properties
of various remedies.—See *T'ien I-yüan* 天 醫 院.

LEI P'ÊNG 雷 鵬.—The god of the star Kou-ch'ên 勾 陳.
A military chief of the imperial armies, killed by Lei Chên-tzŭ
雷 震 子 at Hsi-ch'i 西 岐.

LEI PU 雷 部.—The Ministry of Thunder and Storms. The
first of the celestial Ministries. The *Fêng shên yen i* 封 神 演 義,
gives the names of twenty-four dignitaries composing it. The
principal ones are the Wu Lei-shên 五 雷 神, Five Thunder Spirits:
Lei Tsu 雷 祖, the Ancestor of Thunder (President), Lei Kung
雷 公, the Duke of Thunder, Tien Mu 電 母, the Mother of
Lightning, Fêng Po 風 伯, the Count of Wind, and Yü Shih,
雨 師, the Master of Rain (*q.q.v.*). Three correspond to the Buddhist *asuras* (*q.v.*), the "fourth class of sentient beings, mightiest
of all demons, titanic enemies of the Devas," and the Vedic
Maruta, storm-demons.

In the temples Lei Tsu 雷 祖 is placed in the centre with the
other four to right and left. In Taoist temples, besides the above,
other gods are sometimes represented, namely, three Lei Kung
雷 公 (variations or multiplications of the original): the ordinary
Lei Kung 雷 公; Chiu-t'ien Lei Kung 九 天 雷 公; Wu-fang Lei
Kung 五 方 雷 公 (*q.q.v.*); Hsin T'ien-chün 辛 天 君 and T'ao
T'ien-chün 陶 天 君, both officers of Wên Chung 閗 仲 or Lei Tsu
雷 祖; Ma Yüan-shuai 馬 元 帥 (*q.v.*); Chu T'ien-chün 朱 天 君;
Ch'ên T'ien-chün 陳 天 君; and Chêng T'ien-chün 鄭 天 君.

LEI-TSU 雷 祖.—The Ancestor of Thunder. President of the
Ministry of Thunder (see *Lei Pu* 雷 部). Has three eyes, one in
the middle of his forehead, from which, when open, a ray of light
proceeds to a distance of more than two feet. Mounted on a black
unicorn, he traverses millions of miles in the twinkling of an eye.

His origin is ascribed to a man named Wên Chung 閗 仲,
generally known as Wên Chung T'ai-shih 閗 仲 太 師, the Great
Teacher Wên Chung 閗 仲. He was a minister of the tyrant
king Chou 紂 (1154-1122 B.C.), and fought against the armies of
the Chou 周 dynasty. Being defeated, he fled to Yen Shan 燕 山,
Mount Yen, where he met Ch'ih Ching-tzŭ 赤 精 子, one of the
alleged discoverers of fire, and joined battle with him; the latter,
however, flashed his *yin-yang* 陰 陽 mirror at the unicorn, and
put it out of action. Lei Chên-tzŭ 雷 震 子, one of Wu Wang's
武 王 marshals, then struck the animal with his staff, and severed
it in twain.

Wên Chung 閗 仲 escaped in the direction of the mountains

of Chüeh-lung Ling 絕龍嶺, where another marshal, Yün Chung-tzǔ 雲中子 barred his way. Yün's 雲 hands had the power of producing lightning, and eight columns of mysterious fire suddenly came out of the earth, completely enveloping Wên Chung 聞仲. They were thirty feet high and ten feet in circumference. Ninety fiery dragons came out of each and flew away up into the air. The sky was like a furnace, and the earth shook with the awful claps of thunder. In this fiery prison Wên Chung 聞仲 died.

When the new dynasty finally proved victorious, Chiang Tzǔ-ya 姜子牙, by order of Yüan-shih T'ien-tsun 元始天尊, conferred on Wên Chung 聞仲 the supreme direction of the Ministry of Thunder, appointing him celestial prince and plenipotentiary defender of the laws governing the distribution of clouds and rain. His full title was Celestial and Highly-honoured Head of the Nine Orbits of the Heavens, Voice of the Thunder, and Regulator of the Universe. His birthday is celebrated on the twenty-fourth day of the sixth moon, when incense is burnt to him either in his temple, in shops, or in private houses. Decrees of pardon, bought in shops and countersigned by a priest, are issued in his name, as an easy means of effacing sins. A crime which incurs the penalty of being struck down by Lei Tsu 雷祖 is that of spilling grains of rice on the ground so that they are crushed under foot, because it is one of his duties to make them grow by furnishing the necessary rain. He is often mistaken for Lei Kung 雷公 (q.v.). Lei Tsu 雷祖 is the God of Seedsmen or Cornchandlers and of Innkeepers. Being able to destroy crops at will is propitiated by members of those vocations.—See also *Lei Pu* 雷部.

LI CH'ANG 李昌.—The god of the star Ti-ch'iao 地巧.—See *Ti-sha* 地煞.

LI CHI 李濟.—See *Chiu Yao* 九曜.

LI CH'I 李奇.—See *Wên Pu* 瘟部.

LI CHIN 李錦.—The god of the star Huang-ên 皇恩. An officer of the advance-guard at San-shan Kuan 三山關. Killed before Hsi-ch'i 西岐 by Nan Kung-kua 南宮适, one of Wu Wang's 武王 generals.

LI CHIN-CHA 李金吒.—See *Li No-cha* 李哪吒.

LI CHING 李靖. Li T'ien-wang 李天王, Li, the Heavenly Prince, Prime Minister of Heaven. Guardian of the Gate of Heaven. 12th century B.C. A general who fought for the Chou 周 against the last emperor of the Yin 殷 dynasty. Often referred to as T'o-t'a Li 托塔李, Li, the Pagoda-bearer, from the golden

245

pagoda presented to him by Wên-shu T'ien-tsun 文殊天尊 to ensure the permanency of Li's 李 reconciliation with his son No-cha 哪吒 after the terrific combats which had taken place between father and son on account of the disgrace brought on the family by the latter's slaying of Lung Wang 龍王, the dragon-king's, messenger (see *No-cha* 哪吒). In Buddhist temples he is represented as a richly attired figure holding in his hand a model of a pagoda. He is an assessor of Kuan Yü 關羽 (*q.v.*).

According to a Taoist travesty of the Buddhist legend, his mother gave birth to him in the shape of a ball of flesh, and he became the third son of Vajrapani, the Hindu God of Thunder. The jagged thunderbolt held in the hand of the youthful god was mistaken by Chinese painters for a pagoda.—See also *Jan-têng Fo* 燃燈佛.

"Li the Tower-bearer Heavenly King," T'o-ta Li T'ien-wang 托塔李天王, though of Taoist origin, is found nowadays in nearly all Buddhist temples. As Edkins well remarks, "oriental religions are so mutually complimentary, that they sometimes adopt each other's divinities without scruple."

LI CHUNG 李忠.—The god of the constellation Hsing 星. Alternatively with Lü Nêng 呂能.

LI 黎 (CHUNG-LI 重黎).—See *Huo Pu* 火部.

LI CHÜN 李俊.—See *Li ta T'ien-chün* 李大天君.

LI ÊRH 李耳.—See *Lao Tzŭ* 老子.

LI ÊRH-LANG 李二郎.—See *Êrh-lang* 二郎.

LI FÊNG 李封.—See *Li Yüan-shuai* 李元帥.

LI HSIEN 黎仙.—The god of the star T'ien-fu 天富.—See *T'ien-kang* 天罡.

LI HSIN 李信.—The god of the star Ti-ô 地惡.—See *Ti-sha* 地煞.

LI HSIN 李新.—The god of the star T'ien-an 天暗.—See *T'ien-kang* 天罡.

LI HSIUNG 李雄.—The god of the constellation K'uei 奎. Alternatively with Ma-wu 馬武.

LI HUNG 李弘.—The god of the constellation Niu 牛. Alternatively with Chi Tsun 祭遵.

LI KAO 李杲.—See *Shih Ming-i* 十明醫, 8.

LI KÊN 李艮.—See *Li Liang* 李良.

LI KUANG-PI 李光弼.—An assessor of Kuan Kung 關公. See *Kuan Yü* 關羽.

LI KUNG-JÊN 李公仁.—The god of the star T'ien-shang 天傷.—See *T'ien-kang* 天罡.

LI LAO-CHÜN 李老君.—The God of Farriers, Leather workers, Smelters, and Knife-grinders. Represented as the inventor of alchemy.—See *Lao Tzŭ* 老子.

LI LIANG 李良.—The god of the star Ta-huo 大禍. Real name Li Kên 李艮, the sea-spirit Yaksha, in the service of the dragon-king Ao Kuang 放光. Slain by No-cha 哪吒.

LI MU-CHA 李木吒.—See *Li No-cha* 李哪吒.

LI NO-CHA 李哪吒 (SAN T'AI-TZŬ 三太子).—The third son of Li Ching 李靖 (*q.v.*), whose wife bore him three sons, the eldest Chin-cha 金吒, the second Mu-cha 木吒, and the third No-cha 哪吒, hence generally known as San T'ai-tzŭ 三太子, the Third Prince.

No-cha 哪吒 is one of the most frequently mentioned heroes in Chinese romance; he is represented in one account as being Yü Huang's 玉皇 shield-bearer, sixty feet in height, his three heads with nine eyes crowned by a golden wheel, his eight hands each holding a golden weapon, and his mouth vomiting blue clouds. At the sound of his voice, we are told, the heavens shook and the foundations of the earth trembled. His duty was to bring into submission demons which desolated the world.

No-cha 哪吒 was born after Yin-shih 殷氏, Li-ching's 李靖 wife, dreamed one night that a Taoist priest entered her room. She indignantly exclaimed: "How dare you come into my room in this indiscreet manner?" The priest replied: "Woman, receive the child of the unicorn!" Before she could reply the Taoist priest pushed an object to her bosom.

Yin-shih 殷氏 awoke in a fright, a cold sweat all over her body. Having awakened her husband, she told him what she had dreamed. At that moment she was seized with the pains of childbirth. Li-ching 李靖 withdrew to an adjoining room, uneasy at what seemed to be inauspicious oments. A little later two servants ran to him, crying out: "Your wife has given birth to a monstrous freak!"

Li Ching 李靖 seized his sword and went into his wife's room, which he found filled with a red light exhaling a most extraordinary odour. A ball of flesh was rolling on the floor like a wheel; with a blow of his sword he cut it open, and a babe emerged, surrounded by a halo of red light. Its face was very white, a gold bracelet was on its right wrist, and it wore a pair of red silk trousers, from which proceeded rays of dazzling golden light. The bracelet was "the horizon of heaven and earth," and the two precious objects belonged to the Chin-kuang Tung 金光洞, Golden-light Cave, of T'ai-i Chên-jên 太乙眞人, the priest who had bestowed them upon him when he appeared to his mother during her sleep. The child itself was an avatar of Ling Chu-tzǔ 靈珠子, "the Intelligent Pearl."

On the morrow T'ai-i Chên-jên 太乙眞人 returned and asked Li Ching's 李靖 permission to see the new-born babe. "He shall be called No-cha 哪吒," he said, "and will become my disciple."

At seven years of age No-cha 哪吒 was already six feet in height. Absenting himself one hot day from his house, he went to bathe in a stream. His red trousers caused the waters to boil and shake the foundations of Lung Wang's 龍王 palace. An attendant, sent to ascertain the cause, found only the boy dipping a band of silk in the stream, addressed him rudely, and was about to seize him when No-cha 哪吒 hurled his gold bracelet in the air. It fell on the head of the officer, and No-cha 哪吒 left him for dead. This led to many encounters and marvellous feats between No-cha 哪吒 and Ao Ping 敖丙, the third son of Lung Wang 龍王, the Dragon-king. The latter complained to No-cha's 哪吒 father, Li Ching 李靖, and informed him that he would report his son's crimes to Yü Huang 玉皇. The parents were, however, comforted by their son, who obtained a magic formula from his master T'ai-i Chên-jên 太乙眞人, which rendered him invisible, and enabled him to fell Lung Wang 龍王 to the ground when he was about to enter the gate of Heaven. He also tore off forty scales from his body, but spared his life on his promising to renounce his intention of accusing him before Yü Huang 玉皇.

Numerous other thrilling encounters, accompanied by many wonderful transcendental feats, took place, until No-cha 哪吒, in order to save his parents, committed *hara-kiri*. His soul, on his master's advice, went to beseech his mother to build him a temple, so that he might be reincarnated. This was at length done, but the father, enraged at his son's crimes, destroyed his statue and burnt the temple to the ground. But No-cha's 哪吒 soul was now becoming spiritualized, and T'ai-i Chên-jên 太乙 眞人, from two water-lily stalks and three lotus leaves, produced a new No-cha 哪吒 sixteen feet in height, and furnished him with many magic weapons. There resulted a fierce battle between father and son, the former being saved by Wên-shu T'ien-tsun 文 殊天尊 in the guise of a priest, who imprisoned No-cha 哪吒 and after further vicissitudes, in one of which the father was provided by Wên shu T'ien-tsun 文殊天尊 with a life-preserving pagoda, a reconciliation was at length effected. Li Ching 李靖 became an Immortal, and was thereafter known as Li T'o-t'a 李托塔, Li, the Pagoda-bearer. Finally, Yü Huang 玉皇 appointed him Generalissimo of the Twenty-six Celestial Officers, Grand Marshal

of the Skies, and Guardian of the Gate of Heaven.—See also
Li-Ching 李 靖, *Chiang Tzŭ-ya* 姜 子 牙, and *Werner, Myths,*
pp. 305-19.

LI PA-PAI 李 八 百.—See *Pa Hsien* 八 仙.

LI PAO 李 豹.—The god of the star T'ien-wei 天 威.—See
T'ien-kang 天 罡.

LI PING 李 冰.—See *Kuan-k'ou Shên* 灌 口 神.

LI PING 李 丙.—The Year-god (*q.v.*).

LI P'ING 李 平.—See *Wên Pu* 瘟 部.

LI SAN-I 李 三 益.—See *Chiu Yao* 九 曜.

LI SAN-NIANG 李 三 娘.—The Patron Goddess of Millers.
The wife of Li Chih-yüan 李 知 遠 who afterwards became the
Emperor Kao Tsu 高 祖 (206-194 B.C.) of the Han 漢 dynasty.
When, as a young man, he left her to join the army she was
cruelly treated and made to turn the mill-stones round like
an animal by his elder brother's wife, who tried to drown her
newly-born child. It was, however, saved by a neighbour. Li
San-niang 李 三 娘 became empress and later was worshipped as
the patron Goddess of Millers.

LI-SHIH 力 士, THE GOD OF THE STAR.—See *Wu
Wên--hua* 鄔 文 化.

LI SUI 李 燧.—The god of the star Ti-p'i 地 闢.—See *Ti-sha*
地 煞.

LI TA T'IEN CHÜN 李 大 天 君.—See *Ch'ü-hsieh Yüan*
驅 邪 院.

LI T'AI-PO 李 太 白.—See *Ti-tsang Wang* 地 藏 王, *I Ti* 義 狄,
and *Tu K'ang* 杜 康.

LI TAO-T'UNG 李 道 通.—The god of the constellation
K'ang 亢. Alternatively with Wu Han 吳 漢.

LI T'IEH-KUAI 李 鐵 拐.—See *Pa Hsien* 八 仙.

LI T'IEN 李 欧.—See *Firecrackers, The God of.*

LI T'IEN-WANG 李 天 王.—See *Li Ching* 李 靖, *Li No-cha*
李 哪 吒, and *Chiang Tzŭ-ya* 姜 子 牙.

LI T'O-T'A 李托塔.—See *Li Ching* 李靖.

LI YO 李羅.—The god of the star Ti-mo 地魔.—See *Ti-sha* 地煞.

LI YÜAN-SHUAI 李元帥.—Born A.D. 592 at Chin-chiang K'ou 錦江口. Name Li Fêng 李封. A pirate in the Southern seas, who fled after committing a murder. Received a sword from Lung Wang's 龍王 officers, freed captured victims on a piratical junk and on another occasion jumped overboard and slew seven sea-monsters called *chiang-chu* 江豬, river-pigs (? transcendent porpoises) "as large as mountains and with tails ninety feet long," which were causing disastrous storms. A supernatural being came to thank him, and he was canonized by Yü Ti 玉帝 as Li Yüan-shuai 李元帥, Generalissimo Li, Chief of the Advance Guard, and given two marshals as his assistants.

LIANG-CHIEH CH'AN-SHIH 良价禪師 (38th generation). —A deified Buddhist monk. Ranked seventh in Buddhist School, VI (*q.v.*). Family name Yü 俞. A native of Kuei-chi 會稽, Chêkiang 浙江. Taught first by Ta-wei Ch'an-shih 大潙禪師, and then by T'an-shêng Ch'an-shih 曇晟禪師 (*q.v.*). Became proficient, and opened a school at Tung Shan 洞山, Cave Hill, in the Hsinch'ang 新昌 district, in the same province, where he taught from A.D. 847 to 860. His reputation as a teacher became universal, and spread even beyond China. One day as the bell was being tolled for prayer, he fell into a trance, and seemed almost dead. His disciples burst into tears, but recovering his senses, he begged them to perform during seven days the Buddhist ceremonies for a departing soul, *tso-chai* 做齊 (see Dore, *Recherches*, i, 143). At the end of that time, he died (A.D. 869), aged 63. Posthumous title: Wu-pên Ch'an-shih 悟本禪師, Naturally-clever Monk.

LIANG-SHUA SHIH 掠刷使.—The Grabbing Commissioner. The Gleaner of Merchants' Profits. A man named Wei Yüanfang 韋元方, a resident of Tu-ling 杜陵, Kuangtung 廣東, who had failed to pass the government examinations, met, on the way to Lung-yu 隴右, an officer in uniform, who resembled his cousin Fei P'o 斐璞 (who had died in A.D. 811) so closely that he followed him into the inn, and after assuring himself that he was not mistaken, asked him how it was that, having left this world, he was now here at the head of a body of soldiers. "I am a military officer in the Otherworld," he replied, "that is why you see me in the uniform of a military leader." "What rank are you?" asked Wu Yüan-fang 韋元方. "I am Collecting Commissioner for the three rivers of Lung-yu 隴右," replied the other. "In what does your office consist?" "I grab all the profits made by merchants."

Fei P'o 斐璞 gave Wei Yüan-fang 韋元方 two gold ingots,

mounted his horse and disappeared. Yüan 元 examined the gold and found it to be genuine and of a high grade.

LIANG WU TI 梁 武 帝.—Became a Buddhist priest in A.D. 527 and 529.—See *Lo-han* 羅 漢.

LIAO-I CH'AN-SHIH 了 一 禪 師 (56th generation).—A deified Buddhist monk. Ranked thirty-second in Buddhist School, III (*q.v.*). Family name Yang 楊. A native of Tê-ch'ing 德 清. Being violently repulsed (see *I-hsüan Ch'an-shih* 義 玄 禪 師) when, at seventeen years of age, he desired to study in the school of Yüan-miao Ch'an-shih 原 妙 禪 師 (*q.v.*), he was enlightened after staying seven days at the foot of the mountain, and was then received as Yüan-miao's 原 妙 disciple. When seventy years of age, he withdrew to the Chêng-tsung Ssŭ 正 宗 寺, Chêng-tsung Monastery, in the Shih-tzŭ Lin 獅 子 林, Lion Forest, where he died in the following year.

LIAO-KAI CH'AN-SHIH 了 改 禪 師 (57th generation).—A deified Buddhist monk. Ranked forty-fifth in Buddhist School, VI (*q.v.*). Family name Jên 任. A native of Chin-tien 金 店 in the Sung-yang 嵩 陽 district, Honan 河 南. In A.D. 1398, he entered the Buddhist monastery at Tsu-t'ing 祖 庭, in the same province. Died A.D. 1421, aged 87.

LIAO-YÜAN CH'AN-SHIH 了 元 禪 師 (44th generation).—A deified Buddhist monk. Ranked twenty-eighth in Buddhist School, VI (*q.v.*). Family name Lin 林, personal name Pao-chio 寶 覺. A native of Fou-liang 浮 梁, Kiangsi 江 西. "At the time of his birth, a marvellous light surrounded the house and, strange to say, the hair had already grown on his head, and he had an abundant beard. From the age of two, he studied Buddhist books, and being gifted with a powerful memory, he forgot nothing of what he learned." When grown up, he entered the Pao-chi Ssŭ 寶 積 寺, Monastery of the Precious Granary. His teacher was Fa-hua Ch'an-shih 法 華 禪 師. When fully trained, he went to the K'ai-hsien Ssŭ 開 先 寺, at Lu Shan 廬 山, where Hsien-tao 遷 道 explained the Law; afterwards he became secretary to Yüan T'ung-no 員 通 訥 "For forty years, he roamed from monastery to monastery, and was the friend of every famous teacher of the times." Died A.D. 1098.

LICE, THE GOD OF.—"A famous general who commanded a besieged city, was so busy day and night that he could not change his raiment, and consequently he was covered with 'grey-backs,' which, as the natives say, are generated by perspiration in the pores of the skin; these swarms of little creatures gradually 'drank his blood,' acting as an enemy's sword to the warrior. He was canonized as the god of lice. When our neighbours make a raid on their bodily attendants, they wrap them up in paper and put them under the censer, and the god whisks them to the paradise of insects. When one of the lower classes is seen sitting in the sunshine examining his clothes, and making a hearty meal off the multitude of insects which he finds, we do not wonder that the god of lice is worshipped in this country" (Du Bose, p. 338).

LIEH TZŬ 列 子.—See *Apotheosized Philosophers,* and Finn, ix, 140-1.

LIEH YÜ-K'OU 列禦寇.—See *Apotheosized Philosophers.*

LIEN-CH'IH TA-SHIH 池蓮大師.—A deified Buddhist monk. Ranked eighth in Buddhist School, XVII (*q.v.*). Eighth ancestor. Family name Shên 沈. A native of Jên-ho 仁和, in Ku-hang 古杭, Chêkiang 浙江. Personal name Chu-hung 袾宏 surnames Fo-hui 佛慧 and Lien-ch'ih 蓮池. When his parents died, he entered a monastery, being then 31 years of age. Fascinated by the beauty of the Yün-hsi 雲棲 landscape, he moved there from Hsi-shan 西山, and preached the doctrine for forty years. In A.D. 1615, he visited his family, and exhorted his disciples, saying: "Always fervently invoke the name of Buddha, observe with the greatest fidelity the rules I have given you." Having spoken these words he expired. He was the compiler of of two successful works: *Yün-hsi fa-hui* 雲樓法彙, and *Mi-t'o shu-ch'ao* 彌陀疏鈔.

LIEN-SHÊ TSUNG 蓮社宗.—See *Buddhist Schools,* XVII.

LIGHT OF THE EYE, THE GODDESS OF THE.—See *Yen-kuang P'u-sa* 眼光菩薩.

LIGHTNING, THE GODDESS OF.—See *Tien Mu* 電母.

LIME-BURNERS, THE GODS OF.—See *Ho Ho* 和合.

LIN CH'AN-SHIH 凜禪師.—Included among the saintly Buddhist monks invited to the annual banquet of the gods (see *Hsi Wang-mu* 西王母). Is stated to have been a quack, who endeavoured to administer an antidote to Wu-lieh Ta-ti 武烈大帝 (Ch'ên Kuo-jên 陳果仁, *q.v.*).

LIN-CHI TSUNG 臨濟宗.—See *Buddhist Schools,* V.

LIN-KAO-YÜ CH'AN-SHIH 林臯豫禪師 (68th generation). —A deified Buddhist monk. Ranked sixtieth in Buddhist School, III (*q.v.*) A disciple of Yüan-hsiu Ch'an-shih 圓修禪師 (*q.v.*). Lived in the Chu-lin Ssǔ 竹林寺, Bamboo-forest Monastery, on Chia Shan 夾山, near Chên-chiang (Chinkiang) 鎮江, where he is buried.

LIN SHAN 林善.—The god of the star P'i-ma 披麻. A vassal of Chou Wang 紂王, against whom he revolted and was slain by Lu Jên-chi 魯仁傑 at the siege of Ch'ao-ko 朝歌, the capital.

LIN TS'ÊN 沐澤.—See *Shui Fu* 水府, D (2) (g).

LIN-YEH-CH'I CH'AN-SHIH 林野奇禪師 (68th generation).—A deified Buddhist monk. Ranked fifty-ninth in Buddhist School, III (*q.v.*). Family name Ts'ai 蔡. A native of Chin-tzŭ T'o 金子沱, in the district of Ho-yang 合陽, Ssŭch'uan 四川 His teacher was Yüan-wu Ch'an-shih 圓悟禪師 (*q.v.*). Afterwards he started his own school at Hsi-chên 接真. His tomb is beside the monastery where he taught the Doctrine.

LING-HSING 靈星.—See *Shê Chi* 社稷.

[LING-JUI] HUNG-T'AN CH'AN-SHIH [靈瑞] 弘曇禪師 See *Hung-t'an Ch'an-shih* 弘曇禪師 and *Tzŭ-hsien-chi Ch'an-shih* 子賢祇禪師

LING-KU HOU 靈派侯.—Named Chi Chü-mu 季堀木. Born at Shan-yung 山用, in Wei-chou 衛州. An able marshal in the time of the Emperor Shih Tsung 世宗 (A.D. 954-60) of the Hou-Chou 後周 dynasty. When dying, he said he was going to take up his post of Marshal at Ch'i-ho 漆河, in Shantung 山東. Later on, a temple was erected to him and he received the title of ever Victorious Marquis.—See *Composite Deities*.

LING K'UNG-TZŬ 凌空子.—See *Wu Lao* 五老.

LING MO 靈謨.—The God of the Neck.

LING-PAO TA FA-SHIH 靈寶大法師.—The same as Ling-pao T'ien-tsun 靈寶天尊 (*q.v.*), second member of the Taoist triad. Lived in the Yüan-yang Tung 元陽洞, on K'ung-t'ung Shan 崆峒山, Kansu 甘肅 (? Shantung 山東). Fought for Wu Wang 武王 (1121-1114 B.C.) in the Yin-Chou 殷周 wars.

LING PAO T'IEN-TSUN 靈寶天尊.—*See Ling-pao ta Fa-shih* 靈寶大法師, *San Ch'ing* 三清, *Tao Chün* 道君, *Lao Tzŭ* 老子, *T'ai Ch'ing* 太清, *Shén Pao* 神寶, and *Chén Jên* 眞人.

LING SU-CHIEN 靈素簡.—See *Shui Fu* 水府, C (2) (c).

LING WEI YANG 靈威仰.—See *Jupiter*.

LING-YA HSIEN 靈牙仙.—A white metamorphosed elephant known as "Marvellous Defences," slain whilst fighting on the side of his master T'ung-t'ien Chiao-chu 通天敎主, by P'u

Hsien 普賢, in the historical battle of the Ten Thousand Genii during the Yin-Chou 殷周 wars. Resuming his original form of an elephant he was condemned to serve as his enemy's mount. It is related that at this time the Buddha P'u Hsien 普賢 used to ride a white elephant.

LING-YEN CHU CH'AN-SHIH 靈淡燭禪師 (66th generation).—A deified Buddhist monk. Ranked seventh-ninth in Buddhist School, VI (q.v.). Family name Mao 毛. A native of Shan-yang 山陽, Shensi 陝西. Taught by [Sung-ju] Tao-mi Ch'an-shih [嵩乳] 道密禪師 (q.v.) at P'u-t'i 菩提. In A.D. 1663, opened a school at Hung-fu 洪福. Died in the same monastery twenty years later, aged 74. His tomb is to the left of the monastic tower.

LING-YU CH'AN-SHIH 靈祐禪師 (37th generation).—A deified Buddhist monk. Ranked eighth in Buddhist School, III (q.v.). Founder of the Wei-yang Tsung 潙仰宗, Wei-yang School. A native of Fu-chou 福州, Fukien 福建. Family name Chao 趙. At the age of 23 became disciple of Huai-hai Ch'an-shih 懷海禪師 (q.v.), who trained him with the greatest care, and later appointed him abbot of the Wei Shan 潙山 Monastery, whence his name Wei-shan Ling-yu 潙山靈祐. Died A.D. 840.

LING-YÜAN 靈源.—See Shui Fu 水府, D (1).

LION, THE GREEN.—See Kuan Yin 觀音.

LION, A TRANSCENDENT.—See Ch'iu-shou Hsien 虯首仙.

LION-KING KALA.—See Lo-han 羅漢.

LITERATURE, GODS OF.—See Wên Ch'ang 文昌.

LITERATURE, THE MINISTRY OF.—See Wên Ch'ang 文昌.

LITTLE ORPHAN, THE.—This large rock, or island, in the Yang-tzǔ 揚子 River, known as Hsiao-ku Shan 小孤山, is connected with a story told of Chang Tao-ling 張道陵 (q.v.), who, under the Empire, was closely connected with the government as Chief Exorcist. When he was needed in Peking, he would travel to the capital in state. Popular superstition says, that when his work was completed he would return unseen through the power of his magic.

On one of the trips to Peking 北京, as he passed the Little Orphan, he decided to have some fun at the expense of the spirit of the place. So he stole one of the shoes of the wife of the God of the Little Orphan. This made the god very angry, and there was a battle of magic powers. Chang T'ien-shih 張天師 was defeated, but while fleeing deceived the god by turning the masts of his ship about. The god thinking he was returning waited for him, and did not realize his mistake until Chang 張 had escaped.—See Plopper, p. 210, note *d*.

LIU 柳, THE GOD OF THE CONSTELLATION.—See *Jên Kuang* 任光 and *Wu K'un* 吳坤.

LIU CHIA 劉鉿.—See *Liu-mêng Chiang-chün* 劉猛將軍.

LIU CHIH 柳跖.—One of the Gods of Brigands. The brother of Liu Hsia-hui 柳下惠, the disciple of Confucius. He was generally known as Tao Chih 盜跖, the Brigand Chih, and, aided by his nine thousand fellow-robbers, committed terrible depredations in the State. He is recorded as having had an argument with Confucius, whom he accused of being a hypocrite. Professional brigands sacrifice to him under the name of Liu Chih 柳跖. See also *Wu-tao Chiang-chün* 五盜將軍, *Sung Chiang* 宋江, and *Shih Ch'ien* 時遷.

LIU CHIH 劉直.—The god of the constellation Chên 軫. Alternatively with Hu Tao-yüan 胡道元.

LIU CHIN 劉禁.—See *Chiu Yao* 九曜.

LIU CH'U 六趣.—See *Gati*.

LIU-HAI HSIEN 劉海仙.—The Immortal Liu-hai 劉海. Usually depicted (1) holding in his hand a variegated cord to the end of which is attached a *ch'an* 蟾, three-footed toad; (2) carrying across his shoulder a kind of belt composed of a string of eggs and gold coins. The reason for these is found in the legend associated with his name. As regards the latter, however, there are two versions: (1) that his family name was Liu 劉, and his own name Ts'ao 操; that he was Minister of State under Yeh-lü Cho-li-chih 耶律喋里只 when that Kitan chieftain proclaimed himself emperor under the title I 億 (subsequently canonized as T'ai Tsu 太祖) in A.D. 907; and retired from his Court to a retreat situated between Chung-nan Shan 終南山, Mount Chung-nan, and T'ai-hua Shan 太華山, Mount T'ai-hua, in Hsi-an Fu 西安府, Shensi 陝西; (2) that his family name was Liu-hai 劉海, his personal name Ts'ao 操, and his style Tsung-ch'êng 宗成 (also given as Chao-ta 昭達); a native of Pei-ching (Peking) 北京, Chihli 直隸 (formerly Yen-shan 燕山, in the Kingdom of Yen 燕); became the Minister of Liu Shou-kuang 劉守光, King of Yen 燕.

He was specially given to worshipping the Emperor Huang Ti 黃帝 and Lao Chün 老君. One day he received a visit from

Chêng Yang-tzŭ 正陽子, the Illuminated (*i.e.* Han Chung-li 漢鍾離, *q.v.*). After entering the main hall, the visitor set himself to pile up ten hen's eggs one on the other, placing a gold piece between each. "That's a risky sort of thing your doing," exclaimed Liu-hai 劉海. "Less dangerous than filling the office of Minister to your Prince," replied Chêng 正. Taking the hint, Ts'ao 操 hastened to Kuang 光, King of Yen 燕, who had usurped the title of Emperor, and reproached him with the act. When he found the Emperor would not listen to him he resigned his post, changed his name to Hsüan Ying 玄英, and began to travel in search of perfection. He met Lü Shun-yang 呂純陽 (Lü Tung-pin 呂洞賓—see *Pa Hsien* 八仙), who gave him the recipe for converting the secretions of gold into pills of immortality. He lived some time as an ascetic, and then attained to immortality.

[The title of "King of Yen 燕" had been conferred on Liu Shou-kuang 劉守光 in A.D. 909 by the Emperor T'ai Tsu 太祖 (A.D. 907-15) of the Posterior Liang, Hou Liang 後梁, dynasty, and Liu Shou-kuang 劉守光 had usurped the title of Emperor in A.D. 911.]

The following legend concerning him is quoted by Doré from *Mêng Lai-fu (Fêng-hsia pi-t'an)* 孟籟甫 (豐暇筆譚):—At Su-chou 蘇州, outside the Ch'ang Mên 閶門 (Gate) in the Nan-hao 南濠 suburb, lived a certain Pei Hung-wên 貝宏文, whose family had been occupied in business for generations. In A.D. 1662, a young unknown man, who called himself A-pao 阿保, knocked at the door and offered his services. Being given work, he proved efficient, but at the end of the month, when offered his salary, he refused to accept it. It was also noticed that he would go without nourishment for days without suffering any inconvenience. This caused general astonishment, as did also his turning the night-commodes, when ordered to clean them, inside out as easily as if they had been made of skin instead of earthenware.

On the day of the Feast of Lanterns he disappeared in the crowd with the child of his master, not returning until the third watch of the night. On being scolded by his master, he replied that as the Feast had been poor that year throughout China except at Fu-chou (Foochow) 福州, the capital of Fukien 福建, he had taken the child there to see it. The members of the family being naturally incredulous, the child drew from its breast a bunch of freshly-gathered lichees, and presented them to its parents, asking them to taste them. As the distance from Su-chou 蘇州 to Fu-chou 福州 is several hundred *li* 里, they concluded that they were dealing with an Immortal.

Several months later, when drawing water from the well, Liu-hai 劉海 caught a large three-footed toad. Having tied it to a multi-coloured cord several feet long, he put it on his shoulder and carried it away, leaping for joy. "This animal," he said, "had escaped; I have sought for it unsuccessfully for several years, but only to-day have I been able to find it." The rumour spread about that Liu-hai 劉海 was with the Pei 貝 family, and so many people ran to see him that the crowd was so dense it was impossible to move. Liu-hai 劉海 joined his hands (after the Chinese fashion) to thank Mr. Pei 貝 and, rising into the air from the middle of the courtyard, disappeared. Even at the present day people passing the door point to it as a place whence an Immortal ascended to Heaven.

Liu-hai 劉海 is often represented fishing for the three-footed toad (*ch'an* 蟾), and because he carries a string of coins is invoked for the success of commercial operations. His picture is pasted on the two leaves of a door, one facing the other.

LIU HÊNG 劉衡.—The god of the star Ti-ho 地闔.—See *Ti-sha* 地煞.

LIU-HO 六合, THE GODDESS OF THE STAR.—See *Têng Ch'an-yü* 鄧嬋玉.

LIU-HSIA 流霞, THE GOD OF THE STAR.—See *Wu Jung* 武榮.

LIU HSÜAN-TÊ 劉玄德.—See *Liu Pei* 劉備.

LIU HUAN 劉環.—See *Huo Pu* 火部.

LIU I 劉錡.—An assessor of Kuan Kung 關公.—See *Kuan Yü* 關羽 and *Liu-mêng Chiang-chün* 劉猛將軍.

LIU I 柳毅.—See *Shui Fu* 水府, D (3) (a).

LIU JUI 劉銳.—See *Liu-mêng Chiang-chün* 劉猛將軍.

LIU-LI FO 琉璃佛 or WANG 王.—See *Yao-shih Wang* 藥師王.

LIU LUNG 劉隆.—The god of the constellation Lou 婁. Alternatively with Chang-hsiung Tao-jên 張雄道人.

LIU-MÊNG CHIANG-CHÜN 劉猛將軍.—The Valiant Marshal Liu 劉. Also known as Liu T'ai-wei 劉太尉, the Military Chief Liu 劉. The Protector, or Protecting Spirit, against Grasshoppers or Locusts. One of the Gods of Agriculture. One of the chief gods of the nation. He was a beardless young man, and exceedingly fond of children. The mandarins worship him, his temple is found in every hamlet, theatricals in his honour are quite renowned, and his processions go to every village. His birthday is on the thirteenth of the first moon, and during the following week a long table is placed before his youthful majesty, spread with various kinds of food, fruits, and artificial flowers;

and a retinue of angels bow towards him. He is also worshipped by the coolies; they say, 'Mêng Chiang 猛將 went barefoot, and so do we (with only straw sandals); so we worship him' (Du Bose, pp. 131-2).

Variously said to be:—(1) Liu I 劉錡, a Marshal of the Sung 宋 dynasty, usually called Liu Hsin-shu 劉信叔, of Ch'in Chou 秦州, Kansu 甘肅. Posthumous title: Wu Mu 武穆; (2) Liu Jui 劉銳, younger brother of the above; (3) Liu Chia 劉韐, also called Liu Chung-yen 劉中偃, a native of Ch'ung-an Hsien 崇安縣, Chien-an Fu 建安府, Fukien 福建. Was sent in A.D. 1126 to parley with the invading Mongols, and being retained in their service committed suicide. Posthumous title: Chung Hsien 忠顯, Faithful and Loyal; (4) Liu Tsai (Man-t'ang) 劉宰 (漫塘), whose name was Tsai 宰 and personal name P'ing-kuo 平國. A native of Chin-t'an Hsien 金壇縣, Chên-chiang Fu 鎮江府, Kiangsu 江蘇. Superintendent of Imperial Estates under the Emperor Li Tsung 理宗 (A.D. 1225-65) of the Sung 宋 dynasty. Closed eighty-four illegitimate temples; (5) Liu Ch'êng-ch'ung 劉承忠. Born in the Yüan 元 dynasty at Wu-ch'uan 吳川, Ho-chien Fu 河間府, Chihli 直隸. His presence alone sufficed to pacify a district. Drowned himself in the Chiang 江, and was given the posthumous title of Mêng Chiang-chün 猛將軍.

All these were worshipped as Protectors against grasshoppers or locusts, but in the reign of K'ang Hsi 康熙 (A.D. 1662-1723) of the Ch'ing 清 dynasty a decree was issued abolishing all official sacrifices to Mêng Chiang-chün 猛將軍. Nevertheless, temples still exist in which he is worshipped.—See also *Pa Cha* 叭咋.

LIU PEI 劉備. — The God of Basket-makers, he having followed that avocation in his youth (see *Kuan Yü* 關羽). According to some mythologists, the god of the star Tzŭ-wei 紫微.—See *Po-I K'ao* 伯邑考 and *Composite Deities*.

LIU TA 劉達.—The god of the star T'ien-k'u 天哭.—See *T'ien-kang* 天罡.

LIU T'AI-WEI 劉太尉.—See *Liu-mêng Chiang-chün* 劉猛將軍.

LIU TAO 六道.—See *Gati*.

LIU T'IEN-CHÜN 劉天君.—Name Liu Chün 劉俊. Born on a fishing-boat in A.D. 340 or 400 during the Tung Chin 東晉 dynasty. Was taught to acquire a mysterious power over wind and rain by a recipe called "five thunders" given him by his teacher Lo Chên-jên 羅真人 (*q.v.*). This he used with great benefit to the farmers, who raised a memorial temple to him. He also brought an end to a severe drought in the country round the

Eastern capital, for which deed the Emperor bestowed on him the title of Hsüan-hua Tz'ŭ-chi Chên-chün 玄化慈濟眞君, True and merciful Prince, Benefactor of the Empire, which was ratified by Yü Ti 玉帝, who also granted him as an apanage, The Intendancy of the Five Cereals.

LIU TING 六丁 SPIRITS.—See *Huang-chin Li-shih* 黃金力士.

LIU-TSAI (MAN-T'ANG) 劉宰 (漫塘).— See *Liu-mêng Chiang-chün* 劉猛將軍.

LIU WAN-SU 劉完素.—See *Shih Ming-i* 十明醫, 7.

LIVER, THE GODS OF THE.—The God of the Liver is Lung Yen 龍煙 and his style Han Ming 含明 (*Huang t'ing nei ching* 黃庭內經). The *Yün chi ch'i ch'ien* 雲笈七籤 gives two names; K'ai chün T'ung 開君童, style Tao Ch'ing 道青, height six inches, colour yellowish blue, and Ping Ch'ang, style Tzŭ Yüan 子元.

LO 羅, THE FIVE BROTHERS.—See *Lo Shên* 羅神.

LO-CH'A-P'O 羅叉婆.—See *Rakshasas*.

LO CHING-HSIN 樂靜信.—A name for Yüan-shih T'ien-tsun 元始天尊 (*q.v.*), the Supreme Lord, ruler of the Yü Ch'ing 玉清, Pearly Azure, Heaven.—See also *San Ch'ing* 三清 and *T'ien Pao* 天寶.

LO-HAN 羅漢.—A name derived from the Sanskrit *arhan* or *arhat,* Japanese and Korean *rahan* or *rahat*. The ideal which Sakyamuni taught that every man should strive to attain. An *arhat* is one who has travelled the Eight-fold Path, has reached enlightenment and is saved to all eternity (*Encycl. Sinica*, p. 32, but *v. infra*). The *arhat* is the perfected *arya*. *Arya, lit.* the Reverend, venerable, worthy, deserving of honour, is a title given to those who, by mastering the Four Truths, or Dogmas (of misery, accumulation, extinction, and the path leading to the extinction of passion and existence) have entered the *arya's* path (the *ssŭ tao* 四道) to Nirvana. The last step before perfect salvation is gained. Following this he receives full enlightment and becomes a Buddha, has succeeded in placing himself outside the wheel of Transmigration, and is absolutely free.

The *arhat* is the ascetic, who is freed from all the ten fetters; from all attachment to existence, whether on earth or in heaven; and from all force of Karma (Hardy, *Manual of Buddhism*, p. 38; Williams, *Buddhism*, p. 133). He is the completely freed man, and while still living is completely dead to the world. He has also acquired transcendent powers over Nature, matter, time and space (Eitel, p. 13; Hardy, p. 38; Williams, p. 133; Waddell, p. 141; Geden, p. 576). He can make his body lighter or heavier, smaller or larger than anything in the world; he can reach any place, and assume any shape at will. He has knowledge of all things, and recollection of all previous existences. In short, he is perfectly wise, and has nothing more to learn. His mind is incapable of error upon any subject connected with religious truth, though he may make mistakes upon ordinary subjects (Hardy, p. 38; Williams, p. 133; Geden, p. 577). At death, he will experience no further rebirth, but must either enter Nirvana, or cease to exist. The cause of reproduction—*karma*—being destroyed, it is not possible for him to enter any other mode of existence (Hardy, p. 39; Williams, p. 133). In theory, the *arhat*ship is open to all, laymen as well as monks, and even to women (see below), but practically can only be obtained by those who leave the world, and lead a celibate monastic life. The state of *arhat* can accordingly be attained only by passing through these different degrees of saintship. *Arhat*ship implies, strictly speaking, possession of supernatural powers and successive promotion to Buddhaship and Nirvana. In the *arhans* the worshipper sees those who have become 'venerable' by years, wisdom, and a long course of asceticism.

The *arhan* is only such after passing though three grades of discipleship, which are the first steps on the road to the Nirvana. . . . . They form the ladder of the active world of human life to that cloud-land of abstraction which the contemplative Buddhist hopes to reach at last. But in popular parlance the term *arhan* or *arhat* simply means an advanced disciple of Sakyamuni.

At present, the term *arhan* or *lo-han* 羅漢 is used as a designation of all famous disciples of Sakyamuni, but denotes more especially those five hundred *arhats* who are to re-appear on earth as Buddhas, each assuming then the title *Samantha prabhasa,* or general brightness, *p'u-ming* 普明 (the name under which each of the five hundred *arhats* re-appears as Buddha). The *arhans* are essentially connected with the Hinayana phase of Buddhism.

Sha-tsei 殺賊, destroying the thief (*Kchinas'rava*) and *pu-hsüeh* 不學, exempt from study (*as'aikcha*), attributes of every Buddhist saint, are used as synonym for the term *arhat.*

Later on, the term *arhan* became restricted to those who reached the end of the eightfold path (right belief, resolve, speech, work, livelihood, training, mindfulness, abstract meditation, or mystic concentration of mind-*samadhi*), and were not only perfect themselves, but could teach others how to attain perfection.

He is one distinguished from "his perfect knowledge of the law, its perfect fulfilment, and the practice of the highest degree of *dhyana,* or mystic contemplation, and is more worthy of honour than the generality of *bhikshus,* or mendicant monks. The *lo-han*

羅漢 is the equivalent of the Taoist *chên-jên* 眞人 (*q.v.*). (As LO-HAN to the degree of veneration accorded them, see below.)

The *Fa hua ching* 法華經 says: "The word *arhan* expresses rank, and what follows, character. *Arhan* is variously explained as the 'true man,' or the 'extricated man.' Some say it contains three meanings, *viz.* freedom from birth, killer of robbers in the sense of being delivered from perceptions and sensations, the robbers of the mind, and deserving honour. This is the sense according to the principles of (1) Collection, and (2) Progress. But for the two higher principles, (3) Distinction, and (4) Completion, the word implies, not only the killing of robbers, but of non-robbers, *i.e.* the Nirvana, which in the higher region of these two principles is also deserving of extinction. Freedom from birth expresses their complete rescue from life and death, and that is the meaning of their defects having been obliterated. Because they can give happiness to all the nine classes of beings, therefore they are said to deserve honour. By their embodiment of the religious life, they benefit themselves. By their wisdom, they obtain deliverance from life and death. By expelling ignorance and evil, they kill robbers.

"Interpreting according to the Threefold contemplation, empty, inventive, and medial, the first is exemplified in their wisdom, the second in their expulsion of evil, and the third in their embodiment of the religious life. In the transition from the inventive to the empty, there are also three modifications of the sense, *viz.* arrival at the central point of contemplation, killing the thieves of ignorance, and keeping the heart from a one-sided position.

"Interpreting according to the contemplation of the heart, following the middle path, and taking the correct view, they do not err on the side of the empty or inventive mode of observation. The sorrow of the heart is gone. When a man sees the true moral nature of his mind, that is called the higher state of confirmation. Like a hidden treasure, reserved for myself, is the benefit which the Arhans have obtained."

"The Bodhisattvas and Arhans (Lo-han 羅漢) of oriental religious fiction, correspond to the saints and martyrs venerated in the West" (Edkins). *Arhat*ship is (to be) succeeded either by Buddhaship, or by immediate entrance into Nirvana (Eitel). (The various grades of Buddhist disciples are stated toward the end of this section.)

Finally, among these disciples and saints a certain number were chosen as patrons and guardians of Buddhism throughout the world (Watters). Their number and names have varied in different countries (*v. infra*). In China and Tibet the number eighteen is generally accepted at the present day.

When about to die, Buddha, having reached the age of eighty, entrusted the defence and propagation of his religion to Indra, or Sakra (*q.v.*), and the Four Great Bikshus, Mahakasyapa, Pindola, Kundadhana, and Rahula.

(*Bikshu* is one of the names given to the followers of Buddha generally. They are also called *sha-mên* 沙門 and *ho-shang* 和尚. See also *infra*.)

They were to remain in existence, and not experience Nirvana until the advent of Maitreya, Mi-lo-fo (*q.v.*) 彌勒佛 (Watters). They are the four great Maharajas, who were to maintain the Law and protect the four quarters of the world from demons.

The institution of the Arhat, and his special duty as defender of the Law, is traceable to Gautama. Originating in the "Four Great Bhikshus," or disciples of Buddha, the number of Arhats has varied at different times and in different countries. They may be either 4, 16, 18, 500, 1,000, or 5,000.

Following the group of four is the second traditional group of sixteen. This is unknown in India and Ceylon but is found in all ancient monasteries of China, and is to be seen in Japan and Korea. The sixteen group seems to have originated in Kashmir (*Journal Asiatique*, Sept.-Oct., 1916). This group was in all likelihood built up around the Four Great Disciples (Bikshus), four arhats (*lo-han* 羅漢) being assigned to guard each quarter of the heavens. A single defender of the Law being deemed insufficient, the number was thus increased to sixteen.

The *bikshus* (*bhikchu*) are two classes of *sramanas* (*q.v.*), *viz.* esoteric mendicants (*nei-ch'i* 內乞) who control their nature by the law, and exoteric mendicants (*wei-ch'i* 外乞) who control their nature by diet. Every true bikshu is supposed to work miracles.

The names of the Four Great Bikshus (*p'i-ch'iu* 比丘, one who is completed), to whom Buddha entrusted the propagation and defence of his doctrines are: (1) Mahakasyapa (Ma-ho-chia-yeh 摩訶迦葉), or Kashiapa, the disciple to whom Buddha, before his death, committed the secrets of his mysteries. He was an old Brahman, of Central India, who was anxious to preserve Buddha's teachings. He was the only one who showed attention and pleasure in his countenance when Buddha ascended the platform to give his instructions. Buddha understood what was passing in his mind, and gave him the pure mystery of right doctrine, the secret heart of the Nirvana, that true knowledge of existing things which consists in knowing them not to exist, and the method of enlightenment and reformation (Edkins). He taught at Rajagriha after the Nirvana. He, with the assistance of a thousand Arhans daily supplied with food for a whole summer by King Ajatashatru, was engaged in collecting the books containing the sayings of Buddha, *i.e.* the *Tripitaka*. This was called by Koeppen the First Buddhist Council.

Kashiapa taught for twenty years more, and then entrusted to Ananda the secret of pure doctrine. Later, he proceeded to the four places of pilgrimage to worship, namely, the place of Sakyanumi leaving his home to become a recluse, the place of his becoming Buddha, of his first preaching, and of his entering

Nirvana. (2) Pindola (Pin-tu-lo-Po-lo-to-shih 賓度羅跋囉惰闍: see below). (3) Kundadhana (Kun [chün]-t'ou-p'o-han 君頭波漢), a name representing the Pali Kundo-vahan, "Mungoose-bearing" (see No-chü-lo 諾矩羅, Nakula, *infra*). (4) Rahula (Lo-hu-lo 囉怙羅: see *infra*).

According to the *Record of Duration of the Law, spoken by the great Arhat Nandimitra (Ta-A-lo-han Nan-t'i-mi-to-lo so shuo-fa-chu-chi* 大阿羅漢難提密多羅所說法注記) within eight hundred years from Buddha's decease, but according to Chih P'an's *Fo-tsu-t'ung chi* 佛祖統紀, chapter 33, one hundred years after that event, there was an arhat named Nandimitra at the capital of the King Shêng-chün 勝軍 in the Chih-shih-tzŭ 執師子 country. (Shêng-chün 勝軍 is either Prasenadjit, a king of Kosala, one of the first royal converts to Sakyamuni, and originator of Buddhist idolatry, or Jayasena, and Chih-shih-tzŭ 執師子 probable Simhadvipa.) He reassured his desponding congregation by informing them that Buddhism would continue to exist in the world, since Buddha when about to die had entrusted his religion to sixteen great Arhats. The number sixteen is found for the first time in the *Mahayana-vataraka,* a Mahayana work, translated into Chinese by the monk Tao-t'ai 道台, about A.D. 437 or 439. But this work mentions only two names out of the number of sixteen arhats, namely those of Pindola and Rahula (two of the Four Great Disciples or Bikshus).

These new guardians of Buddha's Law are dispersed all over the world, four being assigned to each quarter of the sphere. They are "to watch over and care for the religious welfare of the lay believers and generally protect the spiritual interests of Buddhism. They are to remain in existence all the long time until Maitreya appears as Buddha and brings in a new system. Then, according to Nandimitra, the Sixteen Arhats will collect all the relics of Sakyamuni and build over them a magnificent tope. Then they will enter an igneous ecstasy and so vanish in remainderless nirvâna" (Watters).

The arhats are the sixteen *Rakan* of the Japanese and Koreans and constitute sixteen of the eighteen Lo-han of the Chinese. They have incense burnt before their images, but generally speaking are not worshipped or consulted like the gods and *p'u sa's* 菩薩 of the temples.

The names of the Sixteen Arhats or Lo-han 羅漢 are now usually given as stated in the *Sutra of the Duration of the Law,* but variations occur. The pictures and images of them are merely symbols and not to be taken as faithful representations of the persons indicated by the names attached to them. Though the number sixteen, as noted above, is first found mentioned in China about A.D. 437 or 439, as noted above, the full list of sixteen names is only given in a translation by Hsüan Tsang 玄奘 in the middle of the seventh century (A.D. 653-4). Their names are given below.

Each of the sixteen has a retinue of from five hundred to sixteen hundred arhats.

1. Pin-tu-lo-po-lo-to-shê 賓度羅跋囉惰闍. Pindola the Bharadvaja. Sometimes styled Pin-t'ou-lo 賓頭羅 or Bharadvaja simply.—The name Pindola is explained in Chinese commentaries as meaning Pu-tung 不動, Unmoved. The Tibetans give "Alms-receiver" as the equivalent, connecting the name with *pinda*, but it may have been derived from the name of a place transcribed Pin-t'ou 賓頭 in Chinese. This was a town or village in the Kosala country in Buddha's time.

According to Nandimitra's account, he resides in the Apara-godhanga region, or "Wheat Continent," to the west. Noted as a successful defender of orthodoxy. Had a voice like the roar of a lion. Was prone to exhibit his magical powers, and was rebuked by the Buddha for floating in the air in a sandal-wood bowl over the heads of a crowd. He was also informed that he was to remain in existence and protect Buddha's system until the coming of Maitreya. He has been living since Buddha's time, and has appeared on several occasions to pious workers for his doctrine. As he has very long eyebrows in his pictures and on his images he has come to be known popularly as Ch'ang-mei sêng 長眉僧, "Long-eyebrowed Monk." (This arose from his having been seen with very long eyebrows and white hair, which he had to hold back with his hands in order to see, when he was summoned by King Asoka to his great assembly, to which he flew swan-like from the Gandhamali or Gandhamadana Mountain, where he was residing with his company of 60,000 arhats.)

When Vasubandhu meditated suicide Pindola by his mystic powers knew the fact and came from Purvavideha to dissuade the pious philosopher from the act.

Pindola came to China in the seventh century and appeared to Tao Hsüan 道宣, the great Vinaya doctor.

"In a far-back existence Pindola had been a bad son and a cruel man, and owing to his bad *karma* he had to suffer in hell for a very long period. Here his food was 'tiles and stones,' and even when he was born to be a pious arhat of wonderful powers, he retained a tendency to live on 'tiles and stones.' We cannot wonder that he was thin and ribbed" (Watters).

He was represented for the first time in art about A.D. 465 or 470. According to a writer in the *Journal Asiatique* (September-October, 1916) he is the only *arhat* who receives special worship.

Some pictures and images represent him sitting and holding a book in one hand and his alms-bowl in the other; others have him holding a book reverently in both hands; and sometimes he is shown with an open book on one knee and a mendicant's staff at his side.

2. Ka [chia] no-ka [chia] Fa-ts'o 迦諾迦伐蹉, Kanaka-Vatsa.—Originally a disciple of Buddha, who heard the Law from

his lips and became a renowned arhat, able to understand all systems, even the most abstruse, good or bad. The Tibetans translate the name as "Golden Calf." Appointed to Kashmir and lives on the Saffron Peak.

3. Ka [chia]-no-ka [chia] Po-li-to-shê 迦諾迦跋釐墮惰闍 Kanaka [or the] Bharadvaya.—Stationed in the Purva-Videha region to the east. Sometimes depicted as a very hairy man; also occasionally as accompanied by a small disciple.

4. Su-p'in-t'ê 蘇頻陀, Subhinda.—His sphere of action is the Kuru (Ultara-kuru) country in the north. Found in temples throughout China, Korea, and Japan. Held by some to be the same as Abhida. In Tibetan the name means "inseparable" or "indissoluble." Represented as a venerable sage with a scroll in his right hand, or as sitting in an attitude of meditation. Also alternatively shown with an alms-bowl and an incense-vase beside him, holding a sacred book in his left hand, while with the right he 'cracks his fingers.' This gesture is indicative of the rapidity with which he attained spiritual insight."

5. No-chü-lo 諾矩羅. Nakula.— His sphere of action is India, to the south. The name (variously written Bakula or Vakula) means a bag made of the skin of the mongoose: hence he is represented in Tibetan temple pictures with a mongoose (or sometimes a three-legged frog) under his arm or in his hand. Otherwise represented as in the act of meditation.

6. Po-t'o-lo 跋陀羅. Bhadra.—Otherwise Tamra Bhadra. Sphere of action, Ceylon. A cousin of the Buddha and one of his great disciples. Represented as accompanied by a tiger, though sometimes without the tiger and merely in an attitude of worship.

7. Ka [chia]-li-ka [chia] 迦理迦. Kalika or Kala.—Resides in the Sêng-ka [chia]-t'a 僧伽茶 (Sanghata) region. Watters says he is apparently the great disciple called "Lion-king Kala" (Shih-tzǔ Wang ka [chia]-lo 師子王迦羅) who attained arhat-ship and was honoured by King Bimbisara. He is represented as studying a scroll or sitting in meditation, or holding a leaf of a tree, or he has extremely long eyebrows which he holds up from the ground.

8. Fa-shê-lo-fu-to-lo 伐闍羅弗多羅. Vajraputra (Vajriputra, Vasuputra).—"Son of the Thunderbolt." Resides in the Po-la-na 鉢刺拏 division of the world (Parana region). Represented as very hairy, or as very lean and ribbed.

9. Shu-po-ka-[chia] 戍博迦. Supaka. (Kou-pa-ka Ch'ü [Kuo]-po-chia 瞿 [國] 波迦, Gopaka.)—"Protector." Resides on the Gandhamadana Mountain. He was a Sthavira or Elder, and expounded the Law at Pataliputra (modern Palibothra, near Patna). Often represented with a small figure of a saint above

his right shoulder, or close to his side, or as holding a book or a fan.

10. Pan-t'o-ka [chia] 半託迦. Panthaka. Pantha.—Called Maha-Panthaka, Great Panthaka, to distinguish him from his twin brother (*infra,* No. 16). The name means "Way" or "Road," or "Born on the road," referring to the two boys having been born on the roadside while their mother was on a journey. Otherwise explained as "continuing the way," *i.e.* propagating Buddhism. Was an intelligent and able disciple, a strenuous expounder and defender of the Law, endowed with extraordinary magic powers, being able to pass through solids and fly through the air, and cause fire and water to appear at pleasure. He could also "reduce his own dimensions until there was nothing left of him." Represented either as sitting under a tree or teaching from an open book, or as holding a scroll, or as sitting in profound meditation with his arms folded, or as in the act of charming a dragon, with his almsbowl.

11. Lo-hu-lo 囉怙羅. Rahula.—One of the Four Great Disciples, or Bikshus (*supra*). The eldest son of Sakyamuni by Yasodhara, also called Rahula-mata, or Rahula's mother. Dwells in the Priyangudvipa region, or "Land of Millet" (some translate "Chestnuts"). Converted to Buddhism, he followed his father as an attendant and disciple. Was distinguished for his diligent study of the Canon and his uncompromising strictness in carrying out the rules of his profession. After his father's death, he became the founder of a philosophical realistic school. It is his lot to die and return to the world as the eldest son of every future Buddha. He is not to pass finally out of existence for many ages. He appeared as a very old bikshu with white bushy eyebrows to a Buddhist layman at a town not very far from Kusinagara sometime before the period of Hsüan Tsang 玄奘 (seventh century A.D.). When the layman gave the old bikshu boiled milk, the latter sighed over it as being as insipid as the river water he once used when attending Buddha, subsequently explaining that he was Rahula. Hsüan Tsang 玄奘, visiting the ruins of Kapilavastu, saw a statue representing him, together with his mother, Rahula-mata. He is often represented in pictures and images as having the large "umbrella-shaped" head, prominent eyes, and hooked nose which some books ascribe to him, but in many cases without any distinctive features or attributes. He is worshipped as the special patron of Buddhist novices.

12. Na-ka [chia]-hsi-na 那迦犀那. Nagasena.—Lives on the Pan-tu-p'o 般度陂, or Pandava, Mountain, in Magadha. Mentioned in the Pali work *Milinda-prasna,* "Questions of Milinda," as the son of the Brahman Sonuttra, a resident of Kajangala, a village near the forest of Himala. Said to have been born in 43 B.C. In early youth, a Buddhist monk taught him the

Maha-vibhasha, an encyclopaedia of Buddhist doctrine, and in later years he became "a learned and subtle arhat," the head of the Church in Milinda's country, and an orthodox expounder of the Hinayana doctrine.

13. Yin-chieh-t'o 因揭陀. Angida or Ingida.—Lived on Kuang-hsieh 廣脅, Broadside Mountain (Vipulaparsva). Said in some legends to be an incarnation of Maitreya. Watters suggests that Angaja and Angila, two of Buddha's great disciples, may have been one person, and identical with this arhat, who, like them, was "perfect in all things." He is said to have preached the Law in the region of Lake Manasrovara. Represented as the fat, jolly Maitreya or his incarnation, he is otherwise represented in pictures and images as a lean old monk holding a staff and a book containing Indian writing.

14. Fa-na-p'o-ssŭ 伐那婆斯. Vanavasa. Varavasa.—Stationed at K'o-chu 可住, Habitable Mountain (Vatsa Mountain). A native of Sravasti. Heard the Law from Buddha himself. Represented in a cave meditating, or with his hands making a *mudra,* magic gesticulation, or as nursing his right knee. Watters surmises that he may be the great disciple called Vanakavasa in Chapter 36 of the *Tsa a han ching* 雜阿漢經.

15. A-shih-to 阿氏多. Asita or Ajita.—The name means "Invincible" or "Unconquered." Resides on the Gridhrakuta Mountain in Magadha. Watters says there is a record of an Asita (阿氏多) who in the remote future is to attain Samyak-sambodhi, that is, to become Buddha. Ajita was at first a *rishi,* or Brahman sage, and later on became a hearer and disciple of Buddha (Waddell). Represented as an old man with very long eyebrows, nursing his right knee or absorbed in meditation.

16. Chu-ch'a (t'a)-Pan-t'o-ka [chia] 注茶半託迦. Chota (Cuda) Panthaka.—Chu-ch'a 注茶 is also given as Chou-li 周利 or Chu-li 祝利 or 朱利. This means "little," to distinguish him from his elder brother, Maha-Panthaka (*supra,* No. 10). Also call-ed Hsiao-lu 小路, "Little Road," the elder brother being Ta-lu 大路, "Great Road." Stationed on Ishadhara Mountain, a part of the Sumeru range (Watters). Others place him on Mount Nemind-hara. At first (as the result of bad *karma*) a dull disciple, but later on mastered the Law and displayed magical powers, on one occasion producing five hundred strange oxen and proceeding to ride on one of them through the air. Represented as an old man sitting under and leaning against a dead tree, one hand holding a fan and the other raised in the attitude of teaching. Also depicted as a venerable sage, sitting on a mat-covered seat and holding a long staff surmounted by a hare's head.

"Besides the 'Four Great Disciples,' or Bikshus, and the group of Sixteen Arhats, that of Eighteen is also traditional, and is generally accepted in China, and often in Tibet, at the present day. There does not seem to be any historical account of the first introduction of the Lohan into the Halls of Buddhist temples, nor can it be ascertained when the number of these guardians was raised from sixteen to eighteen in Chinese temples. The earliest mention of Eighteen Lohan known to the present writer is in the *Fo-tsu-t'ung-chi* 佛祖通紀 (*Bun.* No. 1661), Chapter 33, where there is a reference to the Sixteen Arhats commissioned by Buddha. The author, who lived in the Sung 宋 period, adds 'at present eighteen are talked of'" (Watters). "The group of Eighteen Lo-han, *Shih-pa Lo-han* 十八羅漢, is of later origin than that of Sixteen. So far as can be gleaned from historical records, it [the group of Eighteen] did not exist before the time of the Buddhist poet and painter Kuan-hsiu 貫休, A.D. 832-912 (*Journal Asiatique*, September-October, 1916, pp. 283, 287) . . . . Some fifty years after his death, or about the end of the tenth century, the group of Eighteen was publicly known in China. The portraits made by Kuan-hsiu 貫休 comprised Nandimitra's group of Sixteen, to which two others were added. These latter existed already in popular lore, and were in all likelihood the 'Arhat who subdued the Dragon' and the "Arhat who tamed the Tiger' (*chiang lung fu hu* 降龍伏虎) (*Journal Asiatique*, September-October, 1916, pp. 285-6). The Sixteen were of Hindu origin, and more or less historical (Hackmann, *Buddhism as a Religion*, p. 212, says they are legendary beings, with a historical background); the two added were a purely Chinese conception, and merely symbolical. Both symbolized the superiority of Buddhism over Taoism (*Journal Asiatique*, September-October, 1916, p. 286). In several Buddhist monasteries, this symbolism was ignored, hence later on, Su-shih 蘇軾 (a celebrated statesman, poet, and commentator, A.D. 1036-1101), writing the praises of the Eighteen, assigned the seventeenth place to Nandimitra, and the eighteenth to Pindolo-Bharadvaja, thus ignoring the original symbolism represented by Kuan Hsiu 貫休, namely the "Arhat who subdued the Dragon" and the "Arhat who tamed the tiger," and completing the number by adding the two names above-mentioned.

This solution puzzled the Emperor Ch'ien Lung 乾隆 (A.D. 1736-06). On visiting Hangchou 杭州, Chêkiang 浙江, A.D. 1757, he requested to be shown the Eighteen Arhats of Kuan-hsiu 貫休. Having examined them, he perceived that Pindola's name was used twice, and substituted that of Kasyapa in its stead. The Imperial solution proved also unsatisfactory, and despite the authority of the Emperor, was not generally accepted" (*Journal Asiatique*, September-October, 1916, p. 288; *Doré*, vii 350-1). Watters (pp. 345-6) states: "In some of the temples down to the present time, the number of the Lo-han is still sixteen, *e.g.* in the Pao-ning Ssǔ 寶寧寺, near Mount Omi, visited by Mr. Baber. Some Chinese have supposed that there were formerly eighteen gods regarded as protectors of Buddhist temples, and that the Lohan took their places. But we know nothing about these gods, and the supposition need not be taken into consideration. Another suggestion, and one which seems not improbable, is that the Buddhists in this matter imitated a certain Chinese institution. When we read the history of the reigns of T'ang 唐 Kao Tsu 高祖 (A.D. 618-27) and T'ai Tsung 太宗 (A.D. 627-50), we find the record of an event which may have given the idea of grouping the Lohan in the Chief Hall of a temple and of raising their number to eighteen. In the year 621 T'ai Tsung 太宗 instituted within the palace grounds a very select college composed of eighteen members. These dons were officials of high standing, of sound learning and good literary attainments, and faithful adherents and personal friends of the founder. Among them were such famous men as Tu Ju-hui 杜如晦 and his friend Fang Hsüan-ling 房玄齡; Yü Chih-ning 于志寧, learned scholar and loyal stateman, who wrote the preface to Hsüan Tsang's 玄奘 Hsi-yü-chi 西域記; Lu Tê-ming 陸德明, and K'ung Ying-ta 孔穎達. The members took their turns in batches of three in attending on duty, and while in the college they were liable to be visited and interrogated by the emperor. He had portraits of the members made for the college, and each portrait was furnished with a statement of the name, birthplace, and honours of the original. The merits of each were described in ornate verse by one of the number, Chu Liang 褚亮 (style Hsi Ming 希明). These favoured men were called the *Shih-pa-hsüeh-shih* (十八學士) or Eighteen Cabinet Ministers, and they were popularly said to have *têng Ying-chou* (登瀛州), to have become Immortals. It is this Hall of the Eighteen which I think may have led to the installation of the Eighteen Arhats in Buddha's Hall. The names of these venerable ones are given, and sometimes their stations and retinues are added. There are also temples in which the Lohan are arranged in groups of three.

"But these Eighteen Lohan have never received authoritative recognition, and they are not given even in the modern accepted Buddhist treatises. We find them, however, occasionally in modern Chinese works of art. The South Kensington Museum has a pair of bowls on which they are painted, and the British Museum has them on an incense-vase. This vase is remarkable for departing so far from the established doctrine of the Lohan as to represent three of the eighteen as boys or very young men. The modern Chinese artist, followed by the Japanese, apparently takes the Lohan to be Immortals, and he shows them crossing to the Happy Land of Nirvana or leading lives of unending bliss among the pines of the misty mountain-tops."

"As to the persons who should be admitted as guardian Lohans of Buddha and his religion, there has been a great diversity of opinion, and consequently different worthies have been added in different places"; Nandimitra and a second Pindola being given the seventeenth and eighteenth places respectively; or Liang Wu Ti 梁武帝 (A.D. 502-50); or Kumarajiva; or Maitreya (Mi-lo-fo 彌勒佛) or his supposed incarnation, the Pu-tai ho-shang 布袋和尙, or Calico-bag (cushion) Monk*; the Indian Buddhist Dharmatara (or Dharmatrata), in Chinese Fa-chiu 法救; or Kuan-yin P'u-sa 觀音菩薩 (as Protector of Buddhists and Buddhism); being added as an additional lo-han 羅漢 (Watters, *Journal* R.A.S., April, 1898, pp. 346-7).

The following particulars of the Eighteen Arhats of Wu-wei Chou 無爲州, Anhui 安徽, are abbreviated from Kennelly's descriptions (vii, 356-73):

1. Wu-k'o Ch'an-shih 烏窠禪師.—The Rook-nesting Monk. Family name P'an 潘. Mother's name Chu 朱. He was given the name of Hsiang-kuang 香光, Fragrant Light, because she had borne him after dreaming that a luminous ray from the sun had entered her mouth, a sweet fragrance simultaneously filling the room.

Kennelly (vii, 356-7) relates the following anecdote concerning him:—"In the time of Yao 堯 (2357-2255 B.C.), a certain hermit took up his abode in the branches of trees, and was on this account called Ch'ao-fu 巢父, or the 'Nesting Sage.' The ruler met him one day in the country south of the Lai Ho 淶河, Lai river, and asked him why he chose leading such an eccentric life. 'It is,' replied the hermit, 'in order to avoid the pollution of the world, and also to escape from the great flood, which will soon invade the whole country.' The sage thus foresaw the impending disaster, which marked the close of Yao's 堯 reign, and was finally checked through the labours of Yü the Great, Ta-yü 大禹.

"The 'Nesting Arhat' mentioned here resembles Ch'ao-fu 巢父. He was of Chinese origin and a native of Ching Chou 荆州, in Hupei 湖北. His family name was P'an Hsiang-kuang 潘香光. In early youth he entered the Buddhist monastery of Kuo-yüan, Kuo-yüan Ssŭ 果願寺, but after a few years left for the Ch'in-wang Shan 秦望山, Ch'in-wang Hills, where he took up his abode in the forest that covered the hillside. Ascending a lofty pine-tree, he spent day and night in a nest, which he constructed amidst the branches.

"The scholar Po Lo-t'ien 白樂天, passing one day near the place, wished to pay him a visit, and finding him high up on the tree, exclaimed: 'P'an 潘, your life is exposed in such a lofty position.' 'By no means,' replied the monk, 'I enjoy perfect tranquillity, and can meditate at ease.' 'Then give me some

---

*Pu-tai 布袋 is also called A-mi-t'ê 阿彌陀 or Amitabha and he is represented as seated and holding one end of the bag. Some representations have him in the bag, which is like a cot and three or six "thieves" are drawing it along, or the "thieves," the deadly sins, are young lads with the well-known two tufts of hair on their otherwise bald heads; they are not *ya-t'ou* 了頭 in sense of *slave-girls* or *daughters*.

good advice,' continued the scholar. 'Try to do good and avoid evil,' said the monk. 'But a three-year old child knows all that,' retorted the scholar. 'Yes,' replied the monk, 'but gray heads fail to practise it.'" This arhat died A.D. 824. Is represented in pictures seated on the branch of a tree, his legs hanging down, and an ear-ring on the lobe of his right ear.—See also *Buddhist Schools.*

2. Tzǔ-tsai Ch'an-shih 自 在 禪 師. Isvara.—Came to China from India. Lived in the time of the Yüan 元 dynasty. Used his extraordinary magic powers to prevent a rebellion, for which crime he and a hundred of his followers were buried alive. The executioner then beheaded them, but Tzǔ-tsai's 自 在 head sprang up five times after being severed from the body. Is represented with heavy eyebrows, short hair, bare breast and stomach, and holding a fly-whisk in his right hand.

3. Tao-t'ung Ch'an-shih 道 通 禪 師.—A native of Lu-chiang 廬 江, Anhui 安 徽, Teacher, the famous Buddhist monk Tao-i 道 一 (A.D. 742-56). Lived first on T'zu-yü Shan 紫 玉 山, near Tang-chou 當 州, Ssǔch'uan 四 川. Returned and died there (A.D. 813), aged 83, after visiting Lo-yang 洛 陽, Honan 河 南, in company with Fêng-kan 豐 干 (*infra*). Represented as an old man, with bushy hair and beard, and heavy eyebrows, seated on a mat and nursing his knees.

4. Fêng-kan Ch'an-shih 豐 干 禪 師.—Eighth century A.D. One day, as he travelled to Ch'ih-chêng 赤 城, "Red Wall," a hill about 180 miles S.E. of Hangchou 杭 州, Chêkiang 浙 江, he heard a child wailing by the roadside. He took the infant to the monastery, and had him educated as a monk. This child was later on known as Shih-tê 拾 得, the "Foundling" (*infra*).

Fêng-kan 豐 干 was of giant stature, fully seven feet in height. He spent his life in the Kuo-ch'ing Ssǔ 國 清 寺, Kuo-ch'ing Monastery, on T'ien-t'ai Shan 天 台 山, T'ien-t'ai Hill, Chekiang 浙 江. Whilst there, he cured Lü Ch'iu-yin 閭 邱 胤, Prefect of T'ai Chou 台 州, in the same province, of a violent headache. Of prodigious strength, he habitually rode a tiger, which obeyed him like a lamb, and even occasionally accompanied him into the monastery, to the great consternation of the other monks. He is represented in pictures riding the tiger. Watters notes the resemblance between him and the Hindu arhat Bhadra.

5. Hui-yüan Ch'an-shih 慧 遠 禪 師.—Family name Chia 賈. Born at Yen-mên 雁 門, Shansi 山 西. Soon became a proficient scholar of the classics and of Taoism. Became the disciple of the monk Tao-an 道 安 and took the monastic name of Hui-yüan 慧 遠. Lived for thirty years in the Lu-hsan Ssǔ 盧 山 寺, Kiangsi 江 西, where he gathered round him a large number of followers, and helped much in propagating the Ching-t'u 淨 土, or "Pure

Land," School, also known as the "Lotus School." Toward the end of his life, he had several apparitions of Amitabha, O-mi-t'o Fo 阿彌陀佛. Died about A.D. 454. Represented as a venerable old man, with heavy eyebrows, scanty beard, and a teacher's emblematic staff in his right hand.

6. Shih-tê Tzŭ 拾得子.—The "Foundling."

7. Han-shan Tzŭ 寒山子.—The "Arhat of the Cold Cave."

8. Hui-tsang Ch'an-shih 惠 [慧] 藏禪師.—Born in I-chou 黟州, Anhui 安徽. Lived in early part of seventh century A.D. At Lu-shan 盧山 unearthed a statue of Maitreya, which he set up in a temple, to which pilgrims resorted to worship it. Represented standing, his hands joined, with bare chest, a gold head-band, and a gold ring on his right ear-lobe.

9. Chü-ti Ho-shang 俱胝和伺.—The Monk Gunamati. One of Buddha's chief disciples. A native of Parvata. Author of many *shastras*. Lived in Vallabhi. Chinese Buddhists translate his name as Tê-hui 德慧, "Virtue and Wisdom." Represented as a venerable old man, sitting at the foot of a tree, his right hand raised in the attitude of teaching.

10. Tao-yüeh Ch'an-shih 道月禪師.—The Monk who lived on Golden Island. This is the island near Chên-chiang 鎭江 (Chinkiang), Kiangsu 江蘇. The famous general Yo Fei 岳飛 (A.D. 1103-41), "being opposed to peace with the Kin 金 Tartars, or "Golden Horde," was accused of treasonable designs by the Prime Minister Ch'in-kuei 秦檜. As the General travelled to Chên-chiang 鎭江, on the way to Hangchow 杭州, Chêkiang 浙江, he beheld in a dream a dark cloud covering the heavens, and two dogs which pursued him, forcing him, as it were, to cross the river. Puzzled at such a strange vision, he consulted the monk Tao Yüeh 道月, who then lived on Golden Island, and enjoyed a reputation for supernatural wisdom. The monk explained the dream as follows: Dissecting the character *yü* 獄, prison, 'this pictograph,' said he, 'is composed of yen 言, a word, in the centre, with a dog, '*ch'üan* 犬, standing on each side. Your dream is of evil omen,' continued he; 'you must not proceed further, otherwise you will perish in the coming storm, forecasted by the dark cloud, which you beheld in your dream.'

Yo Fei 岳飛 smiled at this ingenious interpretation, thanked the kind monk, and proceeded on his way to Hangchow 杭州. This happened A.D. 1141. A short time afterwards, the General was cast into prison, and put to death by the order of Ch'in Kuei 秦檜. He is represented seated, his head resting on his right hand. He is dressed in the yellow robes of a Buddhist monk, and seems to be entirely lost in abstract meditation (*dhyana*).

11. Singhalaputra.—Shih-tzŭ-pi-ch'iu Tsun-chê 獅子比丘尊者.— A Brahman arhat from India who afterwards became a Buddhist.

LO-HAN

The name means "Son of a Lion." In early years he went to Kandahar (the country of the Getae, who retreated westward before the Hsiung-nu 匈奴 invasion, 180 B.C., and conquered the Punjab and Kashmir, A.D. 126), and there made numerous converts to the Buddhist Law. He belonged to the Contemplative School, and followed the doctrine of inertia. According to his teaching, the method taught by the Buddhas is none other than this:—Let the mind do nothing, observe nothing, hold fast to nothing. Thus, living in the world, men will have already entered Nirvana. Having reproved some heterodox teachers, he was denounced to the Court, and finally put to death by the king. He is reckoned as the twenty-fourth Indian patriarch of Buddhism, but on account of the above unhappy fate, some hold that the succession was broken off at this point.

Another monk, bearing the name of Shih-tzŭ 獅子, lived in the time of the Ming 明 dynasty, and was associated with Tzŭ-ch'êng 子成, both of whom are said to have combined their labours, and written a short treatise on Buddhism (Wieger, Bouddhisme, i. 132). He is represented standing, dressed in the yellow robe of a Buddhist monk, bearing a mendicant's staff in his left hand, and attended by a disciple, who greets him, and listens attentively to his instructions.

12. Ts'ung-shên Ch'an-shih 從諗禪師.—Ninth century A.D. A native of Ch'ing Chou 青州, in modern Shantung 山東. Lived first in the Sung-shan Ssŭ 嵩山寺, Sung-shan Monastery, Honan 河南, and later established a flourishing school at Chao Chou 趙州, in modern S.W. Chihli 直隸. Hence known as Chao Chou Ch'an-shih 趙州禪師. "Teacher of Chao Chou." Represented standing, his left hand raised in the attitude of teaching, his right holding a broom partly concealed by his long sleeve. This symbol, according to Watters, may have been borrowed from Buddha having given to Cuda-Panthaka the surname of "Sweeping-broom."

13. Rahulata.—Lo-hou-lo-to Tsun-chê 羅睺羅多尊者.—"This Sramana was a native of Kapila. Instructed by Kanadeva, he became an eloquent expounder and defender of the Law. A legend relates that one day he ascended to the heaven of Brahma, to produce rice for a multitude of hearers. After fulfilling his destined work of reformation and instruction, he entered Nirvana, 113 B.C. Rahulata is reckoned the sixteenth patriarch of Indian Buddhism." Represented as an old man, sitting on a crag, and holding a mendicant's staff.

14. Shên-tsan Ch'an-shih 神讚禪師.—Apparently the same as Lan-ts'an 懶殘 q.v.), the lazy glutton monk (A.D. 742), who was a menial in the Hêng-yo Ssŭ 衡嶽寺, Hêng-yo Monastery, Hunan 湖南. When the monks had taken their meal, he greedily devoured the leavings, hence his name. For twenty years he lived

in the monastery cattle-pen. One day, Li Pi 李泌, the famous
scholar and statesman (A.D. 722-89), paid him a visit, and learnt
from him that he was soon to be promoted to the Prime Minister-
ship. Endowed with extraordinary magic powers, he is said to
have moved immense blocks of stone by merely pushing them with
his foot. Represented standing, his mendicant's staff, held in his
right hand, resting on the back of his neck, and his hat hung on
his left shoulder.

15. Kumarajiva.—Chiu-mo-lo-to Tsun-chê 鳩摩羅多尊者.—
or Chiu-mo-lo-shih 鳩摩羅什 (A.D. 360-415). Represented sitting
on a mat, "the upper abdomen ungracefully exposed to view, and
the legs pendent. He bears a rosary in the left hand, and a large
bag lies at his feet. From a critical standpoint, it must be
remarked that this image does not represent the great translator,
but rather the 'Monk with the Calico bag,' who was deemed to
be an incarnation of Maitreya, and to whom he bears a strong
resemblance.

Other illustrations represent Kumarajiva accompanied by a
lion and a dove, both of which emblems refer to a prodigy,
observed in the Imperial Park, a short time before the death of
Lü-tsuan 呂纂.

16. Maha-Kasyapa.—Mo-ho-chia-yeh Tsun-chê 摩訶迦葉尊者.—
"Kasyapa, or as he is more generally called Maha-Kasyapa, the
Great Kasyapa, was a Brahman of Magadha (Bahar), in Central
India, and one of the principal disciples of Buddha. He grasped
readily the teaching of the Master, and practised a severe ascetic
life. Buddha wished him to sit on the same seat as himself, but
to this he would never consent. When Guatama died at Kusinara,
he was apprised of the fact by an earthquake. Immediately afterwards, he convoked an assembly of five hundred Arhats, in the
Sattapanni cave, at Gridkrakuta, and compiled the first Buddhist
Canon. He then expounded the Law during twenty years at
Rajagriha, and being at the point of death, entrusted the deposit
of the doctrine to Ananda."

Kasyapa is held to be the first patriarch of Indian Buddhism.
He is greatly honoured in China. Represented as an old man,
with extremely long eyebrows. Holds a mendicant's staff in his
left hand, and in his right a scroll, symbolical of his great work,
the compilation of the Sutras.

17. Asvagosha.—Ma-ming Tsun-chê 馬鳴尊者.—"The Chinese
name of this arhat, Ma-ming 馬鳴, or the 'Horse's neighing,'
was given him owing to a legend, which states that the Scythian
king Kanishka selected seven horses, and after keeping them
without food for six days, led them to the place where Asvagosha
was preaching, and placed forage before them, but the horses
instead of eating, shed tears on hearing the words of the great
teacher, and refused the food. Asvagosha, therefore, became

celebrated, because the horses understood his voice, and hence he was called in memory of the fact, Ma-ming 馬 鳴, that is, 'a voice like the neighing of a horse.'

"Asvagosha belonged to the Brahman class, and lived not far from the time of Kanishka, which according to Beal was about A.D. 78. He was born at Benares, but taught chiefly at Pataliputra, where he converted in one day five hundred youths of princely families, who forthwith renounced all earthly ties, and became Buddhist monks. (Hereupon the king feared that his realm would become depopulated.) He travelled about, accompanied by a troop of musicians and women, and through these means made many converts to the Law. He was a skilful dialectician, and a great antagonist of Brahmanism. Among his writings are the *Buddha-charita*, or Life of Buddha, written in verse; the *Shastra for Awakening of Faith*, and the *Mahalamkara Sutra*, or series of sixty-six sermons on various subjects. He spent the last years of his life in Kashmir, and died about A.D. 100."

"Asvagosha is held to be the twelfth patriarch of Indian Buddhism. He was, with Nagarjuna, the founder of the Mahayana System, and in conjuction with Aryadeva, opened his way to the spread of the *Yogacarya School.*"

Represented sitting on a crag, his left shoulder slightly bared, and his feet pendent. He wears a ring on his left ear, his left hand is raised, and he gazes at a dragon, the symbol of his powerful genius, disporting itself in the clouds.

18. Pu-tai Ho-shang 布 袋 和 佾, or Pu-tai Ch'an-shih 布 袋 禪 師.—The Monk with the Calico Bag. Lived at the close of the ninth and beginning of the tenth century A.D.

Represented sitting, the upper part of his abdomen exposed to view, and the bag lying at his feet.—*Cf.* No. 15 *supra.*

Dharmatala of Dharmatrata.—Ta-mo-to-lo 達 摩 多 羅.—The Tibetan list has its eighteen Arhats, comprising the sixteen of Su-shih's 蘇 軾 list, and two others added, namely the Upasaka Dharmatala, or Dharmatrata, and Hvashan. The latter corresponds to the "Monk with the Calico Bag" (*supra,* No. 18). Kennelly appends the following short description of Dharmatala: —"This Arhat was born at Gandhara, and seems to be the uncle of Vasumitra. His name is interpreted 'Religious Saviour,' Fa-chiu 法 救. Though he was but an Upasaku, or lay-follower, he wrote several works, of which the principal are the *Udanavarga* (translated by Rockhill), and the *Samyuktabhidharma Shastra,*" translated into Chinese about A.D. 438.

He is represented with long-flowing hair, a bundle of books on his back, and a fly-whisk in his hand. In some pictures, he gazes on a small image of Maitreya.

The Wu-wei Chou 撫 為 州 group is peculiar, as it reduces the number of Hindu names (there are only seven in the Chinese list) already known through Nandimitra's list, and introduces in their stead several lo-han 羅漢 of purely Chinese origin (see Kennelly, vii. 355-6). This list assigns the seventeenth place to Asvagosha and the eighteenth to Pu-tai Ho-shang 布袋和尚. The original idea of Kuan-hsiu 貫休, it would seem, escaped the notice both of Su-shih 蘇軾 and Ch'ien Lung 乾隆, and was ignored even in many Buddhist monasteries. The two added are merely symbolical, and, as noted above, represent in all likelihood the "Arhat who subdued the Dragon," Chiang-lung 降龍, and the "Arhat who tamed the Tiger," Fu-hu 伏虎 (*Journal Asiatique,* September-October 1916, pp. 285-6).

For some of the best known lists, and variations, of the Eighteen Arhats, see Kennelly, vii. 353-6, and pp. 373-6 for particulars regarding groups of 32, 108, 500, 1,000, 1,200, 5,000, etc., Arhats.

For the Sixteen and Eighteen Arhats of Tibet, showing variations from those of Chinese Buddhism, see Waddell, pp. 376-8.

Female arhats.—The rule was that no woman could attain to Buddhahood without being reborn as a man. Women were debarred from Amitabha's paradise. Buddha a misogynist and misogamist, was toward the end of his life persuaded by Ananda to admit some females to the Sangha (*Priesthood*). The first nun was Mahaprajapata, Buddha's nurse. They were placed under the direction of the monks, and were subject to them in all matters of religious discipline.

Arhatship, in theory open to all, could practically only be obtained by those who left the world, and led a celibate, monastic life. Hardy (*Manual of Buddhism,* p. 39) says that in the early phase of Buddhism some females attained to arhatship. The *Avadana-Sataka,* or "Sutra of the Hundred Legends" (a Nepalese work in prose, containing stories of female arhats), mentions ten, who abandoned the world, and entered the path leading to Nirvana. Some even acquired transcendent powers, and could fly through the air at will. The same number of ten is also found in the Pali work, *Sanyutta-Nikaya.* The *Theri-Apadana* and the *Theri-Gatha* also contain legends, the former of forty, the latter of sixty-three female arhats. Kennelly (vii 385-7) gives the names and descriptions, taken from those two works, of the ten female arhats. Three of them are of princely descent, and one is the daughter of a Brahman. Nearly all refused to be married, or renounced the married state. The names are as follows:—

1. Suprabha, or the Brilliant. 2. Supriya, the Dearly-beloved. 3. Sukla or Sukha, the White-robed. 4. Soma, the Moon. 5. Kuvalaya, the Blue Lotus. 6. Kasika-Sundari, the Beautiful Maid of Kasi. 7. Mukta, the Pearl. 8. Kasangala, a slave-woman named after that place. 9. Khema, the Fortunate. 10. Virupa, the Ugly-faced. For short biographical notices of each, see Kennelly, vii, 385-7.

The successive grades of Buddhist disciples are stated by

Kennelly (vii, 333-7) as follows:—Both monks and laymen formed various grades of adherents, of whom the following are the principal.

1. *Upasakas.*—These were mere lay members, who, without entering upon monastic life, observed the five chief rules of conduct. Their practical religion was to give food and clothing to the monks. Wealthy folks built monasteries, or donated parks, gardens, wells and bathing-rooms for the use of the community. They thus acquired merit, and shared in the good works of the monks.

2. *Sramanas,* or *Samanas.*—This term means ascetic, or subject to monastic discipline. It comprised all those who separated themselves from their family and the world, and were admitted into the *Sangha.* (Gautama discouraged solitary asceticism. The true Buddhist leads a celibate monastic life.) All such members were deemed to have entered the stream leading to Arhatship. In former times, they were called Bhikshus, that is, "mendicant monks," because they led a life of poverty, and lived by alms.

3. *Sotapanni.*—Those who through Dhyana, or contemplation, have obtained the first inner perception of truth and sanctity, are called *Sotapanni.* The *Sotapanno* has freed himself from the first three fetters—namely, delusion of self, doubts about Buddha's doctrine, and dependence on external rites. He can only be reborn as a god or man, but not in the four lower phases of sentient beings (as an *asura,* or demon; an animal; a *prêta,* or hungry ghost; or as a being undergoing torments in hell).

4. *Sakad-agami.*—This is the state of the ascetic, who has nearly freed himself from the first five fetters, but has not yet conquered the craving for existence, either on earth or in heaven. This longing is still sufficiently strong to cause one more birth on the earth.

5. *An-agami.*—In this state, the ascetic is quite free from all craving for existence on earth, but not from longing for an immaterial life in the higher heavens. Such a man can only be reborn in a *Brahmaloka,* from which he reaches Nirvana. He is, therefore, called *An-agami,* or "one who will not come back to earth."

6. *Arhats* or *Rahans.*—The Arhat is the ascetic, who is freed from all the ten fetters; from all attachment to existence, whether on earth or in heaven; and from all force of Karma. He is the completely freed man, and while still living is wholly dead to the world. He has also acquired transcendent powers over Nature matter, time and space. He can make his body lighter or heavier, smaller or larger than anything in the world; he can reach any

place, and assume any shape at will. He has knowledge of all things, and recollection of all previous existence. In short, he is perfectly wise, and has nothing more to learn. At deatĥ, he will experience no further rebirth, but must either enter Nirvana, or cease to exist (*cf. supra*).

In theory, this arhatship is open to all, laymen as well as monks, and even to women, but practically can only be obtained by those who leave the world, and lead a celibate monastic life.

7. *Sravakas.*—The term *Sravaka* was used in the Hinayana system, to denote the great disciples of Buddha, and especially those who heard the law from his own lips, and became afterwards renowned Arhats. Among those chief disciples were *Sariputra* and *Maudgalyayana,* who died before the Buddha; and sixteen leaders among the so-called eighty "great disciples," the principal of these being *Mahakasyapa, Upali, Ananda, Anuruddha* and *Katyayana.* At a later time, two chief female disciples, named *Khema* and *Uppalavanna,* were added. Each leading disciple was afterwards called "Sthavira," or Elder.

8. *Pratyeka-Buddha.*—The followers of Buddha thought it desirable to fill up the gap between the ordinary Arhat and the Supreme Buddha, and thus adopted the idea of the *Pratyeka-Buddha.* This *Pratyeka* or *Nidana Buddha* is a solitary saint, who has attained perfection for himself, and through himself alone, and not as a member of a monastic community. He is thus a concentrated, selfish being, the ideal, it is true to state, of the Hinayana system, but quite opposed to the latter development of the Mahayana School. He is not absolutely omniscient, like the Supreme Buddha, and hence does not communicate his knowledge to others. A *Pratyeka-Buddha* never appears on earth at the same time with a Supreme Buddha.

9. *The Supreme Buddha.*—Buddha means the "Enlightened," the "Wise." He is the self-elevated man, perfect in knowledge, and who has by the practice of the ten transcendent virtues, and through the extinction of the passions, and of all desire for existence, reached holiness and the highest summits of Arhatship. He has, however, delayed entering Nirvana, that he may help mortals, and become the Saviour of a suffering world. This is the Supreme Buddha, Guatama, who saves men by teaching them how to save themselves. He is thus immensely superior both to Pratyeka-Buddhas, and the most perfect Arhats.

Sakyamuni, Shih-chia Fo 釋迦佛, is the fourth Buddha of the present kalpa. He will be followed by the fifth Buddha, Maitreya, Mi-lo Fo 彌勒佛, who will appear on earth after a lapse of three thousand years.

The place of the Lohan 羅漢 in Chinese art is described in the following passages from Kennelly (vii, 376-7):—"Chinese pictorial art lavished upon the Lohan 羅漢, much as it did upon Kuan Yin

觀 音, its best inspiration. The groups of sixteen and eighteen were principally represented. These pictures and images, however, are not supposed to be faithful representations of the personages indicated by name. They are to be taken merely as symbols, or fanciful creations of the painter or artist. Waddell says each one has his distinctive symbol or badge. Thus Panthaka sits beneath a tree, the arms folded; Bhadra is accompanied by a tiger; Nakula holds a mongoose, or a three-legged frog under the left arm; Cuda-Panthaka has a broom concealed beneath his mantle. The 'Monk with the Calico Bag' has a sack suspended from a staff placed over the shoulder, or it lies sometimes at his feet. This monk is the patron of tobacco-sellers, and his jolly, fat little image often adorns their shop-fronts. Four of the Arhats, in the Wu-wei Chou 撫 爲 州 list, wear a ring on the ear, as a badge of honour. Incarnations of Maitreya, the Future Buddha, are represented as big-bellied, smiling, and generally in a sitting posture."

Some modern artists seem to confound the Lohan 羅 漢 with the Immortals, and represent them crossing the bitter sea of human life to the happy shores of Nirvana, or enjoying lives of endless bliss amidst groves of pines on misty mountain-tops.

The Lohan 羅 漢 are generally represented as old, with white hair, long-lobed ears, and extremely long eyebrows. The Chinese call Pindola the "long-eyebrowed monk." Some are depicted standing, others sitting on a mat or the ledge of a rock; those who propagated the Law, are represented with a book or scroll in the hand, and a small disciple at the side; others hold in the hand an alms-bowl, a fan, or a mendicant's staff.—For the location of the principal famous pictures, see *ibid.* pp. 377-83.

LO-HOU 羅 睺, THE GOD OF THE STAR.—See *P'êng Tsun* 彭 遵.

LO-HOU-LO-TO TSUN-CHÊ 羅 睺 羅 多 尊 者.—See *Lo-han* 羅 漢.

LO HSÜAN 羅 宣. Huo-tê Hsing-chün 火 德 星 君.—President of the ministry of Fire.—See *Huo Pu* 火 部.

LO-HU-LO 囉 怙 羅.—See *Lo-han* 羅 漢.

LOCHANA.—See *Lu shê na* 盧 舍 那.

LOCUSTS, THE GOD OF.—See *Pa Cha* 叭 咤.

LOCUSTS THE GODDESS OF.—It is said that Chiang T'ai-kung 姜 太 公 divorced his wife in 1122 B.C., and when she was afterwards killed by lightning he made her the Locust-goddess.—See *Pa Cha* 叭 咤.

LOCUSTS, THE GREAT KING OF.—See *Pa Cha* 叭 咤.

LOCUSTS, THE PROTECTING SPIRIT AGAINST.—See *Liu-mêng Chiang-chün* 劉猛將軍.

LOKA.—A world, a division of the universe. In general the *tri-loka* or three worlds are heaven, earth, and hell. Another classification enumerates seven, exclusive of the infernal regions, also seven in number which are classed under Patala (*q.v.*)

LOKAPALAS.—Hu-shih Chê 護世者. — Protectors. *lit.* Guardians of the Universe. A title given to valorous deities and saints.—See *Ssŭ ta T'ien-wang* 四大天王.

LONG-EARED FIX-LIGHT IMMORTAL, THE. — See *Ch'ang-êrh Ting-kuang Hsien* 長耳定光仙.

LONGEVITY, THE GOD OF.—See *Shou Hsing* 壽星.

LONGEVITY, THE STAR OF.—See *Shou Hsing* 壽星.

LORD OF THE BLACK PAVILIONS, THE.—See *Hsüan-t'ien Shang-ti* 玄天上帝.

LO SHÊN 羅神.—The Spirits Lo. The Spirit Oculists. Yen-mu Ssŭ 眼目司 and Yen-mu Hou 眼目侯. In the Ming 明 dynasty, in the reign of the Emperor Shih Tsung 世宗 (A.D. 1522-67), a disgraced Censor Fêng En 馮恩 was exiled to Kuang-tung 廣東 (he was afterwards proved innocent and recalled).
Whilst there he found the people being molested by five brothers named Lo 羅. These later on repented of their sins and committed suicide.
After he left, Fêng En 馮恩 suffered from cataract. In a dream he saw the Spirits of these five men, and on waking found himself completely cured. He accordingly built a temple to them, and all who suffered from eye troubles went there to implore the aid of the Spirit Oculists.

LO-TSU TA-HSIEN 羅祖大仙.—The God of Barbers, Beggars, and Corn-cutters. A disciple of Lao Tzŭ 老子, who "returned to the world" and gained a livelihood as a street barber, using a piece of steel as a razor. Represented in private houses with bare feet, rolled-back sleeves, and a red face, but in temples as holding a work on hair-cutting, entitled *T'i-fa shu* 薙髮書.

LOTUS OR AMIDIST SCHOOL, THE.—See *Buddhist Schools*, XVII.

LOU 婁, **THE GOD OF THE CONSTELLATION.**—See *Liu Lung* 劉隆 and *Chang Hsiung Tao-jên* 張雄道人.

LOU-TZŬ SÊNG 樓子僧.—A saintly Buddhist monk. One of those invited to the annual banquet of the gods (see *Hsi Wang-mu* 西王母).

LU CH'ANG 盧昌.—The god of the star T'ien-chi 天機.—See *T'ien-kang* 天罡.

LU CH'I 盧杞.—See *Wên Ch'ang* 文昌.

LU CHIH 魯芝.—The god of the star Ti-hui 地會.—See *Ti-sha* 地煞.

LU HSIU-TÊ 魯修德.—The god of the star Ti-hsiung 地雄.—See *Ti-sha* 地煞.

LU JÊN-CHIEH 魯仁傑.—See *Wu Tou* 五斗.

LU PAN 魯班.—The God of Carpenters. President of the Celestial Ministry of Public Works. Family name Kung-shu 公輸, personal names Pan 班 and I-chih 依智. Born at Wu-tun Fu 兗州府, Shantung 山東, the ancient feudal kingdom of Lu 魯, whence his name Lu-Pan 魯班, *i.e.* Pan of Lu. His father was Kung-shu Hsien 公輸賢, his mother being of the Wu 吳 family. He was born in 506 B.C. As a youth he practised and became skilled in all kinds of metal, stone and wood work. At 40 years of age he retired to live the life of a hermit on Li Shan 歷山, Mount Li, in Shantung 山東, and was initiated into miracle-working, being able to rise into the air and ride on the clouds. In the reign of Yung Lo 永樂 (A.D. 1403-25) of the Ming 明 dynasty he received the title of Grand Master, Sustainer of the Empire. Artisans who pray to him have their requests granted immediately.

Another biography gives his name as Kung-shu Tzŭ 公輸子, adds that he was called Pan 班 (殷 or 盤), and describes him as a clever man of Lu 魯. Some say he was the son of Mu 穆, duke of Lu 魯. He carved wooden magpies which could float in the air for three days, and constructed a wooden coachman which drove an automobile, as well as engines of war for battering down the walls of cities.

Still another account of his life states that Lu Pan 魯般 belonged to Tun-huang Hsien 燉煌縣, Kansu 甘肅. He made a wooden kite, on which his father could fly long distances in the air. When he flew to Wu-hui 吳會, Kiangsu 江蘇, the people mistook him for a devil and killed him. Angered at this, Pan 般 constructed an Immortal in wood which, on pointing its finger in the direction of the town, caused a drought which lasted three years. When the inhabitants ascertained the cause, they sent him presents to appease him, and he cut off the image's hand, whereupon copious rain fell in Wu 吳.

These differences can only be reconciled by concluding that Lu Pan 魯班 and Kung-shu Tzǔ 公輸子 were two different persons, the one having lived in Shantung 山東 in the time of the Six Kingdoms (3rd cent. B.C.), and the other in Kansu 甘肅 after the time of the Emperor Ming-ti 明帝 (A.D. 58-76) of the Han 漢 dynasty, when Buddhism was officially recognized in China. At the present day, Lu Pan 魯班 is worshipped, without regard to the question whether the name belongs to one man or to two. Temples dedicated to Lu Pan 魯班 are still maintained. He is especially worshipped (on the thirteenth day of the fifth and on the twenty-first day of the seventh moon) by carpenters and varnishers (the latter generally worship his two wives).

He is stated in the *Hsi-yu chi* 西遊記 to have been one of the two Ministers of Public Works of the god Yü Huang 玉皇, being entrusted jointly with his colleague Chang 張 with the building of the Sun-wu Kung 孫悟空 palace in Yü Ti's 玉帝 peach-garden.—See also *Huang Ch'u-p'ing* (皇) 黄初平.

[LU-SHAN] K'UANG-FOU HSIEN-SHÊNG 廬山匡阜先生.
—The name of this Taoist was K'uang-hsü 匡續, his two personal names Chün-p'ing 君平 and Fou 阜. A native of Ch'u 楚. The second of five brothers. Whilst still very young, he conceived the idea of becoming a recluse, refused the offers of office made him by the king, Wu Wang 武王 (1121-1114 B.C.), and returned to the S. of Nan-chang Shan 南障山, Nan-chang Mountain, on the borders of the Hu Ch'i 虎溪, Tiger River, where he built himself a straw hut, living in poverty with his books. Here he was visited by Jung Ch'êng-kung 容成公, under the guise of a young man calling himself Liu-yüeh 劉越, who taught him the secrets of the Immortals.

In the period 1079-1052 B.C. K'uang-hsü 匡續 declared himself a disciple of Lao Tzǔ 老子, who (in a previous existence) taught him some magic formulas. When Lao Tzǔ 老子 withdrew to P'o 亳, K'uang-hsü 匡續 returned to Ch'u 楚 (in the period 1052-1001 B.C.) where he taught his brothers the doctrine of immortality.

Later, he saved the life of the Emperor Wu Ti 武帝 (140-86 B.C.) of the Han 漢 dynasty, under the following circumstances. The Emperor, when passing through P'êng-li 彭蠡 on his return from the Southern Sacred Mountain (Hêng Shang 衡山, in Hunan 湖南), worshipped at a temple dedicated to K'uang-su 匡俗, K'uang-hsü's 匡續 elder brother. Proceeding thence to Hsün-yang Chiang 潯陽江, the sound of a drum on the imperial barge angered a dragon, which raised such huge waves that the vessel was almost submerged. Then a man armed with a bow was seen coming along on the waves and boarding the vessel. He spoke respectfully to the Emperor, saying he had been sent to protect his Majesty by his brother, out of gratitude for the honour done to him in his temple. He then shot the dragon with his arrows; calm supervened at once, and K'uang-hsü 匡續 disappeared. The Taoists having explained the relationship of the two K'uangs 匡, the Emperor canonized K'uang-hsü 匡續 as Nan-chi Ta-ming Kung 南極大明公, Very Illustrious Duke of the South Pole. He also had a temple built to him on the borders of the Tiger River. This temple was later removed by Huan I 桓伊, Prefect of Chiu-yin 舊隱, to Lu Shan 廬山.

K'uang-hsü 匡續 is in charge of the Ministry of Epidemics (see *Ministries*), and protects those who seek his aid in times of drought, inundations, or contagious diseases. The five Marshals of Epidemics were obliged to submit to him and are under his orders. He is gifted with a remarkable power over dragons and tigers, being able to bestride them at will.

The above account, compiled from the *Sou-shên chi* 搜神記 and the *Shên-hsien t'ung-chien* 神仙通鑑, evidently contains errors in dates.

LU-SHÊ-NA 盧舍那.—Lochana.—The reflex, or ideal representation of the universal essence of Buddha. Worshipped by Chinese Buddhist monks. In China, he is represented with a halo round his head, short curly locks, long lobed ears, and arms extended, with the palms of his hands directed downward in an attitude of charity. He is shown in a sitting posture, with one foot showing and folded over the other, which is hidden under his garments.

LU-SHÊN 祿神.—The God of Office (or Official Emoluments). Shih [Tan] Fên 石奮, a scholar of Ho-nei 河内, who became a high official at the Court of the Emperor Ching Ti 景帝 (156-140 B.C.) of the Han 漢 dynasty, was given by the Emperor the honorary title of Wan-shih Chün 萬石君. He was noted for the large amount of emoluments received by him. All the members of his family became very wealthy. He is one of the three gods referred to in the common phrase *Fu-lu-shou san-hsing* 福祿壽三星, the three stars of Happiness, Emoluments, and Longevity, whose pictures and images are seen everywhere in various forms. He is also one of the five Star-spirits in the South Pole Star-group, of which Shou Hsing 壽星, the Star of Longevity, is regarded as the President. See also *Wu Tou* (*Nan Tou*) 五斗 (南斗).

LU T'OU 路頭.—See *Ts'ai Shên* 財神.

LU-YA TAO-JÊN 陸壓道人.—Lived in a cave to the west of K'un-lun 崑崙 Mountains. Fought in defence of Wu Wang 武王. Slew with his sword Yü Yüan 余元, a disciple of T'ung-t'ien Chiao-chu 通天教主, taken captive to Chiang Tzŭ-ya 姜子牙, and split the skull of Pai Li 白禮, fifteenth member of the Ministery of Thunder.

LUCK, THE GOD OF.—"King Wan [萬] is the man; they do not call him 'god of luck,' but 'King Wan's luck.' Only worshipped in times of sickness. They light three sticks of incense when they go to consult the blind fortune-teller, and three sticks when they return" (Du Bose p. 403).

LUNG 龍.—The Chinese rendering (*na-chia* 那 迦, *lung-shên* 龍 神 or *lung-kuei* 龍 鬼), of the Sanscrit *naga*. Dragon-spirits or dragon-demons. Explained as signifying (1) *lung* 龍, *lit.* dragons, (2) *hsiang* 象, *lit.* elephants (*nagaga*), (3) *pu-lai* 不 來, *lit.* persons exempt from transmigration (Eitel, p. 102). Originally "applied to dreaded mountain tribes, and subsequently used to designate monsters generally. The worship of *nagas* (*i.e.* dragons and serpents) is indigenous in China and flourishes even now, dragons being regarded as mountain spirits, as tutelary deities of the five regions (*i.e.* four points of the compass and centre), and as the guardians of the five lakes and four oceans (*i.e.* of all lakes and seas). The worship of *nagas* has been observed as a characteristic of Turanian nations. The Aryan Buddhists, finding it too popular, connived at or adopted this worship. All the most ancient *sutras* and biographies of Buddha mention *nagas*, who washed Buddha after his birth, conversed with him, protected him, were converted by him, and guarded the relics of his body. Chinese Buddhists view mountain *nagas* as enemies of mankind, but marine *nagas* as piously inclined. Whilst the Burmese confound *devas* and *nagas,* the Chinese distinguish them sharply. According to an ancient phrase (*lung, t'ien, pa pu* 龍 天 八 部 *lit. nagas, devas* and others of the eight classes) there are eight classes of beings, always enumerated in the following order, *devas, nagas, rakchas, gandharvas, asuras, garudas, kinnaras, mahoragas.*"

The terms "dragon" and "serpent" were practically synonymous in ancient times. The Dragon standard was adopted by the Emperor of Constantinople from the Assyrians, and it was an especial object of worship by the Babylonians. It was also worshipped both in China and Japan. The great Chinese Dragon was, as in Rome and Babylon, the banner of the Empire, and indicated everything sacred. Just also as the serpent was the insignia of royalty and dominion in Egypt, so the dragon was "the stamp and symbol of royalty in China, and is sculptured in all temples." "The Chinese," writes Cambry, "delight in mountains and high places, because there lives the dragon upon whom their good fortune depends. They call him 'the Father of Happiness.' To this dragon they erect temples shaded with groves." "The dragon," says Mr. Lillie, "represents the Indian cobra as a symbol in China for the supreme god." He is called the "Dragon King," and prayers are regularly offered to him.

Therefore, although the dragon is not actually identified with Amitabha, or Adi Buddha, yet it is plain that he occupies a similar position, and Sangha being at once "the voice, or manifestation, of the dragon," and the incarnation of Amitabha, an intimate connection between the two is implied. This also is the case with Sakyamuni when he takes the place of the mythological Sangha. He is called "the King of the Serpents," "the Tree of Knowledge and the Sun," thus occupying, as Buddha, apparently the same position as the Babylonian Hea, or the prophet Nebo.—Garnier, *The Worship of the Dead,* pp. 108-9, quoting Elliot, *Horæ Apocalypta,* iii. 14; Vossius *De Idol,* iv, liv.; Deane, *Serpent Worship,* pp. 46 69, 70; *Bel and the Dragon;* Stukeley, *Abury,* p. 56; Maurice, *Hist. Hind.,* i. 210; Cambry, *Monuments Celtiques,* p. 163; Lillie, *Buddha and Early Buddhism,* p. 31; Edkins, *Chinese Buddhism,* p. 207.

LUNG AN-CHI 龍安吉.—The god of the star Lan-kan 欄杆. An officer of the advance-guard of the army camped at Ch'uan-yün Kuan 穿雲關. Slain by No-cha 哪吒.

LUNG CH'ÊNG 龍成.—The god of the star Ti-p'ing 地平. —See *Ti-shu* 地帥.

LUNG-CHI KUNG-CHU 龍吉公主.—The goddess of the star Hung-luan 紅鸞. Daughter of Hsi Wang-mu 西王母. Helped to extinguish the incendiary fires at Hsi-ch'i 西岐. Married Hung-chin 洪錦, he and she being slain at T'ung-kuan 潼關.

LUNG CHÜ 龍且.—A celebrated *ch'êng-huang* 城隍, or city-god (of Tan Shiu 灘水). Han 漢 dynasty.

LUNG-HSÜ HU 龍鬚虎.—The god of the star Chiu-ch'ou 九醜. A disciple of Chiang Tzǔ-ya 姜子牙. Slain by Wu Wên-hua 烏文化 at the battle of Mêng-ching 孟津.

LUNG HUAN 龍環.—See *Wu Tou* 五斗.

LUNG TÊ-CHÜ 龍德拘.—See *Gall, The God of the.*

LUNG WANG 龍王; HAI LUNG-WANG 海龍王. The Dragon-kings or Sea Dragon-kings. Tutelary genii of seas, rivers, lakes, and waters generally. The Neptunes of the Chinese. A *naga* (*q.v.*) or dragon-spirit, or genius, one of the snake-gods, with human faces, who live in the lower regions below the earth, or under the waters. The Dragon-kings have their palaces at the bottom of the ocean, north of Mt. Meru.

The Dragon, the most famous of the symbolic animals, "before becoming the symbol of sovereign power, was the emblem of the first royal dynasty, that of the Hsia 夏 (or rather, one of the emblems which tradition ascribed to the Hsia 夏). One of the ancestors of the Hsia 夏 transformed himself into a Dragon in a

Holy Place. This metamorphosis took place after he had been cut to pieces. It is therefore the sequel to a sacrifice. Dragons appeared when there was a renewal or a decline of the generic virtue by which the Hsia 夏 were empowered to reign. One branch of their family had the privilege of breeding dragons and knew the art of making them thrive. One King of the Hsia 夏 fed upon dragons to make his reign prosperous. Finally, two dragon ancestors procured a birth for the descendants of the Hsia 夏. Remarkable to relate: they fought with each other before they disappeared, leaving nothing behind them but a fertilizing foam. Duels between dragons, male and female, were a sign of rain, and had for their stage the marshes formed by two rivers which had overflowed their banks. In such a case it was also said that the rivers were wrestling together, no doubt in sexual duels, for the gods of two rivers which mingle are thought to be of different sexes. Two rivers which mingle are, moreover, a symbol of exogamy. Their junctions were, in fact, places sacred to amorous jousts. In time of spate, the boys and girls believed that by crossing the water they assisted the reincarnations and called down the fertilizing rain. Now it was believed that the crossing of the water by companies, meeting and dancing, was practised in imitation of the duel of the dragons, male and female. They were thus instigated to unite and to send down the fertilizing waters. It is obvious that before becoming the princely emblem, the dragon was the motif of popular dances. The dragons were at first a projection into the mythical world of the rites and games of the seasonal festivals. But as soon as they are regarded as the patrons of a race of Chieftains who alone are able to feed upon them and make them thrive, these dragons, from being simple emanations of the Holy Place, take shape as Ancestors. All the virtue of the Holy Place, all the virtue of the Festivals is in them. It is also present, though diffused, in the race of heroes. It is actually incarnate only in the pair of Great Ancestors who themselves render the incarnations certain, and who, alone, are both dragons and men" (Granet, pp. 181-2).

The dragon in China is a deity, symbolic of fertile rain, rain-sending clouds, thunder and lightning. As a water-god he soars in the clouds, and pours out his blessings on the parched earth (De Groot, III, 1194).

The Dragons live in the heavens in the spring, and return to the deep in the autumn. The Dragon-king, Lung Wang 龍王, has usurped the place of the God of Waters (see Feng-I 馮夷). The Shên Lung 神龍, Spiritual Dragon, controls the streams, floods, seas, and rains. He acts both as a blessing and a curse to man. He moves his head and blows out the clouds, that the earth may be nourished. At other times he returns to his sea home and the clouds retain their moisture. Worshipped on the first and fifteenth of each month. His aid is sought by the people during a drought. He constantly benefits the people. On the other hand, he is blamed for floods, obstructed rivers, and many of the cataclysms of nature. Lung Men 龍門, in Honan 河南, owes its name to the belief that the fish which succeeded in passing the falls there became dragons. The *San Ch'in chi* 三秦記 says, "The fish from the rivers and seas gather together below Lung Men 龍門. Those who can pass on upstream turn into dragons, while those who cannot, bump their heads and bruise their cheeks" (quoted from *P'ei wên yün fu* 佩文韻府, Vol. 13, 2nd part). The saying *Li yü t'iao lung mên* 鯉魚跳龍門, "The carp has leaped through the dragon gate," has long been used in allusion to literary successes, whether in the examinations or elsewhere. The theme, originating in China, was afterwards extensively used in Japanese literature and art (see also *Sagara* and *Virupakcha*).

In China the dragon, except as noted below, is not a power for evil, but a beneficent being producing rain and representing the fecundating principle in nature. By controlling the rain, he "holds in his power prosperity and peace." Generally, the dragons are regarded as protecting and benefiting those who worship them. The evil dragons are those introduced by the Buddhists, who applied the current dragon legends to the *nagas* inhabiting the mountains, these being harmful, as distinguished from the friendly and helpful ones inhabiting lakes and rivers.

The dragon is most generally represented as having the head of a horse and the tail of a snake, with wings on its sides. It has four legs. The imperial dragon has five claws on each foot, other dragons only four. The dragon's "nine resemblances" are as follows:—horns of a deer, head of a camel, eyes of a devil, neck of a snake, abdomen of a large cockle, scales of a carp, claws of an eagle, soles of its feet those of a tiger, and the ears of an ox. Some, however, have no ears, the creature being supposed to hear through its horns.

Other accounts describe it as having a head of a camel, with a pearl in its forehead, with a long beard, behind which are *ni-lin* 逆鱗 (large scales in reverse position, a foot in length; to touch them is death to the offender), and with a sharp sword as a tongue. "He has the horns of a deer, eyes of a rabbit, ears of a cow, neck of a snake, belly of a frog, scales of a carp, claws of a hawk, and the palms of a tiger" (Plopper, p. 48). "It is said that the blood of some dragons is red; of others, black. The saliva of the dragon . . . is purple in colour, and is considered the most fragrant of all perfumes" (Hayes, p. 28). "As he passes from place to place he is royal in his stride and appearance, and receives the homage of all living beings. He has the power of altering his size, becoming exceedingly large or infinitesimally small, at will. He can also make himself visible or invisible, as he chooses" (Plopper, pp. 48-8). This has given rise to many superstitions. Living in the earth and waters, they, if disturbed, bring trouble and misfortune to the locality.

The dragon is usually pictured trying to catch a ball. "This has sometimes been thought to be a pearl or the sun, but is really a spider he fears will enwrap him in his net" (Plopper). However, this explanation seems less plausible than that which interprets the ball as representing the sun: the idea being that swallowing the sun is impossible, and for this reason a dragon trying to swallow the sun used to be painted on the screen in front of a magistrate's or other official yamên, the idea to be conveyed being that it was as impossible for the official to deal unjustly as it was for the dragon to swallow the sun.

"According to Chinese tradition, every dragon possesses and generally wears on his forehead a 'pearl of potentiality'—said by some to be the egg symbol of the dual influences of nature [v. Yin-Yang 陰陽] . . . , and by others to be the symbol of thunder rolling—and if it is lost the dragon is rendered powerless" (Williams, p. 48).

"The small dragon is like a silk caterpillar. The large dragon fills the heaven and the earth." Before the dragon, sometimes suspended from his neck, is a pearl. This represents the sun. There are azure, scaly, horned, hornless, winged, etc., dragons, with apparently evolve one out of the other.

The dragon is also represented as the father of the great emperors of ancient times. He has the power of transformation and of rendering himself visible or invisible at pleasure. In the spring he ascends to the skies, and in the autumn buries himself in the watery depths. Some are wingless, and rise into the air by their own inherent power. There is the celestial dragon, t'ien-lung 天龍, who guards the mansions of the gods and supports them so that they do not fall; the divine or spiritual dragon, shên-lung 神龍, who causes the winds to blow and produces rain for the benefit of mankind; the earth dragon, ti-lung 地龍, who marks out the courses of rivers and streams; and the dragon of the hidden treasures, fu-tsang lung 伏藏龍, who watches over the wealth concealed from mortals.

The Buddhists count their dragons in number equal to the fish of the great deep, which defies arithmetical computation, and can be expressed only by their sacred numerals. The people have a more certain faith in them than in most of their divinities, because they see them so often; every cloud with a curious configuration or serpentine tail is a dragon. He rules the hills, is connected with fêng-shui 風水, dwells round the graves, is associated with the Confuciist worship, is the Neptune of the sea, and appears on dry land.

The dragon of the Chinese "differs from the generally accepted Western idea . . . in appearance, in disposition, and in the regard in which it is held. The European dragon is usually portrayed as a cruel monster, the personification of all that is evil and the enemy of man. The Chinese dragon, on the other hand, is in this very respect very nearly its antithesis. It is a beneficent creature, a friend to man. It brings the rain which produces the crops that in turn supply his food" (L. N. Hayes, quot. Plopper, p. 47, note a).

From the most ancient times, the dragon has been considered the chief of the Four Spiritual Animals (these being Ling 麟, the Unicorn, Fêng 鳳, the Phoenix, Kuei 龜, the tortoise, and Lung 龍, the dragon).

Gifted with an accepted form, which he has the supernatural power of casting off for the assumption of others, the *lung* 龍 has the power of influencing the weather, producing droughts or fertilizing rains at pleasure, of raising tempests and allaying them.

Dragons are referred to in the Classical Books, as *e.g.* "The Emperor K'ung Chia 孔甲, in 1612 B.C., appointed Liu Lei 劉累 to feed the dragons" (*Chu shu* 竹書, xiv, i). Pickled female dragon was served to the same emperor (*ibid, loc. cit.*). Huang Ti 黄帝 (2698-2598 B.C.) had a dragon-like countenance. The mother of Yao 堯 (2357-2258 B.C.) conceived him as a dragon; "After she was grown up, whenever she looked into any of the three Ho 河, there was a dragon following her. One morning the dragon came with a picture and writing. The substance of the writing was—the Red One has received the favour of Heaven. . . . The red dragon made Ch'ing-tu 慶都 pregnant (*ibid.*). When Yao 堯 had been on the throne seventy years, a dragon-horse appeared bearing a scheme, which he laid on the table and went away. The Emperor Shun 舜 (2255-2205 B.C.) also had a "dragon countenance." Green dragons and yellow dragons appeared in the time of Yü 禹 (2205-2197 B.C.). At this time the dragon, one of the twelve symbolical creatures, was recognized as distinct from the serpent, and may have been the alligator. Frequent mention and drawings of the dragon occur in the *Êrh-ya* 爾雅, and in the *Shan-hai ching* 山海經, (where he is represented with horns, wings, and four feet), the *Pên-ts'ao kang-mu* 本草綱目, and eighty pages of the *Yüan-chien-lei han* 淵鑑類函 are devoted to quotations relating to the dragon.

"There are several kinds of dragons. This is due not alone to the fact that nine varieties come from straight propagation, but also because there are other methods of attaining dragonhood. Both the snake and the fish, through patient exertion and much suffering, may ascend to this exalted state. However, this is accomplished only through a long period of time, during which their acts have always been for the good of the world. One can see from this that there must be many dragons. There are; and they serve in many capacities, each having his own place and work. They may be seen in the temple guarding and caring for Buddha's worship. They are to be found in the five different colours, dwelling in the Five Regions of the universe. Each of the Four Seas has its dragon. They are everywhere; in the heavens, on the land, and in the sea, influencing and directing the affairs of all life.

"Although the dragon is found on the earth, and in the skies, his proper element is supposed to be the water. He has a palace in a ten thousand feet deep cave, in the bottom of the sea. No matter where else his work or travels may take him he always wishes to return to his ocean home. In the deep waters, he is in his natural element, and most powerful. It would take a brave man indeed to seek him there. In that his sphere, he is safe from the centipedes, and all other animals that would annoy him. So, naturally, he loves his den in the deep blue sea" (Plopper, pp. 49-52).

"As the dragon was considered the king of the animal creation, he was made the emblem of royalty and the symbol of greatness. The Imperial house, and very high officials only were allowed to wear his picture. A man of great ability or daring was said to be like a dragon (Confucius said that Lao Tzǔ 老 子 was like a dragon). If one had great wealth or power he was envied, and often called one. As education was especially valued, a good writer was said to have a pen which he wielded like one twisting its tail. While the one who successfully passed his *Chü-jen* 與 人 or *Chuang Yüan* 狀 元 examinations was said to have 'leaped the dragon gate.' This often was very difficult, and took years. However, as the Emperor selected his officials from those who successfully passed the examinations and headed the Dragon-tiger list, the graduate was looked upon as one whose future was secure. A new official always took his position on a day governed by the dragon and tiger. Holding the significance it does, there is no greater honour, than for one to have the dragon's name associated with his own, as a title" (*ibid*. pp. 52-3).

"The nine varieties are often given as follows:—(1) The P'u lao 蒲 牢, carved on tops of bells and gongs, in token of its habit of crying out loudly when attacked by its arch-enemy the whale; (2) The Ch'iu niu 囚 牛, carved on the screws of fiddles, owing to its taste for music; (3) The Pi hsi 贔 屭, carved on the top of stone tablets, since it was fond of literature; (4) The Pa hsia 霸 下, carved on the bottom of stone monuments, as it was able to support heavy weights; (5) The Chao fêng 朝 風, carved on the eaves of temples, owing to its liking for danger; (6) The Ch'ih wên 螭 吻, carved on the beams of bridges, because of its fondness for water. It is also placed on the roofs of buildings to keep off fire. Sometimes symbolized by the figure of a fish with uplifted tail; (7) The Suan ni 狻 猊, carved on Buddha's throne, on account of its propensity for resting; (8) The Yai Tzǔ 睚 眦, carved on sword hilts, in memory of its lust for slaughter; (9) The Pi han 狴 犴, carved on prison gates as it was addicted to litigation and quarrelling" (Williams, p. 46).

Wang Ch'ung 王 充 speaks of the dragon: "Nobody has ever seen it. On the faith of an ancient tradition, preserved in the

Book of Mountains and Seas, it is represented with the body of a snake and the head of a horse. It sleeps at the bottom of lakes and wells. The noise of thunder awakens it. It then dashes into the clouds, and causes rain to fall. . . . Wang Ch'ung 王充 says and emphatically repeats that the dragon is not a *shên* 神. For, if it were a *shên* 神, an emanation, a natural force, it would be without form and figure. The dragon is a material being, of the category of scaled reptiles.

"In his seventh chapter, Wang Ch'ung 王充 treats of the popular belief, that the earthen images of dragons, set up on roofs, cause rain to fall. And, in relation to that question, he alludes to several others of great importance. 'The true dragon, he says, causes rain to fall from the clouds, by compressing them, when it rides on them. But its earthen images set on roofs, can obviously not produce the same effect. In general it is useless to hope to obtain a transcendent result, by employing a material medium which cannot normally have that effect. Thus spells and other witchcraft, by means of images and statuettes, are useless and inefficient practices. Useless also" are other practices. . . . "The earthen dragons are set up, when they the people wish for rain. In all these practices the desire is real, the means inept, the result nul. (Chap. 16)" (Wieger, pp. 327-8).

"The dragon is the Great Mystery itself. Hidden in the caverns of inaccessible mountains, or coiled in the unfathomable depths of the sea, it awaits the hour when it shall slowly put itself in motion. It spreads out its coils in the clouds of the tempest, and washes its mane in the darkness of foam-crested whirlpools. Its claws are the prongs of the lightning; its scales gleam in the bark of rain-swept pine trees. Its voice is heard in the hurricane which sweeps away the dead leaves of the forest and quickens a new spring. It is the glorious and symbolic image of that organic elasticity which makes vibrate the inert mass of worn out matter. Coiled upon its strength, it mixes its wrinkled skin in the battle of the elements, and for an instant is seen half revealed by the brilliant shimmer of its scales" (translated from *The Awakening of Japan* by "H.B.C.").

Doré and Kennelly give lists of the various kinds of dragon-kings, *lung-wang* 龍王, taken from Buddhist and other works. The first list, that in the *Miao-fa lien-hua-ching* 妙法蓮花經, records the names of eight dragon-kings, which with the Sanskrit equivalents, are as follows:—1. Nan-t'o 難陀 (Nanda[*]); 2. Pa-nan-t'o 跋難陀 (Upananda); 3. So-chia-lo 娑伽羅 (Sagara); 4. Ho-hsiu-chi 和修吉 (Vasuki); 5. Tê-ch'a-chia 德义伽 (Takshaka); 6. O-na-p'o-ta-to 阿那婆達多 (Anavatapta); 7. Mo-na-ssǔ 摩那斯 (Manasvin); 8. Yu-po-lo 優鉢羅 (Utpolaka).

[*] "Nanda is the chief Naga-raja, and one of the garuda's most formidable enemies. He may have one head, with a serpent crown, and two hands holding a serpent; or have four heads and six arms, two of the hands being employed in drawing a bow."—Getty, *The Gods of Northern Buddhism*, p. 155.

The *Hua-yen ching* 華 嚴 經 (a work of the Mahayana School, attributed to Nagarjuna) contains a list of 10 dragon-kings:— 1. P'i-lou-po-ch'a 毗 樓 博 乂; 2. So-chieh-lo 娑 竭 羅; 3. Yün-yin-miao-ch'uang 雲 音 妙 幢; 4. Yen-k'ou-hai-kuang 烟 口 海 光; 5. P'u-kao-yün-ch'uang 普 高 雲 幢; 6. Tê-ch'a-ch'ia 德 乂 迦; 7. Wu-pien-pu 無 邊 步; 8. Ch'ing-ching-sê 清 淨 色; 9. P'u-yün-ta-shêng 普 運 大 聲; 10. Wu-jê-nao 無 熱 惱.

The *Tu-shu chi shu-lüeh* 讀 書 紀 數 畧, "Abridged Record of Study," by Chên Tê-hsiu 眞 德 秀, mentions 8 classes of dragon-kings:—1. T'ien-lung 天 龍 (Deva Nagas); 2. Yeh-ch'a 夜 乂 (Yakshas); 3. Kan-ta-p'o 乾 達 婆 (Gandharvas); 4. O-hsiu-lo 阿 修 羅 (Asuras); 5. Ch'ia-lou-lo 迦 樓 羅 (Garudas); 6. Chin-na-lo 緊 那 羅 (Vinnaras); 7. Mo-hou-lo-ch'ia 摩 睺 羅 迦 (Mahoragas); 8. Jên-fei-jên-têng 人 非 人 等 (Rakghasas).

The classification most generally adopted by the people in modern times, is that found in the *Hsi-yu chi* 西 遊 記, by Ch'iu Ch'ang-ch'un 邱 長 春:—1. *Ao Kuang* 敖 廣 controlling the Eastern Seas; 2. Ao Ch'in 敖 欽 controlling the Southern Seas; 3. Ao Shun 敖 順 controlling the Northern Seas; 4. Ao Jun 敖 閏 controlling the Western Seas.

Like other kings, dragon-kings live in palaces (*supra*). These are located in the seas, but not confined to them. Prayers, incense, valuable jewels, etc., are offered in thanksgiving to them for marvellous feats attributed to them. When cast into the water, "all these treasures float after some time, and the dragon-king allows the monks to gather them up, and use them for their subsistence and household needs." They are thus provided for by the beneficence of the gods.

Various distinguished persons have been honoured with the title of dragon-king. Examples are given in the *Fêng-shên yen-i* 封 神 演 義 and other works. Doré and Kennelly give the following renderings:—

"The great dragon-king is called Ao Kuang 敖 廣, and his son Ao Ping 敖 丙. During the reign of the tyrant Chou Hsin 紂 辛 (1154-1122 B.C.), last ruler of the Yin 殷 dynasty, the son of General Li Ching 李 靖, known by the name of No-cha 哪 吒 (see Li No-cha 李 哪 吒), fought against Ao Ping 敖 丙, son of the dragon-king, and slew him in the contest. Having defeated him, he plucked out the tendons of his victim, and made therewith a belt, which he wore on special occasions. When Ao Kuang 敖 廣 heard of the death of his son, he became exceedingly angry, and exclaimed: "My son belonged to the race of the genii; he could fly amidst the clouds, and impart life-giving germs to the world; how have you been so rash as to kill him?" Having uttered these words, he engaged in a struggle with No-cha 哪 吒, but was soon cast to the ground.

His adversary trampled on his body, and stripping him of his clothes, found he was covered over with scales, like those of a fish. No-cha 哪 吒 dragged them off till the blood flowed on all sides. Overwhelmed with pain, the dragon-king craved for mercy. No-cha 哪吒 spared his life, but ordered him to be transformed into a little blue snake, which he hid in his sleeve. He then returned to his home."

Ao Kuang 敖廣 inhabits the Eastern Seas, and seems to be the same personage as the Hindu Sagara. Despite his defeat at the hands of No-cha 哪吒, he is worshipped in China as the principle dragon-king, and especially invoked for rain in seasons of drought (Eitel).

The legend of the White Dragon, Pai Lung 白龍, is thus recorded on a stone slab erected in the Temple of the White Dragon, *Pai-lung Shên Miao* 白龍神廟, on Yang Shan 陽山, Mount Yang, five miles north-west of Su-chou Fu 蘇州府 (Soochow), Kiangsu 江蘇. Doré gives the following translation:—

"During the reign of An Ti 安帝 (A.D. 397-419), of the Tung Chin 東晉, Eastern Chin 晉 dynasty, a young girl, who belonged to the Miao [Miu, Mu, Niu] 繆 family, was returning home in the late evening hours. As she travelled on the way, she encountered an elderly man, who inquired her name, and the place where she lived. As rain began to fall, he begged her to stay over with him for the night, and the next morning, she was found to be with child. Upon learning what had taken place, her parents irritated, expelled her from their home, and thus she had to wander about begging her bread from house to house. In the course of a year, she gave birth to a lump of flesh, which she cast out upon the waters. The mass became soon transformed into a white dragon, which advanced toward the young girl, as if it wished to speak to her, but she was so affrighted that she fell to the ground.

"Then, all of a sudden, thunder was heard, flashes rent the clouds, the heavens became obscured, the wind blew with hurricane force, and torrential rain deluged the earth. When the storm was over, the White Dragon ascended to the summit of the hill, and there casting a last glance over the plain, rose higher and higher in the air, till at last it disappeared from mortal gaze. A short time afterwards, the neighbouring folks buried the young girl at the foot of the hill, which is ever since known by the name of the 'Dragon's Peak,' or the sacred palace of the Dragon-king.

"Henceforth a pilgrimage grew up around the spot, and crowds flocked to the place to return thanks, beg favours, consult Fortune, and offer incense in this hallowed spot, which, according to popular belief, gave birth to the White Dragon.

"A temple was also erected on the summit of a hill at Ch'angsha 長沙, in Hunan 湖南, for the purpose of honouring the above Dragon-king, and every year, on the eighteenth of the third moon, the Dragon returns to visit the tomb of his earthly mother. In the Buddhist Calendar, this date is known as the birthday of the white Dragon. The festival is also celebrated throughout Chêkiang 浙江, where the fabulous monster is acknowledged to be nothing else than a white thunder-cloud.

"During the ten previous days, the weather is generally cold and bleak, and rain falls on the hills, but all of a sudden the sky clears up on the birthday of the Dragon-king. Sometimes he may be visibly observed, and is then about ten feet in length; at other times he plays at hide and seek on the hill-tops, or appears occasionally under the shape of a small lizard, such as he is represented in his shrine. From the above facts, one may easily imagine the power he is deemed to wield over storms, winds, thunder and rain."

Chang-lung 張龍, Chang, the Dragon-king, is honoured in a temple specially dedicated to him, and situated about five miles to the East of Ying-chou Fu 潁州府, Anhui 安徽. Doré says: "Chang 張 was born in the early part of the Sui 隋 dynasty (A.D. 589-618), and spent his childhood in the village of Pai-shê 百社, a small locality of the prefecture. At the age of sixteen, he had fully mastered the Classics. During the reign of Chung Tsung 中宗 (A.D. 684) of the T'ang 唐 dynasty, he became district magistrate of Hsüan-ch'êng 宜城, Korea. Here, he displayed much administrative ability, while his wife, who belonged to the Shih 石 family, blessed him with a fine household of nine sturdy boys.

"From Hsüang-ch'êng 宜城 he returned to his native village, where he was wont to spend his leisure hours angling in the stream at Chiao-shih-T'ai 焦氏臺. One day, he beheld near by a small temple, and entering, took up his abode therein. (This was apparently for the purpose of being acknowledged as a genius, and worshipped by the people.) Henceforth, he disappeared every night from the family home, and returned in the morning, wet and shivering with cold. His wife, suspecting something strange, begged him to explain the reason of this sudden change of life. 'I am a dragon,' replied he. 'Chêng Hsiang-yüan 鄭祥遠, of the Liao 蓼 family, is also a dragon, and wants to eject me from the temple, where I have taken up my abode. To-morrow, I shall encounter him in combat, and my nine children must bear assistance in the fray. They will recognize me by seeing a red ribbon in my mouth, while my adversary bears a blue one in his.'

"On the appointed day, the nine children of Chang 張, armed with bows and arrows, shot at the dragon bearing the blue ribbon, and after a short struggle, wounded him and put him to flight. The terrible monster crossed the valley of the Sha Ho 沙河, Sha river, and entered the waters of the Huai Ho 淮河, whence he reached a hill situated to the west of Ho-fei Hsien 合肥縣, in the prefecture of Lu-chou 盧州. Here, exhausted through loss of blood, and the long flight he had accomplished, he expired.

"Henceforth, the hill became known as the 'Dragon's Den,' Lung-hsüeh Shan 龍穴山."

The nine sons of Chang 張 were all transformed into dragons, while their mother was buried in the little island of Kuan-chou

關州. The eldest son held the post of cavalry officer at Ying-shang 潁上, Anhui 安徽, and his descendants inhabit the same place down to the present day.

About A.D. 707, in the reign of Chung Tsung 中宗 (A.D. 684) of the T'ang 唐 dynasty, the inhabitants of the place began to offer sacrifices to him, in the temple of Chiao-shih T'ai 焦氏臺. (This is the temple where he originally took up his abode, with the purpose, as stated above, of being worshipped there.)

In A.D. 894, during the reign of Chao Tsung 昭宗 (A.D. 889-905), a large temple was erected in his honour.

In A.D. 1068, Shên Tsung 神宗 (A.D. 1068-86), of the Pei Sung 北宋, Northern Sung 宋 dynasty, bestowed on him the honorary title of Marquis, Hou 侯, and on his consort that of Noble Lady, Fu-jên 夫人.

In A.D. 1091, during the reign of Chê Tsung 哲宗 (A.D. 1086-1101), also of the Pei Sung 北宋, Northern Sung 宋 dynasty, a great drought occured in the harvest season, whereupon the Prefect of Su-shih 蘇軾, his subordinate officials, and the whole population of the country begged the dragon to end the calamity, and wonderful to say, their prayer was graciously heard by the god. To show their thankfulness for such a favour, they enlarged the former temple, and erected beside it a commemorative slab, recording in full the above event.

Chin-lung Ssŭ Ta Wang 金龍四大王. The Golden Dragon-king, No. 4. This dragon-king "bears the family name of Hsieh 謝, and the surname Hsü 緒. He lived at An-ch'i 安溪, a small village in the district of Ch'ien-t'ang 錢塘, in the province of Chekiang 浙江."

"He was," says Doré, "nephew to the Empress Hsieh 謝, consort of Li Tsung 理宗 (A.D. 1225-65), of the Nan Sung 南宋, Southern Sung 宋, dynasty. When the Mongol troops entered Hangchow 杭州, and led away captive to the North the Empress Hsieh 謝, and her son; the Heir-Apparent, Hsieh Hsü 謝緒, disguised as a Buddhist monk, hid himself in the mountain of the Golden Dragon, Chin-lung Shan 金龍山. Here, in order to avoid falling into the hands of the conquerors, he drowned himself in the T'iao-ch'i 苕溪 stream, which runs close to the district city of Yü-hang 餘杭, in Chêkiang 浙江.

"Before dying, he uttered the following prophetic words: 'When you see the waters of the T'iao 苕 stream revert to their source, I shall have become a genius; when a smiliar phenomenon is observed in the Yellow River, Huang Ho 黄河, the day of vengeance is at hand.' The inhabitants of the country recovered his mortal remains, and laid them to rest at the foot of the Golden Dragon mountain, Chin-lung Shan 金龍山.

"Later on, when Hung Wu 洪武 (A.D. 1368-99), founder of the Ming 明 dynasty, laid siege to the city of Lü-liang 呂梁 (modern Hsü-chou Fu 徐州府, Kiangsu 江蘇), Hsieh Hsü 謝緒 came to his assistance, and hurled a swarm of bees on the Mongol troops, who were thus compelled to retire. Hung Wu 洪武, in thankfulness for this great favour, conferred on him the honorary title of 'Great Golden-king.'"

The reason of his being called Dragon-king, No. 4, is due to the fact that his father had four children, named respectively Chi 紀, Kang 綱, T'ung 統, and Hsü 緒. Hsü 緒, occupying the last place in the series, was called No. 4. There is also a play entitled the "Swarm of bees, that helped to win the battle," *Chü-fêng chu-chan* 聚 蜂 助 戰.

• It is this legendary genius who is generally honoured at the present day, in temples dedicated to dragon-kings, throughout the provinces of Anhui 安 徽 and Kiangsu 江 蘇.

Doré also quotes an instance (said to have occurred in A.D. 1488) of children being transformed into dragon-kings, taken from the *Ming li-chih* 明 禮 志, as follows:—

In the reign of Hsiao Tsung 孝 宗 (A.D. 1488-1506) of the Ming 明 dynasty, "a Buddhist monk was leading a secluded life amidst the wild mountains to the west. One day, two children reached his abode, and requested to be instructed in the Law. A short time afterwards, a terrible drought afflicted the country; the two children went to bathe in a lake, and were transformed into two blue dragons. (In all likelihood, these two children were drowned, but popular legends and superstitious notions transformed them into dragons.) Hereupon, a heavy downpour of rain took place, and the fortunate event was ascribed to the two dragons.

As a reward for the above favour, the monk Lu 盧 received the honorary title of 'Sacrificial genius, who graciously hears all prayers.' Offerings were henceforth made to him, and his statue was placed upon the principal altars. In A.D. 1426, the emperor Hsüan Tsung 宣 宗 erected on the border of the lake a large temple in honour of these dragon-kings, and bestowed on the two children high official rank. Sacrifice is offered to them in spring and autumn, but all in vain, remarks sarcastically the text, as they never hear the prayers addressed to them by the people."

The following dragon-legend of the T'ang 唐 dynasty is quoted by Plopper (p. 92, note *d*): "During the T'ang dynasty (唐 朝), there was a Chin Ko [chio] Lao Lung Wang (金 角 老 龍 王), a Dragon King who controlled the rain. One day the Pearly Emperor (玉 皇 大 帝) gave him the command to make it rain lightly in the cities and heavily in the country. The same day the dragon, in human form visited a fortune teller, named Wang Kuei-ku-tzǔ (王 鬼 谷 子). The fortune teller told him he was a dragon, and had received the orders to make it rain thus in the cities and country. The dragon to show him he was mistaken reversed the order, with the result that several in the cities were drowned. For this disobedience the Pearly Emperor condemned him to death. The dragon went to the fortune teller and asked his help. He was told that a certain official, named Wei

Chêng 魏徵 would be instructed to carry out the sentence, and that if he would go to the Emperor T'ang Ming Wang (唐明王) he would intercede for him with Wei Chêng 魏徵. He saw the Emperor and he agreed to help him. The Emperor called Wei Chêng 魏徵, and made him play chess with him. While doing so, a chessman fell to the floor, and Wei Chêng 魏徵 stooping to pick it up, closed his eyes, his soul went to heaven, received the order, and executed it. (Only as one sleeps can his soul act in this independent capacity.) The Emperor then interceded, but it was too late. That night the soul of the Dragon-king came to the Emperor and quarrelled with him, for breaking his word. The Emperor to make it right, accompanied the Dragon-king into Hell. While there he needed money to settle with the judges. Not having any he was forced to borrow. This he was to repay when he returned to earth. He did so by burning paper money. The custom of burning paper money is said to have its origin in this."—See also *Dragons, Lung* 龍, and *Shui Fu* 水府.

The following incident, which occurred in May 1931, indicates the persistence of the beliefs above noted:

"A scaled and horned dragon, believed by many to be a supernatural creature, has made its appearance in Kiangsi, the communist-ridden province, according to a letter from Mr. Huang Wen-chih, formerly President of the Hankow General Chamber of Commerce.

"Mr. Huang writes from Nanchang saying that the dragon was seen on the Kan River, the principal river in Kiangsi, about half a month ago. He adds that the presence of the dragon is the cause of the flood between Nanchang and Feng-cheng, which are some 200 *li* apart. Most of the houses in that region have been inundated during the past two weeks.

"As the Book of History recorded that some 2,000 years ago the people used to offer the fairest maiden every year to the Ho Po, or the God of the River, to be his concubine, it is now suggested that some suitable sacrifice should be presented to the dragon. It is said that if his wrath is appeased, the flood will subside. On the other hand, if nothing is done to please the creature, it would make the Kiangsi people suffer more besides the flood and the communist uprisings."

LUNG YAO 龍曜.—See *Gall, The God of the*.

LUNG YEN 龍烟.—See *Liver, The Gods of the*.

LUNGS, THE GODS OF THE.—The God of the Lungs is Hao Hua 皓華 and his style Hsü ch'êng 虛成 (*Huang t'ing nei ching* 黃庭內經). The *Yün chi ch'i ch'ien* 雲笈七籤 gives his name as Ch'ing Lung 青龍 and his style as *Yen-lung-tzŭ Fang* 蒸(燕)龍子方; and as Su Ling-shêng 素靈生, with his style as

Tao P'ing 道平, his height as eight and one-tenth inches, and his colour as pure white.

LÜ KUNG-TZǓ 呂公子.—See *Shui Fu* 水府, D (1) (e).

LÜ LING 律令.—Assistant to *Tien Mu* 電母.

LÜ NÊNG 呂能.—The god of the constellation Hsing 星. Alternatively with Li Chung 李忠.

LÜ TSU 呂祖, LÜ YEN 呂喦, or LÜ TUNG-PIN 呂洞賓. —The Patriach Lü 呂. A.D. 755-805. One of the most prominent among the later Taoist patriarchs. One of the Eight Immortals, Pa Hsien 八仙 (*q.v.*). Worshipped by Scholars as a patron god under the designation Shun-yang 純陽, "Pure Essence of the Universe." In the twelfth century temples were erected in his honour. He is worshipped by the fraternity of inkmakers.

Mayers (p. 147) says: "While holding office as magistrate of the district of Têh-hua 德化 (in modern Kiangsi 江西) he encountered, it is said, the immortalized Chung-li Ch'üan 鍾離權 (*q.v.*), among the recesses of the Lu Shan 盧山, and was instructed by him in the mysteries of alchemy and the magic formula of the elixir of life. It is related (in a legend obviously borrowed from a Buddhist prototype), that when the mystic being declared to him who he was, saying: 'I am Yün Fang Hsien-shêng 雲方先生, Lü Yen 呂喦 expressed an ardent desire to fulfil the mission of converting his fellowmen to the true belief, but was preliminarily exposed to a series of temptations, ten in number, all of which he successfully overcame; and hereupon he was invested with the formulas of magic and a sword of super-natural power, with which he traversed the Empire, slaying dragons and ridding the earth of divers kinds of evil, during a period of upwards of four hundred years."

LÜ TSUNG 律宗.—See *Buddhist Schools, XVI.*

LÜ TUNG-PIN 呂洞賓.—See *Lü Tsu* 呂祖 and *Pa Hsien* 八仙.

LÜ TZǓ-CH'ÊNG 呂自成.—The god of the star T'ien-i 天昊.—See *T'ien-kang* 天罡.

LÜ YÜEH 呂岳.—President of the Ministry of Epidemics.— See *Wên Pu* 瘟部.

LYNX-EYE.—See *Ch'ien-li Yen* 千里眼.

M

MA 馬, MADAME.—See *Sao-ch'ing Niang* 掃晴娘.

MA-CHA SHÊN 螞蚱神.—See *Pa Cha* 叭咋.

MA CH'ÊNG-LUNG 馬成龍.—The god of the star Yang-ch'ai 陽差. One of Chou Wang's 紂王 officers. Died on the field of battle during the Yin-Chou 殷周 wars.

MA CHUNG 馬忠.—The god of the star Hsieh-kuang 血光. A sub-officer of Hsü Fang 徐芳, a commander of Chou Wang's 紂王 armies. Burnt to death by No-cha's 哪吒 magic mirror.

MA FANG 馬方.—The god of the star Chu-ch'iao 朱雀 (Red Bird). A subaltern in the Yin 殷 army who was killed by Têng Chiu-kung 鄧九公.

MA-HO-SHÊNG 摩訶乘.—See *Mahayana School*.

MA-HO-YEN-NA 摩訶衍那.—See *Mahayana School*.

MA HSIEN 馬銜.—See *Shui Fu* 水府, C (1) (b).

MA KU 麻姑.—The name of three women who became Immortals. The first and most popular was a native of Tan-ch'êng Hsien 郯城縣, Shantung 山東, and lived in the time of the Emperor Huan Ti 桓帝 (A.D. 147-68) of the Han 漢 dynasty. Her image is presented to married couples on their silver and golden wedding anniversaries. Her adopted brother Wang Fang-p'ing 王方平 also became an Immortal. A sorceress of the second century A.D., said to have reclaimed from the sea a large area on the coast of Kiangsu 江蘇, and transformed it into mulberry

299

orchards by her magic arts. (For a detailed account of their adventures see *Doré*, XII, pp. 1118-24.)

The second Ma Ku 麻 姑 lived in the reign of Chao Wang 趙 王 (A.D. 328-32), King Chao 趙, the founder of the Hou-chao 後 趙 dynasty. Said to be an avatar of the first Ma Ku 麻 姑. She fled from her home, became a hermit on the mountain, and thence ascended to Heaven, after being threatened by her cruel father for having taken pity on his overworked labourers. He only allowed them to stop their work when the cock crew at daybreak, and she had imitated the crowing of a cock to relieve them at an earlier hour. The cruelty of her father Ma Hu-ch'iu 麻 胡 秋, otherwise Ma Ti 麻 狄, was so notorious that it was said that mothers had only to say: "Ma Hu 麻 胡 is coming" to stop their crying. She is said to have returned and restored her father's sight (he having gone blind through weeping over her absence) by giving him some special wine made by her when on the mountains. But when he wished her to remain, she ascended to Heaven on the back of a large bird.

The third Ma Ku 麻 姑 lived in the reign-period A.D. 1111-8 of the Emperor Hui Tsung 徽 宗 (A.D. 1101-26) of the Sung 宋 dynasty. A native of Chien-ch'ang Fu 建 昌 府, Kiangsi 江 西, she lived as a hermit on Ma-yü Shan 麻 餘 山, Shantung 山 東. Was made a Chên Jên 眞 人, Hero, by imperial decree (*Shên hsien chuan* 神 仙 傳).—See also *Composite Deities*.

MA MIEN 馬 面.—See *Ch'êng Huang* 城 隍.

MA-MING TSUN-CHÊ 馬 鳴 尊 者.—See *Lo-han* 羅 漢.

MA SHÊ 馬 社.—See *Ma Wang* 馬 王.

MA SHÊN 麻 神.—The Spirit of Pockmarks. A specialist attached to the celestial Ministry of Medicine. An Assistant to his mother Tou-shên Niang-niang 痘 神 娘 娘(*q.v.*). Worshipped in cases where the skin has become permanently scarred by small-pox, in hope of removal of the disfigurement.—See also *Pan Shên* 瘢 神 and *T'ien I-Yüan* 天 醫 院.

MA SHIH 馬 氏.—The goddess of the star Sao-chou 掃 帚. Daughter of Ma Hung 馬 洪. Wife of Chiang Tzǔ-ya 姜 子 牙, by whom she was divorced, and then married Chang San-lao 張 三 老, an officer of Chou Wang 紂 王 living in the suburbs of the capital Ch'ao-ko 朝 歌. Hanged herself on the approach of Chiang Tzǔ-ya's 姜 子 牙 armies to the capital.

MA SHIH-HUANG 馬 師 皇.—A demi-god. His name was Han Shuai 寒 衰. A colleague of Ch'i Po 岐 伯 (*q.v.*). A celebrated veterinarian and the patron of veterinarians. A member of the commission appointed by Huang Ti 皇 帝 (*q.v.*) to continue and complete the labours of Shên Nung 神農 on natural history and the medicinal properties of plants.

The legend concerning him relates that, when pursued by a dragon, he said that it was following him because it was sick and knew that he could heal him. Accordingly he gave it an injection of liquorice under the lip, and the dragon, healed, carried him away on its back.—See *T'ien I-yüan* 天醫院.

MA TAN 馬丹.—See *Apotheosized Philosophers*.

MA-T'OU NIANG 馬頭娘.—The Horse-head Dame. A composite deity. Also a Goddess of Silkworms.—See *Ts'an Nü* 蠶女 and *Composite Deities*.

MA TSU 馬祖.—The Patriarch Ma 馬. One of the founders of the Nan-yo Ch'êng Tsung 南嶽正宗, School of the Southern Mountain (see *Buddhist Schools*, III). His name in religion was [Chiang-hsi] Tao-i Ch'an-shih [江西] 道一禪師, and he is generally referred to as Ma-tsu Tao-i 馬祖道一, or Tao-i 道一, simply.

"Ma Tsu walked like an ox, had eyes like a tiger's, a tongue that reached beyond the tip of his nose, while a Buddhistic wheel was imprinted by Nature on the soles of his feet" (Johnston, *Buddhist China*, p. 88-9).

The term Ma-tsu 馬祖 is also applied to Ma Wang 馬王 (*q.v.*).

MA WANG 馬王.—The Horse-king. Ma Tsu 馬祖, the ancestor of horses. Said in the *Chou-li* 周禮 Commentary to be the celestial charger of the star Fang 房, the courser of the dragon. The first rearer, Hsien Mu 先牧, was the one who first pastured horses; so in summer he is prayed to to fatten them; in autumn, the first riding-master, Ma Shê 馬社, is prayed to to make them into good saddle-animals; in winter, the prayers are directed to secure their preservation. This explains the passages in the above work which state that in spring the sacrifices are offered to Ma Tsu 馬祖, the Ancestor of Horses, in summer to the First Rearer; in autumn to the First Equerry, and in winter to the Spirit who sends sickness or other maladies to horses.

The Horse-king is worshipped mostly in the North, and is represented in the shape of a three-faced idol symbolizing Ma Tsu 馬祖, Hsien Mu 先母, and Ma Shê 馬社 respectively.

On the *chih-ma* 紙馬, paper prints, burnt in his honour, he is shown as a king accompanied by his officers and is called Ssŭ-ma Ta-shên 司馬大神. He is otherwise represented as a horse, Yüan Ma 元馬, the Original or Ancestral Horse, accompanied by a dragon, a phoenix, and a crane.

MA WU 馬武.—The god of the constellation K'uei 奎. Alternatively with Li Hsiung 李雄.

MA YÜAN-SHAI 馬元帥.—Generalissimo Ma 馬. A three-eyed monster, half-Buddhist, half-Taoist, an avatar of the Spirit Chih Miao-chi 至妙吉, condemned by Ju-lai 如來 to reincarnation for excessive cruelty in the extermination of evil spirits. In order to obey this command he entered the womb of Ma Chin-mu 馬金母 in the form of five globes of fire. Being a precocious youth, he could fight when only three days old, and killed the Dragon-king of the Eastern Sea. From his instructor he received a spiritual work dealing with wind, thunder, snakes, etc., and a triangular piece of stone which he could at will change into anything he liked. By order of Yü Ti 玉帝 he subdued the Spirits of the Wind and Fire, the Blue Dragon, the King of the Five Dragons, and the Spirit of the Five Hundred Fire Ducks, all without injury to himself. For these and many other enterprises he was rewarded by Yü Ti 玉帝 with various magic articles and with the title of Generalissimo of the West, and is regarded as so successful an interceder with Yü Ti 玉帝 that he is prayed to for all sorts of benefits.—See also *Lei Pu* 雷部.

MAHABHARATA.—"The great (war of the) Bharatas." The great epic poem of the Hindus, probably the longest in the world. It is divided into eighteen *parvas* or books, and contains about 220,000 lines. The poem has been subjected to much modification and has received numerous comparatively modern additions, but many of its legends and stories are of Vedic character and of great antiquity. They seem to have long existed in a scattered state, and to have been brought together at different times. Upon them have been founded many of the poems and dramas of later days, and among them is the story of Rama, upon which the *Ramayana* itself may have been based. According to Hindu authorities, they were finally arranged and reduced to writing by a Brahman or Brahmans. There is a good deal of mystery about this, for the poem is attributed to a divine source. The reputed author was Krishna Dwaipayana, the *vyasa*, or arranger, of the *Vedas*. He. is said to have taught the poem to his pupil Vaisampayana, who afterwards recited it at a festival to King Janamejaya. The leading subject of the poem is the great war between the Kauravas and Pandavas, who were descendants, through Bharata, from Puru, the great ancestor of one branch of the Lunar race. The object of the great struggle was the kingdom whose capital was Hastina-pura (elephant city), the ruins of which are traceable fifty-seven miles north-east of Delhi, on an old bed of the Ganges.

MAHAKASYAPA.—See *Lo-han* 羅漢.

MAHAPANTHAKA.—See *Lo-han* 羅漢.

MAHAPRAJAPATA.—See *Lo-han* 羅漢.

MAHARAJAS, THE FOUR.—See *Ssŭ ta T'ien-wang* 四大 天王.

MAHASATTVA. — Ma-ha-sa-tu-ya 嫣哈薩督呀. — The perfected Bodhisattva, as greater (Maha) than any being (sattva) except Buddha, or as using the Mahayana to save other beings.

MAHASTHAMA.—See *Ta-shih-chih* 大勢至.

MAHASTHANA PRATA.—See *Ta-shih-chih* 大勢至.

MAHAYANA SCHOOL. — Ma-ho-yen-na 摩訶衍那 or Ma-ho-shêng 摩訶乘, etc.—The third degree of saintship, the state of a Bodhisattva, who, "being able to transport himself and others to Nirvana, may be compared with a large vehicle (*ta-shêng* 大乘). A school formed by Nagardjuna, which influenced more or less the whole Buddhist church. It is one of the three phases of development" (*v. Triyana*). Its characteristics are "an excess of transcendental speculation tending to obscure nihilism, and the substitution of fanciful degrees of meditation (*Samadhi* and *Dhyana, qq. v.*) in place of the practical asceticism of the Hinayana School. It is not known to Southern Buddhists as a separate system, though it appears to have influenced Singhalese Buddhists, whom Hiuen [Hsüan] Tsang 玄奘 classed among the followers of the Mahayana School."

MAHORAGAS.—Mang Shên 蟒神.—The genii of the large serpent called in Chinese *mang* 蟒. A class of demons shaped like a boa. Dragon-kings.—See *Lung Wang* 龍王.

MAIDEN, THE GREEN.—See *Frost, The Goddess of.*

MAIDEN, THE SOMBRE.—See *Apotheosized Philosophers.*

MAITREYA.—Mi-lo Fo 彌勒佛.—Also called Hsiao Fo 笑佛, the Laughing Buddha. The Coming Buddha, the one met by Sakyamuni in the Tuchita heavens, when he appointed him his successor, to appear as Buddha after 5,000 years. "The world will then have become so corrupt that the Buddhist law will no longer be obeyed, nor even remembered. Maitreya is, therefore, the expected messiah of the Buddhists. Residing at present in the Tuchita heavens, he already watches over and controls the interests of the Buddhist religion. He thus, since Gautama's death, has become a favourite object of worship. He is, besides, the only Bodhisattva worshipped by all Buddhists, whether in the South or in the North" (Monier Williams, *Buddhism,* p. 182; *Doré,* VI, 100-1).

He is the "Buddha Elect." Letters fallen from heaven have frequently announced his coming. Eitel says: "A fictitious

Bodhisattva often called Aditja, a principal figure in the retinue of Sakyamuni, though not a historic disciple . . . The expected Messiah of the Buddhists . . . even now controls the propagation of the faith. A philosophical School (*Wu-hsing Tsung* 五性宗, *lit.* School of the Five-fold Nature) regards him as their founder. Statues were erected in his honour as early as 350 B.C." He is the Buddha who is to establish on earth the lost truths of Buddhism.

He is always represented in a quite peculiar way, a fat, laughing figure, cowering on the ground, so that the left leg lies crosswise in front of the body. The lobes of the ears reach the shoulders (Hackmann, p. 210). "In the Tuchita heavens, Maitreya, Mi-lo Fo 彌勒佛, sits on the right hand of Sakyamuni. He may be well recognized by the laughing expression of his face, flowing hair falls gracefully down on his long-lobed ears. To these characteristics may be added his fat, chubby cheeks, large mouth, breast and upper abdomen exposed to view, all of which impart to him a peculiar aspect among the Buddhas (see also *infra*). He holds in his left hand a mystic bag, containing 'primitive ether,' *ch'i-mu* 氣母, the germ of all past worlds" (*Doré,* VI, 104). "The right hand holds either a rosary or a lotus-bud; the left encircles the mouth of a bag, the so-called bag of the five lucky gifts" (Hackmann, p. 210). "This Buddha is a royal prince, and son of a Cakravarti, Shê-wei ti-t'o 舍衛抵陀 (*q.v.*).

Maitreya, Mi-lo Fo 彌勒佛, bears in his right hand a rosary, each bead of which represents a period of 1000 years, spent by him in doing merciful deeds during preceding existences. In Buddhist temples, he is generally represented sitting, in Hindu fashion, with feet pendent, long flowing locks and smiling face, as befits an inhabitant of the Tuchita heavens, or Buddhist paradise of contented beings" (*Doré,* VI, 78).

"He sits tailor-fashion, with the centre of his body very prominent, and in his hand is a bag; when he was on earth the people called him 'cloth-bag priest,' 'carpet bagger'; his broad, laughing face welcomes the worshipper. At this time Shakyamuni rules the Church; his successor will be Maitreya, and at that time 'the earth with its five evils mingled' will be purified" (Du Bose, p. 236).

Like most of these gods, he is credited with gigantic size, and colossal images of him exist in various parts of China. According to some authorities, he has the special function of a tutelary deity. He is an object of universal reverence among latter-day Buddhists and prayers are addressed to him as to a living and merciful being.

He is also included in a Buddhist triad with Sariputra, one of Sakyamuni's disciples and his right hand attendant, famous for his learning, who died before his master, but is to re-appear as Buddha Padmaprabha (Eitel), and Ju-lai Fo 如來佛, with Sariputra and Yao-shih Fo 藥師佛 (Baishajyaguru); and more generally with Shih-chia Fo 釋迦佛 (Sakyamuni, Gautama), and Kuan Yin 觀音 (Avalokitesvara). He is said to be the nearest approach among the Buddhist gods to Jesus Christ."—See also *Avalokitesvara, Purnamaitrayani, Wên Shu* 文殊, and *Lo-han* 羅漢.

MAJESTIC AND BENEVOLENT MARQUIS, THE.—See *Wei-chi Hou* 威濟侯.

MAKARA.—A huge sea animal, which has been taken to be the crocodile, the shark, the dolphin, etc., but is probably a fabulous animal. It represents the sign Capricornus in the Hindu zodiac, and is depicted with the head and forelegs of an antelope and the body and tail of a fish. It is the vehicle of Varuna, the god of the ocean, and its figure is borne on the banner of Maka-deva, god of love. It is also called Kantaka, Asita-danshtra, "black teeth," and Jala-rupa, "water form."

MALE PRINCIPLE OF NATURE, THE GODDESS OF THE.—She was the Princess Ch'ang Yung 長湧 of the Shang 商 dynasty. "She became an immortal and dwelt on the mountains, and though this maiden lady was aged two hundred, she looked like a damsel in her teens. Walking in the sun she cast no shadow" (Du Bose, pp. 330-1).

MANASVIN.—A dragon-king.—See *Lung Wang* 龍王.

MANG SHÊN 芒神 or **NIU MANG** 牛芒.—The clay herdsman who accompanied the clay ox at the spring sacrifice and beat it (*pien* 鞭—or *ta* 打—*ch'un niu* 春牛) with a branch of willow, so as to stimulate the revival of spring.—See *Cow, The*.

MANG SHÊN 蟒神.—See *Mahoragas* and *Lung* 龍.

MANJUSRI.—See *Wên Shu* 文殊, and *Fa-chao Kuo-shih* 法照國師.

MANTRA.—That portion of the *Veda* which consists of hymns, as distinct from the *Brahmanas*.—See *Veda*.

MANURE, THE GODDESS OF.—Tzŭ Kou 紫姑 "was the concubine of Mr. Li 李 ; incurring the animosity of the head wife she was killed, and was appointed by the Ancient Original as Goddess of Manure. She is much worshipped by the manure hongs" (Du Bose, p. 340).

MANU.—(From the root *man,* to think). "The man." This name belongs to fourteen mythological progenitors of mankind and rulers of the earth, each of whom holds sway for the period called a Manwantara (manu-antara), the age of a Manu, *i.e.* a period of no less than 4,320,000 years. The first of these Manus was Swayam-bhuva, who sprang from Swayam-bhu, the self-existent. The self-existent, as identified with Brahma the creator, divided himself into two persons, male and female. From this pair was produced the male Viraj, and from him sprang the Manu Swayam-bhuva. As the acting creator, this Manu produced the ten Prajapatis or progenitors of mankind, called also Maharshis (maharishis). According to another account, this Manu sprang from the incestuous intercourse of Brahma with his daughter and wife, Sata-rupa. Brahma created himself Manu, "born of and identical with his original self, and the female portion of himself he constituted Sata-rupa," whom Manu took to wife. The law-book commonly known as *Manu* is ascribed to this Manu, and so also is a Sutra work on ritual bearing the same name. The Manu of the present age is the seventh, named Vaivaswata, "sun-born," who was the son of Vivaswat, the sun, and he is a Kshatriya by race. He is also called Satyavrata. There are various legends about his having been saved from a great flood by Vishnu or Brahma.

With the seventh Manu, Vaivaswata, is connected the very curious and interesting legend of the deluge. The first account of this is found in the *Satapatha Brahmana,* of which the following is a summary:—One morning, in the water which was brought to Manu for washing his hands, he caught a fish which spake, and said, "Take care of me and I will preserve thee." Manu asked, "From what wilt thou preserve me?" The fish answered, "A flood will carry away all living beings; I will save thee from that." The fish desired Manu to keep him alive in an earthen vessel, to remove him to a dyke as he grew larger, and eventually to the ocean, "so that he might be beyond the risk of destruction." The fish grew rapidly, and again addressed Manu, saying, "After so many years the deluge will take place; then construct a ship and pay me homage, and when the waters rise, go into the ship and I will rescue thee." Manu did as he was desired, he built the ship, conveyed the fish to the ocean, and did him homage. The flood rose, and Manu fastened the cable of the ship to the fish's horn. Thus he passed over the northern mountain (the Himalaya, as the commentator explains). The fish then desired Manu to fasten the ship to a tree, and to go down with the subsiding waters. He did so, and found that the flood had swept away all living creatures. He alone was left. Desirous of offspring, he offered sacrifice and engaged in devotion. A woman was produced, who came to Manu and declared herself his daughter. "With her he lived, worshipping and toiling in arduous religious rites, desirous of offspring. With her he begat the offspring which is the offspring of Manu."

The story, as told in the *Maha-bharata,* respresents Manu as engaged in devotion by the side of a river, and the fish craving his protection from the bigger fish. Manu placed the fish in a glass vase, but it grew larger and larger till the ocean alone could contain it. Then it warned Manu of the coming flood, and directed him to build a ship and to embark with the seven Rishis. He did so, and fastened his ship to the horn of the fish.

The commentators have given a metaphysical turn to the legend, and endeavoured to illustrate it by philosophical and allegorical interpretations.

MAO 昴, THE GOD OF THE CONSTELLATION.—See *Wang Liang* 王良 and *Huang Ts'ang* 黄倉.

MAO CHUNG 茅衷.—See *San Mao* 三茅.

MAO KU 茅固.—See *San Mao* 三茅.

MAO MÊNG 茅濛.—The god of the planet Jupiter (Mu-hsing 木星), but on his reincarnation at the end of the Chou 周 dynasty Chiang Chun 芘 周 was appointed in his place.

MAO-TUAN 貌端, THE GODDESS OF THE STAR.—See *Chia Shih* 賈氏.

MAO YING 茅盈.—See *San Mao* 三茅.

MARA.—Mo-lo 魔羅 or 末羅.—The God of Lust, Sin and Death, represented with a hundred arms and riding on an elephant. He assumes various monstrous forms, or sends his daughters, or inspires wicked men (like Devadatta, or the Nirgranthas, *qq.v.*) to seduce or frighten saints on earth.

The word *mara* is explained as "he who kills" (*sha-chê* 殺者, the murderer), also as the culprit. The Maras are considered as demons, being enemies of Buddha's doctrine, although they inhabit one of the *lokas,* or heavens of Hindu cosmogony. The king of the maras (Mo Kuei 魔鬼) is called Po Hsün 波旬 and Mo (Ma) Wang 摩王.

MARICHI.—See *Chun T'i* 準提.

MARQUIS, THE MAJESTIC AND BENEVOLENT. See *Wei-chi Hou* 威濟侯.

MARRIAGE, THE GODDESS OF ARRANGERS OF.—See *Nü Wa* 女媧.

MARRIAGE, THE GODS OF.—'Peace and Union are their appropriate names, and they are only worshipped while the marriage ceremony is being performed. Peace and Union are two little boys with straight hair, one holding in his hand a lily, and the other a spherical casket. *Ho* 和 for peace and *ho* 荷 for lily are the same in sound; *ho* 合 for union and *ho* 盒 for casket also sound alike, which symphony is considered very propitious. In contrast to this happy combination, on each side hang the dragon and tiger scrolls as a warning to the happy couple" (Du Bose, pp. 426-7).

MARS, HUO HSING 火星, THE GOD OF THE PLANET.—Known as Ch'ih Ti 赤帝, the Red Ruler, Hsieh-t'ien Chün 謝天君 and Ch'ih-lan Shu 赤熛 [熛] 怒.

MARUTS.—The storm gods of Hindu mythology, who hold a very prominent place in the *Vedas,* and are represented as friends and allies of Indra.

"MARVELLOUS DEFENCES."—See *Ling-ya Hsien* 靈牙仙.

MASONS, THE GOD OF.—His name is Chang Pan 章班. "He was a bricklayer, but afterwards became an immortal. When a house is built they have the two pictures of Lu Pan 魯班 and Chang Pan 章班, and both the owner of the property and the workmen offer a sacrificial feast and engage in worship. These two gods are worshipped in every carpenter's shop and in the guild halls" (Du Bose, p. 334).

MASTER OF THE LILY LAKE.—During the Sung 宋 dynasty "there was a priest collecting for a temple, when, meeting with a tiger, the pious animal offered to be a partner in his firm. Messrs. Priest and Tiger went in company for several years, and the former obtained very liberal subscriptions when the shopmen saw the latter standing guard at the door. After the temple was built, the tiger said to the priest, 'You sit here and chant and I will see you have rice,' so for a long time he collected food for the friar, and at his death the blood-thirsty denizen of the jungle became lord of the lilies" (*Ibid.* p. 318).

MASTER OF RAIN, THE.—See *Shui Fu* 水府.

MATERNITY, THE DEMON OF.—The name of this demon is Shêng-ch'an Kuei 生產鬼.

MATRON WHO BRINGS CHILDREN, THE.—See *Pi-hsia Yüan-chün* 碧霞元君.

MATRON OF GENERATION, THE.—See *Pi-hsia Yüan-chün* 碧霞元君.

MATRON WHO HASTENS CHILD-BIRTH, THE.—See *Ts'ui-shêng Niang-niang* 催生娘娘.

MATRON OF T'AI-SHAN 泰山, THE.—See *Pi-hsia Yüan-chün* 碧霞元君.

MAUDGALYAYANA; MAHAMAUDGALYAYANA; MAUDGALAPUTRA; MOGINLIN.—Mu Lien 目連; Fu-lo-pu 傅羅卜. Derived from Hu-tou 胡豆, Mudga, lentil, because one of his maternal ancestors lived exclusively on lentils. The left-hand disciple of Sakyamuni, also called Kolita, distinguished by magic power (*shên t'ung ti i* 神通第一) by which he viewed Sakyamuni in Tuchita (or transported an artist to that heaven to get a view of the Buddha and make a statue of him, or made it himself).

The *Mu Lien chi* 目連記, *Records of Mu Lien,* (a work written with the object of giving to Ti-tsang Wang 地藏王 a Chinese origin), relates the following legend regarding him.

Mu Lien's 目連 parents were strict vegetarians. On his father's death, the corpse was carried by a stork to the Western Paradise. His mother, whose name was Liu 劉, resenting his fate, exclaimed that if to be devoured by birds was the reward of abstinence, it was hardly worth while striving after perfection.

Her mother, arguing that vegetarianism was not in accordance with the teaching of the ancient sages, Wên Wang 文王, Tsêng Tzǔ 曾子, and Confucius, persuaded her to renounce her former vow and partake of meat food. As however, she still had scruples about taking life, she adopted the following device. She tied a goat up in the centre of a large room, heaped brushwood around him, and set fire to it. Beside the goat she placed a basin of bean-sauce, *chiang-yu* 醬油. Mad with thirst the goat swallowed the sauce, and was roasted alive, pickled with bean-sauce.

Eating this pickled roast goat's flesh gave her such a liking for meat that she frequently transgressed her vegetarian principles, and at length killed and ate her house-dog. To the end of her life she continued eating meat, and was accordingly condemned to be a hungry ghost in Hades, and to be tortured unceasingly by cruel demons.

Mu Lien 目連, learning through revelation of the agonizing torments his mother was undergoing in Hades as a punishment for breaking her vow, was moved with filial piety, and prepared a bowl of rice, which he took to the starving soul of his mother in the nether world. But before she could partake of it, it was seized by the hungry ghosts and either eaten by them or burnt to ashes by the fires of hell. Having made further unsuccessful attempts, he followed his mother from one department of Hades to another, without being able to appease her hunger. On reaching the tenth court she was condemned to be re-born as a dog, and live in a family named Chêng 鄭. On discovering this, Mu Lien 目連 was moved by pity and, weeping, made his way to the Palace of Ju-lai Fo 如來佛.

Having arrived there, he explained the case to the Buddha,

who spoke to him, saying: "Your mother's fate is due to her grievous sin of violating the great precept of the law (not to kill any living thing). You cannot through your own strength rescue her, and she must undergo the series of transmigrations. Only by assembling the monks of the ten quarters and the exercise of their spiritual energy, can deliverance be obtained. On the fifteen day of the seventh moon the monks of the ten quarters should be called together and must prepare every kind of choice food, drink, clothing, bedding, and household articles, and make offerings for the salvation of ancestors who have been in Hades for seven generations. Thus they may be delivered from their torments and he reborn, in a happier state." Mu Lien 目 連 followed those instructions, and thus was enabled to rescue his mother from the torments of hell.

Eitel says this is but an extravagant product of the Yoga School, introduced into China by Amogha, and that Sakyamuni's authority for the deliverance and the ceremony whereby it was accomplished are all forgeries.—See *Ta-shih Chih* 大 勢 至, *Ti-tsang Wang* 地 藏 王 and *Mu Lien* 目 連.

The case of Mu Lien 目 連 is one instance out of many showing that gods do not always retain that dignity. They may be reborn as human or other beings, or die finally (*Cf.* Werner, *The Chinese Idea of the Second Self*).

MEASLES, THE SPIRIT OF.—See *Chên Shên* 疹 神.

MEDICINE, THE CELESTIAL MINISTRY OF.—See *T'ien I-yüan* 天 醫 院.

MEDICINE, KINGS OF.—See *Wei Ku* 韋 古, *Wei-shan Chün* 韋 喜 君, *Pien Ch'iao* 扁 鵲, and *Yao Wang* 藥 王.

MEI HOU-WANG 美 猴 王.—See *Sun Hou-tzŭ* 猻 猴 子.

MEI HSIEN-WÊNG 梅 仙 翁.—See *Ko Hsien-wêng* 葛 仙 翁.

MEI PO 梅 柏.—The god of the star T'ien-tê 天 德. A royal censor burnt alive for criticizing the tyrant Chou Wang 紂 王.

MEI TÊ 梅 德.—The god of the star Ti-k'ung 地 空. An officer of the feudatory prince Ch'ung Hou-hu 崇 侯 虎. Slain during the assault on the capital Ch'ung-ch'êng 崇 城 by Yin Kung 尹 公, one of Wên Wang's 文 王 captains.

MEI T'O 沒 馱.—See *Fo* 佛.

MEI WU 梅 武.—The god of the star T'ien K'ung 天 空. One of Chou Wang's 紂 王 generals, slain by Su Ch'uan-chung 蘇 全 忠, whilst on Ch'ung Hou-hu's 崇 侯 虎 expedition against the vassal Su Hu 蘇 護 at Chi-chou 冀 州.

MÊN-SHÊN 門神.—The Door-gods or Door-spirits. Protectors or Guardians of Doors. The earliest Door-gods are
described in the article Shên T'u Yü Lü 神荼鬱壘 (q.v.), who
in later times were supplanted in popular favour by two ministers
of the Emperor T'ai Tsung 太宗 (A.D. 627-50) of the T'ang 唐
dynasty, by name Ch'in Shu-pao 秦叔寶 and Hu Ching-tê
胡敬德. The former are the family gods of the door; the latter
the gods of official yamêns.

T'ai Tsung 太宗 had fallen sick, and imagined that he
heard demons rampaging in his bedroom. The ministers of
State, on inquiring as to the nature of the malady, were informed
by the physician that his Majesty's pulse was feverish, that he
seemed nervous and saw visions, and that his life was in danger.

The ministers were in great fear. The Empress summoned
other physicians to a consultation, and after the sick Emperor had
informed them that, though all was quiet during the daytime, he
was sure he saw and heard demons during the night, Ch'in Shu-
pao 秦叔寶 and Hu Ching-tê 胡敬德 stated that they would sit
up all night and watch ouside his door.

Accordingly they posted themselves, fully armed, outside the
palace gate all night and the Emperor slept in peace. Next day
the Emperor thanked them heartily, and from that time his sickness diminished. The ministers, however, continued their vigils
until the Emperor informed them that he would no longer impose
upon their readiness to sacrifice themselves. He ordered them to
paint their portraits in full martial array and paste these on the
palace doors to see if that would not have the same effect. For
some nights all was peace; then the same commotion was heard
at the back gates of the palace. The minister Wei Chêng 魏徵
offered to stand guard at the back gates in the same way that his
colleagues had done at the front gates. The result was that in
a few days the Emperor's health was entirely restored.

Thus it is that Wei Chêng 魏徵 is often associated with the
other two Door-gods, sometimes with them, sometimes in place
of them. Pictures of these mên-shên 門神, elaborately coloured,
and renewed at the New Year, are to be seen on almost every door
in China, though the custom has become less prevalent of late
years.

Doré (XI, 978-9) gives the following short biographies taken
from the T'ang-shu 唐書:—(1) Ch'in Shu-pao 秦叔寶 was named
Ch'iung 瓊. A native of Li-ch'êng 歷城, in Shantung 山東. He
followed the Emperor T'ai Tsung 太宗 (A.D. 627-50) of the T'ang
唐 dynasty in his expeditions and rendered him signal services.
He was appointed general-in-chief of the left wing. Died in
A.D. 638, and received the title of Kung 公, Duke. (2) Hu
Ching-tê 胡敬德 or Wei-ch'ih Ching-tê 尉遲敬德 of Shuo Chou
朔州, in Shansi 山西, powerfully aided the Emperor T'ai Tsung
太宗 (A.D. 627-50) of the T'ang 唐 dynasty in his wars against the
rebels. He charged on his horse into the enemy's ranks, and

avoided the blows of his adversaries with such skill that he seemed invulnerable. He died in 659, in the reign of the Emperor Kao Tsung 高宗 (A.D. 650-84) of the T'ang 唐 dynasty, at the age of 74 years. He received the posthumous title of Kung 公, Duke. (3) Wei Chêng 魏 徵, minister of the Emperor T'ai Tsung 太宗 (A.D. 627-50) of the T'ang 唐 dynasty, was born at Ch'ü-yang 曲 陽, in Chihli 直 隸. He received the posthumous title of Wên-chên 文貞.

Doré also, quoting from the *Wu Hsien chih* 吳 縣志, states that the names Wên 温 and Yo 岳, often written in bright colours under the images of the two Door-spirits, are probably those of Wên Yüan-shuai 温 元 帥 and Yo-o Wang 岳鄂王 (*qq.v.*).

The legend of the family door-gods is that there was a peach tree with a limb bent over, thus making an arch, and through this spirits passed and repassed. The two door-gods could subdue these evil spirits, and the Emperor, as his palace was haunted, cut down the peach tree, painted their pictures, and hung them up. The farmers at the new year put them to guard their front doors.

For the meanings of the various emblems of the two Door-spirits see *Doré*, XI, 979-80 (quoting from the *Ch'ing-chia lu* 清嘉錄, bk. 12, p. 26). They are as follows:—The pictures often drawn on the images of the *Mên-shên* 門 神 of a chalice, a stag, a bat, a magpie, a horse, a pearl, a bottle, or a saddle are plays on the words representing the benefits desired: *chüeh* 爵, chalice, for *chüeh* 爵, dignity; *lu* 鹿, stag, for *lu* 祿, official emoluments; *fu* 蝠, bat, for *fu* 福, happiness or good fortune; *ch'iao* 鵲 (*vulg. hsi-ch'iao* 喜 鵲), magpie, for *hsi* 喜, joy. *Ma-pao* 馬寶, horse and precious pearl, are pronounced somewhat like *ma-pao* 馬報, the rapid courier sent by a candidate to inform his family of his success at a public examination. *P'ing-an* 瓶 鞍, bottle and saddle, stand for *p'ing-an* 平 安, peace.—See also *Shên T'u Yü Lü* 神 叔 鬱 壘.

MÊN TAO-CHÊNG 門 道 正.—The god of the the star Ti-fu 地伏.—See *Ti-sha* 地 煞.

MÊNG CH'ANG 孟 昶.—See *Chang Hsien* 張 仙.

MÊNG FEI-CH'ING 孟 非 卿.—See *Hsüan t'ien Shang-ti* 玄 天 上 帝 and *Shih-êrh ting-chia Shên* 十 二 丁 甲 神.

MÊNG K'O 孟 軻.—See *Apotheosized Philosophers*.

MÊNG P'O 孟 婆 or MÊNG-P'O NIANG-NIANG 孟 婆 娘 娘.— Grandmother Mêng. The Buddhist Proserpine. An octogenarian spinster, the presiding goddess of the Hall of Oblivion. Before they leave Hades to pass into a new phase of existence, all souls must enter this Hall, where Mêng P'o 孟 婆 makers them partake of a soup which causes them to forget all previous existences.

The following particulars are given by Du Bose (p. 314):— "Why do not men remember the acts of a previous existence? Buddhism has its answer. Before the metempsychosis, the party is taken to Miss Mang's [Mêng 孟] soup kitchen, and receives a potion which makes him forget all previous events. Miss Mang was a maiden lady of forescore years; in her youth she was an earnest student of Buddhism and an exhorter; in her old age she was appointed a goddess in Tartarus, and compounds this 'forgetful' potion of many different medicines. Scholars arriving at Hades who can repeat the Buddhist chants are beyond the power of King Yama [Yen-lo 閻羅], so they are transferred to Miss Mang's department, return to earth, die just before or immediately after birth, and then they can be brought successively before the ten kings of the dead."

She is said to have been born in the Former Han 漢 dynasty (Ch'ien Han 前漢, 206 B.C.—A.D. 25). All her life she was virtuous and strictly observed the precepts of Buddhism, exhorting people to do good and refrain from taking life. (This is obviously a Buddhist interpolation) Even at eighty years of age she enjoyed the freshness and buoyancy of youth. She refused to marry, preferring a solitary life in the mountains.

Under the Later Han 漢 dynasty (Hou-han 後漢, A.D. 25-221), owing to the escape of some miscreants from Hades and the revelation of some compromising secrets, Yama (q.v.) appointed Mêng P'o 孟婆 a superintendent in Hades, and built for her the Hall of Oblivion, or palace in which the wine of oblivion was made, situated in the Tenth Court. She made this wine from drugs and other substances collected in the world, the decoction of which formed a kind of broth, which was both sweet and bitter. Thereafter, all beings were obliged to partake of this broth before re-incarnation, in order that they might entirely forget all that had happened in their previous existences.

In case a "soul" refused to drink his portion voluntarily, it was administered to him by force by two ferocious demon-attendants. After this, the soul passed on to the "Bridge of Sorrows," K'u-ch'u Ch'iao 苦楚橋, also called the "Bridge across the Styx," Nai-ho Ch'iao 奈河橋, whence they were hurled by two fierce demons, "Short life," Huo-pu-ch'ang 活不長, and "Quick Death," Tsao-kai-ssŭ 早該死, into the foaming dark-red waters of the river, which bore them toward the Four Buddhist Continents, Ssŭ ta chou 四大洲, to another existence, either human, animal, bird, fish or insect.

MÊNG P'O NIANG-NIANG 孟婆娘娘.—See Mêng P'o 孟婆.

MÊNG T'IEN 蒙恬.—The God of Writing-brushes. A man of the time of the Ch'in 秦 State (249-206 B.C.) who conceived the idea of attaching hair taken from stags' tails to the end of a handle of dry wood wound round with goat's hair, and using it as a writing-brush. The implement passed through various stages, taking its present form under the Ch'in 秦 when it also got its name *pi* 筆, pencil or writing-brush.

The invention is otherwise ascribed to the Emperor Shun 舜 (*q.v.*).

Writing-brush shopkeepers of the old style advertize outside their shops that their writing-brushes are *Mêng-shih i-fêng* 蒙氏遺風, made according to the transmitted prescription of the inventor Mr. Mêng 蒙.

MÊNG YÜAN-SHUAI 孟元帥.—Son of Ch'i Hao 其浩. His mother's name was Kuo 郭. He was born on the twelfth day of the eighth moon in the *wu-shên* 戊申 year, probably in the fourth century B.C. He was named Mêng-shan 孟山.

Of a compassionate nature he, when he had become an official, thought frequently of his old mother, and reflecting that the prisoners in the gaol were sad at being parted from theirs, released them all, on the twenty-fifth day of the twelfth moon, on their promise to return on the fifth day of the first moon. This promise was kept, and the same favour was granted them annually.

Reasoning that they were sincere and possessed of filial piety, he released them all finally on their promise to reform. For this he was punished by his superior T'êng 滕, who ordered him to recover the eight hundred liberated prisoners on pain of death. "I will gladly die," said Mêng-shan 孟山, "but to recover the prisoners is impossible." He then seized a lance and tried thrice to transfix himself, but each time the weapon, turned round by some invisible force, only struck him with its butt. He then heard someone outside calling him, and going out found a chariot and horses, all ready with flags and attendants to take him to Heaven. He paid homage to Yü Ti 玉帝, who canonized him as Magnificent Generalissimo of the Chao 趙 Kingdom, and placed on his helmet two flowers of immortality, and also gave him a spear ornamented with a yellow dragon. His chief T'êng 滕 memorialized the Prince of Chao 趙 to erect a temple to him and grant him the title of Marshal. This took place about the time of the rise of the Chao 趙 Kingdom (Circ. 300 B.C.).

MERCHANTS IN GENERAL, GODS OF.—See *Ts'ai Shên* 財神, *Chao Kung-ming* 趙公明, *Hsüan-t'an P'u-sa* 玄壇菩薩, *Tsêng-fu Ts'ai Shên* 增福財神, *Kuan Kung* 關公, *Kuan Yin* 觀音, *Ho Ho* 和合. Besides the gods of special trades, merchants in general sacrifice to Kuan Yin 觀音.

MERCURY, SHUI HSING 水星, THE GOD OF THE PLANET.—Known as Hei Ti 黑帝, the Black Ruler, and Hsieh-kuang Chi 叶光紀. Is worshipped by lighting seven lamps and sacrificing whilst turned toward the west. The God of Winter.

MERCY, THE GODDESS OF.—See *Kuan Yin* 觀 音.

MERU; SUMERU.—Hsü-mi Lou 須 彌 樓; Hsü-mi Shan 須 彌 山; Su-mi Shan 蘇 迷 山; Wu-chiao Shan 沃 焦 山. A fabulous mountain in the navel or centre of the earth, on which is situated Swarga, the heaven of Indra, containing the cities of the gods and the habitations of celestial spirits, it would seem to be some mountain north of the Himalayas. It is also Su-meru, Hemadri, "golden mountain"; Ratnasanu, "jewel pcak"; Karnikachala, "lotus mountain"; and Amaradri and Deva-parvata, "mountain of the gods."

METAL, THE SPIRIT OF.—See *Wu Lao* 五 老.

METAMORPHOSED ELEPHANT, A WHITE.—See *Ling-ya Hsien* 靈 牙 仙.

MI FEI 宓 妃.—See *Shui Fu* 水 府, D (2) (a).

MI-LO-FO 彌 勒 佛.—Maitreya.—During life an Indian prince. After his death Sakyamuni met him in the Tuchita Heavens, and appointed him his successor. The Buddha who is to return after the three-thousand year period of Buddhistic life to explain the Law again and recall men to its observance.

He is "yet to come" ("as the world revolves I will return"). Occasionally letters are said to fall from heaven announcing his speedy coming, and telling men how to prepare for it.

His image is to be found in nearly all temples, in a little shrine, in the centre of the passage, facing the front of the temple. He faces outward, as though eager to welcome the time when he shall come as a Buddha.

Although he is as yet but a Lo-han 羅 漢 (Pu-tai 布 袋), he is thought of as already watching over, and protecting Buddhism.

He has of late been represented with a laughing (*hsiao lo-han* 笑 羅 漢) and hope-inspiring face, but before Sung 宋, or at any rate Yüan 元, times he was represented more in the Kuan Yin 觀 音 style.

He is the God of Goldsmiths and Silversmiths. A small image of this god is placed by these artizans in a glass show-case displaying their goods in the front part of their shops. The origin of this custom is to be found in the legend relating that Mi-lo Fo 彌 勒 佛, when leaving Shih-chia Fo's 釋 迦 佛 (Sakyamuni's) palace, took with him gold and silver ingots, which he coverted into objects of art and sold to get a living. He was thus the first jeweller and the ancestor of jewellers. When, at Shih-chia Fo's 釋 迦 佛 request, he was caught and brought back by Lü Tung-pin 呂 洞 賓, the former gave the latter a magic chain to tie him up with. This wonderful halter is the prototype of the cord from which some copper cash are usually suspended, to be seen hung around the necks of newly-born and young children at the present day. It is the mysterious bond of Buddha, which chains the infant to life. It is called *pai-so shêng* 百 索 繩, "hundred-strand cord," and is plaited with red and green thread, the poorer people using simply cotton.—See also *Tung-fang Shuo* 東 方 朔, *Hua-kuang Fo* 華 光 佛, and *Lo-han* 羅 漢.

MI-LO SHÊN-CHIH 彌 勒 身 智.—One of the twelve divine Buddhist teachers (*Samantabhara*).

MIAO CH'ING 妙 清.—Eldest sister of Kuan Yin 觀 音, Goddess of Mercy. Also Miao Yü 妙 欲.

MIAO CHUANG 妙 莊.—See *Kuan Yin* 觀 音.

MIAO SHAN 妙 善.—The name of Kuan Yin 觀 音 (*q.v.*).

MIAO YIN 妙 音.—Second sister of Kuan Yin 觀 音.

MIAO YÜ 妙 欲.—Eldest sister of Kuan Yin 觀 音. Also Miao Ch'ing 妙 清.

MIDWIFE, THE CELESTIAL.—See *Ko Ku* 葛 姑.

MIDWIVES, THE GODDESS OF.—Mrs. Chieh Sen's [Chieh Shêng 接 生] shrine is in the home of and worshipped by, the female attendants. Both before and after delivery the parents make offerings and vows. Red eggs are used in her worship, which, for good luck, are often stolen by the childless.

MIEH-MO 滅 沒, THE GOD OF THE STAR.—See *Ch'ên Chi-chêng* 陳 繼 貞.

MIEN 免.—See *Shui Fu* 水 府, D (2) (e).

MIGHT, GODS OF.—See *Storm, Gods of the.*

MILLERS, THE PATRON GODDESS OF.—See *Li San-niang* 李 三 娘.

MING CHIH 明 之.—See *Shih Ming-i* 十 明 醫, 8.

MING-FANG CH'AN-SHIH 明 方 禪 師 (65th generation). —A deified Buddhist monk. Ranked fifty-ninth in Buddhist School, VI. Family name Ch'ên 陳. A native of Wu-t'ang 武 塘 He entered a Buddhist monastery at Chia-hsing 嘉 興, Chêkiang 浙 江. His teacher was a monk of Yün-mên 雲 門. He became Principal of monasteries at Hsiang-t'ien 豫 田, Hsien-shêng 顯 聖,

Yü-hang 禹航, Pao-shou 寶壽, Hsüeh-fêng 雲峰 Ch'ang-ch'ing 長慶, etc. Died A.D. 1648. His tomb is at Lung-mên 龍門 Dragon Gate.

MING-PÊN CH'AN-SHIH

MING-FU CH'AN-SHIH 明復禪師 (65th generation).—A deified Buddhist monk. Ranked sixty-first in Buddhist School, VI (*q.v.*). Family name Wang 王, A native of Hui-chi 會稽, Chêkiang 浙江. His teacher was Shan-kung 珊公 (whose name, however, is not included in the list of famous teachers), who instructed him at Ta-tz'ŭ 大慈, whence he passed to Yün-mên 雲門, and there preached the doctrine. Later, he lived in the Kuo-ch'ing Ssŭ 國慶寺, Kuo-ch'ing Monastery, at Tung Shan 東山, East Hill, and in the Mei-yeh Ssŭ 梅野寺, Mei-yeh Monastery. He was twice Superior of the Hsien-shêng Ssŭ 顯聖寺, Hsien-shêng Monastery. In A.D. 1640, he returned to Tung Shan 東山, and died there two years later.

MING-HSÜAN CH'AN-SHIH 明瑄禪師 (62nd generation). A deified Buddhist monk. Ranked fortieth in Buddhist School, III. The legend concerning this monk is that while his teacher Yung-tz'ŭ Ch'an-shih 永慈禪師 (*q.v.*) was engaged in building a monastery, a hatchet fell on the novice Ming-hsüan's 明瑄 foot, causing a deep wound. When the wound was healed, he was sent to help in the kitchen. One day he accidentally burnt his eyebrows, and suffered excruciating pain. Taking up a mirror, he examined his eyes, and was at that moment enlightened on all points of the Doctrine and its interpretation.

MING-HSÜEH CH'AN-SHIH 明雪禪師.—See [*Jui-pai*] Ming-hsüeh Ch'an-shih [瑞白] 明雪禪師

MING-HUI CH'AN-SHIH 明慧禪師 (71st generation).—A deified Buddhist monk. Ranked sixty-seventh in Buddhist School, III. A native of Chia-hsing 嘉興, Chêkiang 浙江. Studied under Ch'ao-pao Ch'an-shih 超寶禪師 (*q.v.*), and was noted for his penmanship and poetic skill. In A.D. 1733, the Emperor Yung Chêng 雍正 (A.D. 1723-36) of the Ch'ing 淸 dynasty conferred on him the honorary title of Wu-hsiu Ch'an-shih 悟修禪師, Intelligent and Accomplished Monk. Later on, he had a monastery built for him, and wrote with his own hand the inscription to be placed on the front: Chio-hai Ssŭ 覺海寺, Monastery of the Vast Ocean. Ming-hui 明慧 died A.D. 1735, aged 72. His tomb is at Lu Shan 盧山, in the Kuang-jên Ssŭ 廣仁寺, Monastery of Vast Benevolence.

MING-PÊN CH'AN-SHIH 明本禪師 (56th generation).—A deified Buddhist monk. Ranked thirty-third in Buddhist School, III (*q.v.*). Family name Sun 孫. A native of Ch'ien-t'ang Hsien 錢塘縣, Chêkiang 浙江. Studied in the school of Yüan-miao Ch'an-shih 原妙禪師 (*q.v.*). Eloquent and virtuous. The emperor

conferred on him the title of P'u-ying Kuo-shih 普應國師, National
Preceptor of Universal Propriety. His tomb is on the T'ien-mu
Shan 天目山, Heavenly-eye Mountain.

MING SHANG 明上.—See *Eye, The Gods of the*.

MING TSAN 明瓚.—See *Lan-ts'an Ch'an-shih* 懶殘禪師.

MING-TS'UNG CH'AN-SHIH 明聰禪師 (64th generation).
—A deified Buddhist monk. Ranked forty-second in Buddhist
School, III (*q.v.*). Family name Hsi 奚. A native of Fukien
福建. His teacher was Pên-jui Ch'an-shih 本瑞禪師 (*q.v.*).
He afterwards opened a school of his own, and taught at the
Lung-ch'üan Ssŭ 龍泉寺, Dragon-spring Monastery, to the end
of his life.

MING WÊN-CHANG 明文章.—See *Hsüan-t'ien Shang-ti*
玄天上帝 and *Shih-êrh ting-chia Shên* 十二丁甲神.

MING-YÜ CH'AN-SHIH 明盂禪師 (65th generation).—A
deified Buddhist monk. Ranked sixtieth in Buddhist School, VI
(*q.v.*). Family name Ting 丁. A native of Ch'ien-t'ang Hsien
錢塘縣, Chêkiang 浙江. Studied under Ch'êng-kung Ch'an-shih
澄公禪師 (whose name, however, is not included in the list of
famous teachers), and afterwards taught at Lung-mên 龍門
and Hua-shan 化山. He then became a Superior, and was head
of several monasteries: Yün-mên 雲門, Chên-chi 眞寂, Fan-shou
梵受 Chu-ming 朱明. Died A.D. 1665. His tomb is at Yün-mên
雲門.

MINISTRIES.—Affairs in the Otherworld are managed by
official Bureaux or Ministries. The *Fêng-shên yen-i* 封神演義
gives full details of their constitution. Their chiefs and staffs
function over the spiritual hierarchies. These Ministries doubtless
had their origin in the Ministries or Boards which at various
periods of history have formed the executive part of the official
hierarchy in China. But, though generally similar, their names
are different and their functions do not coincide.

Generally, the functions of the officers of the celestial Boards
are to protect mankind from the evils represented in the title of
the Board, as, *e.g.* thunder, small-pox, fire, etc. In all cases the
duties seem to be remedial. As the God of War protects people
from the evils of war, so the vast hierarchy of these divinities is
conceived as functioning for the good of mankind. They fall
under the headings of Thunder and Storms, Medicine, Small-pox,
Waters, Fire, Epidemics, Time, the Five Sacred Mountains,
Exorcisms, Literature, War, Finances, and Public Works.—See
Lei Pu 雷部, *T'ien I-yüan* 天醫院, *Tou Shên* 痘神, *Shui Fu*
水府, *Huo Pu* 火部, *Wên Pu* 瘟部, *T'ai Sui* 太歲, *Wu Yo* 五嶽,

Ch'ü-hsieh Yüan 驅邪院, *Wên Ch'ang* 文昌, *Kuan Yü* 關羽, MONKEY-GOD, THE
Ts'ai Shên 財神, and *Lu Pan* 魯班.

MITHRA, MITHRAS. "The Friend."—The Persian god, represented as a military general in Chinese statues. The highest of the second order of deities in the ancient Persian religion. The friend of man in this life and his protector against evil in the next. Sided with Ormuzd against Ahriman, incarnated in the sun, and represented as a youth kneeling on a bull and plunging a dagger into its neck, while he is at the same time attacked by a dog, a serpent, and a scorpion.

MITRA.—Probably connected with the Persian Mithra. A form of the sun. In the *Vedas* he is generally associated with Varuna, he being the ruler of the day and Varuna the ruler of the night. They together uphold and rule the earth and sky, guard the world, encourage religion, and chastise sin. He is one of the Adityas or sons of Aditi.

MO HO CHIA [KA]-YEH TSUN-CHE 摩訶迦葉尊者.— See *Lo-han* 羅漢.

MO-HOU-LO-CHIA [KA] 摩睺羅迦.—A dragon-king.— See *Lung Wang* 龍王.

MO-HUI 莫惠.—See *Wu Yo* 五嶽.

MO-LI CH'ING 魔禮青.—See *Ssŭ ta T'ien-wang* 四大天王.

MO-LI HAI 魔禮海.—See *Ssŭ ta T'ien-wang* 四大天王.

MO-LI HUNG 魔禮紅.—See *Ssŭ ta T'ien-wang* 四大天王.

MO-LI SHOU 魔禮壽.—See *Ssŭ ta T'ien-wang* 四大天王.

MO-LO 魔羅 or 末羅.—See *Mara*.

MO-NA-SSŬ 摩那斯.—A dragon-king.—See *Lung Wang* 龍王.

MO TI 墨翟.—See *Apotheosized Philosophers*.

MO TZŬ 墨子.—See *Apotheosized Philosophers*.

MONKEY-GOD, THE.—"Before heaven, and earth existed, or P'an Ku 盤古 lived, there was the monkey. By taking in the flashes of light from the sun and moon, his animal spirits were made perfect, and at one somersault he could travel one thousand miles. His peregrinations were to the Heavenly Palace, the isles

MONKEY-GOD, THE

of the Immortals, and down to Hades. He stole from the Western Royal Mother (Hsi Wang-mu 西王母) the peach of immortality, defeated the generals of heaven in battle, and stirred up a quarrel in the palace of the Pearly Emperor. At length he was captured by Buddha and shut up within a hill, but was released by the famous traveller Hsüan Tsang 玄奘" (Du Bose, p. 337).—See *Sun Hou-tzŭ* 猴 猴 子.

MONKEY-WOLF, THE—See *Chin-kuang Hsien* 金光仙

MONTH, THE GOD OF THE.—Name Huang Ch'êng-i 黄承乙.—See *T'ai Sui* 太歲.

MOON-GOD, THE.—"At the full harvest moon in the eighth month a nation bows before the heavenly luminary, and each family lights incense made into a vase with gift flowers as an offering. Pictures represent the moon-palace; the hare pestling medicine in a mortar, Mrs. Ch'ang O 嫦娥, who stole the drug of immortality and fled to the moon, and the fragrant tree which one of the genii tries to cut down. The legend affirms that Mrs. Ch'ang O 嫦娥 became changed into a frog, whose outline is traced by the Chinese on the moon's surface. The following written prayer was used: 'Thy nature is effulgent, transparent without spot; thou, the icy-wheel in the milky way along the heavenly street, a mirror always bright; 100,000 classes all receive thy blessings'" (Du Bose, pp. 68-9).—See also *Shên I* 神翼.

MOTHER OF THE BED, THE.—See *Ch'uang Kung Ch'uang P'o* 牀公牀婆.

MOTHER OF BUDDHA, THE.—Her names are stated to be Chên-tê P'u-sa 眞德菩薩 and Hu-shan Ta-shih 護善大士. "She has thirty-four arms and eighteen heads; if her chant is repeated 900,000 times, the four burdens will be taken away and the ten evils avoided" (Du Bose, p. 318).—See also Doré, *Tome* XV.

MOTHER, THE SAINTLY.—See *Pi-hsia Yüan-chün* 碧霞 元君.

MOTHER TORTOISE, THE TRANSCENDENT SAINT-LY.—See *Kuei-ling Shêng-mu* 龜靈聖母.

MOTHER OF THE WATERS, THE OLD.—See *Shui Fu* 水府, D (4).

MOUNTAINS, GODS OF THE.—"There are a million gods of the mountains; for every mountain, hill, peak, knoll, and head-land has its presiding divinity; the greatest among these being the north, south, east, west, and central peaks. The first mountain-god was seen in the days of the Emperor Yao [堯] when the prime minister Pi Ling [邳靈] separated the peaks ot the Ssŭch'uan [四川] province and met the god of the mountain" (Du Bose, p. 72).

MOUNTAINS, THE MINISTRY OF THE FIVE SACRED.—See *Wu Yo* 五嶽.

MOUNTAINS, THE SACRED.—See *Sacred Mountains*.

MOUTH, THE GODS OF THE.—The gods of the sides of the mouth are two named Ch'u Tsai 厨宰; of the middle of the mouth, one named T'ai-i Chün 太一君, whose style is Tan Chu 丹朱.—*Yün chi ch'i ch'ien* 雲笈七籤.

"MR. GOLDEN CUIRASS."—See *Wên Ch'ang* 文昌.

"MR. RED COAT."—See *Wên Ch'ang* 文昌.

MU 木.—See *Feet, The Gods of the*.

MU-CHA 木吒.—See *Li No-cha* 李哪吒.

[MU-CHOU] TAO-MING CH'AN-SHIH [睦州] 道明禪師.—See *Buddhist Schools*, VIII.

MU FÊNG 醒蜂.—See *Teeth, The gods of the*.

MU-FU 木府, THE GOD OF THE STAR.—See *Têng Hua* 鄧華.

MU HSING 木星.—See *Jupiter*.

MU KUNG 木公.—See *Tung Wang-kung* 東王公.

MU LIEN 目連.—The Chinese name of Maudgalyayana, or Moginlin, one of Buddha's disciples.
The Hindu ceremony of *releasing souls out of Hades* was brought to China by Amogha, about A.D. 733. This coinciding with the arrival of the Korean hermit, he was called Mu-lien 目連.—See *Maudgalyayana, Ti-tsang Wang* 地藏王, *Ta-shih Chih* 大勢至, and *Prêtas*.

MU SHÊN 木神.—See *Chin Shên* 金神.

MU T'O 母馱.—See *Fo* 佛.

MU-YÜN-MÊN CH'AN-SHIH 牧雲門禪師 (68th generation).—A deified Buddhist monk. Ranked fifty-sixth in Buddhist School, III (*q.v.*). Family name Chang 張. A native of Ch'ang-shu 常熟, a department of Su-chou (Soochow) 蘇州, Kiangsu 江蘇. Studied under Yüan-wu Ch'an-shih 圓悟禪師 (*q.v.*), and then taught in the Ku-nan-ho Lin 古南鶴林, Old South Crane Forest, where he died. His tomb is on Hsiu Fêng 秀峰, Hsiu Peak, near Su-chou (Soochow) 蘇州.

MUKTA.—See *Lo-han* 羅漢.

MUSICAL INSTRUMENTS, THE GODS OF.—Cha Yung [蔡永] is worshipped by drum and violin shops (Du Bose, p. 336). The god of these instruments are usually stated to be Chin-hua Niang-niang 金花娘娘 and Êrh-lang Yeh-yeh 二郎爺爺; while the god of the latter is also stated to be Pai-yü 伯魚, the son of Confucius.

MUSICIANS, THE GOD OF.—See *Wu-tai Yüan-shuai* 五代元帥.

MUSICIANS, THE THREE.—See *Fêng-huo Yüan T'ien Yüan-shuai* 風火院田元帥.

"MUTE TERRESTRIAL, THE."'—See *Wên Ch'ang* 文昌.

MYTHICAL BUDDHAS, THE TWENTY-FOUR.—See *Jan-têng Fo* 燃燈佛 and (for full lists of names) Doré, VI, 99-102.

N

NA-CHIA 那 伽.—See *Naga*,

NA-CHIA-HSI-NA 那 伽 犀 那.—See *Lo-han* 羅 漢.

NAGA.—A snake, especially the cobra de capello. A mythical semi-divine being, having a human face with the tail of a serpent, and the expanded neck of the cobra. The race of Nagas is said to be a thousand in number, and to have sprung from Kadru, the wife of Kasyapa, for the purpose of peopling Patala, or the regions below the earth, where they reign in great splendour. From the name of their mother they are called Kadraveyas. Their mother is sometimes called Su-rasa. This dominion was taken from them by the Gandharvas, but they recovered it through their sister, the Narmada river, who induced Vishnu to send Pratardana to their assistance. Their females were handsome, and some of them intermarried with men, as Ulupi with Arjuna.

The Nagas, or a people bearing the same name, are historical, and have left many traces behind them. There were mountains so called, and Naga-dwipa was one of the seven divisions of Bharatavarsha. Kings of this race reigned at Mathura, Padma-vati, etc., and the name survives in the modern Nagpur. There are various speculations as to who and what they were, but it seems clear they were a race distinct from the Hindus. The mythological accounts are probably based upon the historical, but they have been mixed up together and confused. The favourite theory is that they were a Scythic race, and probably obtained their name from worshipping serpents or holding them in awe and reverence.

NAGA.—Na chia 那 伽.—A class of snake-gods, with human faces, who live in the lower regions below the earth, or under the waters."—Monier Williams, *Buddhism,* p. 220. "Nagas reside under the rocks supporting Mt. Meru, and are frequently represented with fish-tails, hence the idea of a scaly body."—Grünwedel and Burgess, *Buddhist Art in India,* pp. 43-5.

"Nagas live under the great ocean, and frequent also lakes and rivers. They are believed to control the rainclouds, and hence are appealed to when rain is needed, or is too abundant."—Getty, *The Gods of Northern Buddhism,* p. 49.—See *Lung* 龍 and *Lung Wang* 龍王.

NAGARJUNA.—Lung-shu 龍樹.—The Dragon-tree (Argun or *Pentaptera*). The *arjuna* fourteenth Buddhist patriarch. Author of the *One Hundred Discourses,* one of the most noted of the Buddhist *Shustras.* Wrote also a collection of alchemical formulas. Ko Hung 葛洪 probably learnt his alchemy from this source. His special characteristic is a sophistic nihilism, which admits practically of no ascertained truth whatsoever. He was "a native of Western India, a hermit living under an Arguna tree, until, converted by Kapimala, he became the fourteenth patriarch, famous in Southern India by dialectic subtlety in disputations with heretics. Chief representative of the Mahayana School, first teacher of the Amitabha doctrine, founder of the Madhyamika School, author of some twenty-four works, the greatest philosopher of the Buddhists, viewed as "one of the four suns which illumine the world." He taught that the soul is neither existent nor non-existent, neither eternal nor non-eternal, neither annihilated by death nor non-annihilated. His principal disciples were Deva Bodhisattva and Buddhapalita. In a monastery near Kosala, he cut off his own head as an offering at the request of Sadvasa's son (212 B.C. or A.D. 194). He is now styled a Bodhisattva." (Edkins, p. 210; Eitel, p. 103).

NAGASENA.—See *Lo-han* 羅漢.

NAI-HO CH'IAO 奈河橋.—See *Mêng P'o* 孟婆.

NAKULA.—See *Lo-han* 羅漢.

NAN-AN-I CH'AN-SHIH 南菴依禪師 (66th generation).—A deified Buddhist monk. Ranked seventy-sixth in Buddhist School, VI (*q.v.*). Family name Wu 吳. A native of P'u-t'ien 莆田, Fukien 福建. Obtained his B.A. degree at the age of 12. His brothers and sisters having died, he became a monk in the school of [Sung-ju] Tao-mi Ch'an-shih [嵩乳] 道密禪師 (*q.v.*). He spent part of his life in the Hu-hsin Ssŭ 湖心寺, Hu-hsin Monastery. Died 1683, aged 67. Buried at Hsi-hua Shan 西華山, near Chiang-p'u Hsien 江浦縣, Kiangsu 江蘇.

NAN-CHI HSIEN-WÊNG 南極仙翁.—The Old Immortal

of the South Pole, or Shou Hsing 壽星, the God of Longevity. One of Chiang Tzŭ-ya's 姜子牙 protecting deities. Burnt Chang Shao's 張紹 principal means of defence, namely his three bushels of red sand, whilst Pai-ho T'ung-tzŭ 白鶴童子 despatched him. —See *Chiang Tzŭ-ya* 姜子牙.

NAN-CHI LAO-JÊN 南極老人.—See *Eyebrows, The Gods of the.*

NANDA.—(1) The cowherd by whom Krishna was brought up. (2) A king, or dynasty of kings, of Magadha, that reigned at Patali-putra, and was overthrown by Chandra-gupta the Maurya about 315 B.C. (3) A dragon-king.—See *Lung Wang* 龍王.

NANDI.—The bull of Siva. The *Vayu Purana* makes him the son of Kasyapa and Surabhi. His image, of a milky white colour, is always conspicuous before the temples of Siva. He is the chamberlain of Siva, chief of his personal attendants (*ganas*), and carries a staff of office. He is guardian of all quadrupeds. He is also called Salankayana, and he has the appellations of Nadi-deha and Tandava-talika, because he accompanies with music the *tandava* dance of his master.

NANDIMITRA.—A famous arhat. Author of the *Record of the Law's Duration.*—See *Lo-han* 羅漢.

NAN-HUA CHUANG SHÊNG 南華莊生.—See *Apotheosized Philosophers.*

NAN-SHAN LÜ-TSUNG 南山律宗.—See *Buddhist Schools,* XVI.

NAN-T'O 難陀.—The saintly Hindu monk Dharmananda. Seventh century. One of those invited to the annual banquet of the gods (see *Hsi Wang-mu* 西王母). A native of Kabul. Reached China during the reign of the Emperor Kao Tsung 高宗 (A.D. 650-84) of the T'ang 唐 dynasty. A famous magician. The *Shên-hsien t'ung-chien* 神仙通鑑 says: "He could live in the midst of fire or water, without harm; and could penetrate metal or stone. During his extensive travels he taught his magical arts to a great number of his fellow countrymen. On a visit to Ssŭ-ch'uan 四川 he performed, whilst in a state of intoxication, his trick before the local official of cutting off the heads of the three nuns who accompanied him, but, when about to be seized and punished, raised the corpses from the ground, showing them transformed into three bamboo twigs, the pools of blood on the ground being but wine.

Another of his miraculous feats was enacted when an acquaintance of his named Chang Yen-shang 張延賞, had asked him to dinner. During the meal, the monk ordered the waiters to take off his head and nail it through the ears to the wall. Though this was done, no blood flowed from it. The headless trunk remained sitting at table, and even drank wine poured in through the orifice of the throat. His head, nailed on the wall, assumed a ruddy colour, his lips murmered a chant, and his hands gesticulated. All the guests were astounded. At last the monk arose, took his head down from the wall, and adjusted it on the trunk, without leaving any trace of its having been severed from the body.

He could forecast future events accurately. When he was about to leave a city, the inhabitants closed the gates to prevent his departure, but he walked straight through the walls, leaving only a piece of his gown, torn off by those who had seized it when attempting to stop him. The next day, his features were seen engraved on the wall, and remained there for several days. At the same time, it was reported that he had been seen at P'êng Chou 彭州, Ssŭch'uan 四川. Also a dragon-king.—See *Lung Wang* 龍王.

NAN-YO CHÊNG-TSUNG 南嶽正宗. — See *Buddhist Schools,* III.

NAPE OF THE NECK, THE GOD OF THE.—See *Neck, The Gods of the.*

NARA.—"Man." The original eternal man.

NARAKA.—Hell; the Ming Fu 冥府, Prefecture of Darkness. A place of torture to which the souls of the wicked are sent. *Maru* enumerates twenty-one hells. Other authorities vary greatly as to the numbers and names of the hells. The Buddhist earth-prison, Ti-yü 地獄, the abode of the wicked and of demons. —See *Ti-yü* 地獄.

NATURAL AGENTS, THE FIVE.—See *Wu Hsing* 五行.

NATURAL FORCES, THE FIVE.—See *Wu Hsing* 五行.

NAVIGATORS (OR SAILORS), THE GODDESS OF.—See *T'ien Fei* 天妃.

NAVIGATORS (OR SAILORS), THE GOD OF.—See *Yen Kung* 晏公.

NECK, THE GODS OF THE.—The *Yün chi ch'i ch'ien* 雲笈七籤 states that there are two gods of the "middle" of the neck, whose designation is Shang Chien 上間, and two of the "outside" of the neck, named Yü Nü-chün 玉女君.—See also *Ling Mo* 靈謨.

NEI-CH'I 内乞.—See *Lo-han* 羅漢 and *Sha-mên* 沙門.

NEPTUNE, THE CHINESE.—See *Lung Wang* 龍王.

NET, THE GOD OF THE FISHERMAN'S.—Fu Hsi 伏羲 is the God of the net. He watched the spider weave her web and obtained the idea of catching fish, hares, and birds.

NI 泥.—A Brain-god. See *Chio Yüan-tzŭ* 覺元子.

NIANG-NIANG SUNG-TZŬ 娘娘送子.—See *Pi-hsia Yüan-chün* 碧霞元君.

NI-CHIEN-T'O 泥犍陀.—See *Nirgrantha.*

NIDANA. *Ni-t'o-na* 尼陀那.—Shih-êrh yin yüan 十二因緣. *lit.* the twelve causes of existence. (1) The fundamental dogma of Buddhist thought, the concatenation of cause and effect in the whole range of existence through twelve links (Djaramarana, Djati, Bhava, Upadana, Trichna, Vedana, Sparsa, Chadayatana, Namarupa, Vidjnana, Samskara, and Avidya) the understanding of which solves the riddle of life, revealing the inanity of existence and preparing the mind for Nirvana. (2) All *sutras* or pamphlets written for some special reason (*nidana*), either to answer a query, or to enforce a precept, or to enchance a doctrine (Eitel).

NIDANA BUDDHA.—See *Pratyeka Buddha.*

NINE CARP LAKE, THE IMMORTALS OF THE.—See *Chiu-li Hu Hsien* 九鯉湖仙.

NING SAN-I 寧三益.—The god of the star Ti-yin 地隱.—See *Ti-sha* 地煞.

NING TA T'IEN CHÜN 寧大天君.—See *Ch'ü-hsieh Yüan* 驅邪院.

NIPPLES, THE GODS OF THE.—These are given as Wang Fu Mu 王父母: "On each breast are a *jih* 日, sun, and *yüeh* 月, moon; in these there is one great god each, named Father Wang 王 and Mother Wang 王."—*Yün chi ch'i ch'ien* 雲笈七籤.—See also *Breast, The God of the.*

NIRGRANTHA.—Ni-chien-t'o 泥犍陀.—One who is unfettered by want of food or clothes. Otherwise described as *lu-hsing wai-tao* 露形外道, nude heretics. A *tirthaka* (heretical teacher), a son of Djnati, who taught fatalism, recommended fasting and condemned the use of clothes. Also used for the followers of Nirgrantha.

NIRMANAKAYA.—See *Adi-Buddha.*

NIRVANA.—The Buddhist state of beatitude, *i.e.* extinction of individuality and absorption into the supreme spirit. "As Heaven offered no safe abode for men or gods, Buddha sought some state which would be permanent and enduring; that estate is Nirvana, the doctrine of Buddha's old age when his experience was ripe. It is to get outside of the wheel of life and death, so entering Nirvana one escapes from transmigration. It is the repose of the soul, a passionless condition of body and spirit, an absolute rest obtained by the absorption of the soul into itself." The question comes, What does Buddhism teach of this state? One of Buddha's followers asserted, "Nirvana is"; but if it is a state of being, it is a motionless being, where the heart does not beat, the mind does not think, the soul does not act, the life does not live. There is no thought, personality, or identity—a place where the "I" is lost. It is described as "where the silence lives," a state of "complete silence," a condition of "nothingness," a state of "non-existence." "Nirvana is a state of which nothing can be said, to which no attributes can be given: it is altogether an abstract, devoid of all positive and negative qualities."

If the Chinese equivalents can be relied on, Nirvana means "entire destruction," which is nothing less than annihilation, and it possesses all the qualities we ascribe to annihilation, as it is "the complete extinction of all personal and individual being." In the translations of the Indian *sutras* into Chinese, over and over is Nirvana described as "absolute annihilation."

One might fill pages with the awe-struck and ecstatic praise which is lavished in Buddhist writings on this condition of mind, the Fruit of the fourth Path, the state of an Arahat, of a man made perfect according to the Buddhist faith. But all that could be said can be included in one pregnant phrase—This is Nirvana.

"To him who has finished the Path, and passed beyond sorrow, who has freed himself on all sides, and thrown away every fetter, there is no more fever of grief." "He whose senses have become tranquil, like a horse well broken-in by the driver; who is free from pride and the lust of existence, and the defilement of ignorance—him even the gods envy. Such a one whose conduct is right, remains like the broad earth, unvexed; like the pillar of the city gate, unmoved; like a pellucid lake, unruffled. For such there are no more births. Tranquil is the mind, tranquil the words and deeds of him who is thus tranquillized, and made free by wisdom" (*Dhammapada,* verses 90, 94-96).

"They who by steadfast mind have become exempt from evil desire, and well trained in the teachings of Gautama; they, having obtained the fruit of the fourth Path, and immersed themselves in that ambrosia, have received without price, and are in the enjoyment of Nirvana. Their old *karma* is exhausted, no new *karma* is being produced; their hearts are free from the longing after future life; the cause of their existence being destroyed, and no new yearnings springing up within them, they the wise, are extinguished like this lamp" (*Ratana Sutta*, G, 14). Of Amata, it should be noted that when it was first used of Nirvana, it had acquired the sense of ambrosia, and always alludes to it. Thus we have the Lake of Ambrosia, Fausboll's *Jataka*, v. 25, and "Sweet food and heavenly drink" at *Rat Sutta*, v. 4. "That mendicant conducts himself well, who has conquered error by means of insight, from whose eyes the veil of error has been removed, who is well-trained in religion; and, who, free from yearning, and skilled in the knowledge of, has attained unto, Nirvana" (*Sammaparibbajaniya Suttra*, 14).

What then is Nirvana, which means simply going out, extinction; it being quite clear, from what has gone before, that this cannot be the extinction of a soul? It is the extinction of the sinful, grasping condition of mind and heart, which would otherwise, according to the great mystery of Karma, be the cause of renewed individual existence. That extinction is to be brought about by, and runs paralled with, the growth of the opposite condition of mind and heart, and is complete when that opposite condition is reached. Nirvana is therefore the same thing as a sinless, calm state of mind; and if translated at all, may best, perhaps, be rendered "holiness"—holiness, that is, in the Buddhist sense, perfect peace, goodness, and wisdom.

To attempt translations of such pregnant terms is however always dangerous, as the new word—part of a new language which is the outcome of a different tone of thought—while it may denote the same or nearly the same idea, usually calls up together with it very different ones. This is the case here; our word holiness would often suggest the ideas of love to, and awe in the felt presence of, a personal creator—ideas inconsistent with Buddhist holiness. On the other hand, Nirvana implies the ideas of intellectual energy, and of the cessation of individual existence; of which the former is not essential to, and the latter is quite unconnected with, our idea of holiness. Holiness and Nirvana, in other words, may represent states of mind not greatly different; but these are due to different causes, and end in different results; and in using the words, it is impossible to confine one's thought to the thing expressed, so as not also to think of its origin and its effect.

It is better, therefore, to retain the word Nirvana as one name of the Buddhist *summum bonum*, which is a blissful mental state, a moral condition, a modification of personal character; and we should allow the word to remind us, as it did the early Buddhists, both of the "Path" which leads to the extinction of sin, and also of the break in the transfer of *karma*, which the extinction of sin will bring about. That this must be the effect of Nirvana is plain; for the state of mind which in Nirvana is exinct (*upadana, klesa, trishna*) is precisely that which will, according to the great mystery of Buddhism, lead at death to the formation of a new individual, to whom the *karma* of the dissolved or dead one will be transferred. That new individual would consist of certain bodily and mental qualities or tendencies, enumerated in the five *skandhas* or aggregates. A comprehensive name of all the five is upadi, a word derived (in allusion to the name of their cause, *uparona*), from *upada,* to grasp, either with the hand or the mind. Now, when a Buddhist has become an arahat, when he has reached Nirvana, the fruit of the fourth Path, he has extinguished *upadana,* and *klesa* (error), but he is still alive; the *upadi,* the *skandhas,* his body with all its powers, that is to say, the fruit of his former error, remain. These, however, are impermanent; they will soon pass away. There will then be nothing left to bring about the rise of a new set of *skandhas,* of a new individual; and the arahat will be no longer alive or existent in any sense at all; he will have reached Parinibbana, complete extinction, or *Nir-upadi-sesa-nibbana-dhatu,* extinction not only of *tanha,* and of the fires of passion, but also of the *upadi* and of the five *skandhas.*

The life of man, to use a constantly recurring Buddhist simile or parable, is like the flame of an Indian lamp, a metal or earthenware saucer in which a cotton wick is laid in oil. One life is derived from another, as one flame is lit at another; it is not the same flame, but without the other it would not have been. As flame cannot exist without oil, so life, individual existence, depends on the cleaving to low and earthly things, the sin of the heart. If there is no oil in the lamp, it will go out, though not until the oil which the wick has drawn up is exhausted: and then no new flame can be lighted there. And so the parts and powers of the perfect man will be dissolved, and no new being will be born to sorrow. The wise will pass away, will go out like the flame of a lamp, and their *karma* will be individualized no longer.

As the Chinese proverb says: *pu shêng pu mieh wu jên* 不生不滅無人, so also: "If there were life and death there would not be Buddha": *yu shêng yu mieh fei Fo* 有生有滅非佛.

Stars, long ago extinct, may be still visible to us by the light they emitted before they ceased to burn; but the rapidly vanishing effect of a no longer active cause will soon cease to strike upon our senses; and where the light was, will be darkness. So the living, moving body of the perfect man is visible still, though its cause has ceased to act: but it will soon decay, and die, and pass away; and as no new body will be formed, where life was, will be nothing.

Freedom from the imperfections of finite being is, then, a result of, but it is not Nirvana. The Buddhist heaven is not death, and it is not on death but on a virtuous life here and now, that the *Pitakas* lavish those terms of ecstatic description which they apply to Arhatship, the goal of the Excellent Way, and to Nirvana as one aspect of it.

Thus of the *Dhamma-pada* Professor Max Müller, who was the first to point out the fact, says, "If we look in the *Dhamma-pada* at every passage where Nirvana is mentioned, there is not one which would require that its meaning should be annihilation, while most, if not all, would become perfectly unintelligible if we assigned to the word Nirvana that signification."

The same thing may be said of such other parts of the *Pitakas* as are accessible to us in published texts. Thus the commentator on the *Jatakas* quotes some verses from the *Buddhavansa,* or History of the Buddhas, which is one of the books of the Second *Pitaka.* In those verses we have (*inter alia*) an argument based on the logical assumption that if a positive exists, its negative must also exist; if there is heat, there must be cold; and so on. In one of these pairs we find existence opposed, not to Nirvana, but to non-existence; whilst, in another, the three fires (of lust, hatred, and delusion) are opposed to Nirvana. It follows, I think, that to the mind of the composer of the *Buddhavansa,* Nirvana meant not the extinction, the negation, of being, but the extinction, the absence, of the three fires of passion. It would seem that the word was used in its original sense only, even as late as the time of Buddhagosha; after that time we occasionally (but very seldom, and only when the context makes the modification clear) find Nirvana used where we should expect *anupadisesanibbana* or *parinibbaba*—just as bow is actually used for rainbow, where "in the heaven," or some such expression, is in the context; and it is conceivable that "phrase" might come to be used for "paraphrase."

If we can trust these translations through the Chinese—and I think we may, as far as our purpose requires—the early Sanskrit texts of the Northern Buddhists, like the Pali texts of the *Pitakas,* look upon Nirvana as a moral condition, to be reached here, in this world, and in this life.

In the later Sanskrit books the notices of Nirvana are so meagre that no conclusion can be drawn as to the views of their authors; but it is clear that they use *Parinirvana* and *Anupadhi-sesha Nirvana-dhatu* in the sense of death with no life to follow" (Rhys Davids, pp. 110-17).—See also *Four Fetters, Four Paths,* and *Four Truths.*

NIU 牛, THE GOD OF THE CONSTELLATION.—See *Chi Tsun* 箕 遵 and *Li Hung* 李 弘.

NIU-LAN TA-WANG 牛欄大王.—See *Niu Wang* 牛王.

NIU T'OU 牛 頭.—See *Ch'êng Huang* 城 隍.

NIU-T'OU CHIH 牛 頭 支.—See *Buddhist Schools,* I.

NIU WANG 牛 王.—The God of Oxen. Chin Niu 金 牛, Golden-hair Buffalo. The protecting deity against epidemics which afflict oxen. Originally, a man named Chin Ta-shêng 金大升 of Mei Shan 梅山, Mount Mei. Canonized as the spirit of the star T'ien-wên 天瘟. Is described as being sixteen feet high, with two horns on his forehead, contorted mouth, and pointed ears. Clad in a red gown, wearing a golden helmet and armour, and a three-pointed sword, he rode a unicorn, challenging Wu Wang's 武王 (1121-1114 B.C.) warriors. A fierce battle, lasting some days, ensued, during which the usual marvellous feats and transformations occurred, Chin Ta-shêng 金大升 changing himself back and forth into the form of an ox, as circumstances required. Eventually, he was defeated, decapitated, and his head exposed on a bamboo pole.

His image is placed near stables, as a protecting totem. In his temples, he is worshipped sometimes under the name of Pao-niu Ta-wang 保牛大王, sometimes under that of Niu-lan Ta-wang 牛欄大王. His son, who also has temples dedicated to him, is known as Niu-wang T'ai-tzŭ 牛王太子. An apotheosized golden-haired ox is referred to in the *Shên-hsien t'ung-chien* 神仙通鑑 as having quelled the flood which threatened the district of Ch'ien-t'ang Hsien 錢塘縣, Chêkiang 浙江, in the year A.D. 332 of the reign of the Emperor Ch'êng Ti 成帝 (A.D. 326-43) of the Chin 晉 dynasty. Two temples erected to him bear the names of Chin Hua Chiang-chün Miao 金華將軍廟, Temple of the Illustrious General Chin (though some state that this was first erected in honour of T'sao Kuo 曹杲, a high officer of the Wu-yüeh 吳越 State) and Chin-niu Ssǔ 金牛寺, Monastery of the Golden Ox.

The *Ch'ing-i t'ung-chih* 清一統志 relates that the patron deity of oxen of Mi Hsien 密縣, Honan 河南, is a doctor who lived toward the end of the Sung 宋 dynasty. Being reduced to poverty by the wars which led to the establishment of the Yüan 元 dynasty, about A.D. 1280, he became a ploughman. He never struck his oxen; if they stopped, he knelt before them, and they resumed their work.

NIU-WANG TAI-TZŬ 牛王太子.—See *Niu Wang* 牛王.

NO-CHA 哪吒.—See *Li No-cha* 李哪吒.

NO-CHA SAN-T'AI-TZŬ 哪吒三太子.—See *Li No-cha* 李哪吒.

NO-CHŬ-LO 諾矩羅.—See *Lo-han* 羅漢.

NORTH PLACE, THE GOD OF THE.—Name Yüan Ming 玄冥. Rules draught, flood, war, famine, and pestilence; as well as prosperous years.—See *Wu Fang Shên* 五方神 and *Shui Fu* 水府.

NORTH STAR, THE GODDESS OF THE. — As the pole-star guides the mariner, so its presiding deity, called the "Bushel Mother," is the star of hope to the Chinese. She has four heads and thirty-two hands, and each hand holds a precious substance; *e.g.* the sun's disk, the moon's disk, the five chariots, a spear, a flag, a sword, a pagoda, etc. She occupies the same position in the Taoist religion as Kuan Yin 觀 音 in Buddhism. She rules the books of life and death, and all who wish to prolong their days worship at her shrine. Her devotees abstain from animal food on the third and twenty-seventh of every month. She was said to have been born in India, and her books of devotions are in imitations of the Buddhists'; in times of sickness the Taoist priests are invited to implore the favour of the goddess of the pole-star.—See *Tou Mu* 斗 母.

NORTHERN AND SOUTHERN BUSHELS, THE GODS OF THE.—These are sons of the "Bushel Mother" (Tou Mu 斗 母); the one dressed in red is the Southern Bushel, and rules birth, and the other in white robes is the Northern Bushel, and rules death. A young Esau once found them on the South Mountain, under a tree, playing chess, and by an offer of venison his lease of life was extended from nineteen to ninety-nine years.

NOSE, THE GOD OF THE.—The God of the Nose is Yü Lung 玉 龍, also Yü Lu 玉 廬, and Ch'ung Lung 冲 龍; style Ling Chien 靈 堅 (*Huang t'ing nei ching* 黄 庭 內 經 and *Yün chi ch'i ch'ien* 雲 笈 七 籤). The *Ssŭ ming* 四 命 gives his name as Ch'ung Ling-yü 冲 靈 玉; style Tao Wei 道 微. The *Yu yang tsa tsu* 酉 陽 來 爼 refers to the name Yung Lu 勇 盧 as given in the *Lung yü ho t'u* 龍 魚 河 圖.

NOXIOUS GOD, THE.—"Called the *Sen Shin* [*San Hsing* 三 星], and the time of his worship called the *tsih sen* [*chi san* 祭 三]; the day is fixed two or three weeks after death by the Taoists; this is the most important service during the seven weeks, and is never omitted even by the poorest. The 'noxious god,' who is in the form of a cock, takes the dead man's soul and brings it back home. One feast is spread for the 'noxious god,' and another for the returning soul. Upon the bed in which the man dies must be placed a full suit of clothes. The evil deity brings the man's soul, and it is the part of the Taoist priests to dismiss the 'noxious god' and retain the soul, which after an hour's entertainment is allowed to leave. The day previous all the nails in the house must be covered with red paper, to keep the 'noxious god' from hanging the soul upon a nail" (Du Bose, pp. 438-9).

NÜ 女, THE GOD OF THE CONSTELLATION.—See *Ching Tan* 景 丹 and *Chêng-yüan Tao-jên* 鄭 元 道 人.

NÜ CHIO 女爵.—The Gods of the Back. Two Shao Yin 少陰 and Shao Yang 少陽 spirits; style Nü Chio 女爵.—*Yün chi ch'i chien* 雲笈七籤.

NÜ-HUANG 女皇.—See *Nü Wa* 女媧.

NÜ-MEI 女媒.—See *Nü Wa* 女媧.

NÜ WA 女媧.—The Goddess of Go-betweens, or Arrangers of Marriage. Her mother's name was Chu-ying 諸英, and her father's Shui Ching-tzŭ 水精子, the Spirit of Water. She was born three months after her brother Fu Hsi 伏羲 (2953-2838 B.C.). She had a long head with two fleshy horns, her body resembling that of a snail (*kua* or *wa* 蝸), hence her name Nü Wa 女媧, Snail-maid. She is also depicted with a human head and snake's body. Other names by which she was known are Pao Wa 抱媧 and Nü Hsi 女希. She employed her time in cutting firewood on the mountain near her parent's home at Ch'êng-chi 成紀, Shensi 陝西

When her brother Fu Hsi 伏羲 had become Emperor, she went with him to Ch'ên-ts'ang 陳倉, Shensi 陝西, and later to Wan-ch'iu 宛丘, Honan 河南. There she called his attention to the way in which the young people lived together irregularly, to the great detriment of morality, and advised him to prohibit marriage between members of the same family, to draw up laws of marriage, providing first for betrothal through go-betweens, making rules regarding the purchase-money and presents, the marriage ceremony, and forbidding pre-marital relation. Fu Hsi 伏羲 consented, had the regulations drawn up, and gave Nü Wa 女媧 the title of Go-between Spirit, or Goddess of Go-betweens.

She was afterwards honoured under the names of Kao Mei 臯禖 and Nü Mei 女媒.

She and her brother, together with Ts'ang Chich 倉頡, one of the legendary inventors of writing, Chung Yang 中央 and K'un Wu 昆吾, went and placed themselves under the instruction of the great teacher Yü Hua-tzŭ 鬱華子. The master seated them on a rock, and turning to Nü Wa 女媧 said: "These melted stones can be used to repair a breach in the vault of heaven."

At once the rocks were transformed into stones of five colours. Yü Hua-tzŭ 鬱華子 took his departure, and Fu Hsi 伏羲 died soon after.

After her brother's death, Nü Wa 女媧 reigned as sovereign of the kingdom under the title Nü-huang 女皇. She is described as having the virtuous endowments of a divine sage. Toward the end of her reign there was among the feudatory princes Kung Kung 共工, named K'ang Hui 康回, whose functions were the administration of punishment. Violent and ambitious, he became a rebel, and sought by the influence of water to overcome that of wood (under which Nü Wa 女媧 reigned at Wan-ch'iu 宛丘).

She summoned Mo P'ei 莫坏 a descendant of Chu Jung 祝融, later the God of Fire, to counteract the influence of water, and Kung Kung 共工 flew toward the west. He came to an exceedingly high mountain and ascended to the summit, where the bases of the eight columns of stone supporting the vault of heaven rested. Brooding on the contrast between his former glory and present misery, he at length in desperation seized one of the columns, shook it violently, until it fell in, carrying with it a corner of the celestial vault, and destroying in its fall the southern slope of the mountain. Nü Wa 女媧, however, was able to support it by scaffolding, and Kung Kung 共工, under cover of night, fled to K'un Wu 昆吾, who, however, refused to shelter him. He then went to Li Lien 驪連, who pretended to be willing to help him, but when he was asleep at night bound him with ox-sinews and took him to Nü Wa 女媧, who reproached him for his crimes and killed him with her sword.

The fairy palace which Nü Wa 女媧 then built at Chung-huang Shan 中皇山, Honan 河南, with the materials prepared for her by the spirits of the mountains in a single night, was the prototype of walled cities, being completely surrounded by a wall and moat.

The broken pillar having caused a breach in the vault of heaven, and the corners of the earth to give way, the lopsided mountain to which Kung Kung 共工 had fled was called Pu-chou Shan 不周山, Imperfect Mountain.

It was inaccessibly steep, and the people of that region saw above their heads an enormous black hole, from which violent rain and wind descended. Hereupon Nü-wa 女媧 melted stones of the five colours to repair the heavens, and cut off the feet of the celestial tortoise to set upright the four extremities of the earth. Gathering the ashes of reeds she stopped the flooding waters, and thus rescued the land of Chi 箕, Chi Chou 箕州 (the early seat of the Chinese Sovereignty).

She lived to the age of 143 years. From her beneficient action in causing marriage laws to be introduced she henceforward became the Patron Deity of Go-betweens.

O

O-CHUAN SHIH 阿專師.—A saintly Buddhist monk. Sixth century. One of those invited to the annual banquet of the gods (see *Hsi Wang-mu* 西王母). A contemporary of Bodhidharma (*q.v.*), whom he accompanied after death to Hsi T'ien 西天, the Western Paradise.

O CH'UNG-YÜ 鄂崇禹.—The god of the star T'ien-ma 天馬. A feudatory prince of the tyrant Chou Wang 紂王 in the South. Put to death after having been decoyed to the capital.

O-HSIU-LO 阿修羅.—A dragon-king.—See *Lung Wang* 龍王.

O-MI-T'O FO 阿彌陀佛.—Amitabha.—Fa Pao 法寶, the Precious Law (*Dharma*). The Buddha of Boundless Light. The name Amitabha, O-mi-t'o Fo 阿彌陀佛, was introduced by the Nepalese Mahayana School about A.D. 300, but Amitabha only acquired prominence in the fifth century, when the Western Paradise, Hsi T'ien 西天, a substitute for Nirvana (of which Amitabha is held to be the ruler) was invented. He is a fictitious being and is known only to Northern Buddhism. His birthday is celebrated by Buddhists on the seventeenth day of the eleventh month. Originally conceived of as impersonal, he was early worshipped by the Northern Buddhists as a personal god. Other forms of the name are Amitayus ("Buddha of Boundless Life"), Amitaya, and Amita. In his Bodhisattva form of Avalokitesvara (the Chinese Kuan Yin 觀音) he is the "Buddha of Boundless Compassion." He is also held to be a sun-god, and offspring of the Persian sun-worship (his "Western Paradise" being the place toward which the sun hastens at eventide). Others, again, assert that he was a king in one of the previous *kalpas*; while another legend identifies him with the second son of an Indian Tchakra-vartti Radja, President of the Tenth Court of Hades. Tchakra-vartti, *lit.* a holy king who turns the wheel, a military conqueror of a part or the whole of a universe, whose symbol is the Tchakra or disc of gold, copper, or iron, according to his rank.

Among the various names given to Amitabha, the following are the principal:—Embodiment of the sphere of the Law, Fa-chieh Tsang-shên 法界藏身; Original teacher Upadhyaya, Pên-shih Ho-shang 本師和伺; Sovereign teacher of the Western Paradise, Hsi-t'ien Chiao-chu 西天教主; Guide to the West, Hsi-fang Chieh-yin 西方接引; Boundless Light, Wu-liang Kuang-ming 無量光明; Boundless Age, Wu-liang Shou 無量壽; Great Mercy and Sympathy, Ta-tz'ŭ Ta-pei 大慈大悲.

Of all these, however, the most popular name is Amitabha, O-mi-t'o Fo 阿彌陀佛.

Devout Buddhists repeat constantly this name, and believe they acquire thereby great merit, especially if it is uttered with unflinching faith in this most revered divinity. If a man has no faith, his exercises will be all fruitless. They believe also that their good deeds will be rewarded one day in the Western Paradise, Hsi T'ien 西天.

The powerful name of Amitabha is the mysterious sword, which overcomes all doctrine opposed to that of the Western Paradise; it is the antidote whereby all fear of Hades is banished from the mind; it is the brilliant light which dispels the darkness of the understanding; it is the merciful craft, whereby mortals are wafted across the ocean of misery and suffering, and borne to the happy land of the West.

The Northern Buddhists regard him as the "celestial reflex" of Sakyamuni, the acme of all that is good and beautiful.

The name Amitabha, O-mi-t'o Fo 阿彌陀佛 was first introduced among Chinese Buddhists by the *shaman,* or Buddhist priest, Shirgatchin, Chi-lu-ka-ts'an' or Chi-lou-chia-ch'an 吉甚迦懺, who came to China in A.D. 147 and lived in the Monastery of the White Horse, Pai-ma Ssŭ 白馬寺, in Loyang 洛陽, Honan 河南.

His translations of Buddhist works, together with those accomplished by other *shamans* during the next three centuries, spread the knowledge of the "Merciful Amitabha" and introduced his worship among the Chinese.

"The name of Amitabha is the assured means of ending the fearful series of rebirths; the shield which protects all worshippers from any further death; the mystic power, which enables to lay up merit, and practise the highest perfection.

Amitabha is the heavenly dew, which soothes the hearts of mortals and wins them over to truth; the invocation: "Hail to Amitabha, the Ever-compassionate Lord," *Nan (na)-wu (mo) O-mi-t'o Fo* 南無阿彌陀佛, is the magic passport which opens to all sinners the portals of heaven."

The image of Amitabha is thus described by Johnston (*Buddhist China,* p. 109): "Amitabha is represented seated or standing on a lotus-throne. He has short, curly hair, and long-lobed ears. He bears the *urna* on the forehead. As the guide of souls to the Western Paradise, he has abnormally long arms, and is accompanied by one of his faithful worshippers, standing on the open calyx of a lotus. When a worshipper of Amitabha dies, it is said that Kuan Yin 觀 音 takes the soul, and places it in the heart of a lotus. It is then wafted to the Sacred Lake in the Pura Land, and on awaking, finds itself enjoying the bliss of Paradise."—See also *Hsi T'ien* 西 天 and *San Pao* 三 寶.

O MING 阿 明.—See *Shui Fu* 水 府, C (2) (b).

O-NA-P'O-TA-TO 阿 那 婆 達 多.—A dragon-king. — See *Lung Wang* 龍 王.

O-SÊNG-CHIA 阿 僧 伽.—See *Wu-chê* 無 著 and *Buddhist School,* XV.

O SHUN 鄂 順.—See *Wu Tou* 五 斗.

OATH IN THE PEACH GARDEN, THE.—See *Kuan Yü* 關 羽.

OCULISTS, THE SPIRIT OF.—See *Lo Shên* 羅 神.

OFFICE (OR OFFICIAL EMOLUMENTS), THE GOD OF.—Chinese worship in all its departments is not so much with the view of adoring the deity as of obtaining personal benefit. Literature was the basis of official promotion, and they rose to office by a system of competitive examinations, which were attended with as great excitement as a national election. Confucius was worshipped with the hope of getting office. Office to the Chinese is as heaven to us. The man who bows down before the tablet of the sage had one thought for Confucius and two for himself. When the degrees of A.B., A.M., or LL.D. were conferred the recipients went in state to the Confucian temple, and prostrated themselves in token of the distinctions they had received.—See Du Bose, p. 120, *Lu Shên* 祿 神, and (Star-gods) *Wu Tou* 五 斗 and *Nan Tou* 南 斗.

OLD IMMORTAL OF THE SOUTH POLE, THE.—See *Nan-chi Hsien-wêng* 南 極 仙 翁.

OLD MEN, THE FIVE.—See *Wu Lao* 五 老.

OLD MEN, THE FOUR.—See *Wu Lao* 五 老.

OLD MOTHER OF THE WATERS, THE.—See *Shui Fu* 水府, D (4).

OM.—A Sanskrit word of solemn invocation, affirmation, benediction, and consent, so sacred that when it is uttered no one must hear it. The word is used at the commencement of prayers and religious ceremonies, and is generally placed at the beginning of books. It is a compound of the three letters *a, u, m,* which are typical of the three *Vedas;* and it is declared in the *Upanishads,* where it first appears, to have a mystic power and to be worthy of the deepest meditation. In later times the monosyllable represents the Hindu triad or union of the three gods, *a* being Vishnu, *u* Siva, and *m* Brahma. This monosyllable is called Udgitha.

ONE, THE GREAT.—The first of the celestial spirits.—See *T'ai 1* 太乙.

ORPHAN SPIRITS.—When a child under sixteen years of age dies, it is supposed to sin against the home by doing so. The corpse is not encoffined and no funeral rites are held. The body remains in the home only long enough for it to be put in a rough box or wrapped in a piece of matting. It is then taken out and buried. It has no share in the offerings made to the dead of the home, and becomes an orphan spirit. The names of these, if not already recorded, are not placed on the clan register.

OU-YANG SHUN 歐陽淳.—The god of the star Wang-shên 亡神. A superior officer of Chou Wang's 紂王 armies at Lin-t'ung Kuan 臨潼關. Slain by Jui Chi 芮吉 for refusing to join Chiang Tzǔ-ya 姜子牙.

OU-YANG T'IEN-LU 歐陽天祿.—The god of the star T'ien-hsing 天刑. More usually called Kuei T'ien-lu 桂天祿. A subaltern of Ou-Yang Shun 歐陽渴. Fought at Lin-T'ung Kuan 臨潼關 in the Yin-Chou 殷周 wars. Slain by Li Ching 李靖.

OXEN, THE GOD OF.—See *Niu Wang* 牛王.

OX-HEAD, MR.—See *Ch'êng Huang* 城隍, and *Hades, First Court.*

OX-HEAD KING, THE.—See *Sun Hou-tzǔ* 猻猴子.

P

PA CHA 叭咋 or 虯蜡.—*Cha* sometimes read *Ch'a*. The Spirit of (Protector against) Locusts or Grasshoppers. The most popular God of Locusts, sometimes called Pa-cha Ta-wang 虯蜡大王, Great King Pa Cha. Of unknown origin. He is represented compositely as part human being (arms, chest, upper part of head), part bird (beak, hands and feet), and part bell (from waist down to ankles). Over his ears are the *ya-êrh mao* 壓耳毛, "ear-pressing tufts." The legend says he was born from a bell—the result, probably, of confusing *chung* 鐘 bell, with *ch'ung* 虫, insect. On the bell are the characters *Kuo-t'ai min-an* 國泰民安, "When the kingdom is at peace, the people are tranquil." In one hand he holds a magic gourd, from which he pours a fluid which catches harmful insects and shuts them up in the gourd. In the other, he carries, sometimes an ingot of gold, sometimes a mallet, sometimes a sword, sometimes a banner bearing the characters *Fei-huang t'i-ya* 飛蝗提押, "He summons locusts and imprisons them."

Pa Cha 叭咋 is worshipped also beyond the confines of China Proper. Van Belle relates the Mongol legend of the origin of the Pa Cha Yeh 叭咋爺, Sire Pa Cha 叭咋, as follows:—In a wild valley of Hsin-chiang (Sinkiang) 新疆, in a mountain pass infested by wolves, scorpions, locusts, and other dangerous creatures, lived a peasant who never suffered harm from any of them. The inhabitants were so amazed at this that they used to pray to him as a protecting deity against locusts and savage animals.

The deity is worshipped in the following manner:—The villagers pay a musician to perform the ceremonies, and he erects a tent at the entrance to the main street. In the tent, on the peak of which a flag is fixed, he places images of Kuan Ti 關帝, T'u Ti Lao-yeh 土地老爺, Ts'ai Shên 財神—sometimes also of Yü Huang 玉皇, Tung Yo 東嶽, and Pa Cha 叭咋. The magician beats a drum for half a day, muttering his magic formulas. Groups of children, etc., crowd around him, receive a charm which is fixed over the doors of their homes, and, the ceremony over, he strikes his tent and adjourns to erect it at the next village. The ceremony in many parts is known as Ch'ing-miao Hui 青 苗 會, Green Sprouts Gathering.

Doré gives good reason for supposing that Pa Cha 叭 咤 is either Liu-mêng Chiang-chun 劉 猛 將 軍 (q.v.) or one of his lieutenants.

The Goddess of Locusts or Grasshoppers is Ma-cha Shên 蟆 蚱 神. She was the divorced wife of Chiang Tzŭ-ya 姜 子 牙, who being later on killed by lightning, was canonized as the Goddess of Locusts. She is worshipped largely in the North, where plagues of locusts are frequent, and being able to cause or avert famine, is greatly feared. "Men do not so much seek her help, as they beg to be let alone." A proverb says: "O Locust Goddess, Locust Goddess! eat all our neighbour's crops, but don't touch ours!" (Ma-cha Shên, Ma-cha Shên, pieh ch'ih tsan-ti, ch'ih ssŭ lin 蟆 蚱 神, 蟆 蚱 神, 別 吃 偺 的, 吃 四 鄰).

The eight categories of beings or genii which are either helpful or the reverse in promoting good harvests are:—(1) Hsien Sê 先 嗇, Shên Nung 神 農, the first agriculturist; (2) Ssŭ Sê 司 嗇. Hou Chi 后 稷, the first Minister of Agriculture; (3) Po Chung 百 種, the first sower; (4) Hsien Nung 先 農, the first labourer; (5) Lai Cho 來 啜, the guardian of harvests; (6) Mao Hu 猫 虎, animals, wild beasts (useful or harmful); (7) Shui Fang 水 防, Spirits of banks and dykes; (8) Shui Yung 水 庸, Spirits of canals and rivers.

PA CHA TA-WANG 叭 咤 大 王.—See *Pa Cha* 叭 咤.

PA CHA YEH 叭 咤 爺.—See *Pa Cha* 叭 咤.

PA HSIA 覇 下.—See *Lung Wang* 龍 王.

PA-HSIEN 八 仙.—The Eight Immortals. Also known as Chiu-chung Pa-hsien 酒 中 八 仙, the Eight Inebriated Immortals, or Chiu-chung (酒 鍾) Pa-hsien, Eight Immortals of the Wine-cup. These were men who, for various reasons (detailed below), at different times became Immortals (*hsien jên* 仙 人). Three of them (Chung-li Ch'üan 鍾 離 權, Chang Kuo 張 果, and Lü Yen 呂 嵒) were historical personages; the others are mentioned only in fables or romances.

The legend of the Pa Hsien 八 仙 is certainly not older than the time of the Sung 宋 dynasty (A.D. 960-1280), and is probably (see *T'ung chien* 通 鑑 and other works) to be assigned to that of the Yüan 元 dynasty (A.D. 1280-1368), the emperors of the latter having shown a preference for Taoism, which made rapid progress during their reigns. But some, if not all, of the group seem to have been previously celebrated as Immortals in the Taoist legends. The Yüan 元 emperors bestowed on Han Chung-li 漢 鍾 離, *i.e.* Chung-li Ch'üan 鍾 離 權, the title of True Masculine Principle, and on Lü Tung-pin 呂洞賓 (Lü Yen 呂 喦) that of Pure Active Principle. Ho Hsien-ku 何 仙 姑 was regarded as his pupil, and gradually these designations became the fashion. It was also at this time that the Pa Hsien 八 仙 were introduced into comedies, and for offering congratulations on the attainment of the age of fifty years.

The phrase *Pa Hsien kuo-hai* 八仙過海, the "Eight Immortals crossing the sea," refers to the legend of an expedition made by these deities. Their object was to behold the wondrous things of the sea not to be found in the celestial sphere.

The usual mode of celestial locomotion—by taking a seat on a cloud—was discarded at the suggestion of Lü Yen 呂 喦, who recommended that they should show the infinite variety of their talents by placing things on the surface of the sea and stepping on them.

Li T'ieh-kuai 李 鐵 拐 threw down his crutch, and scudded rapidly over the waves. Chung-li Ch'üan 鍾 離 權 used his feather fan, Chang-kuo Lao 張 果 老 his paper mule, Lü Tung-pin 呂洞賓 his sword, Han Hsiang-tzŭ 韓 湘 子 his flower-basket, Ho Hsien-ku 何 仙 姑 her lotus-flower, Lan Ts'ai-ho 藍 采 和 his musical instrument, and Ts'ao Kuo-chiu 曹 國 舅 his tablet of admission to Court. The popular pictures often represent most of these objects as articles changed into various kinds of sea-monsters. The musical instrument was noticed by the son of the Dragon-king of the Eastern Sea. The avaricious prince conceived the idea of stealing the instrument and imprisoning the owner. The Immortals thereupon declared war, the details of which are described at length by the Chinese writers, the outcome being that the Dragon-king was utterly defeated. After this the Eight Immortals continued their submarine exploits for an indefinite time, encountering numberless adventures.

Either singly or in groups the Eight Immortals are one of the most popular subjects of representation in China; their portraits are to be seen everywhere—on porcelain vases, teapots, teacups, fans, scrolls, embroidery, etc. Images of them are made in porcelain, earthenware, roots, wood, metals. The term "Eight Immortals" is figuratively used for happiness. The number eight has become lucky in association with this tradition, and persons or things eight in number are graced accordingly. Thus we read of reverence shown to the *Pa-Hsien Cho* 八 仙 桌, Eight Genii Table, *Pa-Hsien Ch'iao* 八 仙 橋, Eight Genii Bridge, *Pa Hsien Mien* 八 仙 麵, Eight Genii Vermicelli, *Yin-chung Pa Hsien* 飲 鍾 八 仙, the Eight Genii of the Wine-cup—wine-bibbers of the T'ang 唐 dynasty celebrated by Tu Fu 杜 甫, the poet. They are favourite subjects of romance, and special objects of adoration. In them we see "the embodiment of the ideas of perfect but imagin-

ary happiness which possess the minds of the Chinese people."
Only three of them—as already noted—were historical personages.
The Eight represent all kinds of people—old, young, male, female,
civil, military, rich, poor, afflicted, cultured, noble. They are also
representative of early, middle, and latter historical periods.

Their biographies are usually arranged in the order of their
official eminence or seniority in age. Here, following the precedent of the *Hsiu-hsiang Pa Hsien tung-yu-chi* 修象八仙東遊記,
*An Illustrated Account of the Eight Immortals' Mission to the
East,* they are described in the order in which they became Immortals.

1. LI T'IEH-KUAI 李鐵拐, or T'IEH-KUAI LI 鐵拐李.—
Family name Li 李. Personal name Li Yüan 李玄 (*hsüan* 玄,
now read *yüan*). Also known as K'ung Mu 孔目. He is always
depicted with his crutch and gourd full of magic medicines. Hsi
Wang-mu 西王母 cured him of an ulcer on the leg and taught
him the art of becoming immortal. He was canonized as Rector
of the East. Of commanding stature and dignified mien.
Devoted himself solely to the study of Taoist lore. Hsi Wang-mu
西王母 made him a present of an iron crutch, and sent him to
the capital to teach the doctrine of immortality to Han Chung-li
漢鍾離. He is the emblem or type of sick people, and his image
is habitually used on their signboards, etc., by pharmacists in
China.

He is also identified with Li Ning-yang 李凝陽, to whom Lao
Tzŭ 老子 descended from Heaven in order to instruct him in
the wisdom of the gods. Soon after he had completed his course
of instruction his soul left his body to go on a visit to Hua Shan
華山. Some say he was summoned by Lao Tzŭ 老子, others that
Lao Tzŭ 老子 engaged him as escort to the countries of Hsi-yü
西域. He left his disciple Lang Ling 郎令 in charge of his body,
saying that if he did not return within seven days he was to have
the body cremated. Unfortunately, when only six days had
elapsed the disciple was called away to the death-bed of his
mother. In order to be able to leave at once he cremated the
body forthwith, and when the soul returned it found only a heap
of ashes. Some say the body was not cremated, but only became
devitalized through neglect or through being uninhabited for so
long a time. The object of the setting of the watch was not only
to prevent injury to or theft of the body, but also to prevent any
other soul from taking up its abode in it.

In a forest nearby a beggar had just died of hunger. Finding
his corpse untenanted, the wandering spirit entered it through the
the temples, and made off. When he found that his head was
long and pointed, his face black, his beard and hair woolly and
dishevelled, his eyes of gigantic size, and one of his legs lame, he
wished to get out of this vile body; but Lao Tzŭ 老子 advised
him not to make the attempt and gave him a gold band to keep

his hair in order, and an iron crutch to help his lame leg. On lifting his hands to his eyes, he found they were as large as buckles. That is why he was called Li K'ung-mu 李孔目, "Li Hollow Eyes." Popularly he is known as Li T'ieh-kuai 李鐵拐, "Li with the Iron Crutch."

Elsewhere it is related that Li T'ieh-kuai 李鐵拐, after entering the body of the lame beggar, benevolently proceeded to revive the mother of Lang Ling 郎令, his negligent disciple. Leaning on his iron staff and carrying a gourd of medicines on his back he went to Lang's 郎 house, where preparations were being made for the funeral. The contents of the gourd, poured into the mouth, revived the dead woman. He then made himself known, and, giving Lang 郎 another pill, vanished in a gust of wind. Two hundred years later he effected the immortalization of his disciple.

During his peregrinations on earth he would hang a bottle on the wall at night and jump into it, emerging on the following morning. He frequently returned to earth, and at times tried to bring about the transmigration of others.

An example is the case of Ts'ao Tu 曹杜, the watchman. T'ieh-kuai 鐵拐 walked into a fiery furnace and bade Ts'ao 曹 follow. The latter, being afraid of imitating an act associated with the supernatural world of evil spirits, refused to do so. T'ieh-kuai 鐵拐 then told Ts'ao 曹 to step on to a leaf floating on the surface of the river, saying that it was a boat that would bear him across safely. Again the watchman refused, whereupon T'ieh-kuai 鐵拐, remarking that the cares of this world were evidently too weighty for him to ascend to immortality, stepped on the leaf himself and vanished.

Another account says that he was changed into a dragon, and in that form ascended to Heaven.

His career is by some assigned to the time of the Yüan 元 dynasty.

2. CHUNG-LI CH'ÜAN 鍾離權.—Regarding the origin and life of this Immortal several different accounts are given. One states that his family name was Chung-li 鍾離, and that he lived in the Han 漢 dynasty, being therefore called Han Chung-li 漢鍾離. His cognomen was Ch'üan 權, his literary appellation Chi Tao 及道, and his pseudonyms Ho-ho Tzŭ 和合子 and Wang-yang Tzŭ 王陽子; his style Yün Fang 雲房.

He was born in Hsien-yang Hsien 咸陽縣, Shensi 陝西. He became Marshal of the Empire in the cyclic year 2496. In his old age he became a hermit on Yang-chio Shan 羊角山, Mount Yang-chio, in P'ing-yang Fu 平陽府, Shansi 山西. He is referred to by the title of King-emperor of the True Active Principle.

Another account describes Chung-li Ch'üan 鍾離權 as merely a vice-marshal in the service of Duke Chou Hsiao 周孝. He was defeated in battle, and escaped to Chung-nan Shan 終 南 山, where he met the Five Heroes, the Flowers of the East, who instructed him in the doctrine of immortality. At the end of the T'ang 唐 dynasty, Han Chung-li 漢 鍾 離 taught this same science of immortality to Lü Tung-pin 呂 洞 賓 (see below, 6), and took the pompous title of the Only Independent One Under Heaven. Other versions state that Han Chung-li 漢 鍾 離 is not the name of a person, but of a country; that he was a Taoist priest called Chung Li-tzǔ 鍾 離 子; and that he was a beggar, Chung Li 鍾 離 by name, who gave to one Lao Chih 老 志 a pill of immortality. No sooner had the latter swallowed it than he went mad, left his wife, and ascended to Heaven.

During a great famine he transmuted copper and pewter into silver by amalgamating them with some mysterious drug. This treasure he distributed among the poor, and thousands of lives were thus saved.

One day, while he was meditating, the stone wall of his dwelling in the mountains was rent asunder, and a jade casket exposed to view. This was found to contain secret information as to how to become an Immortal.

When he had followed these instructions for some time, his room was filled with many-coloured clouds, music was heard, and a celestial stork came and bore him away on its back to the regions of immortality.

He is sometimes represented holding his feather-fan, *yü-mao shan* 羽 毛 扇; at other times the peach of immortality. Since his admission to the ranks of the gods, he has appeared on earth at various times as the messenger of Heaven. On one of these occasions he met Lü Yen 呂 嵒 (see below, 6). He is representative of the military type.

3. LAN TS'AI-HO 藍 采 和.—The strolling singer or mountebank of the Immortals. Variously stated to have been a woman, and a hermaphrodite. The type or emblem of the indigent classes. Usually she plays a flute or a pair of cymbals. Her origin is unknown, but her personal name is said to have been Yang-su 養 素, and her career is assigned to the period of the T'ang 唐 dynasty. She wandered abroad clad in a tattered blue gown held by a black wooden belt three inches wide, with one foot shoeless and the other shod, wearing in summer an under-garment of wadded material, and in winter sleeping on the snow, her breath rising in a brilliant cloud like the steam from a boiling cauldron. In this guise she earned her livelihood by singing in the streets, keeping time with a wand three feet long. Though taken for a lunatic, the doggerel verse she sang disproved the popular slanders. It denounced this fleeting life and its delusive pleasures. When given money, she either strung it on a cord and waved it to the time of her song or scattered it on the ground for the poor to pick up.

One day she was found to have become intoxicated in an inn at Fêng-yang Fu 鳳陽府, Anhui 安徽, and while in that state disappeared on a cloud, having thrown down to earth her shoe, robe, belt, and castanets.

According to popular belief, however, only one of the Eight Immortals, namely, Ho Hsien-ku 何仙姑, was a woman, Lan Ts'ai-ho 藍采和 being represented as a young person of about sixteen, bearing a basket of fruit. According to the *Hsiu-hsiang Pa Hsien tung-yu-chi* 修象八仙東遊記, he was Ch'ih-chiao Ta-hsien 赤脚大仙, "the Red-footed Great Genie" incarnate. Though he was a man, adds the writer, he could not understand how to be a man (which is perhaps the reason why he has been supposed to be a woman).

4. CHANG-KUO LAO 張果老.—The type or emblem of an old man. Said to have lived from the middle or close of the seventh to the middle of the eighth century A.D. At first a hermit on Chung-t'iao Shan 中條山, Chung-t'iao Mountain, P'ing-yang Fu 平陽府, Shansi 山西. The Emperors T'ai Tsung 太宗 (A.D. 627-50) and Kao Tsung 高宗 (A.D. 650-84) of the T'ang 唐 dynasty frequently invited him to Court, but he persistently refused to go. At last, pressed once more by the Empress Wu 武 (A.D. 684-705), he consented to leave his retreat, but was struck down by death at the gate of the Temple of the Jealous Woman. His body began to decay and to be eaten by worms, when lo! he was seen again, alive and well, on the mountains of Hêng-chou 恆州 in P'ing-yang Fu 平陽府. He rode on a white mule which carried him thousands of miles in a day, and which, when the journey was finished, he folded up like a sheet of paper and put away in his wallet. When he again required its services, he had only to spurt water upon the packet from his mouth and the animal at once assumed its proper shape. At all times he performed wonderful feats of necromancy, and declared that he had been Grand Minister to the Emperor Yao 堯 (2357-2255 B.C.) during a previous existence.

In A.D. 735, during the reign of the Emperor Hsüan Tsung 玄宗 (A.D. 713-56) of the T'ang 唐 dynasty, he was called to Lo-yang 洛陽, Honan 河南, and elected Chief of the Imperial Academy, with the honourable title of Very Perspicacious Teacher.

It was just at this time that the famous Taoist Yeh Fa-shan 葉法善, thanks to his skill in necromancy, was in great favour at Court. The Emperor asked him who this Chang-kuo Lao 張果老 (the epithet *Lao* 老, "old," is usually added to his name) was. "I know," replied the magician, "but if I were to tell your Majesty I should fall dead at your feet, so I dare not speak unless your Majesty will promise that you will go with bare feet and bare head to ask Chang-kuo 張果 to forgive you, in which case I should immediately revive." Hsüan Tsung 玄宗 having promised, Fa-shan 法善 then said: "Chang-kuo 張果 is a white spiritual bat which came out of primeval chaos." No sooner had he spoken than he dropped dead at the Emperor's feet.

Hsüan Tsung 玄宗, with bare head and feet, went to Chang-kuo 張果 as he had promised, and begged forgiveness for his indiscretion. The latter then sprinkled water on Fa-shan's 法善 face and he revived. Soon after Chang-kuo 張果 fell sick and returned to die in the Hêng-chou 恒州 Mountains during the period A.D. 742-46. When his disciples opened his tomb, they found it empty.

He is usually seen mounted on his white mule, sometimes facing its head, sometimes its tail. He carries a phoenix feather or a peach of immortality.

At his interviews with the Emperor Ming Huang 明皇 (A.D. 713-56) in A.D. 723 (when he was still alive) Chang-kuo 張果 entertained the Emperor with a variety of magical tricks, such as rendering himself invisible, drinking off a cup of aconite, and felling birds or flowers by pointing at them. He refused the hand of an imperial princess, and also declined to have his portrait placed in the Hall of Worthies.

A picture of Chang-kuo 張果 sitting on a donkey and offering a descendant to the newly married couple is often found in the nuptial chamber. It seems somewhat incongruous that an old ascetic should be associated with matrimonial happiness and the granting of offspring, but the explanation may possibly be connected with his performance of wonderful feats of necromancy, though he is said not to have given encouragement to others in these things during his lifetime.

5. Ho HSIEN-KU 何仙姑.—An Immortal represented as a maiden holding in her hand a magic lotus-blossom, the flower of open-heartedness, or the peach of immortality given her by Lü Tung-pin 呂洞賓 in the mountain-gorge as a symbol of identity, playing at times the *shêng* 笙, or reed-organ, or drinking wine.

She lived in the time of the Empress Wu 武 (A.D. 684-705) of the T'ang 唐 dynasty, and was the daughter of Ho T'ai 何泰 of Tsêng-ch'êng Hsien 增城縣, Kuangtung 廣東, though another account says her father was a shopkeeper at Ling-ling 零陵, Hunan 湖南. At her birth six hairs were found growing on the crown of her head, and it is said she never had any more, though the pictures represent her with a full head of hair. She elected to live on Yun-mu Ling 雲母嶺, Mother-of-pearl Range, twenty *li* 里 west of Tsêng-ch'êng Hsien 增城縣. On that mountain was found a stone called *Yün-mu shih* 雲母石, "mother-of-pearl." In a dream she saw a spirit who ordered her to powder and eat one of these stones, by doing which she could acquire both agility and immortality. She complied with this injunction; and also vowed herself to a life of virginity. Her days were thenceforth passed in floating from one peak to another, bringing home at night to her mother the fruits she collected on the mountain.

She gradually found that she had no need to eat in order to live. Her fame having reached the ears of the Empress, she was invited to Court, but while journeying thither suddenly disappeared from mortal view and became an Immortal. She is said to have been seen again in A.D. 750 floating upon a cloud of many colours at the temple of Ma Ku 麻 姑 (*q.v.*), the famous female Taoist magician, and again, some years later, in the city of Kuang-tung 廣 東 (Canton).

She is represented as an extremely beautiful maiden, and is remarkable as occupying so prominent a position in a cult in which no system of female asceticism is developed.

6. Lü Tung-pin 呂洞賓.—Family name Lü 呂; personal name Tung-pin 洞 賓, also Yen 嵒. Pseudonym, Shun-yang Tzŭ 純 陽 子. Born in A.D. 755 at Yung-lo Hsien 永 樂 縣, Ho-chung Fu 河 中 府, Shansi 山 西. He came of an official family, his grandfather having been President of the Ministry of Ceremonies, and his father Prefect of Hai Chou 海州, Kiangsu 江 蘇. He was 5 feet 2 inches in height, and at twenty was still unmarried. At this time he made a journey to Lu Shan 廬 山, Kiangsi 江·西, where he met the Fire-dragon, who presented him with a magic sword, which enabled him at will to hide himself in the heavens.

During his visit to the capital, Ch'ang-an 長 安, in Shensi 陜 西, he met the Immortal Han Chung-li 漢 鍾 離, who instructed him in the mysteries of alchemy and the elixir of life. When he revealed himself as Yün-fang Hsien-shêng 雲 方 先 生, Lü-yen 呂 嵒 expressed an ardent desire to aid in converting mankind to the true doctrine, but was first exposed to a series of ten temptations. These being successfully overcome, he was invested with supernatural powers and magic weapons, with which he traversed the Empire, slaying dragons and ridding the earth of divers kinds of evils, during a period of upward of four hundred years.

Another version says that Han Chung-li 漢 鍾 離 was in an inn, heating a jug of rice-wine. Here Lü-yen 呂 嵒 met him, and going to sleep dreamt that he was promoted to a very high office and was exceptionally favoured by fortune in every way. This had gone on for fifty years when unexpectedly a serious fault caused him to be condemned to exile, and his family was exterminated. Alone in the world, he was sighing bitterly, when he awoke with a start. All had taken place in so short a space of time that Han Chung-li's 漢 鍾 離 wine was not yet hot. This is the incident referred to in Chinese literature in the phrase "rice-wine dream." Convinced of the hollowness of worldly dignities, he followed Han Chung-li 漢 鍾 離 to the Ho-ling. 鶴 嶺 Mountains at Chung Shan 終 山 in Shensi 陜 西, where he was initiated into the divine mysteries, and became an Immortal.

In A.D. 1115 the Emperor Hui Tsung 微 宗 (A.D. 1101-26) of the Sung 宋 dynasty conferred on him the title of Hero of Marvellous Wisdom; and later he was proclaimed King-emperor and Strong Protector. In the Yüan 元 dynasty he received the title of Active Pure Principle.

The legend of Lü Tung-pin 呂洞賓 is variously given by different writers. One of these adds that in order to fulfil his promise made to Han Chung-li 漢鍾離 to do what he could to aid in the work of converting his fellow creatures to the true doctrine, he went to Yüeh-yang 岳陽 in the guise of an oil-seller, intending to immortalize all those who did not ask for additional weight to the quantity of oil purchased. During a whole year he met only selfish and extortionate customers, with the exception of one old lady who alone did not ask for more than was her due. So he went to her house, and seeing a well in the courtyard, threw a few grains of rice into it. The water miraculously turned into wine, from the sale of which the dame amassed great wealth.

He was very skilful in fencing, and is always represented with his magic Excalibur named Chan yao-kuai 斬妖怪, "Devil-slaying Sabre," and in one hand holds a fly-whisk, yün-chou 雲箒, or "cloud-sweeper," in the form of a horse's tail. This is a Taoist symbol of being able to fly at will through the air and to walk on the clouds of Heaven.

A fine scholar, he graduated at the metropolis in 770, took office, and made himself the apostle of practical Taoism. Tradition attributes to him the well-known *Kung kuo ko* 功過格 (analyzed by Wieger, pp. 579-88), a table of merits and demerits, which had an enormous influence on the people's morality. He died in A.D. 805.

Like Kuan Kung 關公, he is shown bearing in his arms a male child—indicating a promise of numerous progeny, including *literati* (Scholars) and famous officials. Consequently he is one of the spiritual beings honoured by the Scholars, and is worshipped, under the title of Lo Tsu 羅祖, the Patriarch Lo, as the God of Inkmakers.

7. HAN HSIANG-TZÜ 韓湘子.—Personal name Ch'ing-fu 清夫. Stated to have been a grand-nephew of Han Yü 韓愈 (A.D. 768-824), the great statesman, philosopher, and poet of the T'ang 唐 dynasty, and an ardent votary of transcendental study. The child was entrusted to his uncle to be educated and prepared for the public examinations. He excelled his teacher in intelligence and the performance of wonderful feats, such as the production from a little earth in a flower-pot of some marvellous flowering plants. He also consoled him during his exile to Ch'ao-chou Fu 潮州府, in Kuangtung 廣東, prophesying his return in perfect health to his family and official dignities—all of which took place exactly as he had predicted.

Another account states that he became the disciple of Lü Tung-pin 呂洞賓, and, having been carried up to the supernatural peach-tree of the genii, fell from its branches, but during his descent attained to the state of immortality. Still another version says that he was killed by the fall, was transformed, and then underwent the above-mentioned experiences with Han Yü 韓愈.

8. Ts'ao Kuo-chiu 曹國舅.—Became one of the Eight Immortals because the other seven, who occupied seven of the eight grottos of the Upper Spheres, wished to see the eighth inhabited, and nominated him because "his disposition resembled that of a genie." He was connected with the imperial family of the Sung 宋 dynasty, and is shown with the tablet of admission to Court in his hand.

The legend relates that the Empress Ts'ao 曹, wife of the Emperor Jên Tsung 仁宗 (A.D. 1023-64) of the Sung 宋 dynasty, had two younger brothers. The elder of the two, Ching-hsiu 景休, did not concern himself with the affairs of State; the younger, Ching-chih 景植, was notorious for his misbehaviour. In spite of all warnings he refused to reform, and being at last guilty of homicide, was condemned to death. His brother, ashamed at what had occurred, went and hid in the mountains, where he clothed his head and body with wild plants, resolved to lead the life of a hermit. One day Han Chung-li 漢鍾離 and Lü Tung-pin 呂洞賓 found him in his retreat, and asked him what he was doing. "I am engaged in studying the Way," he replied. "What way, and where is it?" they asked. He pointed to the sky. "Where is the sky?" they went on. He pointed to his heart. The two visitors smiled and said: "The heart is the sky, and the sky is the Way; you understand the origin of things." They then gave him a recipe for perfection, to enable him to take his place among the Perfect Ones. In a few days only he had reached this much-sought-after condition.

Another version gives fuller details concerning this Immortal. A graduate named Yüan Wên-chêng 袁文正 of Ch'ao-yang Hsien 潮陽縣, in Ch'ao-chou Fu 潮州府, Kuangtung 廣東, was travelling with his wife to take his examinations at the capital. Ts'ao Ching-chih 曹景植, the younger brother of the Empress, saw the lady, and was struck with her beauty. In order to gratify his passion he invited the graduate and his young wife to the palace, where he strangled the husband and tried to force the wife to cohabit with him. She refused obstinately, and as a last resort he had her imprisoned in a noisome dungeon. The soul of the graduate appeared to the imperial Censor Pao Lao-yeh 包老爺 and begged him to exact vengeance for the execrable crime. The elder brother, Ching-hsiu 景休, seeing the case put in the hands of the upright Pao Lao-yeh 包老爺, and knowing his brother to be guilty of homicide, advised him to put the woman to death, in order to cut off all sources of information and so to prevent further proceedings. The young voluptuary thereupon caused the woman to be thrown down a deep well, but the star T'ai-po Chin-hsing 太白金星, in the form of an old man, drew her out again. While making her escape, she met on the road an official procession which she mistook for that of Pao Lao-yeh 包老爺, and, going up to the sedan chair, made her accusation. This official was no other than the elder brother of the murderer. Ching-hsiu 景休, terrified, dared not refuse to accept the charge, but on the pretext that the woman had not placed herself respectfully by the side of the official chair, and thus had not left a way clear for the passage of his retinue, he had her beaten with iron-spiked whips, and she was cast away for dead in a neighbouring lane. This time also she revived, and ran to inform Pao Lao-yeh 包老爺. The latter immediately had Ts'ao Ching-hsiu 曹景休 arrested, cangued, and fettered. Without loss of time he wrote an invitation to the second brother, Ts'ao Ching-chih 曹景植, and on his arrival confronted him with the graduate's wife, who accused him to his face. Pao Lao-yeh 包老爺 had him put in a pit, and remained deaf to all entreaties of the Emperor and Empress on his behalf. A few days later the murderer was taken to the place of execution, and his head rolled in the dust. The problem now was how to get Ts'ao Ching-hsiu 曹景休 out of the hands of the terrible Censor. The Emperor Jên Tsung 仁宗 (A.D. 1023-64), to please the Empress, had a general amnesty proclaimed throughout the Empire, under which all prisoners were set free. On receipt of this edict, Pao Lao-yeh 包老爺 liberated Ts'ao Ching-hsiu 曹景休 from the cangue, and allowed him to go free. As one risen from the dead, he gave himself up to the practice of perfection, became a hermit, and, through the instruction of the Perfect Ones, became one of the Eight Immortals.

LI PA-PAI 李八百.—Li Eight-hundred. An Immortal said to have lived at the end of the Hsia 夏 or beginning of the Chou 周 dynasty. The legend attributes to him a life of eight hundred years' duration. But his name is said to have been derived from his ability to walk 800 *li* (240 miles) at a stretch. He lived sometimes in the cities, sometimes on Hua-lin Shan 華林山, in Kiangsi 江西, and, during the reign of the Emperor Mu Tsung 穆宗 (1001-946 B.C.), on Chin-t'ang Shan 金堂山, in Ssŭch'uan 四川.

Soon after going to offer his services as teacher to T'ang Kung-fang 唐公昉, Prefect of Han-chung Fu 漢中府, in Shensi 陝西, in the reign of the emperor Wang Mang 王莽 (A.D. 68), he found that his whole body was covered with ulcers, and he informed T'ang Kung-fang 唐公昉 that they could only be healed if someone licked them off. T'ang 唐 had them licked by three of his servants. "They should, however," Li 李 added, "be licked not by a servant, but by a sage." T'ang 唐 then licked them himself. But he replied that this would not be sufficient unless T'ang's 唐 wife licked them also. T'ang 唐 accordingly ordered his wife to lick them, but this too was found to be ineffectual. Li 李 then stated that a cure could only be brought about if he bathed his body in (the equivalent measure of) 64,500 gallons of good wine. This being done, he was instantly and completely cured.

"This I did," said Li 李, "to test you. I am an Immortal, and wished to see if you were worthy of my instruction. Now I will teach you the secret of immortality."

He ordered T'ang 唐, his wife, and the three servants to bathe in the wine he had just used, and they emerged from it fresh and rejuvenated. He then gave T'ang 唐 a copy of the *Tan ching* 丹經, *Book of Magic,* or *Elixir Classic,* from which he could learn how to make the drug of immortality. He took the drug on Yün-t'ai Shan 雲臺山, Cloud-terrace Mountain, Pao-ning Fu 保寧府, Ssǔch'uan 四川, and forthwith became immortal.

The worthlessness of this legend historically is shown by the widely-divergent periods (Chou 周, Han 漢, Sung 宋) in which various accounts ascribe to Li 李 the age of eight hundred years. —See also *Journ. N.C.B.R.A.S.,* Vol. XLIX, pp. 53-75.

PA KUA 八卦.—The Eight Diagrams of Fu Hsi 伏羲. They are his explanation of how the creative forces of the universe work, and are worshipped by burning incense and bowing in the direction of the region they are supposed to govern. They were also worshipped yearly, as the Five Planetary Stars, during the service on the Altar of Heaven.

PA-NAN-T'O 跋難陀.—A dragon-king.—See *Lung Wang* 龍王.

PAGODA-BEARER, THE.—See *Li Ching* 李精.

PAI-CHAO CHU 白招矩.—See *Venus.*

PAI CHI 柏姬 or 白雞.—The White Hen. The name given to the young daughter of ten years of age who committed suicide after her father, a Mongol named Pai-t'ieh-mu-êrh 柏帖穆爾, the Governor of Fu-chou 福州, had burnt himself alive when the victorious armies of the Mings 明 were entering the city. After having ordered his wife and two concubines to hurl themselves from the top of the palace walls, there remained the girl above-mentioned, a son of three years, and a girl of one. Having told the child to kneel and pray to Buddha for his salvation, he hurled a sack of rice on to it and suffocated it. He then, before committing suicide, gave a sack of pearls to its nurse, and told her to save the boy as heir to his family.

The people built a temple to the girl after her death and called it Pai Chi 柏姬, but in time this got changed into words of the same sound, *viz.* Pai Chi 白雞, White Hen.

One explanation of the name is that she had a white hen of which she was so fond, that when it fell into a well she jumped in after it and was drowned. Another is that a very old white hen became transcendental and changed itself into a girl who distributed magic medicine during an epidemic, and having cured numberless people flew away into the sky in full daylight, and of course the usual temple was erected to her.—See also *Composite Deities*.

PAI CHUNG 百種.—The first Sower. The *pa cha* 八蜡 sacrifice is offered to this god at the end of the twelfth moon, as one of the above-named eight categories of spirits.

PAI-HO T'UNG-TZǓ 白鶴童子.—The Crane Spirit. This Spirit has been noticed in the account of Chih Nü 織女 (*q.v.*), the Weaver Girl. He also appears in the legend which describes how Pao-chih Ch'an-shih 寶誌禪師 (Chih Kung 誌公) (*q.v.*) was contesting with Pai-ho Tao-jên 白鶴道人 for the possession of Ch'ien Shan 灊山, which the Emperor Wu Ti 武帝 (A.D. 502-50) of the Liang 梁 dynasty had promised to the first occupant.

Pai ho T'ung tzŭ 白鶴童子 was a disciple of Yüan-shih T'ien-tsun 元始天尊, and both of them aided the generals who fought for the establishment of the Chou 周 dynasty. Pai-ho T'ung-tzŭ 白鶴童子 especially distinguished himself in the battle of Huang-ho Chên 黃河陣. When the heroine Ch'iung-hsiao 瓊霄 joined in the fray, Yüan-shih T'ien-tsun 元始天尊 ordered his disciple to throw his magic sceptre *ju-i* 如意 into the air. In falling back it broke Ch'iung-hsiao's 瓊霄 skull. Pi-hsiao 碧霄 came to avenge her sister, and threw into the air her mysterious scissors with the object of slaying Yüan-shih T'ien-tsun 元始天尊, but Pai-ho T'ung-tzŭ's 白鶴童子 *ju-i* 如意 again flew up and struck the scissors so violently that they fell to the earth. Seizing his opportunity, Yüan-shih T'ien-tsun 元始天尊 threw up a magic bottle which he took from his sleeve. Pi-hsiao 碧霄 was imprisoned in it, and thus lost her life in the fight.—*Cf. K'êng-san Ku-niang* 坑三姑娘.

PAI-HU 白虎, WHITE TIGER, THE GOD OF THE STAR.—See *Yin Ch'êng-hsiu* 殷成秀 and *Ch'ing Lung Pai Hu* 青龍白虎.

PAI-I TA-SHIH 白衣大士.—See *Kuan Yin* 觀音.

PAI LAO-YEH 白老爺.—See *Ch'êng Huang* 城隍.

PAI-LIEN T'UNG-TZǓ 白蓮童子.—The Servant of the White Lotus. A disciple of Chieh-yin 接引 (Amida). The latter, having been savagely attacked by the goddess Kuei-ling Shêng-mu 龜靈聖母, The Saintly Mother of the Transcendent Tortoise, threw his Buddhist rosary into the air, and it would have split the goddess' skull, but for her having quickly transformed herself into a tortoise.

Amida called his servant down from Heaven. He came with a bag full of mosquitoes which devoured the flesh of the tortoise, leaving only the carapace. Thus perished Kuei-ling Shêng-mu 龜靈聖母.

PAI LIU-FANG 百流放.—The God of the Throat. Style Tao T'ung 道通. Height 8.8 inches. Clothes of nine colours.— *Yün chi ch'i ch'ien* 雲笈七籤.

PAI LUNG 白龍.—See *Lung Wang* 龍王.

PAI MA 白馬.—See *Sun Hou-tzŭ* 猻猴子.

PAI TI 白帝.—See *Venus*.

PAI YÜ 伯魚.—The God of the Guitar.—See *Musical Instruments, The Gods of*.

PAI YU-HUAN 百有患.—The god of the star Ti-mêng 地猛.—See *Ti-sha* 地煞.

PAN SHÊN 瘢(班)神.—The Spirit of Pustules, or Black Smallpox. A specialist attached to the celestial Ministry of Medicine. An assistant to his mother, *Tou-shên Niang-niang* 痘神娘娘 (*q.v.*). Appealed to especially when smallpox has reached the greyish, or dangerous, stage.—See also *T'ien I-yüan* 天醫院.

PAN-T'O-CHIA 半託迦.—See *Lo-han* 羅漢.

PAN-WO-LÜ CH'AN-SHIH 伴我侶禪師 (66th generation). —A deified Buddhist monk. Ranked seventieth in Buddhist School, VI (*q.v.*). Entered the Pien-shan Ssŭ 弁山寺, Pien-shan Monastery, and was a disciple of [Jui-pai] Ming-hsüeh Ch'an-shih [瑞白] 明雪禪師 (*q.v.*). In A.D. 1649, he preached the doctrine at Yü-ch'i 語溪, and then visited the monasteries at Hu-hsiao 虎嘯, Tzŭ-fu 資福, in Chêkiang 浙江, and Pien-shan 弁山. Died at the latter place.

P'AN CHIN-LIEN 潘金蓮.—The Goddess of Brothels. She was the wife of Wu Ta-lang 武大郎, brother of Wu Sung 武松. Having shortly become a widow, she was working in an upper room when, in opening a window, the cross-bar used to close it fell into the street. A passer-by, a wealthy man named Hsi-mên Ch'ing 西門慶, picked it up and took it to her. So struck was he with her great beauty that he prevailed upon a neighbour Wang P'o-p'o 王婆婆, old Mrs. Wang 王, to arrange another interview, and gradually became on intimate terms with her. On Wu Sung's 武松 return he surprised the couple in *flagrante delicto*. Hsi-mên Ch'ing 西門慶 managed to escape, but Wu

Sung 武松 with one stroke of his sword cut off his sister-in-law's head. In time she came to be worshipped as the Goddess of Brothels. This story is given in the *Shui-hu* 水滸.

Another legend relates:—"It was told the king that there was a female sprite, with a red skirt, dishevelled hair, arms and feet bare, who, travelling as swift as the wind, was corrupting public morals. She was shot through with an arrow and her flesh became a mountain. She is the Goddess of Lasciviousness; she has no temple, image, or picture, but in front of houses of ill-fame courtesans burn incense before the door and make prostrations in her honour" (Du Bose, p. 340).

P'AN KU 盤古.—Variously described as the chiseller of the universe out of chaos, he himself being the offspring of the *yin* 陰 and the *yang* 陽, the dual powers of Nature, and as the actual creator of the universe. Pictured as a dwarf clothed in bearskin, or merely in leaves or with an apron of leaves. He has two horns on his head. In his right hand he holds a hammer and in his left a chisel (sometimes these are reversed). He is also shown as attended in his labours by the four supernatural creatures—the unicorn, phoenix, tortoise, and dragon; others again draw him with the sun in one hand and the moon in the other, some of the firstfruits of his stupendous labours. His task occupied eighteen thousand years, and having finished it he dissolved into the various concrete parts of the visible universe, from constellations to human beings, etc. This Taoist account differs from that given by the Buddhists (see *China Review*, xi, 80-82). The creation myth of P'an Ku 盤古 is, however, of comparatively late origin, and is supposed to date from the fourth century A.D. According to Jên Fang 任昉, the Chinese author, the myth was brought to China by some emissaries when they returned from Siam, in the sixth century A.D., and was only inserted in the *Wai chi* 外記 in the eleventh century by Liu Shu 劉恕.—See also Werner, *Myths*, pp. 76-92, 128-30, and Plopper, p. 20.

P'AN KUAN 判官.—The Decider of Life in Hades. The Chinese Atropos. Records the people's fates in a book. Assisant to the Ch'êng Huang 城隍. The Guardian of the Living and the Dead in the Otherworld. He was originally a scholar who became Minister of Ceremonies. After his death he was appointed to the spiritual post above-mentioned. The term P'an Kuan 判官 is, however, more generally used as the designation of an officer or civil or military attendant upon a god than of any special individual, and the original P'an Kuan 判官 has been gradually supplanted in popular favour by Chung K'uei 鍾馗 (*q.v.*).

P'AN NIANG 潘娘.—See *Vaccination, The Goddess of*; also *Yü Tê* 余德.

P'AN-T'AO HUI 蟠桃會.—The Flat Peach Banquet. Held on the third day of the third moon, the anniversary of Hsi Wang-mu's 西王母 (*q.v.*) birthday.—See also *Sun Hou-tzŭ* 孫猴子.

PANTHA.—See *Lo-han* 羅漢

PANTHAKA.—See *Lo-han* 羅漢

PAO CH'ÊNG 包拯.—See *Yen-lo Wang* 閻羅王.

PAO CHIH 寶誌.—A saintly Buddhist monk. A.D. 425-514. One of those invited to the annual banquet of the gods (see *Hsi Wang-mu* 西王母).—See also *Chih Kung* 誌公.

PAO CHING 寶靜.—A saintly Buddhist monk. Sixth century. One of those invited to the annual banquet of the gods (see *Hsi Wang-mu* 西王母). The teacher of Shên Kuang 神光.—See *Patriarchs: Shên Kuang* 神光.

PAO-KUNG CH'AN-SHIH 寶公禪師.—Little is known about this monk. His secular name is given as Kao-lou Shih 高樓士, a native of Sung Shan 嵩山, Honan 河南. He was much later than the Indian *shaman* Fu T'u-ch'êng 佛圖澄, who reached Lo-yang 洛陽, in the same province, in A.D. 310, was honoured with the title of "Great Monk" by the Turkic emperor Shih Lo 石勒 of the Hou Chao 後趙, Later Chao, State (A.D. 318-52), and died in A.D. 349—since the legend connected with Fu T'u-ch'êng 佛圖澄 states that Kao-lou Shih 高樓士 arrived at a monastery built by the former several years previously. The *Shên-hsien t'ung-chien* 神仙通鑑 surmises that he was identical with Chih Kung 誌公 (*q.v.*), who took the name of Pao Kung 寶公.

The legend of Pao Kung 寶公 is as follows:—On his way to Pai-lu Shan 白鹿山, White Stag Mountain, having passed through Lin-lü 林慮, in Honan 河南, he lost his way. Hearing the sound of a bell, he ascended the hill, and came upon a beautiful monastery which bore the name of Ling-yin chih Ssŭ 靈隱之寺, Monastery of Spiritual Retirement. The gate was guarded by enormous mastiffs with coarse white hair and black snouts. These looked at him so ferociously that he was about to retrace his steps when an Indian monk came out and called to him, but immediately re-entered the monastery, followed by the dogs. When Pao Kung 寶公 turned and approached the gates, he found the inner doors closed, but entering the Great Hall, saw nothing but some beds and seats. In the south-west corner he discovered a small apartment containing a bed, and took up his abode there for the time being.

Presently he heard voices coming from the hall to the east, and observed that there was a large hole in the ceiling. Out of this came fifty or sixty monks, who after soaring through the air (using the transcendent power acquired by arhats) alighted, and arrayed themselves in a line in the hall. Each one asked the other whence he had come. One was from Yü-chang 豫章 (the old name for Kiangsi 江西), a second from Ch'êng-tu 成都, Ssŭch'uan 四川, some from Ch'ang-an 長安 (modern Hsi-an Fu 西安府, Shensi 陝西), others from Chi-lin 吉林 (in Chihli 直隸) or Ling-nan 嶺南 (the southern part of modern Yang Chou 揚州, Kiangsu 江蘇), and even a few from India. At length another arrived, and being asked why he had come so late, replied that he came from Pi-an Ssŭ 彼岸寺, Pi-an Monastery, east of Hsiang Chou 相州, Honan 河南. At a gathering of monks to hear the teacher Chien-ch'an 鑒禪, so many doctrinal problems had been propounded that he had been delayed through trying to solve them.

On hearing the name Chien Ch'an 鑒禪 Pao Kung 寶公 remarked that he (Chien Ch'an 鑒禪) was his venerable master, whereupon all the monks did obeisance to Pao Kung 寶公, after which the whole scene vanished as if by magic, no trace of the monastery remaining. Pao Kung 寶公 looking around, found himself at the foot of a tree; close by was a forest, and before him a mountain, a valley, and some birds flying in the air. Proceeding on his journey, he met Shang-t'ung Fa-shih 伺統法師, Shang-t'ung, Expounder of the Law (an honorary title given to monks engaged in teaching). He told him of his vision, and was informed by him that the monastery dated from the time of Shih Chao 石趙 (A.D. 273-332) and had been built by Fu T'u-ch'êng 佛圖澄. It was inhabited by most extraordinary people, and would become visible at times, and then suddenly vanish, or appear in another place. The tolling of a bell was often heard by people of the neighbourhood, but they could see neither monastery nor monks.

PAO LUNG 鮑龍.—The god of the star Ti-fu 地輔.—See Ti-sha 地煞.

PAO-NIU TA-WANG 保牛大王.—See Niu Wang 牛王.

PAO-P'U-TZŬ 抱朴子.—See Yeh Jên 野人.

PAO WA 抱媧.—See Nü Wa 女媧.

PAO-WEI 豹尾, THE GOD OF THE STAR.—See Wu Ch'ien 吳謙.

PAO YÜAN-CH'ÜAN 寶元金.—See Spleen, The Gods of the.

PAO YÜEH 寶月.—The queen of Ching Tê 淨德.—See Yü Huang 玉皇.

PAPER-MAKERS, THE GOD OF.—See *Ts'ai Lun* 蔡 倫.

PARADISE.—See *Ching T'u* 淨土, *Hsi T'ien* 西天, *K'un Lun* 昆崙, and *P'êng-lai Shan* 蓬萊山.

PARI-NIRVANA.—Complete Nirvana. Absolute stillness. Final termination and emancipation from the bonds of trouble and vexation. The second degree of *Nirvana,* corresponding with the mental process of resigning all thought (*wu-hsiang- mên* 無 想 門). This can only be reached at and through death.—See also *Nirvana.*

PATALA.—The infernal regions of Hindu mythology, inhabited by *nagas* (serpents), *daityas, danavas, yakshas,* and others. They are seven in number, and their names, according to the *Vishnu Purana,* are Atala, Vitala, Nitala, Gabhastimat, Mahatala, Sutala and Patala, but these names vary in different authorities. The sage Narada paid a visit to these regions, and on his return to the skies gave a glowing account of them, declaring them to be far more delightful than Indra's heaven, and abounding with every kind of luxury and sensual gratification.

PATHS, THE FOUR.—See *Four Paths.*

PATRA.—Po-to-lo 波多羅, Po-yü 鉢盂, Po-to-lo 鉢多羅, or Po 鉢 .—The almsbowl of every Buddhist mendicant. The almsbowl (*patera*) of Sakyamuni to be used by every Buddha, first preserved at Vaisali, then taken to Gandhara, Persia, China, Ceylon, to the heaven Tuchita, to the palace of Sagara (at the bottom of the sea), where it awaits the advent of Maitreya, whereupon it will divide into four pieces, each of which is to be guarded by a Maharadja, as with its absolute disappearance the religion of Buddha will perish.

PATRIARCH P'ÊNG 彭, THE.—See *Shou Hsing* 壽星 .

PATRIARCHS. *Tsu* 祖.—A Patriarch is so called because he is above every one else in his attainments. He has magical powers and the keenest mental perceptions, being able to accomplish intellectual feats where others fail. He has an acquaintance with great truths which is beyond measurement and penetrates into Buddha's mind to an unfathomable depth. Possessed of these gifts and qualifications, he is the chief defender of Buddhism against the heretics and opposers of his time. He has no ruling power but is simply a defender, teacher, and example of the Buddhist doctrine and life. Selected by the last patriarch from the crowd of common disciples, he takes the chief place ever after as champion of the Buddhist law and discipline. He cares nothing for luxurious living or social rank. He lives poorly, is meanly clad, and keeps up the dignity of his position by the influence of mind, of character, and of supernatural acts (Edkins).

Buddhist Patriarchs are classified by the Chinese as those of the West, *Hsi-tsu* 西祖 (all of Hindu origin, and bearing Indian names), and those of the East, *Tung-tsu* 東祖, who are Chinese belonging to a later phase of Chinese Buddhism, and are six in number (the Six Patriarchs of Chinese Buddhism, *Tung-t'u Liu Tsu* 東土六祖). For a list of the 28 Patriarchs of Indian Buddhism, see *Doré*, vii, 244-5. Some of the latter, especially Kasyapa Asvagosha, and Nagarjuna (*q.v.*), are worshipped or honoured in Chinese temples.

1. BODHIDHARMA. — Ta-mo-ta-shih 大麛大師; P'u-t'i-to-lo 菩提多羅; P'u-ti-to-na Tsun-chê 菩提多那尊者.—The first patriarch of Chinese Buddhism is Bodhidharma (the 28th Indian patriarch). He was the founder of the Meditative School in China (see *Ch'an* 禪). The name means "Great Teacher Bodhidharma," and is frequently abbreviated to Ta-mo 大廟. His original name, Bodhitara (P'u-t'i to-lo 菩提多羅) was changed by his teacher Panyatara (Pradjnâtara), Pan-jo-to-lo 般若多羅, to Bodhidharma, to mark his unusual penetration (*bodhi*) in religious matters and the Buddhist law (*dharma*). A Kchattriya (or kshatriya, the military caste of warriors and kings) by birth he was the third son of Hsiang Chih 香至, a king in Southern India. The date of his birth is uncertain; but his birthday is celebrated on the fifth day of the tenth moon (which appears to be the anniversary of his death).

Having decided, when already an old man, to leave India, he, after a three years' voyage, reached Canton (Kuang-chou Fu 廣州府) about 527, according to Buddhist tradition, or 520, according to other writers:—*i.e.* either the first *Ta-t'ung* 大通 or the first *P'u-t'ung* 普通 year of Wu Ti 武帝 (A.D. 502-50) of the Liang 梁 dynasty. The first date is probably correct, the error having arisen through confusion of these two periods. He brought with him from India the *patra* (*q.v.*) or sacred alms-bowl of the Patriarchate. After a short stay, he was invited to Nanking, where the Emperor Wu held his court, and explained to him that real merit lay not in works, but solely in purity and wisdom duly combined.

Bodhidharma, being dissatisfied at the emperor remaining unenlightened, left Nanking 南京, and set out for the Wei 魏 kingdom, which then occupied the greater part of Northern China. The emperor, regretting the loss of the great ascetic, sent a messenger to invite him to return. When the officer reached the bank of the Yangtzŭ 揚子 River, he beheld the monk crossing the swollen waters on a reed, bamboo twig, or leaf (as variously represented in this favourite subject of Buddhist art). Bodhidharma refused to return, and proceeded to Loyang 洛陽, Honan 河南. (For his and Buddhism's influence on Wu Ti 武帝, see Edkins, p. 107, and *Doré*, vii, 247-8).

He stayed at Loyang 洛陽 for nine years in the Shao-lin Ssŭ 少林寺, Shao-lin Temple, on Sung Shan 嵩山, Sung Hill, sitting in silent meditation facing a wall, whence the populace called him *P'i-kuan P'o-lo-mên* 壁觀婆羅門, the "Wall-gazing Brahman" (though he was not a Brahman, but belonged, as noted above, to the military caste). For the incident leading to his choice of a successor see *Shên Kuang* 神光, *infra*).

Bodhidharma died (after five attempts by his rivals to poison him) before he could accomplish his purpose of returning to India. He died in A.D. 529 or 535 (see *Doré, Recherches*, vii, 249, and *Manuel des Superstitions*, p. 156). The latter date is probably correct. His desciples buried him on Hsiung-êrh Shan 熊耳山, Bear's Ear Hill, to the W. of Loyang. Eitel says his body rests in the Pao-kuang Ssŭ 寶光寺, two miles W. of Canton.

The *Shên-hsien t'ung-chien* 神仙通鑑 relates that Sung Yün 宋雲, a Wei 魏 official who had been sent to India to procure Buddhist books, reported meeting him on Ts'ung Ling 葱嶺, Onion Range, holding·in his hand a single sandal. To his question as to where he was going, he replied: "To the Western Paradise." His coffin was accordingly opened, but was found to contain nothing but the other sandal. The emperor ordered this to be preserved as a relic in the Shao-lin 少林 Monastery, whence it was stolen in the year A.D. 727, and its whereabouts remains unknown.

In A.D. 587 a special monument was erected by Chü Kung 莒公, the last emperor of the Liang Chi 梁紀, Liang dynasty, on the spot where Boddhidharma had left his footprint in the Shao-lin 少林 Monastery.

Bodhidharma was "a sectarian even in Buddhism." He discouraged the use of the sacred books, images and outward rites, and founded in China the "Meditative School," *Ch'an Mên* 禪門, which taught that religion was not to be learnt from books, but that the Buddha was to be sought by each in his own mind. "Monkish energy was concentrated in mental abstraction from all objects of sense, and even one's own thoughts, thus developing a state of dreamy stillness, mental inactivity, and ecstatic somnolence, falsely called by the adherents of the School enlightenment and right thinking." The system resulted in a general decay of learning and religious zeal, and in a development of laziness and inertia, which gradually led Chinese Buddhism into a state of decadence and torpor, from which it never recovered. "The reading of books was the life and soul of many monasteries." Bodhidharma's system "made the monasteries much less educational, and much more mystical and meditative than before." "It was reserved for the fantastic genius of India to construct a religion out of three such elements as atheism, annihilation, and the non-reality of the material world; and, by the encouragement of mysticism and the monastic life, to make these most ultimate of negations palatable and popular. The subsequent addition of a mythology suited to the tests of the common people was . . . another powerful cause, contributing, in conjunction with these quietest and ascetic tendencies, to spread Buddhism through so great a mass of human kind" (Edkins, pp. 101-2).

"Some contemplative monasteries combined with the Amidist School a form of Buddhist evolution, which strongly appeals to the ignorant. This teaches salvation through faith in Buddha, and holds out the promise of unalloyed happiness in the Western Paradise, where Amithabha reigns in endless glory" (see *Amitabha*). "Nowadays, nearly all Buddhist monasteries adopt and practise both systems," "nearly every contemplative monk is more or less of an Amidist; and most of the large monasteries are perfectly tolerant of the 'Pure hand' teachings" (Johnston, p. 93).

2. SHÊN KUANG 神光, *alias* HUI K'o 慧可.—The second patriarch of Chinese Buddhism, A.D. 487-593. A native of Wu-lao 武牢, Originally named Chi Kuang 姬光, his mother's name being Chi, Chi-shih 姬氏. She conceived one day when a bright cloud passed over her home, and Chi Kuang 姬光 was born in the fifth year (A.D. 487) of Wu Ti 武帝 (A.D. 483-94) of the Ch'i 齊 dynasty. He was called Shên Kuang 神光, "Spiritual Light," in reference to this event. Being an extremely intelligent boy, he studied philosophy and the Buddhist canons, and entering a Buddhist monastery, devoted himself earnestly to the contemplative life. When 40 years of age, as the result of a vision and voice from heaven, interpreted by his teacher, the monk Pao Ching 寶靜, as that of Bodhidharma, he left for the Shao-lin Ssŭ 少林寺, Shao-lin monastery, near Lo-yang 洛陽, Honan 河南, where he received from Bodhidharma the robe and bowl of the Patriarchate. The circumstances leading to this appointment and the instructions as to the nature and duties of the office, as related in the *Chih-yüeh lu* 指月錄, are quoted by Edkins (*Chinese Buddhism*, p. 102-3) as follows:—"The presence [at Lo-yang 洛陽] of the Indian sage [Bodhidharma] excited the more ardent Chinese Buddhists to make great efforts to conquer the sensations. Thus one of them [Shên Kuang 神光], we are told, said to himself, 'Formerly, for the sake of religion, men broke open their bones and extracted the marrow, took blood from their arms to give to the hungry, rolled their hair in the mud, or threw themselves down a precipice to feed a famishing tiger. What can I do?' Accordingly, while snow was falling, he exposed himself to it till it had risen above his knees, when the patriarch observing him, asked him what he hoped to gain by it. The young aspirant to the victory over self wept at the question, and said, 'I only desire that mercy may open a path to save the whole race of mankind.' The patriarch replied that such an act was not worthy of comparison with the acts of

the Buddha. It required, he told him, very little virtue or resolution. His disciple, stung with the answer, says the legend, took a sharp knife, severed his arm, and placed it before the patriarch. The latter expressed his high approval of the deed, and when, after nine years' absence, he determined to return to India, he appointed the disciple who had performed it to succeed him as patriarch in China. He said to him on this occasion: 'I give you the seal of the law as the sign of your adherence to the true doctrine inwardly, and the *kasha* (robe worn by Buddhists) as the symbol of your outward teaching. These symbols must be delivered down from one to another for two hundred years after my death, and then, the law of Buddha having spread through the whole nation, the succession of patriarchs will cease.' He further said: 'I also consign to you the *Lenga Sutra* in four sections, which opens the door to the heart of Buddha, and is fitted to enlighten all living men.'" Ta-mo's 大磨 further instructions are given in detail in the *Chih-yüeh lu* 指月錄.

Perceiving that Shên Kuang 神光 had reached a high degree of virtue, Bodhidharma also changed his name to Hui K'o 慧可, "Intelligent Ability."

Doré adds: Hui K'o 慧可 "begged the Great Teacher to expound the doctrine of all the Buddhas. 'That is a thing quite ignored of mortals,' replied Bodhidharma. 'My heart is not at rest,' added the disciple, 'I pray you to grant me peace.' 'Give me your heart,' replied the patriarch, 'and I will set it at rest.' 'How can I give you my heart?' asked the disciple. 'I bequeath you a prayer to Ju-lai 如來,' replied Bodhidharma. Hereupon, says the legend, foreseeing that his end was drawing near, he appointed Shên Kuang 神光 his successor, and bequeathed to him the secret symbol of the law, and a special prayer to Buddha."

After his appointment, Shên Kuang 神光 travelled throughout the country, associating with the lowest and most debauched classes. Replying to criticism, he asserted: "I cultivate my heart," *i.e.* withdrew his thoughts from the world of sensations. He subsequently taught at the K'uang-chiu 匡救 Temple, where, according to one account, he got into trouble with a rival teacher.

In A.D. 593, the Prefect of Kuan-ch'êng 莞城, disliking his vagrant life, had him severely beaten, a punishment he bore patiently. Shortly afterwards, he returned to his monastery, and died there in A.D. 593 at the age of 107 years.

The Emperor Wên Ti 文帝 (A.D. 581-605) was about to dismiss the Prefect, when it was found that he had died on the same day as the Buddhist monk. The Emperor Tê Tsung 德宗 (A.D. 780-805) of the T'ang 唐 dynasty bestowed upon him the title of *T'ai-tsu Ch'an-shih* 太祖禪師.

3. SENG-TS'AN 僧璨.—The third patriarch of Chinese Buddhism. Little is known of his origin. Having, when more than 40 years of age, introduced himself to Hui K'o 慧可 (*v.*

supra) he, as the result of a conversation with him, chose him for his teacher. Hui K'o 慧可 then gave him a new name (his first is unknown) calling him Sêng Ts'an 僧 璨, "The Monk with a Gem's Lustre." He taught him assiduously, explaining all the rules of his profession, and when dying appointed him his successor.

Sêng Ts'an 僧 璨 lived for more than ten years in seclusion and died in A.D. 606 at Huan-Kung Shan 皖公山, Shu Chou 舒州, Anhui 安徽. He taught that there is no distinction between existence and non-existence. The monk Chih Kung 誌公 is often mistakenly quoted as the third patriarch.

4. TAO-HSIN 道信.—The fourth patriarch of Chinese Buddhism. A.D. 580-651. Surname Ssŭ-ma 司 馬, a native of Ho-nei 河 內., Honan 河南. A precocious youth, he delighted in reading Buddhist books, and in 592 became the disciple of Sêng Ts'an 僧璨 (*v. supra*). This was at a time of fierce persecution and severe restrictions on the teaching of Buddhism. He received instruction in the Law from Sêng Ts'an 僧 璨 for nine years, and being found to have attained to a high degree of virtue, was admitted into the ranks of the Brotherhood, and appointed as his successor. In his zeal for religion he is said never to have lain down for sixty years. Taking up his abode near P'o-t'ou Shan 破頭山, he opened a school there, which became famous. In 617, he and his disciples are said to have raised the siege of Chi Chou 吉州, in Shansi 山西, by inducing the townsfolk to recite the *Prajna Paramita Sutra.* In 624 he returned to Chi 蘄 in Hopei, where he met Hung Jên 弘忍 (*v. infra*). In 643, being threatened with death for thrice refusing Imperial invitations to the Court, he offered his neck to the envoy, and upon this being reported to the Emperor, was allowed to remain in peace. Having appointed Hung Jên 弘忍 as his successor, he died in A.D. 651.

5. HUNG-JÊN 弘忍.—The fifth patriarch of Chinese Buddhism. A.D. 602-675. Often surnamed Ta Man 大 滿. He was the illegitimate son of a girl, named Chou 周, of Huang-mei Hsien 黄 梅 縣, in Hupei 湖北. This is generally described as a miraculous conception, the child being the reincarnation of an aged wood-gatherer who had sought instruction from Tao Hsin 道信, Her parents having driven his mother from their home, she and her son were begging, when they met Tao Hsin 道信, who, from his extensive knowledge of physiognomy, recognized him as his successor. Having received intelligent answers to questions put to the youth, Tao-hsin 道信 proceeded to his home, and obtained his mother's consent to the lad entering a monastery. Tao Hsin 道信 instructed him, gave him the priestly robe, and changed his name to Hung Jên 弘忍, "Vast Endurance."

Toward the end of Kao Tsu's 高祖 (A.D. 618-27) reign, in the fifth month, a bright light appeared in the Tsou-shih Tung 奏石 洞, Musical Stone Grotto, situated at the foot of Fang Shan 房 山,

Mount Fang. In this grotto the Buddhist teacher (*fa-shih* 法師) Ching Wan 靜琬 had hidden a Buddhist prayer-manual, and closed the entrance with a large stone. The third patriarch Sêng Ts'an 僧粲 had often consulted this work, and found therein strength and enlightenment as to how to meet the many adversities of his life. The monk Hsiao Yü 蕭瑀 reported the phenomenon to the Emperor, praying him to cease persecuting Buddhism, and to issue and have engraved on stone an edict in its favour and allowing the dispersed monks to return to their monasteries.

It was Hung Jên 弘忍, and in a still greater degree his disciple Hui Nêng 慧能 (*v. infra*), who founded the sect of Vegetarians.

To choose his successor, Hung Jên 弘忍 held a verse competition of the *gatha* (metrical hymn with a moral purpose) type, among 700 monks. Lu Hui-nêng 盧惠能 (*v. infra*), being adjudged the winner, was chosen as the last Chinese patriarch. Hung Jên 弘忍 thereupon declared that his doctrine was complete, and retired into private life, dying in A.D. 675.

6. HUI NÊNG (慧) 惠能.—The sixth patriarch of Chinese Buddhism. A.D. 637-712. The *Shên-hsien t'ung-chien* 神仙通鑑 uses the character 慧, the *Sou-shên chi* 搜神記 the character 惠. The former gives a detailed, the latter a short account of this patriarch's career.

Descended from the Lu 盧 family, he is frequently referred to as Lu Hui-nêng 盧惠能. His parents were natives of Fan-yang 范陽, in Chih li 直隸, but migrated to the South of the Nan Ling 南嶺, Southern Range. He was born at Hsin-hsing Hsien 新興縣, in Kuangtung 廣東, but his birthplace is also given as Pu-chou Fu 部州府 in the same province, and as Hsin-chou 新州 in Northern China. He is said to have remained in the womb six years, and to have refused his mother's milk, being fed miraculously by angels. The poverty of his parents obliged him to sell in the market firewood gathered by him in a neighbouring forest. During this occupation, he heard a peasant reciting verses of the *Prajnaparamita, Transcendental Wisdom,* known as the *Diamond Sutra, Chin-kang ching* 金剛經. Being thereby attracted toward the Buddhist Law, he proceeded to Shao-chou Fu 韶州府, in Kuangtung 廣東 where he met a Buddhist nun, Wu Chin-ts'ang 無盡藏, who was reciting the *Nirvana Sutra* (an early Buddhist work, translated into Chinese about A.D. 170), *Nieh-p'an ching* 涅槃經, without understanding it. Hui Nêng 惠能 told her that, though he did not know the characters, he could understand the meaning, and, having astonished her by his remarkable intelligence, she summoned the priests from the temple, but he informed them that he was still in search of a teacher, and when fully instructed would return and share his learning with them.

Whilst at Ts'ao-ch'i 曹溪 (in the mountainous region on the frontier between Kuangtung 廣東 and Kuangsi 廣西) he was so charmed with the beauty of the landscape that he selected it as a site for a monastery, and begged the owner to grant him a piece of land for that purpose. He required, he added, only as much as his robe could cover. The owner agreed to the request, whereupon Hui Nêng 惠 能 laid his robe on the ground, and it immediately expanded until it covered an area of eighty Chinese square miles. The present-day monastery on Nan-hua Shan 南 華 山, Nan-hua Hill, occupies the site, and Hui Nêng 惠 能 abode there for several years.

He then continued his wanderings, and about A.D. 674, at Ch'ang-lo Shan 昌 樂 山, met the monk Chih Yüan 智 遠, who sent him to Hung Jên 弘 忍, the fifth patriarch, then living at Huang-mei-shan Ssŭ 黃 梅 山 寺, Monastery of the Yellow Prune Hill, situated in Ch'i Chou 蘄 州, in Hupei 湖 北. Received by him somewhat haughtily on account of the improbability of his native place being likely to produce Buddhas, he nevertheless impressed Hung Jên 弘 忍 by his intelligence in pointing out that "Buddha's doctrine was the same for all," and he was received into the monastery. He was set to hulling rice, and, continuing assiduously at that menial work for eight months, had attained to a high degree of virtue. He was accordingly granted the robe and was instructed in the tenets of the Law.

This was done after the usual intellectual test. The master called his disciples together and ordered them to compose verses indicating the rule of conduct to be followed. The cleverest among them, Shên Hsiu 神 秀, wrote on the well of the lobby the following maxim:—

"The body is comparable to the *p'u-t'i* 菩 提 tree [Bodhi tree, tree of knowledge], the heart resembles the shining surface of a mirror. It must be wiped constantly, in order to remove the dust which accumulates on it."

On reading this quatrain Hui Nêng 惠 能 replied: "This is well expressed, but badly thought out"; a dictum received by all present with derision. But Hui Nêng added to his criticism the following words: *"P'u-t'i* 菩 提 is not a tree, a shining mirror is not a surface, and there being no dust on it, there is no need to wipe it off." After this, the master dismissed the assembled disciples.

Toward midnight Hun Nêng 惠 能 sought his master and begged him to grant him a magic formula and the begging-bowl. The master, on complying with his request, recommended the kneeling monk to hide these insignia of his profession under his robe and keep them secret from the other monks. He then instructed him to proceed to the South to recruit disciples and propagate the doctrine. When about halfway on his journey, a party of aspirants, armed with knives, set upon him, being jealous of him because he had been admitted to the profession in precedence of themselves. Being unable to resist them physically, he adopted the following device. He placed his robe and alms-bowl on a large flat stone, and bade them remove both for their own use. Owing to the influence of the magic formula he had received from Hung Jên 弘忍, the novices were unable to move them or to break the stone, however much they exerted themselves, and at length took their departure, leaving Hui Nêng 惠能 free to continue his journey.

After reaching Huai-chou 懷州, Honei 河內, he crossed the Ai Ling 愛嶺 Range and took up his abode in a grotto on one of the high peaks. This grotto is still known as the "Grotto of the Sixth Patriarch."

Four years later, he set out for Fêng-mao Shan 馮茂山, Fêng-mao Hill, and in 676 (the first year of I-fêng 儀鳳) crossed the Southern Sea, and met the famous monk and teacher Yin-tsung Ch'an-shih 印宗禪師 in the Fa-hsing Ssŭ 法性寺, Fa-hsing Monastery. One evening as they were sitting on the veranda, the wind undulated the banner hoisted in front of the monastery gate. A discussion arose as to whether it was the wind or the banner that moved, but they could come to no agreement. All of a sudden, Hui Nêng 惠能 said: "It is neither the wind nor the banner which moves, but the heart which beats." Struck with this ingenious remark, Yin-tsung 印宗 called together his disciples, and ordered them to salute the incarnate *p'u-t'i* 菩薩 whose acquaintance he had just had the good fortune to make.

Hui Nêng 惠能 returned to Ts'ao-ch'i 曹溪, and lived in the Pao-lin Ssŭ 寶林寺, Pao-lin Monastery, where he gave instruction in the Law, his disciples numbering more than a thousand.

In 705 the Emperor invited him to Court, but he excused himself on the plea of old age. His charming manner on this occasion caused the messenger to make so eulogistic a report that the Emperor sent him an embroidered cope, a monk's begging-bowl, and several other valuable articles.

At this time Shên Hsiu 神秀 (*q.v.*), his contemporary at the time of his novitiate (*v. supra*), was also regarded as the sixth patriarch of Chinese Buddhism. This is why some call Hui Nêng 惠能 the patriarch of the South, and Shên Hsiu 神秀 the patriarch of the North.

Hui Nêng 惠能 is regarded as the real founder of the Vegetarian Sect, Ch'ih-su Chiao 喫素敎 (see *Buddhist Schools,* II). A temple to him still exists 45 *li* 里 N.E. of T'ai-hsing 泰興, Kiangsu 江蘇, where vegetarians go to do him honour. He had a large number of disciples, a good proportion of whom are honoured in Chinese Buddhist temples. The most famous are: Huai Jang 懷讓 (*q.v.*), sometimes described as the seventh patriarch; and Ma Tsu 馬祖 (*q.v.*). Other distinguished disciples were Hsing Ssŭ 行思, Shih T'ou 石頭, and Hsi Ch'ien 希遷. Ma Tsu 馬祖 and Shih T'ou 石頭 were themselves founders of special schools.

Hui Nêng 惠能 named no successor in the patriarchate, as the doctrine was already well established in China, and thus the series of Patriarchs of Chinese Buddhism closes at his death. He rebuked his disciples for weeping over him, and died in the

Kuo-ên Ssŭ 國恩寺, Kuo-ên Monastery, at his native place, where he had caused a dagoba to be prepared for his remains, in A.D. 712. The begging-bowl of Bodhidharma, which had been transmitted from patriarch to patriarch, was buried beside him. The three cities which had been his favourite places of abode, contested the honour of receiving his remains, but he was eventually interred at Ts-ao-ch'i 曹溪 (*supra*).

After his death, his corpse (which was probably lacquered, and thus preserved) is said to have remained incorrupt, and even to have exhaled a sweet fragrance. The chest maintained its natural position, as if he still lived, the skin appearing glossy and flexible. His priestly robe and begging-bowl were taken to the North, but were later on restored to the monastery, where they are still preserved.

In 1276, when the Nan Sung 南宋 dynasty was being over-thrown by the Mongol troops, soldiers violated the tomb of the patriarch, ripping the abdomen open with a sword. Finding the heart and liver in a perfect state of preservation, they were filled with awe, and abstained from further molestation.

The relics of Hui Nêng 惠能, the *Sou-shên chi* 搜神記 states, comprise a richly embroidered cope bestowed on him by the emperor Hsüan Tsung 宣宗 (A.D. 713-56), a begging-bowl made of precious wood, a pair of sandals of unknown material, 16 or 17 pages of the *Saddharma-Pundarika,* or *Fu-hua ching* 法華經, the *Lotus of the Good Law* (one of the canonical books of the Nepalese, and the standard classic of the Lotus School), and some parcels of Buddha's bones contained in a small coffer.

The legend of Hui Nêng 惠能 is as follows:—The inhabitants of the country were greatly afflicted by the misfortunes caused them by a dragon, which abode in a deep lake. Hui Nêng 惠能 promised to assist them, saying: "You will see the dragon become smaller," and it was then seen to become so small that the patriarch received it in a bowl, which he placed in the monastery. In A.D. 1171 the dragon was still to be seen there.

PEACHES, THE FEAST OF.—P'an-T'ao Hui 蟠桃會 —See *Hsi Wang-mu* 西王母.

PEAKS, THE FIVE.—See *Wu Yo* 五嶽.

PEARLY EMPEROR, THE.—See *Yü Huang* 玉皇.

PEI-CHI CH'Ü HSIEH YÜAN 北極驅邪院.—The post-humous title of Yen Chên-ch'ing 顏眞卿 (A.D. 709-85). He lived during the reign of the Emperor Tê Tsung 德宗 (A.D. 780-805) of the T'ang 唐 dynasty. Being a trusted officer of the Emperor, he was sent, in A.D. 783, to fight the rebellious Governor Li Hsi-lieh 李希列. Whilst intoxicated at a farewell banquet given him by his relatives at Ch'ang-lo P'o 長樂坡, he announced that he had formerly met a Taoist named T'ao Pa-pa 陶八八, who had given him the pill of immortality, and had warned him of impending danger. On reaching the Eastern capital he was surrounded and threatened by the rebel forces, but as he remained unperturbed the rebel Governor treated him with honour.

When in the following year, A.D. 784, the rebel proclaimed himself Emperor under the style of Wu Ch'êng 武成, Yen Chên-ch'ing 顏眞卿, then at Ts'ai-chou 蔡州, Honan 河南, wrote warning the Emperor of his approaching death. For this Li Hsi-lieh 李希烈 had him strangled. He was then 77 years of age. The Emperor conferred on him the title of Wên Chung 文忠, Distinguished and Faithful. Before dying, he entrusted to an imperial envoy his gold belt, and instructed him to have his body carefully buried. After his death the body was interred to the south of the city.

In A.D. 787 Li Pi 李泌 begged the Emperor to confer the honour of special obsequies on Yen Lu-kung 顏魯公 (the title which had been bestowed on him by the Emperor) for his patriotic services. The Emperor sent his own son to bring the coffin to the capital. When the Prince had it opened, he found the coffin decayed, but the corpse was intact, of a yellow colour, the hands and feet still flexible, his black hair and beard several feet long, and his hands closed so firmly that the finger-nails had pierced into the palms.

A new coffin was made and the corpse taken to the capital, where ducal obsequies were accorded it. It was then buried at Pei Shan 北山, near Yen-shih Hsien 偃師縣, Honan 河南.

He was canonized by Yü Ti 玉帝 as Pei-chi Ch'ü-hsieh Tso-p'an Kuan 北極驅邪左判官, First Military Officer of the Ministry of Exorcisms of the North Pole. Postmortem apparitions of him are recorded as follows:—A merchant passing Lo-fou Shan 羅浮山 saw two priests playing chess under a tree. One of them asked him whence he came. He replied that he was a trader from Lo-yang 洛陽, Honan 河南. The Taoist wrote a letter and asked him to take it to his family. On returning to Pei Shan 北山, the trader delivered the letter to the guardian of the family tombs, who handed it to the relatives. The latter recognised the writing as his, and on opening the tomb it was found to be empty.

About ten years later a servant of the family, on entering T'ung-tê Ssŭ 同德寺, T'ung-tê Temple, at Lo-yang 洛陽, Honan 河南, saw Yen Chên-ch'ing 顏眞卿 seated there on a Buddhist altar. He went nearer to see him more clearly, but Yen 顏 turned away his head. Each time the servant approached from one side he turned toward the other. Finally, he left the temple and, going into a garden, entered a straw hut. The servant followed him and was questioned by Yen Chên-ch'ing 顏眞卿 regarding news of his family. He then handed him a gold ingot, and enjoined on him not to divulge what had happened. The servant, however, informed the members of the family, who examined the ingot and found it to be of pure gold. They at once mounted horses and galloped to the spot indicated by the servant, but found nothing but a plot of uncultivated ground covered with high grass.

PEI-CHI YU-SHÊNG CHÊN-CHÜN 北極佑聖眞君.—See *Hsüan-t'ien Shang-ti* 玄天上帝.

PEI TOU 北斗.—The Spirits of the Stars of the Northern Dipper (Pei Tou 北斗) record men's actions, both good and evil, and according to one's virtuous deeds, or his sins, they add to or cut off a portion of his life. Those most worshipped of this constellation are the "Three Stars" (representing Happiness, Emoluments, and Longevity). Of these the Star of Longevity is the most important. As the one thing most sought is long life, he is very popular with the people. He is represented as having a large, high forhead. He is always smiling. He carries a large peach in one hand and a staff in the other. There is usually a bat above his head. Temples are erected in his honour.—See Plopper, pp. 40-1 and *T'ou Mu* 北斗.

PEI-TU CH'AN-SHIH 杯渡禪師.—The Cup-boat Monk, or The Monk who crossed Rivers on his Begging-bowl. A staintly Buddhist monk. Sixth century. One of those invited to the annual banquet of the gods (see *Hsi Wang-mu* 西王母).

The origin and name of this monk, and the exact time in which he lived, are unknown. The *Sou-shên chi* 搜神記 says that he was buried in A.D. 426, but the *Shên-hsien t'ung-chien* 神仙通鑑 makes him a contemporary of *Fu Ta-shih* 傅大士 (*q.v.*) and states that he lived during the reign of Wu Ti 武帝 (A.D. 502-50) of the Liang 梁 dynasty. The discrepancy may be due to mistaking or mistranscribing the third year of the period Yüan-chia 元嘉 (426) of the Liu-Sung Chi 劉宋紀, Liu Sung dynasty, for the third year of the period T'ien-chia 天嘉 (562) of the Ch'ên Chi 陳紀, Ch'ên dynasty.

The existing accounts of this monk indicate that they are imitations of those of Bodhidharma (see *Patriarchs*). The following legends concerning him are abridged from the two Chinese works above-mentioned.

The first reference to him shows him living at Chi Chou 冀州, Chihli 直隸, in the house of a peasant, who possessed a golden image of Buddha. One morning, both the monk and the image disappeared, and when pursued by the peasant and several others on horseback, was seen, on reaching the bank of the Mêng-ching 孟津 river, to place his alms-bowl on the water and cross the river on it. Hence the name by which he is known. Landing on the opposite bank, he proceeded to the capital (probably Chien-k'ang 建康, the modern Nanking 南京). Here, though 40 years of age, he went about in ragged garments, and even bathed after breaking the ice on the river, in the coldest water (a custom almost unknown among the Chinese) without suffering any ill effects.

The feat of crossing a river on his alms-bowl was repeated later at the Kua-pu Chiang 瓜步江, and at a village near Kuang-ling 廣陵, (? Kiangsu 江蘇), during the ceremony of *tso-chai* 做齋, releasing souls from Hades. Having placed his basket in the middle of the courtyard, obstructing the passage of the guests, it was found impossible to remove it until Pei-tu 杯渡—having, though in tattered clothes, enjoyed a hearty meal with the guests—easily lifted it after exclaiming: "Four Heavenly Kings." (These are not the same as the Ssŭ-ta T'ien-wang 四大天王 *q.v.*). The basket was seen to contain four richly-dressed and beautiful dwarfs, only a few inches in height. Being asked by Mr. Li 李, the host, to give their names, he said they were Hsi-ts'un 攜寸, Wan-chieh 萬傑, Shu-t'uan 蜀湍, and Chang-ch'i 掌起. After about a hundred days he proceeded to Yen-chou Fu 兖州府, in Shantung 山東, but when the Prefect, Liu Hsing-pai 劉興伯, who had invited him to his official residence, examined his basket, he found in it only an old garment and the monk's alms-bowl.

He returned to Mr. Li's 李 house, and later on was found dead at the foot of a hill, lotus-flowers (the symbol of self-creation) having sprung up around his head and filled the air with an extraordinarily sweet fragrance.

Some days after his burial, Pei-tu 杯渡 was seen carrying his basket and going in the direction of P'êng-ch'êng 彭城, Kiangsu 江蘇. His coffin being opened, it was found to contain nothing but a pair of sandals [as in the case of Bodhidharma]. Pei-tu 杯渡 stayed in P'êng-ch'êng 彭城 for six months with a poor scholar named Huang Hsin 黃欣. Whilst he was his guest, he asked him for the rinds of thirty-six large gourds, each of which he covered over, and on Huang Hsin 黃欣 being told to uncover them they were found to contain over a million ounces of silver. This money the scholar used in promoting good works, thus, according to the Buddhist doctrine, storing up merit and delivering himself from repeated births. A year later, when Pei-tu 杯渡 was leaving, Huang Hsin 黃欣 prepared some provisions for his use on the journey; but on the morrow after his departure they were found intact in the place where the monk had left them.

Another of his miracles was the changing of two pebbles which he had cast into a pond into buffaloes, which broke the nets of a fisherman who had replied with curses to his request for one of the fishes he had caught.

He is also said to have been seen at Yu Chou 有州, Shensi 陝西, and K'ai-fêng Fu 開封府, Honan 河南, at the same time. This is an example of the transcendant power of *arhats* over matter, time and space.

The last prodigy related as being performed by him is that of causing the boat of a rich merchant, Chu Ling-ch'i 朱靈期 of Wu-chün 吳郡, who had been wrecked on a voyage to Korea, to rise in the air, and fly over the trees, first to Shih-t'ou Hui 石頭湫, and then to Chu-ch'iao 朱雀. At the latter place, he and his sailors met Pei-tu 杯渡 riding on horse-back. They fell on their knees and thanked him for his protection. He then boarded their vessel and, reading a letter which he had placed in his alms-bowl and left in the boat with his staff (these being endowed with magic powers), he remarked that he was ordered back to life (thus showing that he regarded himself as still dead), and, taking the bowl, tossed it into the air, catching it again in his hand. "It is forty years since I last saw it," he remarked with joy.

After curing the wife of a scholar named Ch'i Hsieh 齊諧 by reciting a magic formula (in return for which favour the scholar is said to have written Pei-tu's 杯渡 biography), he went on to Ch'ih-shan Hu 赤山湖, Redhill Lake, where he fell ill, and died for the second time (forty years after his first death). Ch'i Hsieh 齊諧 buried him on the Fu-chou Shan 覆舟山, Hill of the Sunken Ship, near Chien-k'ang 建康 (Nanking 南京), Kiangsu 江蘇. After death, he appeared to the scholar, and bade him erect a tower over his remains.

In Chinese art, he is usually represented crossing rivers, etc., on a banana-leaf, or on a reed (after the fashion of Bodhidharma when crossing the Yangtzŭ 揚子 River).

P'EI T'UNG 邳仝.—The god of the constellation I 翼. Alternatively with Wang Chiao 王敫.

PÊN-CHI CH'AN-SHIH 本寂禪師 (39th generation).— A deified Buddhist monk. Ranked ninth in Buddhist School, VI (*q.v.*). Founder of the Ts'ao-tung Mo 曹洞脈, Ts'ao-tung School, a school near Ts'ao Shan 曹山, Mount Ts'ao, in the I-huang 宜黃 district, Fukien 福建 (see *Buddhist Schools,* VII). Family name Huang 黃. A native of P'u-t'ien 莆田, in the same province. At 19 entered the Ling-shih Ssŭ 靈石寺, Mystic-stone Monastery, at Foochow 福州. Studied under Liang-chieh Ch'an-shih 良价禪師 (*q.v.*). Taught at Ts'ao Shan 曹山. Died A.D. 901. Buried at Hsi-lu 西麓, Ssŭch'uan 四川. Posthumous title: Yüan-chêng 元證, Original Testimony.

PÊN-CHING CH'AN-SHIH 本淨禪師.—There is no existing document describing the life of this monk. His virtues alone are are all that his biography records.

He is said to have learnt, when on a visit to the monks of Fukien 福建, who lived in caves, that at Ch'ang-chi 長溪 there were some caves formerly inhabited by *hsien jên* 仙人, Immortals (*q.v.*), and so he went to Hsüeh-t'ung Shan 雪童山, Hsüeh-t'ung Hill, where he built a reed hut to live in.

His transcendental powers were shown in the taming of fierce animals (an enormous dragon, a tiger, etc.) which molested the inhabitants of the district.

One evening, a distinguished stranger spent the night in the monk's hut, but at daybreak both were transformed into cranes, and taking flight (after the manner of Taoist Immortals who fly from place to place seated on the backs of cranes) were never seen again.

PÊN-JUI CH'AN-SHIH 本 瑞 禪 師 (63rd generation).—A deified Buddhist monk. Ranked forty-first in Buddhist School, III (*q.v.*). Family name Chiang 江. Studied under Ming-hsüan Ch'an-shih 明 瑄 禪 師 (*q.v.*), and spent his whole life in the Chung-ling Ssǔ 鍾 陵 寺, Chung-ling Monastery, Kiangsi 江 西.

P'ÊNG CHIU-YÜAN 彭 九 元.—See *Chiu Yao* 九 曜.

P'ÊNG-LAI SHAN 蓬 萊 山.—Among the large number of lesser Paradises of the Taoists (there are supposed to be thirty-six Heavenly Grottoes and seventy-two Happy Lands of the Taoists), the Eastern Isles stand out prominently. Of these P'êng-lai Shan 蓬 萊 山 is the most famous. It is still the home of the Eight Immortals, and a great host of those who have won the blessing of eternal life. The houses are made of gold and silver. The birds and animals are all white. The pearl and coral trees grow there in great profusion. The flowers and seeds all have a sweet flavour. Those who eat them do not grow old nor die. There they drink of the fountain of life, and live in ease and pleasure. The Isles are surrounded with water which has no buoyancy, so it is impossible to approach them. They are inhabited only by the immortals, who have supernatural powers of transportation. The Eastern Isles are a most frequent theme in their literature. They are the goal of many earnest Taoists (Plopper, p. 359).

P'ÊNG SUNG-LIU 蓬 送 留.—The God of the Bowels.—*Yün chi ch'i ch'ien* 雲 笈 七 籤.

P'ÊNG-TSU 彭 祖.—See *Shou Hsing* 壽 星.

P'ÊNG TSU-SHOU 彭 祖 壽.—The god of the star Sui-yen 霞 厭. A feudatory of Chou Wang 紂 王 (1154-1121 B.C.) and Governor of Yen-chou Fu 兗 州 府, Shantung 山 東. Slain at Mêng-ching 津 孟 in fighting the transcendent centipede Wu Lung 吳 龍.

P'ÊNG TSUN 彭 遵.—The god of the star Lo-hou 羅 睺, the star of quarrelling. One of Chou Wang's 紂 王 officers. Hsü Kai's 徐 蓋 aide-de-camp at Chieh-p'ai Kuan 界 牌 關. Killed by Lei Chên-tzŭ 雷 震 子. Canonized by Chiang Tzǔ-ya 姜 子 牙.

PERFECT MATRON, THE.—See *Pi-hsia Yüan-chün* 碧 霞 元 君.

PERFECTED OBSERVATION.—See *Buddhist Schools*, X, and *Chan-jan Tsun-chê* 湛然尊者.

PERFUME SELLERS, THE GODDESS OF FACE-CREAM AND.—See *Hsi Shih* 西施.

PESTILENCE, THE GOD OF.—Originally a literary man. One day, returning from school, he saw a demon about to blow his deadly breath into a well, and reflecting that this was a public well and that a multitude would be poisoned, but that if they saw a dead body in the water no one would drink from it, he leaped into the well. He was appointed the God of Pestilence, and whenever there is an epidemic they take him out in a procession. In some temples represented with a black face. He is one of the four high ministers of Heaven.

PHYSICIANS, THE TEN CELEBRATED.—See *Shih-ming-i* 十明醫.

PI 畢, THE GOD OF THE CONSTELLATION.—See *Ch'ên Chün* 陳俊 and *Chin Shêng-yang* 金繩陽.

PI 壁, THE GOD OF THE CONSTELLATION.—See *Tsang Kuan* 臧官 and *Fang Chi-ch'ing* 方志清.

PI CH'IU 比丘.—See *Lo-han* 羅漢.

PI HSI 蟲屭.—See *Lung Wang* 龍王.

PI-HSIA YÜAN-CHÜN 碧霞元君.—The First Princess of Purple and Azure Clouds. She who presides at confinements and child-births. There are two principal goddesses:—Pi-hsia Yüan-chün 碧霞元君 of Fukien 福建, and Pi-hsia Yüan-chün 碧霞元君 of T'ai Shan 泰山, Mount T'ai. Besides these general names, the goddess is known also as—T'ien Hsien 天仙, the Immortal of Heaven, T'ien-hsien sung-tzǔ 天仙送子, the Celestial Immortal who brings children, Niang-niang sung-tzǔ 娘娘送子, the Matron who brings children, and Shêng Mu 聖母, the Saintly Mother. In Fukien 福建 she is more especially called Ch'ên Fu-jên 陳夫人, Dame Ch'ên, and Chu-shêng Niang-niang 注生娘娘, the Matron of Generation. In the North she is known as T'ai Shan Niang-niang 泰山娘娘, the Matron of T'ai Shan, and Yü Nü 玉女, the Jade Maiden.

Ch'ên Fu-jên 陳夫人 is said to have been Ching Ku 靖姑, born at Ku-t'ien Hsien 古田縣, in Fu-chou Fu 福州府. Her home village was Lin-shui Hsiang 臨水鄉, whence she is also known as Lin-shui Fu-jên 臨水夫人. She was the sister of, and was taught mysterious spirit-controlling incantations by, Ch'ên Shou-yüan 陳守元, the famous magician at the Court of Wang

Yen-chün 王 延 鈞 (Wang Lin 王 鄰), third ruler (died A.D. 935) of the Min 閩 Principality, who canonized her as "The Perfect Matron." She went to live in some unknown place "in the middle of the seas," and her subsequent history is unknown.

This goddess is also said to have been a Fukienese named Chin-ku 進 姑, daughter of Ch'ên Ch'ang 陳 昌, and born in A.D. 767, during the reign of the Emperor Tai Tsung 代 宗 (A.D. 763-80) of the T'ang 唐 dynasty. She is credited with the performance of numerous prodigies, and received honorific titles under the Sung 宋 dynasty.

Another version describes her as the Spirit who stated she was the lady Ch'ên 陳 of Ku-t'ien 古 田 when she suddenly appeared and aided Hsü Ch'ing-sou's 徐 清 叟 daughter-in-law in her confinement, being recognized from her image in the temple, and subsequently worshipped and prayed to by women at the time of their child-bearing.

The Pi-hsia Yüan-chün 碧 霞 元 君 of T'ai Shan 泰 山 is the goddess of the following legend:—So perfect was Chiang T'ai-kung's 姜 太 公 government of the Kuan-t'an 灌 壇 country that it enjoyed such perfect peace that even the wind did not blow there. Wên Wang 文 王 (1231-1135 B.C.) one night dreamt that he saw a woman weeping, who, when asked the cause of her grief, replied that she was the daughter of the God of T'ai Shan 泰 山 and that her husband was a Spirit of the Western Sea. When she travelled, she added, she was usually escorted by the winds and rains, but knowing that Chiang T'ai-kung 姜 太 公 was a man of such great virtue, she did not dare to cross his territory. The next day Wên Wang 文 王 summoned Chiang T'ai-kung 姜 太 公, and a strong wind and heavy rain occurred, showing that the daughter of the god with her escort had been allowed to pass. Thus, Pi-hsia Yüan-chün 碧 霞 元 君 of T'ai Shan 泰 山 is the daughter of the god of this sacred mountain of the East.

The genealogy of the gods of the sacred mountains is given by Doré as follows:—Shao Hai 少 海, a descendant in the fourth generation from P'an Ku 盤 古 (q.v.), married Mi-lun 彌 輪. She gave birth, after dreaming that she had swallowed two suns, to two sons. The elder was named Chin Shan 金 蟬 (=Jan Têng 燃 燈, q.v.). His four sons were—Ch'ung-t'an 崇 覃, the God of Hêng Shan 衡 山, the sacred mountain of the South; Shan-shêng 善 壑, the God of Hua Shan 華 山, the sacred mountain of the West; Ch'ên-ô 彚 夢, the God of Hêng Shan 恒 山 (also called I-wu-lu Shan 醫 無 盧 山), the sacred mountain of the North; and Yün-shan 惲 讋, who with his father Chin Shan 金 蟬 were Gods of Sung Shan 嵩 山, the sacred mountain of the Centre.

The second son, Chin Hung 金 虹, married Shui-i Shih 水 一 氏. He is worshipped as the God of T'ai Shan 泰 山, the sacred mountain of the East. His five sons were:—Hsüan-ling Hou 宣 靈 侯, the Marquis Hsüan-ling; Hui-ling Hou 惠 靈 侯, the Marquis Hui-ling; Chih-shêng Ping-ling Wang 至 聖 炳 靈 王, the most saintly King Ping-ling (San T'ai-tzǔ 三太子, the Third Royal Prince); Chü-jên chin-chien Tsun-shih 居仁盡鑒尊師, the Highly-honoured Master Chin-chien; and Yu-ling Hou 佑靈侯, the Marquis Yu-ling. The daughter of the latter (whose wife was Shu-hui Fu-jên 淑惠夫人) was the famous Yü-nü Ta-hsien 玉女大仙, T'ai Shan Niang-niang 泰山娘娘 (*supra*). She also bears the title Tai-yo T'ai-p'ing hsiang Yü-hsien Niang-niang 岱岳太平項玉仙娘娘, the Immortal Jade Mother of the Sacred Mountain T'ai-shan 泰山. She gave herself up to a life of asceticism on the summit of Lien-hua Fêng 蓮花峰, Lotus-flower Peak, and from her habit of going frequently to wash her hands in the lake situated at the foot of the mountain, it was called Yü-nü Ch'ih 玉女池, Yü-nü's Lake, or the Jade Maiden's Lake.

The Emperor Chên Tsung 眞宗 (A.D. 998-1023) of the Sung 宋 dynasty had a temple built to her on the spot on the borders of the lake where a statue to her had been unearthed, and a new statue erected (see Chavannes, *T'ai-chan*, p. 71).

PI HSIAO 碧瑝.—See *K'êng San Ku-niang* 坑三姑娘.

PI KAN 比干.—See *Wu Tou* 五斗.

PI KAN 豼犴.—See *Lung Wang* 龍王.

PI-K'U (CH'IU) 比丘.—See *Lo-han* 羅漢.

PI-LI-TO 畢利多.—See *Prêtas*.

PI LING 弼璽.—Prime Minister to Yao 堯.

PI-MA WÊN 弼馬溫.—See *Sun Hou-tzǔ* 猻猴子.

PI TÊ 畢德.—The god of the star T'ien-pao 天暴.—See *T'ien-kang* 天罡.

PI YÜAN-SHUAI 畢元帥.—See *T'ien-hua Pi Yüan-shuai* 田華畢元帥.

P'I CHIA-MA 辟假馬.—The God of the Ribs (on each side). Style T'ao Ch'êng 道成. Height 4¹/₁₀ inches. Colour reddish-white.—*Yün chi ch'i ch'ien* 雲笈七籤.

P'I-LOU-PO-CH'A 毗樓博义.—A dragon-king.—See *Lung Wang* 龍王.

P'I-LU FO 毗盧佛. P'I-LU HSIEN 毗盧仙.—Nairotchana or Vairocana. A disciple of Tung-t'ien Chiao-chu 東天教主. Variously rendered as the "Illuminator, he who enlightens all," the "Omnipresent," and the "Omniscient." Originally worshipped as the first of the five Dhyani Buddhas, the Buddhas of Meditation, later on confounded with, and known as Adi-Buddha (*q.v.*), Nirvana Buddha, and Vairocana, or Buddha Supreme and Eternal.

"Dhyani-Buddhas are the outcome of Buddhist mysticism and contemplation. They are pure abstractions, ethereal representations of the transitory earthly Buddhas, fictitious beings invented by the *Mahayana* and Yoga Schools of later Buddhism." The *Dhyani-Buddhas* produce *Dhyani-Bodhisattvas,* which are emanations evolved from themselves, and act as heads and guardians of the Buddhist community in the interval between the death of each human Buddha and the advent of his successor.

To this doctrine an addition was made in the tenth century A.D. by the introduction of an *Adi-Buddha* (*q.v.*), or Primordial Buddha, a Supreme Being, conceived of as a universal essence of pantheistic nature. He was the evolver of the *Dhyani-Buddhas.*

P'i-lu Fo 毗盧佛, the first of the five *Dhyani-Buddhas* (like Amitabha, O-mi-t'o Fo 阿彌陀佛, a fictitious being) was later confounded with Adi-Buddha, Nirvana Buddha, and Vaisocana, and worshipped as the Supreme Being. This was an adaptation of Buddhism to Brahmanism, Adi-Buddha being invented as a counterpart to the One Universal Spirit Brahma.

The Tantra School (see *Buddhist Schools*) adopted the above theory, and gave to each Buddha a triple form of existence: (1) As having entered Nirvana; (2) As existing in an ideal state in the formless worlds of abstract thought; and (3) As having lived on earth in a human form.

The Taoists borrowed this god from Buddhism, and set him up in their temples. In their hierarchy he is the disciple of Tung-t'ien Chiao-chu 東天敎主 (*q.v.*), the Supreme Teacher of the Eastern Heavens (*cf.* Amitabha).

In China, Vairocana is represented seated on a lotus-throne. His hands are joined in the mystic pose of meditation. The lobes of his ears are enormously long. He wears the five-leaved crown of a Bodhisattva, and has the *urna,* or sign of spiritual insight, on his forehead.—See also *P'i-lu Hsien* 毗盧仙 and *Lo-han* 羅漢.

P'I-LU HSIEN 毗盧仙.—The Buddha P'i-lu Fo 毗盧佛 (*q.v.*). Made by the Taoists a disciple of T'ung-t'ien Chiao-chu 通天敎主. After the rout at T'ung-kuan 潼關 he declared himself a disciple of Amida, and became a Buddha.—See also *Lo-han* 羅漢.

P'I-MA 披廟, THE GOD OF THE STAR.—See *Lin Shan* 林善.

P'I-P'U-PO-CH'A T'IEN-WANG 毗普博乂天王.—See *Ssŭ ta T'ien-wang* 四大天王.

P'I-P'U-TUNG-CH'A T'IEN-WANG 毗普動乂天王.—See *Ssŭ ta T'ien-wang* 四大天王.

P'I-SHA MÊN T'IEN-WANG 毗沙門天王.—See *Ssŭ ta T'ien-wang* 四大天王.

P'I-TOU 披頭, THE GOD OF THE STAR.—See *T'ai Luan* 太巒.

PIEN-CH'ÊNG WANG 卞城王.—President of the Sixth Court of Hades (*q.v.*).

PIEN CHI 卞吉.—The god of the star T'ien-sha 天殺. Son of Pien Chin-lung 卞金龍. Fought at Lin-t'ung Kuan 臨潼關 on the side of Chou Wang 紂王 (1154-1121 B.C.). Killed on the pretext of cowardice by two deserting vassals, Têng Kun 鄧昆 and Jui Chi 芮吉.

PIEN CH'IAO 扁鵲.—A demi-god. A member of the commission appointed by Huang Ti 黃帝 (2698-2598 B.C.) (*q.v.*) to continue and complete the labours of Shên Nung 神農 on natural history and the medicinal properties of plants. Chinese authors disagree as to his name. Some state that he was of the Chêng 鄭 Kingdom, his family name being Ch'in 秦 and his personal name Yüeh-jên 越人; others that he was a native of the Lu 盧 Kingdom, the youngest member of the Pien 扁 family (with two elder brothers), his own name being Chio 鵲; and still others that he had a bird's beak and a bat's wings: hence his name Pien-ch'iao 扁鵲.—See also *T'ien I-yüan* 天醫院 and following entry.

PIEN CH'IAO 扁鵲.—One of the Kings of Medicine. A native of the Chêng 鄭 Kingdom. Lived in the Lu 盧 Kingdom, and was known as the Physician of Lu 盧.

He was given by the genie Ch'ang Sang-chün 長桑君 a medicament to be taken in dew. At the end of thirty days this would produce superhuman vision. He also, before disappearing, left him a medical formula. Following the directions, Pien Ch'iao 扁鵲 became spiritualized, could see through walls and into the inner structure of the human body.

By this means he cured, in 521 B.C., Chao Chien-tzŭ 趙簡子, who was seriously ill and had been unconscious for five days. For this he was presented with 40,000 *mu* 畝 of land. He was assassinated out of jealousy by Li Hsi 李醯, a high official of the Academy of Medicine under the Ch'in 秦. He is worshipped by apothecaries and doctors, who offer incense to him as the God of Medicines on the twenty-eighth day of the fourth moon, the anniversary of his birth.—See also *T'ien I-yüan* 天醫院, *Yao Wang* 藥王, *Wei Ku* 韋古, and *Wei Shan-chün* 韋善君.

PIEN CHIN-LUNG 卞金龍.—The god of the star Ssŭ-fu 死符. A subordinate officer slain by Huang Fei-hu 黃飛虎 at Lin-t'ung Kuan 臨潼關 in the Yin-Chou 殷周 wars.

PIEN HO 卞 和.—The God of Jewellers. A native of Ch'u 楚 who was an official in the eight century B.C. in the time of the Chou 周 dynasty. Having found a precious stone on Ching Shan 荆 山, Mount Ching, he offered it successively to Li Wang 厲王, King Li, and to Wu Wang 武王, King Wu, whose advisers having declared it to be false he was ordered to have his left leg, in the first instance, and his right in the second, amputated. Wên Wang 文 王, having heard of the matter, and that Pien Ho 卞 和 had had himself taken to Ching Shan 荆 山 and wept until his eyes bled, ordered the stone to be examined again, when it was found to be genuine and of great value.

The Emperor had it cut in the form of a round tablet called *pi* 璧 and named it Ho-shih chih pi 和 氏 之 璧, "The Precious Stone Tablet of Ho." He bestowed on Ho 和 the title of Ling-yang Hou 零 陽 侯, Marquis of Ling-yang, which Ho 和, however, refused. The Emperor then granted him a life-pension.

Pien Ho 卞 和 having declared that his weeping was not due to the loss of his legs, but because his precious stone had been declared to be a false one, and he had been regarded as an impostor, the jewellers thenceforward adopted him as their patron deity.

PIEN-YIN WU-KUAN 辯 音 五 觀.—One of the twelve divine Buddhist teachers.

PIERCING SIGHT.—See *Ch'ien-li Yen* 千 里 眼.

PIG GOD, THE.—See *Sun Hou-tzŭ* 猻 猴 子.

PIGSTIES, THE GOD OF.—See *Chu-chüan Shên* 猪 櫊 (圈) 神.

PIN-T'OU-LO 賓 頭 羅.—See *Lo-han* 羅 漢.

PIN-TU-LO PO-LO-TO-SHÊ 賓 度 羅 跋 囉 惰 闍.—See *Lo-han* 羅 漢.

PINDOLA.—See *Lo-han* 羅 漢.

PING-FU 病 符, THE GOD OF THE STAR.—See *Wang Tso* 王 佐.

PING-I 冰 夷.—See *Shui Fu* 水 府, D (1) (e).

P'ING TÊNG WANG 平 等 王.—The President of the Ninth Court of Hades (*q.v.*). He is sometimes stated as being President of the Eighth Court.

PLANETS, THE GODS OF THE.—See *Jupiter, Venus, Mars, etc.*

PO CH'I 伯齊.—See *Chih Nü* 織女.

PO HSIEN-CHUNG 柏顯忠.—The god of the star T'ien-pai 天敗. An officer of Hung-ch'in's 洪錦 advance-guard at San-shan Kuan 三山關. Slain at Hsi-ch'i 西岐 by Têng Chiu-kung 鄧九公.

PO I-K'AO 伯邑考.—The god of the Star Tzǔ-wei 紫微. The elder son of Wên Wang 文王 (1231-1135 B.C.). Lute-instructor to Tan Chi 妲己, who fell in love with him and tried to entrap him. Failing in this she accused him of impropriety to her master, the Emperor, who, however, judged him innocent. On a later occasion, having struck Tan Chi 妲己 in a passion with his lute, he was crucified in the palace. Canonized by Chiang Tzǔ-ya 姜子牙 as god of the star Tzǔ-wei 紫微 of the North Pole.

The legend of this god is related as follows:—an Emperor in ancient times had eighteen *chia sha* 袈裟, embroidered copes, made to present to the Eighteen Lô-han 羅漢 (*q.v.*). One of his Ministers was entrusted with delivering them to the lo-han 羅漢 in their palace of the Milky Way. After many years of travelling he reached the palace and found seventeen of the lo-han 羅漢 in the great temple of the central palace. He gave each a cope, and then asked where the eighteenth lo-han 羅漢 was. Being told that he was in the kitchen, he went there and found him dead, his body being already devoured by lice.

This lo-han 羅漢, they told him, was the god of the Tzǔ-wei 紫微 star; since the Minister's departure the Emperor had died and the priest had gone to ascend the throne in his stead. The lice were said to be his ministers, *i.e.* the vermin of the court. The Minister put the cope on the corpse, and asked for a certificate that he had fulfilled his mission. He was given a box, and told that the required proof would be found inside. Returning after many years' journey, he found a new Emperor enthroned, and on handing the box to him, it was found, on being opened, to contain a transcendent crane, which immediately flew back to the palace of the Milky way.

The Taoists locate the palace of T'ien Kuan 天官 in this star, and some modern mythologists maintain that Liu Pei 劉備 (*q.v.*) is its god.

PO-LIN TAO-JÊN 柏林道人.—The god of the constellation Chio 角. Alternatively with Têng Yü 鄧禹.

PO-NAN-T'O 跋難陀.—See *Lung Wang* 龍王.

PO-SHIH 博士, THE GOD OF THE STAR.—See *Tu Yüan-hsien* 杜元銑.

PO SSŬ 波斯.—The patron deity of Candle-merchants or Wax-chandlers. A poor wood-cutter, led by a phoenix, having discovered a white greasy substance, Ta Yü 大禹, Yü the Great (2205-2197 B.C.), made from it the first candles. Consequently, Po Ssŭ 波斯 came to be worshipped as the patron deity of the industry.

PO-T'O-LO 跋陀羅.—See *Lo-han* 羅漢.

PO YAO 伯樂.—The *Shih shih hsing ching* 石氏星經 says this is the name of a star which governs the T'ien Ma 天馬, Heavenly Horse, whose name is given as Pu 步.—See *Cow, The*.

P'O CHIA 婆伽.—The name of King Miao Chuang 妙莊.— (See *Kuan Yin* 觀音).

P'O-HSIU P'AN-T'OU 婆修盤頭.—See *Buddhist Schools,* XIII, 1.

P'O-LO-MÊN 婆羅門.—See *Hsi-yü-sêng Ch'an-shih* 西域僧. 禪師.

P'O-SOU P'AN-TOU 婆藪盤頭.—See *Shih-ch'in P'u-sa* 世親 菩薩.

P'O-SUI 破碎, THE GOD OF THE STAR.—See *Wu Lung* 吳龍.

P'O T'A 勃塔.—See *Fo* 佛.

P'O-YEN-CHI CH'AN-SHIH 破巖繼禪師 (66th generation).—A deified Buddhist monk. Ranked eightieth in Buddhist School, VI (*q.v.*). Family name P'u 濮. A native of Lien-shui 漣水, Kiangsu 江蘇. A B.A. at 17 years of age, at 33 became a Han-lin 翰林 Doctor. Later on became a monk, and was taught by Hsüeh-chiao Hsin-shên 雪嶠信深. At the age of 60, he began expounding the doctrine at Cho-hsi 卓錫. Died A.D. 1686, aged 82. His tomb is on Ch'ing-lung Kang 青龍阿, Blue Dragon Ridge, beside the Cho-hsi 卓錫 monastery.

POCKMARKS, THE SPIRIT OF.—See *Ma Shên* 痳神.

POLE STAR, THE GENIE OF THE.—See *T'ai I* 太一.

POND, THE SPIRIT OF THE HUA-LIN 華林.—See *Shui Fu* 水府, D (2) (g).

PONDS, THE SPIRIT OF THE.—See *Shui Fu* 水府, D (2) (g).

POOL OF BLOOD, THE.—See *Hades*.

POOTOO ISLAND.—See *P'u T'o* 普陀.

POTTERS, THE GODS OF.—See *Ho Ho* 和合.

PRAJA-PATI.—"Lord of creatures," a progenitor, creator. In the *Veda* the term is applied to Indra, Savitri, Soma, Hiranya-garbha, and other deities. In *Manu* the term is applied to Brahma as the active creator and supporter of the universe; so Brahma is the Praja-pati. It is also given to Manu Swayambhuva himself, as the son of Brahma and as the secondary creator of the ten Rishis, or "mind-born sons" of Brahma, from whom mankind has descended. It is to these ten sages, as fathers of the human race, that the name Praja-pati most commonly is given. They are Marichi, Atri, Angiras, Pulastya, Pulaha, Kratu, Vasishtha, Prachetas or Daksha, Bhrigu, and Narada. According to some authorities the Praja-patis are only seven in number, being identical with the seven great Rishis (See *Rishi*). The number and names of the Praja-patis vary in different authorities: the *Maha-bharata* makes twenty-one.

PRAJNA-PARAMITA.—"Transcendent Wisdom," denying the reality of all world phenomena, and the validity of knowledge derived through the senses.

PRATYEKA-BUDDHA.—Pi-lo-chih ti-chia Fo 畢勒支底伽佛.—A degree of saintship (unknown to primitive Buddhism), viewed as one of the three conveyances to Nirvana, and practised by hermits who, as attaining to Buddhaship individually (without teacher and without saving others), are compared with the Khadga and called Eka'sringa richi. As crossing Sansara, suppressing errors, and yet not attaining to absolute perfection, the Pratyeka Buddha is compared with a horse which crosses a river, swimming, without touching the ground. Having mastered the twelve Nidanas, he is also called Nidana Buddha.—See also *Lo-han* 羅漢.

PRÊTA, PRÊTAS.—Pi-li-to 畢利多, etc.—A ghost. An evil spirit animating a dead body, and haunting cemeteries and other places. Hungry ghosts or demons (*ê-kuei* 餓鬼). One of the six Gati (*q.v.*). Thirty-six classes of demons with huge bellies, large mouths, and tiny throats, suffering inappeasable hunger and thirst, but unable to appease either on account of their contracted gullets, and living either in hell, in the service of Yama, or in the air, or among men (but visible only at night). Avaricious persons are to be reborn as prêtas.

"The feeding of hungry ghosts is said to have been instituted by Sakyamuni himself, who directed Moginlin, one of his disciples, to make offerings for the benefit of his mother, who was reborn in this state of existence. The original hungry ghosts were, therefore, Hindu Pretas. In China, the hungry ghosts are the spirits of the dead, especially ancestors. Buddhists are appealed to on behalf of the dead who have no descendants to worship them, and feed them by sacrifices" (Edkins. p. 268). Offerings called *tsu-ya* 做牙 are made to hungry ghosts on the sixteenth day of the first month and may also be made on the second and sixth of every month. Eitel adds: Ananda was "said to have appeased prêtas by food offerings presented to Buddha and Samgha, and Maudgalyayana to have brought back his mother who had been reborn in hell as a prêta."

"This Hindu ceremony [of feeding hungry ghosts] was brought to China by Amogha, about A.D. 733 (*v. infra*). Engrafted upon the native ancestor-worship, it obtained immense popularity, and is nowadays practised by all sects, Confucianists, Taoists, and Buddhists. Food and fruit are offered to the dead, and paper clothes burnt for the benefit of those who have been drowned, all according to an elaborate ritual."

"Although introduced in China in the third century, this ceremonial was popularized only through Amoghavadyra (A.D. 732) and the popular influence of the Yogatcharya School. The whole theory, with its ideas of intercessory prayers, priestly litanies and requiems, is entirely foreign to ancient and Southern Buddhism" (Eitel, p. 186).

The prêtas of Buddhist legend have mouths too small to eat with, and can only emit a thin whistling cry. This whistling sound is often associated with spirits.

In China *kuei* 鬼, demons, are the inhabitants of the *narakas* or subterranean and "other prisons" called *ti-yü* 地獄, hells. Many of them formerly belonged to the world of men. Some are condemned by Yama to certain prisons. Others haunt the graves where their former bodies are interred. The prêtas hunger for food, and hence the custom, so prevalent in China, of feeding the hungry ghosts both of relatives and others.

PRIMARY BUDDHA, THE.—See *Adi-Buddha.*

PRIMORDIAL BUDDHA-GOD, THE.—See *Adi-Buddha.*

PRINCIPLE, THE FIRST.—See *Yüan-shih T'ien-tsun* 元始 天尊.

PRISON, THE GOD OF THE.—In the Han 漢 dynasty Hsiao Wu 蕭武 was directed by the Emperor [Kao Ti 高帝, 206-194 B.C.] to revise the criminal statutes, and at death he was made the God of the Gaol, by the name of Hsiao Wang 蕭王. He was worshipped by the Board of Punishments, the criminal judges, the gaolers, and the prisoners. The latter hope that the gaol-god will keep their guilty consciences at ease, and may open a way to escape. Before execution criminals were dragged into his presence as they were taken from prison, and made to bow to the gaoler of Tartarus (Du Bose).

PROSTITUTION, THE GODDESS OF.—See *P'an Chin-lien* 潘金蓮 and *Kuan Chung* 管仲.

PU 步.—The name of the Horse-god.—See *Po Yao* 伯樂.

PU-FAN HU-YÜ 不返胡余.—See *Shui Fu* 水府, C (2) (d).

PU HSÜEH 不學.—See *Lo-han* 羅漢.

PU K'UNG 不空.—Amoghavarjra or Amogha.—A Singhalese Buddhist priest. The name is taken from *Pu-k'ung chin-k'ang* 不空金剛, the *vadjra* (sceptre) which is not hollow. Eitel says he followed his teacher, Vadjrabodhi, to China (A.D. 719) and eventually succeeded him in the leadership of the Yogatcharya School (A.D. 732). Johnston gives the date of his arrival as about 733. After visiting the Imperial Court at Ch'ang-an 長安, Shensi 陝西, he later followed it to Lo-yang 洛陽, Honan 河南. He is said to have proved his magical skill by taming a herd of wild elephants. His special method of procuring rain was to erect a platform and adorn it with variously coloured cloths. He then made a wooden image six inches high, and recited his formulas over it, until it moved its eyes and showed its teeth, whereupon rain fell in abundance. He used a similar method, with different formulas, to cause it to cease when superabundant; in this case making five or six small clay images of dragons.

Eitel says that from a journey through India and Ceylon (A.D. 741-6), he brought to China more than 500 *sutras* [canonical writings] and *s'âstras* [discourses] previously unknown in China. Besides a large number of *dharanis,* or magic formulas, he also introduced a new alphabet for the transliteration of Sanskrit and published 108 works, mostly translations. He founded the festival of All Souls, or Departed Spirits, known also as that of Feeding the Hungry Ghosts, Yü-lan Hui 盂蘭會 (Sanskrit Ullambana or Ulamba), held annually on the fifteenth day of the seventh moon.

He is the chief representative in China of the Tantra School of Buddhist mysticism, which he succeeded in spreading widely under the patronage of three successive emperors, Hsüan Tsung 玄宗 (A.D. 713-56), who prohibited his retiring to India (749), Su Tsung 肅宗 (756-63), who gave him the title *Tripitaka Bhadanta* (*Ta-kuang-chih San-tsang* 大廣智三藏), and Tai Tsung 代宗 (763-80), who bestowed on him, when he died (774), the rank of a Minister of State and a posthumous title. His translation of the *Manjusri Pariprichchha Sutra* bears the title *Wên-shu wên-ching* 文殊問經. Wieger describes him and Vadjrabodhi as preachers of Tantrism, *Mi-mi-chiao* 密密教, and as making it the fashionable sect. He undoubtedly exercised a profound influence on the Chinese thought of the time.

Pu K'ung 不空 left the Court in A.D. 743 and died in the following year. He is noted for the aphorism: "It is easy to procure rain or sunshine, but difficult to rid the country of evil-doers."—See *Amogha* and *Buddhist Schools*, XIII and XV.

PU SHANG 卜商.—Literary Revisor to Hades. Su Shao 蘇韶 of the Chin 晉 dynasty brought back the information regarding his appointment when he returned to life, stating that he had seen him fulfilling that office in Purgatory.

Pu Shang 卜商 was born in 507 B.C. He was a native of the Wei 衛 State and a disciple of Confucius, who is said to have delivered into his charge the texts of the *Odes* and of the *Annals*. He was first a Magistrate in the Lu 魯 State. When Confucius died, he went into retirement in Shansi 山西, devoting himself to study and teaching, and leading an ascetic life. Posthumously ennobled as Duke. In A.D. 647 his tablet was placed in the Confucian Temple.

PU-TAI CH'AN-SHIH 布袋禪師.—The Monk with the Calico Bag. So called because he always carried a calico bag, containing his belongings and food, hanging from a staff placed over his shoulder. Slept in the open, and indicated coming changes of weather by the kind of shoes he wore. Family name Chang Ting-tzŭ 長汀子. Died A.D. 917. Said to be the last incarnation of Maitreya (see *Mi-lo Fo* 彌勒佛). One of those invited to the annual banquet of the gods (see *Hsi Wang-mu* 西王母).—See also *Lo-han* 羅漢.

PU-TAI HO-SHANG 布袋和尚.—See *Lo-han* 羅漢.

PU-T'ING WEI-YÜ 不廷口余.—See *Shui Fu* 水府, C (2) (d).

PU T'UNG 卜同.—The god of the star *T'ien-p'ing* 天平.—See *T'ien-kang* 天罡.

P'U-AN CH'AN-SHIH 普庵禪師.—A native of P'u-hua 溥化, a village in the I-ch'un 宜春 district of Kiangsi 江西. Born on the twenty-seventh day of the eleventh month, A.D. 1115, in the reign of Hui Tsung 徽宗 (A.D. 1101-26) of the N. Sung, Pei Sung 北宋, dynasty. His secular name was Yin-su 印肅, His father's name was Yü tzŭ 余慈, his mother being of the Hu 胡 family.

It is related that when he was six years of age he dreamt that a monk placed his hand on his heart, saying: "You will under-stand this later on." In the morning his mother found a precious stone of red colour resting on his heart. When grown up, he studied the doctrine in the Buddhist monastery Shou-chiang Yüan 壽降院, and at the age of 18 was received as a full member of the Order.

At 38 years of age, he went to live in the Tz'u-hua Ssŭ 慈化寺, Monastery of Merciful Transformation, and changed his name to P'u-an 普庵. He was a popular preacher, beloved by the people, and is said to have cured sicknesses and diseases, procured fine weather, and destroyed evil spirits haunting temples.

When asked how he had attained to so great virtue and magical power, he wrote signs in the air and chanted a verse. This and other of his compositions became very popular.

He died in A.D. 1170, at the age of 55.

To the posthumous title bestowed upon him soon after his death the Emperor Ch'êng Tsung 成宗 (A.D. 1295-1308) of the Yüan 元 dynasty added, in 1300, the two characters Ta-tê 大德, Great Virtue.

P'U CHI 普寂.—A famous teacher, who conducted a school at Sung Shan 嵩山, the Central Sacred Mountain, in Honan 河南. He is honoured in several Buddhist temples, and is one of those invited to the banquet of the gods (see Hsi Wang-mu 西王母). —See also I-hsing Ch'an-shih 一行禪師.

P'U-CH'IH CH'AN-SHIH 普持禪師 (59th generation).—A deified Buddhist monk. Ranked thirty-seventh in Buddhist School, III (q.v.). Studied many years under Shih-wei Ch'an-shih 時蔚禪師 (q.v.), whom he succeeded as teacher in the same school.

P'U-CHING 普靜.—A saintly Buddhist monk. Third century. A native of Chieh Chou 解州, Shansi 山西. One of those invited to the annual banquet of the gods (see Hsi Wang-mu 西王母).

P'U-CHIO TSÊ-FA 普覺擇法.—One of the twelve divine Buddhist teachers (Samantabhadra).

P'U HSIEN 普賢.—See Buddhist Schools, XV.

P'U-HSIEN HSIN-LI 普賢心雕.—One of the twelve divine Buddhist teachers (Samantabhadra). The Buddha of Universal Kindness. Claimed by the Tantra School as the founder of the Yoga system. His birthday is observed on the twenty-first day of the second moon.

P'U-KAO-YÜN-CH'UANG 普高雲幢.—A dragon-king.— See Lung Wang 龍王.

P'U LAO 蒲牢.—See Lung Wang 龍王.

P'U-SA 菩 薩.—See *P'u-t'i-sa-to* 菩 提 薩 埵.

P'U-T'I 普 提.—The transliteration of the Sanscrit word Bodhi, enlightenment.—See *Fo* 佛.

P'U-T'I-SA-TO 菩 提 薩 埵.— Bodhisattva. Abbreviated in China to P'u-sa 菩 薩. He whose essence (*sattva*) has become intelligence (*bodhi*). Also P'u-sa 菩 薩, the mind of intelligence. The third class of saints who have to pass only once more through human life before becoming Buddhas, including also those Buddhas who are not yet perfected by entering Nirvana (see *Mahasattvas*). Personifications of certain attributes: light, wisdom, mercy, power. They forgo Buddhaship in order to save mortals. One of the three means of conveyance to Nirvana (see *Triyana*), compared with an elephant fording a river (Eitel).

P'U-T'I-TO-LO 菩 提 多 羅.—See *Patriarchs: Bodhidharma*.

P'U-T'I-TO-NA-TSUN-CHÊ 菩 提 多 那 尊 者.—See *Patriarchs: Bodhidharma*.

P'U-T'I TSU-SHIH 普 提 祖 師.—An Immortal. The master of Sun Hou-tzŭ 猻 猴 子.

P'U-T'O or POOTOO 普 陀.—The sacred island of the Buddhists in the Chusan group. The throne of Kuan Yin 觀 音, to which she came floating on a water-lily. The full name is P'u t'o lo ka [chia] 普 陀 洛 伽. The sacred mountain Potaloka is the hill from which Avalokitesvara looks down. The cult of this bodhisattva spread to Tibet, where a second Potaloka was created at Lhasa, and to China where the bodhisattva became Kuan-yin 觀 音 (*q.v.*) and a new Potaloka (P'u-t'o 普 陀) arose.

The fame of P'u-t'o Shan 普 陀 山 dates from A.D. 847, when a Buddhist ascetic from India, worshipping Kuan Yin 觀 音 in the Chao-yin 昭 陰 cave there, beheld a vision of the goddess.

About ten years later a Japanese monk, named Egaku, sent by the Empress-dowager of Japan on a religious mission to China, visited the island. It soon became a favourite resort of devout pilgrims and numerous anchorites lived in solitary hermitages. Not only were other manifestations of the goddess vouchsafed, but miracles of healing took place in the waters of the sacred well near the cave, one as late as the beginning of the sixteenth century. The Sung 宋 emperors were greatly interested in the island, and the Yüan 元 emperors sent presents from time to time. Under the Ming 明 dynasty the monks suffered so much from Japanese pirates that they all removed to the mainland, save one who remained in charge of the ruined buildings.

In 1515 a small monastery was rebuilt, and in 1572 a monk from Wu-t'ai Shan 五 臺 山, with Imperial help, set about rebuilding others.

The Ming 明 Emperor Wan Li 萬曆 (A.D. 1573-1620) presented a complete Buddhist *Tripitaka* to the monks. In 1665 Dutch pirates, driven out of Formosa by Koxinga, plundered the temples at Pu-t'o 普陀, and set fire to many of the buildings. These, with other depredations by Chinese and Japanese pirates, compelled the monks once more to abandon the island. In 1688, however, they returned and under the patronage of K'ang Hsi 康熙 rebuilt many of the monasteries and temples.

In the earlier period, the monks at P'u-t'o 普陀 followed the rules of the Lü 律 or Vinaya school of doctrine, but in 1131 the teaching of the Ch'an 禪 or Dhyana school was introduced, and in the seventeenth century it entirely superseded the Lü 律 rule.

At the present time there are nearly a hundred monasteries and temples on the island, besides a pagoda and sacred rocks, with over a thousand monks. The two principal monasteries are the P'u-chi 普濟 or Ch'un-ssǔ 椿寺 first mentioned in the island records in 1699, and the Fa-yü 法雨 or Hou-ssǔ 後寺. No building is older than the fourteenth century. The T'ai-tsu 太簇 pagoda was erected by a monk in 1334, of stone brought from the neighbourhood of the T'ai Hu 太湖, near Soochow 蘇州. The Fan-yin 梵音 cave is famous for possessing relics of Sakyamuni Buddha placed there by a Benares pilgrim in 1626 (Johnston, *Buddhist China*).— See also *Kuan Yin* 觀音.

P'U-WÊN CH'AN-SHIH 普聞禪師 (45th generation).—A deified Buddhist monk. Ranked twentieth in Buddhist School, III (*q.v.*). Said to have been the son of the Emperor Hsi Tsung 僖宗 (A.D. 874-89) of the T'ang 唐 dynasty, but as his teacher was Ch'u-yüan Ch'an-shih 楚圓禪師 (*q.v.*)., who died A.D. 1041, the dates do not tally. A vegetarian, he abode at the foot of Shao-wu Shan 邵武山, having been captivated by its picturesque site. He protected, by putting in his sleeve, a dragon pursued by its enemies, his reward being a stream of fresh water which the dragon caused to issue from the mountain-side. Here the Lung-hu Ssǔ 龍湖寺, Dragon-pool Monastery, was erected. In it he expounded the Doctrine for thirty years, and there also his ashes repose.

P'U-YEN FA-CHIEH 普眼法界.—One of the twelve divine Buddhist teachers (Samantabhadra).

P'U-YÜAN CH'AN-SHIH 普願禪師 (36th generation).—A deified Buddhist monk. Ranked third in Buddhist School, III (*q.v.*). A native of Hsin-chêng 新鄭, K'ai-fêng Fu 開封府, Honan 河南. Family name Wang 王. Educated first in school of Huai-jang Ch'an-shih 懷讓禪師 (*q.v.*), and later as a fully-trained monk at Sung Shan 嵩山, where he was under the direction of Ma Tsu 馬祖 (*q.v.*). From A.D. 785-805 he lived at Ch'ih-chou 池州, where he died some years later.

P'U-YÜN-TA-SHÊNG 普運大聲.— A dragon-king.— See *Lung Wang* 龍王.

PUBLIC WORKS, THE MINISTRY OF.—See *Lu Pan* 魯班.

PUNCH AND JUDY GOD, THE.—"As fond as the black-haired race is of Punch and Judy, it is not surprising that the large number who play with these wooden men and women should desire a patron for their theatricals. His name is Ch'ên P'ing 陳平, who was the Minister of Han Kao Tsu 漢高祖 and first used a wooden man at the siege of Po-ten."—Du Bose, pp. 338-9.

PURANA.—"Old," hence an ancient legend or tale of olden times. The *Puranas* succeed the *Itihasas* or epic poems, but at a considerable distance of time, and must be distinguished from them. The epics treat of the legendary actions of heroes as mortal men, the *Puranas* celebrate the powers and works of positive gods, and represent a later and more extravagant development of Hinduism, of which they are in fact the Scriptures. The definition of a *Purana* by Amara Sinha, an ancient Sanskrit lexicographer, is a work "which has five distinguishing topics:—(1) The creation of the universe; (2) Its destruction and renovation; (3) The genealogy of gods and patriarchs; (4) The reigns of the Manus, forming the periods called Manwantaras. (5) The history of the Solar and Lunar races of kings." These are the *Pancha-lakshanas* or distinguishing marks, but no one of the Puranas answers exactly to the description; some show a partial conformity with it, others depart from it very widely. The *Vishnu Purana* is the one which best accords with the title. The *Puranas,* although they belong especially to that stage of the Hindu religion in which faith in some one divinity was the prevailing principle, are also a valuable record of the form of Hindu belief which came next in order to that of the *Vedas,* which grafted hero-worship upon the simpler ritual of the latter, and which had been adopted, and was extensively, perhaps universally, established in India at the time of the Greek invasion. Pantheism "is one of their invariable characteristics," and underlies their whole teaching, "although the particular divinity who is all things, from whom all things proceed, and to whom all things return, is diversified according to their individual sectarian bias." The *Puranas* are all written in verse, and their invariable form is that of a dialogue between an exponent and an inquirer, interspersed with the dialogues and observations of other individuals.

PURE AUGUST EMPEROR ON HIGH, THE.—See *Yü Huang* 玉皇.

PURE AUGUST ONE, THE.—See *Yü Huang* 玉皇.

PURE DOCTRINE, THE SECT OF THE.—See *Buddhist Schools*, XVII and *Hsing-ch'ang Lü-shih* 省常律師.

PURE LAND, THE.—See *Buddhist Schools*, XVII.

PURE LAND SCHOOL, THE.—See *Hsi T'ien* 西天 and *Buddhist Schools*, XVII.

PURPLE AND AZURE CLOUDS, THE FIRST PRINCESS OF.—See *Pi-hsia Yüan-chün* 碧霞元君.

PURVEYOR OF CHILDREN, THE.—See *Chang Hsien* 張仙.

PUSTULES, THE SPIRIT OF.—See *Pan Shên* 癍神.

Q

QUEEN CHÊN 甄.—See *Shui Fu* 水 府, D (2) (a).

"QUICK-DEATH."—See *Mêng P'o* 孟 婆.

R

RAHAN.—See *Lo-han* 羅漢.

RAHAT.—See *Lo-han* 羅漢.

RAHULA.—See *Lo-han* 羅漢.

RAHULATA.—See *Lo-han* 羅漢.

RAIN, THE GOD OF.—The officials worshipped tablets in in honour of rain, wind, etc., and lit candles and incense on the first and fifteenth of the moon. They were not considered to worship the common gods who rule over these departments; these *dei minores* were for the vulgar populace (see Du Bose, pp. 72-3). "While the Wind Goddess blesses man by blowing the clouds to the place needing the rain, yet it is a willing God that she helps, for the Rain-god (Yü Shih 雨師) realizes the value of the rain for the people. If there is too much wind in the spring, there will be little rain. So if there is too much wind the people go to her temple and beat her image, in order to make her stop blowing the clouds away." The Rain-god is a benevolent god. "He is pictured holding a vessel of water in one hand, and in the other a sword with seven stars engraved upon it. He is using this sword to scatter the water on the places where he wishes it to rain. In times of drought he is much worshipped by all classes of people, and great processions are organized in his honour. They would in this way regain his favour, and save the country from want and pestilence" (Plopper, p. 55).—See also *Shui Fu* 水府 and *Yü Shih* 雨師.

RAIN CLOTHES DWARF.—"His father died when he was an infant, his mother wept herself blind, and he, the son, a dwarf,

391

became a servant. He dresses in shaggy straw clothes, such as the farmers wear in the fields when it rains, and has on his head an umbrella straw hat."—Du Bose, p. 337.

RAIN-MASTER, THE.—"A divinity identified by the ancient cosmogonists with a son of Kung Kung 共工, bearing the name of 'sombre dark.' Sacrifices by burnt offerings were offered to him in accordance with the ritual of the Chou 周 dynasty. He holds a bowl of water, and if he lets fall only a drop, there is a rainfall of one foot. The Master of Rain rides a white horse over the western sea, followed by twelve boys, and wherever he goes there is rain" (Du Bose, p. 73).—See *Shui Fu* 水府 and *Yü Shih* 雨師.

RAKAN.—See *Lo-han* 羅漢.

RAKSHASAS. — Lo-ch'a-p'o 羅叉婆. Also, K'o-wei 可畏, terrible.—"The aborigines of Ceylon, dreaded as cannibals by ancient mariners, extirpated by Simhala. They and the Asuras were races hostile to the early Hindus. The demons attending Vaisramana, invoked by sorcerers" (Eitel). Man-eating demons, who haunt cemeteries, and waylay travellers in solitary places. A species of demons, resembling the yakshas, but without their power of assuming any shape at pleasure. When they appear to men it must be in their own form. They live in the forest of Himala, and feed on the flesh of the dead (Hardy).

Rakshai, Lo-ch'a-ch'i 羅叉斯, Lo-ch'a-nü 羅叉女, are wives and daughters of rakshasa demons. They are invoked by sorcerers.

These goblins or evil spirits are not all equally bad, but have been classified as of three sorts—one as a set of beings like the the Yakshas, another as a sort of Titans or enemies of the gods, and lastly, in the common acceptation of the term, demons, and fiends (as noted above) who haunt cemeteries, disturb sacrifices, harass devout men, animate dead bodies, devour human beings, and vex and afflict mankind in all sorts of ways.—See also *Lung Wang* 龍王.

RAMAYANA.—"The Adventures of Rama." The eldest of the Sanskrit epic poems, written by the sage Valmiki. It is supposed to have been composed about five centuries B.C., and to have received its present form a century or two later.

RAMPARTS AND DITCHES, THE GOD OF.—See *Ch'êng Huang* 城隍.

RAVANA.—The demon king of Lanka or Ceylon, from which he expelled his half-brother Kuvera. He was son of Visravas by his wife Nikasha, daughter of the Rakshasa Su-mali.

He was half-brother of Kuvera, and grandson of the Rishi Pulastya; and as Kuvera is king of the Yakshas, Ravana is king of the demons called Rakshasas. Pulastya is said to be the progenitor, not only of Ravana, but of the whole race of Rakshasas. By penance and devotion to Brakma, Ravana was made invulnerable against gods and demons, but he was doomed to die through a woman. He was also enabled to assume any form he pleased. All Rakshasas are malignant and terrible, but Ravana as their chief attained the utmost degree of wickedness, and was a very incarnation of evil. For description and details see Dowson, pp. 264-5.

RECORDS, THE GODS OF.—The T'ien Kuan K'ao Chi' 天官考籍 gods are (1) Shang-yüan I-p'in Ta-ti 上元一品大帝; (2) Chung-yüan êrh-p'in Ta-ti 中元二品大帝; and (3) Hsia-yüan San-p'in Ta-ti 下元三品大帝.

RED CHILD DEMON, THE. A demon mentioned in the Monkey-god legend (see Sun Hou-tzu 探猴子). During the travels of the Monkey and his companions they arrived at a great mountain. They saw on the road a red cloud which the Monkey thought must be a demon. It was in fact a demon child who, in order to entrap the Master, had had himself bound and tied to the branch of a tree. The child repeatedly cried out to the passers-by to deliver him. Sun 孫 suspected that it was a trick; but the Master could no longer endure the pitiful wails; he ordered his disciples to loose the child, and the Monkey to carry him.

As they proceeded on their way the Demon caused a strong whirlwind to spring up, and during this he carried off the Master. Sun 孫 discovered that the Demon was an old friend of his, who, centuries before, had pledged himself to eternal friendship. So he consoled his comrades by saying that he felt sure no harm would come to the Master." The Demon subsequently ate the Priest, and a fight occurred. Chu Pa-chieh 猪八戒 was sent to fetch Kuan Yin 觀音, but the Demon played a trick by transforming himself into the shape of Kuan Yin 觀音 and caught Pa-chieh 八戒 in his magic bag, from which he was later released by the Monkey. After many more incidents, tricks and adventures, the Demon was finally overcome, and pardoned and blessed by Kuan Yin 觀音.—Werner, *Myths*, pp. 350-2.

"RED COAT, MR."—See *Wên Ch'ang* 文昌.

RED RULER, THE.—See *Mars*.

REMEDIES, THE KING OF.—See *Yao Wang* 藥王.

RESTING GOD, THE.—See *Chiang Tzǔ-ya* 姜子牙.

REVENGE, THE GOD OF.—"There is nothing so sweet to the Chinese as revenge. The God of Revenge is a *straw man*. When a house has been robbed, or a man has a personal enemy, there is a resort to witchcraft. A straw image of the enemy or the thief is made, and daily worshipped; needles are stuck in the eyes, blood is made to issue from the nose and ears, the arms and body are pierced, and it is confidently believed that this process will send pains, sickness, and probably death on the object of hatred. The practice is universal in China."—Du Bose, p. 339. See also Werner, *China of the Chinese*, p. 247.

RIBS, THE GOD OF THE.—The *Yün chi ch'i ch'ien* 雲笈 七籤 gives the name of the god of the two sets of ribs as P'i Chia-ma 辟假馬, his style as Tao Ch'êng 道成, his height as four inches and one-tenth, and his colour as reddish white.

RICHES, THE GOD OF.—See *Ts'ai Shên* 財神 and *Chang San-fêng* 張三豐.

RIGHT ARM OF THE GOD OF T'AI SHAN 泰山, THE. —See *Wên Yüan-shuai* 溫元帥.

RIGHT KIDNEY, THE GOD OF THE.—See *Hsiang Ti-wu* 象地無.

RISHI.—An inspired poet or sage. The inspired persons to whom the hymns of the *Vedas* were revealed, and under whose names they stand.

RIVER CH'IEN-T'ANG 錢塘, THE GOD OF THE.—The chief God of Rivers. Formerly one of the chief administrators of the Ch'ien-T'ang 錢塘 River.—See *Shui Fu* 水府 and Werner, *Myths,* pp. 218-9.

RIVER-GOD, THE MARRIAGE OF THE.—See *Hsi Mên Pao* 西門豹.

RIVER HAN 漢, THE SPIRIT OF THE.—See *Shui Fu* 水府, D (2) (b).

RIVER HUAI 淮, THE SPIRIT OF THE.—See *Shui Fu* 水府, D (i) (c).

RIVER HUANG 黃 (YELLOW RIVER), THE SPIRIT OF THE.—See *Shui Fu* 水府, D (i) (b).

RIVER YANG-TZǓ 揚子, THE SPIRIT OF THE.—See *Shui Fu* 水府, D (i) (a).

RIVERS, THE PROTECTING DEITY OF.—See *Hsiao Kung* 蕭 公.

RIVERS, THE SPIRITS OF THE. — See *Shui Fu* 水 府, D (1) and (2).

RIVERS CONFINED BY MOUNTAINS, THE SPIRIT OF.
—See *Shui Fu* 水 府, D (2) (h).

ROAD, THE GOD THAT OPENS THE.—The K'ai-lu Shên 開 路 神, known as *fang-hsiang shih* 方 相 氏, "district inspector. Exorcist-in-Chief." His image is carried at the head of funeral processions.—For details see Werner, *Autumn Leaves,* pp. 49-68.

ROAD-GOD, THE.—At first an escort to the wife of the Emperor Hsüan Yüan 軒 轅 (2698-2598 B.C.). The aide-de-camp, Lü Ling 律 令 by name, to the God of Thunder (or, according to some writers, to the Goddess of Lighting), appointed because of his speed. On dangerous roads he grants protection from robbers and wild beasts. Used by metonomy for rapidity by Taoists.

ROADS, THE FIVE SPIRITS OF.—See *Ts'ai Shên* 財 神.

ROBBERS, THE GODS OF.—The names of these are Tu P'ing 杜 平, Li Ssǔ 李 思, Jên An 任 安, Sun Hsüan 孫 玄, and Kêng Yen-chêng 耿 彥 正.

ROYAL FATHER OF THE EAST, THE.—See *Tung Wang-kung* 東 王 公.

ROYAL MOTHER OF THE WEST, THE.—See *Hsi Wang-mu* 西 王 公.

RUKH, THE GREAT GOLDEN-WINGED.—See *Yü-i Hsien* 羽 翼 仙.

RULER OF THE FIRST HEAVEN, THE.—See *Yüan-shih T'ien-tsun* 元 始 天 尊.

RULER OF THE FIVE CELESTIAL SOVEREIGNS, THE.
—See *T'ai I* 太 一.

RURAL PLACES, THE PROTECTING SPIRIT OF.—See *T'u Ti* 土 地.

S

SA CHÊN-JÊN 薩 眞 人.—His name was Sa Shou-chien 薩 守 堅. A native of Hsi-ho 西 河, in Shu 蜀 (modern Ssǔch'uan 四 川) (see *Wang Ling-kuan* 王 靈 官). Practised as a physician, but having caused the death of a patient, fled to Chiang-nan 江 南, hoping to be admitted as a disciple of the Taoist master Hsü Ching 虛 靜 and the famous Lin Ling-su 林 靈 素 and Wang Shih-ch'ên 王 侍 宸; but on reaching Shênsi 陝 西 Province he found his funds were exhausted. Just then he met three Taoists, who informed him that the three men he was looking for had left this earth. To console him in his grief, each of the Taoists gave him a charm. Hsü Ching 虛 靜 gave him a letter written by himself; one of the Taoists gave him a formula by repeating which he could obtain seven cash each time; and the third a charm enabling him to call forth lightning at will.

Leaving these three Taoists, Sa Shou-chien 薩 守 堅, able to procure the means to reach his destination, arrived at the house of the great master in Kiangsi 江 西. He found it in mourning. Hsü Ching 虛 靜 had died a few days before, and when the letter was shown to the family it was recognized as being in his handwriting. Its purport was as follows: I, Hsü Ching 虛 靜 and my two companions Wang Shih-ch'ên 王 侍 宸 and Lin Ling-su 林 靈 素 meeting Sa Shou-chien 薩 守 堅 each gave him a talisman. You need have no hesitation in presenting his name to the Emperor for promotion.

Sa Chên-jên 薩 眞 人 became a renowned magician. Hearing that at Hsiang-yin Hsien 湘 陰 縣, in Ch'ang-sha Fu 長 沙 府, Hunan 湖 南, sacrifices of young boys and girls were made to Ch'êng Huang 城 隍 (*q.v.*), God of the City Moat, in his temple, he declared that he would burn the temple. No sooner had he uttered the words than it was struck by lightning and destroyed,

396

in spite of the efforts made by the inhabitants to save it. It was never rebuilt.

Variations of the legend are given in the *Chia Ch'ing Hu-nan t'ung-chih* 嘉 慶 湖 南 通 志, bk. 171, p. 29, and *Sou-shên chi* 搜 神 記, 上 卷, p. 35. It is there added that, on the spirit of the temple at Hsiang-yin Hsien 湘 陰 縣 repenting of his cruel deeds, Sa Shou-chien 薩 守 堅 petitioned Yü Ti 玉 帝 to accept him as his Marshal, and this was granted. Sa Shou-chien 薩 守 堅 was at Ch'ing-chou 清 州 when a body of celestial functionaries informed him that he was about to be raised to the high rank reserved for him among the Immortals. On hearing this he rose, and was at once changed into an Immortal. It being noticed that the coffin in which his body had been placed was very light, it was opened and found to be empty.

SA CH'IANG 撒 強.—One of the gods of the star San-shih 三 尸. Brother of Sa Chien 撒 堅. An officer in Chou Wang's 紂 王 (1154-1121 B.C.) army, slain on the field of battle.

SA CHIEN 撒 堅.—One of the gods of the star San-shih 三 尸. An officer killed in action during the Yin-Chou 殷 周 wars.

SA-P'O-HSI-TO 薩 婆 委 多.—See *Fo* 佛.

SA SHOU-CHIEN 薩 守 堅.—See *Sa Chên-jên* 薩 眞 人.

SA YUNG 撒 勇.—One of the gods of the star San-shih 三 尸. A younger brother of Sa Chien 撒 堅 and Sa Ch'iang 撒 強. Died on the field of battle during the Yin-Chou 殷 周 wars.

SACRED MOUNTAINS.—See *Wu Yo* 五 嶽, *T'ai Shan* 泰 山, *Hua Shan* 華 山, *Hêng Shan* 恒 山, *Sung Shan* 嵩 山, and *Hêng Shan* 衡 山.

SACRED MOUNTAINS, THE MINISTRY OF THE FIVE. —See *Wu Yo* 五 嶽.

SACRIFICES, THE FIVE DOMESTIC.—See *Ts'ai Shên* 財 神.

SADHYAS.—A *gana* or class of inferior deities; the personified rites and prayers of the *Vedas* who dwell with the gods or in the intermediate region between heaven and earth. Their number is twelve according to one authority, and seventeen according to another, and the *Puranas* make them sons of Dharma and Sadhya, daughter of Daksha.

SAGARA.—A dragon-king.—See *Lung* 龍, *Lung Wang* 龍 王, *Shui Fu* 水 府, and *Virupatcha*.

SAILORS, THE GOD OF.—Called Yang Ssŭ Lao-yeh 楊泗老爺 and Yang Ssŭ Chiang-chün 楊泗將軍, General Yang Ssŭ 楊泗. One of the Gods of Sailors. Controls the surface of the waters. Represented as a child, seven or eight years old. Has a white face and wears white clothing. Carriers an axe in one hand, and grasps a dragon in the other, indicating that he has control over the Dragon-king. Is worshipped on the sixth day of the sixth moon, by all who dwell in boats or are associated with rivers or seas.—See also *Yen Kung* 晏公.

SAILORS, THE GODDESS OF.—See *T'ien Fei* 天妃.

SAINT, THE GREAT BUDDHIST.—See *Ta Shêng* 大聖.

SAINTLY MOTHER, THE.—See *Pi-hsia Yüan-chün* 碧霞元君.

SAINTLY MOTHER TORTOISE, THE TRANSCENDENT.—See *Kuei-ling Shêng-mu* 魁靈聖母.

SAINTS, THE FIVE.—See *Wu Shêng* 五聖.

SAKAD-AGAMI.—See *Lo-han* 羅漢.

SAKRA.—Shih-chia 釋迦 or Ti-shih 帝釋 or Shih 釋 or Shih-chia-p'o 釋迦婆. Nêng T'ien-chu 能天主, *lit.* the mighty Lord (Indra) of Devas, or Shih-chia t'i-p'o 釋迦提婆 (S'akra Devendra) or Shih-t'i huan-yin 釋提桓因, *i.e.* T'ien-ti Shih 天帝釋, *lit.* S'akra the Lord (Indra) of Devas, or Tao-li Ti-shih 忉利帝釋, or Tao-li T'ien-wang 忉利天王, *lit.* king of Trayas-trims'as. Common epithets of Indra (*q.v.*) as ruler of the Devas.

S'AKYA.—Shih-chia [ka] 釋迦. Explained as meaning charity (*jên* 仁) or charitable (*nêng jên* 能仁).—The ancestors and descendants of kings, varying in number from 5 to 15,000 who reigned at Potala, and whose four sons reigned at Kapila-vastu, after the destruction of which four surviving princes founded the kingdoms of Udyana, Bamyan, Himatala, and S'ambi.

SAKYAMUNI.—See *Fo* 佛, *Yü Huang* 玉皇, *San Pao* 三寶, *Buddha, Gautama.*

SALT, THE GOD OF.—The first man who made salt is worshipped as a god. Du Bose (p. 327) says his name is "World Wood."

SALT-PITS OF YÜNNAN 雲南.—See *Yen Tsu* 鹽祖.

SAMANAS.—See *Lo-han* 羅漢.

SAMANTABHADRA.—See *P'u-hsien hsin-li* 普賢心離 and
Buddhist Schools.

SAMANTARAJA.—See *Yen-lo Wang* 閻羅王.

SAMBARA.—In the *Vedas,* a demon, also called a Dasyu, who fought against king Divodasa, but was defeated and had his many castles destroyed by Indra. He appears to be a mythical personification of drought, of a kindred character to Vritra, or identical with him. In the *Puranas* a Daitya who carried off Pradyumna, and threw him into the sea, but was subsequently slain by him.

SAMBHALA.—A mysterious country in Central Asia.

SAMBHOGA-KAYA.—See *Adi-Buddha.*

SAMBODHI.—See *Fo* 佛.

SAMI.—The *Acacia suma* (*Prosopis Spicifera*), the wood of which is used for obtaining fire by friction. So Agni (*q.v.*), or fire, is called Sami-garbha, "having the Sami for its womb." It is sometimes personified and worshipped as a goddess, Sam-devi.

SAN-CH'Ê FA-SHIH 三車法師.—See *Kuei-chi Fa-shih* 窺基法師.

SAN-CHI-FU CH'AN-SHIH 三疾甫禪師 (66th generation). —A deified Buddhist monk. Ranked seventy-second in Buddhist School, VI (*q.v.*). Family name Lü 呂. A native of Shao-hsing 紹興, Chêkiang 浙江. Studied under Mi-yün 密雲 at Chin-su 金栗, and under San-i Ming-yü 三宜明盂 in the Hsien-shêng Ssǔ 顯聖寺, Hsien-shêng Monastery. After finishing his training, he started his own school in the Ch'ing-liang Ssǔ 清涼寺, Ch'ing-liang Monastery, at Wu-hsing 吳興. Died A.D. 1660. Buried by his disciples in the Ning-ts'ui An 凝翠菴, Ning-ts'ui Monastery.

SAN CH'ING 三清.—The Three Pure Ones. The triad of Taoist gods: Yü Ch'ing 玉清, Pearly Azure, Shang Ch'ing 上清, Upper Azure, and T'ai Ch'ing 太清, Supreme Azure.
These deities reside respectively in the three heavens, which correspond with the three divisions into which, in the beginning, the primordial cosmic ether (*t'ai chi* 太極) separated, namely, Ch'ing-wei T'ien 清為天, Yu-yü T'ien 猶宇天, and Ta-shih T'ien 大是天, known also as Yü Ch'ing 玉清, Shang Ch'ing 上清, and T'ai Ch'ing 太清 (*supra*).
In the Pearly Azure Heaven dwells the first god of the triad. He takes his name, Yü Ch'ing 玉清, from it. His throne is on the Jade Mountain, Yü Shan 玉山, and his palace is entered

through the Golden Gate, Chin Mên 金 門. From him, as does light from the sun, proceeds all truth.

His name is variously given as Yüan-shih T'ien-tsun 元 始 天 尊, Beginning, Honoured of Heaven, and Lo Ching-hsin 樂 靜 信, and he is sometimes given the honorary title of T'ien Pao 天 寶, Heavenly Jewel.

In most works, and by the majority of the people, this highest heaven is assigned to Yü Huang 玉 皇 (*q.v.*).

The god who inhabits the second, or Upper Azure (Shang Ch'ing 上 清) Heaven, is known by the name of Ling-pao T'ien-tsun 靈 寶 天 尊, The Mystic Jewel, Honoured of Heaven, or Tao Chün 道 君, Honourable Tao. Of the origin and functions of this god nothing is known. He is supposed to have existed from the beginning of the universe, to calculate time, and to divide it into periods. He dwells beyond the North Pole of the universe and controls the interaction of the *yang* 陽 and *yin* 陰 principles (*q.v.*).

The god of the third, or Supreme Azure (T'ai Ch'ing 太 清) Heaven, is Lao Tzǔ 老 子 (*q.v.*). He is also known as Shên Pao 神 寶, Spiritual Jewel, and is the expounder of the true doctrine emanating from Ling-pao T'ien-tsun 靈 寶 天 尊.

The San Ch'ing 三 清, Three Pure Ones, are the manifestation of Lao Tzǔ 老 子, who was deified for his intellectual and moral qualities. The triad is a modern imitation of that of the Buddhists. The function of this triad is also similar, namely, instruction and benevolent interference for the good of humanity.

SAN HSING 三 星.—See *Noxious God, The.*

SAN-I KO 三 義 閣.—Three Righteousnesses Temple. The Temple of the Three Sworn Brothers. These were Liu Pei 劉 備, Kuan Ti 關 帝, and Chang Fei 張 飛 (*qq.v.*) who swore mutual assistance, in the Peach Garden of the latter, to fight against the Yellow Turbans. Their oath is known as *T'ao-yüan San-chieh-i* 桃 園 三 結 義.

[SAN-I] MING-YÜ CH'AN-SHIH [三 宜] 明 盂 禪 師.—See *Ming-yü Ch'an-shih* 明 盂 禪 師 and *To-fu-ch'i Ch'an-shih* 多 福 啟 禪 師.

SAN KU 三 姑.—See *K'êng san Ku-niang* 坑 三 姑 娘.

SAN KUAN 三 官.—The Three Rulers, Agents, or Transcendent Powers, known also as San Yüan 三 元, The Three Principles, or Epochs, San Kuan Ta-ti 三 官 大 帝, the Three Great Emperors or Officiating Agents, and T'ai-shang San-kuan 太 上 三 官, the Three Supreme Agents, or Venerable Three Rulers. Originally, T'ien Ti Shui 天 地 水, Heaven, Earth, and Water, a triad invented by the early Taoists, who taught that they were three transcendent Powers, bestowing happiness, remitting sins, and protecting from evil, respectively. Each of these powers received the honorary title of Great Ruler, Ta Ti 大 帝.

According to one author, the "Three Rulers," now a peculiar Taoist triad of subordinate divinities, presiding over heaven, earth, and water, said to "send down good and ill fortune on men, and to save the lost," were original vast periods of time, like a geological epoch, but were subsequently personified and deified. They were, however, also embodied in living persons, who were subsequently deified.

Abstinence from animal food in honour of the *San Kuan* 三 官 was observed from the first to the fifteenth day of the first, seventh, and tenth months.

The idea of the San Kuan 三 官 originated with Chang Hêng 張 衡, son of Chang Tao-ling 張 道 陵, in the reign of Ling Ti 靈 帝 (A.D. 168-90) of the Later Han 漢 dynasty. He composed a book of charms, purporting to cure all kinds of diseases. The patient was required to write, on three scrolls, his name and surname and a promise to confess all his sins. One of these was offered to Heaven by being deposited on the summit of a high mountain, another to Earth, by being buried in the ground, and a third to the Water, by being thrown into the sea, a river, etc. The three blessings above-mentioned were thus ensured.

Later on, the idea of the *San Kuan* 三 官 assumed another phase. During the Eastern Chin 晉 dynasty (A.D. 317-420) they became the *San Yüan* 三 元, "Three Periods" of time, or "Epochs." The change was due to the Taoist K'ou Ch'ien-chih 寇 謙 之 (fifth century A.D.; *q.v.*), who divided the year into unequal parts (first to sixth month; seventh to ninth; and tenth to twelfth). In this scheme, the fifteenth day of the first, seventh, and tenth months was sacred to each of the "Three Epochs" or "Principles," *San Yüan* 三 元. The "Ruler of Heaven" became the principal patron of the first period. He, the "First Principal," was called the "Heavenly Ruler presiding over the First Period," *Shang-yüan T'ien-kuan* 上 元 天 官, and was honoured on the fifteenth day of the first month. The "Ruler of Earth" controlled the second period. He, the "Second Principle," was called the "Earthly Ruler controlling the Middle Period," *Chung-yüan Ti-kuan* 中 元 地 官, and was honoured on the fifteenth day of the seventh month. The "Ruler of Water" presided over the last period. He, the "Third Principal," was called the "Ruler of Water presiding over the Last Period," *Hsia-yüan Shui-kuan* 下 元 水 官, and was honoured on the fifteenth day of the tenth month.

These three Rulers are said to "send down good or evil fortune on men, and punish the wicked."

The above two systems (*San Kuan* 三 官 and *San Yüan* 三 元) being found too abstruse for the mass of the people, the Taoists devised one more suitable to the needs of ordinary folk. This is contained in the *Ch'ung tsêng Sou-shên chi* 重 增 搜 神 記 *Records of Gods, New and Enlarged Edition,* divided into three parts, giving the origin of the "Three Rulers," and the advantages derived from worshipping them (the "Ruler of Heaven" granting happiness, the "Ruler of Earth" remitting sins, and the "Ruler of Water" delivering from evil), instances of favours obtained through their intercession (such as healing disease by assuming the forms of three Taoist hermits), and a collection of formularies employed in worshipping them (after abstinence and other preliminaries, including preparatory prayers, reciting the chief prayer for blessings addressed to the "Ruler of Heaven," etc.).

In the Buddhist system, instead of abstract Principles or Records, three of China's legendary rulers, namely, Yao 堯, Shun 舜, and Yü 禹 (*qq.v.*) are worshipped.

The title of the "Three Principles" has also been applied to the Three Genii, T'ang Hung 唐宏, Ko Yung 葛雍, and Chou Wu 周武, Venerable Supreme, Mediate, and Superior Principle respectively, of the Wu State, *Wu k'o san Chên-chün* 吳客三眞君, three canonized personages who had held the office of Censor under King Li, Li Wang 属王 (878-827 B.C.), of the Chou 周 dynasty. See Doré, *Recherches,* vi, 27-8, Kennelly, vi, 34-6, and (for details) *Shên-hsien t'ung-chien* 神仙通鑑, V, iv, 5, where the legend regarding them is related as follows:—

Having, as Censors, in vain upbraided Li Wang 属王 for neglecting the affairs of State, they left Chou 周 for the Wu 吳 State. The Prince of Wu 吳 refusing to receive them, they went to live in the T'ao-hua cave, T'ao-hua Tung 桃花洞, in the Yü-yen Mountains, Yü-yen Shan 玉巖山, but were summoned thence when war broke out with the State of Ch'u 楚. At last, when they had vanquished the enemy, they begged the ruler of Wu 吳 to grant them the Chü-ch'ü mountain, Chü-ch'ü Shan 句曲山, thirty miles south of Nanking 南京 and sacred to the genii. In Taoist lore, it is reckoned as the first of the sacred mountains of the immortals. There they lived as hermits, provided for by the ruler, who also frequently visited them personally. The presence of these transcendent personages overshadowed the influence of the neighbouring princes. Later on, they repaired to the Li-li hills, Li-li Shan 離里山, also known as the National hills, Kuo Shan 國山, near Ch'ang-chou Fu 常州府, Kiangsu 江蘇. As they arrived, the rock split open and disclosed a spacious grotto large enough to accommodate a thousand persons. In the centre of this grotto, a personage lay reclining on a long stone slab. He ordered them to sit down at his feet, and assured them that when the slab would ascend in the air, they would be metamorphosed. Hereupon, they fell into a trance, and became Immortals.

When the Emperor Chên Tsung 眞宗 of the Northern Sung 宋 dynasty, Pei Sung Ch'ao 北宋朝, proceeded, in A.D. 1008, to T'ai Shan 泰山 to offer the *fêng-shan* 封禪 sacrifices to Heaven, the three appeared to him at the Southern Gate of Heaven, Nan-t'ien Mên 南天門, stating that they had been ordered by Heaven to protect him. He thereupon canonized them with the above titles (*T'ang Hung* 唐宏, etc.), and had a eulogy of them, composed by himself, engraved on stone and erected in a temple built in their honour. They thus had conferred on them the power of ruling Heaven, Earth and Water, and became assimilated to the *San Kuan* 三官 (*supra*).

SAN KUAN TA TI 三官大帝.—See *San Kuan* 三官.

SAN LANG 三郎.—See *Huo Pu* 火部.

SAN MAO 三茅.—The Three Brothers Mao 茅. Known as San Mao Chün 三茅君, the Three Princes Mao. Family name Mao 茅. They were respectively, Mao Ying 茅盈 (personal name Shu-shên 叔申), the eldest; Mao Ku 茅固 (personal name Chi-wei 季偉), the second; and Mao Chung 茅衷 (personal name Ssŭ-chih 思知), the youngest. Natives of Hsien-yang 咸陽 (modern Hsi-an Fu 西安府, Shensi 陝西).

They lived toward the end of the Chou 周 dynasty. Their mother was of the Hsü 許 family. Their father, Mao Tsu 茅祚, otherwise Mao Mêng 茅濛, had as his personal name Po-ying 伯英. Their grandfather Mao Hsi 茅焦, whose personal name was Kung-lun 拱倫, had held office under Chuang-hsiang Wang 莊襄王 (249-246 B.C.) of the Ch'in 秦 dynasty, the father of Shih Huang-ti 始皇帝 (221-209 B.C.). As a reward for his services, Mao Hsi 茅焦 was given the honorary title of Magnanimous and Sincere Duke. Their great-great-grandfather, Mao Mêng 茅濛, whose personal name was Ch'u-ch'êng 初成, a famous scholar of Hsien-yang 咸陽 (modern Hsi-an Fu 西安府), became an alchemist on Hua Shan 華山, Mount Hua, dying in 217 B.C.

Mao Ying 茅盈 was born on the third day of the tenth moon in 145 B.C., during the reign of the Emperor Ching Ti 景帝 (156-140 B.C.) of the Han 漢 dynasty. At 18 years of age he went to Hêng Shan 恒山, the sacred mountain of the North, in Shansi 山西. There he became the disciple of Wang Chün 王君, a man who had become a spirit, and learnt from him how to supernaturalize himself, being then independent of the laws of gravitation and nourishment. Hsi Wang-mu 西王母 also taught him the prayer which brings perfection to the deserving.

At 49 years of age, being then proficient in *tao* 道, the science of perfection, he returned to his native place, and, being blamed by his father for lack of filial piety, took up a stick to strike him, but the stick fell to the ground in fragments. He then fled, and later settled at Chü-ch'ü Shan 句曲山, in the former kingdom of Wu 吳 (in modern Kiangsu 江蘇, and called Mao Shan 茅山, on account of its connection with this legend). Here he became further supernaturalized, and was able to float in the air at will.

When his parents died, he returned to Shensi 陝西. In 70 B.C. a celestial messenger came to call him. Bidding his relatives and friends farewell, he said: "I am going to live at Chü-ch'ü Shan 句曲山, in the South-east," and, rising on a cloud, disappeared.

His two brothers, Ku 固 and Chung 衷, who were officials, resigned their posts and went to Chü-ch'ü Shan 句曲山, where Mao Ying 茅盈 taught them how to immortalize themselves. They had to fast for three years, during which time each brother lived on a separate mountain-peak.

The two brothers, seated on yellow cranes, went to Heaven in 64 B.C. They are worshipped on the three peaks above-mentioned.

Mao Ying 茅盈 was afterwards married to Wang Chün's 王君 niece (the famous Pi-hsia Yüan-chün 碧霞元君, q.v.), at T'ai Shan 泰山, and thereafter was accustomed to ride a white crane to and from that mountain and Chü-ch'ü Shan 句曲山. He was canonized in A.D. 976, by the Emperor T'ai Tsung 太宗 (A.D. 976-8) of the Sung 宋 dynasty, as Yu-shêng Chên-chün 佑聖眞君, Loyal Prince and Helper of Saints.

A temple to the San Mao 三茅 was built by the people on the highest point of the three-peaked mountain of Chi-lung Shan 鷄籠山, on the left bank of the Chiang 江, in Anhui 安徽. It can only be reached by means of an iron chain, the two ends of which are fastened into the rocks.

SAN-MAO CHÜN 三茅君.—See *San Mao* 三茅.

SAN PAO 三寶.—The "Three Precious Ones," or "Three Jewels." The Group of Three Venerated objects. A Buddhist triad. The "Three Precious Things," *San Pao* 三寶, or the "Three Holies" (Sanskrit, *Triratna*). Were first only honoured, but subsequently personified and worshipped, being accorded a personality similar to that of the three chief gods of the Hindu pantheon.

The group is also frequently called San-tsun Ta Fo 三尊大佛, the "Three Great Venerable Buddhas."

The first triad is composed of the following: Shih-chia Fo 釋迦佛, Sakyamuni, called Fo Pao 佛寶, The Precious Buddha (Gautama); O-mi-t'o-Fo 阿彌陀佛, Amitabha, called Fa Pao 法寶, The Precious Law (Dharma); Ju-lai Fo 如來佛, called Sêng Pao 僧寶, The Precious Monkhood (Sangha).

These three, the Buddha, his Law, and his Priesthood or Monkhood or Fraternity of Monks, were the first personification of early Buddhism, commonly known as the "Buddhist Triad."

[For developments of this idea and variations of the Triad, see *Doré,* vi, 12-14, and works on Buddhism mentioned in the Bibliography at the end of this dictionary.]

"The Schools of Northern Buddhism were not satisfied with the original Triad of Buddha, the Law, and the Monkhood. They, therefore, invented in addition five Triads, each consisting of a Dhyani-Buddha, a Dhyani-Bodhisattva, and an earthly Buddha. Of all these Triads, the most important and most generally known is that consisting of Amitabha, Avalokitesvara, and the human Buddha, Sakyamuni (see *Adi-Buddha*).

"Others, quoting the historical evolution of Buddhism, say that all modern Triads represent the Buddha of the Past, the Buddha of the Present, and the Buddha of the Future, or Thatagata, Sakyamuni, and Maitreya" (Kennelly, vi, 21).—See also *O-mi-t'o Fo* 阿彌陀佛.

SAN SHÊNG 三聖.—The Three Saints. The eclectic triad, Buddha, Lao Tzŭ, and Confucius (*qq.v.*).

SAN-SHIH 三尸, GOD OF THE STAR.—See *Sa Chien* 撒堅, *Sa Ch'iang* 撒強, and *Sa Yung* 撒勇.

SAN T'AI-TZŬ 三太子.—See *Li No-cha* 李哪吒.

SAN TSUN TA FO 三尊大佛.—The original Buddhist triad.—See *San Pao* 三寶.

SAN YÜAN 三元.—See *San Kuan* 三官.

SANAT-KUMARA.—See *Kumaras,* in *Brahma,* Masculine.

SANDHYA.—"Twilight." It is personified as the daughter of Brahma and wife of Siva. In the *Siva Purana* it is related that Brahma having attempted to do violence to his daughter, she changed herself into a deer. Brahma then assumed the form of a stag and pursued her through the sky. Siva saw this, and shot an arrow which cut off the head of the stag. Brahma then reassumed his own form and paid homage to Siva. The arrow remains in the sky in the sixth lunar mansion, called Ardra, and the stag's head remains in the fifth mansion, Mriga-siras.

SANG CH'ÊNG-TAO 桑成道.—The god of the star Ti-pao 地暴.—See *Ti-sha* 地煞.

SANG-MÊN 喪門, THE GOD OF THE STAR.—See *Chang Kuei-fang* 張桂芳.

SANGHA.—See *Ju-lai Fo* 如來佛, *Sêng Pao* 僧寶, and *San Pao* 三寶.

SANGYOJANAS.—See *Ten Fetters.*

SANI.—The planet Saturn. The regent of that planet, represented as a black man in black garments. Sani was a son of the sun and Chhaya, but another statement is that he was the offspring of Bala-rama and Revati. He is also known as Ara, Kona, and Kroda, and by the patronymic Saura. His influence is evil, hence he is called Krura-dris and Krura-lochana, "the evil-eyed one." He is also Manda, "the slow"; Pangu, "the lame"; Sanaischara, "slow-moving"; Saptarchi, "seven-rayed"; and Asita, "the dark."

SAO-CHOU 掃帚, THE GOD OF THE STAR.—See *Ma Shih* 馬氏 and *Sao-ch'ing Niang* 掃晴娘.

SAO-CH'ING NIANG 掃晴娘:—The Lady who Sweeps [the sky] Clear. The Sky-sweeper. The Goddess of Fine Weather. Also prayed to for rain in times of drought. The spirit of the star Sao-chou 掃帚, the Broom, who is Madame Ma 馬, the wife of Chiang Tzǔ-ya 姜子牙. She refused to accompany him when he joined Wên Wang's 文王 (1231-1135 B.C.) party, and was repudiated by him. When he had become one of Wu Wang's 武王 (1121-1114 B.C.) chief counsellors, she was so filled with remorse that she hanged herself. Chiang Tzǔ-ya 姜子牙 canonized her as the Spirit of the star Sao-chou 掃帚, the Broom.

Her image, representing her holding a broom, cut out of paper, is hung under the roof inside women's apartments, after rainfall.

SAPTARATNA.—See *Ch'i Pao* 七寶.

SARVARTTHASIDDHA.—See *Fo* 佛.

SATURN.—T'u Hsing 土星. The Earth Star. The god of this planet is known as Huang Ti 黃帝, the Yellow Ruler, and Han-shu Niu 含樞紐. Is worshipped by lighting five lamps and sacrificing whilst turned toward the west.—*Cf. Sani.*

SCARLATINA, THE SPIRIT OF.—See *Sha Shên* 痧神.

SCHOOL OF THE SOUTHERN SACRED MOUNTAIN. —See *Buddhist Schools,* III.

SCHOOLS.—See *Buddhist Schools.*

SCORPIONS, THE GOD OF.—Du Bose says this god is much worshipped in Honan 河南 province. "Sometimes a rustic who has caught a basket of scorpions for medicinal use feels on his shoulder the touch of an old man, the god of scorpions, who says: 'Friend, you have taken lives enough, go home.' He is very effective in keeping the houses free from the green intruders."

SEA, THE GODDESS OF THE.—Du Bose says: "She is not only worshipped by 'men that go down to the sea in ships,' but by millions on land. In girlhood she was a Miss Ling 淩, a prophetess whose predictions, whether favourable or adverse, were sure to be fulfilled. 'Her brothers, four in number, were merchants. On one occasion where they were absent on a trading voyage, she fell into a deep trance, from which she was aroused by the loud lamentations of her parents, who supposed her dead. On recovering herself she informed them that she had seen her brothers at sea in a violent storm. Shortly afterwards the youngest son returned home and reported the loss of his elder brothers. He stated that during the storm a lady appeared in mid-heaven, and by means of a rope dragged the ship into a safe position. His sister said she had hastened to the rescue of her elder brothers, but while in the very act of saving them was awakened by the cries of her parents.'

Afterwards old Mr. Ling 凌 was drowned in the sea, and when the affectionate daughter heard the sad tidings she went to the ocean's shore to weep, and her grief being excessive, she threw herself into the foaming deep. Both bodies floated to the shore, and were buried by mourning relatives.

In after years, a mandarin travelling to Korea met with a typhoon, and while all other ships foundered he saw an angel lamp guiding his boat. After going about seven hundred miles he landed at an island, and seeing a temple asked what it was, and was told it was Miss Ling's 凌. She is the guardian protectress of the sailor, and in nights of storm holds out an angel-lantern in the sky to guide the almost shipwrecked mariner."

By her side are images of Ch'ien-li Yen 千里眼 and Shun-fêng Erh 順風耳.—See also *Shui Fu* 水府.

SEAS, THE SPIRITS OF THE FOUR.—See *Shui Fu* 水府, C (2) (b).

SEASONS, THE GODS OF THE FOUR.—The God of Spring is the Green Ruler; of Summer, the Fire, or Red, Ruler; of Autumn, the White Ruler; and of Winter, the Black Ruler.

SECRETARIES AND CLERKS.—These sacrifice to Hsiao Ho 蕭何 and Tsêng Ts'an 曾參.

SEEDSMEN, THE GOD OF.—See *Lei Tsu* 雷祖.

SÊNG-CHIA TA-SHIH 僧迦大師.—See *Ta Shêng* 大聖.

SÊNG PAO 僧寶. The Precious Monkhood. (Sangha).— See *Ju-lai Fo* 如來佛 and *San Pao* 三寶.

SÊNG-PAO CH'AN-SHIH 僧寶禪師 (48th generation).—A deified Buddhist monk. Ranked thirty-sixth in Buddhist School, VI (*q.v.*). Studied under Hsi-pien Ch'an-shih 希辨禪師 (*q.v.*), at Ch'ing-chou 青州, Shantung 山東. In A.D. 1154 went to Ta-ming 大明, Hunan 湖南 (or ? Ta-ming 大名, Chihli 直隸), where he died.

SÊNG-SHÊ 僧 沙.—A saintly Buddhist. Fourth century. Had the power of making rain fall. One of those invited to the annual banquet of the gods (see *Hsi Wang-mu* 西 王 母).

SÊNG-TS'AN 僧 璨.—A saintly Buddhist monk. One of those invited to the annual banquet of the gods (see *Hsi Wang-mu* 西 王 母). The third patriarch of Chinese Buddhism. Died A.D. 606.—See *Patriarchs*.

SERPENTS, KINGS OF.—See *Shê Wang* 蛇 王 and *Shih-hsiang Kung* 施 相 公.

SERVANT OF THE WHITE LOTUS, THE.—See *Pai-lien T'ung-tzŭ* 白 蓮 童 子.

SEVEN TATHAGATA.—Tathagata, in Chinese Ju-lai 如 來, *lit.* "Thus come (or calmly approaching) Buddha." The highest appellation given to a Buddha. The Seven Tathagata (Sapta Tathagata, Ch'i Ju-lai 七 如 來) are the Buddhist substitute for the seven richis of the Brahmans, an arbitrary series of seven (fictitious) Tathagata (See Eitel, p. 148).

SEVEN YOUNG LADIES, THE.—See *Ch'i Ku-tzŭ* 七 姑 子.

SHA 煞.—A character meaning to strike dead, as by some baleful influence, such as malaria or sunstroke; hence, baleful, a baleful person. Sometime before the T'ang 唐 dynasty, a young woman who had been divorced turned into a *sha* 煞, or rather, she turned into a *mên kuei* 門 鬼 able to exercise *sha* 煞 over those she had a grudge against, though it is also stated that the *sha* 煞 is a personal spirit, who can bring *yüan* 冤, wrong, calamity, or vengeance, on his or her enemies.

SHA HO-SHANG 沙 和 尚.—A legendary saintly Buddhist monk. One of those invited to the annual banquet of the gods (see *Hsi Wang-mu* 西 王 母).—See also *Sun Hou-tzŭ* 孫 猴 子.

SHA-MÊN 沙 門.—See *Shramana*.

SHA MO-HAN 沙 漠 汗.—See *Chang Hsien* 張 仙.

SHA SHÊN 痧 神.—The Spirit of Scarlatina, or Benign Measles. A specialist attached to the celestial Ministry of Medicine. An Assistant to his mother Tou-shên Niang-niang 痘 神 娘 娘 (*q.v.*). Worshipped in the temples of Yao Wang 藥 王, the King of Medicine, in cases of a kind of scarlatina which frequently attacks children. (*Sha* 痧 here is not cholera).—See also *Chên Shên* 疹 神 and *T'ien I-yüan* 天 醫 院.

SHA TSEI 殺賊.—See *Lo-han* 羅漢.

SHA WU-CHING 沙悟靜.—See *Sun Hou-tzŭ* 猻猴子.

SHADOWS, THE GOD OF.—This divinity can cause a shadow to turn in the opposite direction (Du Bose, p. 340). His name is

SHAN-CHAO CH'AN-SHIH 善昭禪師 (43rd generation). —A deified Buddhist monk. Ranked sixteenth in Buddhist School, III (*q.v.*). Family name Yü 兪. A native of T'ai-yüan 太原. His novitiate was passed at Shou Shan 首山. Proceeded to Fên-chou 沼州, Shansi 山西, where he lived during the last thirty years of his life. Died A.D. 1023.

SHAN-HUI CHIH-CHÊ 善慧智者.—The Wise Monk Shan-hui 善慧. One of those invited to the annual banquet of the gods (see *Hsi Wang-mu* 西王母).

SHAN-HUI TA-SHIH 善慧大士.—See *Fu Ta-shih* 傅大士.

SHAN SHÊNG 善勝.—See *Hsüan-t'ien Shang-ti* 玄天上帝.

SHAN SHÊNG 靜望.—See *Pi-hsia Yüan-chün* 碧霞元君.

SHAN-SHIH 禪師.—See *Ch'an-shih* 禪師.

SHAN-SHOU CHIEN-SHÊ 善首兼攝.—One of the twelve divine Buddhist teachers (*Samantabhadra*).

SHAN-TAO HO-SHANG 善導和伺.—A deified Buddhist monk. Ranked second in Buddhist School, XVII (*q.v.*). The second ancestor. Buddhist annals describe him as an incarnation of Amitabha, but make no mention of his name or family. There was a pious rivalry between him and Ch'o Ch'an-shih 綽禪師, from Hsi-ho 西河, whom he considered as a living Buddha. "Convinced that without mortification he could never do anything serious for the salvation of mankind, he commenced a life of penance and prayer. He remained in a kneeling posture whole nights and days, reciting prayers in honour of Buddha, and every time he pronounced his name, a beam of vivid light issued from his mouth."

One day, as he ascended a willow-tree, turning his face toward the West, he felt a keen desire to reach, after death, Hsi T'ien 西天, the Western Paradise. In order to hasten that happy moment, he cast himself down, and was killed in the fall. The Emperor Kao Tsung 高宗 (A.D. 650-84) of the T'ang 唐 dynasty conferred on his monastery the honorary title of Kuang-ming 光明, Bright and Illustrious, those characters being thenceforth added to his name.

SHAN TZŬ-KUO 禪子郭.—See *Tsao Chün* 灶(竈)君.

SHANG CHIEN 上間.—See *Neck, The God of the.*

SHANG CH'ING 上清.—The Upper Pure. The Middle Heaven, inhabited by Chên Jên 眞人, Heroes, those who have attained to perfect rule over Nature.—See *San Ch'ing* 三清, *Ling-pao T'ien-tsun* 靈寶天尊, *Tao Chün* 道君, and *Chên Jên* 眞人.

SHANG JUNG 商容.—The god of the star Yü-t'ang 玉堂. A generalissimo under Chou Wang 紂王 (1154-1121 B.C.). Committed suicide at the age of 75 in anticipation of execution.

SHANG TI 上帝.—The Sovereign on high. The apotheosized ancestor. The god of the king or emperor, imposed by the conquering Northerners on the aborigines. The universal Lord and Legislator. His nature is not explained, but he has anthropomorphic characteristics. He governs, predestines, and issues his mandate to the mundane ruler. He is represented as just, providential, as rewarding and punishing, as being worshipped by mortals and as being pleased by offerings and sacrifices. He appears in dreams, grants audiences to the privileged, listens to complaints of the oppressed, blesses and exhorts those who act rightly, is not deceived, wrecks vengeance, is unchanging, unequalled, distinct from the category of transcendent beings, whom he dominates from on high. Nothing is done, or happens, against his will, though he shows anger and pleasure, grief and joy.

Shang Ti 上帝 belongs to the ancestral deities. He was sacrificed to as a vegetation spirit and the remotest ancestor of the dynasty (there seems to be some relationship between Shang Ti 上帝 and Shên Nung 神農, *i.e.* Hsien Nung 先農). "From the sacrificial practice we may conclude that Shang Ti 上帝 was not a so-called *external* vegetation-demon, but an *inherent one,* living within the plant itself. He may be imagined to have originally lived in the rice. . . . Moreover, he also seems to play a part in the commemorative cult." It is an open question what function of Shang Ti 上帝 was the original one, and how the supreme power absorbed all the rest from other deities. His cult sprang from a popular religion. "Opposed to him was an ancient popular deity, the highest in Southern China, 道 *Tao,* a deity originally conceived personal and, apparently, also totemestic. Out of the contest between the two, during the 4th and 3rd centuries B.C. at last came forth the unity 太一 *T'ai-yi,* 'The Great One'" (Schindler, pp. 61, 62, 63).

The idea of this Supreme Being remained substantially the same until the Classical period of Confucius and his disciples. After that, it became somewhat more distant and abstract. In modern times, the state of things is well described by Wieger, as follows: "The world is governed by a supreme Being, who is called Heaven, or Sovereign on high, Pure August, or otherwise. In principle, this supreme Being knows of itself all that takes place on the earth. In practice, he acts as if he did not know, waits till he is informed through some administrative channel, and answers through the same channel, as the emperor of China used to do in the time of the empire. His ministers and officers on the earth, are, from high to low, Kuan Yü 關 羽, an unfortunate general of the third century after Christ, now a great genie, usually called Kuan Kung 關 公 or Kuan Ti 關 帝. Then the hierarchy of the Ch'êng Huang 城 隍, tutelary genii of the cities, governors, prefects and sub-prefects. Then T'u Ti 土 地, the local genie of each village, equivalent to the former Patron of the soil. Finally, in each family, Tsao Chün 竈 君, the Genie of the hearth. The organization of the lower *yin* 陰 world is absolutely identical with that of the upper *yang* 陽 world. The genii of the towns and villages are deceased men. They are promoted, degraded, and subject to the same vicissitudes as their living congeners. Mention is sometimes made of their wives. The temple of the tutelary genie of each city is for the deceased of the district, just as the praetorium of the local mandarin is for the living of the same jurisdiction. These infernal functionaries have their service of satellites, who are as worthless as those of the upper world."—See also *Yao* 堯, *Shun* 舜, *Yü* 禹, *Huang Ti* 皇 帝, *Fo* 佛, and Werner, *China of the Chinese*, pp. 239-40.

SHANG-WÊN 佝 文.—See *Shih Ming-i* 十 明 醫, 5.

SHANG-YÜAN CH'AN-SHIH 上 淵 禪 師 (71st generation). —A deified Buddhist monk. Ranked sixty-eighth in Buddhist School, III (*q.v.*). Family name Ts'ao 曹. A native of Hsin-ho 新 河, in Chi-chou 冀 州. His teacher was Fa-tsang Ch'an-shih 法 藏 禪 師 (*q.v.*). He lived at Ling Fêng 靈 峰, Mystic Peak. Died A.D. 1679. His tomb is on the eastern slope of Ling Fêng 靈 峰.

SHANG-YÜAN T'IEN-KUAN 上 元 天 官.—See *San Kuan* 三 官.

SHAO-K'ANG TA-SHIH 少 康 大 師.—A deified Buddhist monk. Ranked fifth in Buddhist School, XVII (*q.v.*). Fifth ancestor. Family name Chou Shao-k'ang 周 少 康. A native of Hsien-tu 仙 都, Fukien 福 建. He was mute until seven years old, when his mother took him to a Buddhist temple, and kneeling before a statue, asked him whom it represented. "It is Shih-chia Fo 釋 迦 佛" (Sakyamuni), he replied. About A.D. 785, he entered the Pai-ma Ssŭ 白 馬 寺, Monastery of the White Horse, at Lo-yang 洛 陽, Honan 河 南. Being told that a book he saw there, whose characters shone with a brilliant light, was written by the second ancestor, Shan-tao Ho-shang 善道 和 伺 (*q.v.*), he uttered the following prayer: "If I may ever hope to reach the Hsi T'ien 西 天, Western Heaven, may this light shine on me again!" Immediately he was enveloped with the miraculous light. He vowed to persevere in leading the life of a Buddhist monk, and proceeded to the monastery of Shan-tao Ho-shang 善 道 和 伺, the Kuang-ming Ssŭ 光 明 寺, Bright and Illustrious Monastery. There he saw the statue of Shantao 善 道 rise into the air, and say to him: "If you will propagate my doctrine, I will increase your merits, so that you will succeed in attaining to the happiness of the Western Paradise." The monk accordingly zealously preached the doctrine in the Hsin-ting Ssŭ 新 定 寺, Hsin-ting Monastery. Throughout the country he was known only by the name of O-mi-t'o Fo 阿 彌 陀 佛, Amitabha. Every time he pronounced his name, a Buddha was seen to issue from his mouth. Died in the Hsin-ting Ssŭ 新 定 寺, Hsin-ting Monastery.

SHAO-LUNG CH'AN-SHIH 紹 隆 禪 師 (49th generation).— A deified Buddhist monk. Ranked twenty-fifth in Buddhist School, III (*q.v.*). A native of Han Shan 含 山, Anhui 安 徽. His two teachers were Chang Lu-hsin 長 蘆 信 and Yüan-wu 圓 悟. Died A.D. 1136. His tomb is to the S.W. of Hu-ch'iu Shan 虎 丘 山, Tiger Mound Hill.

SHARP EAR.—See *Ch'ien-li Yen* 千 里 眼.

SHÊ CHI 社 稷.—The Gods of the Soil and Harvests (or Grains, *lit.* panicled millet, used for cereals in general). The worship of these deities is both a thanksgiving for past and a prayer for continued blessings. The earth and harvests serve as man's dwelling-place and nourishment, and the soil and millet-crop are taken as representatives of the larger wholes. The spirits of the soil and mil'et were worshipped in the most ancient times, because millet was the first sown, and therefore the first reaped, of all the crops, and because the spirit of the soil, Shê 社, was worshipped by the first Sages as a collective worship of the five Terrestrial Spirits (*shên* 神), of the Mountains and Forests (*shan-lin* 山 林), Rivers and Lakes (*ch'uan-tsê* 川 澤), Tablelands and Hills (*ch'iu-ling* 坵 陵), Mounds and Dikes (*fên-yen* 墳 衍), and Springs and Marshes (*yüan-hsi* 源 隰), respectively.

In course of time human beings were chosen as the Patrons of the soil and agriculture. These are classed as General and Local. As regards the former, K'ang Hui 康 回 (known as Kung Kung 共 工), Minister of Works and a powerful feudatory in the reign of the Emperor Fu Hsi 伏 羲 (2953-2838 B.C.) or of the Emperor Shên Nung 神 農 (2838-2698 B.C.), revolted and was subdued by Nü-wa Shih 女 媧 氏. His son, Kou-lung 句 龍, who distinguished himself in the management of public works,

SHÊ CHI

was worshipped with sacrifices after his death, as the patron deity of the soil. He retained his place under the Shang 商, but the Emperor P'ing Ti 平帝 (A.D. 1-6), of the Han 漢 dynasty, replaced him by Yü Wang 禹王, King Yü 禹, as the Patron of the Soil. Kou-lung 句龍 was, however, reinstated by the T'ang 唐, Sung 宋, and Yüan 元 dynasties, but the Emperor T'ai Tsu 太祖 (A.D. 1368-99) of the Ming 明 dynasty deposed him in favour of his ancestor Jên Tsu 仁祖. In the following reign, that of Hui Ti 惠帝 (A.D. 1399-1403), T'ai Tsu 太祖 himself was the patron deity; and in the reign of Jên Tsung 仁宗 (A.D. 1425-26), T'ai Tsu 太祖 and T'ai Tsung 太宗 shared the honour between them, Kou-lung 句龍 being eventually reinstated by Shih Tsung 世宗 (A.D. 1522-67) of the same dynasty.

As the Emperor alone could worship Sovereign Earth, it was necessary to make provision for the worship of the people. This they did through the worship of the Gods of the Soil, or the Spirits of the Land and Grains, which are but popular titles for Sovereign Earth reduced to a specific locality. (In the sixth year of his reign the Emperor Hui Tsung 徽宗 of the Sung 宋 dynasty gave to Sovereign Earth the title of "Sovereign Earth Imperial God of the Soil," Hou-t'u Huang-ti Ch'i 后土皇地祇; thus clearly identifying the two as one and the same being.) With the Emperor, the worship was of the whole earth, as it was all in his care (t'ien-hsia shê 天下社). The mayor of a city worships the Chou Shê 州社, as it is the part under his control. The people worship their own neighbourhood shê 社 (li shê 里社), as it is the locality they are most interested in. A neighbourhood T'u Ti 土地 is supposed to contain either twenty-five, or one hundred homes, while a Chou Shê 州社 contains twenty-five hundred. While the Emperor sacrificed for the nation, the people worshipped Earth in their own local T'u Ti 土帝.

The most notable altar to the Gods of the Soil is found inside the Forbidden City, in Peking 北京. Upon this altar, the top of which is covered with the five coloured soils, the Emperor worshipped. In addition to it, small temples were erected all over the country. These each contain two small idols, which are now represented as husband and wife. Originally the two represented the God of the Soil and the God of the Grains. The temples vary in size, but on an average are only about four by five feet square. Mencius says, "the people are the most important element in a nation," and "the spirits of the land and grain are the next." Judging by the number of these temples, one would come to the conclusion the people firmly believe his doctrine, for they are thickly scattered over both the cities and the country (Plopper).

Plopper quotes the following legend:—An official named Li 李 had five sons. His wife was a great believer in idols, but he would have nothing to do with them. One day his eldest son became ill, and an idol in a dream told him that if he did not worship him his son would die. He replied, that if it was Heaven's will that he should live, he would live. The boy died. Then three others did likewise. When the fifth became ill, the god came as before in a dream, saying that he had already taken four sons and that if he did not worship he would also lose his last child. The father said, "If he is my son he will not die," and told the idol that because he said he was taking the lives of his children, he would tear down all his temples. This he did. The god then returned and confessed that the boys had died because it was Heaven's will, and that he himself was trying to gain more sacrifices. He begged the official to rebuild his shrines. This Mr. Li 李 finally consented to do, saying he would erect arrow temples. The idol thought that he meant one which would cover the space over which an arrow could fly, but the official meant one as wide and long as an arrow. From that time the temples to the Earth God have been small.

As regards local Patrons, Liu Pang 劉邦 (206-194 B.C.), the founder of the Han 漢 dynasty, decreed that the people themselves should sacrifice to the God of the Soil, according to their means. This is the origin of the T'u-ti Miao 土地廟, temples of the neighbourhood, seen at entrances to villages, and at roadsides throughout the country.

The Earth Gods are apportioned but a small district to control, so necessarily they are localized and numerous. They are: Shê 社, T'u Ti 土地, Shê Shên 社神, T'u Shên 土神, T'u Ti Shên 土地神, T'u Ti P'u Sa 土地菩薩, T'u Ti Lao Yeh 土地老爺, T'u Ti Nai Nai 土地奶奶, Shê Kung 社公, Shê Mu 社母, T'u Ti Kung Kung 土地公公, and T'u Ti P'o P'o 土地婆婆. When going to a new place, one must worship at the temple there, but only the local idol is interested and has power in that neighbourhood. So the stranger feels that as his "feet tread another man's earth," he owes it to the one with whom he lives to worship his gods. Also as he realizes "the T'u Ti 土地 at the east end is powerless at the west end" of a village, he should immediately inquire which temple controls the particular spot of ground in which he is interested. Thus each Locality has its own particular divinity.

Even though the district they control and the temple they live in are small, the Gods are thought to be powerful within their domain. They protect,* care for, and control the locality. . . . They are thought especially to protect their worshippers against

---

* When the community is in danger, these gods are taken from their temples, and placed where they may see all that is happening. They are thus better able to understand the conditions and be readier to assist. Plopper states that during the floods of 1910 in Anhui 安徽, "the little idols in many cases, were taken out and so placed that they could see the danger to the district, and assist the men of the neighbourhood working to save the dykes. Whenever they gave way there was no attempt made to save the gods. They were left to protect themselves."

mildew, locusts, and caterpillars, or to permit the crops of one neglecting them to be destroyed. . . . In popular thought the Gods of the Soil (T'u Ti 土地) have come to be responsible to the City God (Ch'êng Huang 城隍) for their particular district, acting as the middlemen between him and the people. If the land is properly cultivated, they must produce good crops, or they will be held accountable for the failure. Associated with them in managing the affairs of the district is the Demon of the Locality, or Ti Fang Kuei 地方鬼. It is their duty to know all the happenings of their neighbourhood and the actions of their people, and be ready at a moment's notice to render an account of their stewardship to the City God. Holding such a knowledge and relationship they have become most necessary to the daily life of the people (Plopper).

The patron deities of agriculture are:—(1) Shên Nung 神農, the inventer of the plough and the first Chinese agriculturist. Though it is recorded that he went with his people every year in the eleventh moon to worship the Spirits of the Soil and Sowing (showing that an earlier deity existed), he is yet worshipped as the first patron deity of agriculture. (2) Chu 柱, his son, who aided him in his labours, and was worshipped as the patron deity of harvests under the Hsia 夏 dynasty and in later times. (3) Ch'i 棄, or Hou Chi 后稷. When Chu 柱 had been degraded for his incompetency in regard to the drought of 1766 B.C., Ch'i 棄, the son of the Emperor Ti K'u 帝嚳 (2436-2366 B.C.) was appointed in his stead. He was the first ancestor of the Chou 周 dynasty, was a high official under Yao 堯, and a most zealous agriculturist under Shun 舜. He is commonly known as Hou Chi 后稷, Prince Chi, and began to be worshipped under the Hsia 夏 dynasty—though Shên Nung 神農 (2838-2698 B.C.) and his son Chu 柱 were preferred, until the degradation of the latter (as above mentioned), and he continued to hold the position of God of Agriculture under the Chou 周 dynasty. (4) Shu-chün 叔均. Ch'i 棄, having died, was succeeded by his son T'ai-chien 太堅, and then by his grandson Shu-chün 叔均 (known as the Spirit of the Land), who was worshipped as Patron deity of harvests from the time of the Shang 商 dynasty. (5) Liu Pang 劉邦 (247-195 B.C.), in 199-197 B.C., temporarily replaced Hou Chi 后稷 by the star-god Ling Hsing 靈星. (6) Yin-hung 殷洪. After the collapse of the Yin 殷 dynasty, Chiang Tzŭ-ya 姜子牙 canonized Yin-hung 殷洪, the son of the tyrant Chou 紂 (1154-1121 B.C.), as the God of Harvests.

SHÊ CHIANG-CHÜN 佘將軍.—Generalissimo Shê 佘. The sworn brother of Yo Fei 岳飛 (q.v.), at first his enemy, for whose sake he committed suicide when he found he could not avenge his death. He was formerly worshipped in a temple at Shê Shan 佘山, the Mountain of Shê 佘, and numerous temples dedicated to him exist at the present day.—See *Composite Deities*.

SHÊ-MO WANG 蛇 魔 王.—See *Shê Wang* 蛇 王.

SHE-WANG 蛇 王.—The King of Serpents. The celestial King of Serpents is represented in several forms. Commonly, he is shown as a real serpent. This is seen in a temple dedicated to him as the Marshal Serpent at Su-chou Fu (Soochow) 蘇 州 府, Kiangsu 江 蘇, where the boatmen and common people make offerings to him of frogs, special services, with incense, etc., being performed in his honour on the twelfth day of the fourth moon.

The king is otherwise represented by a man named Fang Chêng-hsüeh 方 正 學, a native of Ning-hai Hsien 寧 海 縣. Personal names given variously as Hsiao-ju 孝 孺, Hsi-chih 希 直, and Hsi-ku 希 古. His tongue was said to resemble that of a serpent.

In the reign of the Emperor Hung Wu 洪 武 (A.D. 1368-99) of the Ming 明 dynasty, Hsien 獻, King of Shu 蜀, had appointed him tutor to his son, and he afterwards became counsellor of empire under Hui Ti 惠 帝 (A.D. 1399-1403). The latter having committed suicide, the new Emperor Ch'êng Tsu 成 祖 (Yung Lo 永 樂; A.D. 1403-25) ordered Fang Chêng-hsüeh 方 正 學 to draft an edict, but instead of doing so, he cast his writing-brush on the ground, burst into tears and cursed his new master. For this he was put to death.

The reason why he is regarded as the King of Serpents is to be found in a warning given in a dream to his father the evening before the funeral of his grandfather. He dreamt that an old man advised him to quit the neighbourhood, since a ditch was to be dug on the morrow and the diggers would kill all the serpents they found.

Just at that time Fang Chêng-hsüeh's 方 正 學 mother was with child, and imagined she saw a train of serpents enter and reincarnate themselves in her womb, and to avenge themselves exterminated the descendant of Fang Chêng-hsüeh 方 正 學.

In Chang-chou Fu 漳 州 府, Fukien 福 建, the king is represented as a Buddhist priest. The origin of the idea is ascribed to a man who healed another who had been stung by a serpent.

The Serpent-king is also stated to be Ch'ang Hao 常 昊, the commander of Chou Wang's 紂 王 (1154-1121 B.C.) advance guard. Being a transcendent serpent, he was able by various transformations and marvellous feats to keep his enemies at bay and inflict injuries upon them until finally vanquished by Yang Chien 楊 戩.

Shê-mo Wang 蛇 魔 王, the serpent-king of devils, was a spirit of fire metamorphosed into a serpent. He and the tortoise-king of devils were chained up by Chen Wu's 眞 武 (*q.v.*) orders in a cave, but Yü Ti 玉 帝 took pity on them, ordered them to be set free, and bestowed on the serpent-devil the title of Marshal.

SHEEP, THE GOD OF.—The Sheep-god's name is Huang

Ch'u-p'ing (皇) 黄初平, and he lived near Hangchow 杭州,   SHÊN-HSIU
Chêkiang 浙江. "He told his brother his sheep were on the other
side of the hill, but the latter found only white stones. Huang
Ch'u-p'ing (皇) 黄初平 came and cried, 'Sheep, get up; sheep
get up,' when the whole mountain was covered with his flock. If
a shepherd wishes a large flock, or his sheep are feeble, he
worships the sheep-god" (Du Bose, pp. 324-5).

SHÊN 神.—Usually rendered as spirit, divine, god, without
distinction of its two main uses as indicated below. A term,
dating from the Chou 周 Period, in its original form meaning
lightning. Defined in the *P'ei wên yün fu* 佩文韻府 as *ling* 靈,
spirit. In this work the word is found as an abstract noun, as a
concrete noun, and as an adjective. In the abstract sense the word
means spirit, most frequently the human spirit. In the concrete
sense, it denotes spectre, ghost, genie, and spirit. No instance
justifies the translation "God" in the Christian sense, which has
been given to it by numerous foreign writers. The essence of the
word is thus spirit, whether abstract or concrete, intelligence,
mind, etc., and inscrutable, unfathomable, miraculous, etc., as
though the work of spiritual beings.

A distinction must be made between *shên* 神 during life and
shên 神 after death. The former is one of the *San Hun* 三魂,
the Three Spiritual Energies, which the living man derives from
his *yang* 陽 constituent (his other constituent being his *yin* 陰,
from which he derives the *Ch'i P'o* 七魄, Seven Emotions). The
latter is the result of the separation on death of these *hun* 魂 and
p'o 魄, the *shên* 神 then becoming a spirit, genie, etc., ghost, or
god. (Werner, *The Chinese Idea of the Second Self*).

The *shên* 神 or gods naturally form two distinct categories:
those which inhabit human bodies or have inhabited them—the
souls of living and dead men—and all the rest, forming, in the
widest sense, parts of the universe.. In effect, each member of the
human race, since he has a *shên* 神, is a god, and each god may
become a man by descending into a human body. A man may
be a powerful god if the *shên* 神 or soul which dwells in him be
powerful, in a flourishing state; or, we might say, if the *yang* 陽
substance, composing his soul, be abundant. In fact, to the
Chinese there is no question at all that many a man may, for this
reason, exercise power over the gods, and bend the gods to his
will. The means by which he may do so are numerous; they
may be comprised in the terms worship, invocation, magic. The
term *shên-hsien* 神仙 signifies apotheosized genii or "immortal"
spirits who have left the earth for the Three Islands of the Blessed.
—See De-Groot, *Religion;* Wieger, *Histoire des Croyances,* etc.

SHÊN-HSIU 神秀.—A saintly Buddhist monk. Seventh
century A.D. One of those invited to the annual banquet of the
gods (see *Hsi Wang-mu* 西王母). A native of Wei-hsih Hsien

417

尉 氏 縣. At first a Confucian scholar. Obtained the B.A. degree, but subsequently joined the Buddhist Brotherhood. A contemporary of Hui Nêng 慧 能 (see *Patriarchs*). Was appointed by Kuan Ti 觀 帝, the God of War, guardian of Buddhist temples, thus making him fulfil the functions of a *chia-lan* 伽 藍 (*q.v.*).

SHÊN HSIU-CHIH 沈 秀 之.—A recent god of medicine, worshipped from A.D. 1913 in the Island of Ts'ung-ming 崇 明 and in the country to the S.E. of Hai-mên 海 門. A physician apotheosized by the people for having opposed the authorities and saved them from the extortions of the salt and opium monopolists. Was eventually slain in the temple of Kuan Ti 關 帝, where he had taken refuge, selling his life dearly in a brave fight.

In 1914, the authorities endeavoured to stop the worship performed at his grave by the people by transferring his corpse to the criminals' burying-ground. This proving ineffectual, they weighted it with stones and cast it into the sea. Nevertheless, the people continue to venerate his image in their houses and to make pilgrimages to the shrine where his tablet is exposed.—See also *T'ien I-yüan* 天 醫 院.

SHÊN I 神 羿 (翼).—The Divine Archer. The Emperor Yao 堯, in the twelfth year of his reign (2436 B.C.), one day, while walking in the streets of Huai-yang 淮 陽, met a man carrying a bow and arrows, the bow being bound round with a piece of red stuff. This was Ch'ih-chiang Tzŭ-yü 赤 將 子 輿. He told the Emperor he was a skilful archer and could fly in the air on the wings of the wind. Yao 堯, to test his skill, ordered him to shoot one of his arrows at a pine-tree on the top of a neighbouring mountain. Ch'ih 赤 shot an arrow which transfixed the tree, and then jumped on to a current of air to go and fetch the arrow back. Because of this the Emperor named him Shên I 神 羿, "the Divine Archer," attached him to his suite, and appointed him Chief Mechanician of all Works in Wood. He continued to live only on flowers.

Shên I's 神 羿 great exploits were his vanquishing the Wind-god, dispelling the Nine False Suns, after marrying Ch'ang-O 嫦 娥, the sister of the Water-spirit, slaying various dangerous creatures, building a palace for Chin Mu 金 母, killing Chisel-tooth, visiting the moon after his wife had fled thither, and building a palace for her, where he visited her on the fifteenth day of every moon. On returning to his solar kingdom, he built a wonderful palace, and from that time the sun and moon each had their ruling sovereign. This regime dates from 2309 B.C., the forty-ninth year of Yao's 堯 reign.

When the old Emperor was informed that Shên I 神 羿 and his wife had both gone up to Heaven he was much grieved to lose the man who had rendered him such valuable service, and bestowed upon him the posthumous title of Tsung Pu 總 部,

"Governor of Countries." In the representations of this god and goddess the former is shown holding the sun, the latter the moon. The Chinese add the sequel that Ch'ang O 嫦娥 became changed into a toad, whose outline is traceable on the moon's surface.—See Werner, *Myths,* pp. 180-88.

SHÊN KÊNG 沈 庚.—The god of the constellation Ching 井. Alternatively with Yao Ch'i 姚 期.

SHÊN-KUANG 神光.—A.D. 487-593. A saintly Buddhist monk. One of those invited to the annual banquet of the gods (see *Hsi Wang-mu* 西 王 母). The second patriarch of Chinese Buddhism. Died at the age of 107 years.—See *Patriarchs.*

SHÊN LI 申 禮.—The god of the star T'ien-pai 天 敗.—See *T'ien-kang* 天 罡.

SHÊN LUNG 神 龍.—The spiritual or divine dragon.—See *Lung Wang* 龍 王.

SHÊN NUNG 神農. — 2838-2698 B.C. The Divine Husbandman, the title attributed to the successor of Fu-hsi 伏羲 (2953-2838 B.C.). Said in the *San-huang pên-chi* 三 皇 本 記 to have been the son of a princess named An-têng 安 登, who conceived through the influence of a heavenly dragon and bore her child, the future sovereign, near the Chiang-shui 姜 水, River Chiang 江, whence he derived his surname. Also called Liehshan Shih 烈 山 氏, of the Lieh-shan 烈 山 Clan, *i.e.* Mount Lieh 烈, where he is said to have lived. Personal name I-ch'i 伊 耆. He reigned by the influence of the agent Fire, and is consequently entitled Yen Ti 炎 帝. He first fashioned timber into ploughs, and taught the people the art of husbandry. He discovered the curative virtues of plants, and instituted the practice of holding markets for the exchange of commodities. The extension of the eight diagrams of Fu Hsi 伏 羲 to the number of sixty-four symbols —*liu-shih-ssŭ kua* 六 十 四 卦—is likewise attributed to him.

The Blue Bird is a metamorphosis of the daughter of Shênnung Huang-ti 神 農 黃 帝, who was drowned when crossing the sea to join Ch'ih Sung-tzŭ 赤 松 子. She was changed into a blue bird, and set herself the task of filling up the sea by casting all sorts of things into it. Wang-mu Niang-niang 王 母 娘 娘 (*q.v.*) took pity on her and appointed her caretaker of her garden.

Shên Nung 神 農 is one of the Gods of Apothecaries, he being the first to analyze the useful and harmful properties of plants.— See also *T'ieh-kuai Li* 鐵 拐 李, *Huo Pu* 火 部, *Shê Chi* 社 稷, *Ssŭ Sê* 司 嗇, *Tsao Chün* 灶 (竈) 君, and *Yao Pu* 藥 部.

SHÊN NUNG HUANG-TI 神農黃帝.—See *Shên Nung* 神 農.

SHÊN PAO 神寶.—See *San Ch'ing* 三清, *Lao Tzŭ* 老子, *T'ai Ch'ing* 太清, and *Ling-pao T'ien-tsun* 靈寶天尊.

SHÊN T'U 神茶. YÜ LEI 鬱壘.—In some districts called Shên Shu, Yü Lü. The Door-gods or Door-Spirits. The Protectors of Doors. Also the God of Windows. Originated from one of the five sacrifices of the home. At first it was just the sacrifice to the door. An old legend relates that in the earliest times there grew on Mount Tu-shuo 度朔, in the Eastern Sea, a peach-tree of fabulous size whose branches covered an area of several thousand square *li* 里. The longest branches, which inclined toward the north-east, formed the Door of the Devils (*kuei* 鬼), through which millions of them passed in and out. Two spirits, named Shên T'u 神茶 (or T'u Yü 茶與) and Yü Lei 鬱壘 had been instructed to guard this passage. Those who had done wrong to mankind were immediately bound by them and given over to be devoured by tigers. When Huang Ti 黃帝 heard of this he had the portraits of the two spirits painted on peach-wood tablets and hung above the doors to keep off evil spirits. This led to the suspension of the small figures or plaques on the doors of the people generally. Gradually they were supplanted by paintings on paper pasted on the doors, showing the two spirits armed with bows, arrows, spears, etc., Shên T'u 神茶 on the left, Yü Lei 鬱壘 on the right. In course of time these deities came to be referred to simply as Mên Shên 門神 (*q.v.*), Door-spirits or Door-gods.

These two gods differ from those whose pictures are painted on the doors in front of yamêns and temples. The latter were ministers of state in the T'ang 唐 dynasty, their names being Yü-ch'ih Ching-tê 尉遲敬德 or Yü-ch'ih-kung 尉遲公 (or 恭; *i.e.* Hu Ching-tê 胡敬德) (尉 is pronounced Wei when not a surname), and Ch'in Shu-pao 秦叔寶 (Ch'in Ch'iung 秦瓊), respectively. For the legend see *Mên Shên* 門神, and *Fêng-shên pang* 封神榜.

Other door-gods are Wei Chêng 魏徵 and Wên 溫 (? Wên Yüan-shuai 溫元帥) and Yo 岳 (? Yo O-wang 岳鄂王).

SHÊN-TSAN CH'AN-SHIH 神讚禪師.—See *Lo-han* 羅漢.

SHÊN WAN-SAN 沈萬三.—See *Ts'ai Shên* 財神.

SHÊN YÜEH 沈約.—A celebrated T'u Ti 土地 (*q.v.*).

SHÊNG CH'AN KUEI 生產鬼.—The Demon of Maternity.

SHÊNG JÊN 聖人.—Saints. The highest class of deified mortals. They dwell in the highest region, the Pearly Azure (Yü Ch'ing 玉清) Heaven of Yüan-shih T'ien-tsun 元始天尊 (*q.v.*). —See also *Chên Jên* 眞人 and *Hsien Jên* 仙人.

SHÊNG-KU 聖 (昇) 姑.—A female magician named Li 李, who lived in the time of the T'ang 唐 dynasty. She was credited with being able to walk on water. Her husband put her to death, but her corpse retained its freshness and natural tint for seven centuries. If those who came to pray to her were wanting in respect, they were punished on their return journey by having their boats overturned or delayed by violent winds. Her body was daily bathed, her hair brushed, and her hands manicured. "Her skin is fresh, she appears as if sleeping, she has become immortal." The local topography states that in the reign of the Emperor Tai Tsung 代宗 (A.D. 763-80) of the T'ang 唐 dynasty her tomb was in an enclosure of the Shêng-ku 昇姑 temple on Tung-t'ing Shan 洞庭山, Tung-t'ing Mountain, in T'ai Hu 太湖, Lake T'ai. The priests in charge affirmed that she seemed to be alive, but discouraged inspection, saying that over-curiosity would bring calamity. A certain Li Ch'i-lang 李七郎, however, having been bold enough to open the coffin, saw nothing but a skeleton.

Another legend of a similar character states that Wang Piao-chih 王彪也, an official of the Emperor Mu Ti 穆帝 (A.D. 345-62), who died in A.D. 377 in the reign of the Emperor Hsiao-wu Ti 孝武帝 (A.D. 373-97) of the Chin 晉 dynasty, and was known as White-beard Wang 王 because at the age of 20 his hair and beard were already white, had two daughters. The elder, Shêng-shih 聖始, and the younger, Su-ku 素姑, made shoes of mulberry-tree wood and walked on the water without getting wet. They were accordingly apotheosized and temples erected in their honour. —See also *Composite Deities*.

SHÊNG MU 聖母.—The Goddess of Sorcery (*wu* 筮).—See *Pi-hsia Yüan-chün* 碧霞元君.

SHÊNG [HSING]-NIEN CH'AN-SHIH 省念禪師 (42nd generation).—A deified Buddhist monk. Ranked fifteenth in Buddhist School, III (*q.v.*). Secular name Ti 狄. A native of Lai-chou 萊州, Shantung 山東. Studied in the school of Yen-chao Ch'an-shih 延沼禪師 (*q.v.*). Lived at Shou Shan 首山 until his death in A.D. 993.

SHIH 氏, THE GOD OF THE CONSTELLATION.—See *Chia Fu* 賈復 and *Kao-ping Tao-jên* 高丙道人.

SHIH 室, THE GOD OF THE CONSTELLATION.—See *Kêng Shun* 耿純 and *Kao Chên* 高震.

SHIH-CH'Ê-CH'ÊNG CH'AN-SHIH 石車乘禪師 (68th generation).—A deified Buddhist monk. Ranked fifty-first in Buddhist School, III (*q.v.*). Family name Chu 朱. A native of Chin-hua 金華, Chêkiang 浙江. Studied in the school of Yüan-wu Ch'an-shih 圓悟禪師 (*q.v.*), and afterwards started his own school at Chin-su 金粟, where he taught with great success.

SHIH-CHI NIANG-NIANG 石磯娘娘.—The goddess of the star Yüeh-yu 月遊. Enlisted to avenge the death of her disciple Pi-yün T'ung-êrh 碧雲童兒, slain by No-cha 哪吒, but was in her turn slain by his magic mirror. She then transformed herself into the transcendent stone, Shih-t'ou Ching 石頭精.

SHIH-CH'I-YÜN CH'AN-SHIH 石奇雲禪師 (68th generation.)—A deified Buddhist monk. Ranked fifty-fourth in Buddhist School, III (*q.v.*). A native of T'ai-ts'ang 太倉. Attended the school of Yüan-wu Ch'an-shih 圓悟禪師 (*q.v.*), then withdrew for the remainder of his life to Hsüeh-tou Shan 雪竇山, Snowdrift Mountain.

SHIH-CHIA FO 釋迦佛.—Sakyamuni.—See *Sakyamuni* and *San Pao* 三寶.

SHIH-CHIA-WÊN 釋迦文.—See *Fo* 佛.

SHIH-CHIA-MOU-NI 釋迦牟尼.—See *Fo* 佛.

SHIH CH'IEN 時遷.—One of the Gods of Brigands. A celebrated brigand, a native of Kao-t'ang Chou 高唐州, Shantung 山東. Known for his wonderful skill in burglary. Was a confederate of Sung Chiang 宋江. A temple was erected to him at Hangchou (Hangchow) 杭州, Chêkiang 浙江.—See also *Wu-tao Chiang-chün* 五盜將軍, *Liu Chih* 柳跖, and *Sung Chiang* 宋江.

SHIH CH'IH 視赤.—See *Shui Fu* 水府, C (2) (c).

SHIH-CH'IN 世親.—See *Shih-ch'in P'u-sa* 世親菩薩.

SHIH-CH'IN P'U-SA 世親菩薩 (Vasubandu), *i.e.* the Bodhisattva, Kindred with the World. Also known as Fa-sou P'an-t'ou 法藪盤頭, P'o-sou P'an-tou 婆藪婆豆, Tai-su P'an-tu 伐蘇婆度, P'o-hsiu P'an-t'ou 婆修盤頭, in Chinese Shih-ch'in 世親 or T'ien-chin 天親.—A deified Buddhist monk. Ranked first in Buddhist School, XIII (*q.v.*). Family name Chiao-shih-chia [ka] 嬌尸迦. A native of Radjagriha. A disciple of Nagardjuna (*q.v.*) and, like him, a teacher of the Amitabha doctrine. Laboured until A.D. 117 in Ayodhya (Oude) as twenty-first (or twenty-second) patriarch. Author of thirty-six works. Younger brother of Wu-chê 無著 (Asangha; *q.v.*).

SHIH-ÊRH TA-T'IEN SHIH 十二大天師.—The Twelve Divine Buddhist Teachers (Samantabhadra). (1) Wen-shu yen-k'ung 文殊眼空 (Manjusri); (2) P'u-hsien hsin-li 普賢心離 (Samantabhadra); (3) P'u-yen fa-chieh 普眼法界; (4) Chin-kang-tsan ch'i-hsi 金剛藏起息; (5) Mi-lo shên-chih 彌勒身智 (Maitreya); (6) Ch'ing-ching-hui shuo-fa 清靜慧說法; (7) Wei-tê san-kuan 威德三觀; (8) Pien-yin wu-kuan 辯音五觀; (9) Ching-yeh ch'u-wo 靜業除我; (10) P'u-chio tsê-fa 普覺擇法; (11) Yüan-chio k'o-ch'i 圓覺苤期; (12) Shan-shou chien-shê 善首彙攝.

SHIH-ÊRH TING CHIA-SHÊN 十二丁甲神.—The Twelve Cycle Genii of the Taoists. These are star-gods. There are sixty years in a cycle, and over each of these presides a special star-deity. The one worshipped is the one which gives light on the birthday of the worshipper, and therefore the latter burns candles before that particular image on each succeeding anniversary.

The Taoists' twelve protectors of the cycle—corresponding to the twelve yüan-chia 元甲 of the Buddhist priests and worshipped in a similar manner—are, however, formed on a somewhat different method. Instead of combining the shih kan 十干, ten celestial stems, with the shih-êrh chih 十二支, twelve terrestrial branches, they use only the two characters ting 丁 and chia 甲 of the former, combining the ting 丁 stem with the first six ti-chih 地支, terrestrial branches, and then the chia 甲 stem with the six last ones. They thus obtain six ting 丁 genii and six chia 甲 genii. There remains only for them to add to each combination the name of the genie. The result is shown in the following lists.

I. The six ting 丁 genii.

Name of cycle.		Name of person.	
Ting-mao Shên	丁卯神	Ssŭ-ma Ch'ing	司馬卿
Ting-chou Shên	丁丑神	Chao Tzŭ-jên	趙子壬
Ting-hai Shên	丁亥神	Chang Wên-t'ung	張文通
Tin-yu Shên	丁酉神	Tsang Wên-kung	臧文公
Ting-wei Shên	丁未神	Shih Shu-t'ung	石叔通
Ting-ssŭ Shên	丁巳神	Ts'ui Shih-ch'ing	崔石卿

II. The six chia 甲 genii.

Chia-tzŭ Shên	甲子神	Wang Wên-ch'ing	王文卿
Chia-hsü Shên	甲戌神	Chan Tzŭ-chiang	展子江
Chia-shên Shên	甲申神	Hu Wên-ch'ang	扈文長
Chia-wu Shên	甲午神	Wei Shang-ch'ing	衛上卿
Chia-ch'ên Shên	甲辰神	Mêng Fei-ch'ing	孟非卿
Chia-yin Shên	甲寅神	Ming Wên-chang	明文章

Generally these are all represented as masculine, but some Taoist writers describe the first six as feminine and the last six as masculine.

These cycle gods, who play an important part in the composition of charms and talismans, are represented by most grotesque images: "white, black, yellow, and red; ferocious gods with vindictive eyeballs popping out and gentle faces as expressive as a lump of putty; some looking like men and some like women." In one temple one of the sixty was in the form of a hog, and another in that of a goose. "Here is an image with arms protruding out of his eye-sockets, and eyes in the palms of his hands, looking downward to see the secret things within the earth. See that rabbit, Minerva-like, jumping from the divine head; again a mud-rat emerges from his occipital hiding-place, and lo! a snake comes coiling from the brain of another god—so the long line serves as models for an artist who desires to study the fantastic" (Du Bose).

SHIH-ÊRH YÜAN-CHIA 十二元甲.—The characters used in the cyclic computation of years (said to have been invented in 2637 B.C.) represent twelve gods, or genii, who preside over the year. They are represented in a sitting posture, holding in their hands the *hu* 笏 , or badge of honour distinctive of eminent personages. The process of deification is ascribed to Buddhism, which invented twelve genii as rulers of the cycle—the twelve *yüan-chia* 元甲 . (For an explanation of the Chinese or *yüan ch'ên* 元辰 cycle of 60 years see *Encyclopaedia Sinica,* p. 137, and Peter Huang, *A Notice of the Chinese Calendar,* p. 6.) Thus, the twelve cyclic symbols were deified, a god or genius presiding over each month, hour, and day, and being supposed to hear prayers, grant protection or special favours, and cure diseases.

The legend as to the origin of the "heavenly stems," *t'ien kan* 天干, and "earthly branches," *ti-chih* 地支, the combination of which forms the means of reckoning the cycle, is as follows:—The Heavenly Ruler, T'ien Huang 天皇 (*q.v.*), had 12 brothers, 10 of whom were kings, while the Earthly Ruler, Ti Huang 地皇, also had 10 brothers. Toward the close of his life, the former said to the latter: "Let us combine the brothers of our two families, and thus establish a chronological order for naming months, days and hours. [The symbols at first designated only days and hours. In the Han 漢 dynasty, 206 B.C., they were first used to mark years.] My 10 brothers will be the heavenly stems, and your 10 the earthly branches. But 2 are wanting to represent the series of the 12 months, so my 2 extra brothers may be taken to complete the cycle." The matter was thus arranged. The 10 brothers of the Heavenly Ruler became the heavenly stems, and the 10 brothers of the Earthly Ruler bcame the earthly branches, to which were added the 2 younger brothers of the Heavenly Ruler, thus completing the duodenary cycle of 12 months.

"It was Ta-nao 大撓 , Minister to Huang-ti 黃帝 (2698-2598 B.C.), who combincd the various symbols, and worked out this cumbrous system" (Mayers).

The names of the 12 Genii ruling the cycle are as follows:— SHIH-ÊRH
YÜAN-CHIA

I. The 10 Earthly Brothers.

Name of Genie.			*Earthly branch ruled.*	
1. K'un-tun	困	敦	Tzŭ	子
2. Ch'ih-fên-jo	赤	奮 若	Ch'ou	丑
3. Shê-t'i-ko	攝	提 格	Yin	寅
4. Tan-ô	單	閼	Mao	卯
5. Chih-hsü	執	徐	Ch'ên	辰
6. Ta-huang-lo	大	荒 落	Ssŭ	巳
7. Tsan-tsang	敦	牂	Wu	午
8. Hsieh-hsia	協	洽	Wei	未
9. Chün-t'an	涒	灘	Shên	申
10. Tso-ô	作	噩	Yu	酉

II. The 2 Brothers of the Heavenly Ruler.

11. Yen-mao	閹	茂	Hsü	戌
12. Ta-yüan-hsien	大	淵 獻	Hai	亥

III. The 10 Brothers of the Heavenly Ruler, forming the 10
heavenly stems, T'ien-kan 天 干.

Name of Genie.			*Heavenly stems ruled.*	
1. Ô-fêng	閼	逢	Chia	甲
2. Chên-mêng	旃	蒙	I	乙
3. Jou-chao	柔	兆	Ping	丙
4. Chiang-yü	疆	圉	Ting	丁
5. Chu-yung	著	雍	Wu	戊
6. T'u-wei	屠	維	Chi	己
7. Shang-chang	上	章	Kêng	庚
8. Chung-kuang	重	光	Hsin	辛
9. Hsüan-yi	玄	默	Jên	壬
10. Chao-yang	昭	陽	Kuei	癸

The names of these genii are employed constantly in Chinese
works, for indicating the year of the cycle; the Scholars and
chroniclers employ them also in dating official and other documents. The people use them generally in a superstitious manner,
with reference to births, deaths, marriages, and various important
events of life. Models of letter-writing contain full directions for
the use of these cyclic characters.

The cyclic characters are used also to denote the 12 Chinese
hours of the day, and the 12 points of the compass. A Chinese
hour corresponds to 2 hours according to European notation.

In the Imperial Calendar, *huang-li* 皇 歷, the first character
of the cycle, *chia-tzŭ* 甲 子, indicates the Genie who presides over
the year, and hence should be invoked on New Year's Day and
on other festivals, in order to enjoy happiness and prosperity.

Prayers for children are made before pictures of the 12 Cyclic Genii in Buddhist temples, known as "Halls of the Hundred children," *Po-tzŭ T'ang* 百子堂. The prayers are addressed to Chang Hsien 張仙, Chang the Immortal, or some other divinity. The child born in that cyclic year is placed under the special protection of the god who presides over it. It is usual with parents to inform their children of the name of the animal (tiger, dragon, rat, monkey, etc.) that influences the year (Doré; Kennelly; Hwang).

SHIH-FAN CH'AN-SHIH 師範禪師 (53rd generation.)—A deified Buddhist monk. Ranked twenty-ninth in Buddhist School, III (*q.v.*). Family name Yung 雍. A native of Tzü-chou 梓州, Ssŭch'uan 四川. He studied under Tsu-hsien Ch'an-shih 祖先禪師 (*q.v.*), and later taught at Ching Shan 徑山. Died A.D. 1248.

SHIH FÊN 石奮.—See *Wu Tou* 五斗.

SHIH HSIANG-KUNG 施相公.—A man who became a Spirit after being put to death on suspicion of possessing undesirable supernatural powers. Name Pai-ch'êng 伯成. Became a Spirit at nine years of age. Was canonized as Marquis by the Emperor Li Tsung 理宗 (A.D. 1225-65) of the Sung 宋 dynasty, the Ming 明 dynasty adding the title of Protector of the Realm and Guardian of the Seas. Many prodigies occur in the temples dedicated to him.

The legend relates that one day as he was walking on the mountain, he picked up an egg, from which emerged a serpent, which grew larger and took up its abode in a bamboo tube. Whilst he was absent in the capital in order to undergo the examination for his degree, the people of the place saw the serpent, in the form of a spirit in golden armour, in Shih Hsiang-kung's 施相公 house. It refused to be ousted, defending itself vigorously and succeeding in defeating their intention to slay it. When the local official brought his soldiers, it defeated them also. On Shih Hsiang-kung's 施相公 return, he informed them that it belonged to him and that they need have no fear. It obeyed when he ordered it to re-enter the tube. Thereupon the terrified local official memorialized the Emperor, saying that a man with such power would be capable of anything, and Shih Hsiang-kung 施相公 was immediately put to death.

In revenge, the serpent bit many people, and none was able to slay it. The local official accordingly requested the Emperor to bestow the above title—Marquis Protector of the Realm and Guardian of the Seas—on the deceased, and when this was done and proper sacrifices of loaves of the kind specially liked by the deceased offered, the serpent curled itself up on them and died.

At the present time, figures are made of a serpent coiled upon a loaf, which is commonly called the dragon's bread-plate. Shih Hsiang-kung 施相公, who is supposed to have lived in the latter part of the reign of the the Emperor Li Tsung 理宗 (*supra*), is known as "The Young General."

SHIH HSÜAN-HÊNG 石玄恒.—See *Wu Yo* 五嶽.

SHIH HU SHIH 石尸史.—The wife of the dragon-king, Chang Lung 張龍.

SHIH KAN-TANG 石敢當.—The Stone which dares to undertake (defence against malign influences). The Transcendent and Preservative Stone. The origin of the custom of placing this stone at places subject to evil influences is traced to the time of the Wei 衞, Chêng 鄭, Chou 周, and Ch'i 齊 feudal States, when certain residents of each of those States named Shih 石 adopted as their family motto the words *Kan-tang* 敢當, "Dare-all." The character *shih* 石 meaning stone, the combination was applied also to stones used for the above-mentioned purpose. The bravery originally existing in some courageous person is supposed to be transferred to this sculptured stone. The head of the stone is usually carved to represent a tiger's head on whose forehead is cut the character Wang 王, king. This is the royal transcendent tiger, the emblem of the power of the spirit-protector, Shih kan-tang 石敢當. A large number of these stones are engraved with an appeal to the protecting spirit of the Sacred Mountain of the East, T'ai Shan 泰山, the inscription then reading *T'ai Shan shih kan-tang* 泰山石敢當.

The use of these stones is mentioned as occurring in the T'ang 唐 dynasty, about A.D. 770, in the reign of the Emperor Tai Tsung, 代宗 (A.D. 763-80), and also in the reign-period A.D. 1041-9 of the Emperor Jên Tsung 仁宗 (A.D. 1023-64) of the Sung 宋 dynasty.

The custom of bestowing honorific titles (such as marquis) on stones as well as other inanimate objects has existed from the time of the earliest dynasties.

SHIH-K'OU CH'AN-SHIH 師備禪師 (40th generation.)—A deified Buddhist monk. Ranked fifteenth in Buddhist School, VI (*q.v.*). Family name Hsieh 謝. A native of Fukien 福建. Studied under I-ts'un Ch'an-shih 義存禪師 (*q.v.*), and practised great mortification. His teacher called him K'ou T'ou-t'o 傳頭陀, Kou, incarnation of T'ou-t'o. Opened a school with the monk Hsüan-sha 玄沙, who lived in the P'u-ying Ssŭ 普應寺, P'u-ying Monastery. Died A.D. 906, aged 70.

SHIH KUEI 施檜.—The god of the star T'ien-hsiung 天雄.—See *T'ien-kang* 天罡.

SHIH LIANG-SHIH 始梁時.—See *Tongue, The God of the.*

SHIH MING I 十明醫.—The Ten Celebrated Physicians, assessors of Yao Wang 葉王, the King of Medicines. They are: —

1. Chang Chi 張機.—Personal name Chung-ching 仲景. Born at Nan-yang 南陽, Honan 河南, during the reign-period Yüan-chia 元嘉 (A.D. 151-3) of the Emperor Hsiao Huan Ti 孝桓帝 (A.D. 147-68) of the Han 漢 dynasty. Was Prefect of Ch'angsha 長沙, Honan 河南. Taught by Yang Li-kung 陽勵功. Composed works on medicine. Effected celebrated cures of the Emperor and others, and was rewarded with office, but later resigned and went to live in seclusion on the mountain at Shaoshih 少室, where he wrote further medicinal treatises. His ultimate fate is unknown.

2. Huang Pu 皇甫.—A native of An-ting 安定, Shensi 陝西. Name Ching 靜. Personal name Shih-hung 士宏. The family name Huang 皇 was changed by imperial decree to Mi 謐. Lived in the time of the Tung Chin 東晉 dynasty (A.D. 317-420). Wrote on cauterization.

3. Ch'ien I 錢乙.—A native of Ch'ien-t'ang 錢塘, Chêkiang 浙江. Personal name Chung-yang 仲陽. Celebrated, in the time of the Sung 宋 dynasty, for his medicial skill and writings.

4. Chu Chên-hêng 朱震亨.—A native of I-wu 義烏, Chêkiang 浙江. Personal name Yen-hsiu 彦修. Taught by Hsü Chien 許謙. Famous as a physician and inventor of a new method, during the reign-period A.D. 1333-41 of the Emperor Shun Ti 順帝 (A.D. 1333-68) of the Yüan 元 dynasty. Kuei Ku-tzŭ 鬼谷子 (q.v.) appeared to him in a vision, taught him some medical secrets, and changed his name to Tan Hsi-shêng 丹溪生.

5. T'ao Hua 陶華.—A native of Yü-hang 餘杭, Chêkiang 浙江. Also known as Shang Wên 尚文 and Chieh Yen 節菴. A famous physician and medical writer of the Ming 明 dynasty.

6. Wang Shu-ho 王叔和.—A native of Kao-p'ing 高平, Shansi 山西. A member of the Academy of Medicine under the Chin 晉 dynasty, and a noted medical author.

7. Liu Wan-su 劉完素.—A Ho-chien 河間, Chihli 直隸, scholar and medical writer in the time of the Kin 金 dynasty. Often called Shou Chên 守眞.

8. Li Kao 李杲.—A native of Chên-ti 鎮地, near Tung-yüan 東垣, Honan 河南. Named Ming-chih 明之. Lived during the reign of the Emperor Shun Ti 順帝 (A.D. 1333-68). Famous as a writer on medicine, and commentator and continuator of the works of Chang Chi 張機 (supra).

9. Wu Shu 吳恕.—A native of Jên-ho 仁和, Chêkiang 浙江. Personal names Ju-hsin 如心 and Mêng-ch'i 蒙齊. A medical writer under the Yüan 元 dynasty.

10. Hsieh Chi 薛巳.—A native of Wu-chün 吳中, Kiangsu 江蘇. Personal names Hsin-pu 新甫 and Li-chai 立齋. A celebrated physician and surgeon of the Ming 明 dynasty.—See also T'ien I-yüan 天醫院.

SHIH NIANG 十娘.—See Ch'ing-wa Shên 青蛙神.

SHIH-O 十惡, THE GOD OF THE STAR.—See Chou Hsin 周信.

SHIH PA KUNG (CHING CHIEH) 十八公 (勁節).—See Wu Lao 五老.

SHIH-PA LO-HAN 十八羅漢.—See Lo-han 羅漢.

SHIH SHU-T'UNG 石叔通.—See Hsüan t'ien Shang-ti 玄天上帝 and Shih-êrh t'ing-chia Shên 十二丁甲神.

SHIH TA T'IEN CHUN 卅十十尹   See Ch'ii hsieh Yüan 驅邪院.

SHIH TA TUNG T'IEN 十大洞天.—The ten great Cave-Heavens of Taoist mythology. Serve as dwelling places of the genii of earth. Situated in ten of the mountains of China. Each is presided over by a Taoist Immortal. There are said to be thirty-six smaller Cave-heavens, situated in other mountains, and many legends are narrated concerning these mystic abodes.

SHIH TÊ 拾得.—See Ho Ho (êrh hsien) 和合 (二仙).

SHIH-TÊ TZǓ 拾得子.—See Lo-han 羅漢.

SHIH-T'I CH'AN-SHIH 師體禪師 (49th generation).—A deified Buddhist monk. Ranked thirty-seventh in Buddhist School, VI (q.v.). A disciple of Sêng-pao Ch'an-shih 僧寶禪師 (q.v.). "One day, as a sparrow was picking up some grains in the yard of the monastery, the young novice clapped his hands to frighten it away. His teacher thereupon gave him a slap, which suddenly illumined him, so that he was able to understand the doctrine of the Law" (cf. I-hsüan Ch'an-shih 義玄禪師). He lived ten years in the monastery.

SHIH-TIEN YEN-WANG 十殿閻王.—The Ten Demon-Rulers (or kings) of Hades. Lit. The Ten Palaces of Kings of Hell.

SHIH-T'OU 石頭.—See Patriarchs: Hui Nêng 慧能.

SHIH-TZǓ KUO 獅子國.—The Lion Kingdom. A rendering of the Sanskrit Sinhala or Simhala, whence Singhalese. A kingdom in Ceylon, founded by Simha Sêng Ho 僧訶 or Seng Chia 僧伽 or Shih Tzŭ 獅子, a merchant of Ceylon, who was ensnared by Avalokitesvara (appearing as a magic horse). One Rakchasi having followed him to India and slain the king of that country, Simhala, his son, succeeded to the throne, led an army to Ceylon and destroyed all the Rakchasis there.

SHIH-TZŬ-PI-CH'IU TSUN-CHÊ 獅子比丘尊者. — See *Lo-han* 羅漢.

SHIH-TZŬ WANG CHIA-LO 獅子王迦羅.—See *Lo-han* 羅漢.

SHIH-WEI CH'AN-SHIH 時蔚禪師 (58th generation).—A deified Buddhist monk. Ranked thirty-sixth in Buddhist School, III (*q.v.*). Family Chin 金. A native of Lo-ch'ing 樂清, in Wên-chou 溫州, Chêkiang 浙江. Studied under Yüan-chang Ch'an-shih 元長禪師 (*q.v.*). Died A.D. 1381.

SHIH-YÜ CHANG-LI 是禹帳里.—See *Shui Fu* 水府, C (2) (c).

SHIH YÜAN-SHUAI 石元帥.—Generalissimo Shih 石. His father's name was Wên Fu 文甫, and his mother's Han 韓. He was born in 833 B.C. in Hsiang-ch'i 相溪, Kansu 甘肅, amid auspicious signs in the heavens, and was named Shên-yü 神毓. He studied in Kuan-chung 關中, Shensi 陝西, under Yin Yü 尹于.

After he had settled at Mei Shan 眉山 he was besought by the peasants to find a means of ending the severe drought. He bathed, changed his clothes, burnt incense, and prayed with the people, whereupon rain fell. During the prayer he was suddenly changed into an Immortal, his clothes only remaining on the spot where he had been.

He was reported to have been seen by some travellers riding toward the east, with an escort of a hundred standard-bearers, and begged the travellers to thank the people and say that Yü Ti 玉帝 had entrusted him with an important mission.

Shang Ti 上帝 granted him the office of Overseer of the Ministry of Thunder, with the duty of rewarding the good and punishing the bad.

SHINING-GOLD IMMORTAL, THE.—See *Chin-kuang Hsien* 金光仙.

SHOE MAKERS.—These sacrifice to Sun Pin 孫臏.

"SHORT-LIFE."—See *Mêng P'o* 孟婆.

SHOU CH'ANG 壽長.—See *Hair, The God of the*.

SHOU CHÊN 守眞.—See *Shih Ming-i* 十 明 醫, 7.

SHOU HSING 壽 星.—The Star of Longevity. The God of
Longevity. First a stellar deity, later on represented in human
form. It was a constellation formed of the two star-groups
Chio 角 and K'ang 亢, the first two on the list of twenty-
eight constellations. Because of this precedence it was called the
Star of Longevity. When it appears the nation enjoys peace,
when it disappears there will be war. Ch'in Shih Huang-ti 秦 始
皇 帝, the First Emperor, was the first to offer sacrifices to this
star, the Old Man of the South Pole, at Shê-po 社 毫, in 246 B.C.
Since then the worship has been continued pretty regularly until
modern times.

But desire for something more concrete, or at least more personal, than a star led to the god's being represented as an old man.
Connected with this is a long legend which turns on the point
that after the father of Chao Yen 趙 顏 had been told by the
celebrated physiognomist Kuan Lo 管 輅 that his son would not
live beyond the age of nineteen, the transposition from *shih-chiu*
十 九, nineteen, to *chiu-shih* 九 十, ninety, was made by one of
two gamblers, who turned out to be the Spirit of the North Pole,
who fixes the time of decease, as the Spirit of the South Pole does
that of birth.

The deity is a domestic god, of happy mien, with a very high
forehead, usually spoken of as Shou-hsing Lao T'ou-tzŭ 壽 星
老 頭 子, "Longevity Star Old-pate," and is represented as riding
a stag, with a flying bat above his head. He holds in his hand
a large peach, and attached to his long staff are a gourd and a
scroll. The stag and the bat both indicate *fu* 福, happiness. The
peach, gourd, and scroll are symbols of longevity. Sometimes he
is represented as travelling in the rain.

Two small images, five or six inches in height, are sometimes
placed by the side of incense-burners in temples. They are called
Shou-shan fu-hai 壽 山 福 海, *i.e.* longevity as high as a mountain,
happiness as deep as the sea, and are the images of the two Spirits
of Longevity and Happiness. It was deemed best thus to divide
them into two, instead of combining them into one. The two
titles represent P'êng Tsu 彭 祖 and Fu Hai 福 海, respectively.

P'êng Tsu 彭 祖, the Patriarch P'êng 彭, a legendary person,
the Taoist Mathuselah, the type of longevity, was a distant
descendant of the Emperor Chuan Hsü 顓 頊 (2514-2436 B.C.).
His father was Lu Chung 陸 終. Having become an orphan at
three years of age, and a refugee to Hsi-yü 西 域 for ten years,
he later so efficiently served the Emperors Yao 堯 and Yü 虞
(Shun 舜) that he was granted the fief of P'êng 彭. His
instructor in "the knowledge of the doctrine" was Pai Shih 百 石,
who lived on Yün-mu Shan 雲 母 山, and had the appearance of
a man of forty years of age. But when asked his age by Pêng Tsu
彭 祖 he replied that he had already lived two thousand years

before P'êng 彭 was born. P'êng 彭 at that time was seven hundred and sixty years of age. He afterwards became, in 1324 B.C., a high officer of State, but he preferred to retire and, in 1258 B.C., eloped with a lady of the palace named Ts'ai-nü 采女 to Nan-mên Shan 南門山, Southgate Hill, and married her after changing his name to Yen-shêng Tzŭ-kao 延生子高. They had two sons: Wu 武 and I 夷. He married nineteen women, and survived fifty-four sons, having lived about a thousand years. The mountain where he made his home was named Wu-i Shan 武夷山 after the first two.—See also *Wu Tou* 五斗.

SHOU I-CH'ÜN 壽逸羣.—See *Wu Yo* 五嶽.

SHOU-SHAN FU-HAI 壽山福海.—See *Shou Hsing* 壽星.

SHOU SHÊN 守神.—See *Mouth, The Gods of the.*

SHOU-TUAN CH'AN-SHIH 守端禪師 (46th generation). —A deified Buddhist monk. Ranked twenty-first in Buddhist School, III (*q.v.*). Family name Ko 葛. A native of Hêng-yang 衡陽. Studied in the school of Fang-hui Ch'an-shih 方會禪師 (*q.v.*). Known as Wu-tsu 五祖, the Fifth Patriarch. Died A.D. 1072, aged 48.—See *Yüan-miao Ch'an-shih* 原妙禪師.

SHRAMANA, S'RAMANA.—Shramanas are disciples of Buddha. Chinese *sha-mên* 沙門; also *sang-mên* 桑門; *ho-shang* 和佝. Shramana means the "quieting of the passions"; in Chinese *hsi-hsin* 息心, restful, or to put the mind at rest, or *chih-hsi* 止息, to stop the breath. *Bikshu* (*q.v.*) is one of the names given to the followers of Buddha generally. *Sha-mên* 沙門 originated in Kashiapmadanga, "the most ancient of translators," using *sha-mên* 沙門 in the "Sutra of Forty-two Sections," and "thus originating that name, to be used ever after as the designation of the members of the Buddhist community in China" (Edkins, p. 416). The term is explained by *ch'u-chia jên* 出家人, *lit.* monastics, or by *chin-lao* 勤勞, *lit.* toiling, or as above. Ascetics of all denominations. Buddhist monks and priests who "have left their families and quitted the passions."—See also *Lo-han* 羅漢.

SHU-CHÜN 叔均.—See *Shê Chi* 社稷.

SHU KUNG 樞公.—See *Knee, The God of the.*

SHU-PO-CHIA 戊博迦.—See *Lo-han* 羅漢.

SHU-YÜAN 屬原.—See *Shui Fu* 水府, V, a, 1.

SHUANG I 雙以.—See *Kidneys, The Gods of the.*

SHUI-CHING TZǓ 水精子.—See *Wu Lao* 五老.

SHUI FANG 水 防.—The God of Embankments and Dykes. One of the eight categories of beings or genii who can assist or retard the growth of crops.—*Cf. Shui Yung* 水 鄘, *Hsien Nung* 先 農, etc., and See *Shui Fu* 水 府.

SHUI FU 水 府.—The Treasury (or Palace) of Waters. The main divisions of this Ministry are:—A. The Supreme Council. —B. The Body of Ministers.—C. Ministry of Salt Waters, comprising (1) The General Department of Salt Waters (presided over by four dragon-kings). (2) The Special Department of Salt Waters.—D. The Department of Sweet Waters, comprising (1) Spirits of the Four Great Watercourses, (2) Spirits of Various Bodies of Water, (3) Spirits of Indefinite Jurisdiction, and (4) Shui-mu Niang-niang 水 母 娘 娘, the Old Mother of the Waters.

A. The Supreme Council.—The President is the Dragon-saint, Honoured of the Heavens of the Dawn and Greatly Venerated Cavern, of the Luminous Valley, of the Rising Sun.

B. The Body of Ministers is composed of the Dragon-kings of the Four Seas:—(1) Kuang-tê Lung-wang Ta-ti 廣 德 龍 王 大 帝, the Dragon-king of the Eastern Sea; (2) Kuang-li Lung-wang Ta-ti 廣 利 龍 王 大 帝, the Dragon-king of the Southern. Sea; (3) Kuan-jun Lung-wang Ta-ti 廣 潤 龍 王 大 帝, the Dragon-king of the Western Sea; and (4) Kuang-tsê Lung-wang Ta-ti 廣 澤 龍 王 大 帝, the Dragon-king of the Northern Sea.

C. The Ministry of Salt Waters.

(1) General Department of Salt Waters.

(*a*) Yang Hou 陽 侯, a Marquis of the Yang 陽 State, who was drowned, and became the Spirit of the Sea. Is also referred to as the Genie of the Waves.

Ch'in-shih Huang-ti 秦 始 皇 帝, the First Emperor's, visit to this genie is described as follows:—Po-shih 博 士, a Taoist priest, told the Emperor that an enormous oyster vomited from the sea a mysterious substance which accumulated in the form of a tower, and was known as "the market of the sea" (Chinese for "mirage"). Every year, at a certain period, the breath from his mouth was like the rays of the sun. The Emperor expressed a wish to see it, and Po-shih 博 士 said he would write a letter to the God of the Sea, and the next day the Emperor could behold the wonderful sight.

The Emperor then remembered a dream he had had the year before in which he saw two men fighting for the sun. The one killed the other, and carried it off. He therefore wished to visit the country where the sun rose. Po-shih 博 士 said that all that was necessary was to throw rocks into the sea and build a bridge across them. Thereupon he rang his magic bell, the earth shook, and rocks began to rise up; but as they moved too slowly he struck them with his whip, and blood came from them which left red marks in many places. The row of rocks extended as far as the shore of the sun-country but to build the bridge across them was found to be beyond the reach of human skill.

So Po-shih 博 士 sent another messenger to the God of the Sea, requesting him to raise a pillar and place a beam across it which could be used as a bridge. The submarine spirits came and placed themselves at the service of the Emperor, who asked for an interview with the god. To this the latter agreed on condition that no one should make a portrait of him, he being very ugly. Instantly a stone gangway 100,000 feet long rose out of the sea, and the Emperor, mounting his horse, went with his courtiers to the palace of the god. Among his followers was one Lu Tung-shih 魯 董 師, who tried to draw a portrait of the god by using his foot under the surface of the water. Detecting this manœuvre, the god was incensed, and said to the Emperor: "You have broken your word; did you bring Lu 魯 here to insult me? Retire at once, or evil will befall you." The Emperor, seeing that the situation was precarious, mounted his horse and galloped off. As soon as he reached the beach, the stone causeway sank, and all his suite perished in the waves. One of the Court magicians said to the Emperor: "This god ought to be feared as much as the God of Thunder; then he could be made to help us. To-day a grave mistake has been made." For several days after this incident the waves beat upon the beach with increasing fury. The Emperor then built a temple and a pagoda to the god on Chih-fu Shan 之 罘 山 and Wên-têng Shan 文 登 山, respectively; by which act of propitiation he was apparently appeased.

(*b*) Ma-hsien 馬 銜, a Spirit of the Sea, represented as a uni-corned dragon.

(*c*) In a legend referring to the time of the Emperor Wu Tsung 武 宗 (A.D. 1506-22) of the Ming 明 dynasty, the Spirit of the Sea is represented as a bewitching young lady.

Ch'êng Tsai 程 宰, a native of An-hui 安 徽, having gone to Liao-yang 遼 陽, Shansi 山 西, and from being wealthy become poor, was forced to enter the service of a merchant. Twelve years later, during a violent storm, he went to bed and slept. On starting up from his sleep, he found his room lit up as bright as day, and saw three beautiful women with rose-coloured complexions, green hair, and fine head-dresses ornamented with blue feathers. They were accompanied by hundreds of hand-maids. One of the three approached his bed and requested him to let her live with him as his wife. The other two suddenly disappeared with all their followers. The one who remained said to Ch'êng 程 : "I am not an Immortal, I am the Spirit of the Sea. We are predestined to live together, and that is why I have come to seek you to-day."

At cock-crow she took her departure, but returned every night, disappearing at dawn.

(d) The Spirit of the Sea, according to another legend, is named Chao Hung 晁 閎. Jui I 如 意, King of Chao, assuming a tangible form in order to avenge himself on Lü-shih 呂 氏 removed a tide-dam on the edge of Chiung Ch'ih 邛 池, Lake Chiung, thus causing the death of more than two thousand persons. This being reported by Chao Hung 晁 閎 to ShangTi 上 帝, the latter punished Jui I 如 意 by changing him into the dragon of Chiung Ch'ih 邛 池, removing from him all power over rain and lake waters, so that the lake began to dry up. The dragon, exposed to the rays of the sun and suffering internally from intense heat, found that a worm had formed under each of his 84,000 scales, which caused him intolerable torture.

One morning, the clouds were lit up by brilliant colours, and a person of noble bearing with violet-coloured hair and a face shining like the moon, appeared in them. The Spirits of the Mountains and the Waters bowed before him, the air was filled with the odour of fragrant incense, and a rain of flowers fell from the sky.

The dragon raised its head and implored the help of this transcendent being. The celestial troop informed him that he was the Buddha Shih-chia-wên 釋 迦 文, then on a mission to the East. The Buddha granted his prayer, on condition that he would give up all idea of vengeance and repair his fault. He was then allowed to be reborn in human form, in the house of Chang Yü 銀 禹, an official of Yang-chou 揚 州, Kiangsu 江 蘇. The new-born one was given the name of Chang Hsün 銀 勳, magistrate of Yang Chou 揚 州, and became magistrate of Ch'ing-ho Hsien 淸 河 縣, in the same province, where he acquired a reputation for benevolence and probity.

(2) Special Department of Salt Waters.

(a) The four Dragon-kings.—Each of the these exercises jurisdiction over one of the four seas.

The Shên-hsien t'ung-chien 神 仙 通 鑑, mentioning the Buddhist dragon-kings, Ao-kuang 敖 廣, Ao-ch'in 敖 欽, Ao-shun 敖 順, and Ao-jun 敖 潤, relates the following legend, describing the Taoists at war with the Buddhist enemy Ao-ch'in 敖 欽 and his armies:—Once the Eight Immortals (see Pa Hsien 八 仙) were on their way to Ch'ang-li Shan 長 離 山 to celebrate the birthday anniversary of Hsien Wêng 仙 翁, the God of Longevity. They had with them a servant who bore the presents they intended to offer to the god. When they reached the seashore the Immortals walked on the waves without any difficulty, but Lan Ts'ai-ho 藍 采 和 remarked that the servant was unable to follow them, and said that a means of transport must be found for him. So Ts'ao Kuo-chiu 曹國舅 took a plank of cypress-wood and made a raft. But when they were in mid-ocean a typhoon arose and upset the raft, and servant and presents sank to the bottom of the sea.

Regarding this as the hostile act of a water-devil, the Immortals said they must demand an explanation from the Dragon-king, Ao-ch'in 敖欽. Li T'ieh-kuei 李鐵拐 took his gourd, and, directing the mouth toward the bottom of the sea, created so brilliant a light that it illuminated the whole palace of the Sea-king. Ao-ch'in 敖欽, surprised, asked where this powerful light originated, and deputed a courier to ascertain its cause.

To this messenger the Immortals made their complaint. "All we want," they added, "is that the Dragon-king shall restore to us our servant and the presents." On this being reported to Ao-ch'in 敖欽 he suspected his son of being the cause, and, having established his guilt, severely reprimanded him. The young Prince took his sword, and, followed by an escort, went to find those who had made the complaint to his father. As soon as he caught sight of the Immortals he began to inveigh against them.

Han Hsiang-tzŭ 漢湘子, not liking this undeserved abuse, changed his flute into a fishing-line, and as soon as the Dragon-prince was within reach caught him on the hook, with intent to retain him as a hostage. The Prince's escort returned in great haste and informed Ao-ch'in 敖欽 of what had occurred. The latter declared that his son was in the wrong, and proposed to restore the shipwrecked servant and the presents. The Court officers, however, held a different opinion. "These Immortals," they said, "dare to hold captive Your Majesty's son merely on account of a few lost presents and a shipwrecked servant. This is a great insult, which we ask permission to avenge." Eventually they won over Ao-ch'in 敖欽, and the armies of the deep gathered for the fray. The Immortals called to their aid the other Taoist Immortals and Heroes, and thus two formidable armies found themselves face to face.

Several attempts were made by other divinities to avert the conflict, but without success. The battle was a strenuous one. Ao-ch'in 敖欽 received a ball of fire full on his head, and his army was threatened with disaster when Tz'ŭ-hang Ta-shih 慈航大士 appeared with his bottle of lustral water. He sprinkled the combatants with this magic fluid, using a willow-branch for the purpose, thus causing all their magic powers to disappear.

Shui Kuan 水官, the Ruler of the Watery Elements, then arrived, and reproached Ao-ch'in 敖欽 ; he assured him that if the matter were to come to the knowledge of Shang Ti 上帝, the Supreme Ruler, he would not only be severely punished, but would risk losing his post. Ao-ch'in 敖欽 expressed penitence, restored the servants and the presents, and made full apology to the Eight Immortals.

(b) The Spirits of the Four Seas: (1) O-ming 阿明, the Spirit of the Eastern Sea; (2) Chü-ch'êng 互乘, the Spirit of the Southern Sea; (3) Chu-liang 祝良, the Spirit of the Western Sea; (4) Yü-chiang 禺疆, the Spirit of the Northern Sea. These are but variations on the names given below under (e). Having borrowed the names of four of the Spirits of the Five Cardinal Points to form the Spirits of the Four Seas, the Taoists further transformed them into a new series:—O-ming 阿明 becoming Kou-mang 勾芒; Chü-ch'êng 互乘, Ju-shou 蓐收; and Yü-chiang 禺疆, Hsüan-ming 玄冥, making them Governors of the seas situated in the territories ruled over by them.

(c) Fêng Hsiu-ch'ing 馮修凊 is the sovereign lord of the Eastern Seas; his wife is Chu Yin-ê 朱隱娥. Shih-ch'ih 視赤, of the Southern Seas; his wife is I I-liao 翳逸寥. Kou-ta Ch'iu-po 勾大邱百, of the Western Seas; his wife is Ling Su-chien 靈素簡. Shih-yü Chang-li 是禺帳里, of the Northern Seas; his wife is Chieh Lien-ch'iao 結連翹.

(d) The Spirit Yü Hao 禺貔 (䝁), son of Yü Yang 禺陽, and grandson of Huang Ti 黃帝, lives on an island of the Eastern Sea. He has a human face set on a bird's body, two yellow serpents form his ear-rings, and two other serpents of the same colour form his footstool.

The Spirit Pu-t'ing Wei-yü 不廷口余 lives on an island of the Southern Sea. He has a human form, ear-rings of two blue serpents, and two red serpents as a foostool. He is also called Pu-fan Hu-yü 不返胡余.

The Spirit Yen Tzǔ 弇兹 lives on an island in the Western Sea. He has a human face, a bird's body, two azure serpents as ear-rings, and two red serpents as a footstool.

The Spirit Yü Ch'iang 禺疆 lives on an island in the Northern Sea. He has a human face and a bird's body, two azure serpents as ear-rings, and two red serpents as a footstool.

(e) Chu-jung 祝融 is the Spirit of the Southern Sea. Kou-mang 勾芒 is the Spirit of the Eastern Sea. Ju-shou 蓐收 is the Spirit of the Western Sea. Hsüan-ming 玄冥 is the Spirit of the Northern Sea. (See above, (b), and *Wu-fang Shêng* 五方神.)'

D. Department of Sweet Waters.

(1) Ssǔ-tu Shên 四瀆神.—The Spirits of the Four Water-courses. These are:—The Dragon-king Kuang-yüan 廣源, Lord of the Yang-tzǔ Chiang 揚子江, Yang-tzǔ River; the Dragon-king Ling-yüan 靈源, Lord of the Huang Ho 黃河, Yellow River; the Dragon-king Ch'ang-yüan 長源, Lord of the Huai Ho 淮河, River Huai, and the Dragon-king Ch'ing 凊, Lord of the Chi 濟, River Chi.

The Spirits have been personified as follows:—

(*a*) The Spirit of the Yang-tzǔ Chiang 揚子江 is Shu-yüan 屬原, of the Ch'u 楚 State, under which he held a high official post. Canonized under the T'ang 唐 and Sung 宋 dynasties. Under the Ming 明 dynasty he received the rank of Wang 王, King. His honorific posthumous title is Kuang-yüan Shun-chi Wang 廣源順濟王.

(*b*) The Spirit of the Yellow River is Ch'ên Hsü 陳胥, who lived under the Han 漢 dynasty. To the two-character title bestowed on him by the T'ang 唐 the Sung 宋 added two more, and under the Ming 明 he became a king with the posthumous title of Ling-yüan Hung-chi Wang 靈源宏濟王.

(*c*) The Spirit of the Huai 淮 River is Fei Yüeh 斐說, who lived under the T'ang 唐 dynasty, and was canonized under that and the Sung 宋 dynasty. The Ming 明 made him a king with the posthumous title of Ch'ang-yüan Chi-chi Wang 長源疾濟王.

(*d*) The Spirit of the Chi 濟 River is a high official of the Ch'u 楚 State (1078-223 B.C.). He received honorary titles from the T'ang 唐 and the Sung 宋 emperors, the Ming 明 granting him the rank of Wang 王, King, with the title Ch'ing-yüan Han-chi Wang 清源漢濟王.

(*e*) Certain Spirits and Spirits' Palaces are attached to these river dragon-gods. To those of the Yang-tzǔ Chiang 揚子江: Chi-hsiang 奇相, Chiang-nan Po 江南伯, Yang-tzǔ Chiang San-shui Fu 揚子江三水府. To those of the Huang Ho 黃河: Fêng-i 馮夷, Lü Kung-tzǔ 呂公子, Wu-i 無夷, Ping-i 冰夷, and the latter metamorphosed into a white dragon. To those of the Huai 淮: Wu Chih-ch'i 無 (or 巫) 支祁.

The legend relating to the latter is as follows:—In the course of his great work of conserving the land from floods, Ta Yü 大禹, the Great Yü, thrice visited T'ung-po Shan 桐柏山, Mount T'ung-po, where the Huai 淮 takes its rise, in order to regulate the course of that river. The Spirit of the river having raised such a storm that the work had to be given up, Yü 禹, infuriated, seized the Spirit of the Huai 淮 and one of its affluents, the Kuo 渦, the latter being named Wu Chi-ch'i 無 (or 巫) 支祁. He had the flattened face of a monkey, high forehead, grey hair, gold-coloured eyes in a white head, and snow-white teeth. His neck was more than a hundred feet long, and his strength was greater than that of nine elephants. He was a loquacious talker, and knew everything about the depth, etc., of all the places in the Huai 淮 and the Kuo 渦.

Yü 禹 handed him over to Hou Chi 后稷 (*q.v.*), who chained him by the neck to Kuei Shan 龜山, Mount Kuei, in Ssŭ Chou 泗州, Anhui 安徽, attaching a gold bell to his nose. From that time the Huai 淮 flowed peacefully on its course.

In the period A.D. 765-6, during the reign of the Emperor Tai Tsung 代宗 (A.D. 763-80) of the T'ang 唐 dynasty, a fisherman, casting in his line at night on the S.W. side of the mountain, felt himself dragged into the water, and, sinking, found a long chain bound round the base of the mountain. A monster resembling a monkey was sitting there motionless, as if intoxicated, a horror-inspiring filthy slaver running from his jaws.

In A.D. 765, Li T'ang 李 湯, a Sub-prefect of Shan-yang Hsien 山 陽 縣, Kiangsu 江 蘇, had the chain dragged up by a team of fifty oxen. At the end of it was seen a monkey more than fifty feet high, who plunged back into the water, dragging in the oxen after him. (See also *Shui-mu Niang-niang* 水 母 娘 娘).

A Spirit of the Sung Chiang 凇 江, River Sung, Sung-chiang Yu-i Shên 凇 江 遊 突 神, is mentioned in the *Sou-shên chi* 搜 神 記, 上 卷, p. 51.

(2) Spirits of Various Bodies of Water.—

(*a*) The Lo 洛. The Spirit of this river, an affluent of the Huang Ho 黄 河, is Mi Fei 宓 妃, daughter of Mi Hsi 宓 羲 or Fu Hsi 伏 羲. She drowned herself in that river and became its Spirit. But the one who is always regarded as the Spirit of the Lo 洛 is Queen Chên 甄. In A.D. 227-33, during the reign of the Emperor Ming Ti 明 帝 (A.D. 227-40), a scholar named Hsiao Kuang 蕭 曠 was going along the bank of the Lo 洛, and stayed the night in a pavilion attached to an inn. The moon and breeze inspiring him, he began playing his lute, when he heard sighs coming from the river, and soon a beautiful lady appeared.

On being asked her name, she said she was the female Spirit of the Lo 洛, and asked him if he did not know that Ch'ên-ssŭ Wang 陳 思 王 [the posthumous title of Ts'ao Chih 曹 植 (Ts'ao Tzŭ-chien 曹 子 建), brother of Wên Ti 文 帝, who reigned from A.D. 220-227] had composed a poem in her honour.

"That is true," replied the scholar, "but I have heard that Queen Chên 甄 is the Spirit of the Lo 洛. Ch'ên-ssŭ Wang 陳 思 王 having met her soul on the river, dedicated to her a poem entitled *Kan-chên fu* 感 甄 賦, 'A Tribute of Love to Queen Chên.' Then, reflecting on the impropriety of his action, he changed the title to *Lo-shui Shên fu* 洛 水 神 傳, 'An Elegy to the Spirit of the Lo.' His first idea was not to dedicate it to Mi Fei 宓 妃."

"I am Queen Chên 甄," answered the lady. "To punish him for having too greatly enjoyed the poetry of Ch'ên-ssŭ Wang 陳 思 王, the Emperor Wên Ti 文 帝 caused me to die in a dungeon. My soul, separated from my body, met Ch'ên-ssŭ Wang 陳 思 王 on the waters of the Lo 洛, and on hearing of my misfortune his love expressed itself in poetical songs. Then, noticing the incorrectness of his conduct, he changed the title of his elegy."

Ch'ên-ssŭ Wang 陳 思 王, the lover of Queen Chên 甄 and author of the amorous poem, was the brother of the Emperor Wên Ti 文 帝, Queen Chên 甄 being thus his sister-in-law. This explains the indignation of Wên Ti 文 帝 and the motive prompting Ch'ên-ssŭ Wang 陳 思 王 to change the title of his poem.

(*b*) The Han 漢, a large affluent of the Yang-tzǔ 揚 子. The Spirit is a female genie named Ho Ku 河 姑.

(*c*) The Spirit of the T'ai Hu 太 湖, Lake T'ai 太, is commonly stated to be Shui-p'ing Wang 太 平 王, the God of Tranquil Waters, a son of a concubine of Hou Chi 后 稷 (*q.v.*). He greatly aided Yü 禹 (*q.v.*) in his labours, and taught the people to dig canals, being worshipped after his death.

Others state that the Spirit of this lake is Yu Shih 郁 使, a Prefect of Yung Chou 雍 州, Shensi 陝 西. The Spirit is otherwise stated to have been a native of Su Chou 蘇 州, in Kiangsu 江 蘇. The Emperor Hui Ti 惠 帝 (194-187 B.C.) of the Han 漢 dynasty granted him the Prefecture of Yung Chou 雍 州, which he administered so justly that the people worshipped him after his death.

In A.D. 924 T'ai Tsu 太 祖, the Emperor of Wu-yüeh 吳 越, bestowed on him the posthumous title of King, and that of Marshal on his two sons.

(*d*) The Spirit of the Tsê 澤 Lakes is an aquatic serpent (*shê* 蛇) called *wei* 蝛 (or 蜎), generally spoken of as *wei-shê* 蝛 (or 蜎) 蛇. It is described as being as large round as the nave of a chariot wheel, as long as a carriage shaft, and as wearing violet clothes and a red hat. The sound of thunder frightens it, causing it to assume an erect position and hold its head (possibly a kind of saurian).—See also (*f*) infra.

(*e*) The Spirit of the Dried-up Lakes is called Mien 晃. It is a two-headed serpent, and mottled in five colours. It responds to its name when called, and can be sent to find gold and silver.

(*f*) The Spirit of the Former Beds of Rivers is the serpent Wei 蜎, which has one head and two bodies, and is eight feet long. It responds to its name when called, and can be sent to catch fish and tortoises.

(*g*) The Spirit of Ponds, *ch'ih* 池, is Lin Ts'ên 淋 涔, as described in the legend stating that the Emperor Hsiao Wu Ti 孝 武 帝 (A.D. 373-97) of the Chin 晉 dynasty one evening, whilst intoxicated, saw from a northern window of his palace a being dressed in a single garment, ornamented with a yellow ribbon between two white borders, his body streaming with water. It gave its name as Lin Ts'ên 淋 涔 and said that it was the Spirit of the Hua-lin Ch'ih 華 林 池, Hua-lin Pond. It promised protection and happiness to whomever should worship it. The Emperor seized a sword and tried to strike it a great blow, but the weapon only passed through the air and did not wound the Spirit.

(*h*) The Spirit of Rivers confined by Mountains is stated in a   SHUI FU
Taoist work to be Chên Yü-nü 眞玉女. This refers to the twelve
rivers called Ch'i 溪.

(*i*) The Spirit of Waves of the Sea is Yang Hou 陽侯, who is
also a Spirit of the sea. Since it was he who let loose the waves
of the sea after his animated interview with Ch'in Shih-huang
秦始皇, and as he is not said to have troubled the waves of rivers,
he is to be regarded as the Spirit of the Waves of the Sea.

The Spirit of Waves of Rivers is Wu Tzŭ-hsü 伍子胥, a
native of the Ch'u 楚 Kingdom. His personal name was Yüan
員. He was minister to the two Kings of Wu 吳: Ho Lü 闔閭
and Fu Ch'ai 夫差. In 483 B.C. the latter ordered him to commit
suicide, and had his corpse sewn up in a skin sack and thrown
into the Yang-tzŭ 揚子 River. In revenge, Wu Tzŭ-hsü 伍子胥
raised the waves and thereby caused the death of numerous people.
To appease him, temples were erected to him on the banks of the
Ch'ien-t'ang 錢唐 and Chê-chiang 浙江 Rivers. He is worshipped under the title of the Spirit of the Waves, and has the
honorary title of Ling Hsü 靈胥, Hsü the Marvellous.

(*j*) The Spirits of Wells are to be found in the following
Taoist legend:—One day Chang Tao-ling 張道陵, the "father of
modern Taoism," was on Ho-ming Shan 鶴鳴山, Mount Ho-
ming, with his disciple Wang Ch'ang 王長. "See," he said, "that
shaft of white light on Yang Shan 陽山 yonder. There are
undoubtedly some bad spirits there. Let us go and bring them to
reason." When they reached the foot of the mountain they met
twelve women who had the appearance of evil spirits. Chang
Tao-ling 張道陵 asked them whence came the shaft of white
light. They answered that it was the *yin* 陰, or female, principle
of the earth. "Where is the source of the salt water?" he asked
again. "That pond in front of you," they replied, "in which lives
a very wicked dragon." Chang Tao-ling 張道陵 tried to force
the dragon to come out, but without success. Then he drew a
phoenix with golden wings on a charm and hurled it into the
air over the pond. Thereupon the dragon took fright and fled,
the pond immediately drying up. After that Chang Tao-ling
張道陵 took his sword and stuck it in the ground, whereupon a
well full of salt water appeared on the spot.

The twelve women each offered Chang Tao-ling 張道陵
a jade ring, and asked that they might become his wives. He took
the rings, and pressing them together in his hands made of them
one large single ring. "I will throw this ring into the well," he
said, "and the one of you who recovers it shall be my wife." All
the twelve women jumped into the well to get the ring; whereupon Chang Tao-ling 張道陵 put a cover over it and fastened
it down, telling them that henceforth they should be the spirits of
the well and would never be allowed to come out.

Shortly after this Chang Tao-ling 張道陵 met a hunter. He exhorted him not to kill living beings, but to change his occupation to that of a salt-burner, instructing him how to draw out the salt from salt-water wells. Thus the people of that district were advantaged both by being able to obtain the salt and by being no longer molested by the twelve female spirits. A temple, called Temple of the Prince of Ch'ing Ho 淸河, was built by them, and the territory of Ling Chou 陵州 was given to Chang Tao-ling 張道陵 in recognition of the benefits he had conferred upon the people.

(3) Spirits with undefined jurisdiction.

(a) Liu I 柳毅, the Immortal of the Waters. The legend of this Spirit describes how a graduate named Liu I 柳毅, in the reign-period A.D. 676-9 of the Emperor Kao Tsung 高宗 (A.D. 650-84) of the T'ang 唐 dynasty, having failed in his examination for his licentiate's degree, when passing through Ching-yang Hsien 涇陽縣, in Ch'ang-an Fu 長安府, Shensi 陝西, on his way home, saw a young woman tending goats by the roadside. She said to him: "I am the youngest daughter of the Dragon-king of the Tung-t'ing 洞庭 Lake. My parents married me to the son of the god of the River Ching 涇, but my husband, misled by the slanders of the servants, repudiated me. I have heard that you are returning to the Kingdom of Wu 吳, which is quite close to my native district, so I want to ask you to take this letter to my father. To the north of the Tung-t'ing 洞庭 Lake you will find a large orange-tree, called by the natives Protector of the Soil. Strike it three times with your girdle and some one will appear."

Some months later the graduate went to the spot, found the orange-tree, and struck it three times, whereupon a warrior arose from the lake and, saluting him, asked what he wanted. "I wish to see your king," the graduate replied. The warrior struck the waters, opening a passage for Liu I 柳毅, and led him to a palace. "This," he said, "is the palace of Ling Hsü 靈虛." In a few minutes there appeared a person dressed in violet-coloured clothes and holding in his hand a piece of jade. "This is our King," said the warrior. "I am your Majesty's neighbour," replied Liu I 柳毅. "I spent my youth in Ch'u 楚 and studied in Ch'in 秦. I have just failed in my licentiate examination. On my way home I saw your daughter tending some goats; she was all dishevelled, and in so pitiable a condition that it hurt me to see her. She has sent you this letter."

On reading the letter the King wept, and all the courtiers followed his example. "Stop wailing," said the King, "lest Ch'ien-t'ang 錢唐 hear." "Who is Ch'ien-t'ang 錢唐?" asked Liu-I 柳毅. "He is my dear brother," replied the King; "formerly he was one of the chief administrators of the Ch'ien-t'ang 錢唐 River; now he is the chief God of Rivers." "Why are you so afraid that he might hear what I have just told you?" "Because he has a terrible temper. It was he who, in the reign of Yao 堯, caused a nine years flood."

Before he had finished speaking, a red dragon, a thousand feet long, with red scales, mane of fire, bloody tongue, and eyes blazing like lightning, passed through the air with rapid flight and disappeared. Barely a few moments had elapsed when it returned with a young woman whom Liu I 柳毅 recognized as the one who had entrusted him with the letter. The Dragon-king, overjoyed, said to him: "This is my daughter; her husband is no more, and she offers you her hand." Liu 柳 did not dare to accept, since it appeared that they had just killed her husband. He took his departure, and eventually married twice, his wives dying one after the other. He at length agreed to marry a young widow, the daughter of a former Magistrate of Ch'ing-liu 清流, in Anhui 安徽. Her husband's name had been Chang 張, and her mother's Chêng 鄭.

At the end of a year they had a son. She then said to her husband: "I am the daughter of the King of the T'ung T'ing 洞庭 Lake. It was you who saved me from my miserable plight on the bank of the Ching 涇, and I swore I would reward you. Formerly you refused to accept my hand, and my parents decided to marry me to the son of a silk-merchant. I cut my hair, and never ceased to hope that I might some time or other be united to you in order that I might show you my gratitude."

In A.D. 712, in the reign of the Emperor Hsüan Tsung 玄宗 (713-756) of the T'ang 唐 dynasty, they both returned to the Tung-t'ing 洞庭 Lake; but the legend says nothing further with regard to them.

Shang Ti 上帝, the Supreme Ruler, conferred on Liu I 柳毅 the title of Chin-lung Ta-wang 金龍大王, Golden Dragon Great Prince.

(*b*) The title Hsüan Ming 玄冥 came to be given to the Spirit of the Waters, it being the official designation of an office of canal and irrigation works. Hsiu 修 and Hsi 熙, the two uncles of Shao Hao 少曎 (? 昊) (2598-2514 B.C.) were the incumbents of this office and were posthumously honoured as spirits of these watercourses. With the lapse of time, the title was transferred to the Spirit of the Waters.

(*c*) The subtile and transcendent spirit or element of water Wang Hsiang 罔象. He is represented as a child of dark skin and red eyes, with large ears and long claws.

Another name for this element is Ch'ing Chi 慶忌. It has a human figure, and travels in a chariot a thousand *li* 里 a day. On request, it dives into the water and brings out fish.

(*d*) The Count of Waters is T'ien Wu 天吳. Personal name Ku-shên 谷神, Spirit of the Valleys. He has a tiger's body and nine heads with human faces, eight feet, and eight or even ten tails.

(*e*) The Female Immortal of the Waters is Ho Ku 郝姑. She was almost contemporary with Mi Fei 宓妃 (*supra* D. 2), having lived in the reign of the Emperor Ming Ti 明帝 (A.D. 227-40) of the Wei 魏 Kingdom. Between the years A.D. 233-7 a girl named Ho Ku 郝姑 of the family of Ho Chao 郝昭, an official of Ch'ên-ts'ang 陳倉, went to live at Chi Chou 冀州. Whilst gathering flowers one day on the banks of the Ou-i Hsieh 漚漢洩, three youths appeared and informed her that the Duke of the Eastern Seas had chosen her as his wife, and requested her to go to him. They spread a carpet on the surface of the water, on which she walked across. Her companions ran to inform her parents, but she requested the latter not to worry on her account, as she had become the Immortal of the Waters. She added that she would send some *tao* 刀 fish to bring them news of herself in the fourth month of every year. Having said this she glided along the surface of the waters and disappeared. In the following year enormous numbers of these fish were seen in the waters and even up to the banks of the river.

A memorial temple was built to her on the spot where she had received the message, and the local authorities first pray to her in the open air before sacrificing in the temple. The latter is forty-five *li* 里 N.W. of Chi Chou 冀州. She is also officially sacrificed to under the designation of Nü Chün 女君.

(4) Shui-mu Niang-niang 水母娘娘.—The Old Mother of the Waters is the Spirit of Ssŭ Chou 泗州, in Anhui 安徽. To her is popularly ascribed the destruction of the ancient city of Ssŭ Chou 泗州, which was completely submerged by the waters of the Hung-tsê 洪澤 Lake in A.D. 1574.

One author states that this Goddess of the Waters is the younger sister of the White Spiritual Elephant, a guardian of the Door of Buddha. This elephant is the "subtile principle of metamorphosed water."

Doré (X. 796-8) relates the legends he had heard with regard to this deity. One of these is as follows:—

A report was presented to Yü Huang 玉皇, Lord of the Skies, begging him to put an end to the inundations of Ssŭ Chou 泗州 caused by Shui-mu Niang-niang 水母娘娘 almost every year. These inundations devastated the country and cost many lives. Yü Huang 玉皇 commanded the Great Kings of the Skies to raise troops and capture this goddess. But her tricks triumphed over force, and the city continued to be devastated by inundations.

One day Shui-mu Niang-niang 水母娘娘 was seen near the city gate carrying two buckets of water. Li Lao-chün 李老君 suspected some plot, but an open attack being too risky, he preferred to adopt a ruse. He went and bought a donkey, led it to the buckets of water, and let it drink their contents. Unfortunately the animal could not drink all the water, so that a little remained at the bottom of the buckets. Now these magical buckets contained the sources of the five great lakes, which held enough water to inundate the whole of China. Shui-mu Niang-niang 水母娘娘 with her foot overturned one of the buckets, and the water that had remained in it was enough to cause a formidable flood, which submerged the unfortunate town, and buried it for ever under the immense sheet of water called the lake of Hung-tsê 洪澤.

So great a crime deserved an exemplary punishment, and accordingly Yü Huang 玉皇 sent reinforcements to his armies, and a pursuit of the goddess was methodically organized.

Sun Hou-tzǔ 猻猴子 (*q.v.*), the rapid courier, started in pursuit and caught her up, but the astute goddess was clever enough to slip through his fingers. Sun Hou-tzǔ 猻猴子, furious at this setback, went to ask Kuan-yin P'u-sa 觀音菩薩 to come to his aid. She promised to do so. The furious race she had had to escape from her enemy had given Shui-mu Niang-niang 水母娘娘 a good appetite. Exhausted with fatigue, and with an empty stomach, she caught sight of a woman selling vermicelli, who had just prepared two bowls of it and was awaiting customers. Shui-mu Niang-niang 水母娘娘 went up to her and began to eat the strength-giving food with avidity. No sooner had she eaten half of the vermicelli than it changed in her stomach into iron chains, which wound round her intestines. The end of the chain protruded from her mouth, and the contents of the bowl became another long chain which welded itself to the chain which stuck out beyond her lips. The vermicelli-seller was no other than Kuan-yin P'u-sa 觀音菩薩 herself, who had conceived this stratagem as a means of ridding herself of this evil-working goddess. She ordered Sun Hou-tzǔ 猻猴子 to take her down a deep well at the foot of a mountain in Hsü-I Hsien 盱眙縣 and to fasten her securely there. It is there that Shui-mu Niang-niang 水母娘娘 remains in her liquid prison. The end of the chain is to be seen when the water is low.

Doré gives the following as the constitution of the Ministry of Waters, as shown in the canon of Chiang T'ai-kung 姜太公, it being still in force in some temples:—

President: Lu Hsiung 魯雄, Stellar Sovereign of the Virtue of Water, Shui-tê Hsing-chün 水德星君. Members of the Ministry: Yang Chên 楊眞, Spirit of the constellation Chi 箕, the Leopard (δγ of Sagittarius). Fang Chi-ch'ing 方吉淸, Spirit of the constellation Yü 獝, the Porcupine (γ of Pegasus). Sun Hsiang 孫祥, Spirit of the constellation Shên 參, the Gibbon (Rigel of Orion). Hu Tao-yüan 胡道元, Spirit of the constellation Chên 軫, the Earth-worm (γε of the Crow). These are all stellar gods, formerly employed as high functionaries of the Emperor Chou 紂 (1154-1121 B.C.). After their death, and after the accession of Wu Wang 武王 (1121-1114 B.C.) to the throne, Chiang Tzǔ-ya 姜子牙 conferred on them the title of Spirits of the Waters. The four stars assigned as a palace to the members of the Ministry of the Waters form part of the twenty-eight Chinese constellations.

The *Sou-shên chi* 搜神記 gives Hai Jo 海若 as the Spirit of the Waters of the Sea; Wu Tzǔ hsü 吳子胥 as the Spirit of Tides; Yü Chiang 禹彊 as the Spirit of Waters; and Ch'uan Hou 川后 as the Spirit of Waves.

SHUI-FU 水府, THE GOD OF THE STAR.—See *Yü Yüan* 余元.

SHUI HSING 水星.—See *Mercury*.

SHUI-HUO T'UNG-ÊRH 水火童兒.—A disciple of T'ung-t'ien Chiao-chu 通天敎主.—Not to be confused with Shui-huo T'ung-tzǔ 水火童子 (*q.v.*).

SHUI-HUO T'UNG-TZǓ 水火童子.—A disciple of Chun-t'i Tao-jên 準提道人. When Wu-yün Hsien 烏雲仙, a disciple of T'ung-t'ien Chiao-chu 通天敎主, had changed himself into an *ao* 鰲, large tortoise, Chun-t'i Tao-jên 準提道人 ordered his disciple to mount on the reptile's back. It immediately shot through the air like an arrow, and bore him away to the Western Paradise. Not to be confused with Shui-huo T'ung-êrh 水火童兒 (*q.v.*).

SHUI KUAN 水官.—See *Shui Fu* 水府, C (2) (a).

SHUI KUAN CHIEH Ô 水官解厄.—The Water Ruler who delivers from calamity.—See *San Kuan* 三官.

SHUI-MU NIANG-NIANG 水母娘娘.—See *Shui Fu* 水府, D. (4).

SHUI-P'ING WANG 水平王.—See *Shui Fu* 水府, D. (2) (c).

SHUI SHÊN 水神.—See *Fêng I* 馮夷.

SHUI YUNG 水庸.—The Gods of Canals and Rivers.—One of the eight categories of beings or genii who can assist or retard the growth of crops.—*Cf. Hsien Nung* 先農, *Shui Fang* 水防, etc., and see *Shui Fu* 水府.

SHUN 舜.—The Successor of Yao 堯. 2317-2208 B.C. He was born, according to one account, at Yü-mu 虞幕, in Honan 河南. His father having a favourite son by a second marriage took a dislike to Shun 舜 and several times tried to kill him. Shun 舜, however, by his conduct toward his father and step-mother, has gained a place among the twenty-four examples of filial piety. He attracted the notice of the Emperor Yao 堯 who made him his heir, setting aside his own unworthy son, and moreover gave to Shun 舜 his two daughters as wives. He was first associated with Yao 堯 in the rule and later succeeded to the throne. It is said of him that he had double pupils to his eyes. The title Ch'ung Hua 重華 bestowed on him signifies that he rivalled Yao 堯 in virtue. He was canonized with the title Yü Ti Shun 虞帝舜 (*Encyclopaedia Sinica*). Worshipped as one of the San Kuan 三官 (*q.v.*). The reported inventor of the writing-brush (see *Mêng-t'ien* 蒙恬).

SHUN-FÊNG ÊRH 順風耳.—See *Ch'ien-li Yen* 千里眼.

SHUN I FU-JÊN 順懿夫人.—The Goddess of Drought (or Famine) and Flood.

SI-DA-GAM.—See *Su-da-wan*.

SIDDHARTA.—See *Fo* 佛.

SILK, THE GOD OF.—His name is Hsi Ling-ssŭ 西林司 and he is worshipped by silk merchants, and by silk and satin weavers. Before his time men dressed in linen (Du Bose, p. 335).

SILKWORMS, THE GODS OF.—See *Ch'ing-i Shên* 青衣神. *Ma-t'ou Niang* 馬頭娘, and *T'ien-ssŭ Fang* 天駟房.

SILKWORMS, THE GODDESS OF.—See *Ts'an-nü* 蠶女.

SILVERSMITHS, THE GOD OF.—See *Mi-lo Fo* 彌勒佛, *Tung-fang Shuo* 東方朔, and *Hua-kuang Fo* 華光佛.

SIMHA.—See *Shih-tzŭ Kuo* 獅子國.

SIMHALA.—See *Shih-tzŭ Kuo* 獅子國.

SINGHALAPUTRA.—See *Lo-han* 羅漢.

SINHALA.—See *Shih-tzŭ Kuo* 獅子國.

SINLO (HSIN-LO) 新羅.—A small Kingdom in south-east Korea.—See *Ti-tsang Wang* 地藏王.

SIVA.—The name Siva is unknown to the *Vedas,* but Rudra, another name of this deity, and almost equally common, occurs in the *Veda* both in the singular and plural, and from these the great deity Siva and his manifestations, the Rudras, have been developed. In the *Rig-veda* the word Rudra is used for Agni, and the Maruts are called his sons. In other passages he is distinct from Agni. He is lauded as "the lord of songs, the lord of sacrifices, who heals maladies, is brilliant as the sun, the best and most bountiful of gods, who grants prosperity and welfare to horses and sheep, men, women, and cows; the lord of nourishment, who drives away diseases, dispenses remedies, and removes sin; but, on the other hand he is the wielder of the thunderbolt, the bearer of bow and arrows, and mounted on his chariot is terrible as a wild beast, destructive and fierce."

SIX PATHS, THE.—See *Gati*.

SIX PATRIARCHS, THE.—See *Patriarchs*.

SIX PLACES, THE.—See *Gati*.

SKAMBHA.—"The Supporter." A name sometimes used in the *Rig-veda* to designate the Supreme Deity. There is considerable doubt and mystery about both this name and deity. "The meaning of the term," says Goldstücker, "is 'the fulcrum,' and it seems to mean the fulcrum of the whole world in all its physical, religious, and other aspects."

SKANDA.—In Hindu mythology, the God of War.—See *Karttikeya*.

SKIN, THE GOD OF THE.—The name of this god is T'ung Chung-chung 通衆仲; style Tao Lien 道連; height 1½ inches; colour yellow.—*Yün chi ch'i ch'ien* 雲笈七籤.

SKY-SWEEPER, THE.—See *Sao-ch'ing Niang* 掃晴娘.

SMALLPOX, THE DAME WHO CONTROLS.—See *Tou-shên Niang-niang* 痘神娘娘.

SMALLPOX, THE MINISTRY OF.—See *Tou Shên* 痘神.

SMALLPOX, THE SPIRIT OF.—See *Tou-shên* 痘神.

SMELTERS, THE GOD OF.—See *Li Lao-chün* 李老君.

SNAKES, THE GODS OF.—"The image of the snake-god has sometimes a man's head and a snake's body. If a snake is found on the premises the tenant immediately repairs to the snake-god's temple; also he rubs out his tracks with manure. At the feast in the fifth moon they mark all little children's foreheads with the word 'king' (*wang* 王), and put yellow paint on their legs, as a charm against snakes and centipedes. Live snakes are still carried in processions in some parts of China, for luck, in honour of the serpent-king.

"The Holding-snakes God was twenty feet high; a very powerful giant. His father's name was Hsin 信, Faith. Wherever he went there was a drought, so studying the subject he became convinced that drought came from the sun, and he must try and destroy the sun. For three months beside the Yellow River he studied the art of flying, and taking a green snake in one hand and a yellow one in the other, he followed the sun in his circuit, but overcome with thirst and heat he died. Afterwards sacrifices were offered to him" (Du Bose, pp. 325-6).—See also *Shê Wang* 蛇王.

SNORTER, THE.—See *Hêng Ha êrh chiang* 哼哈二將.

SNOW, THE GOD OF.—His name is Tung Lu 冬魯. "A prince fond of hunting goes to the forest for game. A giant asks the beasts, 'Would you prefer to die by the knife or by an arrow?' An aged deer begs the giant to save him from the prince, and he is directed to pray to Tung Lu 冬魯 for snow, so that hunters cannot go out for game" (Du Bose, p. 75).

SO-CHIA-LO 娑伽羅.—A dragon-king.—See *Lung Wang* 龍王.

SO-CHIEH-LO 娑竭羅.—A dragon-king.—See *Lung Wang* 龍王.

SODOMY, THE GOD OF.—See *Chou Wang* 紂王.

SOIL AND HARVESTS, GOD OF.—See *Shê Chi* 社稷.

SOMA.—The juice of a milky climbing plant (*Asclepias acida*), extracted and fermented, forming a beverage offered in libations to the deities, and drunk by the Brahmans. Its exhilarating qualities were grateful to the priests, and the gods were represented as being equally fond of it.

In later times, the name was appropriated to the moon, and some of the qualities of the soma juice have been transferred to the luminary, who is Oshadhi-pati, or lord of herbs. So Soma is considered the guardian of sacrifices and penance, asterisms and healing herbs.—See also *Lo-han* 羅漢.

"SOMBRE MAIDEN," THE.—See *Hsüan Nü* 玄女. The Sombre or Mysterious Maiden seems to have been a very early impersonation of some solar influence which aided the Emperor Huang Ti 黃帝 in his contest with rebellious powers. The beginning of history in many countries recounts a struggle between solar light and darkness of the abyss (Meade, p. 198).

"SOMBRE YOUTH," THE.—See *Wên Ch'ang* 文昌.

SORCERY, THE GODDESS OF.—The Goddess of Sorcery is Shêng Mu 聖母.

SORROWS, THE BRIDGE OF.—See *K'u-ch'u Ch'iao* 苦處橋 and *Mêng P'o* 孟婆.

SOTAPANNI.—See *Lo-han* 羅漢.

SOUL.—See *Kuei* 鬼 and *Shên* 神.

SOUTH PLACE.—The God of the South Place is Chu Fung 祝融, the Fire-god.

SOUTH POLE, THE OLD IMMORTAL OF THE.—See *Nan-chi Hsien-wêng* 南極仙翁.

SOUTHERN SACRED MOUNTAIN, THE SCHOOL OF THE.—See *Buddhist Schools,* III.

SOVEREIGN EARTH, THE.—See *Hou T'u* 后土.

SOVEREIGN EMPEROR OF THE GOLDEN PALACE, THE.—See *Chin-ch'üeh Shang-ti* 金闕上帝.

SOVEREIGN EMPEROR OF THE JADE PALACE, THE. —See *Chin-ch'üeh Shang-ti* 金闕上帝.

SPECTACLE-MERCHANTS, THE GOD OF.—See *Hsüan Yüan Huang-ti* 軒轅黃帝 and *Kuei Ku-tzǔ* 鬼谷子.

SPIRIT OF EARTH, THE.—Huang Lao 黃老.—See *Wu Lao* 五老.

SPIRIT OF FIRE, THE.—Ch'ih Ching-tzǔ 赤精子.—See *Wu Lao* 五老.

SPIRIT OF METAL, THE.—See *Wu Lao* 五老.

SPIRIT OCULISTS, THE.—See *Lo Shên* 羅神.

SPIRIT OF THUNDER, THE.—See *Hsin-hsing Kou Yüan-shuai* 辛興苟元帥 and *Ministries.*

SPIRIT TING 丁, THE.—See *T'ieh Yüan-shuai* 鐵元帥.

SPIRIT OF WATER, THE.—Shui Ching-tzǔ 水精子.—See *Wu Lao* 五老 and *Shui Fu* 水府.

SPIRIT OF WOOD, THE.—See *Wu Lao* 五老.

SPIRITS OF DOORS, THE.—See *Shên T'u Yü Lei* 神茶
鬱壘 and *Mén Shên* 門神.

SPIRITS OF THE FIVE NATURAL AGENTS, THE.—
See *Wu Lao* 五老.

SPIRITS OF THE SEA.—See *Shui Fu* 水府.

SPLEEN, THE GODS OF THE.—The God of the Spleen is
named Huang T'ing 黄庭; his style is Fei Huang-tzŭ 飛黄子.
Another god is named Pao Yüan-ch'üan 寶元全; style, Tao Ch'ien
道騫, height, 7³⁄₁₀ths inches; colour, pure yellow (*Yün chi ch'i
ch'ien* 雲笈七籤). The *Huang t'ing nei ching* 黄庭內經 says
the God of the Spleen is Ch'ang Tsai 常在, and his style Hun
T'ing 魂停.

SRAMANAS.—Those subject to monastic discipline.—*See
Lo-han* 羅漢.

SRAVAKAS.—The great disciples of Buddha.—See *Lo-han*
羅漢.

SSŬ-CH'I 死炁, THE GOD OF THE STAR.—See *Ch'ên
Chi-chêng* 陳季貞.

SSŬ CHIN-KANG 四金剛.—*Vajrapani*. The Thunderbolt-
handed. The personification of force. In Northern Buddhist
countries, a powerful subduer of evil spirits. The second Dhyani-
Bodhisattva. Also the ferocious emanation of Vajrahara (a kind
of supreme Buddha). A product of the Mahayana and Tantra
Schools. Identified by some with Indra, the Hindu god of rain.

SSŬCH'UAN 四川, THE SPIRIT OF.—See *Chang Hsien*
張仙.

SSŬ-FEI 四廢, THE GOD OF THE STAR.—See *Yüan
Hung* 遠洪.

SSŬ-FU 死符, THE GOD OF THE STAR.—See *Pien Chin-
lung* 卞金龍.

SSŬ LAO 四老.—See *Wu Lao* 五老.

SSŬ-MA CH'ING 司馬卿.—See *Hsüan-t'ien Shang-ti* 玄天
上帝, and *Shih-êrh ting-chia·Shên* 十二丁甲神.

SSŬ-MA HSIANG-JU 司馬相如.—One of the Patron Deities

of Wine-merchants. Lived in the time of the Emperor Wên Ti 文帝 (179-156 B.C.) of the Han 漢 dynasty. Was a scholar of Ssŭch'uan 川四. Eloped with the daughter of a millionaire named Cho Wang-sun 卓王孫, and was obliged to sell wine for a living. Not liking to see his daughter in that position, her father presented her husband with a million taels and a hundred servants. Died 117 B.C. Wine merchants worship him in the hope of attracting like good fortune.—See also *Tu K'ang* 杜康.

SSŬ-MA TA-SHÊN 司馬大神.—See *Ma Wang* 馬王.

SSŬ-MING-FU CHÜN 司命福君.—See *Tsao Chün* 灶 (竈) 君.

SSŬ SÊ 司嗇.—The first Minister of Agriculture Hsien Sê 先 嗇 is Shên Nung 神農, the first agriculturist, Hou Chi 后稷 the patron deity of harvests.—See *Hou Chi* 后稷 and *Shên Nung* 神農.

SSŬ TA CHIN-KANG 四大金剛.—See *Ssŭ ta T'ien-wang* 四大天王.

SSŬ TA T'IEN-WANG 四大天王. — The Four Great Heavenly Kings or Kings of Heaven, also known as the Four Great Diamond Kings, Ssŭ ta Chin-kang 四大金剛. The Four Maharajas, not properly gods, but genii, or minor divinities. Buddhist protectors, or tutelary genii. They belong to the class of Lakapalas, Hu-shih-chê 護世者, guardians of the universe. They are: To Wên 多聞 (Vraisravana), Tsêng Ch'ang 增長 (Virudhaka), Ch'ih Kuo 持國 (Dhritarashtra), and Kuang Mu 廣目 (Virupaksa). These are some of the various Hindu gods, etc., borrowed by Buddhism from Brahmanism, and admitted into its pantheon. They seem to have assisted at every important event of Gautama Buddha's life.

"In China, they are especially guardians of temples (having been demon-kings, afterwards converted and made protectors of the homes of the gods) but symbolize also the seasons, and control the four elements, fire, air, earth, and water. As guardians, they are placed at the outer entrance to temples, two on each side. They are immense, grotesque figures, in full armour, standing, and bearing their respective symbols. These symbols vary in India, Tibet, China, and Japan. Their purpose seems to be largely connected with elemental phenomena, such as producing rain, thunder, storms, and even universal darkness. Taoists perverted these symbols to purely magic purposes, as may be seen in the battle of the Four Genii" (Kennelly, vii, 407, summarizing Edkins, Hackmann, Eitel, and Getty). They are but seldom worshipped, incense being occasionally burnt before them by devotees of other idols. They are supposed to have bodies, minds, and a faith as strong as steel, because of their pure living.

According to the Buddhist account, they were originally four demon-kings, who having been converted were assigned the guardianship of the four sides of Mount Meru (or Sumeru) against *asuras* and other noxious influences. Hence they were called *lokapalas,* protectors, or tutelary deities. In other accounts their protection extends to the Four Continents, which surround Mount Meru on the four points of the compass.

They reside in their palaces on Hsü-mi Shan 須彌山, Mount Hsü-mi (Sumeru), the centre of the Universe. It is 3,360,000 li 里 (about a million miles) high. Its eastern slope is of gold, its western of silver, its south-eastern of crystal, and its north-eastern of agate.

These four Great Kings are evidently the Taoist reflection of the four Chin-kang 金剛 (*q.v.*) of Buddhism. By the Taoists they are known by the names Li 李, Ma 馬, Chao 趙, and Wên 溫, represented as holding a pagoda, sword, two swords, and spiked club respectively.

The *Sou-shên chi* 搜神記 gives their names as follows: (1) P'i-p'u-tung-ch'a T'ien-wang 毘普動叉大王; (2) P'i-p'u-po-ch'a T'ien-wang 毘普博叉天王; (3) T'i-t'ou-lai-ch'a T'ien-wang 提頭賴吒天王, and (4) P'i-sha-mên T'ien-wang 毘沙門天王.

The *Hsi-yu chi* 西遊記 adds the names of two other Kings of Heaven: Tsêng-chang T'ien-wang 增長天王 and T'o-t'a-Li T'ien-wang 托塔李天王. The latter (*q.v.*) has become the most popular of all.

In a later phase of evolution, especially in China and Japan, they are considered as presiding over the four quarters of the universe and the four seasons (Getty; Hackmann). As elemental genii, they are said to be surrounded by thirty generals, and to have each ninety sons (Beal; Johnston). They thus symbolize the ancient division of the year into 12 months of 30 days each, each season comprising 3 months, or 90 days. (The Brahmanical year was divided into 12 months of 30 days each.) In the *Chin-kuang ming-ching* 金光明經 (a translation from the Sanskrit), they are described as actively interfering in the affairs of the world. They protect individuals, households, and kingdoms that have adopted the Buddhist Law, but kings and nations who neglect it lose their protection. They bestow happiness, however, on those who honour the Three Treasures: the Buddha, the Law, and the Brotherhood (or Priesthood) (Edkins). (See *San Pao* 三寶.) Their worship was introduced into China from Ceylon by Amogha in A.D. 733. But being genii and not gods proper, they are not worshipped by prayers and thanksgiving, but only by incense being occasionally burnt before them. Their images are generally placed at the outer entrance to Buddhist temples. They are described and represented as follows:—

1. To Wên 多聞, One who hears much, or One who hears everywhere. Originally Kuvera, the Brahmanic God of Wealth,

and regent of the North, the place of fabulous treasures. Converted to Buddhism, he received the name of Vaisravana. The king who watches over the North, and presides over autumn.

In China, his colour is black, and he is sometimes called the Black Warrior. His symbol is a pearl and a snake. Commands an army of Yakshas, or good genii.

2. Tsêng Chang 增長.—Increased Grandeur, Virudhaka. Presides over the South. God of Spring. His colour is red. He holds an umbrella, the raising of which induces a violent thunder and rain storm or, according to other accounts, universal darkness. Attended by an army of Kubhandas, deformed demons.

3.—Ch'ih Kuo 持國.—He who governs a kingdom. Dhritarashtra. Presides over the East. God of Summer. His colour is blue. Touches with his right hand the chords of a guitar held in his left. Commands an army of Gandharas, musicians, and Pisatchas, powerful vampires.

4. Kuang Mu 廣目.—Large-eyes. Virupaksa. Presides over the West. God of Winter. His colour is white. Leads an army of *nagas,* or serpent-gods. Holds a sword in his left hand.

Borrowing the idea from Buddhism, the Taoists have also their Four Great Kings, or Genii. "Some general features and symbols are retained, but new names have been substituted for those given them by the Buddhists." The following particulars concerning them are given in the *Fêng-shên yen-i* 封神演義:—

Mo Li-ch'ing 魔禮青.—The eldest of the four, 24 feet high. Features of a crab. Beard like brazen spikes. Fights on foot, carrying a magic lance, known as Blue Cloud, inscribed with the characters *ti, shui, huo, fêng* 地, 水, 火, 風, earth, water, fire, wind. As an elemental god, his function is especially to rule the winds and produce storms. This he does by wielding his lance, by which he also causes fire, fills the air with fiery snakes, produces columns of smoke from the ground, to blind and consume the enemy's troops.

Mo Li-hung 魔禮紅.—Is represented (as in Buddhism) holding a magic umbrella, on which are inscribed the characters *chuang-tsai-ch'ien-k'un* 裝載乾坤, shut and open heaven and earth." It is adorned with gems, precious stones, and mother-of-pearl. By moving it slightly, he causes the earth to quake to its centre; by merely raising it, he obscures the sun and the moon, and covers the universe with darkness.

Mo Li-hai 魔禮海.—Carries a guitar. Sometimes represented with a lance as well. By the former, he exerts a transcendent influence over the four elements: earth, water, fire, air. In order to raise a storm, he has merely to touch one of the chords.

Mo Li-shou 魔禮壽.—Holds a magic whip, and carries a bag containing a monster resembling a white rat, called by Taoists *hua-hu tiao* 花狐貂, literally, a sable that can assume the form of a speckled fox. When set at liberty, it becomes a winged white elephant, which devours everything it encounters. "This is a pure fancy of the Taoist brain, which seems to ignore altogether the Buddhist symbolism of the ichneumon" (Kennelly, vii, 397).

The word *mo* 魔 in these names means a malignant spirit. It enters into the composition of the word *Mora,* the Buddhist god of lust, sin, and death. The Taoists have converted him into a Genie (Monier Williams).

After describing these Four Genii the *Fêng-shên yen-i* 封神演義, *The Art of Deification,* a fabulous tale of the adventures of Wu Wang 武王 (1121-1114 B.C.), founder of the Chou 周 dynasty, in his battles with Chou Hsin 紂辛, the last ruler of the House of Yin 殷, details the many exciting incidents, battles, and marvellous feats which followed the entry of the Four Genii Mo 魔 into the contest at the request of the Generals fighting for the House of Yin 殷. The following extract summarizes the portion dealing with the Four Diamond Kings.—"At the time of the consolidation of the Chou 周 dynasty in the twelfth and eleventh centuries B.C., Chiang Tzŭ-ya 姜子牙, chief counsellor to Wên Wang 文王 (1231-1135 B.C.), and general Huang Fei-hu 黃飛虎 were defending the town and mountain of Hsi-ch'i 西岐. The supporters of the house of Yin 殷 appealed to the four genii Mo 魔, who lived at Chia-mêng Kuan 佳夢關, praying them to come to their aid. They agreed, raised an army of 100,000 celestial soldiers, and traversing towns, fields, and mountains arrived in less than a day at the north gate of Hsi-ch'i 西岐, where Mo-li Ch'ing 魔禮青 pitched his camp and entrenched his soldiers.

"Hearing of this, Huang Fei-hu 黃飛虎 hastened to warn Chiang Tzŭ-ya 姜子牙 of the danger which threatened him. 'The four great generals who have just arrived at the north gate,' he said, 'are marvellously powerful genii, experts in all the mysteries of magic and use of wonderful charms. It is much to be feared that we shall not be able to resist them.'

"Many fierce battles ensued. At first these went in favour of the Chin-kang 金剛, thanks to their magical weapons and especially to Mo-li Shou's 魔禮壽 Hua-hu Tiao 花狐貂, who terrorized the enemy by devouring their bravest warriors.

"Unfortunately for the Chin-kang 金剛, the brute attacked and swallowed Yang Chien 楊戩, the nephew of Yü Huang 玉皇. This genie, on entering the body of the monster, rent his heart asunder and cut him in two. As he could transform himself at will, he assumed the shape of Hua-hu Tiao 花狐貂, and went off to Mo-li Shou 魔禮壽, who unsuspectingly put him back into his bag.

"The Four Kings held a festival to celebrate their triumph, and having drunk copiously gave themselves over to sleep. During the night Yang Chien 楊戩 came out of the bag, with the intention of possessing himself of the three magical weapons of the Chin-kang 金剛. But he succeeded only in carrying off the umbrella of Mo-li Hung 魔禮紅. In a subsequent engagement No-cha 哪吒, the son of Vadjrapani, the God of Thunder, broke the jade ring of Mo-li Ch'ing 魔禮青. Misfortune followed misfortune. The Chin-kang 金剛, deprived of their magical weapons, began to lose heart. To complete their discomfiture, Huang T'ien-hua 黃天花 brought to the attack a matchless magical weapon. This was a spike 7½ inches long, enclosed in a silk sheath, and called 'Heart-piercer.' It projected so strong a ray of light that eyes were blinded by it.

"Huang T'ien-hua 黄天花, hard pressed by Mo-li Ch'ing 魔禮青, drew the mysterious spike from its sheath, and hurled it at his adversary. It entered his neck, and with a deep groan the giant fell dead.

"Mo-li Hung 魔禮紅 and Mo-li Hai 魔禮海 hastened to avenge their brother, but ere they could come within striking distance of Huang T'ien Hua 黄天花 his redoubtable spike reached their hearts, and they lay prone at his feet.

"The one remaining hope for the sole survivor was in Hua-hu Tiao 花狐貂. Mo-li Shou 魔禮壽, not knowing that the creature had been slain, put his hand into the bag to pull him out, whereupon Yang Chien 楊戩, who had re-entered the bag, bit his hand off at the wrist, so that there remained nothing but a stump of bone.

"In this moment of intense agony Mo-li Shou 魔禮壽 fell an easy prey to Huang T'ien-hua 黄天花, the magical spike pierced his heart, and he fell bathed in his blood. Thus perished the last of the Chin-kang 金剛."

They were canonized by Chiang Tzŭ-ya 姜子牙, acting on behalf of Yüan-shih T'ien-tsun 元始天尊 (*q.v.*), being raised to the rank of Heavenly Kings, appointed advisers on Buddhism, rulers of the universe, and controllers of the four elements (fire, air, earth, and water), "for the greater prosperity of the world, and the welfare of mankind." They were thenceforth to rule the winds, and distribute rain to all the peoples of the earth, thus becoming finally elemental gods, as they were in Buddhism.

The annexed table, epitomizing the particulars regarding them, indicates also the variation in minor details as given by different English and Chinese authorities:—

Chinese Buddhist Name	*Sanskrit Name*	*Taoist Name*	*Presides over*
1. To Wên 多聞 "One who hears much."	Originally Kuvera. Vaisravana.	Mo-li Shou 魔禮壽	North.

God of	Colour	Symbol	In Japan
Winter.	Black (Tibet: yellow).	Pearl and snake (India and Tibet: flag, ichneumon, jewel).	Bishamon, God of Good Fortune.

Chinese Buddhist Name	Sanskrit Name	Taoist Name	Presides over
2. Tsêng Chang 增長 "Increased Grandeur."	Virudhaka.	Mo-li Hung 魔禮紅	South.

God of	Colour	Symbol	In Japan
Summer.	Red (Tibet: green).	Umbrella (Tibet: sword and helmet, made of skin of elephant's head).	Komoku, the Heavenly Guardian of the South.

Chinese Buddhist Name	Sanskrit Name	Taoist Name	Presides over
3. Ch'ih Kuo 持國 "Ruler of Kingdom."	Dhritarashtra.	Mo-li Hai 魔禮海	East.

God of	Colour	Symbol	In Japan
Spring.	Blue or green (Tibet and India: white).	Guitar.	Worshipped under the name of Jikoku.

Chinese Buddhist Name	Sanskrit Name	Taoist Name	Presides over
4. Kuang Mu 廣目 "Large eyes."	Virupaksa.	Mo-li Ch'ing 魔禮青	West.

God of	Colour	Symbol	In Japan
Autumn.	White (Tibet and India: red).	Sword.	Worshipped under the name of Zocho.

Variations occur in the representations in different places. To Wên 多聞 is sometimes shown with a pink face, no beard, holding an umbrella in his right hand and a rat in his left. Tsêng Chang 增長 is shown with a white face, short beard, and holding a guitar. Ch'ih Kuo 持國 is shown with a black face, a long black beard, a sword in his right hand, and a golden ring in his left, and Kuang Mu 廣目 is shown with a red face, no beard, a snake or dragon in his right hand, and his left raised in the air and holding a jewel. The seasons over which these four gods preside are also sometimes varied as autumn, spring, summer, and winter for Mo-li Shou 魔禮壽, Mo-li Hung 魔禮紅, Mo-li Hai 魔禮海, and Mo-li Ch'ing 魔禮青, respectively.

These four Kings are frequently represented in Chinese painting and sculpture. The earliest known statues date from the first century B.C. Pictures and frescoes have been found at Tun-huang 敦煌 in Chinese Turkestan, and at Turfan, respectively.

Their worship appears to be due to their auspicious appearance and aid on various critical occasions in the dynastic history of the T'ang 唐 and Sung 宋 dynasties. In the reign of the Emperor T'ai Tsung 太宗 (A.D. 627-50), whose name was Li Shih-ming 李世明, of the T'ang 唐 dynasty, as he was fighting to consolidate the dynasty founded by his father, a genie descended from Heaven and said: "I am P'i-sha-mên T'ien-wang 毘沙門天王, and will aid you in restoring peace to the Empire." He was holding a monster with a pig's head and elephant's trunk; his presence alone sufficed to restore peace in any place it came to. When Li Shih-ming 李世明 had succeeded to the throne, he promulgated an edict ordering all the officials of the Empire to offer sacrifices to P'i Sha-mên 毘沙門, T'ien-wang 天王, King of Heaven.

In the T'ien-pao 天寶 period (A.D. 742-56) of the Emperor Hsüan Tsung 玄宗 (A.D. 713-56) of the T'ang 唐 dynasty, Tu-chien 獨健, the second son of P'i-sha-mên T'ien-wang 毘沙門天王, appeared from Heaven dressed in a golden suit of armour and routed the Barbarians who were attacking the capital, Kuan-nei 關內, now the city of Hsi-an Fu 西安府, Shensi 陝西.

An order was issued, at the beginning of his reign, by the Emperor Jên Tsung 仁宗 (A.D. 1023-64) of the Sung 宋 dynasty to build temples to the same deity and to inscribe the characters T'ien-wang 天王, King of Heaven, over the entrances. A large number were accordingly erected throughout the Empire.

SSŬ YU-FÊN 死有分.—Death has its part. One of the Demons which, when the soul is on the floating Bridge of Sorrows (K'u-chu fou-ch'iao 苦竹浮橋 or K'u ch'u Ch'iao 苦處橋), suddenly jumps upon and rocks the bridge so that the soul slips off into the red stream and goes out into the world, to its new body. His colleague is Uncertain Life, Huo-wu-ch'ang 活無常. Cf. Huo-wu-ch'ang 活無常, K'u-ch'u Ch'iao 苦處橋, and Mêng P'o 孟婆.

STAR CHANG 張, THE SPIRIT OF THE.—See *Chang Hsien* 張仙.

STAR-GODS.—Besides the Sun and the Moon, the stars have become objects of common worship. They are supposed to have their own individualities, powers, likes and dislikes. There are those whose influence is for good, and those whose is for evil. Each day is governed by a constellation, but those most worshipped are the Northern and Southern Dippers. The former is supposed to control death, the latter life. The people burn incense and place a peck measure of rice before their tablet as an offering. They also light a lamp which is not allowed to go out for three days. The Spirits of the stars of the Northern Dipper (Pei Tou 北斗) record men's actions, both good and evil, and according to one's virtuous deeds, or his sins, they add to or cut off a portion of his life. Those most worshipped of this constellation are the "Three Stars." Of these the star of Longevity is the most important (see *Pei Tou* 北斗).

Prominent among the stars worshipped are the Five Planetary Stars, the homes of the Five Emperors. About 2500 B.C. the Emperor Chuan-Hsü Kao-Yang Shih 顓頊高陽氏 appointed six princesses to govern the Five Regions of the universe, together with the five elements of which it is composed. These officials were later deified as the Five Emperors presiding over these regions. Their spirits, because they at times reside in the Five Stars are also called the Gods of the Five Planetary Stars (see Plopper, pp. 39-43).—See also *Erh-shih-pa Hsü* 二十八宿. For lists of stars and constellations see Morrison, *Dictionary of the Chinese Language,* Pt. II, Vol. I pp. 1063-81.

STATIONERS, THE GOD OF.—This god is Wên-ch'ang Ta-ti 文昌大帝.

STOMACH, THE GOD OF THE.—Name *T'ung Lai-yü* 同來育; style Tao Huan 道還; 7 inches high; colour, yellow.— *Yün chi ch'i ch'ien* 雲笈七籤.

STONE, THE TRANSCENDENT AND PRESERVATIVE. —See *Shih Kan-tang* 石敢當.

STONE LION, THE.—"In front of every official yamên there are a pair of stone lions, who guard, as Cerberus, the courts of justice. It is believed that at night they are living lions, and are seen roaming around. They are accordingly worshipped by those residing in the neighbourhood (Du Bose, p. 344).

STORM-GODS.—Invisible gods, manifesting great strength, worshipped from fear of their destructive actions.—See *Lei Pu* 雷部, *Fêng Po* 風伯, etc.

STORMS, THE MINISTRY OF.—See *Lei Pu* 雷部.

STORMS, THE MINISTRY OF THUNDER AND.—See *Lei Pu* 雷部.

STOVE, THE GOD OF THE.—See *Tsao Chün* 灶 (竈) 君.

STRANGE-WINGS IMMORTAL, THE.—See *Yü-i Hsien* 羽翼仙.

STRENGTH, GODS OF.—A class of fabulous beings believed to be superior to men.—See *Garudas*.

STROLLING SINGERS, THE GOD OF.—See *Chêng Yüan-ho* 鄭元和.

SU CHI-LI 蘇吉利.—See *Tsao Chün* 灶 (竈) 君.

SU CHIEN 蘇緘.—A celebrated *ch'êng huang* 城隍, or city-god (of Nan-ning Fu 南寧府). Sung 宋 dynasty.

SU CH'ÜAN-CHUNG 蘇全忠.—See *Wu Tou* 五斗.

SU HU 蘇護.—See *Wu Tou* 五斗.

SU LING-SHENG 素靈生.—See *Lungs, The Gods of the,* and *Ch'ing Lung* 青龍.

SU-P'IN-T'Ê (T'O) 蘇頻陀.—See *Lo-han* 羅漢.

SU TING-FANG 蘇定方.—An assessor of Kuan Kung 關公, —See *Kuan Yü* 關羽.

SU YÜAN TAO-JÊN 蘇元道人.—The god of the constellation Hsin 心. Alternatively with K'ou Hsün 寇恂.

SUAN-NI 狻猊.—See *Lung Wang* 龍王.

SUBHAKARA.—(Shan 善, Virtuous and) Wu-wei 無畏, Fearless. A priest and scholar of Nalanda, descendant of Amritodana. Translated five works (A.D. 716-24).—See *Buddhist Schools,* XV and *Wu-wei Ch'an-shih* 無畏禪師.

SUBHAVYUHA.—Miao Chuang Yen Wang 妙莊嚴王.——(1) A king, during the Priyadarsana kalpa, of Vairotchanarasmipratimandita, who, converted, together with his wife Vimaladatta, by his sons Vimalagarbha and Vimalanetra, was reborn in the time of Sakyamuni as Padmasri Bodhisattva, and is to reappear, during the Abhyudga radja kalpa, in Vistirnavati as Salendra radja. (2) The father of Kuan Yin 觀音 *(q.v.).*

SUBHINDA.—See *Lo-han* 羅漢.

SU-DA-WAN.—One of the four grades of discipleship, or

"fruits" (*i.e.* the attainment of a certain amount of enlightenment in the Buddhist doctrine), the others being *Si-da-gam, A-na-gam,* and *A-la-han*; they are also called the Four Paths (*q.v.*) of Nirvana.

SU-DYUMNA.—See *Ida.*

SUI-HSING 歲刑, THE GOD OF THE STAR.—See *Hsü Fang* 徐芳.

SUI K'UNG-TZǓ 隨孔子.—See *Foot, The Gods of the.*

SUI-P'O 歲破, THE GOD OF THE STAR.—See *Ch'ao T'ien* 晁天.

SUI-SHA 歲殺, THE GOD OF THE STAR.—See *Ch'ên Kêng* 陳庚.

SUI-YEN 歲厭, THE GOD OF THE STAR.—See *P'êng Tsu-shou* 彭祖壽.

SUKHA.—See *Lo-han* 羅漢.

SUKHAVATI.—Hsi fang chi-lo-shih-chieh 西方極樂世界. —The Paradise in the West, or Ching T'u 淨土, the Pure Land. A land, in some universe in the West, the Nirvana of the common people, where the saints revel in physical bliss for aeons, until they re-enter the circle of transmigration.—See *Hsi T'ien* 西天.

SUKLA.—See *Lo-han* 羅漢.

SUKRA.—In Hindu mythology, the planet Venus and its regent.

SUMERU.—See *Meru.*

SUMMER, THE GOD OF.—The colour red, south, fire, and summer are all connected in the Chinese mind. The Fire Official, Huo Chêng 火正, the Red Emperor, Ch'ih Ti 赤帝, Chu Jung 祝融, and Mars are all worshipped in times of great heat or danger from fire.

SUN CHI 孫吉.—The god of the star Ti-tsei 地賊.—See *Ti-sha* 地煞.

SUN HO 孫合.—The god of the star Wu-ch'iung 五窮. K'ung Hsüan's 孔宣 aide-de-camp at San-shan Kuan 三山關. Slain by Wu Chih 武志 on the field of battle, during the Yin-Chou 殷周 wars.

SUN HOU-TZǓ 猻猴子.—Sun the Monkey, or Monkey Sun. A monkey who became a god. The popular hero of the *Hsi-yu chi* 西遊記, "The Record of a Journey to the Western Paradise." This work is a dramatization of the introduction of Buddhism into China. Widely diffused among the Chinese, it is a mythological account of the adventures of Hsüan [Yüan] Tsang 元奘 (*v. infra*), a Buddhist monk, and his associates, who went to India in the seventh century, and returned after a sojourn of seventeen years with 657 Buddhist books, pictures and relics. The reputed author is Ch'iu Ch'ang-ch'un 邱長春, 1148-1227, a Taoist master, who was sent to India during the early years of the Yüan 元 dynasty on a similar mission, and on his return wrote a journal of his travels with the same title as the above. This work is not to be confounded with the valuable geographical document bearing the title *Hsi-yü chi* 西域記, a description of the journey of the monk Hsüan Tsang 玄奘 to India, A.D. 629-45.

Doré quotes the following brief sketch of the *Hsi-yu chi* 西遊記: "In A.D. 629, being the second year of T'ai Tsung 太宗 (A.D. 627-50) of the T'ang 唐 dynasty, the monk T'ang Sêng 唐僧 set out from Hsi-an Fu 西安府, the then capital of the State, and travelled to India for the purpose of visiting its holy places, and bringing back copies of the sacred books of Buddhism. Kuan-yin P'u-sa 觀音菩薩, the Goddess of Mercy, associated with him the Buddhist monks Sha Ho-shang 沙和尚 and Chu Pa-chien 猪八戒; also the son of the Dragon-king of the Western Seas, who assumed the form of a white horse, Pai Ma 白馬, and bore T'ang Sêng 唐僧 on the way . . . The central hero of the novel, the man fertile in resources, and finding expedients in the most distressful circumstances, is Sun Hou-tzŭ 猻猴子."

Sun Hou-tzŭ's 猻猴子 alternative designations are: Sun Hsing-chê 孫行者, Sun Wu-k'ung 孫悟空, Mei-hou Wang 美猴王 King of the Handsome Monkeys, Ch'i-t'ien Ta-shêng 齊天大聖, Great Saint ruling the Heavens, and Pi-ma Wên 弼馬溫, Grand Master of the Heavenly Stud, the last-mentioned recalling the derisive dignity conferred on him by Yü Huang 玉皇, the Pearly Emperor, to keep him out of mischief.

His origin is described as follows:—Beyond the seas, in Shêng-shên Chou 勝神州, the Eastern continent, in Ao-lai Kuo 傲來國, the Kingdom of Ao-lai, is Hua-kuo Shan 花果山, Hua-kuo Mountain. On a rocky point on the steep sides of this mountain an egg formed and, fructified by the breath of the wind, gave birth to a stone monkey. The newly-born saluted the four points of the horizon; from his eyes shone golden streaks of lightning, which filled the palace of the North Pole Star with light. This light subsided as soon as he was able to take nourishment.

"To-day," said Yü Huang 玉皇 to himself, "I am going to complete the wonderful diversity of the beings engendered by Heaven and earth. This monkey will skip and gambol to the highest peaks of mountains, jump about in the waters, and, eating the fruit of the trees, will be the companion of the gibbon and the crane. Like the deer he will pass his nights on the mountain slopes, and during the day will be seen leaping on their summits or in their caverns. That will be the finest ornament of all for the mountains!"

The creature's exploits soon caused him to be proclaimed king of the monkeys. He then began to try to find some means of becoming immortal. Having acquired human attributes and transcendent powers, he, now faithful, now restive and undisciplined, was always in the end triumphant over the eighty-one fantastical tribulations which beset the travellers on their journey. Having eventually joined the holy religion of Buddhism, endeavoured to suppress evil and cherish virtue, he was rewarded, at a meeting of the Immortals presided over by Mi-lo Fo 彌 勒 佛, the Coming Buddha, by being appointed God of Victorious Strife. He is the patron deity of official couriers.

Sha Ho-shang 沙 和 尚, Priest Sha, also known as Sha Wu-ching 沙 悟 静, Sha, Seeker after Peace, was one of the chief of Sun's 孫 fellow servants. He was originally Grand Superintendent of the Manufactory of Stores for Yü Huang's 玉 皇 palace. During the P'an-t'ao Hui 蟠 桃 會, Flat-peach Festival, banquet to all the gods and Immortals of the Taoist Olympus, he let fall a crystal bowl, which was smashed to atoms. Yü Huang 玉 皇 caused him to be beaten with eight hundred blows, drove him out of Heaven, and exiled him to earth. He lived on the banks of the Liu-sha Ho 流 沙 河, Liu-sha River, where every seventh day a mysterious sword appeared and wounded him in the neck. Having no other means of subsistence, he used to devour the passers-by.

When Kuan Yin 觀 音 passed through that region on her way to China to find the priest who was predestined to devote himself to the laborious undertaking of the quest of the sacred Buddhist books, Sha Ho-shang 沙 和 尚 threw himself on his knees before her and begged her to put an end to all his woes.

The goddess promised that he should be delivered by the priest, her envoy, provided he would engage himself in the service of the pilgrim. On his promising to do this, and to lead a better life, she herself ordained him priest. In the end it came about that Hsüan Tsang 玄 奘, when passing the Sha-ho 沙 河, took him into his suite as coolie to carry his baggage. Yü Huang 玉 皇 pardoned him in consideration of the service he was rendering to the Buddhist cause.

He is frequently represented wearing a necklace of nine skulls, these being the remnants of nine Chinese delegates sent in former times to India, and whom he devoured when on their return they tried to cross the Liu-sha 流 沙 River.

Having repented, he was received by Kuan Yin 觀 音 as a Buddhist monk. At the meeting of the Immortals after the return to the capital he was elevated to the rank of Golden Body Perpetual Saint.

Chu Pa-chieh 猪八戒, the Pig Fairy, is a grotesque, even gross, personage, exhibiting the lowest instincts of the animal whose name he bears. Having been appointed Superintendent of the navigation of the Milky Way, he one day, when intoxicated, abused the daughter of Yü Huang 玉皇, the Pearly Emperor. The latter ordered him to be punished with two thousand blows of a heavy iron mallet. He then banished him to earth, until he should enter a new phase of existence through metempsychosis.

When his time came to be reborn, he by mistake entered the body of a sow, whence he emerged half-man half-swine, having the head and ears of a pig and a human body. The first act of his new life was to kill and eat his mother; his next, to devour the rest of the litter born with him. After this, he betook himself to the wild Fu-ling Shan 福陵山, where he attacked passers-by with his iron rake, even killing some of them.

He was afterwards appointed by Mao Erh-chieh 卯二姐, the inhabitant of the Yün-chan Tung 雲栈洞, Yün-chan Grotto, steward of all his property, which in course of time he inherited.

Owing to the exhortations of Kuan Yin 觀音, he renounced his dissolute habits and became a Buddhist monk. The goddess named him Chu 猪, Pig, and added the surname Wu-nêng 悟能, Seeker after Strength. He accompanied T'ang Sêng 唐僧 on his journey to India, and on the return of the party was rewarded for his assistance in propagating the Buddhist doctrine by being taken to Hsi T'ien 西天, the Western Paradise. For his repentance, and for his assistance to his Master, he was eventually appointed Head Altar-washer to the Gods. This was the highest office for which he was eligible, on account of his inherent greed.

T'ang Sêng 唐僧. Better known by his religious name of Hsüan Tsang 玄奘 or Yüan Tsang 元奘. The Buddhist monk (A.D. 602-4), the principal character in the *Hsi-yu chi* 西遊記.

In the family annals of the sect, his name is said to be Ch'ên 陳. He was a native of Hou-shih 緱氏, in the district of Lo-yang 洛陽, Honan 河南. In A.D. 629, he begged the emperor T'ai Tsung 太宗 (A.D. 627-50), of the T'ang 唐 dynasty, to allow him to proceed to India, and bring back Buddhist books. The emperor refused his demand. He set out, however, at his own risk, passed through the Yü-kuan 玉關, Pearly Pass, and reached Hsi-yü 西域, the distant countries of the West, visiting 130 kingdoms. After sojourning abroad sixteen years, he returned with 657 Buddhist works. An official, named Fang Hsüan-ling 房玄齡, informed the Emperor of his arrival, and he was summoned to the palace, for the purpose of translating his Hindu treasures. He erected a tower, and placed there all the Buddhist works brought from India. Died A.D. 664. Before expiring, he begged all those present to invoke the name of Tz'ŭ-shih Ju-lai 慈氏如來.

464

The legend of this priest is as follows:—

In the reign of the emperor T'ai Tsung 太宗 (A.D. 627-50) of the T'ang 唐 dynasty, Ch'ên Kuang-jui 陳光蕊, a graduate of Hai-chou 海州, Kiangsu 江蘇, in his examination for the doctor's degree came out as *chuang-yüan* 狀元, first on the list. Wên-chiao 渭嬌 (also named Man-t'ang Chiao 滿堂嬌), the daughter of the minister Yin K'ai-shan 殷開山, meeting the young academician, fell in love with him, and married him. Several days after the wedding the Emperor appointed Ch'ên Kuang-jui 陳光蕊 Governor of Chiang Chou 江州 (modern Chên-chiang Fu 鎮江府), in Kiangsu 江蘇. After a short visit to his native town he started to take up his post. His old mother and his wife accompanied him. When they reached Hung Chou 洪州 his mother fell sick and they were forced to stay for a time at the Wan-hua Tien 萬花店, Inn of Ten Thousand Flowers, kept by one Liu Hsiao-êrh 劉小二. Days passed; the sickness did not leave her, and as the time for her son to take over the seals of office was drawing near, he had to proceed without her.

Before his departure he noticed a fisherman holding in his hand a fine carp; this he bought for a small sum to give to his mother. Suddenly he noticed that the fish had a very extraordinary look, and, changing his mind, he let it go in the waters of the Hung-chiang 洪江, afterwards telling his mother what he had done. She congratulated him on his action, and assured him that the good deed would not go unrewarded.

Ch'ên Kuang-jui 陳光蕊 re-entered his boat with his wife and a servant. They were stopped by the chief waterman, Liu Hung 劉洪, and his assistant. Struck with the great beauty of Ch'ên Kuang-jui's 陳光蕊 wife, the former planned a crime which he carried out with the help of his assistant. At the dead of night he took the boat to a retired spot, killed Ch'ên Kuang-jui 陳光蕊 and his servant, threw their bodies into the river, seized his official documents of title and the woman he coveted, passed himself off as the real *chuang-yüan* 狀元, and took possession of the magistracy of Chiang Chou 江州. The widow, who was with child, had two alternatives—silence or death. Meantime she chose the former. Before she gave birth to her child, T'ai-po Chin-hsing 太白金星, the Spirit of the South Pole Star, appeared to her, and said he had been sent by Kuan Yin 觀音, the Goddess of Mercy, to present her with a son whose fame would fill the Empire. "Above all," he added, "take every precaution lest Liu Hung 劉洪 kill the child, for he will certainly do so if he can." When the child was born the mother, during the absence of Liu Hung 劉洪, determined to expose it rather than see it slain. Accordingly she wrapped it up carefully in a shirt, and carried it to the bank of the Yangtzŭ 揚子 River. She then bit her finger, and with the blood wrote a short note stating the child's origin, and hid it in its breast. Moreover, she bit off the infant's left little toe, as an indelible mark of identity. No sooner had this been done than a gust of wind blew a large plank to the river's edge. The poor mother tied her infant firmly to this plank and abandoned it to the mercy of the waves. The waif was carried to the shore of the isle of Chin Shan 金山, on which stands the famous monastery of Chin-shan Ssŭ 金山寺, near Chin-kiang Fu, Chên-chiang Fu 鎭江府, Kiangsu 江蘇. The cries of the infant attracted the attention of an old monk named Chang Lao 長老, who rescued it and gave it the name of Chiang-liu 江流, "Waif of the River." He reared it with much care, and treasured the note its mother had written with her blood. The child grew up, and Chang Lao 長老 made him a priest, naming him Hsüan Tsang 玄奘 on the day of his taking the vows. When he was eighteen years of age, having one day quarrelled with another priest, who had cursed him and reproached him with having neither father nor mother, he, much hurt, went to his protector Chang Lao 長老. The latter said to him: "The time has come to reveal to you your origin." He then told him all, showed him the note, and made him promise to avenge his assassinated father. To this end he was made a roving priest, went to the official Court, and eventually got into touch with his mother, who was still living with the prefect Liu Hung 劉洪. The letter placed in his bosom, and the shirt in which he had been wrapped, easily proved the truth of his statements. The mother, happy at having found her son, promised to go and see him at Chin Shan 金山. In order to do this she pretended to be sick, and told Liu Hung 劉洪 that formerly, when still young, she had taken a vow which she had not yet been able to fulfil. Liu Hung 劉洪 himself helped her to do so by sending a large gift of money to the priests, and allowed her to go with her servants to perform her devotions at the Chin-shan Ssŭ 金山寺. On this second visit, during which she could speak more freely with her son, she wished to see for herself the wound she had made on his foot. This removed the last shadow of doubt.

She told Hsüan Tsang 玄奘 that he must first of all go to Hung Chou 洪州 and find his grandmother, formerly left at the Wan-hua Tien 萬花店, Inn of Ten Thousand Flowers, and then on to Ch'ang-an 長安 to take to her father Yin K'ai-shan 殷開山 a letter, putting him in possession of the chief facts concerning Liu Hung 劉洪, and praying him to avenge her.

She gave him a stick of incense to take to her mother-in-law. The old lady lived the life of a beggar in a wretched hovel near the city gate, and had become blind from weeping. The priest told her of the tragic death of her son, then touched her eyes with the stick of incense, and her sight was restored. "And I," she exclaimed, "have so often accused my son of ingratitude, believing him to be still alive!" He took her back to the Wan-hua Tien 萬花店, Inn of Ten Thousand Flowers, and settled the account, then hastened to the palace of Yin K'ai-shan 殷開山. Having obtained an audience, he showed the minister the letter, and informed him of all that had taken place.

The following day a report was presented to the Emperor, who gave orders for the immediate arrest and execution of the murderer of Ch'ên Kuang-jui 陳 光 蕊.

Yin K'ai-shan 殷 開 山 went with all haste to Chên-chiang 鎮 江 (Chinkiang), where he arrived during the night, surrounded the official residence, and seized the culprit, whom he sent to the place where he had committed the murder. His heart and liver were torn out and sacrificed to the victim.

Now it happened that Ch'ên Kuang-jui 陳 光 蕊 was not dead after all. The carp released by him was in fact no other than Lung Wang 龍 王, the God of the River, who had been going through his kingdom in that guise and had been caught in the fisherman's net. On learning that his rescuer had been cast into the river, Lung Wang 龍 王 had saved him, and appointed him an officer of his Court. On that day, when his son, wife, and father-in-law were sacrificing the heart of his assassin to his *manes* on the river-bank, Lung Wang 龍 王 ordered that he return to earth. His body suddenly appeared on the surface of the water, floated to the bank, revived, and came out full of life and health. The happiness of the family reunited under such unexpected circumstances may well be imagined. Ch'ên Kuang-jui 陳 光 蕊 returned with his father-in-law to Chên-chiang 鎮 江 (Chinkiang), where he took up his official post, eighteen years after his nomination to it.

Hsüan Tsang 玄 奘 became the Emperor's favourite priest. He was held in great respect at the capital, and had innumerable honours bestowed upon him, and in the end was chosen for the journey to Hsi T'ien 西 天, the Western Paradise, where Buddha in person handed him the sacred books of Buddhism. On his return he was rewarded by Mi-lo Fo 彌 勒 佛, the President of the gathering of the gods, by being appointed Controller of Sacrifices to his Supreme Majesty Yü Huang 玉 皇, the Pearly Emperor.

Pai Ma 白 馬. The White Horse. When he left the capital, Hsüan Tsang 玄 奘 had been presented by the Emperor with a white horse to carry him on his long pilgrimage. One day, when he reached Shê-p'an Shan 蛇 盤 山, near a torrent, a dragon emerged from the deep river-bed and devoured both the horse and its saddle. Sun Hou-tzŭ 孫 猴 子 tried in vain to find the dragon, and at last had to seek the aid of Kuan Yin 觀 音.

Now Yü-lung san T'ai-tzŭ 玉 龍 三 太 子, son of Ao-jun 敖 閏, Dragon-king of the Western Sea, having burnt a precious pearl on the roof of his father's palace, was denounced to Yü Huang 玉 皇, who had him beaten with three hundred blows and suspended in the air. He was awaiting death when Kuan Yin 觀 音 passed on her way to China. The unfortunate dragon requested the goddess to have pity on him, whereupon she prevailed upon Yü Huang 玉 皇 to spare his life on condition that he served as steed for her pilgrim on the expedition to the Western Paradise. The dragon was handed over to Kuan Yin 觀音, who showed him the deep pool in which he was to dwell while awaiting the arrival of the priest. It was this dragon who had devoured Hsüan Tsang's 玄奘 horse, and Kuan Yin 觀音 now bade him change himself into a horse of the same colour to carry the priest to his destination. He had the honour of bearing on his back the sacred books that Buddha gave to T'ai Tsung's 太宗 deputy, and the first Buddhist temple built at the capital bore the name of Pai-ma Miao 白馬廟, Temple of the White Horse.

On the return of the pilgrims to China, Pai Ma 白馬 was led by a god down the Spirit Mountain, to the banks of the Pool of Dragon Transformation. Pai Ma 白馬 plunged in, and changed at once into a four-footed dragon, with horns, scales, claws, and wings complete. From this time he became the chief of the celestial dragon tribe.

For a full account of the various episodes and adventures of the journey, see the *Hsi-yu chi* 西遊記, and Werner, *Myths and Legends,* pp. 325-69.

SUN HSIANG 孫祥.—The god of the constellation Ts'an 參. Alternatively with Tu Mao 杜茂. Also the god of the star Ti-ying 地英.—See *Ti-sha* 地煞.

SUN HSING-CHÊ 孫行者.—See *Sun Hou-tzŭ* 猻猴子.

SUN HSÜAN 孫玄.—One of the Gods of Robbers. Others are: Tu P'ing 杜平, Li Ssŭ 李思, Jên An 任安, and Kêng Yen-chêng 耿彦正.

SUN I 孫乙.—The god of the star T'ien-mêng 天猛.—See *T'ien-kang* 天罡.

SUN PAO 孫寶.—See *Wu Tou* 五斗.

SUN PIN 孫臏 (賓).—The God of Cobblers, Shoemakers, and Harness-makers. A disciple of Kuei Ku-tzŭ 鬼谷子 who had his legs cut off by his erstwhile friend and sworn brother Pang Chüan 龐涓 through jealousy when Sun Pin 孫臏 had been given an official post by the King of Wei 魏. It is said that in reality his toes only were amputated, and that he made himself leather shoes to hide the deformity. Hence the worship accorded him by the handicraftsmen above-mentioned.

SUN SSŬ-MIAO (MO) 孫思邈.—The God of Druggists.

SUN TZŬ-YÜ 孫子羽.—See *Wu Tou* 五斗.

SUN WU-K'UNG 孫悟空.—See *Sun Hou-tzŭ* 猻猴子.

SUN YEN-HUNG 孫焰紅.—The god of the star Hsieh-kuang 血光. Could vomit flames which burnt his enemies. A subaltern officer of Têng Chiu-kung 鄧九公, who afterwards joined the forces fighting for the Chou 周 dynasty.

SUN, THE GOD OF THE.—With the worship of Heaven and Earth there came the belief in the supernatural powers of the Sun, the Moon, and the Stars. They were worshipped by the Emperor on the second terrace of the Round Altar at the time of the winter sacrifices. While they are inferior to and dependent on Heaven, they are not to be neglected, as much that man has is due to their good offces.

The Sun and Moon are the friends of man. The Sun-god is looked upon as the one who, in conjunction with the Moon-goddess, brings the cold and hot weather. On this account, they are both loved and feared. They are believed to be impartial in their service, shining upon good and evil. They not only help in gaining the increase from the Earth, but also they would protect their people against evil influences. They desire to serve all, but at times their benevolence is thwarted by clouds and storms. They are thought occasionally to do wrong, at which time their sin becomes apparent, as the Heavenly Dog attempts to devour them (an eclipse being supposed to be caused by it attempting to swallow the sun or moon). However, because they have constantly befriended man, the people both high and low immediately come to their rescue, and do not rest until they have saved their benefactors. By the burning of incense, by the firing of fire-crackers, and by the beating upon anything that will make a noise, they finally frighten away the Heavenly Dog, and feel proud and happy in having rescued their friends. Thus the friendship, help, and protection of the gods and man for the·gods is mutual. The practice, however, is less observed than formerly.

At one time there were supposed to be a number of moons. However, they have all been swallowed up by the Black Moon, or the Heavenly Dog, with the exception of the present one. For this reason the people fear for her safety, and exert themselves to protect her.

The Chief of the Three Great Lights is the Sun (Jih 日, or Yang 陽). Being the Yang 陽 (see *Hou I* 后羿), he rules the day. The special festival held in his honour, is on his birthday, the nineteenth of the third moon. At this time the people greet him in the early morning with incense, in the open courts and in front of their homes. During the day they flock to his temple, and there worship his idol. The first of the second month and the nineteenth of the eleventh month are also set aside for his service.

From the *Li chi* 禮記 it is evident that the worship of the Sun goes back to at least the Chou 周 dynasty. In the time of Yao 堯 (2357-2255 B.C.) there were ten suns, but they burnt up the trees and were more than man could endure. The life of each sun was bound up in a large crow (*wu* 烏). Hou I 后羿 took his bow and arrows and killed nine of these crows, whereupon their respective suns disappeared, leaving only the present one to bless mankind.—*Plopper*, p. 34-7. See also *Moon, the Goddess of the*.

SUNG CHIANG 宋江.—One of the Gods of Brigands. Commonly known as Sung Chiang 宋江 the Black, from his swarthy countenance. He was of small stature, a native of Yün-ch'êng Hsien 鄆城縣, Shantung 山東, his personal name being Kung-ming 公明. After ravaging the country in A.D. 1121, during the reign of the Emperor Hui Tsung 徽宗 (A.D. 1101-26) of the Sung 宋 dynasty, he was captured by the government troops under the Prefect Chang Shu 張叔. Eventually he was given the title of Celestial Protector of Liang Shan 梁山, Mount Liang, by Yü Huang 玉皇. His innumerable escapades and adventures form the theme of the celebrated romance *Shui-hu* 水滸.—See also *Wu-tao Chiang-chün* 五盜將軍, *Liu Chih* 柳跖, and *Shih Ch'ien* 時遷.

SUNG-CHIANG YU-I SHÊN 淞江遊奕神.—See *Shui Fu* 水府, D (1).

SUNG KÊNG 宋庚.—The god of the constellation Wei 胃. Alternatively with Wu Ch'êng 烏成.

SUNG-LI 嵩里, THE YOUNG GENTLEMAN OF.—See *Sung-li Hsiang-kung* 嵩里相公, *Lei Pu* 雷部, and *Yüan Ch'ien-li* 袁千里.

SUNG-LI HSIANG-KUNG 嵩里相公.—The Young Gentleman of Sung-li 嵩里. Family name Chao 趙, a native of Sung-li Ts'un 嵩里村, Shensi 陝西. Dashed his skull to pieces on the palace steps, because the Emperor took no heed of his suggestions. Is known by the people as Hsiang-kung 相公. In A.D. 712 was given the posthumous title of "Completely Frank Marquis" by the Emperor Jui Tsung 睿宗 (A.D. 710-3) of the T'ang 唐 dynasty.—See also *Composite Deities*.

SUNG LU 宋祿.—The god of the star Ti-ch'iu 地囚.—See *Ti-sha* 地煞.

SUNG SHAN 嵩山, THE GOD OF.—See *Pi-sha Yüan-chün* 碧霞元君 and *Wu Yo* 五嶽.

SUNG TA T'IEN CHÜN 宋大天君.—See *Ch'ü-hsieh Yüan* 驅邪院.

SUNG-TI WANG 宋帝王.—The President of the Third Court of Hades (*q.v.*).

SUNG T'OU-T'O 嵩頭陀.— A saintly Hindu Buddhist monk, who came from India toward the middle of the sixth century A.D., and abode with T'an-yin 曇隱 (*q.v.*) at the foot of Chung Shan 鍾山, Bell Mountain, near Nanking 南京, Kiangsu 江蘇. One of those invited to the annual banquet of the gods (see *Hsi Wang-mu* 西王母).

SUNG-TZŬ NIANG-NIANG 送子娘娘.—See *Chang Hsien* 張仙 and *Pi-hsia Yüan-chün* 碧霞元君.

SUNG WU-CHI 宋無忌.—The God of the Flame.

SUNG-YO FU-SÊNG CH'AN-SHIH 嵩岳伏僧禪師.—In a famous monastery on the sacred Sung Yo 嵩岳, Mount Sung, in Honan 河南, lived a hermit monk named P'o-tsao-to 破竈墮. The only statue adorning the sanctuary was one of Tsao Chün 竈君 (*q.v.*), the God of the Hearth. Several prodigies were ascribed to this statue, and sacrifices daily offered to it by the people.

When Fu-sêng 伏僧 arrived in the temple, he struck the statue with his staff, saying: "Tsao Chün 竈君 is but a mud god seated on a pile of bricks; whence comes the transcendent power ascribed to him?" He then again struck the statue, three hard blows, shattering it to pieces. Thereupon a genie, dressed in blue, appeared and, prostrating himself before Fu-sêng 伏僧, said: "I am Tsao Chün 竈君, the God of the Hearth; for long I have been confined in penance, but to-day you have released me from my corporeal prison and I can now ascend to heaven (namely, that of Yü Huang 玉皇, *q.v.*). I am grateful to you for liberating me." Having said this he disappeared.

Fu-sêng's 伏僧 disciples asked him what means he had employed to enable the god to ascend to heaven. He answered: "I merely said to him: 'You are nothing but a mass of mud and bricks.'" As they remained silent, Fu-sêng 伏僧 added: "Do you know how to cast off the bodily envelope?" "No," they replied, looking ashamed. "Then you are ignorant of your own nature," he said; "it must be broken before rebirth can take place." (Death being the gateway to a new metamorphosis, the soul wanders through creation, until it is purified enough to be reabsorbed into the One, Universal, Impersonal Spirit, with which the whole visible world is identified.) The disciples thus understood how, in breaking up the statue, Fu-sêng 伏僧 had delivered Tsao Chün 竈君 from his captivity. Literally, the phrase means: "In breaking up (the god) Tsao, I restored him to a new life": a play on the characters composing the name P'o-tsao-to 破竈墮 and *p'o*

破, to break to pieces, *to* 墮, to be reborn in a new phase of existence.

SUPAKA.—See *Lo-han* 羅漢.

SUPRABHA.—See *Lo-han* 羅漢.

SUPREME BUDDHA, THE.—See *Lo-han* 羅漢 and *Adi-Buddha*.

SUPRIYA.—See *Lo-han* 羅漢.

SURAS.—In the *Vedas,* a class of beings connected with Surya, the sun. The inferior deities who inhabit Swarga; a god in general. According to some, the word is allied to *swar,* "heaven"; others think it to have sprung from the derivation assigned to *asura,* and as *a-sura* is said to signify "not a god," *sura* has come to mean "god."

SURYA.—The sun or its deity. He is one of the three chief deities in the *Vedas,* as the great source of light and warmth, but the references to him are more poetical than precise.

SUTRA.—"A thread or string." A rule or aphorism. A verse expressed in brief and technical language—a very favourite form among the Hindus of embodying and transmitting rules. There are *sutras* upon almost every subject, but "the *sutras*" generally signify those which are connected with the *Vedas*.

SWORN BROTHERS, THE THREE.—*See San-i Ko* 三義 閣.

T

TA-CHIH CH'AN-SHIH 大志禪師 —A monk of the Ku 顧 family. A native of Hui-chi 會稽. His name, Ta-chih 大志, Vast Disposition, was given to him by his teacher in recognition of his intelligence whilst in the Buddhist monastery he had entered in early youth. Possessed of a fine voice, he delighted in chanting the *Fa-hua ching* 法華經, *Saddharma Pundarika, Lotus of the Good Law*.

When, later on, he went to the Kan-lu Ssŭ 甘露寺, Sweet Dew Monastery, on Lu Shan 廬山, he lived most abstemiously, constantly reciting the Buddhist prayers. Eventually he became abbot of the Fu-lin Ssŭ 福林寺, Happy Forest Monastery.

During the reign of Yang Ti 煬帝 (A.D. 605-17) of the Sui 隋 dynasty, when, it is alleged, that Emperor decided to persecute Buddhism, Ta-chih 大志 donned mourning garments and wept in the temple for three days. He then proceeded to Lo-yang 洛陽, Honan 河南, the eastern capital, and presented a petition to the Emperor, offering himself to be burnt alive on Sung Shan 嵩山, if His Majesty would spare the lives of his co-religionists.

His offer being accepted, he proceeded to Sung Shan 嵩山, where, after fasting for three days, he wrapped cloth around his body, seated himself in a stove, poured wax all around and set it alight, the flames illuminating the whole mountain. He, however, in spite of the lamentations of the spectators, remained perfectly calm, reciting prayers, invoking the Buddha, and preaching the doctrine. When the wax was burnt out, he descended from the stove and sat down, crossing his legs in the Buddhist fashion. He survived for seven days.

Tradition has made him a martyr in the cause of Buddhism, and in the pictorial representations he is always shown seated burning in a stove or urn.

473

TA-HAO 大耗, THE GOD OF THE STAR.—See *Ch'ung Hou-hu* 崇侯虎.

TA-HUO 大禍, THE GOD OF THE STAR.—See *Li Liang* 李良.

TA LU 大路.—See *Lo-han* 羅漢.

TA-MO TA-SHIH 大磨大師.—See *Patriarchs: Bodhidharma*.

TA-MO-TO-LO 達摩多羅.—See *Lo-han* 羅漢.

TA-NAI FU-JÊN 大奶夫人.—The Greatly Honoured Dame. The real Matron who Hastens Child-birth (see *Ts'ui-shêng Niang-niang* 催生娘娘). One of the specialists attached to the celestial Ministry of Medicine. A daughter of Ch'ên Chien-i 陳諫議, an official of the Revenue Board. Her mother was of the Ko 葛 family. Lived at Hsia-tu 下渡, in Lo Hsien 羅縣, Fu-chou Fu 福州府 (Foochow), Fukien 福建. Her two brothers were Ch'ên Êrh-hsiang 陳二相 and Ch'ên Hai-ching 陳海清.

Kuan Yin 觀音, when passing over Fu-chou 福州, noticing a diabolical emanation rising into the air, cut off one of her fingers and changed it into a ray of light which entered the womb of Mrs. Ko 葛, Ch'ên Chien-i's 陳諫議 wife, and caused her to give birth, amid many miraculous signs from Heaven, to a girl child. The latter was named Chin-ku 進姑, "Girl introduced by the Gods," on this account. This was in A.D. 766.

In A.D. 417, an evil spirit appeared in the form of a serpent called Shê Mu 蛇母, the Mother of Serpents, in Ling-ch'i Ta-tung 靈氣大洞, in Ku-t'ien Hsien 古田縣, Fukien 福建, and devoured many people. The inhabitants of Lin-shui Ts'un 臨水村 built a temple to her, and annually on the ninth day of the ninth moon sacrificed a boy and a girl to stop her ravages.

Êrh-hsiang 二相 was requested to free the place of this monster, but being drunk at the time, his transcendent soldiers were called to arms in vain, and the serpent was about to devour him. At this juncture, Yü Chia 瑜珈, Êrh-hsiang's 二相 master, appeared in the air, and let fall a gold bell, which encompassed Êrh-hsiang 二相, so that the serpent could not bite him. But he was unable to get out.

His sister, Chin-ku 進姑, or Ta-nai Fu-jên 大奶夫人, at once fetched Chiu-lang Fa-shih 九郎法師 (*q.v.*) from Lü Shan 閭山, who by a mysterious process manipulated the thunder to strike the serpent dead and deliver her brother.

For safely and painlessly delivering the Empress of an heir to the throne the Emperor bestowed on Ta-nai Fu-jên 大奶夫人 the title of Greatly Honoured Dame, Protectress of the Realm, Miraculous Benefactor of Humanity. He also had a temple built to her at Ku-t'ien 古田, so that she might continue to protect humanity from the young transcendent serpents, the progeny of this slain mother.

She was canonized under the title of Ts'ui-shêng Shêng-mu 催生聖母, the Saintly Mother who hastens Childbirth, her relatives and assistants also receiving posthumous honorary titles.

Two acolytes are represented beside her in the temples: P'ei-t'ai Niang-niang 培胎娘娘, the Lady who Promotes Conception, and Yin-mêng Niang-niang 引蒙娘娘, the Lady who Brings Children. —See also T'ien I-yüan 天醫院.

TA-P'ÊNG CHIN-CH'IH NIAO 大鵬金翅鳥.—See Yü-i Hsien 羽翼仙.

TA SHÊNG 大乘.—"The Great Conveyance." The Mahayana School of Buddhism.

TA SHÊNG 大聖.—The Great (Buddhist) Saint. Sêng-chia Ta-shih 僧伽大師, the Great Buddhist Teacher. A Hindu rishi, or monk. A native of the West, Hsi-yü 西域 (probably Khotan or Turkestan). Popularly known as Ho 何. His Indian name is unknown. When asked what it was, he stated that he was called Ho 何, and that he came from the country of Ho 何.

Arrived from India in A.D. 705, when Chung Tsung 中宗 (A.D. 705-10) of the T'ang 唐 dynasty had been proclaimed Emperor in place of the usurper Wu Hou 武后 (A.D. 684-705), the Dowager-Empress Wu 武. It is surmised that he may have accompanied the monk I-ching 義淨, who returned from India to China A.D. 695, bringing with him 400 sutras, an image of Indra, and 300 relics. But according to a writer in the New China Review, July 1919, p. 222, as he died in A.D. 710, at the age of 83, and lived in China fifty-three years, he must have arrived in A.D. 657 (v. infra).

He abode at first in the Lung-hsing Ssŭ 龍興寺, Lung-hsing Monastery, at Huai-an 淮安, Kiangsu 江蘇, but afterward went to Lin-an Hsien 臨安縣, a sub-district in Ssŭ-chou 泗洲, Anhui 安徽.

He begged the inhabitants to grant him a piece of land whereon to build a monastery. When they had acceded to his request, he erected a tall mast on the site, and during the excavations preparatory to building, a temple servant or lay helper or helpers unearthed from beneath the mast a stone slab belonging to the ancient Hsiang-chi Ssŭ 香積寺, Monastery of Copious Incense, and a golden statue bearing the characters P'u-chao Wang Fo 普照王佛, Buddha, the World-illuminating King.

In the meanwhile, the prince imperial having been killed in a battle, the Emperor Chung Tsung 中宗 (A.D. 705-10) sent for the Hindu monk Ho 何 to perform the funeral rites for the deceased prince. He was taken to Lo-yang 洛陽, Honan 河南, in an imperial carriage, and received with great honour. The Emperor

conferred on him the title of Kuo-shih 國師, State Preceptor—
whence the inscription frequently seen on popular images:—*Ta
Shêng Kuo-shih Wang* 大聖國師王, "Great Saint Prince and
State Preceptor."

At Lo-yang 洛陽 he resided in the Chien-fu Ssŭ 薦福寺,
"Prosperity-bringing Monastery," where the priest Wan-hui
萬迴, who had been invited some years previously by Wu Hou
武后 (A.D. 684-705), the Empress-Dowager Wu, also dwelt.
Though Wan-hui 萬迴 treated the new arrival with honour and
respect, the latter gave him a hint that he need not prolong his
stay. Wan-hui 萬迴 preferring to remain, however, a separate
cell was assigned to Ho 何 (this was in A.D. 708), and it is alleged
that he had on the top of his head a hole, which he kept closed
during the day with cotton-wool. At night-time, when he
removed the wad, a sweet fragrance escaped, and perfumed all
the rooms. At dawn the delicious odours re-entered the hole in
his head. Water in which he had washed his feet was eagerly
sought after, and sick people who drank it were all cured.

A severe drought devasting the country at that time, the
Emperor requested the priest to put a stop to the scourge. He at
once caused abundant rain to fall, by sprinkling the ground by
wetting a willow branch with lustral water from a phial which
he always carried with him (*v. infra*). To reward him, the
Emperor wrote with his own hand an inscription for his monastery
at Lin-hui, Lin-hui Ssŭ 臨淮寺.

In A.D. 710, seating himself cross-legged in Indian fashion in the
Chien-fu Ssŭ 薦福寺, he expired on the twelfth day of the third
moon, at the age of 83, having been fifty-three years in China.

The Emperor ordered his corpse to be embalmed, and exposed
in the temple for the veneration of the people. However, a violent
wind suddenly arose, and a foetid odour infected the whole town.
The Court officials represented to the Emperor, Chung Tsung
中宗 (A.D. 705-10), that apparently the monk wished his body to
be taken to his former monastery at Lin-hui Hsien 臨淮縣. No
sooner had the Emperor resolved in his mind to agree to their
suggestion than an agreeable prefume replaced the nauseating
odour.

This was taken as indicating the deceased monk's pleasure at
the Emperor's decision, and in the fifth moon his remains, after
having been escorted with honour by all the high officials as far
as the gate of the capital, were transported to Lin-hui Hsien
臨淮縣, where, by the Emperor's order, a tower was erected to
commemorate his life and work. A tower is nearly always
printed on the *chih-ma* 紙馬* used in religious ceremonials in

---

* These are portraits of deceased persons printed on small sheets of thin
unmounted paper, generally used by the poorer classes. The portrait having
been placed in a suitable place, the Spirit is supposed to descend from
heaven and take up its temporary abode in it. After he has been worshipped,
the paper portrait is burnt and he is sent back to heaven.

his honour. His Majesty enquired of his companion Wan-hui 萬迴 who this extraordinary monk was. Wan-hui 萬迴 replied: "He was an incarnation of Kuan Yin 觀音." The willow-branch and phial of water noted above as being habitually carried by Ta Shêng 大聖, are well-known symbols of the Goddess of Mercy (see *Kuan Yin* 觀音).

Some variations of detail in the above account are found in the *Sou-shên chi* 搜神記. The chief of these are:—the date of his arrival in China is given as in the reign of Kao Tsung 高宗 (A.D. 650-84), and the day of his death as the third day of the third moon in A.D. 710.

Of the shrines erected to his memory, one of the most famous is that on Lang Shan 狼山, Wolf Hill, five miles S.W. of T'ung Chou 通州, N. Kiangsu 江蘇. It is said to be so called because of its resemblance to a wolf sitting on its haunches, but another account states it was formerly the home of a white wolf, from the ravages of which Ta-shêng 大聖 delivered the inhabitants of that district.

On reaching Lang Shan 狼山, the monk had begged the people to grant him a site for the erection of a monastery. This is said to have been the origin of this famous shrine, which annually attracts thousands of pilgrims from the neighbouring towns and villages. For a detailed description of it, see Doré, *Superstitions,* vii, 267-70.

Among the legends related concerning him, transmitted verbally from generation to generation, the most popular one in that locality is as follows:—

The great Buddhist Saint, Ta Shêng 大聖, lived in a temple situated in the large village of Hsi-ch'i 西岐, beyond the Grand Canal, in Hsia-ho 下河 (Tung-t'ai 東臺), Kiangsu 江蘇. One fine morning, he left the monastery, carrying on his shoulders two trays (or sections) of a steamed-bread basket (*mo-lung* 饃籠, a kind of oval basket, with a tier of shelves or sections, on which the loaves are placed and steamed in the vapour of boiling water rising from the pot placed underneath and penetrating to all the superimposed sections). The monk bore on his shoulders what seemed to be two of these sections. He proceeded on the way to Li-fa Ch'iao 立發橋, a village situated on the N.W. frontier of the sub-prefecture of Ju-kao 如皋, in N. Kiangsu 江蘇. On reaching the stone crossing which spanned the canal, he enquired whether the bridge could bear him. Bystanders laughingly told him that hundreds of people crossed it every day, and that none had ever doubted its security. The monk accordingly started to cross it, but when he reached the central arch the bridge swayed and seemed about to collapse. At that moment Kuan Yin 觀音, the Goddess of Mercy, appeared walking on the water, and with her hand supported the arch until the monk had passed over in safety. But no sooner had he set foot on the bank than the bridge collapsed, and from that day it has been impossible to rebuild it.

But when, after Ta Shêng's 大聖 departure the inhabitants of Hsi-ch'i 西岐 examined the tower built near their local monastery, they were astonished to see that the two upper storeys had disappeared. They then knew that the two sections of the *mo-lung* 窣籠 which the monk had carried on his shoulders were these two storeys beneath whose enormous weight the Li-fa 立發 bridge had collapsed.

TA-SHIH-CHIH 大勢至 (Mahasthama or Mahasthanaprata, a Bodhisattva belonging to the retinue of Amitabha).—The Bodhisattva who has obtained great strength. Perhaps a deified form of Maudgalyayana, the right-hand disciple of Sakyamuni. Famous for his magic powers. Released his mother from Hades, where she was suffering as a hungry ghost (*prêta*). His birthday is celebrated on the thirteenth day of the seventh month.—See *Maudgalyayana* and *Mu-lien Ti-tsang Wang* 目連地藏王.

TA-SHIH T'IEN 大是天.—T'ai Ch'ing 太清, the Supreme Azure. One of the three divisions into which the primordial cosmic ether separated. Populated by the *hsien-jên* 仙人 (*q.v.*), human souls endowed with divine powers.—See *San Ch'ing* 三清.

TA-TU 大度.—A saintly Buddhist monk. One of those invited to the annual banquet of the gods (see *Hsi Wang-mu* 西王母).

TA-YIN CH'AN-SHIH 大音禪師 (66th generation).—A deified Buddhist monk. Ranked sixty-sixth in Buddhist School, VI (*q.v.*). Family name Yao 姚. A native of Yü-ch'i 語溪 Chêkiang 浙江. Trained at Pien Shan 弁山 under [Jui-pai] Ming-hsüeh Ch'an-shih [瑞白] 明雪禪師 (*q.v.*). Later, he was appointed Superior of the monastery, and died there. His tomb is on the Pei Wu 北塢, one of the peaks of Pien Shan 弁山.

TAI LI 戴禮.—The god of the star Huang-wu 荒蕪. The transcendent dog, a genie of Mei Shan 梅山, Mount Mei, incarnated in human form. One of Yüan Hung's 袁洪 officers at Mêng-ching 孟津. Slain, after several encounters, by Yang Chien 楊戩 in the Yin-Chou 殷周 wars.

TAI-SU P'AN-TU 代蘇盤度.—See *Shih-ch'in P'u-sa* 世親菩薩.

TAI-YO T'AI-P'ING HSIANG YÜ-HSIEN NIANG-NIANG 岱岳太平頊玉仙娘娘.—See *Pi-hsia Yüan-chün* 碧霞元君.

T'AI CHI 太極.—The Great Extreme. The Great Ultimate. The Grand Ridge-pole. The Primal Monad (a mingled potentiality of Form, Breath, and Substance). Synonymous with Hun-tun 渾沌, chaos. The Ultimate Ground of Existence. The insufficiency of the dualism which finds expression in the contrast of the *yang* 陽 and *yin* 陰 principles, led to a gradual tendency toward monism. The *yang* 陽 and *yin* 陰 are thought to have originated in a process of differentation through the T'ai-i 太易, Great Change, T'ai-ch'u 太初, Great Starting, T'ai-shih 太始, Great Beginning, T'ai-su 太素, Great Blank, and Liang I 兩儀, two primary symbols representing *Yin* 陰 and *Yang* 陽, from the T'ai Chi 太極, which is "the Grand Origin," *der Urgrund,* the source of existence. Gabelentz translates it, *das Urprinzip,* Legge and other English sinologists, "the Grand Terminus," or "the Grand Extreme." Its symbol is a circle, thus: O (see Werner, *The Chinese Idea of the Second Self*).

T'AI-CHIEN 太堅.—Son of Ch'i 棄, son of the Emperor Ti K'u 帝嚳.—See *Shê Chi* 社稷.

T'AI CH'ING 太清.—Great Pure. The Heaven inhabited by the *hsien jên* 仙人, human souls endowed with divine powers. —See *San Ch'ing* 三清, *Lao Tzŭ* 老子, *Shên Pao* 神寶, *Ling-pao T'ien-tsun* 靈寶天尊, and *Hsien Jên* 仙人.

T'AI HU 太湖 LAKE, THE SPIRIT OF THE.—See *Shui Fu* 水府, D (2) (c).

T'AI I 太一.—The Great One. The Great Unity. This conception has taken various forms in the course of ages. Temples are found in various parts dedicated to T'ai I 太一. When the Emperor Wu Ti 武帝 (140-86 B.C.) of the Han 漢 dynasty was in search of the secret of immortality, and various suggestions had proved unsatisfactory, a Taoist priest, Miao-chi 謬忌, told the Emperor that his want of success was due to his omission to sacrifice to T'ai I 太一, the first of the celestial spirits, quoting the classical precedent of antiquity found in the *Shu-ching* 書經, *Book of History.* The Emperor, believing his word, ordered the Grand Master of Sacrifices to re-establish this worship at the capital. He followed carefully the prescriptions of Miao-chi 謬忌. This enraged the Scholars (Literati), who resolved to ruin him. One day, when the Emperor was about to drink one of his potions, one of the chief courtiers seized the cup and drank the contents himself. The Emperor was about to have him slain, when he said: "Your Majesty's order is unnecessary; if the potion confers immortality, I cannot be killed; if, on the other hand, it does not, Your Majesty should recompense me for disproving the pretensions of the Taoist priest." The Emperor, however, was not convinced.

One account represents T'ai I 太一 as having lived in the time of Shên Nung 神農 (2838-2698 B.C.), the Divine Husbandman, who visited him to consult with him on the subjects of diseases and fortune. He was Hsüan Yüan's 軒轅 (2698-2598 B.C.) medical preceptor. His medical knowledge was handed down to subsequent generations. He was one of those who, with the Immortals, was invited to the great Peach Assembly of Hsi-wang Mu 西王母, the Western Royal Mother.

As the spirit of the star T'ai I 太一 he resides in the Eastern Palace, listening for the cries of sufferers in order to save them. For this purpose he assumes numberless forms in numerous regions. With a boat of lotus-flowers of nine colours he ferries men over to the shore of salvation. Holding in his hand a willow-branch, he scatters from it the dew of the Doctrine.

T'ai I 太一 is represented as the highest of the Heavenly Genii, the Ruler of the Five Celestial Sovereigns: Green of the East, Red of the South, White of the West, Black of the North, and Yellow of the Centre. Hence he is of the same rank as Shang Ti 上帝, the Supreme Being.

After a request for the abolition of the worship of T'ai I 太一, on account of its being unclassical, in the reign of Yüan Ti 元帝 (48-32 B.C.) of the Han 漢 dynasty, the worship declined, and sacrifices to him are not again mentioned, at least officially, until the reign of the Emperor Hsüan Tsung 玄宗 (A.D. 713-56) of the T'ang 唐 dynasty.

T'ai I 太一 is also represented as Cosmic Matter before it congealed into concrete shapes. From that process resulted the Heaven and the earth; its revolutions constituted the *Yin* 陰 and *Yang* 陽 (*q.v.*); its changes produced the four seasons; and from the subordination of its parts the *Shên* 神, Genii, and the *Kuei* 鬼, dependants, were born (see *Shên* 神).

Another representation of T'ai I 太一 is as the Triune Genie of Heaven, regarded as one if taken separately, and as three entities, if regarded together with the entity Heaven and the entity Earth. Thus Heaven, Earth, and T'ai I 太一 form a triad, of which the single Genie is the Great One or Unity. In ancient times, according to the Taoists, the Emperor sacrificed an ox every three years to the One and Triune Genie: the Heaven One, the Earth One, and the Great One. This view was sanctioned by the Emperor Wu Ti 武帝 (140-86 B.C.) of the Han 漢 dynasty.

The *Ming shih* 明史 (bk. 49, p. 18) states that it is not known which genie is designated by the term T'ai I 太一, then in general use. The term, according to the *Yüan chien lei han* 淵鑑類函 and the *Wên hsien t'ung k'ao* 文獻通考, is also applied to the Genie of the Pole Star, who had taken up his abode in that luminary; and also to the Genie of the first of the nine constellations, known as the star T'ien-p'êng 天蓬.

The Emperor Hsüan Tsung 玄宗 (A.D. 713-56) of the T'ang 唐 dynasty, was deceived by the Taoists into sacrificing to the Genii of the Nine Constellations. His son, the next Emperor,

T'AI-P'ING HSIANG
OF THE SACRED
MOUNTAIN T'AI-
SHAN, THE
IMMORTAL JADE
MATRON OF

Su Tsung 肅宗 (A.D. 756-63) worshipped T'ai I 太一 separately at a special altar.

The Emperor Jên Tsung 仁宗 (A.D. 1023-64) instituted the T'ai I 太一, Great One, of the West; and Shên Tsung 神宗 (A.D. 1068-86) of the Sung 宋 dynasty, instituted the T'ai I 太一 of the Centre, giving him the title of Wu Fu 五福, Five Blessings. Further, he raised the number of T'ai I 太一 genii to ten. The Emperor Hui Tsung 徽宗 (A.D. 1101-26) of the Sung 宋 dynasty instituted the T'ai I 太一 of the North.

The Ten T'ai I 太一 Genii are the T'ai I 太一 of (1) the Five Blessings; (2) the Prince; (3) the Officials; (4) the People; (5) the nine agents of nature; (6) the great voyages; (7) the small voyages; (8) the Four Genii; (9) the Heaven Unity; and (10) the Earth Unity.

In spite of a strong protest raised by his minister Mou Tzŭ-ts'ai 牟子才 against the erection of a temple to T'ai I 太一 in the West and his worship there in A.D. 1252 by the Emperor Li Tsung 理宗 (A.C. 1225-65) of the Nan Sung 南宋, Southern Sung, dynasty, T'ai I 太 continued to be worshipped under the Yüan 元, and also under the Ming 明 dynasty, though the procedure was opposed, during the latter period by the Minister of Rites, resulting in the worship being carried on, not as before on a separate altar, but on that of the celestial Genii-agents of the wind, clouds, thunder, and rain.

Practically, however, the Taoists confine their T'ai I 太一 to T'ai I Chên-jên 太一眞人 (q.v.), in which Perfect Man they personify the abstract philosophical notions. (See also *Babylonian and Oriental Record*, VI, 145-50; Doré, IX, 557-62).

T'AI-I CHÊN-JÊN 太一眞人.—See *T'ai I* 太一.

T'AI-I CHÜN 太一君.—See *Mouth, The Gods of the.*

T'AI-I HUANG-JÊN 泰壹皇人.—An emperor who lived in the fabulous times after the Jên Huang 人皇, the family of Human Sovereigns. He was elected emperor because of his special ability for governing, and is said to have reigned four hundred years. He had two sons the elder named Tu 都, and the younger Chang 章. He studied the science of Immortality on O-mei Shan 峨帽山, Mount O-mei.—See also *Chên-yüan Hsien* 蕻元仙.

T'AI LUAN 太鸞.—The god of the star P'i-t'ou 披頭. An officer under the command of general Têng Chiu-kung 鄧九公. Having, with his chief, joined the party of Wu Wang 武王 (1121-1114 B.C.), was killed by Yü Ta 余達, a leader of the hostile troops.

T'AI-P'ING HSIANG 太平項 OF THE SACRED MOUNTAIN T'AI-SHAN 泰山, THE IMMORTAL JADE MATRON OF.—See *Pi-hsia Yüan-chün* 碧霞元君.

T'AI-PO CHIN-HSING 太白金星.—The god of the planet Venus (Chin Hsing 金星). But Tung-fan Shuo 東方朔 (*q.v.*) is more generally worshipped as such.

T'AI SHAN 泰山, THE GOD OF.—See *Pi-hsia Yüan-chün* 碧霞元君 and *Wu Yo* 五嶽.

T'AI SHAN 泰山, THE GODDESS OF.—See *Pi-hsia Yüan-chün* 碧霞元君 and *Ts'ai Shên* 財神.

T'AI-SHAN 泰山, THE MATRON OF.—See *Pi-hsia Yüan-chün* 碧霞元君.

T'AI SHAN NIANG-NIANG 泰山娘娘.—See *Pi-hsia Yüan-chün* 碧霞元君.

T'AI-SHAN SHIH KAN-TANG 泰山石敢當.—See *Shih Kan-tang* 石敢當.

T'AI-SHAN WANG 泰山王.—The President of the Seventh Court of Hades (*q.v.*).

T'AI-SHANG SAN KUAN 太上三官.—See *San Kuan* 三官.

T'AI-SHÊNG 胎神, THE GOD OF THE STAR.—See *Chi Shu-li* 姬叔禮.

T'AI SUI 太歲.—The President of the Ministry of Time. Also the Ministry of Time itself. The celestial Spirit who presides over the year. The Spirit of the Year. Whoever offends against this god is sure to be destroyed. He strikes when least expected to. The members of the Ministry, 120 in number, are set over time, years, months, and days. The conception is said to be of Chaldeo-Assyrian origin.

The god T'ai Sui 太歲 is not mentioned in the T'ang 唐 and Sung 宋 rituals, but in the Yüan 元 dynasty sacrifices were offered to him in the College of the Grand Historiographer whenever any work of importance was about to be undertaken. Under this dynasty the sacrifices were offered to T'ai Sui 太歲 and to the ruling gods of the months and of the days. But these sacrifices were not offered at regular times: it was only at the beginning of the Ch'ing 清 (Manchu) dynasty that it was decided to offer the sacrifices at fixed periods.

T'ai Sui 太歲 corresponds to the planet Jupiter. He travels across the sky, passing through the twelve sidereal mansions. He is a stellar god. Therefore an altar is raised to him and sacrifices are offered on it under the open sky. This practice dates from the beginning of the Ming 明 dynasty, when the Emperor T'ai Tsu 太祖 (A.D. 1368-99) ordered sacrifices to this god to be made throughout the empire. According to some authors, he corresponds to the god of the twelve sidereal mansions. He is also variously represented as the moon, which turns to the left in the sky, and the sun, which turns to the right. The diviners gave to T'ai Sui 太歲 the title of Grand Marshal, following the example of the usurper Wang Mang 王莽 (A.D. 9-23) of the Western Han 漢 dynasty, who gave that title to the year-star.

The *Fêng shên yen i* 封神演義 gives the composition of the Ministry of Time as follows: — President: Yin Chiao 殷郊. Members: (1) Spirit for Day Service, Wên Liang 溫良; (2) Spirit for Night Service, Chiao K'un 喬坤; (3) Spirit who Accumulates Happiness, Han Tu-lung 韓毒龍; (4) Spirit who Bears Misfortunes, Hsieh O-hu 薛惡虎; (6) Spirit who Acts as Guide, Fang Pi 方弼; (6) Spirit who Acts as Herald, Fang Hsiang 方相; (7) Spirit who Superintends the Year (Chih-nien 值年), Li Ping 李丙; (8) Spirit who Superintends the Month (Chih-yüeh 值月), Huang Ch'êng-i 黃承乙; (9) Spirit who Superintends the Day (Chih-jih 值日), Chou Têng 周登; (10) Spirit who Superintends the Period (Chih-shih 值時), Liu Hung 劉洪.

The last four officials of the Ministry (*Ssǔ ta kung-ts'ao* 四大功曹) all perished in the great battle of the Ten thousand Genii, *Wan-hsien Chên* 萬仙陣.

The worship of T'ai Sui 太歲 is first noted in the reign of the Emperor Shên Tsung 神宗 (A.D. 1068-86) of the Sung 宋 dynasty, and was continued during the remainder of the Monarchical Period (to A.D. 1912). The object of the worship is to avoid calamities, T'ai Sui 太歲 being a dangerous spirit who can do injury to palaces and cottages, to people in their houses as well as to travellers on the road. But he has this peculiarity, that he injures persons and things not in the district in which he himself is, but in those districts which adjoin it. Thus, if some constructive work is undertaken in a region where T'ai Sui 太歲 happens to be, the inhabitants of the neighbouring districts take precautions against his evil influence. This they generally do by hanging out the appropriate talisman. In order to ascertain in what region T'ai Sui 太歲 is at any particular time, an elaborate diagram is consulted. This consists of a representation of the twelve terrestrial branches or stems, *ti-chih* 地支, and the ten celestial trunks, *t'ien kan* 天干, indicating the cardinal points and the intermediate points, north-east, north-west, south-east, and south-west. The four cardinal points are further verified with the aid of the Five Natural Forces, the Five Colours, and the Eight Trigrams. By using this device, it is possible to find the geographical position of T'ai Sui 太歲 during the current year, the position of threatened districts, and the methods to be employed to provide against danger.

The legend of T'ai Sui 太歲 relates that he was the son of the Emperor Chou 紂 (1154-1121 B.C.) of the Yin 殷 dynasty. His mother was Queen Chiang 姜. When he was born he looked like a lump of formless flesh. The infamous Ta Chi 妲己, the famous concubine of this wicked Emperor, at once informed him that a monster had been born in the palace, and the over-credulous sovereign ordered that it should immediately be cast outside the city. Shên Chên-jên 申眞人, who was passing, saw the small abandoned one, and said: "This is an Immortal who has just been born." With his knife he cut open the caul which enveloped it, and the child was exposed.

His protector carried him to the cave Shui-lien 水濂, where he led the life of a hermit, and entrusted the infant to Ho Hsien-ku 賀仙姑 (see *Pa-hsien* 八仙), who acted as his nurse and brought him up.

The child's hermit name was Yin [chin] Ting-nu 唫叮哣, his ordinary name Yin [Chin] No-cha 金哪吒, but during his boyhood he was known as Yin-chiao 殷郊, *i.e.* "Yin the Deserted of the Suburb." When he had reached an age when he was sufficiently intelligent, his nurse informed him that he was not her son, but really the son of King Chou 紂, who, deceived by the calumnies of his favourite Ta Chi 妲己, had taken him for an evil monster and had him cast out of the palace. His mother had been thrown down from an upper storey and killed. Yin-chiao 殷郊 went to his rescuer and begged him to allow him to revenge his mother's death. The Goddess T'ien Fei 天妃 (*q.v.*), the Heavenly Concubine, picked out two magic weapons from the armoury in the cave, a battle-axe and club, both of gold, and gave them to Yin-chiao 殷郊. When the Yin 殷 army was defeated at Mu-yeh 牧野, Yin-chiao 殷郊 broke into a tower where Ta Chi 妲己 was, seized her, and brought her before the victor, King Wu 武, who gave him permission to split her head open with his battle-axe. But Ta Chi 妲己 was a spiritual hen-pheasant (some say a spiritual vixen). She transformed herself into smoke and disappeared. To reward Yin-chiao 殷郊 for his filial piety and bravery in fighting the demons, Yü Ti 玉帝 canonized him with the title T'ai Sui 太歲, Marshal Yin 殷.

Another version describes Yin-chiao 殷郊 as fighting on the side of the Yin 殷 against Wu Wang 武王 (1121-1114 B.C.), and after many adventures being caught by Jan-têng 燃燈 (*q.v.*) between two mountains, which he pressed together, leaving only Yin-chiao's 殷郊 head exposed above the summits. The general Wu Chi 武吉 promptly cut it off with a spade. Chiang Tzŭ-ya 姜子牙 subsequently canonized Yin-chiao 殷郊.

T'AI TSU 太祖.—See *Shê Chi* 社稷.

T'AI TSUNG 太宗.—See *Shê Chi* 社稷.

T'AI-YANG 太陽 (the sun), THE GOD OF THE STAR.— See *Hsü Kai* 徐蓋.

T'AI-YIN 太陰 (the moon), THE GODDESS OF THE STAR.—See *Chiang* 姜.

T'AI-YIN SHÊN 太陰神.—See *Chin, The Gods of the.*

TAILORS, THE GOD OF.—Hsüan Yüan 軒轅 (Huang Ti 黃帝) (2698-2598 B.C.) is worshipped as their god by tailors. Before his time men wore raiment of fig leaves, and he first taught them to wear clothing.—See *Hsüan-yüan Huang-ti* 軒轅黃帝 and *Yen-kuang P'u-sa* 眼光菩薩.

TAKSHAKA.—A dragon-king.—See *Lung Wang* 龍王.

TAMRA BHADRA.—See *Lo-han* 羅漢.

TAN CHU 丹朱.—See *Teeth, The God of the.*

TAN HSI-SHÊNG 丹溪生.—See *Shih Ming-i* 十明醫, 4.

TAN LING-CHIH 丹靈峙.—See *Wu Yo* 五嶽.

TAN PAI-CHAO 單百招.—The god of the star T'ien-chiu 天究.—See *T'ien-kang* 天罡.

TAN YÜAN 丹元.—See *Heart, The Gods of the.*

T'AN-HUA CH'AN-SHIH 曇華禪師.—A saintly Buddhist monk. Fifth century. Taken by Ch'ih Sung-tzǔ 赤松子 to the Hsiao 蕭 family (see *Ch'ang-yang* 菖陽), where he found means of entering a new phase of existence, being reborn about the time of the reign of the Emperor Wu Ti 武帝 (A.D. 483-94) of the Ch'i 齊 dynasty. One of those invited to the annual banquet of the gods (see *Hsi Wang-mu* 西王母).—See also following paragraph.

T'AN-HUA CH'AN-SHIH 曇華禪師 (50th generation).—A deified Buddhist monk. Ranked twenty-sixth in Buddhist School, III (*q.v.*). Family name Chiang 江. A native of Ch'i-chou 蘄州, Hupei 湖北. Studied the Doctrine under Shao-lung Ch'an-shih 紹隆禪師 (*q.v.*) at Hu-ch'iu Shan 虎丘山, where he taught until his death in A.D. 1164. He was buried on T'ai-pai Fêng 太白峰, one of the highest peaks of the T'ien-t'ung Shan 天童山, Heavenly-lad Mountains.

T'AN-SHÊNG CH'AN-SHIH 曇晟禪師 (37th generation). —A deified Buddhist monk. Ranked fifth in Buddhist School, VI (*q.v.*). Family name Wang 王. A native of Chien-ch'ang Hsien 建昌縣, Ssǔch'uan 四川. Said when born to have had on his back the outlines of a Buddhist cope. Studied under

Huai-hai Ch'an-shih 懷海禪師 (*q.v.*), and remained with him for twenty years. Later, attended the school of Wei-yen Ch'an-shih 惟儼禪師 (*q.v.*), became most proficient in the doctrine, and taught at Yün-yen 雲巖, Shansi 陝西. Died A.D. 841.

T'AN-WU-CHIEH CH'AN-SHIH 曇無竭禪師.—A monk of the Li 李 family, known as Shih-t'an-wu-chieh Fa-yung 釋曇無竭法勇, *i.e.* Fa-yung, Strength of the Law. He was born at Huang-lung 黃龍, Yu-chou 幽州, Chihli 直隸. The dates of his birth and death are not recorded. Entering the monastery at an early age, he soon won his teacher's praise for his fervency in religious observances.

In A.D. 420, he left with Sêng-mêng 僧猛 and other monks for Honan 河南, and proceeded by way of Yarkand to the Karakorum Mountains and through to Kashmir. After further extensive travels and studies in India and other countries, he returned to Kuang-chou 廣州 (modern Canton), where he translated the *Kuan-yin ching* 觀音經, the Kuan-yin (Goddess of Mercy) Sutra.

T'AN-YIN 曇隱.—A saintly Hindu Buddhist monk. Sixth century. Caused a dragon to procure rain by inhaling ink. One of those invited to the annual banquet of the gods (see *Hsi Wang-mu* 西王母).

TANG YÜAN-SHUAI 黨元帥.—Generalissimo Tang 黨. Born at Huai-chou 懷州, Honan 河南, in the reign-period A.D. 1086-94 of the Emperor Chê Tsung 哲宗 (A.D. 1086-1101) of the Sung 宋 dynasty. His mother's name was Ch'ên 陳; his father's posthumous title—Ho-chia Tsai-hsiang 何家宰相, Prime Minister of the Ho 何 family—only is known. Remarkable prodigies accompanied his birth. Thirty children carrying flags and a newly-born child appeared, and announced that it was called I-lu fu-hsing 一路福星, the Star of Happiness throughout the Journey. The child had a black complexion. Throughout his life he was absolutely incorrupt, and was regarded by the people as a synonym for justice, his name being embodied in that sense in their popular ditties.

He died at the age of 97, and was canonized by Yü Ti 玉帝. He is shown carrying a long, clubbed staff, for use in punishing evil-doers. This, and rewarding good deeds, are the functions he performs.

T'ANG CH'ÊNG 唐臣.—See *Wu Yo* 五嶽.

T'ANG HUNG 唐宏.—See *San Kuan* 三官.

T'ANG KUNG-FANG 唐公昉.—See *Li Pa-pai* 李八百.

T'ANG SÊNG 唐僧.—See *Sun Hou-tzŭ* 孫猴子 and *Buddhist Schools*, XIV.

T'ANG T'IEN-CHÊNG 唐天正.—The god of the star T'ien-sun 天損.—See *T'ien-kang* 天罡.

TANTRA.—Rule, ritual. The title of a numerous class of religious and magical works, generally of later date than the *puranas,* and representing a later development of religion, although the worship of the female energy had its origin at an earlier period. The chief peculiarity of the *tantras* is the prominence they give to the female energy of the deity, his active nature being personified in the person of his Sakti, or wife. There are a few *tantras* which make Vishnu's wife or Radha the object of devotion, but the great majority of them are devoted to one of the manifold forms of Devi, the *sakti* (the wife or female energy) of Siva, and they are commonly written in the form of a dialogue between these two deities. Devi, as the *sakti* of Siva, is the especial energy concerned with sexual intercourse and magical powers, and these are the leading topics of the *tantras.* There are five requisites for *tantra* worship, the five *makaras* or five *m's*— (1) *madya,* wine; (2) *mansa,* flesh; (3) *matsya,* fish; (4) *mudra,* parched grain and mystic gesticulations; (5) *maithuna,* sexual intercourse. Each *sakti* has a twofold nature, white and black, gentle and ferocious. Thus Uma ("Light") and Gauri ("Brilliant") are gentle forms of the *sakti* of Siva, while Durga ("Inaccessible") and Kali ("Black") are fierce forms. The *saktas* or worshippers of the *saktis* are divided into two classes, Dakshinacharis and Vamacharis, the right-handed and the left-handed, *i.e.* forms of *sakta* worship. The worship of the right-hand *saktas* is comparatively decent, but that of the left-hand is addressed to the fierce forms of the *saktis,* and is most licentious. The female principle is worshipped, not only symbolically, but in the actual woman, and promiscuous intercourse forms part of the orgies. *Tantra* worship prevails chiefly in Bengal and the Eastern provinces.

Tantra and Tantra School. Shên-pien 神變.—Supernatural formulæ (generally either in Sanskrit or Tibetan) of mystic or magic efficacy, and necromantic books, taught by the Yogatcharya School. The School of demonistic Buddhism. Its germs are to be found in the Yoga (*q.v.*) system, which, influenced by Sivaism, added monstrous forms to the gods, peopled the universe with all kinds of disaster-bringing evil spirits, leading to an immense development of exorcism and witchcraft as counter-agents. "Tantra gods often have several heads, and always more than two arms." The cult developed an organized ecclesiastical ritual with its accessories. As, in India, in the middle of the seventh century A.D. Buddhism began to be replaced by Hinduism, though the old gods Siva and Vishnu remained supreme, Siva was generally represented by the phallic emblem and Vishnu by images. But the gods now came to be looked on as inaccessible, and each to be represented by his *sakti* (energy), or wife, who acted for him, and was approachable by mankind. This gave rise to a new sect, the Saktas, which soon divided into two groups, called the right and left-hand, who respectively in a respectable and immoral manner, worshipped Kali as the emanation of Siva of the phallic emblem. Their manuals are called *tantra* (the looms), and the Tantrika Schools thus set up spread widely, especially in Tibet, where they still exist. The more sensual characteristics were not adopted by its Chinese adherents.

The Yoga or Yogachara school is also called the Tantra school, because it taught the use of magic formulæ or unintelligible charms used for rain, for protection in storms, etc. They are written in Sanskrit or Tibetan letters.—See also *P'i-lu Fo* 毗盧佛, *P'u-hsien Hsin-li* 普賢心離, *Yoga,* Kennelly, vi. 132-3, and *Buddhist Schools,* XIII and XV.

TAO 道.—The Way. The Way that cannot be walked.—See *Lao Tzŭ* and (for the genealogy of Taoism) Finn, IX, 6-7.

TAO-CHÊN 刀砧, THE GOD OF THE STAR.—See *Ch'ang Hao* 常昊.

TAO-CH'IN CH'AN-SHIH 道欽禪師 (38th generation).— A deified Buddhist monk. Ranked seventh in Buddhist School, I (*q.v.*). A native of K'un Shan 崑山, a district dependent on Su-chou 蘇州. Family name Chu 朱. Of the literary class. A pupil of Hsüan-su Ch'an-shih 玄素禪師 (*q.v.*), who kept a school near Ho Lin 鶴林, Crane Forest. Having completed his education, he was sent to Ching Shan 徑山 to preach the doctrine, and made many disciples.

The Emperor T'ai Tsung 太宗 (A.D. 627-50) of the T'ang 唐 dynasty, summoned him to Court, and conferred on him the honorary title of Kuo I 國一, First Man of the Nation. On returning to Ching Shan 徑山, he died A.D. 792. His posthumous title is Ta-chio Ch'an-shih 大覺禪師.

TAO CHÜN 道君.—The Honourable Tao 道.—See *San Ch'ing* 三淸 and *Ling-pao T'ien-tsun* 靈寶天尊.

TAO-HSIN 道信.—A.D. 580-651. A saintly Buddhist monk. One of those invited to the annual banquet of the gods (see *Hsi Wang-mu* 西王母). The fourth patriarch of Chinese Buddhism. He heard the Law from Sêng-ts'an 僧璨 (*q.v.*).

TAO-HSING T'IEN-TSUN 道行天尊.—An inhabitant of the Yü Tung 玉洞, Jade Grotto, on Chin-t'ing Shan 金庭山, Mount Chin-t'ing. Was ordered by Lao Tzŭ 老子 to dismantle the Chu-hsien Chên 誅仙陣, Slay-immortals Tower. He removed the magic swords hung above the doors to drop on the heads of those brave enough to enter. Known as the propagator of the True Doctrine, and worshipped as a demi-god.

TAO-HSÜAN LÜ-SHIH 道宣律師. Tao-hsüan, Teacher (or Master) of the Vinaya.—A deified Buddhist monk. Ranked first in Buddhist School, XVI (q.v.). The father of this monk, whose name was Ch'ien Shên 錢申, was President of the Board of Rites. His mother saw in a dream a monk, who foretold that her child would be an incarnation of a legist named Yu 祐, who lived in the time of the Liang 梁 dynasty. When the child had grown up, he wished to become a monk, and proceeded to Chung-nan Shan 終南山, taking Lü 律 (i.e. Vinaya) as his personal name. His life was a series of prodigies, his food being brought to him by heavenly genii, a heavenly messenger presenting him with a tooth of Buddha, etc. Died A.D. 667. Composed eighty-one volumes of commentaries and prayer-formulas.

TAO-I CH'AN-SHIH 道一禪師 (35th generation).—A deified Buddhist monk. Ranked second in Buddhist School, III (q.v.). Family name Ma 馬. Generally designated by the title of Ma Tsu 馬祖, Patriarch Ma (see Ma Tsu 馬祖 and Hui-nêng 慧能). A native of Shih-fang Hsien 什方縣 in Han-chou 漢州, in Ch'êng-tu Fu 城都府, Ssŭch'uan 四川. For some time lived at Hêng Shan 衡山, where Huai-jang Ch'an-shih 懷讓禪師 (q.v.) entrusted to his care the K'ai-yüan Ssŭ 開元寺, K'ai-yüan Monastery. He died in A.D. 788. The Emperor Hsien Tsung 憲宗 (A.D. 806-21) of the T'ang 唐 dynasty conferred on him the honorary title of Ta-chi Ch'an-shih 大寂禪師, Monk of Vast Stillness. For a description of Ma Tsu's personal appearance, see Ma Tsu 馬祖.

TAO-K'AI CH'AN-SHIH 道楷禪師 (45th generation).—A deified Buddhist monk. Ranked twenty-ninth in Buddhist School, VI (q.v.). Family name Ts'ui 崔. A native of I-chiang 沂江, (? Kuei chou 貴州). At first a hermit on I yang Shan 伊陽山, I-yang Mountain. His teacher was I-ch'ing Ch'an-shih 義青禪師 (q.v.), in the Hai-hui Ssŭ 海會寺. When trained, he went to the T'ien-ning Ta-kuan Ssŭ 天寧大觀寺, T'ien-ning Ta-kuan Monastery, at Tung-ching 東京 (? Fêng-t'ien 奉天), and died there in A.D. 1118.

TAO KUNG 道公.—See Diaphragm, The God of The.

TAO-MI CH'AN-SHIH 道密禪師 (65th generation).—A deified Buddhist monk. Ranked sixty-fourth in Buddhist School, VI (q.v.). Family name T'ang 唐. A native of Ssŭ-chou 泗州 Hunan 湖南. Studied at the Ching-hui Ssŭ 景會寺, Ching-hui Monastery, under Yün-mên Ch'êng 雲門澄. Later, he lived in seven different monasteries, and taught there. Died A.D. 1658, aged 71. His tomb is at P'u-t'i Shê 菩提社.

TAO-MIN CH'AN-SHIH 道忞禪師 (68th generation).—A deified Buddhist monk. Ranked fifty-fifth in Buddhist School, III (*q.v.*). Family name Lin 林. A native of Ling-nan 嶺南. Studied under Yüan-wu Ch'an-shih 圓悟禪師 (*q.v.*), and then started his own school at P'ing-yang 平陽. Treated with great respect by the Emperor Shun Chih 順治 (A.D. 1644-62). His tomb is at P'ing-yang 平陽. Posthumous title: Hung-chio Ch'an-shih 弘覺禪師.

TAO-MING CH'AN-SHIH 道明禪師 (38th generation).—A deified Buddhist monk. Ranked ninth in Buddhist School, III (*q.v.*). Family name Ch'ên 陳. A native of Mu-chou 睦州. At his birth, an extraordinary light illumined the paternal home. He had double eyeballs, and seven pimples, like stars, on his face. After visiting the K'ai-yüan Ssŭ 開元寺, K'ai-yüan Monastery, he studied at the school of Hsi-yün Ch'an-shih 希運禪師 (*q.v.*), who appointed him Principal over all the monks. Later, he returned to the K'ai-yüan Ssŭ 開元寺, and worked at making straw sandals, which he sold in order to maintain his aged parents. At this time, he saved Mu-chou 睦州 from being captured by a band of brigands by suspending a straw sandal on the city-gate.

His corpse was cremated, a shower of precious stones falling from the heavens during the process. He was 89 years of age. His image was placed in the monastery.

TAO MU 道母.—See *Tou Mu* 斗母.

TAO-P'EI CH'AN-SHIH 道丕禪師 (40th generation).—A deified Buddhist monk. Ranked thirteenth in Buddhist School, VI (*q.v.*). Family name and place of birth not recorded. Taught in the T'ung-an Ssŭ 同安寺, United Peace Monastery, at Hsi-fêng Shan 樓鳳山, Roosting Pheasant Mountain, in Hung-chou 洪州, Kueichou 貴州, where he died and was buried.

TAO-SHÊNG CH'AN-SHIH 道盛禪師 (65th generation).— A deified Buddhist monk. Ranked sixty-third in Buddhist School, VI (*q.v.*). Family name Chang 張. A native of Chê-p'u 柘浦, Kiangsi 江西. Studied at Tung-yüan 東苑 under Yüan-ching Ch'an-shih 元鏡禪師 (*q.v.*). After living at Lo Shan 羅山 (A.D. 1619) he roamed from one monastery to another. Died A.D. 1659. His tomb is at Shê Shan 攝山.

TAO-SUI TSUN-CHÊ 道遂尊者.—A deified Buddhist monk. Ranked ninth in Buddhist School, X (*q.v.*). Family name and birthplace unknown. Between A.D. 766 and 780 visited Chan-jan Tsun-chê 湛然尊者 (*q.v.*) at Fu-lung 佛隴, and became his disciple. In A.D. 805, was appointed teacher at T'ien-t'ai 天台 to Tsui-ch'êng 最澄, a Japanese monk (Kobô Daishi), and, when the latter returned to his native country, withdrew to, and propagated the doctrine at, a mountain he called T'ien-t'ai 天台, his disciples being numerous and the sect becoming highly popular.

Tsui-ch'êng 最澄 had returned to Japan in A.D. 806, and introduced there the doctrine of the T'ien-t'ai 天台 School, known as the Shingon sect, or the Mantra School of Japan, of which Tao-sui Tsun-chê 道邃尊寺 was held to be the founder.

TAO-T'UNG CH'AN-SHIH 道通禪師.—See *Lo-han* 羅漢.

TAO-WU CH'AN-SHIH 道悟禪師 (36th generation).—A deified Buddhist monk. Ranked fourth in Buddhist School, VI (*q.v.*). Family name Chang 張. A native of Tung-yang 東陽, in the department of Wu-chou 婺州, Chêkiang 浙江. At 14 years of age became a disciple of Hsi-ch'ien Ch'an-shih 希遷禪師 (*q.v.*). Later, opened a school at T'ien-huang 天皇. Died A.D. 807.

TAO-YIN CH'AN-SHIH 道間禪師 (63th generation).—A deified Buddhist monk. Ranked sixty-second in Buddhist School, VI (*q.v.*). Family name Fu 傅. A native of Hsin-chou 信州, Ssŭch'uan 四川. Taught by a Po Shan 博山 instructor. After living for some time in the Ying-shan Ssŭ 瀛山寺, Ying-shan Monastery, he was appointed Superior at Po Shan 博山. He then visited the monasteries at Hu-p'ao 虎跑 and Miao-hsing 妙行, finally returning to Ying-shan 瀛山, where he died, A.D. 1637.

TAO-YING CH'AN-SHIH 道膺禪師 (39th generation).—A deified Buddhist monk. Ranked eleventh in Buddhist School, VI (*q.v.*). Family name Wang 王. A native of Yü-t'ien 玉田, in the Yu-chou 幽州 department, Kiangsi 江西 (? Kiangsu 江蘇 or Fukien 福建). Studied under Liang-chieh Ch'an-shih 良价 禪師 (*q.v.*). At the age of 25, he was already famous, and being appointed President of all the monks, taught for more than thirty years at Yün-chü 雲居 in the same province. His school was attended by 1,500 disciples. Died A.D. 902. Posthumous title: Hung-chio Ch'an-shih 弘覺禪師, Monk of Vast Intelligence.

TAO-YÜEH CH'AN-SHIH 道月禪師.—See *Lo-han* 羅漢.

T'AO HUA 陶華.—See *Shih Ming-i* 十明醫, 5.

T'AO-HUA 桃花, THE GODDESS OF THE STAR.—See *Kao Lan-ying* 高蘭英.

T'AO T'IEN-CHÜN 陶天君.—See *Hsin T'ien-chün* 辛天君.

TATHAGATA.—Tan-t'o-i-to 怛佗議多, or Ju-lai 來如, etc. *Lit.* One who (in coming into the world) is like the coming (of his predecessors). The highest epithet of a Buddha.—See also *Seven Tathagatas*.

TÊ-CH'A-CH'IA 德义迦.—A dragon-king.—See *Lung Wang* 龍王.

TÊ-PAO CH'AN-SHIH 德寳禪師 (65th generation).—A deified Buddhist monk. Ranked forty-third in Buddhist School, III (*q.v.*). Family name Wu 吳. A native of Chin-ling (Kinling) 金陵 (modern Nanking 南京). Suddenly became enlightened in the Doctrine while he was cleaning the vegetables for the monk's dinner (*cf. Ming-hsüan Ch'an-shih* 明瑄禪師).

TÊ-SHAO KUO-SHIH 德韶國師 (43rd generation).—A deified Buddhist monk. Ranked twenty-fourth in Buddhist School, VI (*q.v.*). Family name Ch'ên 陳. A native of Ch'u-chou 處州, in the Lung-ch'üan 龍泉, Dragon Spring, district, Chêkiang 浙江. His teacher was Wên-i Ch'an-shih 文益禪師 (*q.v.*), who esteemed him highly. He went to T'ien-t'ai 天台, in the same province, and lived there with Chih-chê Ta-shih 智者大師 (*q.v.*). Died A.D. 972. His tomb is on T'ien-t ai Shan 天台山, Heaven-terrace Mountain.

TEA, THE GODS OF.—Lo Yü, of the T'ang 唐 dynasty is worshipped as the God of Tea; in the north Ching Ling Tzǔ 京陵司, and in south China, Sung Su-kung 宋叔公.

TEATS, THE GODS OF THE.—The *Yün chi ch'i ch'ien* 雲笈七籤 states that under the two nipples are a *jih* 日, sun, and a *yüeh* 月, moon, and that in the centre of each is a *t'ai shên* 太神, great god, Wang Fu 王父, Father Wang, 王, and Wang Mu 王母, Mother Wang 王, respectively; usually spoken of conjointly as Wang Fu Mu 王父母.

TEETH, THE GODS OF THE.—The *Yün chi ch'i ch'ien* 雲笈七籤 states that the God of the Teeth (*ch'ih* 齒) is Tan Chu 丹朱. The *Huang t'ing nei ching* 黃庭內經 names the god of the lower teeth (*ya* 牙) as Hao Hua 皓華; style Hsü Ch'êng 虚成; the God of the *ch'ih* 齒, upper teeth, as Mu Fêng 耀鋒, style Lo Ch'ien 羅干.

TEMPLES, A PROTECTING DEITY OF.—See *Hua-kuang Fo* 華光佛.

TEN FETTERS, THE.—The ten errors or evil states of mind conquered in the course of the four Paths (see *Four Paths*) are the ten *Sangyojanas* or Fetters, which are:—

1. Delusion of self. 2. Doubt. 3. Dependence on Works. 4. Sensuality, bodily passions. 5. Hatred, ill-feeling. 6. Love of life

on earth. 7. Desire for life in heaven. 8. Pride. 9. Self-righteousness. 10. Ignorance.

When the first five fetters are completely broken, the converted Buddhist has become an Arahat, and has entered the fourth path; when the other five are broken, he has become Asekha, and thus put an end to all delusion and to all sorrow.—See *Four Truths, Four Paths,* and *Dhyana.*

TEN T'AI I 太一 GENII, THE.—See *T'ai I* 太一.

TÊNG CH'AN-YÜ 鄧嬋玉.—The goddess of the star *Liu-ho* 六合.—See *T'u Hsing-sun* 土行孫.

TÊNG CHIU-KUNG 鄧九公.—The god of the star Ch'ing-lung 青龍. Commander-in-chief of the imperial troops at San-shan Kuan 三山關. Deserted Chou Wang 紂王 (1121-1114 B.C.), was made prisoner, and condemmed to death by order of Ch'iu Yin 邱引.

TÊNG HSIU 鄧秀.—The god of the star Wu-kuei 五鬼. The son of general Têng Chiu-kung 鄧九公 (*q.v.*). Went over to the side of Wu Wang 武王 (1121-1114 B.C.), and fought for the new dynasty.

TÊNG HUA 鄧華.—The god of the star Mu-fu 木府. A disciple of Yüan-shih T'ien-tsun 元始天尊. Killed by lightning.

TÊNG-KUAN P'U-SA 燈官菩薩.— A Lamp-god. — See *Lamp, The God of the.*

TÊNG WEI-T'ING 澄渭亭.—See *Wu Yo* 五嶽.

TÊNG YÜ 鄧玉.—The god of the star T'ien-chieh 天捷. —See *T'ien-kang* 天罡.

TÊNG YÜ 鄧禹.—The god of the constellation Chio 角. Alternatively with Po-lin Tao-jên 柏林道人.

T'ÊNG-SHÊ 螣蛇, THE GOD OF THE STAR.—See *Ch'ang Shan* 張山.

THEATRE, THE GOD OF THE.—This god is worshipped by actors, "to keep them from laughing when on the stage." He was T'ang Ming Huang 唐明皇.

THIRD LADY (OR MISS) OF THE LATRINE.—See *Tzŭ-ku Shên* 紫姑神.

THIRTY TEACHERS, THE.—Among the seventy-two teacher-gods (see *Forty Masters*) are thirty medicine-gods worshipped by sufferers from special maladies, whose functions are indicated as follows:—Headache, Chills, Liver, Diarrhoea, Dropsy, Cough, Stomach-ache, Colic, Eye disease (the Divine Oculist), Ear disease (the Divine Aurist), Small-pox, Sores, Consumption, Animal spirits, Ague, Losing the soul sickness, Pestilence, Stop-pestilence God, Acupuncture, Haemorrhage, Drugs, Weakness, Dyspepsia, Diseases of the hands and feet, of the Breast, Poison, Toothache, the Criminal Judge of Pestilence, and the Ruler of the thirteen kinds of doctors. The number thirty is made up by multiple offices.

THOUSAND-LI 里 EYE.—See *Ch'ien-li Yen* 千里眼.

THREE AGENTS, THE.—See *San Kuan* 三官.

THREE DEIFIED MORTALS, THE.—See *San Kuan* 三官.

THREE EPOCHS, THE.—See *San Kuan* 三官 and *San Yüan* 三元.

THREE GENII OF THE WU 吳 STATE, THE.—See *San Kuan* 三官.

THREE GREAT BUDDHAS, THE.—See *San-tsun ta Fo* 三尊大佛.

THREE GREAT RULERS, THE.—See *San Kuan* 三官.

THREE LEGENDARY RULERS, THE.—See *San Kuan* 三官.

THREE LOWER PATHS, THE.—See *Gati*.

THREE PRECIOUS ONES, THE.—See *San Pao* 三寶.

THREE PRINCIPLES, THE.—See *San Kuan* 三官.

THREE PURE ONES, THE.—See *San Ch'ing* 三清.

THREE RULERS, THE.—See *San Kuan* 三官.

THREE SAGES, THE.—See *San Shêng* 三聖.

THREE SOURCES, THE.—See *San Kuan* 三官.

THREE SWORN BROTHERS, THE TEMPLE OF THE.—See *San-i Ko* 三義閣.

THREE TRANSCENDENT POWERS, THE.—See *San Kuan* 三官.

TI MU

THREE-WAGON TEACHER, THE.—See *Kuei-chi Fa-shih* 窺基法師.

THROAT, THE GOD OF THE.—The name of this god is Pai Liu-fang 百沐放; style Tao T'ung 道通; height 8.89 inches; coloured clothes.—*Yün chi ch'i ch'ien* 雲笈七籤.

THUNDER, THE SPIRIT OF.—See *Hsin-hsing Kou Yüan-shuai* 辛興苟元帥 and *Lei Pu* 雷部.

THUNDER AND STORMS, THE MINISTRY OF.—See *Lei Pu* 雷部.

TI 地.—See *Hou T'u* 后土 and *Wên Ch'ang* 文昌.

TI-CH'E 帝車, THE GOD OF THE STAR.—See *Chiang Huan-ch'u* 姜桓楚.

TI CH'ING 狄青.—An assessor of Kuan Kung 關公.—See *Kuan Yü* 關羽.

TI-HOU 地后, THE GODDESS OF THE STAR.—See Huang 黃.

TI HSIEN 地仙.—Genii upon earth—human beings who have attained to immortality in the existing world.

TI HUANG 地皇. The Earthly Ruler.—See *Shih-êrh Yüan-chia* 十二元甲.

TI-KANG 地綱, THE GOD OF THE STAR.—See *Chi Shu-chi* 姬叔吉.

TI KUAN SHÊ TSUI 地官赦罪.—The Earth Ruler who remits and effaces punishments.—See *San Kuan* 三官.

TI-K'UNG 地空, THE GOD OF THE STAR.—See *Mei Tê* 梅德.

TI-LU 地轆, THE GOD OF THE STAR.—See *Ting Ts'ê* 丁策.

TI LUNG 地龍.—The Earth-dragon.—See *Lung Wang* 龍王.

TI MU 地母.—See *Wên Ch'ang* 文昌.

TI-SHA 地煞.—Seventy-two stars of evil influence, opposed to the thirty-six T'ien-kang 天罡 (*q.v.*). The wicked genii of these stars are cast out and slain by *t'ung-tzǔ* 童子 magicians, who impale them on forks and shut them up in earthen jars, then take them to waste lands, throw them into fires, and surround the spot with a circle of lime, which is supposed to prevent any spirit which may have survived the burning from getting out of it.

The names of these stars, followed by those of their stellar spirits included in brackets, are as follows:—Ti-an 地暗: Earth's Obscurity (Yü Chung 余忠).—Ti-ch'a 地察: Earth's Examination (Chang Huan 張煥).—Ti-ch'ang 地猖: Earth's Madness (Ch'i Kung 齊公).—Ti-chên 地鎮: Earth's Domination (Chiang Chung 姜忠).—Ti-chêng 地正: Earth's Rectitude (K'ao Ko 考扁).—Ti-chi 地羈: Earth's Halter (K'ung T'ien-chao 孔天兆).—Ti-ch'i 地奇: Earth's Prodigy (Wang P'ing 王平).—Ti-ch'iang 地强: Earth's Strength (Hsia Hsiang 夏祥).—Ti-ch'iao 地巧: Earth's Skill (Li Ch'ang 李昌).—Ti-chieh 地傑: Earth's Heroes (Hu Pai-yen 呼百顏).—Ti-chieh 地捷: Earth's Triumph (Kêng Yen 耿顏).—Ti-chien 地健: Earth's Hardness (Yeh Ching-ch'ang 葉景昌).—Ti-chin 地進: Earth's Entry (Hsü Chi 徐吉).—Ti-chio 地角: Earth's Horn (Lan Hu 藍虎).—Ti-ch'iu 地囚: Earth's Prisoner (Sung Lu 宋祿).—Ti-chou 地周: Earth's Circumference (Yao Chin-hsiu 姚金秀).—Ti-ch'ou 地醜: Earth's Ugliness (Hsü Shan 徐山).—Ti-chün 地俊: Earth's Wisdom (Yüan Ting-hsiang 袁鼎相).—Ti-ch'üan 地全: Earth's Totality (K'uang Yü 匡玉).—Ti-chuang 地壯: Earth's Strength (Wu Yen-kung 武衍公).—Ti-fei 地飛: Earth's Flying (Yeh Chung 葉中).—Ti-fu 地輔: Earth's Aid (Pao Lung 鮑龍).—Ti-fu 地伏: Earth's Ambush (Mên Tao-chêng 門道正).—Ti-hao 地耗: Earth's Destruction (Yao Hua 姚燁).—Ti-ho 地閤: Earth's Closing (Liu Hêng 劉衡).—Ti-hsing 地刑: Earth's Punishment (Ch'in Hsiang 秦祥).—Ti-hsiung 地雄: Earth's Male (Lu Hsiu-tê 魯修德).—Ti-hui 地會: Earth's Meeting (Lu Chih 魯芝).—Ti-hui 地慧: Earth's Intelligence (Chê K'un 車坤).—Ti-i 地異: Earth's Wonder (Yü Chih 余知).—Ti-kou 地狗: Earth's Dog (Ch'ên Mêng-kêng 陳夢庚).—Ti-ku 地孤: Earth's Orphan (Wu Ssǔ-yü 吳四玉).—Ti-k'uang 地狂: Earth's Tyranny (Ho Chih-yüan 霍之元).—Ti-k'uei 地魁: Earth's First (Chên Chi-chêng 陳繼貞).—Ti-k'ung 地空: Earth's Void (Hsiao-tien 蕭電).—Ti-li 地理: Earth's Right (T'ung Chêng 童貞).— Ti-lieh 地劣: Earth's Weakness (Fan Pin 范斌).—Ti-ling 地靈: Earth's Efficiency (Kuo-chi 郭巳).—Ti-lo 地樂: Earth's Joy (Wang Hsiang 王祥).—Ti-man 地滿: Earth's Fullness (Cho Kung 卓公).—Ti-mêng 地猛: Earth's Fierceness (Pai Yu-huan 百有患).—Ti-ming 地明: Earth's Brightness (Fang Chih 方志).—Ti-mo 地默: Earth's Meditation (Chou Kêng 周庚).—Ti-mo 地魔: Earth's Devil (Li Yo 李躍).—Ti-nu 地奴: Earth's Slave (K'ung Tao-ling 孔道靈).—Ti-ô 地惡: Earth's Evil (Li Hsin 李信). Ti pao 地暴: Earth's Violence (Sang Ch'êng-tao 桑成道).—Ti-p'i 地闢: Earth's

Opening (Li Sui 李燧).—Ti-p'i 地僻: Earth's Depravity (Tsu-lin 祖林).—Ti-p'ing 地平: Earth's Justice (Lung Ch'êng 龍成).—Ti-sha 地殺: Earth's Executioner (Huang Ching yüan 黃景元).—Ti-shou 地獸: Earth's Animal (Chin Nan-tao 金南道).—Ti-shu 地數: Earth's Number (Ko Fang 葛方).—Ti-su 地束: Earth's Rapidity (Hsing San-luan 刑三鸞).—Ti-sui 地遂: Earth's Obsequiosity (K'ung Ch'êng 孔成).—Ti-sun 地損: Earth's Hurt (Huang-wu 黃烏).—Ti-ts'ang 地藏: Earth's Abyss (Kuan Pin 關斌).—Ti-tsei 地賊: Earth's Thief (Sun Chi 孫吉).—Ti-tso 地佐: Earth's Left (Huang Ping-ch'ing 黃丙慶).—Ti-tsou 地走: Earth's Walk (Ku Tsung 顧宗).—Ti-tuan 地短: Earth's Brevity (Ts'ai Kung 蔡公).—Ti-t'ui 地退: Earth's Recoil (Fan Huan 樊煥).—Ti-wei 地威: Earth's Majesty (Hsü Ch'êng 須成).—Ti-wei 地徵: Earth's Hiding-place (Ch'ên Yüan 陳元).—Ti-wên 地文: Earth's Elegance (Ko Kao 革高).—Ti-yao 地妖: Earth's Imp (Kung Ch'ien 龔倩).—Ti-yin 地隱: Earth's Depth (Ning San-i 寧三益).—Ti-yin 地陰: Earth's Shadow (Chiao Lung 焦龍).—Ti-ying 地英: Earth's Beauty (Sun Hsiang 孫祥).—Ti-yu 地佑: Earth's Right (Chu ... Ch'i ...).—Ti-yu 地幽 Earth's Entrails (Chia Ch'ing 賈清).—Ti-yung 地勇: Earth's Bravery (Chia Ch'êng 賈成).—Cf. T'ien-kang 天罡.

TI SHÊ 地社.—An Assessor who is placed on the right of Kuan Kung 關公.—See Kuan Yü 關羽.

TI-TSANG CHIN 地藏金.—See Ti-tsang Wang 地藏王.

TI-TSANG CHING 地藏經.—See Ti-tsang Wang 地藏王.

TI-TSANG WANG 地藏王.—The King of the Underworld. The Chinese manifestation of Kshitigarbha, the Buddha of the Nether Regions. The Master of the Six Worlds of Desire. The great Earth God. In China, King of Hades. Ruler or Overlord of Hell. The Hell-god. Senior to Yen-lo Wang 閻羅王 (Yama) with his ten judges. Also known, from the inscription on the banner carried by his attendants, as Yu-ming Chiao-chu Ti-tsang Wang P'u-sa 幽冥教主地藏王菩薩, Lord and Teacher of Hades, Bodhi king of the Earth's Matrix (or Earth's Treasure)—the World of Shadow, or Hades of Spirits.

Thus Ti-tsang Wang 地藏王 is the Earth Spirit, who delivers souls from the Buddhist Naraka or earth- prison, Ti Yü 地獄. He is a "mere abstraction, a symbol, the flash of Buddha's compassion for the suffering souls of Hades." The "Saviour and Deliverer," who visits Hell on errands of love and mercy, and leads souls to the Heaven of Amitabha. Especially popular as a god in Anhui 安徽 and Western Kiangsu 江蘇, where numerous temples are dedicated to him. Not to be identified with Yen-lo Wang 閻羅王 (Yama) (q.v.).

He is represented as round-faced, bearing a staff or crozier topped with six rings, in one hand, and a miraculous jewel in the other, with the one, he opens Hades, and with the other he lights up the dark abode of suffering souls.

In China, as noted above, he is held to be the Over-Lord of Hell, while Yama, Yen-lo Wang 閻羅王, with his ten judges, holds a subordinate position under him; but in Indian Buddhism, though connected with the Underworld, he is not the the ruler of Hades, nor identified with Yama. His merit was so great that he would have been promoted to Buddhahood, had he not vowed to rescue from hell all orphan spirits and devils, so he is still engaged on that task in the infernal regions. He is said to sleep 359 days, and only awakes on his birthday; if there are only twenty-nine days in that month he sleeps for another year. On that night the candles lit in front of every door are placed on the curb stones. He is worshipped on the thirtieth day of the seventh moon.

This Buddhist Ti-tsang Wang 地藏王 is associated in Chinese mythology with Chiu Hua Shan 九華山 (v. infra), originally Chiu Tzŭ Shan 九子山, the Mountain of the Nine Philosophers,* one of the most famous of China's sacred mountains, situated on the South bank of the Yangtzŭ 揚子 River, a little west of Ch'ih-chou Fu 池州府, in Anhui 安徽.

Here crowds of worshippers intercede for their ancestors in Hades and endeavour to avert a like fate for themselves. The pilgrimages take place chiefly from September to November. The prayers, theatricals and ceremonies performed by the pilgrims and monks relate principally to inducing Ti-tsang Wang 地藏王 to pity the dead and deliver the souls from Hades. This association arose from the arrival there during the reign of the Emperor Su Tsung 肅宗 (A.D. 756-63) of the T'ang 唐 dynasty, of a foreigner, named Chin Ch'iao-chio 金喬覺, clad as a Buddhist monk, who came from Sin [Hsin]-lo 新羅 (a small kingdom in South-eastern Korea), and landing on the coast of Kiangsu 江蘇, proceeded thence to the mountain. (His name is otherwise given as Fu Lo-pu 傅羅卜, a native of Wang-shê Ch'êng 王舍城, a city of the wild Hsi Jung 西戎 tribes of W. China. His religious name was Mu Lien 目連 (q.v.). This Chinese name Mu Lien 目連 was given him because his arrival in China coincided with that of Amogha (q.v.) about A.D. 733. It is also suggested that he was a T'ai 大 Prince, who entered China through Yünnan 雲南.

Temples dedicated to Ti-tsang Wang 地藏王 are found in Kiangsu 江蘇 and some other provinces. Though his principal

---

* The change of name is ascribed by Johnson (*Buddhist China*, p. 216-7) to the poet Li T'ai-po 李太白, who, "having caught sight of its peaks from his boat on the Yangtze River, likened them to the upturned petals of the lotus." The legend of Li T'ai-po 李太白 saving Ti-tsang Wang 地藏王 from drowning is obviously false.

shrine is at Chiu-hua Shan 九華山, he has a shrine in almost every Chinese temple.

Through the propaganda fictions of the Buddhist monks, who described him as heir to the throne of Sin-lo 新羅, his fame spread throughout the district. The monks stated that he had fled from the realm accompanied by the Prime Minister Wei-t'o 韋陀. [It seems, however, that the latter did not come from Korea.] This explains the latter's presence in all temples dedicated to Ti-tsang Wang 地藏王.

He became famous as an ascetic devoting all his time to the service of Buddha, living a life of extreme austerity, and had a following of devoted disciples, who came to listen to his teachings, and built him a monastery. At the age of 99 he died, sitting cross-legged in his coffin and surrounded by his followers. When his coffin was opened three years later his corpse was found as fresh as when he died. Buddha made him king of the Earth's Matrix and Over-lord of the Underworld, and the ten assistant judges of hell (see *Shih tien Yen-wang* 十殿閻王) made him obeisance. The birthday of Ti-tsang Wang 地藏王 is celebrated on that day (thirtieth of seventh month). His disciples gave him the title of Chin Ti-tsang 金地藏, Chin 金 being the clan or family name of the hermit prince, and Ti-tsang Chin 地藏金, an incarnation of the Buddhist god Ti-tsang Wang 地藏王, the title of deification bestowed on him by the Chinese. Chin Ti-tsang 金地藏, has had several incarnations in past *kalpas*.

In the *Mu Lien chi* 目連記, *Records of Mu Lien* 目連, an endeavour is made to give him a Chinese origin. A legend relates that he was saved whilst crossing the Yangtzü 揚子 River during a storm by the spirit of Li T'ai-po 李太白, the poet, but it is discredited by an anachronism in dates (as noted above).

For the Chinese version of the legend (of his delivering his mother from Hades) applied to Ti-tsang Wang 地藏王, see *Maudgalyayana* and Plopper, pp. 159-60, note *g*. For Ti-tsang Wang 地藏王 as an avatar of Chin Ch'an-tzü 金蟬子 see *Jan-têng* 燃燈.

TI YÜ 地獄 (*Maraka*).—The Chinese Hades or Earth-prison. "According to Buddhist cosmogony, the existing universe consists of an infinite number of vast circular planes rising in tiers above Mount Meru (Sumeru), the ideal centre of this fabulous world. The hells lie deep down in the system, and are situated 20,000 Yoganas, or Yodjanas (280,000 miles) below the earth. Outside, there are mountains, a wide sea, and a circular mass of iron. This Hindu hell was too far from China, so it was resolved to place it in one of the provinces, namely Ssǔch'uan 四川. A legend relates that in the Ming 明 dynasty, during the reign of Shên Tsung 神宗 (A.D. 1573-1620), the governor of the province, named Kuo 郭, forced entrance into the side of a high mountain, near the city of Fêng-tu Hsien 酆都縣, and visited the lower regions, being let down in a strong box, and on his return erecting a monument relating his experience at Kuei-chou Fu 夔州府, a city in the north-east of Ssŭch'uan 四川. At night the cries of the tortured souls can be heard arising from the regions below. Some accounts relate that he proceeded along an underground passage which led from the city temple of Fêng-tu 酆都 to the nether world, and came to a city full of light, broad streets, and storied houses. He was only allowed to go as far as the fifth hell or hall of justice. The account of the city is said to be "an Indo-Chinese production; an attempt to combine the Chinese doctrine of the *Yang* 陽 and *Yin* 陰 with the Indian tenets of the 'earth-prison.'"

The administrative divisions of Hades number, in Brahmanism, twenty-one, in Buddhism, originally eight, to which the Northern, *Mahayana,* School added eight more, thus making the "eight hot and eight cold hells"—*jê-yü* 熱獄 and *han-yü* 寒獄 (the idea of cold being naturally alien to the Hindu mind, the cold hells were an invention of the Northern Buddhists). To these sixteen some writers add eight "frontier (tchakravalas) hells" ("hells of utter darkness"). These are also called "vivifying hells" (*huo-yü* 活獄) because any being, dying in the first of these hells, is at once reborn in the second, and so forth, life lasting five hundred years in each.

Hades is stated by others to have 136 divisions, one for each class of offenders. This number is increased to 138 by addition of the special "hell for females" and the "city of suicides."

Besides the hot, cold, and dark hells there are the cold Lokantarika hells (*pien-yü* 邊獄, *lit.* hells on the edge, *sc.* of the universe), ten in number, but each having one hundred millions of smaller hells attached, all being situated outside of the Tchakravalas (the circle of mountains forming the outer periphery of every universe). Finally, there are the 84,000 Lokantarika hells (*pien hsiao ti-yü* 邊小地獄, *lit.* small hells on the edge), divided into three classes, as situated on mountains, on water, or in deserts. Each universe has the same number of hells, distributed so that the northern continent contains no hell at all, the two continents E. and W. of the Meru have only the small Lokantarika hells, and all the other hells are situated under the southern continent (Djambudvipa). Chinese fancy has added a special hell for females (*hsieh-p'an ch'ih* 血盤池, *lit.* placenta tank), consisting of an immense pool of blood. From this hell, it is said, no release is possible, but all the other hells are mere purgatories, release being procured when sin has been sufficiently expiated or through intercession of the priesthood.

The torments and length of abode differ in each. Yama and his lictors rule over the victims and decree the various degrees of torture. His sister, Yami, performs the same duties in regard to female criminals.

The Buddhist hell or purgatory is not a place of final retribution, but one of the six phases of transmigration, or conditions in which sentient beings may find a new existence. The six spokes of the wheel of metempsychosis represent the six different regions in which one may find a new existence: the heavens, the titanic world, the man-world, the animal-world, the region of ghosts, and hell.—See also *Yama*.

T'I-T'OU LAI-CH'A T'IEN-WANG 提頭賴吒天王.—See *Ssŭ ta T'ien-wang* 四大天王.

TIAO-K'O 吊客, THE GOD OF THE STAR.—See *Fêng Lin* 風林.

TIDES, THE GODS OF THE.—These two gods were Wu (Yüan) Yün 伍員 (Wu Tzŭ-hsü 伍子胥), of the kingdom of Wu 吳, whose capital was Soochow 蘇州, Kiangsu 江蘇, and Wên Chung 開仲, of the kingdom of Yüeh 越, whose capital was Hangchow 杭州, Chêkiang 浙江. They were enemies during life, but now exercise joint sovereignty over the tides; perhaps to account for the ebb and flow the Chinese regard it as necessary to have two opposing gods.

T'IEH-KUAI LI 鐵拐李.—One of the most popular Gods of Apothecaries.—See also *Pa Hsien* 八仙, *Shên Nung* 神農, and *Yao Pu* 藥部.

T'IEH T'OU 鐵頭.—See *T'ieh Yüan-shuai* 鐵元帥.

T'IEH YÜAN-SHUAI 鐵元帥.—Generalissimo T'ieh 鐵. Non-historical. An incarnation of the Spirit Ting 丁 (see *Shih-êrh yüan-chia* 十二元甲). T'ai-i Chên-jên 太乙眞人 was ordered by Yü Ti 玉帝 to send to earth one of the six Ting 丁 Spirits to be incarnated in the womb of a woman of the Yen 顏 family. She was his mother, but he had no father. The date of his birth is given as the seventh day of the fifth moon in the year *ping-wu* 丙午 of the Emperor Hsin 辛 of the Shang 商 dynasty, but the omission of the first character of the Emperor's dynastic title makes it uncertain to which of the four Hsin 辛 reference is made. He was given the name of T'ieh-t'ou 鐵頭, Ironhead, and was noted for his bravery and strength, being able to throw down nine oxen.

His various exploits include the slaying of a demon to the S. of Shui-ying 水頭, taming a fiery horse to the N. of Yin-shan 陰山, killing a demon at Yeh-huo Miao 野火廟, capturing a transcendent fox at Tzŭ-hsü Lou 紫虛樓, and destroying a transcendent snake of the Chiang 江.

His bravery was rewarded by Yü Ti 玉帝 with the appointment of Administrator of the North, with the title Fierce and Impetuous Generalissimo, T'ieh 鐵

TIEN MU 電 母.—The Mother of Lightning. Represented as a female figure, gorgeously apparelled in blue, green, red, and white, holding in either hand a mirror from which proceed two broad streams or flashes of light. Lightning, say the Chinese, is caused by the rubbing together of the *yin* 陰 and the *yang* 陽, just as sparks of fire may be produced by the friction of two substances.

Tung Wang-kung 東 王 公, the King of the Immortals, was playing at pitch-pot (the game of throwing arrows from a distance into a narrow-necked jar) with Yü Nü 玉 女. He lost; whereupon Heaven smiled, and from its half-open mouth a ray of light came out. This was lightning; it is regarded as feminine because it is supposed to come from the earth, which is of the *yin* 陰, or female, principle.—See also *Lei Pu* 雷 部.

The particular work of Shan-tien P'o-tzŭ 閃 電 婆 子, Goddess of Lightning, is to assist the God of Thunder, by revealing to him the hearts of men, that he may be just in his punishments. For this reason she is often called, by the people, the Mirror of the God of Thunder. She is represented holding one in each hand, by the use of which she sends forth lightning, the so-called "golden snakes." No one can escape her searching light. She faithfully and impartially carries out her task of helping Heaven's messenger (Plopper, pp. 55-6).—See also *Lei Pu* 雷 部 and *A Hsiang* 阿 香.

TIEN T'UNG 典 通.—The god of the star T'ien-k'ung 天 空. —See *T'ien-kang* 天 罡.

T'IEN 天.—The material heaven. Afterwards personified. Until recently, supposed to represent an "early anthropomorphic picture of the Deity" (which Deity?), the "Great 大 One 一," or the "One 一 Great 大 Thing," but shown by Werner (*China of the Chinese,* pp. 235-9) to have been originally a picture of the "great dome" 大 冂 of heaven 冂, the semicircle having in time become shortened into a straight line. Later on, through the confusion of primitive language (as seen universally), the material heaven was mistaken in speech for the spirits which were supposed to reside there, and heaven itself thus came to be worshipped.

At the Old Year's feast, during the New Year's holidays, and on a wedding day, heaven and earth are worshipped. During the 1st Moon, the 9th day is heaven's birthday, and the 10th day is earth's birthday, when incense is burned towards heaven in the open courts of the houses. The official worship of heaven was, however, reserved for the Emperor, the "Son of Heaven." The two great thoughts engraved on the Chinese mind are the duties of honouring the father and mother, and of worshipping heaven and earth, the great father and mother of the universe.—See also *Deva,* and for Heaven and Earth worship generally, Plopper, pp. 23-34.

T'IEN CHIH-PIAO 田智彪.—See *Fêng-huo Yüan T'ien Yüan-shuai* 鳳火院田元帥.

T'IEN-CH'IN 天親.—See *Shih-ch'in P'u-sa* 世親菩薩.

T'IEN-CH'IN 天禽.—See *Tou Mu* 斗母.

T'IEN-CHU 天柱.—See *Tou Mu* 斗母.

T'IEN-CHUNG-T'IEN 天中天.—See *Fo* 佛.

T'IEN-CH'UNG 天冲.—See *Tou Mu* 母斗.

T'IEN FEI 天妃. Also called T'ien Hou 天后 and T'ien-hou Niang-niang 天后娘娘.—The Heavenly Concubine, the Concubine of Heaven, the Empress of Heaven, or the Lady Empress of Heaven. The Goddess of Sailors. A goddess worshipped by navigators for safety during voyages; also to obtain children.

The origin of this goddess is differently stated by different Chinese writers. There is uncertainty as to the name of her father (a petty official named Lin Yüan 林願, or the Taoist Lin Ling-su 林靈素, or a man named Ts'ai 蔡, an inhabitant of a small island off the coast of Fukien 福建); her mother's name is variously given as Ch'ên 陳 and Wang 王; her birthplace as either Fukien 福建 or Chêkiang 浙江; and the date of her birth as either in the period A.D. 713-56, 907-60, 960-77, or 1101-26.

The author of the *Lang-ya tai tsui pien* 琅琊代醉編 explains the appellation T'ien Fei 天妃, Concubine of Heaven, by saying that "Heaven is regarded as the Emperor, because he is the greatest and noblest; after Heaven comes the earth, and the Spirit of the earth is the Empress, who ranks immediately after the Emperor. The third dignity is reserved for the Spirit or Spirits of the Waters, and these female Spirits are the concubines of the Emperor, or of Heaven." This view, however, is not generally accepted.

The worship of this divinity may be an imitation of that rendered to the Apsaras, feminine water-spirits, in Indian Vedantism.

T'IEN FU 天輔.—See *Tou Mu* 斗母.

T'IEN HOU 天后.—See *Tou Mu* 斗母 and *T'ien Fei* 天妃.

T'IEN-HOU NIANG-NIANG 天后娘娘.—See *T'ien Fei* 天妃.

T'IEN-HSI 天喜, THE GOD OF THE STAR.—See *Chou Wang* 紂王.

T'IEN HSIEN 天仙.—Celestial gods: those who have attained to consummate purity and perpetual life in heaven.—See *Pi-hsia Yüan-chün* 碧霞元君.

T'IEN HSIEN SUNG-TZǓ 天仙送子.—See *Pi-hsia Yüan-chün* 碧霞元君.

T'IEN HSIN 天心.—See *Tou Mu* 斗母.

T'IEN-HSING 天刑, THE GOD OF THE STAR.—See *Ou-yang T'ien-lu* 歐陽天祿.

T'IEN HSÜN-LIU 田荀留.—See *Fêng-huo Yüan T'ien Yüan-shuai* 風火院田元帥.

T'IEN HUA, PI YÜAN-SHUAI 田華畢元帥.—The Generalissimo T'ien-hua, Pi of the Ministry of Thunder (see *Lei Pu* 雷部). It is related that he sprang from terrestrial electricity, which assumed human form in the middle of a meadow, during a terrific thunder and rain storm. He appeared seated on the back of a huge serpent, and bees came and fed him with honey.

Family name T'ien 田, Field; personal name Hua 華, Glory. To this he added that of Pi 畢, because of the grass in the meadow. He thus became known as T'ien Hua, Pi 田華畢 (*v. infra*).

After becoming a hermit at Lu-lu Yen 轆轤岩, Lu-lu Cliff, he helped Nü Wa 女媧 (*q.v.*) to repair the Heavens by combining the essence of fire and that of water with the primeval essence drawn from flint (or rock).

Later on, he assisted Hsüan Yüan 軒轅 (*q.v.*) (2698-2598 B.C.) to subdue the rebel Ch'ih Yu 蚩尤 by overwhelming him with a shower of five-coloured fire in the midst of a terrific wind and thunder storm. For this Huang Ti 皇帝 bestowed on him the title and office of Master-dragon. However, refusing these unsuitable dignities as being incompatible with his hermit status, he withdrew to the retreat of Hua-hsü 華胥; and it was then that he added its name to his own, being thenceforth known as T'ien Hua, Pi 田華畢.

During the reign of the Emperor Yao 堯 (2357-2255 B.C.), when diabolical monsters and the ten suns were spreading terror and trouble throughout the land, Yü Ti 玉帝 granted to T'ien Yüan-shuai 田元帥 by edict the right to drive his thunder-chariot over the skies, sun, and moon, bearing his thunder-flag in his hand.

When a like calamity occurred during the Han 漢 dynasty, Yü Ti 玉帝 canonized T'ien Hua 田華 as Lei-mên Pi Yüan-shuai 雷門畢元帥, Pi, Generalissimo of Thunder (of the Ministry of Thunder), and appointed him superintendent of the twelve subdivisions of that Ministry to help Chên Wu 眞武 (*q.v.*) subdue the demons of epidemics, take charge of droughts and floods, and put public malefactors to death.

T'IEN HUANG 天皇.—The Heavenly Ruler. The head of the family of fabulous sovereigns who succeeded P'an Ku 盤古, the "first development out of chaos."—See also *Shih-êrh yüan-chia* 十二元甲.

T'IEN HUNG-I 田洪義.—See *Fêng-huo Yüan T'ien Yüan-shuai* 風火院田元帥.

T'IEN-I 天醫, THE GOD OF THE STAR.—See *Ch'ien Pao* 錢保.

T'IEN I-YÜAN 天醫院.—The Celestial Ministry of Medicine. Composed of three main divisions comprising: (1) the Ancestral Gods of the Chinese race; (2) the King of Remedies, Yao Wang 藥王; and (3) the Specialists and Celebrities.

The chief gods of medicine are the mythical kings P'an Ku 盤古, Fu Hsi 伏羲, Shên Nung 神農, and Huang Ti 黃帝. The first two, being by different writers regarded as the progenitor or creator of the Chinese people, are alternatives, so that Fu Hsi 伏羲, Shên Nung 神農, and Huang Ti 黃帝 may be said to be a sort of ancestral triad of medicine-gods, superior to the actual God or King of Medicine, Yao Wang 藥王 (*q.v.*).—See *P'an Ku* 盤古, *Fu Hsi* 伏羲, *Shên Nung* 神農, *Huang Ti* 黃帝, *Yao Wang* 藥王, *Ts'ang Chieh* 倉頡, the President of the commission of learned men appointed by Huang Ti 黃帝, and members of that commission, namely, *Yü Fu* 兪跗, *Wu (?Hu) P'êng* 巫彭, *Lei Kung* 雷公, *Ch'i Po* 岐伯, *Kuei Ku-tzŭ* 鬼谷子, *T'ung Chün* 桐君, *Pien Ch'iao* 扁鵲, *Ma Shih-huang* 馬師皇, and *Wang Ping* 王冰. For the Specialists see *Hua T'o* 華陀, *Yen-kuang P'u-sa* 眼光菩薩, *Ts'ui-shêng Niang-niang* 催生娘娘, *Ta-nai Fu-jên* 大奶夫人, *Ko Ku* 葛姑, *Tou-shên Niang-niang* 痘神娘娘, *Pan Shên* 瘢 (班) 神, *Chên Shên* 疹 (症) 神, *Sha Shên* 痧 (莎) 神, *Ma Shên* 痲神, *Wu-fang Shên* 五方神, and *Shên Hsiu-chih* 沈秀之.

Doré (X. 756), stating that the Taoist books disagree as to the names of the chief dignitaries of the Celestial Ministry of Medicine, gives the following list, taken from the work *T'ai-shang wu-chi tung-tz'ŭ chên-yüan t'ien-hsin pao-chan* 太上無極洞慈真元天心寶懺, bk. 30, p. 5b:—President, (Lu) Pien-ch'iao (盧) 扁鵲; Senior Assistant, Sun Chên-jên 孫眞人; Junior Assistant, Wei Chên-jên 韋眞人; two Superintendents of Pharmacies, Li 李 and Chu 朱; the Grand Master of the Medical Formulary, Chao 趙; the Grand Master, the Pillar of Humanity, Hsü 許; the Grand Master of Diagnostics, Kao 高; the Grand Officer of the Ministry, T'ao 陶; the Infallible Doctor, a member of the same Ministry, Ma 馬; the Grand Master of Therapeutical Clinic, Wang 汪; the Celestial Doctor of Decoctions and of Acupuncture, Shih Fan-wu 石泛杵.

T'IEN-JÊN 天任.—See *Tou Mu* 斗母.

T'IEN-JUI 天芮.—See *Tou Mu* 斗母.

T'IEN-KANG 天罡.—Thirty-six stars of the Great Bear which revolve around the pivotal star. The gods of these stars (all stars of good omen) are all heroes who fell on the field of battle in the epic combat known as *Wan-hsien Chên* 萬仙陣, "The Battle of the Myriad Genii."

The names of the stars, followed by those of their stellar spirits included in brackets, are as follows:—T'ien-an 天暗: Heaven's Mystery (Li Hsin 李新).—T'ien-chi 天機: Heaven's Motor (Lu Ch'ang 盧昌).—T'ien-ch'iao 天巧: Heaven's Artifice (Ch'êng San-i 桯三益).—T'ien-chieh 天捷: Heaven's Victory (Têng Yü 鄧玉).—T'ien-chien 天間: Heaven's Middle (Chi Ch'ang 紀昌). —T'ien-chien 天劍: Heaven's Sword (Wang Hu 王虎).—T'ien-chiu 天究: Heaven's Examination (Tan Pai-chao 單百招).— T'ien-fu 天富: Heaven's Fortune (Li Hsien 黎仙).—T'ien-hsiung 天雄: Heaven's Male (Shih Kuei 施檜).—T'ien-hsüan 天玄: Heaven's Profundity (Wang Lung-mao 王龍茂).—T'ien-hui 天慧: Heaven's Wisdom (Chang Chih-hsiung 張智雄)—T'ien-i 天異: Heaven's Prodigy (Lü Tzŭ-ch'êng 呂自成).—T'ien-kang 天罡: Heaven's *kang* stars (Huang Chên 黄眞).—T'ien-ku 天孤: Heaven's Orphan (Chan Hsiu 詹秀).—T'ien-k'u 天哭: Heaven's Moaning (Liu Ta 劉達).—T'ien-kuei 天貴: Heaven's Nobility (Ch'ên K'an 陳坎).—T'ien-k'uei 天魁: Heaven's First (Kao Yen 高衍).—T'ien-k'ung 天空: Heaven's Void (Tien T'ung 典通). —T'ien-lao 天牢: Heaven's Granary (Wên Chieh 開傑).—T'ien-man 天滿: Heaven's Fullness (Fang Pao 方保).—T'ien-mêng 天猛: Heaven's Fierceness (Sun I 孫乙).—T'ien-pai 天敗: Heaven's Defeat (Shên Li 申禮).—T'ien-pao 天暴: Heaven's Cruelty (Pi Tê 畢德).—T'ien-p'ing 天平: Heaven's Balance (Pu T'ung 卜同).—T'ien-sha 天殺: Heaven's Executioner (Jên Lai-p'in 任來聘).—T'ien-shang 天傷: Heaven's Wound (Li Hung-jên 李洪仁).—T'ien-shou 天壽: Heaven's Longevity (Ch'i Ch'êng 戚成).—T'ien-su 天速: Heaven's Rapidity (Wu Hsü 吳旭).—T'ien-sun 天捐: Heaven's Hurt (T'ang T'ien-chêng 唐天正).—T'ien-tsui 天罪: Heaven's Offence (Yao Kung 姚公).— T'ien-t'ui 天退: Heaven's Recoil (Kao K'o 高可).—T'ien-wei 天威: Heaven's Majesty (Li Pao 李豹).—T'ien-wei 天微: Heaven's Hiding (Kung Ch'ing 龔清).—T'ien-ying 天英: Heaven's Heroes (Chu I 朱義).—T'ien-yu 天佑: Heaven's Aid (Hsü Chêng-tao 徐正道).—T'ien-yung 天勇: Heaven's Valour (Yao Kung-hsiao 姚公孝).—*Cf. Ti-sha* 地煞.

T'IEN-KOU 天狗, THE GOD OF THE STAR.—See *Chi K'ang* 季康.

T'IEN KUAN SHANG FU 天官賜福.—The Heaven Ruler who grants happiness.—See *San Kuan* 三官.

T'IEN-KUEI 天貴, THE GOD OF THE STAR.—See *Chi Shu-ch'ien* 姬叔乾.

T'IEN-K'UNG 天空, THE GOD OF THE STAR.—See *Mei Wu* 梅武.

T'IEN-LING CHÜN 天靈君.—See *Eyebrows, The Gods of the*.

T'IEN-LO 天羅, THE GOD OF THE STAR.—See *Ch'ên T'ung* 陳桐.

T'IEN LUNG 天龍.—The Celestial Dragon.—See *Lung Wang* 龍王.

T'IEN LUNG 天聾.—See *Wên Ch'ang* 文昌.

T'IEN-MA 天馬, THE GOD OF THE STAR.—See *O Ch'ung* 哦腔洵.

T'IEN MU 天母 (or 姆).—See *Tou Mu* 斗母.

T'IEN NÜ 天女.—Female devas. Apsaras. Attendants on the regents of sun and moon, wives of Gandharvas, and other female devas.

T'IEN-PAI 天敗, THE GOD OF THE STAR.—See *Po Hsien-chung* 柏顯忠.

T'IEN PAO 天寶.—The Treasure of Heaven. The heavenly Jewel. See *San Ch'ing* 三清, *Yüan-shih T'ien-tsun* 元始天尊, and *Lo Ching-hsin* 樂靜信.

T'IEN P'ÊNG 天蓬.—See *Tou Mu* 斗母.

T'IEN-SHA 天殺, THE GOD OF THE STAR.—See *Pien Chi*. 卞吉.

T'IEN SHAN 天山.—The Celestial Mountains of Central Asia. The Ch'i-lien Shan 祁連山 range which formed the centre of the country of the Hsiung-nu 匈奴, in whose language Ch'i-lien 祁連 signified Heaven.

T'IEN-SHÊ 天赦, THE GOD OF THE STAR.—See *Ch'ao Chi* 晁蓋.

T'IEN-SSŬ 天嗣, THE GOD OF THE STAR.—See *Huang Fei-pao* 黃飛豹.

T'IEN-SSŬ FANG 天駟房.—A Star-god. One of the Gods of Silkworms. A composite deity.—See *Composite Deities* and *Cow, The*.

T'IEN-T'AI CHIAO 天台教.—See *Buddhist Schools*, X.

T'IEN-T'AI TSUNG 天台宗.—See *Buddhist Schools*, X.

T'IEN-TÊ 天德, THE GOD OF THE STAR.—See *Mei Po* 梅柏.

T'IEN-WÊN 天瘟, THE GOD OF THE STAR.—See *Chin Ta-shêng* 金大升 and *Niu Wang* 牛王.

T'IEN WU 天吳.—See *Shui Fu* 水府, D (3) (d).

T'IEN YING 天英.—See *Tou Mu* 斗母.

T'IEN-YÜ-PAO CH'AN-SHIH 天愚寶禪師 (66th generation).—A deified Buddhist monk. Ranked seventy-third in Buddhist School, VI (*q.v.*). Family name Ou 歐. A native of Hsin-ch'êng 新城, Kiangsi 江西. He studied first under [Chu-mo] Ta-yin Ch'an-shih [久墨] 大音禪師 (*q.v.*) in the Pien-shan Ssŭ 弁山寺, Pien-shan Monastery, and after his death under [Shih-yü] Ming-fang Ch'an-shih [石雨] 明方禪師 (*q.v.*). In A.D. 1656, he began teaching at Yü-hang 禹航. Having lived successively in the monasteries of Nan-shan 南山, Yüeh-chou 越州, Hsien-shêng 顯聖, Chia-ho 嘉禾, Hsing-shan 興善, and Tzŭ-yün 紫雲, at Hangchow 杭州, he died in A.D. 1675, aged 67. His tomb is on Nan Shan 南山, South Hill.

T'IEN-YÜ YÜAN-SHUAI 田雨元帥.—Generalissimo T'ien-yü 田雨. The son of the Green Dragon. The dragon, pursued by Tz'ŭ-chi Chên-chün 慈濟眞君, fled to Ssŭch'uan 四川 and hid in the Huang-sha Tung 黃沙洞. He married a beautiful woman named P'ang 龐, but when she was about to give birth to a child, Tz'ŭ-chi Chên-chün 慈濟眞君 arrived, and the Green Dragon had to flee. His wife hid in a field, but Tz'ŭ-chi Chên-chün 慈濟眞君 found her, and, pointing at her his flying sword, amid terrific rain and violent thunder she was delivered of a child. The child had a human body and a dragon's head. Tz'ŭ-chi Chên-chün 慈濟眞君, though he continued his pursuit of the Green Dragon, was always careful not to harm either the child or its mother. The child was given the family name T'ien 田, because it was born in a field, and Yü 雨 as its personal name, in reference to the rain which fell at the time of its birth.

At six years of age it was entrusted to Chang Chên-jên 張眞人 to be educated. He taught it the science of thunder, and gave it the antonym Ch'üan Ling 全靈, Complete Spirituality.

When at Tzŭ-hua Shan 紫華山, he enquired of an old Taoist as to his origin, and learnt that his father was the Green Dragon and that his blind mother was living at Lung-yu 隴右 in Ssŭ-ch'uan 四川.

Deeply grieved, he left in two years' time to find his mother and avenge his father. Making a battle-flag out of the cloth of his tent, he searched the skies for his enemy. His saliva formed clouds and the waving of his flag made a sound like thunder. An encounter with twelve devils who obstructed his way proved indecisive.

Yü Ti 玉帝 then informed him that he should not show hostility either to Tz'ŭ-chi Chên-jên 慈齊眞人 or to the twelve devils, because the former, by driving away the Green Dragon, was benefiting the people, and the latter, although deserving death for preventing him from executing vengeance, yet wished to become his followers and serve him.

Yü Ti 玉帝 then canonized him as Hsiang-yao ch'ü-hsieh Yüan-shuai 降妖祛邪元帥, Generalissimo who conquers demons and drives away evil influences. He is represented holding the thunder-stone in his left hand and a yellow flag in his right, and is a member of the Ministry of Exorcisms (see *Ministries*).

T'IEN YÜAN-SHUAI 田元帥.—See *Fêng-huo Yüan T'ien Yüan-shuai* 風火院田元帥.

TIME, THE MINISTRY OF.—See *T'ai Sui* 太歲.

TING-CHIA SHÊN 丁甲神.—See *Shih-êrh ting-chia Shên* 十二丁甲神.

TING-CHOU SHÊN 丁丑神.—See *Shih-êrh ting-chia Shên* 十二丁甲神.

TING 丁 GODS, THE.—Six gods who assisted Yü 禹 the Great in his labours. Chang 張, the Taoist Pope, can summon them at his will, and the priests rely on the Ting 丁 gods to expel demons. On the land they can subdue tigers and panthers, and in the water overcome dragons.

TING-HAI SHÊN 丁亥神.—See *Shih-êrh ting-chia Shên* 十二丁甲神.

TING-KUANG FO 定光佛.—See *Jan Têng Fo* 燃燈佛.

TING-MAO SHÊN 丁卯神.—See *Shih-êrh ting-chia Shên* 十二丁甲神.

TING 丁 SPIRIT, THE.—See *T'ieh Yüan-shuai* 鐵元帥.

TING-SSŬ SHÊN 丁巳神.—See *Shih-êrh ting-chia Shên* 十二丁甲神.

TING TS'Ê 丁策.—The god of the star *Ti-lu* 地輅. A general of Chou Wang 紂王 (1121-1114 B.C.). Killed by No-cha 哪吒 during the attack on the capital Ch'ao-ko 朝歌.

TING-WEI SHÊN 丁未神.—See *Shih-êrh ting-chia Shên* 十二丁甲神.

TING-YU SHÊN 丁酉神.—See *Shih-êrh ting-chia Shên* 十二丁甲神.

TO-FU-CH'I CH'AN-SHIH 多福啟禪師 (66th generation). A deified Buddhist monk. Ranked seventy-fourth in Buddhist School, VI (*q.v.*). Family name Ch'ên 陳. A native of Ch'ient'ang Hsien 錢塘縣, Chêkiang 浙江. Studied first under [Shih-yü] Ming-fang Ch'an-shih [石雨] 明方禪師 (*q.v.*) and then under [San-i] Ming-yü Ch'an-shih [三宜] 明孟禪師 (*q.v.*). The latter taught at the Hsien-shêng 顯聖 Monastery. Afterwards, he led a solitary life at Fêng Shan 鳳山, Phoenix Hill, and was much esteemed for his virtue. Died A.D. 1674. His tomb is on the same hill.

TO-PAO TAO-JÊN 多寶道人.—A disciple of T'ung-t'ien Chiao-chu 通天教主. Was captured at the battle of Chieh-p'ai Kuan 界牌關 by the Ting-chia 丁甲 genii and taken to Lao-tzŭ 老子 as a prisoner of war.

TO WÊN 多聞.—See *Ssŭ ta T'ien-wang* 四大天王.

T'O-T'A LI 托塔李.—See *Li Ching* 李靖.

TONGUE, THE GODS OF THE.—The God of the Tongue is Shih Liang-shih 始梁峙; style Tao Ch'i 道岐; height 7 inches; colour red (*Yün chi ch'i ch'ien* 雲笈七籤). In the *Huang t'ing nei ching* 黃庭內經 the name is given as T'ung Ming 通命; style Chêng Lun 正倫.

TORTOISE, THE TRANSCENDENT.—See *Wu-yün Hsien* 烏雲仙 and *Shui-huo T'ung tzŭ* 水火童子.

TORTOISE, THE TRANSCENDENT SAINTLY MOTHER. —See *Kuei-ling Shêng-mu* 龜靈聖母.

TORTOISE SPIRIT, THE.—See *Ch'ing-wa Shên* 青蛙神.

TOU 斗, THE GOD OF THE CONSTELLATION.—See *Chu Yu* 朱祐 and *Yang Hsin* 楊信.

TOU-FU T'IEN-TSUN 斗父天尊.—See *Tou Mu* 斗母.

TOU JUNG 竇榮.—See *Wu Tou* 五斗.

TOU MU 斗母 (or 姆 or 姥), T'IEN MU 天母, TAO MU 道母.—The Bushel Mother, or Goddess of the North Star. The Indian Maritchi (said by Georgi to be a Chinese transcription of the Christian holy virgin Mary). The Chinese Buddhists's Goddess of Light who holds aloft the sun and the moon, the protectress against war. Also styled T'ien Hou 天后, Queen of Heaven, T'ien Mu 天母, Mother of Heaven, and Tao Mu 道母, Mother of the Way. The Chinese Taoists use the term T'ien Hou 天后, and locate her, her husband Tou-fu T'ien-tsun 斗父天尊, Father of the Bushel Honoured of Heaven, and their nine sons (*v. infra*), in Sagittarius.

Tou Mu 斗母 was born in T'ien-chu Kuo 天竺國, India. She married Ch'ên Chi-tsung (or ts'ung) 辰祭從, king of the northern realm of Chou yü 周御. They had nine sons—Jên Huang 人王, or Human Sovereigns, of fabulous antiquity, who succeeded the lines of Celestial and Terrestrial Sovereigns. The names of the sons were:—1. T'ien-ying 天英. 2. T'ien-jên 天任. 3. T'ien-chu 天柱. 4. T'ien-hsin 天心. 5. T'ien-ch'in 天禽. 6. T'ien-fu 天輔. 7. T'ien-ch'ung 天沖. 8. T'ien-jui 天芮. 9. T'ien-p'êng 天蓬.

She occupies in the Taoist religion the same relative position as Kuan Yin 觀音 (*q.v.*). Having attained to a profound know-ledge of celestial mysteries, she shone with heavenly light, could cross the sea, and pass from the sun to the moon. She also, like Kuan Yin 觀音, "the heart of Buddhism," had a kind heart for the sufferings of humanity.

Having trained her sons in all transcendental wisdom, she, owing to the sparse population of the northern regions, went with them to the south and settled on Chih-hsiu Shan 指修山. When the inhabitants of those parts saw their fine clothes, chariots, etc., they took them for genii and elected the elder, T'ien-ying 天英, as their king. He is often called Chiu-t'ou Shih 九頭氏, "the elder of the nine," but more usually by the generic name Jên Huang 人皇, "Human Sovereign."

Yüan-shih T'ien-tsun 元始天尊 came to earth to invite her, her husband, and nine sons to enjoy the delights of Heaven. He placed her in the palace Tou-shu 斗樞, the Pivot of the Pole, because all the other stars revolve around it, and bestowed upon her the title Queen of the Doctrine of Primitive Heaven. This is the origin of the appellation Tou Mu 斗母, Mother of the North Star. Her honorary title is Tou-mu T'ien-tsun 斗母天尊, Heaven-honoured Mother of the Pole Star. Her husband inhabited the same palace, her nine sons having their palaces in the neigh-bouring nine stars.

Tou Mu 斗母 wears the Buddhist crown, is seated on a lotus throne, has three eyes, eighteen arms, and holds various precious objects in her numerous hands, such as a bow, spear, sword, flag, dragon's head, pagoda, five chariots, sun's disk, moon's disk, etc. She has control of the books of life and death, and all who wish to prolong their days worship at her shrine. Her devotees abstain from animal food on the third and twenty-seventh day of every month.

Of her sons, two are the Northern and Southern Bushels; the latter, dressed in red, rules birth; the former, in white, rules death. "A young Esau once found them on the South Mountain, under a tree, playing chess, and by an offer of venison his lease of life was extended from nineteen to ninety-nine years."

TOU-MU T'IEN-TSUN 斗母天尊.—See *Tou Mu* 斗母.

TOU-MU YÜAN-TSUN 斗母元尊.—See *Tou Mu* 斗母.

TOU SHÊN 痘神.—The Spirit of Smallpox. Name Yü Hua-lung 余化龍. He and his five sons (Ta 達, Chao 兆, Kuang 光, Hsien 先, and Tê 德) constitute the Ministry of Smallpox. The father was the military governor of the important fortress of T'ung-kuan 潼關, in the bend of the Huang Ho 黃河, Yellow River, in Shensi 陝西, in the reign of Chou Wang 紂王 (1154-1121 B.C.), the last king of the Yin 殷 dynasty. After he had made an unsuccessful attempt to dislodge Chiang Tzŭ-ya 姜子牙, the Chou 周 Generalissimo, his son Tê 德, during the night, scattered five bushels of smallpox pustules in the enemy's camp. Wu Wang 武王 (1121-1114 B.C.), King Wu 武, Chiang Tzŭ-ya 姜子牙, and all his soldiers caught it, General Yang Chien 楊戩, who was absent, alone escaping. Chiang Tzŭ-ya 姜子牙 then sent to Fu Hsi 伏羲 for an antidote, and the latter ordered Shên Nung 神農 to transmit to him three magic pills. "The first," he said, "will cure Wu Wang 武王, the second Chiang Tzŭ-ya 姜子牙, and by dissolving the third in water and sprinkling the camp with the liquid, the virus will be expelled therefrom. This was done, and all were healed, but, being enraged at finding all who had contracted the disease pockmarked, Chiang Tzŭ-ya 姜子牙 ordered a mass attack on the T'ung-kuan 潼關 fortress. This resulted in the death of Yü Hua-lung's 余化龍 five sons, whereupon the father committed suicide.

After defeating the Yin 殷, Chiang Tzŭ-ya 姜子牙 canonized Yü Hua-lung 余化龍 as First Sovereign Prince of Smallpox. His five sons also received titles: True Spirit of Smallpox in the East, West, South, North, and Centre, respectively.—See also *Tou-shên Niang-niang* 痘神娘娘, *Chang Yüan-shuai* 張元帥, and *Small-pox, The God of*.

TOU-SHÊN NIANG-NIANG 痘神娘娘.—The Dame who

controls Smallpox. One of the specialists attached to the celestial Ministry of Medicine. A Taoist goddess, rarely represented as a god. She had four sons; one of them had black smallpox, the second smallpox (variola), the third scarlatina, and the fourth a face deeply scarred from the disease. All four were canonized by Shang Ti 上帝, who granted them the power of protecting mankind against this scourge.

The goddess is variously represented; sometimes wearing a large shawl to protect her infected skin from cold.

This is a variation of the legend of Yü-hua Lung 余化龍 (see *Tou Shên* 痘神).—See also *Pan Shên* 瘢神, *Chên Shên* 疹神, *Sha Shên* 痧神, *Ma Shên* 痲神, and *T'ien I-yüan* 天醫院.

TRADES, THE GODS OF.—Each different trade in China has its own patron god. Usually it is a deified man who was especially proficient in that particular profession. These are often carried through the streets in the parades organized by the various guilds. They are as numerous as the various pursuits of man, and each belongs to its particular line of business.

TRANSCENDENT LION, A.— See *Ch'iu-shou Hsien* 虬首仙.

TRANSCENDENT SAINTLY MOTHER TORTOISE, THE.—See *Kuei-ling Shêng-mu* 龜靈聖母.

TRANSCENDENT TORTOISE, THE.—See *Wu-yün Hsien* 烏雲仙 and *Shui-huo T'ung tzŭ* 水火童子.

TRAVEL, THE GODDESS OF.—This goddess is said to have been the wife of the Emperor Hsüan Yüan 軒轅. The latter went on a journey to Mount T'ai 泰 to place a handful of earth on the top as an offering to Heaven, and a clod on a clean spot on the level ground as an offering to the mountain, and the Empress dying en route he appointed her the Goddess of Travel (Du Bose).

TREASURE OF HEAVEN, THE.—See *Yüan-shih T'ien-tsun* 元始天尊.

TREASURY OF MEDICINAL HERBS, THE.— See *Yao-shih Fo* 藥師佛.

TREES, THE GODS OF.—"The god of trees is only worshipped when an oak of the forest is to be felled with the woodman's axe. Notice is duly served throughout the neighbourhood, announcing at what time the tree is to be cut down, so that those who live near may remain indoors, as the tree-god

TREES, THE GODS OF is to be robbed of his roost, and may avenge himself upon the neighbours. Every tree has its separate individual deity" (Du Bose). A very polytheism of the forest.

TRIADS.—Groups of three gods or saints, or both. The groupings of the numerous Buddhist Triads differ in China, Mongolia, and Tibet.—See *San Shêng* 三 聖, *San Ch'ing* 三 淸, *San-tsun ta Fo* 三 尊 大 佛, *San Pao* 三 寶, *San Kuan* 三 官, and *Wu-k'o san Chên-chün* 烏 窠 三 眞 君.

TRI-KAYA.—See *Adi-Buddha*.

TRI-MURTI.—Triple form. The Hindu triad. This was foreshadowed in the Vedic association of the three gods Agni, Vayu, and Surya. The triad consists of the gods Brahma, Siva, and Vishnu, the representatives of the creative, destructive, and preservative principles.

TRIUNE GENIE OF HEAVEN, THE.—See *T'ai I* 太 一.

TRIYANA.—San shêng 三 乘, San chü chih chiao 三 車 之 敎, or San shêng fa mên 三 乘 法 門.—(1) three vehicles (*sc.* across Sansara into Nirvana), sheep (*a*), *i.e.* S'ravakas, (*b*) deer, *i.e.* Pratyeka Buddhas, (*c*) oxen, *i.e.* Bodhisattvas; salvation by three successive degrees of saintship. (2) The three principal Schools of Buddhism, *viz.* the Mahayana, Hinayana, and Madhyimayana (Eitel).

TROUBLED ORIGINS, THE GOLDEN BUSHEL OF.—See *K'êng san Ku-niang* 坑 三 姑 娘.

TRUE WORDS, THE SCHOOL OF.—See *Buddhist Schools, XV*.

TRUTHS, THE FOUR.—See *Four Truths, The*.

TS'AI KUNG 蔡 公.—The god of the star Ti-tuan 地 短.—See *Ti-sha* 地 煞

TS'AI LUN 蔡 倫.—The God of Paper-makers or Stationers. Personal name, Ching-chung 敬 仲. A native of Kuei-yang 桂 陽, Honan 河 南. Held an important post in the reign of the Emperor Ho Ti 和 帝 (A.D. 89-106) of the Han 漢 dynasty. Learnt to make paper (theretofore unknown) from the bark of trees, hemp, bits of cloth, and old fishing nets. In the period A.D. 114-20 was given the title of Marquis of Lung-t'ing 龍 亭 by the Emperor Hsiao-an Ti 孝 安 帝 (A.D. 107-26) of the Han dynasty, and was universally known as the Marquis Ts'ai 蔡.

TS'AI SHÊN 財 神.—The Spirit or God of Riches or Wealth. As with many other Chinese gods, the proto-being of the God of

Wealth has been ascribed to several persons. The original and best known until later times, was Chao Kung-ming 趙公明 (beginning of Chou 周 dynasty). The accounts of him differ also, but the following is the most popular:—When Chiang Tzŭ-ya 姜子牙 was fighting for Wu Wang 武王 (1121-1114 B.C.) of the Chou 周 dynasty against the last of the Yin 殷 emperors, Chao Kung-ming 趙公明, then a hermit on Mount O-mei 峨嵋, took the part of the latter. He performed many wonderful feats. He could ride a black tiger and hurl pearls which burst like bomb-shells. But he was eventually overcome by the form of witchcraft known in Wales as *Ciurp Creadh*. Chiang Tzŭ-ya 姜子牙 made a straw image of him, wrote his name on it, burned incense and worshipped before it for twenty days, and on the twenty-first shot arrows made of peach-wood into its eyes and heart. At the same moment Chao Kung-ming 趙公明, then in the enemy's camp, felt ill and fainted, and uttering a cry gave up the ghost.

Later on Chiang Tzŭ-ya 姜子牙 persuaded Yüan-shih T'ien-tsun 元始天尊 to release from the Otherworld the spirits of the heroes who had died in battle, and when Chao Kung-ming 趙公明 was led into his presence he praised his bravery, deplored the circumstances of his death, and canonized him as President of the Ministry of Riches and Prosperity.

Another God of Wealth is Chao Kung-ming 趙公明 of the time of the Three Kingdoms, San Kuo 三國 (A.D. 220-80). His name was Lang 朗, and he was the younger brother of Chao Tzŭ-lung 趙子龍, the legendary hero of the Three Kingdoms, commonly known as Chao Yün 趙雲. Died A.D. 229, and was posthumously honoured.

The Mohammedan Hsüan (Yüan)-t'an P'u-sa 玄(元)壇菩薩 is also worshipped as a God of Riches. His name means the P'u-sa 菩薩 of the North Terrace, *hsüan-t'an* 玄壇, *hsüan,* black, being the colour of the North (see *Wu-fang Shên* 五方神), the sacrifices to him being offered on the North Terrace. There are thus two persons thus designated: Chao Kung-ming Hsüan-t'an Chên-chün 趙公明玄壇眞君, canonized by Chiang Tzŭ-ya 姜子牙 and the Hsüan-t'an 玄壇, above-mentioned. Universally worshipped in every house, he is shown riding a tiger or a dragon; holds in his hand a knotted stick, and has at his feet the magic bowl *chü-pao p'ên* 聚寶盆, from which ingots sprout in proportion as they are taken out of it. The peasants sacrifice a cock to him, spreading some of its blood on their door-sills and on the foot of the god's image, and let off large quantities of crackers.

Lu T'ou 路頭 is the God of Riches of roads (or cross-roads) worshipped by merchants on the fifth day of the first moon to ensure success during the year. (See also next paragraph).

Wu-lu Ts'ai-shên 五路財神, the God of Riches of the Five Roads (or the Five Directions, *v. infra*) was originally a man named Ho Wu-lu 何五路, who was slain by brigands toward the end of the Yüan 元 dynasty and afterwards apotheosized. But the term as used later, and quite unconnected with the above, refers to the five sons of Ku Hsi-fêng 顧希馮 (personal name Yeh-wang 野王), a native of Su-chou 蘇州, Kiangsu 江蘇, and a eunuch in the palace of the Ch'ên 陳 emperors. He died in A.D. 581 during the reign of the Emperor Hsüan Ti 宣帝 (A.D. 569-83), and received the posthumous title of Wang 王, King. His five sons, named respectively Hsien-ts'ung 顯聰, Hsien-ming 顯明, Hsien-chêng 顯正, Hsien-chih 顯直, and Hsien-tê 顯德, were honoured with the title of Hou 侯, Marquis, and a temple was built and dedicated to them. At the end of the Ming 明 dynasty this temple was known as the Temple of the Five Brilliances. They were worshipped as the Five Saints, Wu Shêng 五聖, this title being changed in the reign of K'ang Hsi 康熙 (A.D. 1662-1723) to the Five Penetrating Ones, Wu Hsien 五顯, and finally to Lu T'ou 路頭 and Ts'ai Shên 財神 (*supra*). Lu T'ou 路頭 indicates the Five Directions: North, South, East, West, and Centre. The Five Spirits of Roads are one of the five categories of Spirits honoured by the five domestic sacrifices, namely, Hu 戶, the Spirit of the House, Tsao 灶, the Spirit of the Stove, Mên 門, the Spirit of the Door, Hsing 行, the Spirit of the Alley, and Chung 中, the Spirit of the Centre of the dwelling.

Shên Wan-san 沈萬三, a native of Nanking 南京, Kiangsu 江蘇, originally a fisherman, is another God of Riches. One day he fished up a valuable casket or bowl (*chü- pao p'ên* 聚寶盆, *supra*). This magic article he presented to the Emperor Hung Wu 洪武 (A.D. 1368-99), who used it to blow down the city-gate of Nanking 南京, which he was then besieging. For this he was canonized as Guardian of the Territory of the Capital.

Kuan Kung 關公 (see *Kuan Yü* 關羽) is also honoured as Wu Ts'ai Shên 武財神, the Military God of Riches, and the Goddess of T'ai-shan 泰山 (see *Pi-hsia Yüan-chün* 碧霞元君) as the Goddess of Riches in addition to the deities abovementioned.

In Buddhist temples a large paunched figure resembling the Maitreya is worshipped as the God of Riches. He bears in his hand an ingot and has at his feet the *chü-pao p'ên* 聚寶盆 (*supra*).

The God of Riches is universally worshipped in China; images and portraits of him are to be seen everywhere. He is a special patron deity of merchants in general. Talismans, trees of which the branches are strings of cash, and the fruits ingots of gold, to be obtained merely by shaking them down, a magic inexhaustible casket full of gold and silver—these and other spiritual sources of wealth are associated with this much-adored deity. He himself is represented in the guise of a visitor accompanied by a crowd of attendants laden with all the treasures that the hearts of men, women, and children could desire.

The celestial Ministry of Finance is composed of the President, Chao Kung-ming 趙公明, and the two ministers: Hsiao Shêng 蕭昇 and Ts'ao Pao 曹寶. They were canonized after death as members of the Ministry of Riches. The peasants worship them also under the name of Ho Ho 和合 (*q.v.*).

Two other members of the Ministry are Ch'ên Chiu-kung 陳九公 and Yao Shao-ssŭ 姚少司, two of Chao Kung-ming's 趙公明 subalterns, who fought with him in Chou Wang's 紂王 army, and were slain by Yang Chien 楊戩 and No-cha 哪吒 respectively. They are commonly designated under the title of Chao-ts'ai li-shih 招財利市, He who brings Riches, and He who brings Gain, and are usually represented as the God of Riches (see *Ts'ai Shên* 財神, *supra*).

TS'AN 參, THE GOD OF THE CONSTELLATION.—See *Tu Mao* 杜茂 and *Sun Hsiang* 孫祥.

TS'AN-CH'U 蠶畜, THE GOD OF THE STAR.—See *Huang Yüan-chi* 黃元濟.

TS'AN NÜ 蠶女.—The Goddess of Silkworms. This divinity is variously considered to be: (1) a young lady changed into a silkworm; (2) a star-deity—the star T'ien-ssŭ 天駟; (3) the first man to breed silkworms; (4) the wife of Huang Ti 黃帝, the Emperor Huang (2698-2598 B.C.).

The legend of the Silkworm Maiden is that in the Kingdom of Shu 蜀 (modern Ssŭch'uan 四川), in the time of Kao Hsin-shih 高辛氏 (2436-2366 B.C.), a band of robbers kidnapped the father of Ts'an Nü 蠶女. A whole year elapsed, and the father's horse still remained in the stable as he had left it. The thought of not seeing her father again caused Ts'an Nü 蠶女 such grief that she would take no nourishment. Her mother did what she could to console her, and further promised her in marriage to anyone who would bring back her father. But no one was found who could do this. Hearing the offer, the horse stamped with impatience, and struggled so much that at length he broke the halter by which he was tied up. He then galloped away and disappeared. Several days later, his owner returned riding the horse. From that time the horse neighed incessantly, and refused all food. This caused the mother to make known to her husband the promise she had made concerning her daughter. "An oath made to men," he replied, "does not hold good for a horse. Is a human being meant to live in marital relations with a horse?" Nevertheless, however good and abundant food they offered him, the horse would not eat. When he saw the young lady he plunged and kicked furiously. Losing his temper, the father discharged an arrow and killed him on the spot; then he skinned him and spread the skin on the ground outside the house to dry. As the young lady was passing the spot the skin suddenly moved, rose up, enveloped her, and disappeared into space. Ten days later it was found at the foot of a mulberry tree; Ts'an Nü 蠶 女 changed into a silkworm, was eating the mulberry-leaves, and spinning herself a silken garment.

The parents of course were in despair. But one day, while they were overwhelmed with sad thoughts, they saw on a cloud Ts'an Nü 蠶 女 riding the horse and attended by several dozens of servants. She descended toward her parents, and said to them: "The Supreme Being, as a reward for my martyrdom in the cause of filial piety and love of virtue, has conferred on me the dignity of Concubine of the Nine Palaces. Be reassured as to my fate, for in Heaven I shall live for ever." Having said this she disappeared into space.

In the temples her image is to be seen covered with a horse's skin. She is called Ma-t'ou Niang 馬頭娘 (q.v.), 'the Lady with the Horse's Head,' and is prayed to for the prosperity of mulberry trees and silkworms. The worship continues even in modern times. The sacrifice is performed on the third day of the third moon. It dates from the Chou 周 dynasty, or earlier.

TSANG KUAN 臧官.—The god of the constellation Pi 壁. Alternatively with Fang Chi-ch'ing 方吉清.

TSANG WÊN-KUNG 臧文公.—See *Hüan-t'ien Shang-ti* 玄天上帝 and *Shih-êrh ting-chia Shên* 十二丁甲神.

TS'ANG CHIEH 倉頡.—A demi-god. The president of a commission of learned men appointed by Huang Ti 黄帝 (q.v.) to continue and complete the labours of Shên Nung 神農 on natural history and the medicinal properties of plants.—See *T'ien I-yüan* 天醫院.

TSAO CHÜN 灶 (竈) 君.—The God of the Stove. The God of the Hearth. The Kitchen-god. A Taoist invention, but universally worshipped by all families in China—about sixty millions of pictures of him are regularly worshipped twice a month—at new and full moon. "His temple is a little niche in the brick cooking-range; his palace is often filled with smoke; and his Majesty sells for one farthing."

"There is some reason to believe that the Hearth God was once regarded as an anonymous ancestor of the family, though, nowadays, this relationship is ignored" (Johnston, *Lion and Dragon in Northern China*).

The origin of his worship, according to the legend, is that a Taoist priest, Li Shao-chün 李少君 by name, of the Ch'i 齊 State, obtained from the Kitchen-god the double favour of exemption from growing old and of being able to live without eating. He then went to the Emperor Hsiao Wu-ti 孝武帝 (140-86 B.C.) of the Han 漢 dynasty, and promised that credulous monarch that he should benefit by the powers of the god provided that he would consent to patronize and encourage the religion. It was by this means, he added, that the Emperor Huang Ti 皇帝 (2698-2598 B.C.) obtained his knowledge of alchemy, which enabled him to make gold.

The Emperor asked the priest to bring him his divine patron, and one night the image of Tsao Chün 灶君 appeared to him.

Deceived by this trick, dazzled by the ingots of gold which he too should obtain, and determined to risk everything for the pill of immortality which was among the benefits promised, the Emperor made a solemn sacrifice to the God of the Kitchen.

This was the first time that a sacrifice had been offered to this new deity.

Li Shao-chün 李少君 gradually lost the confidence of the Emperor and, at his wits' end, conceived the plan of writing some phrases on a piece of silk and then causing them to be swallowed by an ox. This done, he announced that a wonderful script would be found in the animal's stomach. The ox being killed, the script was found there as predicted, but Li's unlucky star decreed that the Emperor should recognize his handwriting, and he was forthwith put to death. Nevertheless, the worship of the Kitchen-god continued and increased, and has existed in full vigour down to the present day.

Between the Han 漢, and the Sung 宋 dynasties the Prince of the Furnaces (Tsao Chün 竈君), whose powers were connected with alchemy, was transformed into the God of the Hearth, Tsao Shên 竈神, the word *tsao* meaning both 'furnace' and 'hearth.' There are no records of the way in which this change took place, but probably it was during the T'ang 唐 dynasty when the process of creating new deities by the Taoists, and of ascribing new powers to deities already known, flourished at the height of its popularity. The first historical reference to the universality of the worship of the god of the hearth at the close of the year occurs in a collection of poems called Shih Hu Tz'ǔ 石湖詞, by Fan Ch'êng-ta 范成大, who lived in the reign of the emperor Kao Tsung 高宗 (A.D. 1127-62) of the S. Sung 宋 dynasty. The poet says that every family made presents to this god preparatory to his departure to present his report of family affairs to the Ruler of Heaven, but no account of the origin of the custom is given. The poet refers to the custom of worshipping this god as being universal in the country at that time. It needed no explanation to those for whom the poem was written.

This deity has power over the lives of the members of each family under his supervision, distributes riches and poverty at will, and makes an annual report to the Supreme Being on the conduct of the family during the year, for which purpose he is usually absent for from four to seven days. Some hold that he also makes these reports once or twice or several times each month. Various ceremonies are performed on seeing him off to Heaven and welcoming him back. One of the former is to regale him with honey, so that only sweet words may be spoken by him while up aloft!

There are more than forty different stories of the origin of the Kitchen-god, and of the men deified to take this responsible position. Perhaps the most popular one is that of Chang Tsao-wang 張繼王. He married a young lady by the name of Kuo Ting-hsiang 郭丁香, who was very virtuous and brought good luck to his home. But in a short time he tired of her, and fell in love with a fast girl named Li Hai-t'ang 李海棠. She persuaded him to put away his wife and marry her. When Ting-hsiang 丁香 returned to her parents' home the prosperity of her husband left him. Li Hai-t'ang 李海棠 forsook him and returned to her former method of life. Conditions went from bad to worse. He lost his eyesight and became a beggar. When seeking alms, without realizing it, he came to the home of Ting-hsiang 丁香. She recognized him, admitted him to the house, and gave him a dish of macaroni, his favourite dish. This recalled to his memory his former wife and their happy, prosperous condition together. He began to cry, and said, "My good wife cooked just this way." She then said, "Chang Lang 張郎, Chang Lang 張郎, open your eyes." At this he recovered his sight, and seeing her was so filled with shame for the way he had treated her that he tried to hide behind the stove. In his effort to escape he jumped into the stove, not knowing there was fire in it. Ting Hsiang 丁香, in trying to save him, grasped his leg and attempted to pull him out. The leg parted from the body. From that time the wooden rake used to pull the ashes out of the stove has been called Chang Lang's 張郎 leg. Ting Hsiang 丁香 mourned for him, and placed his tablet over the stove, as the place where he lost his life, and there worshipped him. From this came his worship as the Kitchen-god.

Extreme divergence of opinion is shown by Chinese authors as to the name of the person to whom the title of Tsao Chün 灶君 is given. The following are only some out of a lengthy list:—An old female cook, who in early times specialized in cooking; a saint of antiquity, noted for his virtuous life; Yen Ti 炎帝 (Shên Nung 神農), on account of his predilection for fire; Huang Ti 黃帝, who was the first to erect stoves; Chung Li 重黎 (see *Huo Pu* 火部); Wu Hui 吳回 (see *ibid.*); Su Chi-li 蘇吉利 and his wife Wang-shih 王氏 (see *ibid.*); a goddess named Chi 觺; a god named Shan Tzǔ-kuo 禪子郭, who when a man, died on the day *jên* 壬, on which day, therefore, stoves must not be erected; a beautiful maiden named Kuei 隗; Chang Tan 張單, named Tzǔ-kuo 子郭, whose wife was Ch'ing-chi 卿忌; he is also referred to by the name of Jang-tzǔ 壤子; an old woman of unknown origin who lived on K'un-lun Shan 崑崙山, the K'un-lun Mountains, and was deputed by the seven rulers of the Pole Star to govern human beings; etc.

There are also Tsao Chün 灶 君 of the East, with grey face; of the South, with red face; of the West, with white face; of the North, with black face; and of the Centre, with yellow face; each with a goddess, his wife. There are Tsao Chün 灶 君 of the Heavens, and of the kitchens on earth, and all their ancestors to the third generation, their fathers, mothers, wives, sons, grandsons, sisters, daughters-in-law, etc., and numerous others (for particulars see *Doré*, XI. 901-4).

The chief duty of this god is to determine (as he sees fit) the length, whether long or short, of the lives of the members of the family over which he presides. Hence his alternative designation of Ssŭ-ming fu-chün 司 命 府君, Official Superintendent of Lives. Next, to distribute riches or poverty to the members, as he deems best. Finally, to keep a record of the good or bad acts of the members in order to report them to the Supreme Being.

This report he makes (according to different authors) at midnight on the fifteenth day of each month; on the last day of the month; on each *kêng* 庚 and *shên* 申 day of the month; the first and fifteenth day of the month. But all agree that at the end of each year (either on the twenty-third, twenty-fourth, or twenty-sixth day of the twelfth month) he reports to the Supreme Being on the family for the whole year. He returns on the thirtieth, sometimes a little later.

Some days after the fixed date Buddhist or Taoist priests are engaged by the family to wish the god a pleasant journey and to welcome him back when he returns. The ceremony is known as *Sung Tsao* 送 灶, seeing off, or accompanying, Tsao Chün 灶 君 when leaving. The family burns the old image of Tsao Chün 灶 君, and an address in an envelope is also burnt to convey the wishes to the god.

Crackers are let off to ensure his safety as he sits on his cloud-chariot drawn by the horses of the wind on the journey to heaven, and (as stated above) a dainty meal consisting of meats, well sugared rice-balls, and sacrificial wine is offered to him. Sometimes his horse is also fed and watered.

On the evening of the thirtieth day of the twelfth month a new image of Tsao Chün 灶 君 is placed over the stove, the action being accompanied by the letting-off of more crackers, and a second address, welcoming him back, is burnt. This ceremony is called *Chieh Tsao* 接 灶, Receiving Tsao.

The festival of the god is celebrated on his birthday, the third day of the eighth moon; that of his wife, the goddess, on the twenty-fourth of the same moon.

For further devotional observances in honour of Tsao Chün 灶 君 see *Doré*, IX, 913, and for numerous other practices of the cult, as also for the various days fixed for the cleaning of kitchen utensils, *ibid*. XI, 909-12.

TSAO-KAI-SSŬ 早 該 死.—See *Mêng P'o* 孟 婆.

TSAO SHÊN 灶 (竈) 神.—See *Tsao Chün* 灶 (竈) 君.

TSAO WANG 灶 (竈) 王.—See *Tsao Chün* 灶 (竈) 君.

TS'AO KUO 曹果.—See *Ch'ing-wa Shên* 青 蛙 神.

TS'AO KUO-CHIU 曹國舅.—See *Pa Hsien* 八仙.

TS'AO PAO 曹寶.—See *Ministries (Finance)*.

TS'AO PIN 曹彬.—An assessor of Kuan Kung 關公.—See *Kuan Yü* 關羽.

[TS'AO-SHAN] PÊN-CHI CH'AN-SHIH [曹山] 本嶽禪師. See *Buddhist Schools*, VII.

TS'AO-TUNG MO 曹洞脈.—See *Buddhist Schools*, VII.

TSÊ 澤 LAKES, THE SPIRITS OF THE.—See *Shui Fu* 水府, D (2) (d).

TSÊ-LUNG 宅龍, THE GOD OF THE STAR.—See *Chi Shu-tê* 姬叔德.

TS'ÊN P'ÊNG 岑彭.—The god of the constellation Wei 尾. Alternatively with Chu Chao 朱昭.

TSÊNG CHANG 增長.—See *Ssŭ ta T'ien-wang* 四大天王.

TSÊNG-FU TS'AI-SHÊN 增福財神.—A God of Riches. Worshipped by merchants in general.

TSOU SHANG 鄒尚.—See *Wu Yo* 五嶽.

TSOU-SHU 奏書, THE GOD OF THE STAR.—See *Chiao K'o* 膠鬲.

TSOU WU-CH'ANG 走無長—See *Wu-ch'ang Kuei* 無長鬼.

TSU-CH'IN CH'AN-SHIH 祖欽禪師 (54th generation).— A deified Buddhist monk. Ranked thirtieth in Buddhist School, III (*q.v.*). A disciple of Shih-fan Ch'an-shih 師範禪師 (*q.v.*). Spent his early years at Lung-hsing 龍興. Died at Yang Shan 仰山, in the Yüan-chou 袁州 Department.

TSU-HSIEN CH'AN-SHIH 祖先禪師 (52nd generation).— A deified Buddhist monk. Ranked twenty-eighth in Buddhist School, III (*q.v.*). Family name Wang 王. A native of Kuang-an 廣安. His teacher was Hsien-chieh Ch'an-shih 咸傑

禪師 (*q.v.*). He spent the greater part of his life in the Ling-yin Ssŭ 靈隱寺 (*q.v.*). His tomb is in the Hsiu-fêng Ssŭ 秀峰寺, Hsiu-fêng Monastery, at Su-chou (Soochow) 蘇州, Kiangsu 江蘇.

TSU LIN 祖林.—The god of the star Ti-p'i 地僻.—See *Ti-sha* 地煞.

TSUAN-KU 鑽骨, THE GOD OF THE STAR.—See *Chang Fêng* 張鳳.

TSUI 觜, THE GOD OF THE CONSTELLATION.— See *Fu Chün* 傅俊 and *Fang Kuei* 方蕢.

TS'UI FU-CHÜN 崔府君.—A husbandman of Ku Hsien 鼓縣, Ch'i Chou 祁州, Chihli 直隸, who, having reached the age of fifty without having a son, made a pilgrimage to Hêng Shan 衡山, Mount Hêng, the Sacred Mountain of the North, to pray for an heir. After their return, both dreamt that a young man offered them a box and told them to eat the contents, saying it was a present sent by Yü Ti 玉帝. The box contained two fine precious stones. They each ate one, and the next morning the wife found herself with child. The child was born in A.D. 607 in the reign of the Emperor Yang Ti 煬帝 (A.D. 605-17) of the Sui 隋 dynasty, and was named Chio 珏, *i.e.* two precious stones joined together. His personal name was Tzŭ-yü 子玉, Jade Son. He grew to be an intelligent youth, and after passing the examinations was appointed Sub-Prefect of Ch'ang-yü Hsien 長于縣, or Lu-chou 潞州, Shansi 山西, where he became noted for his uprightness, so much so that he was regarded as a god. Many examples are given of his wonderful penetration and supernatural powers, exercised over animals and human beings alike, a temple being built to him by the people of the locality concerned on quite a large number of occasions. Instances are also quoted of his assisting human beings after his death, notably the Emperor Kao Tsung 高宗 (A.D. 1127-63) of the Sung 宋 dynasty, when His Majesty's horse died as he was fleeing from his enemies on the road between Chên-chiang (Chinkiang) 鎮江, Kiangsu 江蘇, and Chü-lu 鉅鹿, Chihli 直隸. For this service the Emperor had a temple erected to Ts'ui Fu-chün 崔府君 and the characters Hsien-wei 顯衞, Miraculous, inscribed over its portals. Another account says that he was canonized by K'ang Wang 康王, who escaped capture when on the borders of the Chiang 江 through the horse of the temple of Ts'ui Fu-chün 崔府君 coming to his assistance, and carrying him over on its back.—See also *Composite Deities.*

TS'UI-SHÊNG NIANG-NIANG 催生娘娘.—The Matron who Hastens Child-birth. One of the specialists attached to the celestial Ministry of Medicine, and an official attendant on Pi-hsia

Yüan-chün 碧霞元君, the Goddess of T'ai Shan 泰山, Mount T'ai 泰. Represented in temples in company with Kuan-yin P'u-sa 觀音菩薩 and Yen-kuang P'u-sa 眼光菩薩 (q.v.). A Taoist invention. Prayed to by women for protection and assistance during confinement. Represented carrying a child on her left arm and a twig of cinnamon in her right hand. The child is shown with a flute in its right, and a lotus-flower in its left hand. These, by a play on the words *lien shêng kuei tzǔ* 蓮笙桂子, lotus, flute, cinnamon, son, indicate the desire *lien shêng kuei tzǔ* 連生貴子, continuously to give birth to noble sons.

The real incumbent of this office is Ta-nai Fu-jên 大奶夫人 (q.v.).—See also *T'ien I-yüan* 天醫院.

TS'UI SHIH-CH'ING 崔石卿.—See *Hsüan-t'ien Shang-tı* 玄天上帝 and *Shih-êrh ting-chia Shên* 十二丁甲神.

TS'UI YING 崔英.—See *Wu Yo* 五嶽.

TS'UN-CHIANG CH'AN-SHIH 存獎禪師 (39th generation). In the genealogical table, his name is given as Ts'un-i 存嶭.—A deified Buddhist monk. Ranked twelfth in Buddhist School, III (q.v.). Trained by I-hsüan Ch'an-shih 義玄禪師 (q.v.). Died about A.D. 926, sitting cross-legged, after receiving no reply from his disciples to his question as to whether they still recognized him. Posthumous title: Kuang-chi Ch'an-shih 廣濟禪師.

TSUNG-KAO CH'AN-SHIH 宗杲禪師 (49th generation). —A deified Buddhist monk. Ranked twenty-fourth in Buddhist School, III (q.v.). Family name Hsi 奚. A native of Hsüan-ch'êng 宣城. His teacher was K'o-ch'in Ch'an-shih 克勤禪師 (q.v.). At Chang Wei-kung's 張魏公 invitation he settled at the foot of Ching Shang 徑山, Mount Ching, where he founded a school attended by more than 2,000 pupils. Unjustly accused to the Emperor, he was later restored to his former privileges. Died A.D. 1164. Posthumous title: P'u-chio Ch'an-shih 普覺禪師.

TSUNG-KUAN 總管.—Governors. Probably Governors of cities, to whom temples, etc., have been dedicated, but whose names have been forgotten or gradually fallen out of use. Various names are, however, attached to the title in different localities, e.g. a man named Chin Ch'ang 金昌, his son Yüan-ch'i 元七 having the posthumous title of Li-chi Hou 利濟侯. Their country of origin is variously stated to have been Tien-shan 澱山, west of Sung-chiang Fu 松江府, Kiangsu 江蘇, and Honan 河南 Province. Their genealogy is traced back to the Chin 金 family of Pien Liang 汴梁 (K'ai-fêng Fu 開封府), of the latter Province.

In the Yüan 元 dynasty at Yang-chou Fu 揚州府, Kiangsu 江蘇, and Hang-chou Fu 杭州府, Chêkiang 浙江, there was a

Tsung-kuan 總管 instead of the usual Prefect. There is also a record during the same dynasty of a man named Wang-chi Wêng 王積翁 who was called Tsung-kuan 總管.

In Hang-chou 杭州, Shao-hsing 紹興, etc., there are numerous temples dedicated to Tsung-kuan 總管. Pictures often show Tsung-kuan fu-tzŭ 總管父子, Tsung-kuan and his son together, without indicating any name.—See also *Composite Deities*.

TSUNG-MI CH'AN-SHIH 宗密禪師.—A deified Buddhist monk. Ranked fifth in Buddhist School, XI (*q.v.*). A certain Mr. Ho 何 of Kuo-chou 果州, Ssŭch'uan 四川, set out in A.D. 807 to present himself for the public literary examination. At Sui-chou 遂州, in the same province, he met Tao-yüan Ch'an-shih 道圓禪師, the monk Tao-yüan, who took him to his monastery, where he donned the Buddhist habit. One day, during the ceremony of delivering departed souls, *tso-chai* 做齋, in the family of Jên Kuan 任灌, he received a book entitled *Yüan-chio ching* 圓覺經, *Sutra of Perfect Learning*. Before he had finished reading it, his mind was fully enlightened. His teacher said to him. "It is undoubtedly Buddha himself who has given you this book." He also held the *Hua-yen ching* 華嚴經 in great esteem. His second teacher was Ch'êng-kuan Kuo-shih 澄觀國師 (*q.v.*).

The Emperor Wên Tsung 文宗 (A.D. 827-41) of the T'ang 唐 dynasty presented him with a violet cope. He was the author of ninety works and prayer-formulas. At his burial, *shê-li* 舍利, precious relics (*cf. Kuang-hsiu Tsun-chê* 廣修尊者), fell from the sky. The tower erected over his remains bears the inscription, Ting-hui 定慧, Fixed Intelligence.

TSUNG-PÊN CH'AN-SHIH 宗本禪師 (45th generation).— A deified Buddhist monk. Ranked thirtieth in Buddhist School, VI (*q.v.*). Family name Kuan 管. A native of Wu-hsi 無錫, a district dependent on Ch'ang-chou 常州, Kiangsu 江蘇. Studied at Ch'ih-yang 池陽, Shensi 陝西, under I-huai Ch'an-shih 義懷禪師 (*q.v.*), and soon became famous. His tomb is at Ling-yen 靈巖, near Su-chou (Soochow) 蘇州, Kiangsu 江蘇.

TSUNG-SHU CH'AN-SHIH 宗書禪師 (61st generation).— A deified Buddhist monk. Ranked forty-ninth in Buddhist School, VI (*q.v.*). Family name Li 李. A native of Shun-tê Fu 順德府, Chihli 直隸. Taught for many years in the Shao-lin Ssŭ 少林寺, Few Forests Monastery. At the end of his life withdrew to Tsung-ching 宗鏡, where he died, A.D. 1567.

TS'UNG HEI-HU 崇黑虎.—See *Wu Yo* 五嶽.

TS'UNG-SHÊN CH'AN-SHIH 從諗禪師 (37th generation). —A deified Buddhist monk. Ranked seventh in Buddhist School, III (*q.v.*). Family name Ho 郝. A native of Ts'ao-chou 曹州,

where he entered a monastery. Later proceeded to Ch'ih-chou 池州, where he followed the teaching of P'u-yüan Ch'an-shih 普顧 禪師 (*q.v.*). Received as a fully-trained monk in a monastery of Sung Shan 嵩山, the Central Sacred Mountain, and spent the remainder of his life explaining the Doctrine in the Kuan-yin Yüan 觀音院, Kuan-yin Monastery. Died A.D. 897, at the age of 120 years. Posthumous title: Chên-chi Ta-shih 眞際大師, True and Sublime Teacher.—See also *Lo Han* 羅漢.

TU CHIEN 獨健.—See *Ssŭ ta T'ien-wang* 四大天王.

TUCHITA, TUSHITA. Now pronounced Tu-shih-to (or t'o) 都史多 (or 陀) or Tou-shih-to 兜師 (or 駛 or 史)多.—The heavens (fourth Devaloka) where all Bodhisvattvas are reborn before finally appearing on the earth as Buddha. Life in Tuchita lasts 400 years, twenty-four hours being equal to 400 years on earth.—See also *Jan-têng Fo* 燃燈佛.

TU-HUO 獨火, THE GOD OF THE STAR.—See *Chi Shu-i* 姬叔義.

TU K'ANG 杜康.—One of the Gods of Wine-merchants. Both Tu K'ang 杜康 and I Ti 儀狄 (of Chêkiang 浙江) are regarded by the Chinese as the inventors of wine. The latter was banished by Yü 禹 (2205-2197 B.C.) for offering him ferment of rice, which the Emperor regarded as a beverage likely to harm the people.

Tu K'ang 杜康, who was of the later Chou 周 period, discovered a means of manufacturing wine. He died on the *yu* 酉 day of the cycle, and consequently distillers refrain from making wine on that day. To manufacture it, he is supposed to have used the water of the spring called Tu K'ang 杜康 in the temple of Shun 舜 at Chi-nan Fu 濟南府, Shantung 山東.—See also *Ssŭ-ma Hsiang-ju* 司馬相如.

TU MAO 杜茂.—The god of the constellation Ts'an 參. Alternatively with Sun Hsiang 孫祥.

TU-Ô CHÊN-JÊN 度厄眞人.—Inhabited the Pa-pao Yün-kuang Tung 八寶雲光洞. Was instructor to Li Ching 李靖 (T'o-t'a Li T'ien-wang 托塔李天王). He and his disciple performed feats of gallantry on behalf of Wu Wang 武 (1121-1114 B.C.). Worshipped as a demi-god.

TU P'ING 杜平.—One of the Gods of Robbers. Others are Li Ssŭ 李思, Jên An 任安, Sun Hsüan 孫玄, and Kêng Yen-chêng 耿彥正.

TU-SHUN HO-SHANG 杜順和尚.—A deified Buddhist monk. Ranked first in Buddhist School, XI (*q.v.*). Family name

Tu 杜. A native of Wan-nien 萬年, in Chang-an Fu 長安府, Shensi 陝西. The first patriarch of the Hua-yen Tsung 華嚴宗, Hua-yen School. At the age of 18, he entered the I-shan Ssǔ 義善寺, I-shan Monastery, at Yung-chou 雍州. His life abounded in prodigies: he had extraordinary power over insects, animals, demons, rivers, etc., and effected marvellous cures. The emperor T'ai Tsung 太宗 (A.D. 627-50) of the T'ang 唐 dynasty conferred on him the honorary title of Ti-hsin 帝心, Imperial Heart. Died A.D. 640. His corpse exhaled a sweet fragrance. He is said to have been reincarnated as Wên-shu 文殊 (Manjusri, *q.v.*) at Chung-nan Shan 終南山, Chung-nan Mountain.

TU-TI WANG 都帝王.—The President of the Eighth Court of Hades (*q.v.*). He is sometimes stated as being President of the Ninth Court.

TU T'IEN 都天.—The god, Tu-t'ien Pu-sha 都天菩薩 worshipped in the Tu-t'ien Miao 都天廟, Tu-t'ien temples, is Chang Hsün 張廵 a native of Nan-yang Hsien 南陽縣, Honan 河南. Lived in the reign of the Emperor Hsüan Tsung 玄宗 (A.D. 713-56) of the T'ang 唐 dynasty. A scholar and brave, but cruel warrior. A rain-god. On one occasion, when besieged and his soldiers were dying of hunger, he killed his concubines to feed them. Was slain in battle at the age of 49 years, and subsequently canonized and worshipped. Processions in his honour, or to induce him to bring rain, now obsolete or very rare, have been known to cost as much as $50,000.—See *Composite Deities* and *Journal N.C.B.R.A.S.*, XLIX, pp. 86-92.

TU YÜAN-HSIEN 杜元銑.—The god of the star Po-shih 博士. Grand Preceptor to Chou Wang 紂王 (1154-1121 B.C.). Put to death for having reproached him for his irregularities.

T'U-FU 土府, THE GOD OF THE STAR.—See *T'u Hsing-sun* 土行孫.

T'U HSING 土星.—See *Saturn*.

T'U HSING-SUN 土行孫.—The god of the star T'u-fu 土府. A disciple of Chü Liu-sun 拘留孫. Married Têng Ch'an-yu 鄧嬋玉, daughter of General Têng Chiu-kung 鄧九公. Was killed by Ch'ang K'uei 長奎 at the battle of Chia-lung Shan 夾龍山. His wife was killed by the female genie Kao Lan-ying 高蘭英 at the battle of Min-ch'ih Hsien 澠池縣.

T'U TI 土地.—The Protecting Spirit of Rural Places. Differs from the Shê 社 (see *Shê Chi* 社稷) in the limited extent of his jurisdiction, which is confined to a small section of territory, whereas the Shê 社 controls a sub-prefecture, prefecture, or even a province.

T'u Ti 土 地 are divided into five families of protecting spirits: the Green T'u Ti 土 地 of the Eastern circuit, the Red of the Southern, the White of the Western, the Black of the Northern, and the Yellow of the Centre.

Shrines to these Spirits, colloquially called T'u-ti Lao-yeh 土 地 老 爺, are to be seen in every village, along roads, on the banks of canals, etc., and incense is burnt in them by those seeking aid. Any person may be elected to this spiritual office after his death. Usually it is conferred on those who have rendered local public service, but if the spiritual duties are not properly fulfilled, the god may be relieved of his post and another appointed in his stead.

During the Ming 明 dynasty the custom arose of placing the image of the T'u-ti Lao-yeh 土 地 老 爺 on the ground, without any stand or platform. The reason for this is that when the Emperor T'ai Tsu 太 祖 (A.D. 1368-99) was on his travels, he found all the tables in the inn occupied by guests, except the one on which the T'u-ti Lao-yeh's 土 地 老 爺 image was exposed. He had the image placed on the ground, and said to it: "Give me your place." He then began his dinner. The innkeeper later replaced the image on the table, but the spirit appeared to him in a dream and told him that he did not dare to contravene the Emperor's order, and this story being spread abroad the custom arose of placing the image on the ground, without any stand, chair, or other support.

Among the celebrated T'u Ti 土 地 mentioned in Chinese literature are the following:—Chiang Tzǔ-wên 蔣 子 文, end of Han 漢 dynasty; Shên Yüeh 沈 約, of the Ch'i 齊 and Liang 梁 dynasties; Yo Fei 岳 飛 of the Sung 宋 dynasty; Ch'un Shên-chün 春 申 君, who from being a Ch'êng Huang 城 隍, was afterwards degraded; and Yang Wên-ch'ang 楊 文 昌, of the Sung 宋 dynasty.

T'U-TI LAO-YEH 土 地 老 爺.—See *T'u Ti* 土 地.

T'U-TI MIAO 土 地 廟.—See *Shê Chi* 社 稷.

TUNG CHUNG 董 忠.—See *Wu Tou* 五 斗.

TUNG CHUNG-SHU 董 仲 舒.—Said to have been a native of Kuang-ch'uan 廣 川, in Chihli 直 隸. According to the *Ch'un-ch'iu* 春 秋 he became an official at an early age, and a sage in the time of the Emperor Ching Ti 景 帝 (156-140 B.C.) of the Ch'ien Han 前 漢 dynasty. He investigated the laws of nature by examining inauspicious and unusual events. His system is a mixture of theism and naturism, of Confuciism mixed with Taoism, but he was more of an orator than a philosopher.

TUNG-FANG SHUO [SO] 東 方 朔.—First of the Moon East. A patron deity of goldsmiths and silversmiths. A star-spirit, an avatar of the star Sui-hsing 歲星, and alternatively a reincarnation of the Spirit of the planet Venus, Chin-hsing 金星. A man of the Chang 張 family. Personal name Shao-p'ing 少平. Father's name Chang I 張夷, a native of Lei-tz'ŭ 頪次, in P'ing-yüan 平原, Shantung 山東, his mother being of the T'ien 田 family. The *Shên-hsien t'ung chien* 神仙通鑑 gives a long account of his life, adventures, and subsequent apotheosis. His name Shuo 朔 was given him because he was born on the first day of the eleventh moon. Owing to his mother's death three days later, his father threw him out on to the road, but he was rescued by an old woman of the neighbourhood, who brought him up as her own son. The first two characters, Tung-fang 東方, were added because, when the old lady found him, a bright light dawned in the east. His other name was Man-ch'ing 曼倩. His father left the district in the following year.

The child showed remarkable intelligence, and related to his mother several supernatural events which happened to him during his unauthorized absences from the house. On one of these expeditions an old man named Huang Yüeh 黃月 told him that he (the child) was the Spirit of the planet Venus (Chin-hsing 金星). For this reason goldsmiths and silversmiths adopted him as their patron deity.

Later on, Tung-fang Shuo 東方朔, owing to his ready wit, gained the approbation of the Emperor Wu Ti 武帝 (140-86 B.C.) of the Han 漢 dynasty, received an official post and presents, and was even invited to the Emperor's table. Through his skill in argument he saved the life of the Emperor's nurse and others who had been condemned to death. One of his answers to the Emperor is frequently quoted. It was on the occasion when he had imbibed copiously from the jars of the wine of immortality presented to the Emperor. Hearing of this, the Emperor was so enraged that he ordered him to be executed. Tung-fang Shuo 東方朔 pleaded guilty, but added: "This wine is all-powerful. If your Majesty kill me, I cannot die; if, however, your Majesty succeeds in putting me to death, then this wine is not one which can confer immortality!" Being amused at his clever reply, the Emperor pardoned him.

In 103 B.C. he brought back with him from a journey to Hsi-na-hsieh 西那邪 ten sonorous trees, nine feet high. Their branches, when moved by the wind, gave forth sounds like jade-stones tapping together. When the wood sweated, he was told, people fell ill; when it broke, it presaged death. Tung-fang Shuo 東方朔 presented the trees to the Emperor who, however, instructed him to retain one of them. When, in 93 B.C., the latter broke, Tung-fang Shuo 東方朔 knew that his end was near. He accordingly summoned his three sons, Ch'i 齊, Chi 極, and T'an 坦, and said to them: "You will retain the family name Chang 張, and T'an 坦 will take Tung-fang 東方 as his family name." A green dragon then descended from the sky, took Tung-fang

Shuo 東方朔 on its back, and flew away up to the heavens. Before his death he had told the Emperor that Ta-wu Kung 大伍公 alone knew his origin, and the latter stated that the star Sui-hsing 歲星 had not been seen in the sky for sixty-nine years, but that it had reappeared on the day of Tung-fang Shuo's 東方朔 death. Thus it was known that he was a reincarnation of the star Sui-hsing 歲星. (He had, however, several rebirths.) The Emperor had his hat and clothes buried on Chung-ch'iu 重丘 Hill at P'ing-yüan 平原.—See also *Mi-lo Fo* 彌勒佛 and *Hua-kuang Fo* 華光佛.

TUNG-HUA TI-CHÜN 東華帝君.—See *Tung Wang-kung* 東王公.

[TUNG-SHAN] LIANG-CHIEH CH'AN-SHIH [洞山] 良价禪師.—See *Buddhist Schools*, VII.

TUNG-T'IEN CHIAO-CHU 東天教主.— The Supreme Teacher of the Eastern Heavens. A tutelary genie of the Shang 商 dynasty, but being defeated by Chun T'i 準提, P'i-lu Fo 毗盧佛 abandoned him, and accompanied Chun T'i 準提 to the Western Paradise, where he subsequently became a Buddha.—See *Chun T'i* 準提, *P'i-lu Fo* 毗盧佛, *Hsi-t'ien Chiao-chu* 西天教主 and *Adi-Buddha*.

TUNG TSU 東祖.—See *Patriarchs*.

TUNG-T'U LIU-TSU 東土六祖.—The six Patriarchs of Chinese Buddhism.—See *Patriarchs*.

TUNG WANG-FU 東王父.—See *Head, The Gods of the*.

TUNG WANG-KUNG 東王公.—The God of the Immortals. Several Chinese works, *e.g.* the *T'ai-p'ing kuang chi* 太平廣記, state that Tung Wang-kung 東王公 is also called Mu Kung 木公, and the *Hsü Wên-hsien t'ung-k'ao* 續文獻通考 adds the further names I 倪 and Chün-ming 君明. Sometimes also we find the appellations Yü-huang Chün 玉皇君, Prince Yü-huang, and Tung-hua Ti-chün 東華帝君.

The primitive vapour congealed, remained inactive for a time, and then produced living beings, beginning with the formation of Mu Kung 木公, the purest substance of the Eastern Air, and sovereign of the active male principle *yang* 陽 and of all the countries of the East. His palace is in the misty heavens, violet clouds form its dome, blue clouds its walls. Hsien T'ung 仙童, the Immortal Youth, and Yü Nü 玉女, the Jade Maiden, are his servants. He keeps the register of all the Immortals, male and female.— See also *Hsi Wang-mu* 西王母.

T'UNG CHENG 童貞.—The god of the star Ti-li 地理.—
See *Ti-sha* 地煞.

T'UNG-CH'IU-YÜ CH'AN-SHIH 童求昱禪師 (67th generation).—A deified Buddhist monk. Ranked eighty-fourth in
Buddhist School, VI (*q.v.*). Family name Chang 張. Born at
Nanking 南京 in A.D. 1638. Taught by the monk Hsi Hsia-i
棲霞依. When his training was finished, he went to Fukien
福建, and taught at Mêng-pi 夢筆, where he visited the
monasteries of Hu-hsin 湖心, Pao-ên 報恩, and Chien-chou 建州.
Died A.D. 1685. His tomb is on Hsi-wu Shan 西塢山, West Store
Hill.

T'UNG CHÜN 桐君.—A demi-god. A member of the commission appointed by Huang Ti 黄帝 (*q.v.*) to continue and
complete the labours of Shên Nung 神農 on natural history and
the medicinal properties of plants. Determined these properties
of several plants and minerals.—See *T'ien I-yüan* 天醫院.

T'UNG CHUNG-CHUNG 通衆仲.—See *Skin, The God of
the*.

T'UNG-HSIU CH'AN-SHIH 通琇禪師 (68th generation).
—A deified Buddhist monk. Ranked sixty-first in Buddhist
School, III (*q.v.*). Family name Yang 楊. A native of Chên-
chiang (Chinkiang) 鎭江. Studied under Yüan-hsiu Ch'an-shih
圓修禪師 (*q.v.*), and then started his own school at Pao-ên Ssŭ
報恩寺, Thanksgiving Monastery. The Emperor Shun Chih
順治 (A.D. 1644-62) of the Ch'ing 淸 dynasty, summoned him to
Court, and conferred on him the title of Ta-chio Kuo-shih 大覺
國師, Highly Intelligent State Preceptor. He died in A.D. 1674.
His tomb is at Tung-wu 東塢, on Hsi T'ien-mu Shan 西天目山,
West Heavenly-eye Mountain.

T'UNG-HSÜAN CH'AN-SHIH 通玄禪師.—A monk of the
Li 李 family, who lived to the north-east of T'ai-yüan Fu 太原府,
Shansi 山西. He was noted for his unusual physical appearance
and for his extraordinary literary knowledge. He is described as
being seven feet in height, with features of a pale violet colour, a
heavy moustache, long drooping eyebrows, and curly reddish hair.
He was thoroughly versed in the Confuciist and Buddhist books.
In A.D. 719, he left Ting-hsiang 定襄, in the same province, for
Mêng Hsien 孟縣, Honan 河南, where he gave up his whole time
to writing essays and chanting the *Hua-yen ching* 華嚴經, *Hua-
yen* sutra, a work of the Mahayana School, containing mythological abstractions which are deemed to lead to salvation. He lived
abstemiously and in retirement for twenty or thirty years.
   The *Sou-shên chi* 搜神記 relates of him that he once tamed a
tiger he met on his way to Han-shih Chuang 韓十莊 by rubbing

its neck, the tiger afterwards accompanying him and carrying his parcels of literary and ecclesiastical writings on its back.

When during the night the light failed, he produced two streams of bright light from his writing-brush merely by placing it between his teeth. Fairies would wait upon him and supply him with writing materials and food.

He is credited with forty volumes of essays, eighty books of prayers, and ten of annotations.

When he foretold his death to the villagers who flocked to see him in the monastery, clouds enveloped the mountain-top and a beam of white light ascended from the monastery tower toward the sky.

He died in A.D. 730 at the age of 96, and was buried in a stone vault to the north of T'ai Shan 泰 山.

T'UNG-JUNG CH'AN-SHIH 通容禪師 (68th generation).
—A deified Buddhist monk. Ranked fifty-second in Buddhist School, III (*q.v.*). Family name Ho 何. A native of Fu-ch'ing 福清, Fukien 福建. His first teacher was Chan-jan 湛然, and he completed his studies under Yüan-wu Ch'an-shih 圓悟禪師 (*q.v.*). Having been repulsed and beaten (see *I-hsüan Ch'an-shih* 義玄禪師) so violently that blood flowed from his head (which test, however, he patiently endured), he was suddenly enlightened on the Doctrine.

T'UNG-KUNG 通公.—A saintly Buddhist monk. One of those invited to the annual banquet of the gods (see *Hsi Wang-mu* 西王母). Lived about the time of the Emperor Chien Wên 簡文 (A.D. 550-1) of the Liang 梁 dynasty. Greatly feared by the rebel Hou Ching 侯景.

T'UNG LAI-YÜ 同來育.—See *Stomach, The God of the*.

T'UNG MING 通命.—See *Tongue, The Gods of the*.

T'UNG-MING CH'AN-SHIH 通明禪師 (68th generation).
—A deified Buddhist monk. Ranked fiftieth in Buddhist School, III (*q.v.*). Family name Chien 蹇. A native of Ssǔch'uan 四川. One day, after being so affected by the perusal of a ditty composed by Chih-kung 誌公 (*q.v.*), *Chih-kung Ch'üan-shih ko* 誌公勸世歌, that he wept for joy, withdrew to P'o-t'ou Shan 破頭山, Bald-head Mountain, and lived there for three years. Subsequently, he became a disciple of Chan-jan 湛然, at Yün-mên Shan 雲明山, Cloud-gate Mountain, and then of Yüan-wu Ch'an-shih 圓悟禪師 (*q.v.*), at T'ien-t'ung Shan 天童山, Heavenly-lad Mountain, where he became enlightened on the Doctrine. At the close of his life, he returned to Ssǔch'uan 四川, and propagated there the Buddhist faith.

T'UNG-T'IEN CHIAO-CHU 通天教主.— The Supreme Teacher of the Eastern Heaven. A tutelary deity of the Shang 商 dynasty. Also called T'ung-t'ien Chiao-tsu 通天教祖. In modern Taoism the first of the Patriarchs (q.v.), and one of the most powerful genii of the sect. His master was Hung-chün Lao-tsu 洪鈞老祖. He wore a red robe embroidered with white cranes, and rode a *k'uei niu* 夔牛, a monster resembling a buffalo, with one long horn like a unicorn. His palace, the Pi-yu Kung 碧遊宮, was situated on Tzŭ-chih Yai 紫芝崖, Tzŭ-chih Mountain.

This genie took the part of Chou Wang 紂王 (1154-1121 B.C.) and helped him to resist Wu Wang's 武王 (1121-1114 B.C.) armies. First he sent his disciple To-pao Tao-jên 多寶道人 to Chieh-p'ai Kuan 界牌關. He gave him four precious swords and the plan of a fort which he was to construct and to name Chu-hsien Chên 誅仙陣, the Citadel of all the Immortals.

To-pao Tao-jên 多寶道人 carried out his orders, but he had to fight a battle with Kuang Ch'êng-tzŭ 廣成子, and the latter, armed with a celestial seal, struck his adversary so hard that he fell to the ground and had to take refuge in flight.

T'ung-t'ien Chiao-chu 通天教主 came to the defence of his disciple and to restore the morale of his forces. Unfortunately, a posse of gods arrived to aid Wu Wang's 武王 powerful general, Chiang Tzŭ-ya 姜子牙. The first who attacked T'ung-t'ien Chiao-chu 通天教主 was Lao Tzŭ 老子, who struck him several times with his stick. Then came Chun T'i 準提, armed with his cane. The buffalo of T'ung-t'ien Chiao-chu 通天教主 stamped him under foot, and Chun T'i 準提 was thrown to the earth, and only just had time to rise quickly and mount into the air amid a great cloud of dust.

There could be no doubt that the fight was going against T'ung-t'ien Chiao-chu 通天教主; to complete his discomfiture Jan-têng Tao-jên 燃燈道人 cleft the air and fell upon him unexpectedly. With a violent blow of his "Fix-sea" staff he cast him down and compelled him to give up the struggle.

T'ung-t'ien Chiao-chu 通天教主 then prepared plans for a new fortified camp beyond T'ung-kuan 潼關, and tried to take the offensive again, but again Lao Tzŭ 老子 stopped him with a blow of his stick. Yüan-shih T'ien-tsun 元始天尊 wounded his shoulder with his precious stone Ju-i 如意, and Chun-t'i Tao-jên 準提道人 waved his "Branch of the Seven Virtues." Immediately the magic sword of T'ung-t'ien Chiao-chu 通天教主 was reduced to splinters, and he saved himself only by flight.

Hung-chün Lao-tsu 洪鈞老祖, the master of these three genii, seeing his three beloved disciples in the *mêlée*, resolved to make peace between them. He assembled all three in a tent in Chiang Tzŭ-ya's 姜子牙 camp, made them kneel before him, then reproached T'ung-t'ien Chiao-chu 通天教主 at length for having taken the part of the tyrant Chou 紂, recommended them in future to live in harmony. After finishing his speech, he produced three pills, and ordered each of the genii to swallow one. When they had done so, Hung-chün Lao-tsu 洪鈞老祖 said to them: "I have given you these pills to ensure an inviolable peace among you. Know that the first who entertains a thought of discord in his heart will find that the pill will explode in his stomach and cause his instant death."

Hung-chün Lao-tsu 洪鈞老祖 then took T'ung-t'ien Chiao-chu 通天敎主 away with him on his cloud to Heaven.—See also P'i-lu Fo 毗盧佛 and *Amitabha*.

T'UNG-T'IEN CHIAO-TSU 通天敎祖.—See *T'ung-t'ien Chiao-chu* 通天敎主.

T'UNG-WÊN CH'AN-SHIH 通問禪師 (68th generation). —A deified Buddhist monk. Ranked sixty-second in Buddhist School, III (*q.v.*). Family name Yü 兪. A native of Sung-ling 松陵. His teacher was Yüan-hsiu Ch'an-shih 圓修禪師 (*q.v.*). He lived successively in the monasteries of Ch'ing Shan 磬山, Chia Shan 夾山, and Lou Tsê 漏澤. Died A.D. 1715. Was then teaching in the Ying-t'ien Ssŭ 應天寺, Ying-t'ien Monastery, at Wu-chiang 吳江. His tomb is at Nan-chien 南澗.

T'UNG YUNG 董永.—Han 漢 dynasty. The husband of Chih Nü 織女 (*q.v.*).

TWELVE CELESTIAL OFFICERS UNDER HSÜAN T'IEN 玄天, THE.—See *Pa Hsien* 八仙 and *Hsüan-t'ien Shang-ti* 玄天上帝.

TWELVE DIVINE BUDDHIST TEACHERS, THE.—See *Shih-êrh ta T'ien-shih* 十二大天師.

TWELVE RIVERS CH'I 溪, THE SPIRIT OF THE.—See *Shui Fu* 水府, D (2) (h).

TWO IMMORTALS HO HO 和合, THE.—See *Ho Ho* (*êrh-hsien*) 和合 (二仙).

TZŬ-CHIO CH'AN-SHIH 自覺禪師 (46th generation).—A deified Buddhist monk. Ranked thirty-first in Buddhist School, VI (*q.v.*). Family name Wang 王. A native of Ch'ing-chou 青州, Shantung 山東. Fond of study from his youth, it was only when he was getting old that he begged Tao-k'ai Ch'an-shih 道楷禪師 (*q.v.*) to admit him as a disciple. Summoned by the emperor Hui Tsung 徽宗 (A.D. 1101-26) of the Sung 宋 dynasty to Ching-yin 淨因 (the name of a temple in Kiangsu 江蘇), then went thence in 1115 to Lu-mên 鹿門, Shansi 山西. Died A.D. 1117. Buried at Ch'ing-chou 清州.

TZŬ-HSIEN-CHI CH'AN-SHIH 子賢紀禪師 (67th generation).—A deified Buddhist monk. Ranked eighty-fifth in Buddhist School, VI (q.v.). Born A.D. 1635. Taught at Pao-ên 報恩 by [Ling-jui] Hung-t'an Ch'an-shih [靈瑞] 弘曇禪師 (q.v.), and at the Cho-hsi 卓錫 Monastery by P'o-yen-chi Ch'an-shih 破巖繼禪師 (q.v.) in A.D. 1669. Afterwards opened his own school in the Tou-shuai 兜率 and Cho-hsi 卓錫 Monasteries. "The dragons and elephants, states the legend, flocked in crowds to listen to his lessons."

TZŬ-KU SHÊN 紫姑神.—The Violet Lady Spirit. The Goddess of Latrines. Also known as K'êng San-ku 坑三姑, the Third Lady or Miss (of the family—third in order of the daughters) of Latrines (or Cesspools). Family name Ho 何, her own name Mei 媚, and first name Li-ch'ing 麗卿. Born at Lai-yang Hsien 萊陽縣, Shantung 山東. After having studied with success during her youth she became the concubine of the Sub-Prefect Li Ching 李景 of Shou-yang Hsien 壽陽縣, Shansi 山西. This was in the period A.D. 685-9 of the reign of the Empress Wu Hou 武后 (A.D. 684-705) of the T'ang 唐 dynasty. She having been murdered out of jealousy in a latrine by Li Ching's 李景 wife, the Supreme Being took pity on her and conferred on her the title of Spirit of Latrines. The people made images of her and sacrificed to them at night in the latrines or in a corner of the pigsties. Women, whilst doing so, repeat the words: "The son-in-law Tzŭ-hsü 子胥 is dead, the legitimate wife has disappeared, you may come out, my pretty lady." When the dung-basket which the young women hold appears to move, the Spirit is supposed to have arrived, and all kinds of requests are made to it. Women also offer sacrifices to it at the New Year. On the evening of the twenty-ninth day of the twelfth moon a dung-basket decorated with earrings, hairpins and flowers, is placed in the corner of the latrine, and some young girls of about ten years of age are chosen to hold the basket in their hands before a table on which candles and incense have been set out around a spread of pounded rice. When the time for the sacrifice has come, a child makes prostrations. They then with a silver hairpin draw outlines in the rice of various articles, such as scissors, knives, flowers, etc., at the same time asking the Spirit if the New Year harvest will be abundant, what percentage of grain will be reaped, etc. The dung-basket is then supposed to make a certain number of raps in answer. This, the girls affirm, moves in spite of themselves and becomes so much heavier that they are not strong enough to hold it up. The heavier it grows the more questions they put to the Spirit regarding the future.

This ceremony is practised only by women, never by men. No temples to this goddess exist, but she was canonized by the Empress Wu Hou 武后 (A.D. 684-705) of the T'ang 唐 dynasty as the Spirit of Latrines.

Two other divinities.—Hsü T'ien-chu 項天竺 and Kuo-têng 郭登 are mentioned in the *Yu-yang tsa-tsu* 酉陽雜俎 and the *Hsü Wên-hsien t'ung-k'ao* 續文獻通考 as Divinities of the Latrine, but the only one worshipped in China is K'êng San-ku 坑三姑 (*supra*).—See also *K'êng san Ku-niang* 坑三姑娘.

TZǓ-TSAI CH'AN-SHIH 自在禪師.—See *Lo-han* 羅漢.

TZǓ-T'UNG SHÊN 梓潼神.—See *Wên Ch'ang* 文昌.

TZǓ-T'UNG TZǓ 梓潼子.—See *Wên Ch'ang* 文昌.

TZǓ-WEI HSING 紫微星, THE GOD OF THE STAR.—See *Po I-k'ao* 伯邑考.

It is this star Tzǔ-wei 紫微 which is supposed to be incarnated in the person of the Emperor. Hence the saying that when an Emperor has died: "A star has fallen from Heaven." The image of the star, the incarnation of the reigning emperor, was placed in the imperial palace.

TZǓ-YEN CH'AN-SHIH 子巖禪師 (56th generation).—A deified Buddhist monk. Ranked forty-fourth in Buddhist School, VI (*q.v.*). Family name Fan 樊. A native of Kou-shih Hsien 緱氏縣, Honan 河南. Studied under Fu-yü Ch'an-shih 福裕禪師 (*q.v.*). The Emperor Hung Wu 洪武 (A.D. 1368-99) of the Ming 明 dynasty appointed him governor of the Shao-lin Ssǔ 少林寺, Few-Forests Monastery, at Sung Yo 嵩嶽, the Sacred Peak of the South.

TZ'Ǔ-ÊN CHIAO 慈恩敎.—See *Buddhist Schools*, XIV.

TZ'Ǔ-SHAN CHANG TA-TI 祠山張大帝.—The God of Tz'ǔ Shan 祠山, Mount Tz'ǔ 祠. Family name Chang 張, personal names P'o 渤 and Pai-ch'i 伯奇. A native either of Wu-hsing 吳興, Chêkiang 浙江, or of Wu-ling 武陵, Hunan 湖南. Born in 58 B.C., during the reign of Hsiao Hsüan Ti 孝宣帝 (73-48 B.C.) of the Han 漢 dynasty. The work he undertook of digging a canal between Ch'ang-hsing Hsien 長興縣 and Ching-ch'i 荆溪 and extending it to Kuang-tê Chou 廣德州 in Anhui 安徽, was only half finished when he retired to Hêng Shan 橫山, where a temple in which his image was worshipped, was constructed. Sacrifices have been offered to him from the time of the Han 漢 dynasty to the present day, and it was because, in the period A.D. 742-56 that he was supposed to have caused the cessation of a drought, that he was given the title of second assistant to the Shui Pu 水部, Ministry of Waters, and the name of Hêng-shan 橫山 changed to Tz'ǔ-shan 祠山. He was thenceforth known as Tz'ǔ-shan Chang Ta-ti 祠山張大帝. Various other titles were conferred on him during subsequent dynasties.

Legend has been busy in embroidering the meagre facts of his
life with transcendental events, of which the following is a brief
summary. To dig the canal above-mentioned he employed
soldiers from the infernal regions, and having raised a mound
near a maple-tree he placed on it a gong, and made a secret
agreement with his wife that each time she brought him his repast
she should strike the gong thrice and he would come and fetch
the food, but she was not to enter the work-yard. One day, after
she had placed the victuals on the gong, some crows came and
pecked it. Hearing the sound of the gong, the husband hastened
to the mound, only to find that he and his food had been taken
in by the birds.

The next time his wife came and struck the gong he, thinking
it was the crows again, did not go to fetch the food. His wife,
seeing that he did not come, went to look for him in the work-
yard, where she saw him, transformed into a large pig, directing
the soldiers digging the canal. Ashamed that his wife should
have seen him in that guise, he refused thenceforth to have
anything to do with her, stopped the work, and fled to Hêng Shan
橫 山, Mount Hêng 橫, 100 *li* 里 west of Kuang-tê 廣 德, Anhui
安 徽. The inhabitants built a temple to him there, on the west side
of the mountain. His wife was changed into a stone statue two *li*
里 to the east of Kuang-tê 廣 德, where a temple was erected to
her in the Han 漢 dynasty.—*Cf.* the legend of Ta Yü 大 禹
changed into a bear, which, *mutatis mutandis,* is identical with the
above, the mountain being Huan Yüan 轅 轅 in Honan 河 南, his
wife, T'u-shan 塗 山, being changed into stone at the foot of Sung
Kao 嵩 高 Mountain, where she gave birth to a son, Ch'i 啟. Yü
禹 said to her: "This child belongs to me," whereupon he split the
side of the stone statue, and she brought forth Ch'i 啟. It is
recorded that when Wu Ti 武 帝 (140-86 B.C.) of the Han 漢
dynasty visited the central mountain he went to see the stone
mother, Yü's 禹 wife.

The attribution of the title *ti* 帝, god, to Yü 禹 is a mistake
(he having never officially been appointed anything but *wang* 王,
king), grounded on the following legend. When Liu Wêng
劉 翁, the celestial Emperor, wished to slay his enemy Chang
Wêng 張 翁, the latter, having made his adversary drunk, rode
up to Heaven on a dragon and annexed his kingdom. Chou
Hsing 周 興 after his death was ordered to appear at the celestial
palace, but first made enquiries as to whether the reigning celestial
Emperor was the same as Chang 張, and was informed that he
had became an Immortal, and that the actual Emperor was Ts'ao
Ming 曹 明.

Chang Wêng 張 翁 and Chang P'o 張 渤, whom some writers
have attempted to identify, were two distinct persons, but those
attempts led to Chang Wêng 張 翁 being styled Chang Ta-ti
張 大 帝. Chang Wêng's 張 翁 personal name was Chien 堅, his
other name being Tz'ŭ-k'o 刺 渴. He was a native of Yŭ-yang

漁陽, the modern Yü Chou 漁州, Chihli 直隸. In his youth he had led an irregular life. One day he caught a white bird to which he took a fancy. At night, he dreamt he saw Liu Wêng 劉翁, the Emperor of Heaven, who reprimanded him angrily, but each time the latter attempted to slay him his white bird protected him.

Liu Wêng 劉翁 came down from Heaven to see him, and Chang Wêng 張翁 prepared a feast in his honour. Then, making an excuse, he left the dining-hall, and mounting his guest's dragon rode off to Heaven. Liu Wêng 劉翁 mounted another dragon and pursued him, but could not catch him up. Chang Wêng 張翁 reached the celestial palace, blocked up the North gate, and appointed his white bird Grand Minister of the Empire, with the title of Duke. Liu Wêng 劉翁, deprived of his sceptre, took up his abode on the five sacred mountains and lived by cheating and gambling. Chang Wêng 張翁 out of pity for him, nominated him Guardian of the Sacred Mountain of the East and Curator of the Registers of the Living and the Dead.

Chang P'o 張渤 was first worshipped in the Hêng-shan 橫山 temple at Kuang-tê Chou 廣德州, on occasions of droughts and floods. Oxen were sacrificed to him in large numbers, a canal or ditch being dug in the temple grounds and the bodies placed in them overnight, but pigs were never used, for a reason which is obvious from the legend above-related. Parents tied up their children and struck them, as the gong had been struck in the legend, to obtain favours from the god. In spite of attempts made by the local officials to put a stop to these practices, they continued until modern times.—See also *Composite Deities*.

TZ'Ŭ-SHIH JU-LAI 慈氏如來.—See *Buddhist Schools*, XIV.

UDGITHA.—See *Om*

ULAMBA.—The Buddhist festival of the benefit of the *prêtas*, or hungry ghosts.—See *Yü-lan Hui* 盂 蘭 會.

UNCERTAIN LIFE.—See *Huo-wu-ch'ang* 活 無 長.

UNDEFINED JURISDICTION, WATER SPIRITS WITH. —See *Shui Fu* 水 府, D (3).

UPANADA. UPANANDA.—An arhat, disciple of Sakya-muni. A dragon-king.—See *Lung Wang* 龍王.

UPANISHADS.—"Esoteric doctrine." The third division of the *Vedas* attached to the Brahmana portion, and forming part of the *Sruti* or revealed word. The *Upanishads* are generally written in prose with interspersed verses, but some are wholly in verse. There are about one hundred and fifty of these works, probably even more. They are of later date than the *Brahmanas*, but it is thought that the oldest may date as far back as the sixth century B.C. The object of these treatises is to ascertain the mystic sense of the text of the *Veda*, and so they enter into such abstruse questions as the origin of the universe, the nature of the deity, the nature of soul, and the connection of mind and matter. Thus they contain the beginnings of that metaphysical inquiry which ended in the full development of Hindu philosophy.

UPASAKA.—Wu-p'o-so 烏 波 索 (or so 娑) chia 迦. Lay-members of the Buddhist church who, without entering upon monastic life, vow to keep the five principal commandments. If females, they are called Upasika. Their practical religion was to

UPASAKA

give food and clothing to the monks. Wealthy folks built monasteries, or donated parks, gardens, wells and bathing-rooms for the use of the community. They thus acquired merit, and shared in the good works of the monks.—See also *Lo-han* 羅漢.

UTPOLAKA.—A dragon-king.—See *Lung Wang* 龍王.

V

VACCINATION, THE GOD AND GODDESS OF.—Yü Tê 余 德, the God of Vaccination, was born in the Yin 殷 dynasty in the province of Shensi 陝 西. He was the fifth son of his father, Yü Hua-lung 余 化 龍, a brigade-general at the city of T'ung Kuan 潼 關, in the same province. The Goddess, P'an Niang 潘 娘, is not related to him.

VAIDURYA BUDDHA.—See *Yao-shih Wang* 藥 師 王.

VAIROCANA.—Originally worshipped as the first of the five Dhyani (*q.v.*) Buddhas of the actual universe, and is best known under that form.—See *P'i-lu Fo* 毗 羅 佛.

VIRUPAKCHA.—See *Lung* 龍, *Lung Wang* 龍 王, *Sagara,* and *Shui Fu* 水 府.

VAISRAMANA.—The God of Riches, Ts'ai Shên 財 神 (Kuvera), of ancient Brahmanism. Also a god of modern Brahmanism; and a guardian of the North and king of Yakchas and Rakshasas (*qq.v.*).—See also *Ssŭ ta T'ien-wang* 四 大 天 王.

VAJRABODHI.—See *Chin-kang Chih* 金 剛 智 and *Buddhist Schools,* XV.

VAJRAHARA.—A kind of Supreme Buddha, identified in Tibet with the Primordial Buddha, Adi-Buddha (*q.v.*).

VAJRAMATI.—See *Chin-kang Chih* 金 剛 智.

VAJRAPANI.—See *Ssŭ Chin-kang* 四 金 剛:

VAJRAPUTRA.—See *Lo-han* 羅 漢.

541

VAJRIPUTRA.—See *Lo-han* 羅漢.

VANAKAVASA.—See *Lo-han* 羅漢.

VANAVASA.—See *Lo-han* 羅漢.

VARAVASA.—See *Lo-han* 羅漢.

VARIOUS BODIES OF WATER, SPIRITS OF THE.—See *Shui Fu* 水府, D (2).

VARNISHERS, THE GODS OF.—See *Lu Pan* 魯班 and *Yü Pai-ya* 俞伯牙.

VARUNA.—"The universal encompasser, the all-embracer." One of the oldest of the Vedic deities, a personification of the all-investing sky, the maker and upholder of heaven and earth. As such he is king of the universe, king of gods and men, possessor of illimitable knowledge, the supreme deity to whom especial honour is due. He is often associated with Mitra, he being the ruler of the night and Mitra of the day; but his name frequently occurs alone, that of Mitra only seldom. In later times he was chief among the lower celestial deities called Adityas, and later still he became a sort of Neptune, a god of the seas and rivers, who rides upon the *maraka* (a huge sea animal, probably fabulous). This character he still retains. His sign is a fish. He is regent of the west quarter and of one of the *nakshatras* or lunar mansions.

VASU.—The *Vasus* are a class of deities, eight in number, chiefly known as attendants upon Indra. They seem to have been in Vedic times personifications of natural phenomena. They are *Apa* (water), *Dhruva* (pole-star), *Soma* (moon), *Dhara* (earth), *Anila* (wind), *Anala* (fire), *Prabhasa* (dawn), and *Pratyusha* (light). According to the *Ramayana* they were children of Aditi (infinity; the boundless heaven; called the "mother of the gods").

VASUBANDU.—See *Shih-ch'in P'u-sa* 世親菩薩.

VASUKI.—A dragon-king.—See *Lung Wang* 龍王.

VASUPUTRA.—See *Lo-han* 羅漢.

VEDA.—Root, vid, "know." "Divine knowledge." The *Vedas* are the holy books which are the foundation of the Hindu religion. They consist of hymns written in an old form of Sanskrit, and according to the most generally received opinion they were composed between 1500 and 1000 B.C. But there is no direct evidence as to their age, and opinions about it vary considerably.—See *Wei T'o* 韋陀.

VEDANTA.—The orthodox school of philosophy. See *Darsana,* the six schools of Hindu philosophy, in Dowson, pp. 80-83.

VEGETARIAN SCHOOL, THE.—See *Buddhist Schools,* II.

VENERABLE FU 傅, THE.—See *Fu Ta-shih* 傅大士.

VENERABLE THREE RULERS, THE.—See *San Kuan* 三官.

VENUS, THE GOD OF THE PLANET.—The God of Autumn. Chin Hsing 金星. Known as Pai Ti 白帝, the White Ruler, and Pai-chao Chü 白招炬. The god descends to this earth on the fifteenth day of each month.—See also *T'ai-po Chin-hsing* 太白金星.

VIHARAPALA.—P'i-ho-lo-po-lo 毗阿羅波羅 or Hu-ssŭ 護寺.—A title given to patrons and tutelary deities of Buddhist monasticism and Daré, XII, ᴌᴀᴛᴛ ᴌᴌ

VINAYA SCHOOL.—See *Buddhist Schools,* XVI.

VINNARAS.—See *Lung Wang* 龍王.

VIOLET LADY, THE.—See *Tzŭ-ku Shên* 紫姑神.

VIROCHANA.—A *danava* (*q.v.*), son of Prahlada, and father of Bali. He is also called Drisana. When the earth was milked, Virochana acted as the calf of the *Asuras. Cf.* Prithi, called the first king, from whom the earth received her name Prithivi.

VIRUDHAKA.—See *Ssŭ ta T'ien-wang* 四大天王.

VIRUPA.—See *Lo-han* 羅漢.

VIRUPAKSA.—See *Ssŭ ta T'ien-wang* 四大天王.

VISHNU.—Root, wish, "to pervade." The second god of the Hindu triad. In the *Rig-veda* Vishnu is not in the first rank of gods. He is a manifestation of the solar energy, and is described as striding through the seven regions of the universe in three steps, and enveloping all things with the dust (of his beams). These three steps are explained by commentators as denoting the three manifestations of light—fire, lightning, and the sun; or the three places of the sun—its rising, culmination, and setting. In the *Veda* he is occasionally associated with Indra. He has very little in common with the Vishnu of later times, but he is called "the unconquerable preserver," and this distinctly indicates the great preserving power which he afterwards became.

VISHNU

The worshippers of Vishnu recognize in him the supreme being from whom all things emanate. In the *Maha-bharata* and in the *Puranas* he is the Prajapati (creator) and supreme god.

Vishnu's preserving and restoring power has been manifested to the world in a variety of forms called *Avataras*, literally "descents," but more intelligibly "incarnations," in which a portion of his divine essence was embodied in a human or supernatural form possessed of superhuman powers. The *Avatara* is the Chinese *a-po-to-lo* 阿 跋 多 羅 = *hua-shêng* 化 生, metamorphosis; the Brahminical idea of incarnation. All these *Avataras* (ten in number) became manifest for correcting some great evil or effecting some great good in the world.

As preserver and restorer, Vishnu is a very popular deity, and the worship paid to him is of a joyous character.

VRAISRAVANA.—See *Ssŭ ta T'ien-wang* 四 大 天 王.

W

WAN 九.—A Brain-god.—See *Chio Yüan-tzŭ* 覺元子.

WAN HSIEN CHÊN 萬仙陣.—The famous Battle of all the Immortals, one of the numerous encounters during the wars which preceded the accession of the Chou 周 dynasty in 1122 B.C.

WAN HSIU 萬修.—The god of the constellation Chang 張. Alternatively with Hsieh Ting 薛定.

WAN-HUI 萬回.—See *Ho Ho (êrh-hsien)* 和合 (二仙).

WAN-HUI 萬迴.—A priest invited to China by Wu Hou 武后 (A.D. 684-705), the Empress-Dowager Wu 武, in the seventh century A.D. (see *Ta Shêng* 大聖). A saintly Buddhist monk. One of those invited to the annual banquet of the gods (see *Hsi Wang-mu* 西王母).

WAN-JU-WEI CH'AN-SHIH 萬如衛禪師 (68th generation). (The character which should follow *wei* 衛 is missing in the original document).—A deified Buddhist monk. Ranked fifty-seventh in Buddhist School, III (*q.v.*). Family name Chang 張. A native of Ho-chung 禾中. His teacher was Yüan-wu Ch'an-shih 圓悟 禪師 (*q.v.*). He afterwards started his own school at Lung-ch'ih Shan 龍池山, Dragon-pool Mountain, where he died and is buried.

WANG CH'ANG 王長.—See *Wang Ta-hsien* 王大仙.

WANG CHIAO 王蛟.—The god of the constellation I 翼. Alternatively with P'ei T'ung 邳仝.—See *Huo Pu* 火部.

WANG CH'U 王儲.—See *Chiu Yao* 九曜.

WANG CHÜN 王潛.—An assessor of Kuan Kung 關公.—See *Kuan Yü* 關羽.

WANG FANG-P'ING 王方平.—See *Ma Ku* 麻姑.

WANG FÊNG 王封.—See *Chiu Yao* 九曜.

WANG FU MU 王父母.—See *Teats, the Gods of the*.

WANG HSIANG 汪祥.—The god of the star Ti-lo 地樂.—See *Ti-sha* 地煞.

WANG HSIANG 罔象.—See *Shui Fu* 水府, D (c) (3).

WANG HU 王虎.—The god of the star Yüeh-p'o 月破. A commander of troops under Chou Wang 紂王 (1154-1121 B.C.). Slain by No-cha 哪吒. Also the god of the star T'ien Chien 天劍.—See *T'ien-kang* 天罡.

WANG KAO ÊRH YÜAN-SHUAI 王高二元帥.—The two Generalissimos Wang 王 and Kao 高. Named respectively Wang-t'ieh 王鐵, Iron Wang, and Kao-t'ung 高銅, Copper Kao. The former came from the S. of Jung-ch'êng 榕城, and the latter from the N. of Chi-yung 薊雍. Both were born in 839 B.C. They held several official posts, but resigned because Han Wang 韓王, King Han, took no notice of their advice.

They are noted in Chinese lore for their sworn brotherhood and bravery. For the latter they were rewarded by Yü Ti 玉帝 conferring on them the title of Superintendents of the Tiger Hills.

WANG LIANG 王良.—The god of the constellation Mao 昴. Alternatively with Huang Ts'ang 黃倉.

WANG LING-KUAN 王靈官. WANG YÜAN-SHUAI 王元帥.—The Taoist counterpart of the Chia-lan 迦藍 (*q.v.*) of Buddhist temples. A mediate disciple of the celebrated Lin Ling-su 林靈素 (*q.v.*) of the Sung 宋 dynasty, whose methods he transmitted, his fame resting only on this, the people believing in him without giving any reason.

The Taoists state that Sa Shou-chien 薩守監 was a disciple of Lin Ling-su 林靈素, and Wang Ling-kuan 王靈官, the celestial Marshal of the Ministry of Fire, was a disciple of Sa Shou-chien 薩守監, and Chou Ssŭ-tê 周思得, of Hang-chou 杭州, in Chêkiang 浙江, famous at the Court of the Emperor Yung Lo 永樂 (A.D. 1403-25) of the Ch'ing 清 dynasty, was a pupil of Wang Ling-kuan 王靈官. Details are wanting, but the Emperor Hsien Tsung 憲宗 (A.D. 1465-88) of the Ming 明 dynasty changed the name

Temple of the Virtue of Fire to that of Palace of the Virtue of Fire, and added to Wang Ling-kuan's 王靈官 title the two characters Hsien-ling 顯靈, Miraculous.

The raiments on his image were changed every three months; every three years some of his robes were burnt and replaced by new ones, richly ornamented with precious stones, silks, etc. Great expenses were also incurred in the annual celebration of his birthday. Sacrifices were offered by the officials on the first day of the year, at the winter solstice, and on the festival of the apparition of the two Spirits Wang Ling-kuan 王靈官 and Sa Shou-chien 薩守監. This went on until a great disturbance was caused by Ku Chio 顧珏 and his son Ku Lun 顧倫 passing themselves off as being possessed by these two Spirits, for which imposture they were officially exiled.

The worship was denounced by the Ming 明 dynasty Board of Rites, but nevertheless the sacrifices were not entirely abolished, because several emperors had caused temples to be built and dedicated to them, and it was forbidden to burn the old garments.

In modern (mostly Taoist, but also Buddhist) temples Wang Ling-kuan 王靈官 often fulfils the office of gatekeeper, sometimes alone, sometimes in company with Chia-lan 迦藍 or Wei T'o 韋馱. He holds a knotty staff to drive away evil spirits.—See also *Sa Chên-jên* 薩眞人.

WANG LUNG-MAO 王龍茂.—The god of the star T'ien-hsüan 天玄.—See *T'ien-kang* 天罡.

WANG-MU 王母.—See *Wu Lao* 五老.

WANG Ô 王亞.—See *Wang Yüan-shuai* 王元帥.

WANG PA 王霸.—The god of the constellation Kuei 鬼. Alternatively with Chao Pai-kao 趙白高.

WANG PA-PA 王爸爸.—Du Bose describes this god as "the chief of police in the land of shades. The owners of lost property make application to him for recovery of goods, sometimes sticking a list of valuables on his person. Notices of 'Man Lost,' with the character 'Man' turned upside down, are at times pasted to his clay raiment."

WANG PAO 王豹.—The god of the star Chi-tu 計都. He was companion in arms to P'êng Tsun 彭遵 (*q.v.*), and officer of Chou Wang's 紂王 (1154-1121 B.C.) advance guard, under Hsü Kai 徐蓋, at Chieh-p'ai Kuan 界牌關. Slain by No-cha 哪吒. Canonized by Chiang Tzŭ-ya 姜子牙.

WANG PING 王冰.—A demi-god. A colleague of Ch'i Po 岐伯 (*q.v.*). Studied the nervous system. Kept his knowledge to himself until the beginning of the T'ang 唐 dynasty, when he gave it forth for the benefit of mankind. A member of the commission appointed by Huang Ti 皇帝 (*q.v.*) to continue and complete the labours of Shên Nung 神農 on natural history and the medicinal properties of plants.—See also *T'ien I-yüan* 天醫院.

WANG P'ING 王平.—The god of the star Ti-ch'i 地奇.—See *Ti-sha* 地煞.

"WANG 王 THE PURE."—See *Gamblers, The God of*.

WANG-SHÊN 亡神, THE GOD OF THE STAR.—See *Ou-yang Shun* 歐陽濬.

WANG-SHIH 王氏.—See *Tsao Chün* 灶(竈)君.

WANG SHIH-CH'ÊN 王侍宸.—Shih-ch'ên 侍宸 is the name of his official post, his own name being Wang Wên-ch'ing 王文卿. He was born at Lin-ch'uan 臨川 during the Sung 宋 dynasty, and was of unusual mien. He travelled widely, and one day met a magician who gave him a formula by which he could unloose the winds and produce thunder. He became the protegé of the Emperor Hui Tsung 徽宗 (A.D. 1101-26) of the Sung 宋 dynasty, who bestowed on him the title of Tao-shih 道士 of the Palace, and frequently made him presents, which, however, he declined.

He put an end to a drought in the Yang Chou 揚州 district by seizing his magic sword and blowing water from his mouth, thus causing the Yellow River to rise three feet.

Some days later the Magistrate of that place reported to the Emperor that rain of a yellow colour had fallen.

In the Ta-yüan 大元 period (Yüan 元 dynasty) a temple was built to him in the city of Chien-ch'ang Fu 建昌府.

WANG SHU-HO 王叔和.—See *Shih Ming-i* 十明醫, 6.

WANG-SSǓ CH'ÊNG 枉死城.—The City of Suicides. Situated on the right of the Ninth Court of Hades (*q.v.*). Here are tormented those who commit suicide in a fit of passion, or for merely trivial motives. Suicides for reasons of filial piety, love of chastity or justice, fidelity, etc., are not punished in this hell.

WANG TA HSIEN 王大仙.—A disciple of Chang Tao-ling 張道陵, named Wang Ch'ang 王長, whose aid is invoked against white ants and the *mêng ch'ung* 蠓虫, sand flies or dung flies, which attack rice. Pilgrimages are made to his shrine at Tê-hsing Hsien 德興縣, on the borders of Anhui 安徽 and Kiangsi 江西.

WANG TSO 王佐.—The god of the star Ping-fu 病符. In command of the advance-guard under general Chang K'uei 張奎 at Mien-ch'ih Hsien 澠池縣. Killed by general Nan Kung-kua 南宮适 (Yin-Chou 殷周 wars).

WANG WÊN-CHÊNG 王文正.—See *Hsing-ch'ang Lü-shih* 省常律師.

WANG WÊN-CH'ING 王文卿.—See *Wang Shih-ch'ên* 王侍宸, *Hsüan-t'ien Shang-ti* 玄天上帝, and *Shih-êrh ting-chia Shên* 十二丁甲神.

WANG YEN-CHANG 王彥章.—An assessor of Kuan Kung 關公.—See *Kuan Yü* 關羽.

WANG YÜAN-SHUAI 王元帥.—Generalissimo Wang 王. Posthumous son of Wang Ch'ên 王臣 and Chao-shih 邵氏. Born A.D. 636. Called Wang Ô 王惡; personal name Tung-ch'êng 東誠. His parents lived in La-li 凇村, at Hsiang-yang 州卅, Hupei 湖北. Being extremely muscular and discinclined to study, he enlisted and put down some disturbances in the Marches. Later on his name Wang Ô 王惡 was falsely assumed by a man named Wang Hei-hu 王黑虎, Black Tiger Wang, who oppressed the people, the latter fearing to take any action in the belief that he was the real Wang Ô 王惡, whose name inspired great terror on account of his prowess. Wang Ô 王惡 having killed the pretender and being found guilty by the Magistrate, attacked and nearly killed the latter. He, however, escaped and went to Ching-hsiang 荆襄, where he learnt that a river-devil was casting spells on the people and causing them to sacrifice annually a large number of animals to his image, on the pretext of warding off epidemics. Thus the people were becoming pauperized, and were even reduced to selling their children in order to pay the levies made for this purpose.

Wang Ô 王惡 burnt the temple which had been erected to the demon, whereupon the latter raised a violent wind, but Sa Chên-jên 薩眞人 (*q.v.*) having appeared and dissipated it, the evil spirit took to flight.

Wang Ô 王惡 was canonized by Yü Ti 玉帝 as Wang 王, the Perspicacious Generalissimo, and was also appointed Spirit Protector of the Capital of the Empire. He has his post near the gate of Heaven, and when ordered by Yü Ti 玉帝 to redress the wrongs of humanity, he immediately departs to fulfil his mission. Owing to his irascible disposition, the people take care not to offend him.—See also *Wang Ling-kuan* 王靈官.

WAR, THE GOD OF.—See *Kuan Yü* 關羽.

WAR, THE MINISTRY OF.—See *Kuan Yü* 關羽.

WATER, THE SPIRIT OF.—Shui ching-tzŭ 水精子.—See *Wu Lao* 五老.

WATER, THE SPIRIT OF THE SUBTILE ELEMENT OF.—See *Shui Fu* 水府, D (3) (c).

WATER, THE SPIRITS OF VARIOUS BODIES OF.—See *Shui Fu* 水府, D (2).

WATER-GOD, THE.—For the various gods of the waters see *Shui Pu* 水部. Du Bose gives the generic Chinese description of the "water-god" as having a tiger's body, a man's face of green and yellow colour, eight hands, eight feet, and eight tails. He adds: "One of the emperors saw another of the water-gods near Tsingki'angpu (Chinkiang: Chên-chiang 鎮江, Kiangsu 江蘇), where the Grand Canal crosses the old bed of the Yellow River. In the time of a flood he came floating down like a log of wood; he was ten feet long, with a sounding voice; in colour he was black, with the appearance of a monkey; in strength equal to nine elephants: all who gazed at him became blind. The Emperor called to his aid one of the *ting* 丁 gods, who caught him, and confined him in a cave at the source of the river, with a great stone resting upon him, so that the waters could not again come with a great flood."—*Cf. Shui Fu* 水府, D (1) (e).

WATERS, THE COUNT OF.—See *Shui Fu* 水府, D (3) (d).

WATERS, THE FEMALE IMMORTAL OF THE.—See *Shui Fu* 水府, D (3) (e).

WATERS, THE GOD OF.—See *Fêng I* 馮夷.

WATERS, THE OLD MATRON OF.—See *Shui-mu Niang-niang* 水母娘娘.

WATERS, THE OLD MOTHER OF THE.—See *Shui Fu* 水府, D (4).

WATERS, THE SPIRIT OF THE.—See *Shui Fu* 水府, D (3) (b).

WATERS, THE TREASURY OF.—See *Shui Fu* 水府.

WAVES OF RIVERS, THE SPIRIT OF THE.—See *Shui Fu* 水府, D (2) (i).

WAVES OF THE SEA, THE SPIRIT OF THE.—See *Shui Fu* 水府, D (2) (i).

WAX-CHANDLERS, THE PATRON DIETY OF.—See *Po-Ssŭ* 波斯.

WEALTH, THE GOD OF.—Yüan Tan 元澹, the true God of Wealth, now occupies a secondary place, having been supplanted by Ts'ai Shên 財神 (*q.v.*). He lived during the time of Chiang T'ai-kung 姜太公. Some of his exploits were riding a tiger and hurling a pearl which burst like a bomb. He was overcome by witchcraft: a straw man was made to represent him, and its eyes and heart were pierced with darts. After death he was appointed the god of wealth.—See *Ts'ai Shên* 財神.

WEAVER-GIRL, THE.—See *Chih Nü* 織女.

WEAVERS, THE GODDESS OF.—See *Chih Nü* 織女.

WEI 危, THE GOD OF THE CONSTELLATION.—See *Chien Tan* 堅鐔 and *Hou T'ai-i* 侯太乙.

WEI 尾, THE GOD OF THE CONSTELLATION.—See *Ts'ên P'êng* 岑彭 and *Chu Chao* 朱昭.

WEI 胃, THE GOD OF THE CONSTELLATION.—See *Wu Ch'êng* 烏成 and *Sung Kêng* 宋庚.

WEI 蠳 or 蠍.—See *Shui Fu* 水府, D (2) (f).

WEI-CHI HOU 威濟侯.—The Majestic and Benevolent Marquis. A man of T'ung-chuang 童莊, Chang-hsing Hsien 長興縣, Chi Chou 吉州, Shansi 山西. Born in A.D. 1104, during the reign of the Emperor Hui Tsung 微宗 (A.D. 1101-26) of the Sung 宋 dynasty. When dying at the age of 18, said that he was leaving for Chiao-hsi 膠西, Shantung 山東, and would return a few years later.

He was a man of affable manners and great intellectual powers, being able to warn his fellow-countrymen of impending calamities, and after his apotheosis was prayed to for good harvests, rain, fine weather, success in silkworm-rearing, etc. Titles of high degree including that of Marquis, were conferred on him during the Sung 宋 dynasty. On the *chih-ma* 紙馬, "paper horses," he is represented attended by two servants and accompanied by two dukes on horseback, the inscription being *San-wei Kung-hou* 三位公侯, "Dukes and Marquis, three persons." Those *chih-ma* 紙馬 are used by the natives when about to move house. They are first pasted in the old house, and then removed to the new one, some being stuck on the walls of the latter and some burnt.—See also *Composite Deities*.

WEI [YÜ]-CH'IH CHING-TÊ 尉遲敬德.—An assessor of

Kuan Kung 關公.—See *Kuan Yü* 關羽 and *Shên T'u Yü Lei* 神荼鬱壘.

WEI-CHUNG-FU CH'AN-SHIH 位中符禪師 (66th generation).—A deified Buddhist monk. Ranked seventy-fifth in Buddhist School, VI (*q.v.*). Family name Liu 劉. A native of Lu-ling 廬陵, Kiangsi 江西. Instructed by [Hsüeh-kuan] Tao-yin Ch'anshih [雪關] 道誾禪師 (*q.v.*) at Po-shan 博山, and then by [Shih-yü] Ming-fang Ch'an-shih [石雨] 明方禪師 (*q.v.*). In A.D. 1641, he withdrew to Pai-yen 白巖, in Chêkiang 浙江, where he lived for some years. "His reputation attracted all the monks of the neighbourhood, as the ocean attracts the rivers." His tomb is on Pai-yen Shan 白巖山, Pai-yen Hill, to the right of the monastery.

WEI KU 韋古.—One of the Kings of Medicine. Of Indian birth, a native of Hsi-yü 西域. Bhaishajyaraja, the Buddha whose festival is observed on the fifteenth day of the fourth moon. Specially honoured by the bonzes under the name of Yao-wang P'u-sa 藥王菩薩. His Taoist name was Kuei-ts'ang 歸藏. He came to the capital during the K'ai-yüan 開元 period (A.D. 713-42) of the reign of the Emperor Hsüan Tsung 玄宗 (A.D. 713-56) of the T'ang 唐 dynasty. He went about wearing a gauze headdress, a woollen robe, carrying a staff, and with dozens of gourds strung on his waistbelt and back, from which he distributed remedies liberally to the sick. The Emperor summoned him to Court, and bestowed on him the title of Yao Wang 藥王, King of Remedies. —See also *T'ien I-yüan* 天醫院, *Yao Wang* 藥王, *Wei Shan-chün* 韋善俊, and *Pien Ch'iao* 扁鵲.

WEI PI 魏賁.—The god of the star Huang-fan 黃旛. Joined the party of Chiang Tzŭ-ya 姜子牙. Was killed by P'êng Tsun 彭遵 at Chieh-p'ai Kuan 界牌關, in the Yin-Chou 殷周 wars.

WEI SHAN-CHÜN 韋善俊.—One of the Kings of Medicine. A native of Hsi-an Fu 西安府, Shensi 陝西. Lived a strict life as a Taoist in the time of the usurping Empress Wu Hou 武后 (A.D. 684-705) of the T'ang 唐 dynasty. He was always accompanied by a black dog called the "black dragon," and was known by the People as Yao Wang 藥王, the King of Medicines.

The legend relates that Dr. Han I 韓億, a high official at the Court of the Emperor Chên Tsung 眞宗 (A.D. 998-1023) of the Sung 宋 dynasty, had been afflicted with a severe illness since the age of six years. One day, when about to take his medicine, he said: "A Taoist leading a black dog has given me a remedy which has cured me instantly." Thereupon he had the portrait of the Taoist drawn and sacrifices offered to it.—See also *T'ien I-yüan* 天醫院, *Yao Wang* 藥王, *Wei Ku* 韋古, and *Pien Ch'iao* 扁鵲.

WEI SHANG-CH'ING 衞上卿.—See *Hsüan-t'ien Shang-ti*   WEI T'O
玄天上帝 and *Shih-êrh ting-chia Shên* 十二丁甲神.

WEI-TÊ SAN-KUAN 威德三觀.—One of the twelve divine
Buddhist teachers (*Samantabhadra*).

WEI T'O 韋陀.—Veda. Viharapala (*q.v.*). A Hindu god.
Deva protector of the Law of Buddha and Buddhist temples.
His image is placed behind that of Maitreya, the future Buddha.
Wei T'o 韋陀 is accompanied and assisted (*chia-li* 加力) by a
tutelary deity, Chia-lan 伽藍 (*q.v.*). In Hindu mythology, a
deity who protects three of the four continents into which the
world is divided (Remusat). A *deva* (inhabitant of heaven)
defender of the Buddhist faith (*hu-fa wei-t'o* 護法韋陀) and
Buddhist monasteries. General-in-chief under the Four Great
Heavenly Kings, Ssŭ ta T'ien-wang 四大天王 (*q.v.*) who guard
the world from the attacks of Asuras (*q.v.*) and watch over every
Buddhist temple. "Regularly invoked by the Chinese Buddhists
for monastic supplies and as protector of monasteries" (Waddell)
"A tutelary *Deva* borrowed from India and Tibet" (Edkins; Eitel;
Hackman). He is represented clad completely in armour,
holding a sceptre-shaped defensive weapon usually resting on the
ground, but often a sword placed crosswise on his folded arms.
He stands facing inward, opposite the principal sanctuary. Sometimes his image is placed in small shrines at turning points of long
roads, to protect pilgims from evil influences. It is also placed on
small tablets attached to portable shrines carried by begging
monks. In Chinese works Wei-t'o 韋陀 is referred to as a *deva*,
t'ien shên 天神, spirit of heaven. His worship, as heavenly protector, and erection of statues to him became general in Buddhist
monasteries in the time of Kao Tsung 高宗 (A.D. 650-84) of the
T'ang 唐 dynasty. As a tutelary deity, he generally accompanies
Kuan Yin 觀音, the Goddess of Mercy. In some editions of the
Buddhist sutras, the name is corrupted to Wei T'o 韋馱 and
Chien T'o 建馱 and it has thence been inferred that he is entirely
a fictitious deity.

"Wei-T'o," 韋陀, says Plopper, "sometimes erroneously called
Wei-T'o Buddha, is one of the lesser Bodhisattva." He is shown
standing in the temples, facing the inner courts. "He thus shows
his position as Defender of the Law and of Buddhism. He was
originally a Chin-kang 金剛, but on account of his zeal and goodness he was advanced to the P'u-sa 菩薩 state. He is thought to
protect against and destroy demons. He stands, holding the
Chin-kang's 'diamond club,' ready instantly to avenge any slight
to the Buddhist faith."

The *Shên-hsien t'ung-chien* 神仙通鑑 gives the following
legend concerning him:—Ju-lai 如來 having invited all the
Buddhas to a banquet in the Lei-yin Kung 雷音宮, Thunder
Palace, of the Western Heavens, Wei T'o Chiang-chün 韋陀將軍,

General Wei T'o, was ordered to receive them. Wearing his armour, with his sword placed across his joined hands, he introduced the guests to the banquet hall.

Jan-têng Fo 燃燈佛 (*q.v.*), addressing the Buddhas, said: "This is Wei T'o 韋陀, my disciple, who has practised virtue from his youth up. He is now General-in-chief under the Four Heavenly Kings. In one day he can visit three continents of the Buddhist world. His power is unlimited. He assists all who pray to him. He is the valiant protector of Buddhism in the three continents of the present *kalpa,* and is called T'ien-tsun 天尊, Honoured of Heaven. His mercy and love for suffering mortals is proclaimed by all."

For the short local legend of the market town of Chia-li 加力, the place where Buddha, the world-illuminating king, P'u-chao Wang 普照王, helped Wei T'o 韋陀, see Doré, vii, 209.—See also *Ti-tsang Wang* 地藏王.

WEI T'O 韋馱.—See *Wei T'o* 韋陀.

WEI-TSÊ CH'AN-SHIH 維則禪師 (57th generation).—A deified Buddhist monk. Ranked thirty-fourth in Buddhist School, III (*q.v.*). Family name T'an 譚. A native of Chi-an 吉安. His teacher was Ming-pên Ch'an-shih 明本禪師 (*q.v.*). In A.D. 1342, he lived in the Chêng-tsung Ssŭ 正宗寺, Chêng-tsung Monastery, in Shih-tzŭ Lin 獅子林 (*q.v.*). He died there, but the year of his death is unknown.

WEI-YANG TSUNG 溈仰宗.—See *Buddhist Schools*, IV.

WEI-YEN CH'AN-SHIH 惟儼禪師 (36th generation).—A deified Buddhist monk. Ranked third in Buddhist School, VI (*q.v.*). Family name Han 韓. A native of Chiang-chou 絳州. Entered a Buddhist monastery at the age of 17. Intelligent and well-behaved. Studied under Hsi-ch'ien Ch'an-shih 希遷禪師 (*q.v.*), and then under Ma Tsu (*q.v.*). After returning to Shih-t'ou 石頭, founded a school at Yo Shan 藥山. Died A.D. 834. Posthumous title: Hung-tao Ta-shih 弘道大師, Master of Vast Intelligence.

WELL-GOD, THE.—Du Bose says that this god, who is a little boy, has no image, but his picture is put beside the well at the new year, and a sacrifice in the form of a feast is made to him. —See *Shui Fu* 水府 and Werner, *Myths,* p. 217.

WELLS, THE SPIRITS OF.—See *Shui Fu* 水府, D (2) (j).

WÊN CH'ANG 文昌.—The God of Literature. The God of Stationers. His name was Chang Ya 張亞. He was born during the T'ang 唐 dynasty in the kingdom of Yüeh 越 (modern

Chêkiang 浙 江) and went to live at Tzŭ-t'ung 梓 潼, in Ssŭch'uan 四 川. There he was subsequently worshipped as a god. He was a brilliant writer, and held an appointment in the Board of Rites. In his latter days he suddenly disappeared, or was killed in battle. Rulers of the T'ang 唐 dynasty canonized him, and those of the Sung 宋 and Yüan 元 dynasties bestowed on him various other honorary titles.

This is the account accepted as historically authentic, but other versions exist. One refers to him as the God or Spirit (*Shên* 神) of Tzŭ-t'ung 梓 潼, and states that he was a man named Chang Ya-tzŭ 張 亞 子 who held office in the Chin 晉 dynasty (A.D. 265-316), and was killed in a fight. Another again states that under the Sung 宋 dynasty (A.D. 960-1280), in the third year (A.D. 1000) of the reign-period Hsien-p'ing 咸 平 (A.D. 998-1004) of the Emperor Chên Tsung 眞 宗 (A.D. 998-1023), he repressed the revolt of Wang Chün 王 均 at Ch'êng Tu 成 都 in Ssŭch'uan 四 川. General Lei Yu-chung 雷 有 終 caused to be shot into the besieged town arrows to which notices where attached inviting the inhabitants to surrender. Suddenly a man mounted a ladder, and pointing to the rebels cried in a loud voice: "The Spirit of Tzŭ-t'ung 梓 潼 has sent me to inform you that the town will fall into the hands of the enemy on the twentieth day of the ninth moon, and not a single person will escape death." Attempts to strike down this prophet of evil were in vain. for he had already disappeared. The town was captured on the day indicated. The general, as a reward, caused the temple of the Tzŭ-t'ung 梓 潼 Spirit to be repaired, and sacrifices offered to it.

The object of worship nowadays in the temples dedicated to Wên Ch'ang 文 昌 is Tzŭ-t'ung Ti-chün 梓 潼 帝 君, the God of Tzŭ-t'ung 梓 潼. The convenient elasticity of dualism enabled Chang 張 to have as many as seventeen reincarnations, which ranged over a period of some three thousand years.

The title bestowed on him by the Emperor Jên Tsung 仁 宗 (A.D. 1312-21) in A.D. 1314, was "Supporter of the Yüan 元 dynasty, Diffuser of Renovating Influences, Ssŭ-lu 司 錄 of Wên Ch'ang 文 昌, God and Lord." He was thus apotheosized, and took his place among the gods of China.

The date of his birth is given differently in different works. Some assign it to the Chin 晉 dynasty (fourth century A.D.) as stated above; others even as early as the Ch'in 秦 dynasty (third century B.C.).

It should be noted, in view of what follows, that though the literati of Ssŭch'uan 四 川 venerated Chang Ya 張 亞 as their master, and as a mark of affection and gratitude built a temple to him, they had no intention of making him the God of Literature.

A scholar, Chung K'uei 鍾 馗 by name, having been admitted as first academician at the metropolitan examination, presented himself according to custom to the Emperor to receive the rose of gold bestowed on the successful candidate. He was, however, of such repulsive mien that the Emperor refused the reward, and Chung K'uei 鍾旭 in despair went and threw himself into the sea. Just as he was drowning, however, a sea-monster (an *ao* 鼇 or "kraken") raised him on his back to the surface, and ascending to Heaven he became arbiter of the destinies of men of letters. His abode was said to be the star K'uei 奎 (the stellar "mansion" of Andromneda and Pisces). Scholars soon began to worship and sacrifice to K'uei 奎 as the God of Literature.

As time went on, there was a general demand for a sensible, concrete representation of this star-god, and eventually there was substituted for the star-group K'uei 奎 another star-group K'uei 魁, which is the square part of the constellation Dipper, or Great Bear. Yet, even for this no satisfactory personal representation could be found, and accordingly a drawing was made from the character itself, representing a *kuei* 鬼 (or disembodied spirit) with its foot raised, and bearing aloft a *tou* 斗 (bushel measure). This is the image which was most frequently worshipped by the literati. The worship properly belonging to the constellation Andromeda and Pisces was thus transferred to the square portion of the constellation Dipper, or Great Bear.

There remains to be explained how Chang Ya 張亞 came to have the honorific title of Wên Ch'ang 文昌, God of Literature. This was due to a Taoist subterfuge. The Taoists, to whom an invention of the legend of Chung K'uei's 鍾旭 rescue by the sea-monster is ascribed, gave out that Shang Ti 上帝, the Supreme Ruler, had entrusted Chang Ya's 張亞 son with the management of the palace of Wên Ch'ang 文昌, the square or oblong part of the Dipper. Then scholars gradually acquired the habit of saying that they owed their success to the spirit of Tzǔ-t'ung 梓潼 which they falsely represented as being an incarnation of the star-group Wên Ch'ang 文昌. Thus though Chang Ya 張亞 belonged to Ssǔch'uan 四川 and his worship should be confined to that province, he came to have the honorific title of Wên Ch'ang 文昌; and the personality of the deified mortal canonized as the Spirit of Tzǔ-t'ung 梓潼 was combined with the personality of the patron of literature enthroned in the star-palace of the Dipper, or Great Bear. Imperial sanction being obtained for this stroke of priestly cunning, the composite deity was fully recognized in the State ceremonial.

Nevertheless, the independent existence of the stellar spirit is sedulously maintained, and wherever Wên Ch'ang 文昌 is worshipped there is also found a separate representation of K'uei Hsing 魁星 and the ancient stellar deity largely monopolizes the popular idea of a guardian of literature and study, notwithstanding that the deified recluse of Tzǔ-t'ung 梓潼 has been added in this capacity to the State pantheon for more than five hundred years.

Wên Ch'ang 文昌 is popularly represented as attended by four acolytes. Behind him stand a servant and a groom. These are colloquially known as T'ien Lung 天聾, Deaf Celestial or Heaven-deaf, and Ti Ya 地啞, Mute Terrestrial, or Earth-dumb (or "Deaf as Heaven" and "Mute as Earth"). Their names are Hsüan T'ung-tzŭ 玄童子, "Sombre Youth," and Ti Mu 地母 "Earth Mother," respectively. They are thus unable to disclose the secrets of their master (or to act unfairly). The services of the groom are necessary because Wên Ch'ang 文昌 on his journeys rides a white horse.

In front of Wên Ch'ang 文昌, on his left, stands K'uei Hsing 魁星. He is represented as of diminutive stature, with the visage of a demon, holding a writing-brush in his right hand and a *tou* 斗 in his left, one of his legs kicking up behind—the figure being obviously intended as an impersonation of the character *k'uei* 魁. He is regarded as the distributor of literary degrees, and was invoked above all in order to obtain success at the competitive examinations. His images and temples are found in all towns. In the temples dedicated to Wên Ch'ang 文昌 there are always two secondary altars, one of which is consecrated to his worship.

The other is dedicated to Chu I 朱衣, "Mr. Redcoat." He and K'uei Hsing 魁星 are represented as the two inseparable companions of the God of Literature. The legend related of Chu I 朱衣 is as follows:—

During the T'ang 唐 dynasty, in the reign-period Chien-chung 建中 (A.D. 780-4) of the Emperor Tê Tsung 德宗 (A.D. 780-805), the Princess T'ai Yin 太陰 noticed that Lu Ch'i 盧杞, a native of Hua Chou 滑州, had the bones of an Immortal, and wished to marry him.

Ma P'o 麻婆, her neighbour, introduced him one day into the Crystal Palace for an interview with his future wife. The Princess gave him the choice of three careers: to live in the Dragon Prince's Palace, with the guarantee of immortal life, to enjoy immortality among the people on the earth, or to have the honour of becoming a minister of the Empire. Lu Ch'i 盧杞 first answered that he would like to live in the Crystal Palace. The young lady, overjoyed, said to him: "I am Princess T'ai Yin 太陰. I will at once inform Shang Ti 上帝, the Supreme Ruler." A moment later the arrival of a celestial messenger was announced. Two officers bearing flags preceded him and conducted him to the foot of the flight of steps. He then presented himself as Chu I 朱衣, the envoy of Shang Ti 上帝.

Addressing himself to Lu Ch'i 盧杞, he said: "Do you wish to live in the Crystal Palace?" The latter did not reply. T'ai Yin 太陰 urged him to give his answer, but he persisted in keeping silent. The Princess in despair retired to her apartment, and brought out five pieces of precious cloth, which she presented to the divine envoy, begging him to have patience a little longer and wait for the answer. After some time, Chu I 朱衣 repeated his question. Then Lu Ch'i 盧杞 in a firm voice answered: "I have consecrated my life to the hard labour of study, and wish to attain to the dignity of minister on this earth."

T'ai Yin 太陰 ordered Ma P'o 麻婆 to conduct Lu Ch'i 盧杞 from the palace. From that day his face became transformed: he acquired the lips of a dragon, the head of a panther, the green face of an Immortal, etc. He took his degree, and was promoted to be Director of the Censorate. The Emperor, appreciating the good sense shown in his advice, appointed him a minister of the Empire.

From this legend it would seem that Chu I 朱衣 is the purveyor of official posts; however, in practice, he is more generally regarded as the protector of weak candidates, as the God of Good Luck for those who present themselves at the examinations with a somewhat light equipment of literary knowledge. The special legend relating to this rôle is known everywhere in China. It is as follows:—

An examiner, engaged in correcting the essays of the candidates, after a superficial scrutiny of one of the essays, put it on one side as manifestly inferior, being quite determined not to pass the candidate who had composed it. The essay, moved by some mysterious power, was replaced in front of his eyes, as if to invite him to examine it more attentively. At the same time a reverend old man, clothed in a red garment, suddenly appeared before him, and by a nod of his head gave him to understand that he should pass the essay. The examiner, surprised at the novelty of the incident, and fortified by the approval of his supernatural visitor, admitted the author of the essay to the literary degree.

Chu I 朱衣, like K'uei Hsing 魁星, is invoked by the literati as a powerful protector and aid to success. When anyone with but a poor chance of passing presents himself at an examination, his friends encourage him by the popular saying: "Who knows but that Mr. Redcoat will nod his head?"

Chu I 朱衣 is sometimes accompanied by another personage, named Chin Chia 金甲, "Mr. Golden Cuirass." Like K'uei Hsing 魁星 and Chu I 朱衣 he has charge of the interests of scholars, but differs from them in that he holds a flag, which he has only to wave in front of a house for the family inhabiting it to be assured that among their descendants will be some who will win literary honours and be promoted to high offices under the State.

Though Chin Chia 金甲 is the protector of scholars, he is also the redoubtable avenger of their evil actions: his flag is saluted as a good omen, but his sword is the terror of the wicked.

Other patron deities of literature are the God of War (see *Kuan Yü* 關羽) and Lü Tung-pin 呂洞賓 (see *Pa Hsien* 八仙).

WÊN CHIEH 聞傑.—The god of the star T'ien-lao 天牢.
—See *T'ien-kang* 天罡.

WÊN CHUNG 聞仲.—See *Lei Tsu* 雷祖.

WÊN-I CH'AN-SHIH 文益禪師 (42nd generation).—A deified Buddhist monk. Ranked twenty-first in Buddhist School, VI (*q.v.*). Founder of the Fa-yen Mo 法眼脈 (Buddhist School, IX), Eye of the Law School, a branch school which originated in the ninth generation from Hui-nêng 慧能 (see *Patriarchs*). Family name Lu 魯. A native of Yü-hang 餘航, Chêkiang 浙江. His teacher was Kuei-ch'ên Ch'an-shih 桂琛禪師 (*q.v.*). He took part thrice in the ceremonies performed at the capital, Chin-ling 金陵 (modern Nanking 南京, Kiangsu 江蘇). Seeing his end approaching, he had his head shaved, took a bath and expired, A.D. 958. Posthumous title: Ta Fa-yen Ch'an-shih 大法眼禪師, Great Monk who was the Eye of the Law.

WÊN P'IN 聞聘.—See *Wu Yo* 五嶽.

WÊN PU 瘟部.—The Ministry of Epidemics. The gods of epidemics, etc., belong to the ninth, ninth, second, and third celestial Ministries. The composition of the Ministry of Epidemics is arranged differently in different works as Epidemics (regarded as epidemics on earth, but as Demons in Heaven) of the Centre, Spring, Summer, Autumn, and Winter, or as the Marshals clothed in yellow, green, red, white, and blue respectively, or as the Officers of the East, West, South, and North, with two additional members: a Taoist who quells the plague, and the Grand Master who exhorts people to do right.

With regard to the Ministry of Seasonal Epidemics, it is related that in the sixth moon of the eleventh year (A.D. 599) of the reign of the Emperor Kao Tsu 高祖 (A.D. 589-605) of the Sui 隋 dynasty, five stalwart persons appeared in the air, clothed in robes of five colours, each carrying different objects in his hands: the first a spoon and earthenware vase, the second a leather bag and sword, the third a fan, the fourth a club, the fifth a jug of fire. The Emperor asked Chang Chü-jên 張居仁, his Grand Historio-grapher, who these were and if they were benevolent or evil spirits. The official answered: "These are the five powers of the five directions. Their appearance indicates the imminence of epidemics, which will last throughout the four seasons of the year." "What remedy is there, and how am I to protect the people?" inquired the Emperor. "There is no remedy," replied the official, "for epidemics are sent from Heaven." During that year the mortality was very great. The Emperor built a temple to the five persons, and bestowed upon them the title of Marshals to the five Spirits of the Plague. During that and the following dynasty sacrifices were offered to them on the fifth day of the fifth moon.

The different compositions of the Ministry, according to the *Sou-shên chi* 搜神記 and the *Fêng-shên yen-i* 封神演義 respectively, are as follows:—*Sou-shên chi* 搜神記: *Shih Wên-yeh* 史文業, the Central Plague: President; Chang Yüan-po 張元伯, the Spring Plague; Hsiang Yüan-ta 鄉元達, the Summer Plague; Chao Kung-ming 趙公明, the Autumn Plague; Chung Shih-kuei 鍾仕貴, the Winter Plague. *Fêng-shên yen-i* 封神演義: President: Lü Yo 呂岳; Chou Hsin 周信, Overseer of Epidemics of the East; Li Chi 李奇, Overseer of Epidemics of the West; Chu T'ien-lin 朱天麟, Overseer of Epidemics of the South; Yang Wên-hui 楊文輝, Overseer of Epidemics of the North. Attachés to the Ministry: Ch'ên Kêng 陳庚, the *Tao-shih* 道士 who allays the plague; Li P'ing 李平, the Grand Master who exhorts to good.

The President of the Ministry, Lü Yo 呂岳 (*supra*) was an old Taoist hermit, living at Chiu-lung Tao 九龍島, Nine-dragon Island, who became an Immortal. The four members of the Ministry were his disciples. He wore a red garment, had a blue face, red hair, long teeth, and three eyes. His war-horse was named the Myopic Camel. He carried a magic sword, and was in the service of Chou Wang 紂王 (1154-1121 B.C.), whose armies were concentrated at Hsi-ch'i 西岐. In a duel with Mu-cha 木吒, brother of No-cha 哪吒, he had his arm severed by a sword-cut. In another battle with Huang T'ien-hua 黃天化, son of Huang Fei-hu 黃飛虎, he appeared with three heads and six arms. In his many hands he held the celestial seal, plague microbes, the flag of plague, the plague sword, and two mysterious swords. His faces were green, and large teeth protruded from his mouths. Huang T'ien-hua 黃天化 threw his magic weapon, *huo-lung piao* 火龍標, and hit him on the leg. Just at that moment Chiang Tzǔ-ya 姜子牙 arrived with his goblin-dispelling whip and felled him with a blow. He was able, however, to rise again, and took to flight.

Resolved to avenge his defeat, he joined General Hsü Fang 徐芳, who was commanding an army corps at Ch'uan-yün Kuan 嶂雲關. Round the mountain he organized a system of entrenchments and of infection against their enemies. Yang Chien 楊戩 released his celestial hound, which bit Lü Yo 呂岳 on the crown of his head. Then Yang Jên 楊任, armed with his magic fan, pursued Lü Yo 呂岳 and compelled him to retreat to his fortress. Lü Yo 呂岳 mounted the central raised part of the embattled wall and opened all his plague-disseminating umbrellas, with the object of infecting Yang Jên 楊任, but the latter, simply by waving his fan, reduced all the umbrellas to dust, and also burned the fort, and with it Lü Yo 呂岳.

Similar wonderful achievements are related in short notices in the *Fêng-shên yen-i* 封神演義 of the four other officers of the Ministry.

Chou Hsin 周信 is described as having a green face, red gold eyes, and large teeth. He wore a grey-green robe, hemp shoes, and a transcendent sword. He was killed by a blow from Yang

Chien's 楊戩 sword after his neck had been bitten by the latter's celestial hound.

Li Chi's 李奇 hair stood up in two horns on his head. He wore a light yellow robe, had a white face, pig's eyes, long whiskers and long beard, and carried a sword. He died through being speared by Li No-cha 李哪吒, after being felled by the latter's magic bracelet.

Chu T'ien-lin 朱天麟 had a violet-hued face, wore a Taoist hat with pearl pendants, a red gown, hemp shoes, and a sword. He was slain through having his skull split by the transcendent sword hurled into the air by Yü-ting Chên-jên 玉鼎眞人 (q.v.).

Yang Wên-hui 楊文輝 had a violet face, his hair stood up like spikes, he wore a golden hat ornamented with a fish's tail, a black gown, straw shoes, and a transcendent sword. He was killed through being struck on the head by the demon-smashing staff hurled into the air by Wei Hu 韋護 (q.v.), a disciple of Tao-hsing T'ien-tsun 道行天尊 (q.v.).

Ch'ên Kêng 陳庚. Was burnt to death by the flames produced by Yang Jên's 楊任 magic fan, when fighting for his friend Lü Yo 呂岳 against the tyrant Chou Wang 紂王, King Chou (1154-1121 B.C.).

Li P'ing 李平, Lü Yo's 呂岳 friend, met a like fate after having tried to induce the latter to abandon the cause of the Yin 殷 dynasty for that of the Chou 周.

For a case in which the unsuperstitious Magistrate Chang Tzŭ-chih 張子智 of Ch'ang-chou Fu 常州府, Kiangsu 江蘇, in A.D. 1195 destroyed a temple dedicated to the Spirits of Epidemics, see Doré, X, 816-7.

In Doré's *Recherches sur les Superstitions en Chine* is given an interesting legend concerning five other gods of epidemics. These gods are called the Wu Yo 五岳, Five Mountains, and are worshiped in the temple San-i Ko 三義閣 at Ju-kao 如臯, especially in outbreaks of contagious diseases and fevers. A sufferer goes to the temple and promises offerings to the gods in the event of recovery. The customary offering is five small wheaten loaves, called *shao-ping* 燒餅, and a pound of meat.

The Wu Yo 五岳 are stellar devils whom Yü Huang 玉皇 sent to be reincarnated on earth. Their names were T'ien Po-hsüeh 田伯雪, Tung Hung-wên 董宏文, Ts'ai Wên-chü 蔡文舉, Chao Wu-chên 趙武眞, and Huang Ying-tu 黄應度, and they were reincarnated at Nan-ch'ang Fu 南昌府, Chien-ch'ang Fu 建昌府, Yen-mên Kuan 雁門關, Yang Chou 揚州, and Nan-ching 南京 (Nanking), respectively. They were all noted for their brilliant intellects, and were clever scholars who passed their graduate's examination with success.

When Li Shih-min 李世民 ascended the throne, in A.D. 627, he called together all the Scholars of the Empire to take the Doctor's Examination in the capital. The five graduates started for the capital, but, losing their way, were robbed by brigands, and had to beg help in order to reach the end of their journey. By good luck they all met in the temple San-i Ko 三 義 閣 , and related to each other the various hardships they had undergone. But when they eventually reached the capital the examinations were over, and they were out in the streets without resources. So they took an oath of brotherhood for life and death. They pawned some of their clothes, and buying a drum, a seven-stringed guitar, a mandolin, and a clarinet, formed themselves into a band of strolling musicians. The fifth and youngest composed songs.

Their melodies having come to the ears of Li Shih-min 李 世 民 he ordered them to be brought into his presence, and after hearing them play and sing appointed them to his private suite, and henceforth they accompanied him wherever he went.

The Emperor bore malice toward Chang T'ien-shih 張 天 師 , the Master of the Taoists, because he refused to pay the taxes on his property, and conceived a plan to bring about his destruction. He caused a spacious subterranean chamber to be dug under the reception-hall of his palace. A wire passed through the ceiling to where the Emperor sat. He could thus at will give the signal for the music to begin or stop. Having stationed the five musicians in this subterranean chamber, he summoned the Master of the Taoists to his presence and invited him to a banquet. During the course of this he pulled the wire, and a subterranean babel began.

The Emperor pretended to be terrified, and allowed himself to fall to the ground. Then, addressing himself to Chang T'ien-shih 張 天 師 , he said: "I know that you can at will catch the devilish hobgoblins which molest human beings. You can hear for yourself the infernal row they make in my palace. I order you under penalty of death to put a stop to their pranks and to exterminate them."

Having spoken thus, the Emperor rose and left. The Master of the Taoists brought his projecting mirror, and began to seek for the evil spirits. In vain he inspected the palace and its precincts; he could discover nothing. Fearing that he was lost, he in despair threw his mirror on the floor of the reception-hall.

A minute later, sad and pensive, he stooped to pick it up; what was his joyful surprise when he saw reflected in it the subterranean room and the musicians! At once he drew five talismans on yellow paper, burned them, and ordered his celestial general, Chao Kung-ming 趙 公 明 , to take his sword and kill the five musicians. The order was promptly executed, and Chang T'ien-shih 張 天 師 informed the Emperor, who received the news with ridicule, not believing it to be true. He went to his seat and pulled the wire, but all remained silent. A second and third time he gave the signal, but without response. He then ordered his Grand Officer to ascertain what had happened. The officer found the five graduates bathed in their blood, and lifeless.

562

The Emperor, furious, reproached the Master of the Taoists. "But," replied Chang T'ien-shih 張天師, "was it not your Majesty who ordered me under pain of death to exterminate the authors of this pandemonium?" Li Shih-min 李世民 could not reply. He dismissed the Master of the Taoists and ordered the five victims to be buried.

After the funeral ceremonies, apparitions appeared at night in the place where they had been killed, and the palace became a babel. The spirits threw bricks and broke the tiles on the roofs.

The Emperor ordered his uncomfortable visitors to go to Chang T'ien-shih 張天師 who had murdered them. They obeyed, and, seizing the garments of the Master of the Taoists, swore not to allow him any rest if he would not restore them to life.

To appease them the Taoist said: "I am going to give each of you a wonderful object. You are then to return and spread epidemics among wicked people, beginning in the palace and with the Emperor himself, with the object of forcing him to canonize you.

One received a fan, another a gourd filled with fire, the third a metallic ring to encircle people's heads, the fourth a stick made of wolves' teeth, and the fifth a cup of lustral water.

The spirit graduates left full of joy, and made their first experiment on Li Shih-min 李世民. The first gave him feverish chills by waving his fan, the second burned him with the fire from his gourd, the third encircled his head with the ring, causing him violent headache, the fourth struck him with his stick, and the fifth poured out his cup of lustral water on his head.

The same night a similar tragedy took place in the palace of the Empress and the two chief imperial concubines.

T'ai-po Chin-hsing 太白金星, however, informed Yü Huang 玉皇 what had happened, and, touched with compassion, he sent three Immortals with pills and talismans which cured the Empress and the ladies of the palace.

Li Shih-min 李世民, having also recovered his health, summoned the five deceased graduates and expressed his regret for the unfortumate issue of his design against Chang T'ien-shih 張天師. He proceeded: "To the south of the capital is the temple San-i Ko 三義閣. I will change its name to Hsiang-shan Wu-Yüeh Shên 香山五岳神, Fragrant Hill of the Five Mountain Spirits. On the twenty-eighth day of the ninth moon betake yourselves to that temple to receive the seals of your canonization." He conferred upon them the title of Ti 帝, Emperor (Doré).

WÊN-SHU 文殊.—See *Fa-chao Kuo-shih* 法照國師 and following paragraph.

WÊN-SHU YEN-K'UNG 文殊眼空.—Manjusri, Manjusiri, or Manjugosha.—One of the twelve divine Buddhist teachers

(Samantabhadra). The Buddhist Apollo. The God of Transcendent Wisdom. His duty is to turn the Wheel of the Law for the salvation of the Chinese. His birthday is celebrated on the fourth day of the fourth month.

WÊN-T'AI CH'AN-SHIH 文泰禪師 (53rd generation).—A deified Buddhist monk. Ranked forty-first in Buddhist School, VI (*q.v.*). Family name Wei 魏. A native of Yang-ch'êng 陽城. Shansi 山西. Studied successively under Hsüeh-fêng Hêng 雪峰恒 and T'ai-yüan Shên 太原深, but finding them uncongenial, went to the school of Fu-yü Ch'an-shih 福裕禪師 (*q.v.*), at Hsüeh-t'ing 雪庭, Hupei 湖北, and remained in his service for ten years.

WÊN-TSAI CH'AN-SHIH 文載禪師 (60th generation).— A deified Buddhist monk. Ranked forty-eighth in Buddhist School, VI (*q.v.*). Family name Wang 王. A native of Kuang-ning 廣寧, in the Wei-chou 蔚州 department, Chihli 直隸. Studied under K'o-ts'ung Ch'an-shih 可從禪師 (*q.v.*). In A.D. 1506, the Emperor Wu Tsung 武宗 (A.D. 1506-22) of the Ming 明 dynasty appointed him Superior of the Shao-lin Ssŭ 少林寺, Few Forests Monastery, situated at the foot of Sung Yo 嵩嶽, the Sacred Peak of the South. His disciples "equalled in number the clouds of heaven." He erected a monastery at San-shih-liu Fêng 三十六峰, Thirty-six Peaks.

WÊN-TS'AI CH'AN-SHIH 文才禪師 (55th generation).— A deified Buddhist monk. Ranked forty-eighth in Buddhist School, VI (*q.v.*). Family name Wang 姚. A native of Kuang-ning 臨汾, in P'ing-yang Fu 平陽府, Shansi 山西. In A.D. 1324, he lived at Shao-lin 少林, and died there in 1352, aged 80. His tomb is beside that of Fu-yü Ch'an-shih 福裕禪師 (*q.v.*).

WEN-YEN CH'AN-SHIH 文偃禪師 (40th generation).—A deified Buddhist monk. Ranked fourteenth in Buddhist School, VI (*q.v.*). Founder of the Yün-mên Mo 雲門脈, Cloud Sect School (Buddhist School VIII), a branch of the Southern Buddhist Schools. Family name Chang 張. A native of Chia-hsing 嘉興, Chêkiang 浙江. Remarkably intelligent, he visited the monk Tao-ming Ch'an-shih 道明禪師 (*q.v.*), at Mu-chou 睦州, in the same province, and begged to be admitted as a disciple. "Three times the door was closed against him, but on the last occasion, his foot was crushed, and he found himself suddenly illumined." He afterwards studied under I-ts'un Ch'an-shih 義存禪師 (*q.v.*), and then opened his own school at Yün-mên 雲門, a mountain in Shantung 山東. Died A.D. 954. Buried at Lingshu 靈樹, in the same province. Posthumous title: Ta-tz'ŭ Yün-k'uang Chên-hung-ming Ch'an-shih 大慈雲匡眞弘明禪師, Great merciful, cloud-regulating, orthodox, vast and illustrious monk.

WÊN YÜAN-SHUAI 溫元帥.—Also called Fou-yu Wên
Yüan-shuai 孚祐溫元帥. An avatar of a *chia* 甲 Spirit (*v. Shih-
ërh Yüan-chia* 十二元甲). The right arm of the god of T'ai
Shan 泰山. Born in the market-town of Pai-shih Ch'iao 白石橋,
Whitestone Bridge, in Wên Chou 溫州, Chêkiang 浙江.
Though of plebian origin, his father had obtained a degree.
Having no child, he went with his wife, Chang-shih 張氏, named
Tao-hui 道輝, to pray to Hou T'u 后土 (*q.v.*) in her temple.
During the night, his wife dreamt that she saw a Spirit in golden
armour, holding a large axe in one hand and presenting her with
a shining pearl which he held in the other.

He informed her that he was one of the six Chia-shên 甲神
and a Marshal of Yü Ti 玉帝, that he wished to be reincarnated
as a man, and asked if she was willing to become his mother.
Chang-Shih 張氏 agreed, saying that he being a wise majestic
saint and she only a poor uneducated woman, she could not of
course refuse. The Spirit then placed the pearl in her womb
and she awoke. She remained pregnant for twelve months, and
the child was born on the fifth day of the fifth moon of the year
in the reign of the Emperor Shun Ti 順帝 (A.D. 126-45) of the
Han 漢 dynasty. When the babe was being washed, her cousin
remarked that it had twenty-four talismans written in unknown
characters on its left side, and sixteen on its right. However, all
trace of them soon disappeared. His mother having, in another
dream, seen a Spirit offering her a precious stone and a bracelet,
gave the infant the name of Huan 環, Bracelet, and as its
first name Tzǔ-yü 子玉, Child of the Precious Stone.

A precocious youth, he understood the Classics, historical
annals, astronomy, etc., but at 19 and 26 he failed in the civil and
military examinations respectively. He then made up his mind to
lead a hermit's life, and whilst he was meditating on this course,
a dragon appeared and dropped a pearl at his feet. He seized the
pearl and put it in his mouth to swallow it. The dragon started
dancing in front of him. Wang Yüan-shuai 王元帥 seized it
and curled it up, twisting its tail round his hand. Immediately
his face turned grey, his hair red, and his body blue, assuming a
terrifying aspect. Learning of his formidable transformation, the
god of T'ai Shan 泰山, the Southern sacred mountain, nominated
him his assessor in the government of that mountain, in which
office he acquired much merit.

Yü Huang 玉皇 canonized him first as the Great Spirit with
the Heart of Gold, and secondly, as Marshal, Chief of all the
Spirits, Director of all the functionaries of T'ai Shan 泰山. He
made him a present of a bracelet, a flower cut out of precious
stone, and a free pass of entry and exit. In his left hand he holds
a bracelet of precious stones, and in his right a *t'ieh-chien* 鐵簡,
spiked club.

His image appears in the temple of the god of T'ai Shan 泰山,

sometimes accompanied by two attendants and a horse.—See also *Mên Shén* 門 神.

WEST, THE GOD OF THE.—This god is Ju Shou 蓐 收, the Spirit of the first month of Spring (*mêng ch'un* 孟 春).

WESTERN AIR, THE SOVEREIGN OF THE.—See *Hsi Wang-mu* 西 王 母.

WESTERN PARADISE.—See *Hsi T'ien* 西 天.

WESTERN ROYAL MOTHER, THE.—See *Hsi Wang-mu* 西 王 母 and Du Bose, pp. 394-5.

WHEAT, THE GODDESS OF.—Du Bose (p. 76) says: "A merchant of North China in 1873 met a fair maiden with twin stalks of wheat growing from one grain, which he told her was an auspicious omen. She replied that she was going to the city of T'ung Chou 通 州 to order the harvest. The merchant, reporting the fact to the prefect, the latter had an image of the wheat-goddess made like this maiden with the twin stalks in her hand, and at the wheat harvest there are annual theatricals in her honour."

WHITE, MR.—See *Ch'êng Huang* 城 隍.

WHITE ANTS, THE GOD OF.—See *Wang Ta-hsien* 王 大 仙.

WHITE DRAGON.—See *Shui Fu* 水 府, D (1) (e).

WHITE HEN, THE.—See *Pai Chi* 柏 姬 or 白 鷄.

WHITE LOTUS, THE SERVANT OF THE.—See *Pai-lien T'ung-tzŭ* 白 蓮 童 子.

WHITE METAMORPHOSED ELEPHANT, A.—See *Ling-ya Hsien* 靈 牙 仙.

WHITE RULER, THE.—See *Venus*.

WHITE TIGER GOD, THE.—"The Emperor Hsüan Yüan 軒 轅 (2698-2598 B.C.) saw a god riding on a white tiger, and coming to his palace. The Western Royal Mother appointed the White Tiger God as ruler of the world" (Du Bose, p. 396).—See *Ch'ing-lung Pai-hu* 青 龍 白 虎.

WIG-MAKERS, THE GODDESS OF.—See *Chao San-niang* 趙 三 娘.

WILLOW, THE GOD OF THE.—"Twigs of the weeping willow are favourite emblems in the hands of gods and goddesses. A Mr. Lee (Li 李), walking through a willow-grove, was accosted by the willow-god, who told him to dye his clothing blue, as he would soon be the highest scholar in the empire. The prophecy was fulfilled by his appointment as Senior Wrangler at the Han-lin 翰林 College, Peking" (Pei-ching 北京, Chihli 直隸).—*Du Bose,* pp. 75-6.

WIND, THE GODS OF.—There are two Gods of Wind, namely, Fei Lien 飛廉 and Chi Po 箕伯. A Spiritual bird is mentioned in the *Yu hsüeh* 幼學 as the Wind-god. She is the spirit of the constellation Chi Shu-k'un 姬叔坤, and so is called Chi P'o 姬婆 (Fêng lao p'o p'o 風老婆婆).—See also *Fêng Po* 風伯.

WITCHES, THE GOD OF.—"He stands as a mediator beside the 'Five Holy Ones.' When one is afflicted with epilepsy the witches say, 'The Five Holy Ones call him,' and will advise appealing to the god of witches to intercede for him with these deities, and he will get well."—*Du Bose,* p. 394.

WINE-MERCHANTS, THE GODS OF.—See *Tu K'ang* 杜康 and *Ssŭ-ma Hsiang-ju* 司馬相如.

WOMB, THE GODDESS OF THE.—Name Mang Chin-i 芒金衣. Three inches in height. Worshipped to ensure safe child-birth.

WOMEN IMMORTALS, THE THREE.—See *Ma Ku* 麻姑.

WOOD, THE SPIRIT OF.—See *Wu Lao* 五老.

WORSHIP OF ANCESTORS.—This, in China, as in all other countries, is the root of religion, and is rightly described as the religion of China. It originates in the idea of the second self, or double, which gives rise to the idea, first of a concrete double, and later of a spiritual double or soul. This being propitiated and worshipped, leads to universal ancestor-worship.—See Werner, *The Chinese Idea of the Second Self* and *China of the Chinese,* Chap. VIII.

WRITING, THE GOD OF.—Ts'ang Chieh 倉頡 together with Tsu Sung 沮誦 was reputed as the inventor of the art of writing in the period of the Emperor Huang Ti 黃帝 (2698-2598 B.C.). He is said to have elaborated the art of forming written characters by imitating the footprints of birds. He was given the title Shih Huang 史皇, Prince of Scribes. The reverence for the written character was a kind of idolatry. Printed paper was sacred, the sin first mentioned is its misuse, and its preservation the first among meritorious actions. Waste paper was gathered up and burnt in the "Pity the Written Character" furnace. The ashes were sent to a port and carried out to sea, to be thrown overboard in a storm, so as to cause the waves to be stilled. These furnaces or altars were, and still are, often connected with temples, and large sums of money were thus expended. It was considered an offering to Confucius, and to the God of Literature.

WRITING-BRUSH, THE GOD OF THE.—See *Mêng T'ien* 蒙恬 and *Shun* 舜.

WU-CH'ANG KUEI 無常鬼.—Messengers of Yen Wang 閻王, King of Hell. When the years of a man's life are accomplished, the King sends his messengers to summon him to the Otherworld. There is a Yang Wu-ch'ang 陽無常, represented as a man, and a Yin Wu-ch'ang 陰無常, represented as a woman. Their images are to the right and left of Yen Wang 閻王 in Ch'êng Huang's 城隍 temple. The two, accompanied by the demons Horse Face (Ma Mien 馬面) and Ox Head (Niu T'ou 牛頭), call for the soul of the one dying. The local Earth-god escorts them to the house, where the spirit is given over into their hands by the Kitchen-god and the Earth-gods of the home. They then take it bound before the City-god, and from his court to that of the God of the Eastern Peak, Huang Fei-hu 黃飛虎. Here his good and evil deeds are passed upon, and he is then carried off to Hades. No one can escape these demons.

Yang Wu-ch'ang 陽無常, or Pai Lao-yeh 白老爺, is white; while Yin Wu-ch'ang 陰無常, or Hei Lao-yeh 黑老爺, is black. The Yang Wu-ch'ang 陽無常 takes those under fifty years of age, the Yin Wu-ch'ang 陰無常 those over fifty. Idol processions usually carry both. Yang Wu-ch'ang 陽無常 usually wears a long, pointed, high hat with the sentence *i chien ta chi* 一見大吉, "to see me is great fortune," written upon it.

At times, when one dies the *yang* 陽 breath does not scatter, and the demons are not able to take the soul to Hell. In this case the assistance of a "Walking Wu-ch'ang," Tsou Wu-ch'ang 走無常, is called upon. This is the spirit of some living being who has entered into a trance, and so is able to leave its body and perform this service. At times the souls of those living enter Hell to assist the judges as officials (*tso yin kuan* 做陰官), or for various other purposes.

When Wu-ch'ang 無常 comes for a soul he is led to the home by the Earth-god who, for this reason, is called the leader of the little demons.

Wu-ch'ang 無常 is a personification of the Buddhist doctrine of impermanency. There is growth and decay in everything. There is life and death for all creatures. Thoughts arise and vanish. Nothing is constant or unchanging. This is the principle of Wu-ch'ang 無常. However, the Wu-ch'ang 無常 are not thought of in this way by the common people. They know them as the demon messengers of Yen Wang 閻王.

WU-CHÊ 無著, *i.e.* Having no Attachment.—A deified Buddhist monk. Ranked second in Buddhist School, XII (*q.v.*). Asangha or Asamgha 阿 僧 伽, Elder brother of Vasubandu (*q.v.*). Also known as O-sêng-chia 阿 僧 迦. A native of Fu-lou sha-fu-lin 富 婁 沙 富 林, Gandhara. Lived mostly in Ayodhya (Oude). Was one of the early (some regard him as the principal) founders of the Yogachara, or Tantra School (see *Buddhist School,* XV), toward the close of the second century A.D. According to Eitel, he is said to have lived about A.D. 550. (It is possible that misprints have occurred with regard to Vasubandu's lifetime. Edkins, *Ch. Buddhism,* p. 278, note 2, says: "Eitel separates Vasubandu from Asengha by an interval of some centuries. My authority for making them brothers is the introduction to *Ch'êng-wei-shi-lun* [成 唯 識 論]. They were natives of Purusha in Grandhara— north end of the Punjab.")

He composed 500 works of commentaries on the Mahayana system, and 500 others on the Hinayana school, hence he is called "the author of a thousand discourses." His teachings received wide acceptation among early Buddhists, owing to the belief that he had been transported to the Tuchita heavens, where Maitreya taught him the principles of the Yogachara School. He is honoured in Chinese Buddhist temples.

WU CH'ÊNG 烏 成.—The god of the constellation Wei 胃. Alternatively with Sung Kêng 宋 庚.

WU-CHIAO SHAN 沃 焦 山.—See *Meru.*

WU CH'IEN 吳 謙.—The god of the star Pao-wei 豹 尾, Sworn brother of Huang Fei-hu 黄 飛 虎 and his companion in arms during the war against the tyrant Chou Wang 紂 王 (1154-1121 B.C.)

WU CHIH-CH'I 無 (巫) 支 祁.—See *Shui Fu* 水 府, D (1) (e).

WU CHIN-TSANG 無 盡 藏.—A saintly Buddhist monk. Eight century A.D. One of those invited to the annual banquet of the gods (see *Hsi Wang mu* 西 王 母 and *Hui Nêng* 慧 能).

WU-CH'IUNG 五 窮, THE GOD OF THE STAR.—See *Sun Ho* 孫 台.

WU-FANG LEI-KUNG 五 方 雷 公.—The Thunder-god of the Five Cardinal Points. An ugly monster invented as a fellow to Chiu-t'ien Lei-kung 九 天 雷 公 (*q.v.*).—See also *Lei Pu* 雷 部.

WU-FANG SHÊN 五 方 神.—The Spirits of the Five Cardinal Points. Specialists attached to the celestial Ministry of

Medicine. At the side of the altar to Yao Wang 藥王, the King of Medicine, is placed a small table on which are five images. These were originally titles of administrative offices (*v. infra*). In the centre, as President, is the image of *T'ai-i Chên-jên* 太乙 眞人 (*q.v.*). When Taoist priests are called in cases of sickness they place these small statues in the room, in the northern, southern, eastern, and western parts, with the fifth in the centre.

The legend relates that in the wars between the Yin 殷 dynasty and Wu Wang 武王 (1121-1114 B.C.), the founder of the Chou 周 dynasty, at a time when the ground was thickly covered with snow, five men, wearing clothes of five different colours, some on horseback, others in chariots, came to the door of the palace and requested an interview with the King. Wu Wang 武王 surprised, asked his minister, Chiang Tzŭ-ya 姜子牙, who these men were. The minister replied that they were named Chu-jung 祝融, Hsüan-ming 玄冥, Kou-mang 勾芒, and Ju-shou 蓐收, the Spirits of the South, North, East, and West, and were the four Great Protectors of his Majesty. Lung 龍, the son of Kung Kung 共工, was the protector of the territory. These are the Spirits of the Five Cardinal Points. The difference in the colour of their garments was of no significance.

The King having summoned them by name and asked them their mission, they replied that Heaven having decreed that the power was to pass to the Chou 周, all the Spirits should place themselves at his Majesty's service, and they had therefore come to receive his orders. The King, however, having protested his unworthiness, Chiang Tzŭ-ya 姜子牙 lodged them in the palace, and treated them with great deference.

During their long stay they made it known that the crimes of Chou 紂, the last Emperor of the Yin 殷, had caused to be let loose on earth the six demon-kings with their infernal legions, but that Chên Wu 眞武, the celestial envoy, wearing golden armour, and flying his black banner, had just gained a signal victory over them. He had crushed under his feet two infernal kings who had transformed themselves into a serpent and a tortoise, the victor ascending to Heaven to receive the title of honour bestowed upon him for his bravery.

The origin of these five Spirits is explained as follows:—From early times the Chinese had used the five forces or agents *chin* 金, metal, *mu* 木, wood, *shui* 水, water, *huo* 火, fire, and *t'u* 土, earth, to indicate the four cardinal points and the centre. Later on, these same characters were to distinguish the five classes of government Ministries, which received special names and were in the charge of high functionaries.

Thus the prefecture of *huo* 火, fire, was called Chu-jung 祝融 and was entrusted to Kao-hsin Shih 高辛氏 (2436-2366 B.C.), the grandson of Chuan Hsü 顓頊 (2514-2436 B.C.). The four uncles of Shao Hao 少昊 (2598-2514 B.C.) shared the other Ministries between them. That of *chin* 金, metal, called Ju-shou 蓐收, was administered by Kai 陔; that of *mu* 木, wood, called Kou-mang 勾芒, by Chung 重; that of *shui* 水, water, called Hsüan-ming 玄冥, by the two other brothers Hsiu 修 and Hsi 熙; that of *chung-yang* 中央, the centre, or of the earth (the territory) by Li 李, the grandson of Chuan Hsü 顓頊, son of Kung Kung 共公.

Thus, as stated above, these names of the Spirits of the Five Cardinal Points were not originally names of persons, but of offices or ministries. The Presidents of these Ministries gradually came to be regarded as Spirits and the names of their offices transferred to themselves. The Taoists invested these new Spirits with the jurisdictions of the Five Cardinal Points indicated by the five characters above-mentioned.—See also *T'ien I-yüan* 天醫院.

WU-FÊNG-HSÜEH CH'AN-SHIH 五峰學禪師 (68th generation).—A deified Buddhist monk. Ranked forty-eighth in Buddhist School, III (*q.v.*). Family name Ch'ang 常. A native of P'u-pan 蒲阪, Ho-tung 河東, Shansi 山西. He became a ⸬⸬⸬ ⸬ ⸬⸬ ⸬⸬ ⸬ ⸬⸬⸬⸬. His teachers were, first Chih-t'o 祇阤, and afterwards Yüan-wu Ch'an-shih 圜悟禪師 (*q.v.*) He lived in the Chi-shêng An 濟生庵, Chi-shêng Convent, until his death. His tomb is at Chin-ling (Kinling) 金陵 (modern Nanking 南京, Kiangsu 江蘇).

WU HAN 吳漢.—The god of the constellation K'ang 亢. Alternatively with Li Tao-t'ung 李道通.

WU HSIEN 五顯.—See *Wu Shêng* 五聖.

WU HSING 五行.—The Five Elements, or Natural Forces, of which the universe is composed or which operate in it. They are wood, fire, earth, metal, and water. Their combinations are the source of everything, even to the happiness or distress of a human life. They mutually cause each other, in rotation. Wood produces fire, fire earth, earth metal, metal water, water wood, and so on. From the opposite viewpoint, these elements are opposed to each other and mutually destructive. Wood overpowers earth, earth conquers water, water vanquishes fire, fire conquers metal, and metal overpowers wood. These when properly united, create an influence which creates peace and prosperity, or when incorrectly jointed, result in one which brings suffering and calamity to those living in that neighbourhood. They affect a person only while he remains in that locality. Should he move, he would put himself under the control of a different combination. Thus the five forces, from which everything comes, affect all life.

About 2500 B.C. the Emperor Chuan Hsü 顓頊 (2514-2436 B.C.) appointed six princes to govern the Five Regions of the universe, together with the five elements of which it is composed. These officials were later deified as the Five Emperors presiding over these regions. Their spirits, because they at times reside in

the Five Stars are alse called the Gods of the Five Planetary Stars.
—See Plopper, pp. 42-3, *Huo Pu* 火 部, and Doré, X, 801.

WU HSÜ 吳 旭.—The god of the star T'ien-su 天 速.—See
T'ien-kang 天 罡.

WU HUI 吳 回.—See *Huo Pu* 火 部 and *Tsao Chün* 灶 (竈) 君.

WU I 無 夷.—See *Shui Fu* 水 府, D (1) (e).

WU-JÊ-NAO 無 熱 惱.—A dragon-king.—See *Lung Wang*
龍 王.

WU JUNG 武 榮.—The god of the star Liu-hsia 流 霞. One
of Wu Wang's 武 王 generals. Slain by Ma Yüan 馬 元 at the
siege of Hsi-ch'i 西 岐 during the Yin-Chou 殷 周 wars.

WU-K'O CH'AN-SHIH 烏 窠 禪 師.—A deified Buddhist
monk. Ranked eighth in Buddhist School, I (*q.v.*).—See also
Lo-han 羅 漢.

WU-K'O SAN CHÊN-CHÜN 吳 客 三 眞 君.—The Three
Genii of the Wu 吳 State.—See *San Kuan* 三 官.

WU-KU 五 谷, THE GOD OF THE STAR.—See *Yin Hung*
殷 洪.

WU-KUAN WANG 五 官 王.—The President of the Fourth
Court of Hades (*q.v.*).

WU-KUEI 五 鬼, THE GOD OF THE STAR.—See *Têng
Hsiu* 鄧 秀.

WU K'UN 吳 坤.—The god of the constellation Liu 柳.
Alternatively with Jên Kuang 任 光.

WU-KUNG CHING 娛 蚣 精.—The Centipede Spirit. One
of the seven devils of Mei Shan 梅 山, Mount Mei, who placed
themselves at the service of the tyrant Chou Wang 紂 王 (1154-
1122 B.C.). An officer of the advance-guard, he changed himself
into a centipede and killed P'êng Tsu-shou 彭 祖 壽, Count of Yü
Chou 豫 州. After various successful ruses, he was eventually
slain by Yang Chien 楊 戩.

WU LAO 五 老.—The Five Old Men.—The Spirits of the
Five Natural Agents or Forces: metal, wood, water, fire, earth.
They were among the first human beings who appeared on the
earth.

1. The Spirit of Metal is Wang Mu 王母 or Chin Mu 金母. WU (?HU) P'ÊNG
She was born on K'un-lun Shan 昆崙山, the K'un-lun Mountains, of the *yin* 陰 and the *yang* 陽. At birth, her hair was in a
topknot on the top of her head, she had tiger's teeth, and a necklace of jade resting on a background of mulberry leaves (*cf. Hsi
Wang-mu* 西王母).

2. The Spirit of Wood is Mu Kung 木公, the God of the
Immortals. Born of the primeval air in the Wei-ling 危嶺 country
in the East. He made himself clothes of hawthorn leaves (*cf.
Tung Wang-kung* 東王公).

3. The Spirit of the Water is Shui Ching-tzǔ 水精子.
Born at Ts'ang-lang 滄浪 in the Northern regions. Very handsome. Made himself clothes of ebony-bark.

4. The Spirit of Fire, Ch'ih Ching-tzǔ 赤精子, first appeared
at Shih-t'ang Shan 石塘山, in the South. He also came from
the *yin* 陰 and the *yang* 陽. He resembled a man of fire, and
~~made himself clothes of red leaves.~~ He came down from a star
in the form of a streak of light.

5. The Spirit of the Earth is Huang Lao 黃老. He appeared
suddenly in the Southern regions, a product of moisture and heat.

The Wu Lao 五老 are also variously named as follows:
Shih-pa Kung (ching-chieh) 十八公 (勁節), Ku-chih Kung
孤直公, Ling K'ung-tzǔ 凌空子, Fu Yün-sou 拂雲叟, and
Hsing Hsien 杏仙.

In modern times it is customary to omit Wang Mu 王母, and
to speak of and represent only Ssǔ Lao 四老, the Four Old Men.
The Four and the Five Old Men are frequently depicted by
Chinese artists.

WU LEI-SHÊN 五雷神.—See *Lei Pu* 雷部.

WU-LU TS'AI-SHÊN 五路財神.—See *Ts'ai Shên* 財神.

WU LUNG 吳龍.—The god of the star P'o-sui 破碎. The
transcendent serpent. The vanquisher of P'êng Tsu-shou 彭祖壽
(*q.v.*). Slain by Yang Chien 楊戩, who transformed himself
into a cock and cut him in two with one peck of his beak.

WU-MU WANG 武穆王.—A title of Yo Fei 岳飛 (*q.v.*).

WU (?HU) P'ÊNG 巫彭.—A demi-god. A member of the
commission appointed by Huang Ti 黃帝 (*q.v.*) to continue and
complete the labours of Shên Nung 神農 on natural history and
the medicinal properties of plants. He specialized in surgery and
acupuncture.—See *T'ien I-yüan* 天醫院.

WU-PIEN-PU 無 邊 步.—A dragon-king.—See *Lung Wang* 龍王.

WU SHÊNG 五 聖.—The Five Saints. Composite deities. Also called Wu Hsien 五 顯, the Five Shining Ones, and Wu T'ung 五 通, the Five Penetrating or Intelligent Ones. The origin of these saints is to be traced to an incident which occurred in the year A.D. 885 of the reign of the Emperor Hsi Tsung 僖 宗 (A.D. 874-89) of the T'ang 唐 dynasty. A man named Wang Yü 王 喻 owned a garden outside the northern wall of the city. One evening, a blaze of light illumined the sky. The people ran to find out what had happened, and saw five Spirits in human form descending from the sky. They asked for Wang Yü 王 喻 and said to him: "By celestial mandate we have come here to receive sacrifices, for which we will give protection and happiness to the people." Wang Yü 王 喻 accordingly sacrificed to them, and they re-ascended to heaven. The people at once built a temple, in which they placed the images of the Five Spirits. They were at first known as the Wu T'ung 五 通. They were canonized and temples erected to them under the Sung 宋, Yüan 元, and Ming 明, dynasties, but were officially discountenanced under the Ch'ing 清 dynasties, though they were still worshipped and sacrificed to for relief in any kind of sickness.—See also *Composite Deities*.

WU SHU 吳 怨.—See *Shih Ming-i* 十 明 醫, 9.

WU SSǓ-T'U 五 司 徒.—See *Yang Chou wu ssŭ-t'u* 揚 州 五 司 徒.

WU SSǓ-YÜ 吳 四 玉.—The god of the star Ti-ku 地 孤.—See *Ti-sha* 地 煞.

WU TA CHIA 五 大 家.—See *Five Animals, The*.

WU TAI YÜAN-SHUAI 五 代 元 帥.—The Marshal of the Five Dynasties. The God of Musicians. This god had his origin in a practical joke played by his school-fellows on a young scholar who lived in the time of the Five Dynasties (A.D. 907-60). Whilst he was taking a siesta they drew a picture of a crab on his forehead, and stuck two willow-branches (sometimes represented as pheasant's tail-feathers) behind his ears. When he awoke he was so chagrined that he committed suicide.

This Spirit, honoured at Fu-chou (Foochow) 福 州, Fukien 福 建, under the name of Wu Tai Yüan-shuai 五 代 元 帥, Marshal of the Five Dynasties, is the same as Lei-hai Ch'ing 雷 海 青, of the T'ang 唐 dynasty, worshipped at several cities in Fukien 福 建. The character *hsieh* 蟹, crab, has approximately the same sound locally as *hai* 海, sea, and the willow-branches symbolize verdure, *ch'ing* 青. Lei Hai-ch'ing 雷 海 青 was a musician, and is popularly referred to in the district as Marshal. He died cursing robbers, and for that reason temples were erected to him. Thus the young scholar became apotheosized owing to this play on words having the same or similar sounds. He is represented as attended by two male and two female instrumentalists, holding respectively a mandolin, a lute, a violin, and a tambourine.

To evoke the Spirit, his image is placed on a raised platform, its forehead is dabbed with red, it is prayed to and candles and incense burnt before it. The priests kneel in front of it, and then rise, skipping about with dishevelled hair and staring eyes. Crying out that the Spirit has come, they scratch their tongues and write charms with the blood. When incense has been lit in the four corners of the room, everyone can ask of the Spirit what he wants, and the answer is explained by the accompanying musicians. He is frequently prayed to to remove abscesses, boils, etc., from children.

WU TANG SHÊNG-MU 武 當 聖 母.—A disciple of T'ung-t'ien Chiao-chu 通 天 教 主. After the battle of the Ten Thousand Genii, the T'ung-kuan 潼 關 Pass was taken by assault by Chiang Tzŭ-ya's 姜 子 牙 troops, the hostile armies were cut to pieces, the spirits and genii had to submit to their captors, and Wu-tang Shêng-mu 武 當 聖 母 took to flight.

WU-TAO CHIANG-CHÜN 五 盜 將 軍.—The Five Brigand Marshals. Their names were Tu P'ing 杜 平, Li Ssŭ 李 思, Jên An 任 安, Sun Li 孫 立, and Chung-ho 鍾 和. As they were terrorizing the country in the reign of the Emperor Fei Ti 廢 帝 (A.D. 465) of the Liu Sung 劉 宋 dynasty, the Emperor sent his general Chang Hung 張 洪 to exterminate them. After death they became ghosts, and the only way for the people to appease them was to sacrifice to them and address them as Marshals. Temples are to be seen dedicated to them in regions where travellers are exposed to danger from robbers, etc.—See also *Liu Chih* 柳 跖 and *Sung Chiang* 宋 江.

WU-TI 五 帝.—The Five Emperors. The Five Sovereigns of Heaven. In ancient times Shang Ti 上 帝 (*q.v.*) was sacrificed to as the sole protector of the four regions of the Empire, on a mound in each of those regions—*i.e.* the Centre, South, East, and West. These being designated by colours, there arose the designations: Yellow Sovereign, Red South, Green East, and White West respectively.

Ch'in Shih Huang-ti 秦 始 皇 帝 (221-209 B.C.), the First Emperor, said to his Ministers that he had heard there were five Sovereigns in Heaven, and that the gods must have been waiting to make him the fifth. Accordingly he created the Black Sovereign of the North, and gave orders that sacrifices should be performed to him on the Northern mound. His younger son (who became the Emperor Wên Ti 文帝) for the first time offered the sacrifice *chiao* 郊, in the suburb, to Yung 雍 and paid his respects to the Five Sovereigns. In spite of the remonstrances of the Scholars, who protested that there was only one Heaven, he erected a special temple to the Five Sovereigns to the North of the river Wei 渭. From that time, not a single Sovereign, but five distinct Sovereigns of Heaven were worshipped. In spite of the suppression in 32 B.C. of this worship by the Emperor Ch'êng Ti 成帝 (32-6 B.C.) it was restored by the Emperor Ai Ti 哀帝 (6 B.C.—A.D. I) in the year 5 B.C., and has continued down to modern times.—See also *Composite Deities*.

WU TING 五丁 SPIRITS, THE.—See *Huang-chin Li-shih* 黄金力士.

WU TOU 五斗.—The Five Bushels, Houses, or Constellations of the Five Directions: North, South, East, West, and Centre (corresponding to the terrestrial Wu Fang 五方). The gods of these, who were all officers of the armies of the Yin 殷 and the Chou 周 who died in the war which resulted in the placing of Wu Wang 武王 (1121-1114 B.C.) on the throne, are:—

Tung Tou 東斗, Eastern constellation: Su Hu 蘇護, Chin K'uei 金奎, Chi Shu-ming 姬叔明, and Chao Ping 趙丙.

Hsi Tou 西斗, Western Constellation: Huang T'ien-lu 黄天祿, Lung Huan 龍環, Sun Tzǔ-yü 孫子羽, Hu Shêng 胡升, and Hu Yün-p'êng 胡雲鵬.

Chung Tou 中斗, Central Constellation: Lu Jên-chieh 魯仁傑, Ch'ao Lei 晁雷, and Chi Shu-shêng 姬叔昇.

Nan Tou 南斗, Southern Constellation: Chou Chi 周紀, Hu Lei 胡雷, Kao Kuei 高貴, Yü Ch'êng 余成, Sun Pao 孫寶, and Lei K'un 雷昆.

Pei Tou 北斗, Northern Constellation: Huang T'ien-hsiang 黄天祥, Pi Kan 比干, Tou Jung 寶榮, Han Shêng 韓昇, Han Pien 韓變, Su Ch'üan-chung 蘇全忠, O Shun 鄂順, Kuo Ch'ên 郭宸, and Tung Chung 董忠.

More generally, the six gods are given as Shou Hsing 壽星 (Longevity), Kuo Tzǔ-i 郭子儀 (Happiness), Shih Fên 石奮 (Rank), Ch'ien Wu-su 錢武肅 (Peace), Kao Po-kung 高伯恭 (Rest), and Fêng Wên-i 馮文懿.

In popular ceremonial, there are seven gods of the Pei Tou 北斗, Great Bear, and six only of the Nan Tou 南斗, Southern constellation. Shou Hsing 壽星, the God of Longevity, is the chief of the star-gods of the South, and the ruler of waters, the third person of the San Kuan 三官 (*q.v.*) is the presiding deity of the stars of the Great Bear.

WU-TS'AI SHÊN 武財神.—See *Ts'ai Shên* 財神.

WU T'UNG 五通.—See *Wu Shêng* 五聖.

WU-TZŬ HSÜ 伍子胥.—The Yang-tzŭ 揚子 River Genius. Name Wu Yüan (or Yün) 伍員. A native of the Ch'u 楚 State. Minister of State in the time of the Wu Kuo 吳國, Kingdom of Wu. This kingdom comprised all Chêkiang 浙江, part of Kiangsu 江蘇, and extended west to the P'o-yang 鄱陽 Lake. Prince P'ing 平 of Ch'u 楚 having killed his father Wu Ch'ê 伍奢 and his brother Wu Shang 伍尙, he went over to Wu 吳 in 522 B.C., seeking to avenge them.

On his way thither he stopped by a river to drink, and asked a maiden for something to eat. She gave him food and then disappeared in the water. Later on, when he had made a position for himself, he returned and threw some gold pieces into the river as payment to his mysterious benefactress. Rising to eminence in the service of the Wu 吳 State, he urged the viscount of Wu 吳 to invade Ch'u 楚 (506 B.C.) and conducted expeditions against his native country. Prince P'ing 平 having died, Wu Tzŭ-hsü 伍子胥 had his corpse disinterred and flogged. He served Wu 吳 under three successive dynasties.

Finally Fu Ch'ai 夫差 (the last ruler of the house of Wu 吳), advised by Pai Pi 伯嚭, sent him a handsomely-carved sword, with which he committed suicide (484 B.C.). Fu Ch'ai 夫差, to prevent reprisals, had his body put in a leathern sack and buried in the sea (some say in the river near the modern city of Soochow, Su-chou 蘇州, Kiangsu 江蘇). Hence he became, in legend, a genie of the waters, and temples were dedicated by the people to his memory. He is the personification of vengeance, a thing sacred in China. Died 483 B.C.—See also *Shui Fu* 水府, D (2) (i).

WU-WAI TSUN-CHÊ 物外尊者.—A deified Buddhist monk. Ranked eleventh in Buddhist School, X (*q.v.*). Family name Yang 楊. A native of Hou-kuan 候官, Fukien 福建. Taught by Kuang-hsiu Tsun-chê 廣修尊者 (*q.v.*), under whom he studied the *Chih-kuan* 止觀, Perfected Observation. Died A.D. 885. His tomb is beside that of Chih-chê Ta-shih 智者大師 (*q.v.*).

WU-WEI CH'AN SHIH 無畏禪師.—The Fearless Monk. Abhayagiri the Fearless? A saintly Buddhist monk. Eighth century A.D. A contemporary of Vajramati. Born in India, he renounced a throne to become a Buddhist. In his native country, he was held in great esteem on account of his virtue and wisdom. Whenever he preached prodigies took place. He arrived in China with his companion Chin-kang San-ts'ang 金剛三藏 (see *Chin-kang Chih* 金剛智) during the reign of Hsüan Tsung 玄宗 (A.D. 713-56) of the T'ang 唐 dynasty. Wu-Wei's 無畏 Indian name is unknown. The Emperor held him in great esteem, and said: "You, who come from so far, where do you wish to dwell?"

"I wish to live in the Hsi-ming Ssŭ 西明寺" [Monastery of Western Brightness], he replied.

During his residence in that monastery he defied the abbot, Hsüan 宣, a strict disciplinarian, by breaking the rules as to abstaining from meat and strong drink. Furthermore, his speech and demeanour were rather lax. When intoxicated, he became uproarious and upset everything in his cell. The abbot, who on this account held him in abhorrence, proceeded one night to his cell with the intention of giving him a thrashing. Wu-wei 無畏, however, in drunken tones asked him if he wished to kill the child of Buddha. This caused the abbot to change his mind, and instead of punishing him he adopted him as his teacher.

At Lo-yang 洛陽, Honan 河南, a snake 100 feet long was terrorizing the whole neighbourhood, and Wu-wei 無畏 prophesied that it prognosticated a great calamity to the city. He therefore recited some prayers, which caused a strong gust of wind to bring the snake to him. The snake was so overcome by the reproof administered to him, that he fell dead on the spot. Shortly afterwards, the rebel general, An Lu-shan 安祿山, captured Lo-yang 洛陽, and destroyed all the monasteries and part of the city. Thus the monk's prophecy was fulfilled.

Other accomplishments of his were the procuring and stopping of rain as ordered by the Emperor Ming Huang 明皇 (A.D. 713-56) of the T'ang 唐 dynasty, and the rescue of a prayer manual from the back of a snake swimming in a stream, for which meritorious act Lung Wang 龍王, the Dragon-king, invited him to his palace for three days and three nights. When he returned from the water, the manual was found not to have suffered in any way from its long immersion.

A few days afterwards he said to Chin-kang San-ts'ang 金剛三藏: "I am the first to go." With these words, he expired peacefully.

He is portrayed by Chinese artists with features exhibiting little of his Indian origin. He is one of the guests at the annual banquet of the gods (see *Hsi Wang-mu* 西王母).—See also *Buddhist Schools*, XV.

WU WÊN-HUA 鄔文化.—The god of the star Li-shih 力士. Grand Marshal of the royal armies in the Yin-Chou 殷周 wars. Decoyed by Chiang Tzŭ-ya 姜子牙, to P'an-lung Ling 蟠龍嶺, the P'an-lung Range, and there burnt alive.

WU YEN-KUNG 武衍公.—The god of the star Ti-chuang 地壯.—See *Ti-sha* 地煞.

WU YO 五嶽. — The Five Peaks. The Five Sacred Mountains. The Ministry of the Five Sacred Mountains. To the original four, *viz.* North: Hêng Shan 恒山, in Shansi 山西 (?Chihli 直隸); South: Hêng Shan 衡山, in Hunan 湖南; East:

T'ai Shan 泰 山, in Shantung 山東; and West: Hua Shan 華 山, in Shensi 陝 西, there was in course of time added a fifth, *viz.* that of the Centre: Sung Shan 嵩 山, in Honan 河南.

Under the T'ang 唐 dynasty, Hêng Shan 衡 山, in Hunan 湖 南 being found too inaccessible, Ho Shan 霍 山, in Anhui 安徽, was substituted for it. From that time, Ho Shan 霍 山 has sometimes been called Hêng Shan 衡 山, and sometimes Nan Yüeh 南嶽, the sacred Mountain of the South.

The worship of these mountains dates at least from the time of Yao 堯 (2357-2255 B.C.) and probably from that of Huang Ti 黃 帝 (2698-2598 B.C.). It had a politico-religious significance. Ch'in Shih Huang-ti 秦始皇帝, the First Emperor, inaugurated, in 219 B.C., the ceremony of canonizing the sacred mountains by performing the supernatural investiture at T'ai Shan 泰 山 (for details see *Chavannes, Le T'ai Shan,* and for a historical summary, *Doré,* X, 834-9; 841-5). Temples to the sacred mountains began to be erected in A.D. 396, the practice continuing at intervals during subsequent epochs nearly all, however, being built during the T'ang 唐 dynasty.

The names of the Spirits of the Five Sacred Mountains are given in two lists in the *Yüan-chien lei-han* 淵 鑑 類 函 as follows: —Yüan Ch'ang-lung 圓常龍, the Spirit of the East; Tan Ling-chih 丹靈峙, the Spirit of the South; Hao Yü-shou 浩鬱狩, the Spirit of the West; Têng Wei-t'ing 澄渭亭, the Spirit of the North; and Shou I-ch'ün 壽逸羣, the Spirit of the Centre.

The second list is:—Marshal T'ang Ch'ên 唐 臣, the Spirit of the East; Marshal Chu Tan 朱 丹, the Spirit of the South; Marshal Tsou Shang 鄒 佝, the Spirit of the West; Marshal Mo Hui 莫 惠, the Spirit of the North; and Marshal Shih Hsüan-hêng 石玄恒, the Spirit of the Centre.

A further list is given in the *Fên-shên yen-i* 封神演義. It contains the names of generals or statesmen who rendered distinguished service in the wars which put an end (1121 B.C.) to the Yin 殷 dynasty, were canonized by Chiang Tzŭ-ya 姜子牙, and are generally accepted by the people as the gods of the five sacred mountains. It is as follows:—Huang Fei-hu 黄飛虎 became god of the Eastern Peak; Ts'ung Hei-hu 崇黑虎 became god of the Southern Peak; Wên P'in 聞聘 became god of the Central Peak; Ts'ui Ying 崔英 became god of the Northern Peak; and Chiang Hsiung 蔣雄 became god of the Western Peak.

The God of T'ai Shan 泰 山 predominates over the rest. He is, on earth, the *alter ego* of Yen Wang 閻王 (*q.v.*), the King of the Hells. Hence life, death, reincarnation, the government of men, of spirits, etc., can be appealed to the sacred peak of T'ai Shan 泰 山, the seat of the God's authority. He fulfils the same role with the Taoists as Ti Tsang-wang 地藏王 with the Buddhists, and is also worshipped by the latter.

Du Bose (p. 387) adds some interesting particulars:—"The 'Eastern Peak' is Mount T'ai 泰, and this is the god of that mountain; his reputation having rapidly increased during the last century. The Chinese have not very distinct ideas about the rulers of Tartarus, so among others he is now considered the 'god of the Judgment Day.' At the 'Fall Judgment' the Taoists issue proclamations, calling on all the orphan spirits to assemble and receive sentence, as he holds in his hand the awards of good and evil, but he considers the hypocrite who pays his fee as a good man.

"The rank of the Eastern Peak among the long columns of native gods is as high as the lofty summit of Mount T'ai 泰 among the ranges of Chinese hills. One feature of his worship in some places differs from others, in that the temples belong to families and have no priesthood, so the devotees are both men and women who mingle in the nocturnal devotions. At a Hangchou 杭 州, Chêkiang 浙 江, temple it has been computed that £200 every night of the worship season was spent in burning paper money, contributed by the gentry and by pilgrims. At this time also the sick are brought for healing, and lunatics in his presence are cured by casting out of devils. In this temple the processions with torches and lanterns, the tinsel and embroidery, the solemn prostrations and the mimic of a royal pantomime, are as gorgeous as Chinese art can devise."

For a still further list of the gods of the sacred mountains, see *Pi-hsia Yüan-chün* 碧 霞 元 君.

The Spirit of the Eastern Sacred Mountain fixes the day of birth and death; distributes riches and honours; and has a branch of Yen Wang's 閻 王 court on Mount T'ai Shan 泰 山. The Spirit of the Southern Sacred Mountain controls the stars incarnated (according to the Taoist doctrine) in humanity; and aquatic animals, etc. The Spirit of the Central Sacred Mountain administers the affairs relating to lands, lakes, water courses, valleys, canals, hills, mountains, forests, and the vegetable kingdom. The Spirit of the Western Sacred Mountain is in charge of metals, their fusion and fabrication, and also of volatile substances. The Spirit of the Northern Central Mountain is superintendent of rivers, streams, tigers, leopards and all quadrupeds, reptiles, and worms.

WU-YÜN HSIEN 烏 雲 仙.—The *ao* 鰲 or Transcendent Tortoise.—See *Shui-huo T'ung-tzŭ* 水 火 童 子.

Y

YAKCHA.—See *Yaksha*.

YAKSHA. YAKCHA.—Yeh Ch'a 夜又.—A species of demons living in the earth and waters, often represented as malignant toward men and devouring them. When moving fast, they resemble shooting stars or comets. Dragon-kings. They are otherwise described as a class of good genii, ruled over by Kuvera (Vaisramana), the Hindu God of Wealth. Authorities differ as to their origin. "They have no very special attributes, but they are generally considered as inoffensive, and so are called Punya-janas, 'good people,' but they occasionally appear as imps of evil. It is a Yaksha in whose mouth Kali-dasa placed his poem *Megha-duta* (cloud messenger)" (*Dowson*).—See also *Lung Wang* 龍王.

YAMA.—The King of the Demons. In Hindu mythology the ruler of the dead (*v. infra*). From his office as judge of future punishments, his name constantly occurs in the conversation of the common people in China. He is called Yen-mo-lo-shih 閻摩羅士 (formerly Jam-ma-la-ja＝Yeh-ma-lu-chia 夜摩盧迦), which is abbreviated to Yen-lo 閻羅. The usual Hindoo name may be recognized in Yen-ma 閻摩 and Yeh-ma 夜摩, which are other designations applied to him in Chinese books. Jam-ma-raja means the "Royal pair," a brother and sister, who judge men and women respectively. Associated with Yen-lo 閻羅 are nine kings who preside together over the state of the dead. His image is placed with theirs in temples, accompanied with various representations suited to remind the spectator of the world of torment. In the *Ti-tsang* 地藏 *Sutra*, he is described as coming from the iron mountain wall where the Buddhist hell is situated, to the Ta-li 達利 heaven, to hear Sakyamuni Buddha deliver a *sutra* there. He is classed among the sons of Devas, and is attended by many thousand kings of demons. He may be pointed to as the most remarkable example of the influence of Hindu mythology on the popular mind of China. The common people all expect to meet Yen-lo Wang 閻羅王 (Yama) after death, and be judged by him with the strictest impartiality. They believe that he fixes the hour of dissolution, and that the decision once made, nothing can alter or postpone it (See *Yen-lo Wang* 閻羅 王).

In the *Vedas* (Yama, 'Restrainer,' Pluto, Minos) is god of the dead, with whom the spirits of the departed dwell. He was the son of Vivaswat (the Sun), and had a twin-sister named Yami or Yamuna. These are by some looked upon as the first human pair, the originators of the race; and there is a remarkable hymn, in the form of a dialogue, in which the female urges their cohabitation for the purpose of perpetuating the species. Another hymn says that Yama "was the first of men that died, and the first that departed to the (celestial) world." He it was who found out the way to the home which cannot be taken away: "Those who are now born (follow) by their own paths to the place whither our ancient fathers have departed." "But," says Dr. Muir, "Yama is nowhere represented in the *Rig-veda* as having anything to do with the punishment of the wicked." So far as is yet known, "the hymns of that *Veda* contain no prominent mention of any such penal retribution . . . . Yama is still to some extent an object of terror. He is represented as having two insatiable dogs with four eyes and wide nostrils, which guard the road to his abode, and which the departed are advised to hurry past with all possible speed. These dogs are said to wander about among men as his messengers, no doubt for the purpose of summoning them to their master, who is in another place identified with death, and is described as sending a bird as the herald of doom."

In the epic poems Yama is the son of the Sun by Sanjna (conscience), and brother of Vaivaswata (Manu). Mythologically he was the father of Yudhi-shthira. He is the god of departed spirits and judge of the dead. A soul when it quits its mortal form repairs to his abode in the lower regions; there the recorder, Chitra-gupta, reads out his account from the great register called Agra-sandhani, and a just sentence follows, when the soul either ascends to the abodes of the Pitris (Manes), or is sent to one of the twenty-one hells according to its guilt, or it is born again on earth in another form. Yama is regent of the south quarter and as such is called Dakshinasa-pati. He is represented as of a green colour and clothed with red. He rides upon a buffalo, and is armed with a ponderous mace and a noose to secure his victims.

In the *Puranas* a legend is told of Yama having lifted his foot to kick Chhaya, the handmaid of his father. She cursed him to have his leg affected with sores and worms, but his father gave him a cock which picked off the worms and cured the discharge. Through this incident he is called Sirna-pada, 'shrivelled foot.'

Yama had several wives, as Hemamala, Su-sila, and Vijaya. He dwells in the lower world, in his city Yamapura. There, in his palace called Kalichi, he sits upon his throne of judgment, Vichara-bhu. He is assisted by his recorder and councillor, Chitra-gupta, and waited upon by his two chief attendants and custodians, Chanda or Mahachanda, and Kala-pursusha. His messengers, Yama-dutas, bring in the souls of the dead, and the door of his judgment-hall is kept by his porter, Vaidhyata.

Yama has many names descriptive of his office. He is Mrityu, Kala, and Antaka, 'death'; Kritanta, 'the finisher'; Samana, 'the settler'; Dandi or Danda-dhara, 'the rodbearer'; Bhimasasana, 'of terrible decrees'; Pasi, 'the noose-carrier'; Pitripati, 'lord of the manes'; Preta-raja, 'king of the ghosts'; Sraddha-deva, 'god of the exequial offerings'; and especially Dharma-raja, 'king of justice.' He is Audumbara, from Udumbara, 'the fig-tree,' and from his parentage he is Vaivaswata. There is a *Dharma-sastra* (law-book or code of laws) which bears the name of Yama.

YAMI.—The goddess of the Yamuna river. Sister of Yama (*q.v.*).

YANG 陽.—See *Yin* 陰 and *Yang* 陽.

YANG-CH'AI 陽差, THE GOD OF THE STAR.—See *Ma Ch'êng-lung* 馬成龍.

YANG CHÊN 楊眞.—The god of the constellation Chi 箕. Alternatively with Fêng I 馮異.

YANG CH'ÊNG 楊成.—See *Ts'ai Shên* 財神.

YANG CHIEN 楊戩.—Nephew of Yü Huang 玉皇. A genie capable of marvellous feats, which he used to great advantage in the wars which took place during the consolidation of the Chou 周 dynasty.—See Werner, *Myths,* pp. 122, 123, 147, 162 *seq.,* and 242.

YANG CHING 羊精.—The Goat Spirit. The presiding deity of the star Fan-yin 反吟. Yang Hsien 楊顯 (*q.v.*) of Mei Shan 梅山 was a transcendent goat. His face was white, his head furnished with horns, he wore a long beard and a special kind of head-dress. Being beheaded by Yang Chien 楊戩 in one of the innumerable combats of the unsettled period at the end of the Yin 殷 and beginning of the Chou 周 dynasties, the former ran and notified Chiang Tzŭ-ya 姜子牙 that he had just slain one of the "destructive devils" who were obstructing his military measures for the overthrow of his enemies. He is also worshipped as a god in Mongolia. In the pictorial representations he does not follow the analogy of the Dog Spirit (see *Kou Ching* 狗精 and *Composite Deities*) by being shown as a composite creature, though he is depicted with two horns on his head, or his hair done in the shape of two short horns.

YANG CHOU 揚州, THE FIVE DIRECTORS OF.—See *Yang Chou wu Ssŭ-t'u* 揚州五司徒.

YANG CHOU WU SSŬ-T'U 揚州五司徒.—The Five Directors of Yang Chou 揚州. The five illustrious presidents of the Ministry of Agriculture, Mao 茅, Hsü 許, Huang 況, Chiang 蔣, and Wu 吳, sworn brothers, lived a long while in Yang Chou 揚州, Kiangsu 江蘇. They were brave hunters with supernatural influence over wild animals. A temple was erected in their honour. The Emperor Yang Ti 煬帝 (A.D. 605-17) of the Sui 隋 dynasty bestowed on them the title of Ssŭ-t'u 司徒, or President of Ministry, for safeguarding his equipage from attack, and under the Sung 宋 Emperor Li Tsung 理宗 (A.D. 1225-65) they received the title of Marquis. They are also styled Wang 王, Kings. Invoked in cases of drought or excessive rainfall.—See also *Composite Deities*.

YANG HOU 陽侯.—See *Shui Fu* 水府, C (1) (a) and D (2) (i).

YANG HSIEN 楊顯.—The god of the star Fan-yin 反吟. The transcendent goat, a genie of Mei Shan 梅山 in the service of Yüan Hung 袁洪 at Mêng-ching 孟津, during the Yin-Chou 殷周 wars. Being frightened by Yang Chien 楊戩 who had transformed himself into a tiger, he fled, and was cut to pieces by the enemy's soldiers.—See also *Yang Ching* 羊精.

YANG HSIN 楊信.—The god of the constellation Tou 斗. Alternatively with Chu Yu 朱祐.

YANG-JÊN 羊刃, THE GOD OF THE STAR.—See *Chao Shêng* 趙昇.

YANG LI-KUNG 陽勵公.—A famous (apotheosized) physician and surgeon. Second century A.D.

YANG SHIH 楊氏.—The goddess of the star Hung-yen 紅艷. A concubine of the tyrant Chou Wang 紂王 (1154-1121 B.C.). She hanged herself in anticipation of the punishment she feared for saving the lives of the two sons of Queen Chiang 姜.

YANG-SHIH (LI-CHUNG) 楊峙 (立中).—See *Ch'ing-wa Shên* 青蛙神.

YANG SSŬ CHIANG-CHÜN 楊四將軍.—General Yang Ssŭ 楊 四. Worshipped by boatmen, managers of rafts, and wood-merchants, as the protector of the rafts of timber which are floated down the rivers. In one hand he holds a dragon, as a sign of his power over waters and storms, in the other an axe, the emblem of workers in wood.

He is one of Lung Wang 龍 王, the dragon-king's, generals, and is in control of the policing of the waters. His image is to be seen in many temples.

YANG TA T'IEN-CHÜN 楊大天君.—See *Ch'ü-hsieh Yüan* 驅邪院.

YANG TÊ-TSU 楊 德 祖.—See *Chieh K'ung* 解空.

YANG-TZŬ CHIANG SAN-SHUI FU 揚 子 江 三 水 府.— See *Shui Fu* 水 府, D (1) (a).

YANG-TZŬ RIVER GENIUS, THE. See *Wu-tzŭ Hsü* 伍 子 胥.

YANG WÊN-CH'ANG 楊文昌.—A celebrated T'u Ti 土 地 (*q.v.*).

YANG WÊN-HUI 楊 文 輝.—See *Wên Pu* 瘟 部.

YANG YÜAN-SHUAI 楊 元 帥.—The son of Yang 楊, his mother being Hsü 徐. He was born during the Han 漢 dynasty, and named Piao 彪, Tiger-cat, a tiger having been seen a few minutes before his birth. Having become an official, he persuaded the Emperor to pardon a robber condemned to death, and refused a large bribe offered him by the local officials.

Appointed to Yang Chou 揚 州, Kiangsu 江 蘇, he became famous for his courage and honesty. Shang Ti 上 帝 bestowed on him the dignity of Terrestrial Spirit, with a military subordinate, and power in this world over retribution of the good and bad actions of human beings and over the demons of the mountains and sea; in the other world, jurisdiction over the devils of the five directions and ten princes of hell (see *Hades*).

YAO 堯.—The legendary Emperor of China's "golden age." He had a miraculous birth and ascended the throne 2357 B.C. and after reigning seventy, or as others say ninety-eight, years, abdicated in favour of Shun 舜.—See also *San Kuan* 三 官.

YAO CH'I 姚 期.—The god of the constellation Ching 井. Alternatively with Shên Kêng 沈 庚.

YAO CHIN-HSIU 姚 金 秀.—The god of the star Ti-chou 地 周. —See *Ti-sha* 地 煞.

YAO CHUNG 姚 忠.—The god of the star Yüeh-yen 月 厭. A subordinate officer of Chou Wang's 紂 王 armies. Fought under general Tu Jung 竇 榮 at Yu-hun Kuan 遊 魂 關, during the Yin-Chou 殷 周 wars.

YAO HSÜAN 堯 喧.—See *Ch'ü-hsieh Yüan* 驅 邪 院.

YAO HUA 姚 燁.—The god of the star Ti-hao 地 耗.—See *Ti-sha* 地 煞.

YAO KUAI 妖 怪.—A special category of malevolent beings. They assume all kinds of forms. It is believed that extreme age generates soul substance, and the spirits thus produced are called *yao kuai* 妖 怪.

YAO KUNG 姚 公.—The god of the star T'ien-tsui 天 罪.— See *T'ien-kang* 天 罡.

YAO KUNG-HSIAO 姚 公 孝.—The god of the star T'ien-yung 天 勇.—See *T'ien-kang* 天 罡.

YAO KUNG-PO 姚 公 伯.—The god of the constellation Fang 房. Alternatively with Kêng Yen 耿 弇.

YAO SHAO-SSǓ 姚 少 司.—See *Ministries: Finance.*

YAO-SHIH FO 藥 師 佛.—The Healing Teacher, Supreme Physician, Medical (or Doctor) Buddha (Baishajyaguru). Also called Yao-shih Wang 藥 師 王 and Liu-i Fo (or Wang) 琉 璃 佛 (or 王), Vaidurya (*v. infra*). He is worshipped in China, Japan, Tibet and Manchuria. He is supposed to have lived in a previous *kalpa*. His birthday is celebrated on the twenty-eighth day of the fourth month. Having received his power of healing from Gautama, he dispenses spiritual medicine, when properly worshipped. The widespread superstition of healing resulting from touching a saint's image is here illustrated afresh, the process being for the sufferer to touch the eye, ear, or other part of the image and then to apply his finger to the corresponding affected part of his own body—a sort of inverted form of the "king's touch" of English history. "In China and Japan he is generally represented in bronze, but in paintings the colour must be blue."

Yao-shih Fo 藥 師 佛 is the ruler of a world situated in endless space somewhere to the East. It is composed of lapis-lazuli (hence the name Liu-li Wang 琉 璃 王), its walls and palaces of the seven precious stones and metals, and its streets of gold. Between it and our world there intervene kingdoms of Buddhas to the number of the grains of sand of the Ganges.

Yao-shih Fo 藥 師 佛 has two assistant Bodhisattvas to help him in removing suffering: Yao Tsang 藥 藏, the "Treasury of

Medicinal Herbs," also called *Jih-kuang pien-chao* 日光遍照, "All pervading light of the Sun," and Yao-wang 藥王, the "King of Medicinal Herbs," also known as *Yüeh-kuang pien-chao* 月光遍照, the "All pervading light of the Moon."—See also *Yao Wang* 藥王.

YAO-SHIH WANG 藥師王.—Vaidurya Buddha. Known as Liu-li Fo 琉璃佛, or Wang 王, Crystal Buddha, or King, and worshipped in China as a god of healing.—See *Yao-shih Fo* 藥師佛.

YAO SHU-LIANG 姚庶良.—The god of the star Fu-yin 伏吟. The Marquis of Tso-po 左伯. Joined battle with Ch'ang Hao 常昊 at Mêng-ching 孟津 in the Yin-Chou 殷周 wars. Was at first victorious, but suddenly Ch'ang Hao 常昊 transformed himself into a serpent, flew into the air, and descending on the marquis from above, unhorsed him, he being immediately killed by a lance-thrust.

YAO TSANG 藥藏.—See *Yao-shih Fo* 藥師佛.

YAO WANG 藥王.—The King of Medicines or Remedies. Family name Sun Ssŭ-miao 孫思邈. Personal name Chih-wei 知微. Born at Hua-yüan 華原, Shensi 陝西. Showed marked ability at a very early age, being able to learn a thousand characters a day. Withdrawing to live a hermit's life on T'ai-po Shan 太白山 on account of the disturbances which took place in the reign of Hsüan Wang 宣王 (827-721 B.C.), he was initiated by Chiu Chên-jên 仇眞人 (*q.v.*) into the secrets of the *yin* 陰 and the *yang* 陽, the science of immortality, etc. Leaving to go on a journey, he saw on the way a shepherd trying to kill a snake. He saved the reptile by giving his cloak to the shepherd, healed its wounds, and let it go into the grass. Ten days later, when on one of his journeys, a horseman dressed in white met him, dismounted, and saluting him respectfully said: "My father has sent me to request you to go to him to receive his thanks." He made him mount his horse, and almost immediately they reached a magnificent city. The rider bade him enter the door of an imposing palace. He was received by a person of noble bearing and dress, followed by a large suite, who said to him: "I sent my son to invite you here in order that I may offer you my sincerest thanks." The next moment a young woman brought an infant dressed in blue, and said to him: "My child had gone out alone to play, when a shepherd struck him roughly. You redeemed him by surrendering your cloak, and so saved his life. Allow me to express my most profound gratitude." Sun Ssŭ-miao 孫思邈 then recalled the incident of the shepherd and the snake on his previous journey.

Enquiring of the officers who this personage, whom they addressed as king, was he was informed that he was King Ching Yang 涇 陽, of the Palace of the Waters, *i.e.* Lung Wang 龍王, the Dragon-king. (On the day in question the son of Lung Wang 龍 王 was strolling about in the form of a snake. At other times he moved in the waters in the form of a carp.)

The King having prepared a banquet in his honour, Sun Ssŭ-miao 孫 思 邈 asked to be excused, as he lived only on air, but added that he drank wine. Accordingly, he was fêted for three days, after which the King presented him with silks, embroideries, gold and pearls. These Sun Ssŭ-miao 孫 思 邈 refused. The King then ordered his attendants to present him with thirty chapters of the work *Lung-ts'ang* 龍 藏, *The Secrets of the Dragon,* which would be of use to him in benefiting humanity. He then had a horse saddled, and Sun Ssŭ-miao 孫 思 邈 was escorted back. He at once added these thirty chapters of marvellous recipes to his great work, *Ch'ien-chin chien-i-fang* 千 金 簡 易 方. This celebrated work is composed of thirty books, each containing a chapter of *The Secrets of the Dragon.*

On another occasion Sun Ssŭ-miao 孫 思 邈 met a tiger, which seemed to be imploring his help, a bone having stuck in its throat. Sun Ssŭ-miao 孫 思 邈 having extracted it by use of a forceps, the tiger wagged its tail as a sign of gratitude, and then placed itself at his service to guard his gate.

Sun Ssŭ-miao 孫 思 邈 refused the title of Doctor of the Realm bestowed on him by the Emperor Wên Ti 文帝 (A.D. 590-605) of the Sui 隋 dynasty, in recognition of his knowledge of the secrets of the dragon and the tiger, saying that in fifty years' time he would become a saint. On the expiration of that time he was given an honourable post in the palace, and treated with with great respect by the Emperor, who wished to retain him as physician to the metropolis.

For curing, during the reign-period A.D. 674-6, the Emperor Kao Tsung 高宗 (A.D. 650-84) of the T'ang 唐 dynasty, of a bad headache he was presented with a fine horse and the district of Pan-yang 郫 陽, after having refused an imperial censorship. Later on, he cured the same Emperor of dysentery, after opposing the views of the most celebrated physicians of the time as to the seat of the malady, they contending that the stomach required strengthening, he, that the kidneys were at fault.

Sun Ssŭ-miao 孫 思 邈 was the friend, counsellor, and physician of all the chief personages of that epoch. He died in A.D. 682, his body remaining in a perfect state of preservation for a whole month. When about to be placed in the coffin, it was found that the corpse had disappeared, the clothes only remaining.

He is represented in pictures and images as attended by two youthful servants, the one carrying his gourd full of his wonderful pills, and the other presenting him with a leaf of a medicinal herb.—See also *T'ien I-yüan* 天 醫 院, *Wei Ku* 韋 古, *Wei Shan-*

chün 韋善俊, *Pien Ch'iao* 扁鵲, *Shih Ming-i* 十明醫, and *Yao-shih Fo* 藥師佛.

YEAR, THE GOD OF THE. — Name Li Ping 李丙. —

A son of the Emperor Shou 受 (1154-1122 B.C.), named Yin-chou 殷紂. His father, the abandoned tyrant, killed Yin-chou's 殷紂 mother at the instigation of a concubine, and was about to kill the son, when he fled, and one of the genii took him for a disciple. Afterwards in battle he was defeated, and Jan Têng 燃燈 Buddha caused two hills to meet and hold him as in a vice. Chiang T'ai-kung 姜太公 made him the T'ai Sui 太歲 god. He is one of the fiercest gods in China. Worshipped by the officials at the reception of spring.—See *T'ai Sui* 太歲.

YEH CH'A 夜叉.—A dragon-king.--See *Lung Wang* 龍王 and *Yaksha*.

YEH CHUNG CHANG 葉 中 正. The god of the star Ti-chien 地健.—See *Ti-sha* 地煞.

YEH CHUNG 葉中.—The god of the star Ti-fei 地飛.—See *Ti-sha* 地煞.

YEH JÊN 野人.—The Desert Savage. A disciple of Ko Hung 葛洪, *alias* Pao P'u-tzŭ 抱朴子 (*q.v.*), the celebrated Taoist teacher of the fourth century A.D. Honoured as a genie by the Taoists. He became a terrestrial Immortal through eating one of the pills of immortality hidden by his master, before passing on to the next life, in a stone column on Lo-fou Shan 羅浮山, Mount Lo-fou. He is seen by travellers, completely naked except for long hair covering his body, on that mountain, and passes his time wandering about and singing cheerful ditties.

YELLOW RULER, THE.—See *Saturn*.

YEN-CHAO CH'AN-SHIH 延沼禪師 (41st generation).—

A deified Buddhist monk. Ranked fourteenth in Buddhist School, III (*q.v.*) Family name Liu 劉. A native of Yü-hang 餘杭, Studied for six years under Hui-yung Ch'an-shih 慧顒禪師 (*q.v.*), and became highly proficient in the Doctrine. Died A.D. 973, aged 78.

YEN CHÊN-CH'ING 顏眞卿.—See *Pei-chi Ch'ü Hsieh-yüan* 北極驅邪院.

YEN CHÜN-P'ING 嚴君平.—Born at Lin-chiung 臨邛, Ssŭch'uan 四川. His first name was Tsun 遵. In the *I-ching* 易經 it is stated that he practised as a diviner in the streets of

Ch'êng-tu 成都, the capital of the province. As soon as he had received ten copper coins he returned to his house. In his youth he had as master the hermit Yang Jung 楊雄, who lived on the south of Min Shan 岷山, Mount Min, in Ssǔch'uan 四川, during the reign-period Yüan-ting 元鼎 (116-110 B.C.) of the Emperor Wu Ti 武帝 (140-86 B.C.) of the Ch'ien-Han 前漢, Former Han, dynasty.

YEN-K'OU-HAI-KUANG 焰口海光.—A dragon-king.—See Lung Wang 龍王.

YEN-KUANG P'U-SA 眼光菩薩.—The Goddess of the Light of the Eye. One of the specialists attached to the celestial Ministry of Medicine. Is represented holding an eye in her two hands; sometimes the eye is placed in a dish at her feet. Worshipped by those with eye troubles and by those who wish to avoid them. Her image is to be seen in all the temples dedicated to the medicine-gods. She was formerly represented in company with the Goddess of T'ai Shan 泰山, Mount T'ai 泰, the Goddess of the Dawn (see Chun T'i 準提), to whom she is the chief assistant. But as the worship of Kuan Yin 觀音 (q.v.) extended at the expense of that of the Goddess of T'ai Shan 泰山 (Pi-hsia Yüan-chün 碧霞元君), Kuan Yin 觀音 was given the chief place of honour, Yen-kuang P'u-sa 眼光菩薩 being placed on her left, and Tou Shên 痘神, the Goddess of Smallpox, on her right.

Yen-kuang P'u-sa 眼光菩薩 is also worshipped at T'ai-hsing 泰興, Kiangsu 江蘇, as the God of Tailors.

Spade-workers occupied in ground-excavations for the construction of buildings, etc., believing that their operations offend and molest the spirits of the land or their descendants (see T'ai Sui 太歲), and that they are therefore punished with eye-diseases, pray to her and to the Goddess of the Dawn to have compassion on and cure all those who come and burn incense at their shrines. For the names of her six acolytes and for the ceremonial of worship in towns and villages, see Doré, X. 737-9.—See also T'ien I-yüan 天醫院 and Hsüan-yüan Huang-ti 軒轅黃帝.

YEN KUNG 晏公.—The God of Sailors. The date and place of his birth are variously given as follows:—In the period A.D. 238-51 the Emperor Ta Ti 大帝 (A.D. 222-52) of the Wu 吳 Kingdom built a temple to Yen Kung 晏公 outside the West gate of Shanghai 上海. Yen Kung 晏公 protected that city from the attacks of rebels in the reign of the Emperor Shih Tsung 世宗 (A.D. 1522-67) of the Ming 明 dynasty.

Yen Kung 晏公 is otherwise said to have lived during the Sung 宋 dynasty. His name is given as Tun Fu 敦復, and his personal name as Ching-ch'u 景初, a native of Fu-chou 撫州, in Kiangsi 江西. He was a Censor in the period A.D. 1131-8, and was famous for his integrity. He resigned, and died at the age of 71 whilst returning to his native place. He was post-humously honoured with the title of Marquis, and a temple was erected to him at Jao-chou Fu 饒州府, Kiangsi 江西.

Another version is that he lived under the Yüan 元 dynasty, and was a native of Ch'ing-chiang Hsien 清江縣, Kiangsi 江西. His surname was Yen 晏, and his personal name Hsü-tzǔ 戌仔. At the beginning of the dynasty he was appointed Superintendent of Belles-lettres in the palace, but, falling ill, was drowned in a storm on a voyage to his home. His body was buried by his attendants, but he was seen on the same day by the inhabitants of his native district, and when his coffin arrived it was found to be empty. A temple was then built in his honour. To cause storms, etc., to abate, it is only necessary for sailors to seek his aid by prayer.

The events resulting in the canonization of Yen Kung 晏公 are related as follows:—He saved the life of the Emperor Hung Wu 洪武 (A.D. 1368-99) whose name was Chu 朱, of the Ming 明 dynasty, when the latter was crossing the Yang-tzǔ 揚子 with the object of besieging the cities of Chên-chiang 鎮江 (Chin-kiang) and Ch'ang-chou 常州, both in Kiangsu 江蘇. After the Emperor's position on the throne had been firmly established, complaints were made that the banks of the Yang-tzǔ 揚子 were undermined by a creature called the pig-dragon of the waves. The Emperor's name being Chu 朱, which has the same sound as chu 猪, pig, his name was changed to Yüan 黿, or dragon. Now the name of the dynasty, Yüan 元, having the same sound, orders were issued for the extermination of all the *yüan* 黿.

An old fisherman described these creatures as having four feet, with which it dug in the ground. As they were of prodigious strength, the only way to take them, he said, was to bait a hook with a piece of boiled pork, and to pass the line tied to the hook through a bottomless earthenware jar. When the creature bit, the jar was to be slid down over its head and neck, which would cause it to use its feet to free itself. It being thus unable to dig them into the ground, it could be dragged ashore and so slain. This method proved successful. On being asked his name, the old fisherman replied that it was Yen 晏. The Emperor, being informed, exclaimed: "Why, that is he who saved me from being drowned." Consequently he bestowed on him the title of Ch'i-hsiu Lei-kao 七修類藁, Marshal of the Metropolis, and ordered a temple to be built to him and sacrifices offered in his honour.

YEN-LO WANG 閻羅王.—The President of the Fifth Court of Hades (*q.v.*). Originally President of the First Court, Yen-lo Wang 閻羅王 was degraded to this Court for overleniency in allowing souls to return forthwith to life. Buddhism borrowed this god and his functions from Brahmanism, Yen-lo Wang

閻羅王 being the same as Yama (*q.v.*), the Vedic god of the dead. As a human monarch, he is said to have been ruler of the kingdom of Vaisali, in Northern India. In danger of defeat in a war with the ruler of a neighbouring State he swore that if the Powers of the Underworld would give him the victory, he and his officers would agree to be reborn in hell. The battle being won by the help of heavenly warriors sent to his assistance, he was reborn as Yama, the principal king of Hades, his eighteen officers and 80,000 men becoming his assistant rulers, jailers, etc. "His palace, made of copper and iron, is at the extremity of the earth, southward, and floating on the waters" (Getty). He controls the male offenders, his sister Yami the female ones. Every eight hours a band of devils torture him and his officers and followers by pouring molten copper down their throats, as a punishment for their former crimes; this does not interfere with their prospects of attaining to Buddhahood, and they will be saved eventually, and Yen-lo Wang 閻羅王 reborn as Samantaradja, the Universal King, P'u Wang 普王.

In the Sung 宋 dynasty, the Supreme Taoist god, Yü Huang 玉隍 (*q.v.*), was made the ruler of Hades, with Ch'êng Huang 城皇 (*q.v.*) and T'u-ti Lao-yeh 土地老爺 (*q.v.*) as his subordinate administrators.

In China, Yama is a subordinate to Ti-tsang Wang 地藏王. According to another legend, Huang Fei-hu 黃飛虎, one of Chou Wang's 周王 Generals, is also named as ruler of Hades, having been appointed by Chiang Tzŭ-ya 姜子牙 (*q.v.*). Others are Pao Ch'êng 包拯 (Pao Lao-yeh 包老爺, died A.D. 1062), Han Ch'in-hu 韓擒虎 (A.D. 527-93), and K'ou Chun 寇準 (died A.D. 1023).

All these rulers and their subordinates are considered by popular tradition as subject to Yü Huang 玉皇 (see *Yü Ti* 玉帝).

YEN-SHOU CH'AN-SHIH 延壽禪師 (44th generation).— A deified Buddhist monk. Ranked twenty-seventh in Buddhist School, VI (*q.v.*). Family name Wang 王. A native of Yü-hang 餘航, Chêkiang 浙江. Studied at T'ien-t'ai 天台, in the same province, in the T'ien-chu Fêng Ssŭ 天柱峰寺, Heaven's-pillar Peak Monastery, his teacher being Tê-shao Kuo-shih 德韶國師 (*q.v.*), who, "struck with his brilliant genius, predicted he would one day become eminent." He remained a year in the Ling-yin Ssŭ 靈隱寺, Monastery of Mystic Retirement, at Ching Shan 徑山, Chêkiang 浙江, whither he had been invited by Chung I-wang 忠懿王, but then withdrew to the Yung-ming Ssŭ 永明寺, Monastery of Perpetual Brightness, where he died in A.D. 975. He was buried at Ta-tz'ŭ 大慈, but his remains were afterwards transferred to the Yung-ming Ssŭ 永明寺.

The emperor T'ai Tsung 太宗 (A.D. 976-98) of the Sung 宋 dynasty, as a tribute to the monk's life and work, bestowed upon the place the title of Shou-ning Yüan 壽寧院, Convent of Longevity and Tranquillity.—See also *infra*.

YEN-SHOU CH'AN-SHIH 延壽禪師.—Sixth ancestor of the Amidist School (see *Buddhist Schools*, XVII). A deified Buddhist monk. Belonged to the Ch'ing-yüan Tsung 青原宗, Ch'ing-yüan School (see *Buddhist Schools*, VI). This shows that the two schools intermingled, and how the other sects were influenced by Amidism.

YEN TI 炎帝.—See *Tsao Chün* 灶 (竈) 君.

YEN TSU 鹽祖.—The patron deity of the salt-pits of Yünnan 雲南. His name is Li A-t'ai 李阿台. The King of the Nan Chao 南詔 caused these pits to be dug, about A.D. 779, on information furnished by this hermit priest, a native of Ta-li Fu 大里府.

YEN TZŬ 兮 蟲. See *Shui Fu* 水 府, C (a) (d).

YEN WANG 閻王.—See *Yen-lo Wang* 閻羅王 and *Wu-yo* 五嶽.

YIN 陰 and YANG 陽.—The negative and positive principles of universal life. These words meant originally the dark and bright sides of a sunlit bank, and occur on the stone Drums (eighth century B.C.). By the time of Confucius they had acquired a philosophical significance as the two aspects of the duality which Chinese thinkers perceived in all things. Traces of the dual notion occur in the "Great Plan" of the *Shu ching* 書經, but the actual words Yin 陰 and Yang 陽 as used in this sense occur first in the pseudo-Confucian commentaries on the *I Ching* 易經.

In this way Yang 陽 came to mean Heaven, Light, Vigour, Male, Penetration, The Monad. It is symbolized by the Dragon and is associated with azure colour and oddness in numbers. In Fêng-shui 風水 (the outward and visible signs of celestial *Yin* 陰 and *Yang* 陽) raised land forms (mountains) are Yang 陽.

Similarly Yin 陰 stands for Earth (the antithesis of Heaven), Darkness, Quiescence, Female, Absorption, The Duad. It is symbolized by the Tiger and is associated with orange colour and even numbers. Valleys and streams possess the Yin 陰 quality.

The two are represented by a whole and a broken line respectively, thus:—Yang — Yin — — .

Groups of three such lines are known as "trigrams," groups of six as "hexagrams," and the *I ching* 易經 is classified under the sixty-four possible hexagrams.

In connection with the five elements (or natural forces), the Yin 陰 and Yang 陽 have been for at least two thousand years

YIN AND YANG

used to interpret the processes of nature and they are the funda-mental feature in the theories which underlie *Fêng-shui* 風水, Astrology, Divination, and Medicine.

The Yin 陰 and Yang 陽 principles have been deified as Tung Wang-kung 東王公, the Royal Father of the East, and his consort Hsi Wang-mu 西王母, the Royal Mother of the West. The Royal Father lives in a kind of a Paradise in the Eastern Ocean. The Royal Mother rules in the K'ung Lun 崑崙 Mountains, which are said to be the junction point between Heaven and Earth, and the place where the Yin 陰 and Yang 陽 vapours are harmonized. Once each year Hsi Wang-mu 西王母 goes to her husband, crossing over the back of a gigantic bird, which is said to overshadow them, and they spend a short space of time in each other's company. The bird is known as the "rare bird, *hsi yu* 希圖." On his back is a small place where there are no feathers. He covers the royal pair with his left and right wing respectively.

T'ai 太 (Great) Yang 陽 means the Sun, T'ai Yin 太陰 the Moon, Shao 少 (Lesser) Yang 陽 the fixed stars and Shao Yin 少陰 the planets, these four being supposed to be the four primary combinations (Hsiang 像) of Yin 陰 and Yang 陽.

Yin 陰 and Yang 陽 are themselves supposed to have proceeded from a "Great Ultimate," T'ai Chi 太極 . (Carus, *Chinese Philosophy; Ency. Sinica, Suzuki.*).—See also *San Ch'ing* 三清 and Werner, *The Chinese Idea of the Second Self*.

YIN CH'ÊNG-HSIU 殷成秀.—The god of the star Pai-hu 白虎 (White Tiger). Son of Yin P'o-pai 殷破敗. Killed at Hsi-ch'i 西岐 by Chiang Wên-huan 姜文煥.

YIN CHIEH-T'O 因揭陀.—See *Lo-han* 羅漢.

YIN HUNG 殷洪.—The god of the star Wu-ku 五谷. Second son of the tyrant Emperor Chou 紂 (1154-1121 B.C.). Slain by Ch'ih Ching-tzŭ 赤精子, who reduced him to ashes by striking him with his magic seal *T'ai-chi t'u* 太極圖.—See also *Shê Chi* 社稷.

YIN P'O-PAI 殷破敗.—The god of the star Hsiao-hao 小耗. One of Chou Wang's 紂王 generals, who lost his life at the hands of Chiang Wên-huan 姜文煥 during the assault on the capital Ch'ao-ko 朝歌, during the Yin-Chou 殷周 wars.

YIN SHÊN 陰神.—The God of the Element Earth.—See *Wu Hsing* 五行.

YIN-SU 印肅.—See *P'u-an Ch'an-shih* 普庵禪師.

YIN-TS'O 陰錯, THE GOD OF THE STAR.—See *Chin Ch'êng* 金成.

YIN-TSUNG 印宗.—A saintly Buddhist monk. Seventh century A.D. One of those invited to the annual banquet of the gods (see *Hsi Wang-mu* 西王母). He had a discussion on the cause of movement with Hui Nêng 慧能 (*q.v.*).

YIN YÜAN-SHUAI 殷元帥.—Generalissimo Yin 殷. A member of the Ministry of Thunder and President of the Ministry T'ai Sui 太歲. An example of the holding of two or more posts by the same deity, so frequently found in the Spirit world.—See also *Lei Pu* 雷部.

YING MING 英明.—See *Eye, The Gods of the.*

YO FEI 岳飛.—A celebrated T'u Ti 土地 (*q.v.*). Born at T'ang-yin Hsien 湯陰縣, Honan 河南. Personal name P'êng-chü 鵬舉. Titles Yo-ô Wang 岳鄂王, Yo 岳, King of O 鄂, and Wu-mu Wang 武穆王, Venerable Warrior-king.

At his birth, a large bird, like a swan, flew over the house and screamed, hence he was given the name Fei 飛, to fly. Distinguished himself by victories over the Tartar invaders, but was at length put to death through the jealousy of Ch'in Kuei 秦檜, in spite of his baring his shoulders and showing the Emperor the characters *chin chung pao kuo* 盡忠報國, Perfectly Loyal in the Country's Service, tattooed thereon.

The Emperor Hsiao Tsung 孝宗 (A.D. 1163-90) of the Sung 宋 dynasty restored his honours, a temple was built to his memory, and he received the posthumous title of Chung Lieh 忠烈, Loyal and Valiant, the other titles above-mentioned being bestowed in A.D. 1179 and 1211 respectively.—See also *Composite Deities.*

YO-Ô WANG 岳鄂王.—A title of Yo Fei 岳飛 (*q.v.*).—See also *Mên Shên* 門神.

YOGA.—Yü-chia 瑜伽 or Yü-chia [ka] 迦.—Ecstatic union of the individual soul with the world-soul. A pantheistic cult, which superseded the early system of Buddhist salvation through good works, and the performance of moral duties. "The ancient practice of ecstatic meditation [as a means of obtaining spiritual or magic power], revived by the Yogatcharya School, and vulgarly abused for purposes of exorcism, sorcery and jugglery" (Eitel). The fundamental idea of Yoga of the highest type is the conception of Prakriti and Purusha, which may be loosely described as objective and subjective Reality, the unintelligent, unchanging, and eternal primal causes. It is abstract meditation, consisting in mental fixity, neither thought nor annihilation of thought; religious ecstacy, mystic union of the individual with the Universal Spirit. Arising about A.D. 500, it was grafted on the theistic Mahayana doctrine of a Supreme universal, impersonal Spirit, into which all beings were finally absorbed, and was introduced by Vajrabodhi into China in A.D. 720, and carried to Japan toward the end of the eighth or in the early part of the ninth century.

In the state of abstraction resulting from the absorption of the individual in the divine Universal Spirit, the body becomes ethereal, and enjoys the power of performing wonderful feats, such as flying through the air, etc.

The first Yoga school was founded by Asangha (Asamgha, Aryasamgha), a native of Peshawar (Gandhara, an ancient kingdom in the north of the Punjab), whose birth is variously stated as A.D. 400 (Eitel), 500 (Grünwedel), etc., but the Northern Buddhists attribute the principles of the sect to Samantabhadra (*q.v.*), the Buddha of religious ecstasy, and the Japanese sects to Vairocana (*q.v.*). "The Yoga (Tantra, or Mantra) system was made known in China (A.D. 647) by Hsüan Tsang's 玄奘 translation of the *Yogatcharya bhumi s'astra,* on which basis Amoghavadjra (A.D. 720) established the Chinese branch of the Yoga School which was popularized chiefly by the labours of Vadjra Bodhi (A.D. 732)" (Eitel). (See also Edkins, p. 132).

"This Pantheistic cult was imported into Buddhism and Yoga was invented as a method of obtaining the mystic union of the individual with the Universal Spirit. Yoga may thus be called 'contemplative Mahayana,' religious ecstasy, mystic union in which the individual is absorbed in the unfathomable depths of the divinity" (Waddell; Monier Williams; Getty).

The first Yoga School was followed by the Mahayana School. Asangha is said to have been transported to the Tuchita heaven, where he received the principles of the system from Maitreya himself.

YOGACHARA SCHOOL.—See *Buddhist Schools,* XIII.

"YOUNG GENERAL, THE."—See *Shih Hsiang-kung* 施相公.

YOUNG GENTLEMAN OF SUNG-LI 嵩里, THE.—See *Sung-li Hsiang-kung* 嵩里相公.

YOUNG LADIES, THE SEVEN.—See *Ch'i Ku-tzŭ* 七姑子.

YU HUN 尤渾.—The god of the star Chüan-shê 卷舌. A companion in arms of Fei Chung 費仲 (*q.v.*), and shared the same fate.

YU-MING CHIAO-CHU 幽冥敎主.—See *Ti-tsang Wang* 地藏王.

YU-MING CHIAO-CHU TI-TSANG WANG P'U-SA 幽冥敎主地藏王菩薩.—See *Ti-tsang Wang* 地藏王.

YU PIAO-CHO 郵 [? 亢] 表啜.—See *Lai-cho* 來啜 and *Pa Cha* 八蜡.

YU-PO-LO 優鉢羅.—A dragon-king.—See *Lung Wang* 龍王.   YÜ CHIANG

YU SHIH 郁使.—See *Shui Fu* 水府, D (2) (c).

YU-YÜ T'IEN 猶宇天.—Shang Ch'ing 上淸, "The Upper Azure." One of the three divisions into which the primordial cosmic ether separated.—See *San Ch'ing* 三淸.

YUGA.—An age of the world. Each of these ages is preceded by a period called its *sandhya* or twilight, and is followed by another period of equal length called *sandhyansa*, 'portion of twilight,' each being equal to one-tenth of the *yuga*. The *yugas* are four in number, and their duration is first computed by years of the gods (see *Dowson*, pp. 381-2).

YUNG LU 勇廬.—See *Nose, The Gods of the*.

YUNG-TZǓ CH'AN-SHIH 永慈禪師 (61st generation).—A deified Buddhist monk. Ranked thirty-ninth in Buddhist School, III (*q.v.*). Family name Ch'ien 錢. A native of Ch'ang Chou 常州, a dependent department of Su Chou 蘇州. His teacher was Hui-chao Ch'an-shih 慧照禪師 (*q.v.*). He spent his whole life in the Tung-ming Ssŭ 東明寺 (*v. ibid.*), and his tomb is to the east of the same place.

YÜ 禹.—Generally referred to as Ta Yü 大禹, Yü the Great. Was minister to the Emperors Yao 堯 (2357-2255 B.C.) and Shun 舜 (2255-2205 B.C.). According to the records (which are, however, not historical) he was appointed by the latter to drain the great floods, a task he is said to have successfully accomplished after nine years' incessant labour. Succeeded Shun 舜 in 2205 B.C. as first Emperor of the Hsia 夏 dynasty, the feudal empire then becoming hereditary. Died 2197 B.C. Worshipped as one of the San Kuan 三官 (*q.v.*).
He, with Yao 堯 and Shun 舜, was substituted by the priests for the abstract or time principles (see *San Kuan* 三官). The Scholars (Literati) proud of the apotheosis of their ancient rulers hastened to offer incense to them, and temples, San Kuan Kung 三官宮, arose in many parts of the Empire. For the legend of Yü's 禹 transformation into a bear, see *Tzŭ Shan Chang Ta-ti* 祠山張大帝.—See also *San Kuan* 三官.

YÜ CH'ÊNG 余成.—See *Wu Tou* 五斗.

YÜ-CHIA CHIAO 瑜伽敎.—See *Buddhist Schools*, XV.

YÜ CHIANG 禹彊.—See *Shui Fu* 水府, C (2) (b) (4) and C (2) (d).

YÜ-CH'IEH SHANG-TI 玉闋上帝.— See *Chin Ch'ieh Shang-ti* 金闋上帝.

YÜ CHIH 余知.—The god of the star Ti-i 地異.—See *Ti-sha* 地煞.

YÜ-CH'IH CHING-TÊ 尉遲敬德.—See *Wei-ch'ih Ching-tê* 尉遲敬德.

YÜ-CH'IH KUNG 尉遲公.—Alias *Hu Ching-tê* 胡敬德. A door-god.—See *Mên Shên* 門神.

YÜ CH'ING 玉清.—The Heaven of the first member of the Taoist triad. He inhabits the Jade Mountain (Yü Shan 玉山). The entrance to his palace is named the Golden Door (Chin Mên 金門). He is the source of all truth, as the sun is the source of all light.—See *San Ch'ing* 三清, *Shêng Jên* 聖人, and *Yüan-shih T'ien-tsun* 元始天尊.

YÜ CHUNG 余忠.—The god of the star Ch'u-sha 除殺. An officer of the army of the feudatory prince Ou Shun 鄢順, who joined the confederates. Bitten to death at Mêng-ching 孟津 by Chu Tzǔ-chên 朱子眞, the transcendant pig, in the Yin-Chou 殷周 wars. Also the god of the star Ti-an 地暗.—See *Ti-sha* 地煞.

YÜ FU 兪跗.—A demi-god. A member of the commission appointed by Huang Ti 黃帝 (*q.v.*) to continue and complete the labours of Shên Nung 神農 on natural history and the medicinal properties of plants. He specialized in exteriorizing internal maladies.—See *T'ien I-yüan* 天醫院.

YÜ HAO 嵎虩 (HAO 號).—See *Shui Fu* 水府, C (2) (d).

YÜ HUA 余化.—The god of the star Ku-ch'ên 孤辰. An officer and magician. Popular name, "Seven-headed Commander." A disciple of Yü Yüan 余元. Fought at Fan-shui Kuan 氾水關, and was killed by Yang Chien 楊戩 during the Yin-Chou 殷周 wars.

YÜ HUA-LUNG 余化龍.—See *Tou Shên* 痘神.

YÜ HUANG 玉皇.—The Jade Emperor. The Pure August One (jade symbolizing purity). Also called Yü-huang Shang-ti 玉皇上帝, the Pure August Emperor on High. The Supreme Lord of the physical world, and the saviour of men. In the Taoist pantheon he corresponds to the Confucian Shang Ti 上帝 (*q.v.*), though he is much more humanized; and to the Buddhist Fo 佛, or Sakyamuni (*q.v.*). Worshipped as the ancestor of jade.

The history of this deity, who later received many honorific titles and became the most popular god, a very Chinese Jupiter, is related as follows: The Emperor Chên Tsung 眞宗 (A.D. 998-1023) of the Sung 宋 dynasty having been obliged in A.D. 1005 to sign a disgraceful peace with the Tunguses or Kitans, the dynasty was in danger of losing the support of the nation. In order to hoodwink the people the Emperor constituted himself a seer, and announced with great pomp that he was in direct communication with the gods of Heaven. In doing this he was following the advice of his crafty and unreliable minister Wang Ch'in-jo 王欽若, who had often tried to persuade him that the pretended revelations attributed to Fu Hsi 伏羲, Yü Wang 玉王 and others were only pure inventions to induce obedience. The Emperor, having studied his part well, assembled his ministers in the tenth moon of the year 1012, and made to them the following declaration: "In a dream I had a visit from an Immortal, who brought me a letter from Yü Huang 玉皇, the purport of which was as follows: 'I have already sent you by your ancestor Chao [T'ai Tsu] 趙 [太祖] two celestial missives. Now I am going to send him in person to visit you.'" A little while after, his ancestor T'ai Tsu 太祖, the founder of the dynasty, came according to Yü Huang's 玉皇 promise, and Chên Tsung 眞宗 hastened to inform his ministers of it. This is the origin of Yü Huang 玉皇. He was born of a fraud, and came ready-made from the brain of an emperor.

Fearing to be admonished for the fraud by another of his ministers, the scholar Wang Tan 王旦, the Emperor resolved to put a golden gag in his mouth. So one day, having invited him to a banquet, he overwhelmed him with flattery and made him drunk with good wine. "I would like the members of your family also to taste this wine," he added, "so I am making you a present of a cask of it." When Wang Tan 王旦 returned home, he found the cask filled with precious pearls. Out of gratitude to the Emperor he kept silent as to the fraud, and made no further opposition to his plans, but when on his death-bed he asked that his head be shaved like a priest's and that he be clothed in priestly robes so that he might expiate his crime of feebleness before the Emperor.

The Emperor K'ang Hsi 康熙 (A.D. 1662-1723) of the Ch'ing 清 dynasty, who had already declared that if it is wrong to impute deceit to a man it is still more reprehensible to impute a fraud to Heaven, stigmatized him as follows: "Wang Tan 王旦 committed two faults: the first was in showing himself a vile flatterer of his Prince during his life; the second was in becoming a worshipper of Buddha at his death."

The legend of Yü Huang 玉皇 relates that in ancient times there existed a kingdom named Kuang-yen Miao-lo Kuo 光嚴妙樂國, whose king was Ching Tê 淨德, his queen being called Pao Yüeh 寶月. Though getting on in years, the latter had no

YÜ HUANG

son. The Taoist priests were summoned by edict to the palace to perform their rites. They recited prayers with the object of obtaining an heir to the throne. During the ensuing night the Queen had a vision. Lao Chün 老君 appeared to her, riding a dragon, and carrying a male child in his arms. He floated down through the air in her direction. The Queen begged him to give her the child as an heir to the throne. "I am quite willing," he said. "Here it is." She fell on her knees and thanked him. On waking she found herself *enceinte*. At the end of a year the Prince was born. From an early age he showed himself compassionate and generous to the poor. On the death of his father he ascended the throne, but after reigning only a few days abdicated in favour of his chief minister, and became a hermit at P'u-ming 普明, in Shensi 陝西, and also on Mount Hsiu-yen 秀巖, in Yünnan 雲南. Having attained to perfection, he passed the rest of his days in curing sickness and saving life; and it was in the exercise of these charitable deeds that he died. The emperors Chên Tsung 眞宗 (A.D. 998-1023) and Hui Tsung 徽宗 (A.D. 1101-26) of the Sung 宋 dynasty, loaded him with all the various titles associated with his name at the present day.

Both Buddhists and Taoists claim him as their own, the former identifying him with Indra, in which case Yü Huang 玉皇 is a Buddhist deity incorporated into the Taoist pantheon, the qualification Yü 玉 being added to Ti 帝, or Ti 帝 substituted for the synonym Huang 皇. He has also been taken to be the subject of a "nature myth." The king Ching Tê 淨德 his father, is the sun, the Queen Pao Yüeh 寶月 the moon, and the marriage symbolizes the rebirth of the vivifying power which clothes nature with green plants and beautiful flowers.

In A.D. 1013, the Emperor Chên Tsung 眞宗 (A.D. 998-1023) of the Sung 宋 dynasty had a statue of Yü Huang 玉皇 cast and placed in the Yü-ch'ing Kung 玉清宮, Palace of Pure Jade, and worshipped it with all his Court.

In A.D. 1015, the same Emperor conferred on him the title of Highest Author of Heaven, of the Whole Universe, of Human Destinies, of Property, of Rites, and of the Way, Very August One, Grand Sovereign of Heaven.

In A.D. 1115, the Emperor Hui Tsung 徽宗 (A.D. 1101-26) of the Sung 宋 dynasty had a magnificent temple constructed in his honour, and he was granted the right to wear the robe of an emperor. Orders were also issued for temples to be built to him all over the empire and statues of him cast. The highest title of all, Shang Ti 上帝, was conferred on him by this Emperor, thus putting him on the same level as the Sovereign on High, August Heaven, of the Scholars (Literati).

From that time Yü Huang 玉皇 became the most popular god of the people. For them generally, Yü Huang 玉皇 was God. [Hence the mistake of calling the Christian God Shang Ti 上帝, since that is the appellation commonly given by the people to Yü Huang 玉皇.] The Taoists and all the people considered Yü Huang 玉皇 as a personal god, who had his Court, palace, ministers, received delegations from other gods his subordinates, and intimated to them his orders.—See also *Yü Ti* 玉帝 and *San Ch'ing* 三清.

YÜ-HUANG CHÜN 玉皇君.—See *Tung Wang-kung* 東王公.

YÜ-HUANG SHANG-TI 玉皇上帝.—See *Yü Huang* 玉皇.

YÜ-I HSIEN 羽翼仙.—The Strange-wings Immortal. A denizen of P'êng-lai 蓬萊 Island, Shantung 山東. A mysterious bird named *Ta-p'êng chin-ch'ih niao* 大鵬金翅鳥. The Great golden-winged rukh. Having assumed human form, he became a spirit in the epoch of the T'ien Huang 天皇, Celestial Sovereigns. Fought against Wu Wang 武王 (1121-1114 B.C.) in the Yin-Chou 殷周 wars. Jan-têng Tao-jên 燃燈道人 gave him an attack of colic by changing 108 beads of his rosary into 108 nice-looking loaves of bread. Jan-têng Tao jên 燃燈道人 advised him to vomit them up, but the loaves having become joined together by an iron chain, Jan-têng Tao jên 燃燈道人, seizing the end of it, was able to lead him away as his prisoner. His life was spared on his promising to become a disciple of Buddha, on whose images the representation of this bird always appears. During the Sung 宋 dynasty it was reincarnated in the person of Yo Fei 岳飛.

YÜ-LAN HUI 盂蘭會.—The Festival of the *Prêtas,* or Hungry Ghosts. It takes place on the fifteenth of the seventh moon, and is the time of their special sacrifices. The gates of Hell are opened and all the demons are allowed to return to earth for the space of thirty days. Offerings of rice, incense, paper money, and fruit are made within the home to the departed relatives, and at the same time similar presents are placed just outside the door for the orphan spirits. Processions are organized in the towns and suburbs. Paper or reed boats containing small lamps are floated in thousands on large stretches of river or in harbours, and on land thousands of lamps made of cotton wool dipped in oil are placed along the roads as guides to the hungry spirits. In the temples and on the streets, the priests pray for their release from punishment. These festivals continue until Ti Tsang's 地藏 birthday, at which time the ghosts are compelled to return to the Underworld. As there is a great deal of danger from their presence, the people treat them most courteously during this period. Providing of food or money for them at any time is a work of merit.

YÜ LU 玉壘.—See *Nose, The Gods of the.*

YÜ LÜ [LEI] 鬱壘.—See *Shên T'u Yü Lei* 神荼鬱壘.

YÜ LUNG 玉龍.—See *Nose, The Gods of the.*

YÜ NÜ 玉女.—See *Pi-hsia Yüan-chün* 碧霞元君.

YÜ NÜ CH'IH 玉女池.—See *Pi-hsia Yüan-chün* 碧霞元君.

YÜ-NÜ CHÜN 玉女君.—See *Neck, The Gods of the.*

YÜ NÜ TA-HSIEN 玉女大仙.— See *Pi-hsia Yüan-chün* 碧霞元君.

YÜ PAI-YA 兪伯牙.—The God of Varnishers. His name was Yü Jui 兪瑞, and he was a high official in the time of Chao Wang 昭王 (1052-1001 B.C.), King Chao 昭. A skilled lutist, he found that only a woodcutter named Chung Hui 鍾徽 could rightly interpret his music. When Chung Hui 鍾徽 died, he dashed his lute on the ground and broke it, but afterwards glued it together again with Chinese varnish.—See also *Lu Pan* 魯班.

YÜ SHAN 玉山.—The Jade Mountain.—See also *San Ch'ing* 三清.

YÜ SHIH 雨師.—The Master of Rain. Represented as clad in yellow scale-armour, with a blue hat and yellow busby, standing on a cloud and from a watering-can pouring rain upon the earth. Otherwise shown as holding a plate, on which is a small dragon, in his left hand, while with his right he pours down the rain. The Parjanya of Vedism.

Native writers say he is Ch'ih Sung-tzǔ 赤松子, who appeared during a terrible drought in the reign of Shên Nung 神農 (2838-2698 B.C.), and owing to his reputed magical power was requested by the latter to bring rain from the sky. "Nothing is easier," he replied; "pour a bottleful of water into an earthen bowl and give it to me." This being done, he plucked from a neighbouring mountain a branch of a tree, soaked it in the water and with it sprinkled the earth. Immediately clouds gathered and rain fell in torrents, filling the rivers to overflowing. Ch'ih Sung-tzǔ 赤松子 was then honoured as the God of Rain, and his images show him holding the mystic bowl. He resides in the K'un-lun 崑崙 Mountains, and has many extraordinary peculiarities, such as the power to go through water without getting wet, to pass through fire without being burned, and to float in space.

The Rain-god also appears in the form of a silkworm chrysalis. He possesses (according to this account) a concubine who has a black face, holds a serpent in each hand, and has other serpents, red and green, resting on her right and left ears respectively; also a mysterious bird, with only one leg, the *shang yang* 商羊, which can change its height at will and drink the seas dry.

The legend of the One-legged Bird states that at the time when Hsüan-ming Ta-jên 玄冥大人 instructed Fei Lien 飛廉 in the secrets of magic, the latter saw a wonderful bird which drew in water with its beak and blew it out again in the shape of rain. Fei Lien 飛廉 tamed it, and would take it about in his sleeve.

Later on a one-legged bird was seen in the palace of the Prince of Ch'i 齊 walking up and down and hopping in front of the throne. Being much puzzled, the Prince sent a messenger to Lu 魯 to enquire of Confucius concerning this strange behaviour. "This bird is a *shang-yang* 商羊," said Confucius; "its appearance is a sign of rain. In former times the children used to amuse themselves by hopping on one foot, knitting their eyebrows, and saying: 'It will rain, because the *shang-yang* 商羊 is disporting himself.' Since this bird has gone to Ch'i 齊, heavy rain will fall, and the people should be told to dig channels and repair the dykes, for the whole country will be inundated." Not only Ch'i 齊, but all the adjacent kingdoms were flooded; all sustained grievous damage except Ch'i 齊, where the necessary precautions had been taken. This caused Duke Ching 景 to exclaim: "Alas! how few listen to the words of the sages!"—See also *Lei Pu* 雷部.

YÜ-T'ANG 玉堂, THE GOD OF THE STAR.—See *Shang Jung* 商容.

YÜ TÊ 余德.—Born in the Yin 殷 dynasty, in modern Shensi 陝西. The fifth son of Yü Hua-lung 余化龍, who was a Brigadier-General at T'ung Kuan 潼關. Became the God of Vaccination.—See *Vaccination, The God and Goddess of*.

YÜ TI 玉帝.—The Pearly Emperor. The chief god of the Taoist pantheon. Incorporated, though inferior to Sakyamuni and the Buddhist saints, into the Buddhist pantheon. In Buddhist temples is assigned a position inferior to Brahma (*q.v.*). Confused with Indra (*q.v.*) through use of the same name, Yü Ti 玉帝. The full title—Yü-huang Shang-ti 玉皇上帝—is found only in T'ang 唐 dynasty and later works. Generally designated by the expression Yü Huang 玉皇. Corresponds to the Buddhist Fo 佛, or Sakyamuni, and to the Confuciist Shang Ti 上帝, but in a more anthropomorphic form than the later developments. According to popular ideas, he commands all Buddhas, spirits, genii, and the Ten Kings of Hades (*q.v.*), and metes out justice to mortals.

In tradition, he represents Ti-shih 帝釋, Indra (Lord, Ruler) or Sakra (the Indra of the Devas), the Vedic nature-god, and personifies the sky, thunder, rain, etc. The Jupiter (or Dies-piter) of the Romans, and Zeus of the Greeks.

Buddha's mother having died seven days after his birth, was deprived of the advantage of his instruction. To compensate her, Buddha ascended to the heaven of Indra, and preached the law to her for three months. "His return to earth was effected by means of a ladder made for him by Indra" (Monier Williams). For this and other services, he was admitted into the pantheon of early Buddhism, but as inferor to Gautama and all the Buddhist Saints. "Armed with his Vajra, or thunderbolt, he became a powerful tutelary god, and is deemed to protect Buddhism throughout the world, keeping the *asuras* at a respectful distance" (Doré, vii. 211-2).

"The popular divinity, Yü-huang Shang-ti 玉皇上帝, is an ancient magician, exalted to this dignity probably by the Taoist writers of the T'ang 唐 dynasty. In the *Pên-hsing ching* 本性經 of the Taoist collection it is said, that a magician of the Chang 張 family was the son of a king in a former *kalpa,* who, instead of succeeding his father, became a hermit, and after 800 *kalpas,* and much patient endurance of injuries, attained to the rank of the 'Golden Immortals' (Chin Hsien 金仙), and at the same time a Buddha with a special title, Ching ching tzǔ-jan-chio ju-lai 清淨自然覺如來, 'The pure, calm, and spontaneously perceiving ju-lai.' After a million more *kalpas* he became Yü Ti 玉帝, or Yü Huang Ta-ti 玉皇大帝, 'Emperor of all the Immortals.'

The title Yü Ti 玉帝 occurs in Taoist books earlier than the T'ang 唐 dynasty, but not the full title with four characters. This belongs evidently to the T'ang 唐 dynasty, the age of Buddhist influence, and to the belief in metamorphoses, and a former life, borrowed from India.

Yü Ti 玉帝 is also represented as a female. This is explained by the Taoists by saying that Yü Ti 玉帝 was a female in a previous state of existence, but in a later transmigration was born a man.—See also *Fan Wang* 梵王, *Brahma,* and *Yü Huang* 玉皇.

YÜ-TING CHÊN-JÊN 玉鼎眞人.—A genie who lived in the Chin-hsia Tung 金霞洞, on Yü-ch'üan Shan 玉泉山. Killed Chu T'ien-lin 朱天麟, one of Chou Wang's 紂王 (1154-1121 B.C.) officers, who was canonized as the third member of the Ministry of Epidemics. Worshipped as a demi-god.

YÜ YANG 禹陽.—See *Shui Fu* 水府, C (2) (d).

YÜ YÜAN 余元.—The god of the star Shui-fu 水府. Lived on the Isle of P'êng-lai 蓬萊. A disciple of T'ung-t'ien Chiao-chu 通天敎主. Was put to death by order of Chiang Tzǔ-ya 姜子牙.

YÜAN 黿.—See *Yen Kung* 晏公.

YÜAN-CHANG CH'AN-SHIH 元長禪師 (57th generation). —A deified Buddhist monk. Ranked thirty-fifth in Buddhist School, III (*q.v.*). Family name Tung 董. A native of Hsiao-shan 蕭山, Shao-hsing Fu 紹興府, Chêkiang 浙江. One of his disciples was Ming-pên Ch'an-shih 明本禪師 (*q.v.*), with whom he afterwards abode for three years. In the last year of his life, A.D. 1357, he lived at Lung-yüan 龍元.

YÜAN CH'ANG-LUNG 圓常龍.—See *Wu Yo* 五嶽.

YÜAN-CHAO LÜ-SHIH 元昭律師.—A deified Buddhist monk. Ranked second in Buddhist School, XVI (*q.v.*). Family name T'ang Chan-jan 唐湛然. A native of Yü-hang 餘杭, Chêkiang 浙江. At 18, became a monk, and studied the *P'i-ni* 毘尼. Later, he followed the teaching of Ch'u-ch'ien Fa-shih 處謙法師 at T'ien-t'ai 天台. Regarded as the second founder of the school, and the successor of the first founder, Tao-hsüan Lü-shih 道宣律師 (*q.v.*). After his death, fishermen heard heavenly genii singing in the air.

YÜAN-CH'ÊNG CH'AN-SHIH 圓澄禪師 (64th generation). —A deified Buddhist monk. Ranked fifty-fourth in Buddhist School, VI (*q.v.*). Family name Hsia 夏. A native of Hui-chi 會稽, Chêkiang 浙江. Studied under Fang-nien Ch'an-shih 方念禪師 (*q.v.*), having entered the Buddhist monastery at Chih-fêng T'u 止風塗 in A.D. 1591. He taught there for thirty years, having a following of 8,000 disciples. Died A.D. 1626. Buried on Nan Shan 南山, Southern Mountain.

YÜAN-CHIEH-JUNG CH'AN-SHIH 元潔瑩禪師 (66th generation).—A deified Buddhist monk. Ranked sixty-eighth in Buddhist School, VI (*q.v.*). Family name Chuang 莊. A native of Wei-yang 維揚, in Yang Chou 揚州, Kiangsu 江蘇. Studied in the Chieh-chu Ssŭ 戒珠寺, Chieh-chu Monastery, under [Jui-pai] Ming-hsüeh Ch'an-shih [瑞白] 明雪禪師 (*q.v.*). He lived in the monastery for twelve years, and afterwards visited the monasteries of Ku-tung Shan 古洞山, Yün-yen 雲巖, Pien-shan 弁山, and Hsien-shêng 顯聖. He died in the latter, A.D. 1671. Buried by his disciples on Yün-yen Shan 雲巖山, Yün-yen Mountain, in Kiangsi 江西.

YÜAN CH'IEN-LI 袁千里.—A functionary of the Celestial Ministry of Thunder (see *Lei Pu* 雷部). The third (?second) military officer of its administration. Born at Nan-fêng 南豐, Kiangsi 江西. Personal name Shêng 勝. Said by some to have been a nephew of Wang Shih-ch'ên 王侍宸. His father gave him a magic recipe for procuring thunder, and he went through Kiangsi 江西 Province exterminating devils. In A.D. 1234-7, during the reign of the Emperor Li Tsung 里宗 (A.D. 1225-65) of the Sung 朱 dynasty, he was living in the house of a man named Tai Tien 戴顛. One day he said to his host: "I am about to die; after my death have my body cremated." This was done, and during the cremation of the corpse a flag was seen in the flames inscribed in gold letters *Lei-t'ing ti-san p'an-kuan Yüan Ch'ien-li* 雷霆

YÜAN CH'IEN-LI

第三判官袁千里, *i.e.* Yêan Ch'ien-li, the third military officer of the Ministry of Thunder. Another account says "second" instead of "third," that he ascended to heaven in a column of smoke during the cremation, and that his host's name was Tai Yung 戴顒.—See also *Composite Deities*.

YÜAN-CHING CH'AN-SHIH 元鏡禪師 (64th generation).— A deified Buddhist monk. Ranked fifty-sixth in Buddhist School, VI (*q.v.*). Family name Fêng 馮. A native of Chien-yang 建陽, Fukien 福建. Studied under Shou-ch'ang 壽昌. In 1618, he lived at Tung-yüan 東苑. Died A.D. 1630.

YÜAN-CHIO K'O-CH'I 圓覺尅期.—One of the twelve divine Buddhist teachers (*Samantabhadra*).

YÜAN-HSIEN CH'AN-SHIH 元賢禪師 (64th generation). —A deified Buddhist monk. Ranked fifty-seventh in Buddhist School, VI (*q.v.*). Family name Ts'ai 蔡. A native of Chien-yang 建陽, Fukien 福建. Studied under Shou Ch'ang 壽昌. In A.D. 1634, he was teaching at Ku Shan 鼓山, Drum Hill. Later, lived at the monasteries of K'ai-yüan 開元, Pao-shan 寶山, and Chên-chi 眞寂. Died A.D. 1657.

YÜAN-HSIN CH'AN-SHIH 圓信禪師 (67th generation).— A deified Buddhist monk. Ranked forty-seventh in Buddhist School, III (*q.v.*). Family name Chu 朱. A native of Yin Hsien 鄞縣, near Ning-po 寧波, Chêkiang 浙江. At twenty years of age, he shaved his head, and wandered from one monastery to another, spending the night in some sheltered corner of a ruined temple. One day, he noticed an extremely long hand issuing from the clouds, and seizing him so violently by the nose that the bridge was broken. Simultaneously, his mind was illumined by another light, and he found himself able to grasp the full essence of the Doctrine. Thenceforth he worked with Chêng-ch'uan Ch'an-shih 正傳禪師 (*q.v.*). His tomb is on the slope of Yün-mên Shan 雲門山, Cloud-gate Mountain.

YÜAN-HSIU CH'AN-SHIH 圓修禪師 (67th generation).— A deified Buddhist monk. Ranked forty-sixth in Buddhist School, III (*q.v.*). Family name Min 閔. Brought up by his mother (of the P'an 潘 family), his father having died while the son was still young. A native of Ching-ch'i 荊溪. He followed the school of Chêng-ch'uan Ch'an-shih 正傳禪師 (*q.v.*). In later years, he taught in the Pao-ên Ssŭ 報恩寺, Thanksgiving Monastery, at the foot of Ch'ing Shan 磬山, Mount Ch'ing. Here he died, and his tomb is on the mountain-side.

YÜAN-HSIU TSUN-CHÊ 元琇尊者.—A deified Buddhist monk. Ranked twelfth in Buddhist School, X (*q.v.*). A native of T'ien-t'ai 天台, Chêkiang 浙江. Studied, under Wu-wai

Tsun-chê 物外尊者 (*q.v.*), the doctrine and the *chih-kuan* 止觀, Perfected Observation. "One day, while he was expounding the Law, ten unknown monks of majestic bearing appeared to him and offered him presents. After being thanked, they withdrew. Yüan-hsiu 元琇 sent a messenger after them, begging them to return, but he perceived that they had taken their flight heavenwards, meanwhile saluting and thanking him. During the troublous times of Hsi Tsung 僖宗 (A.D. 874-89) and Chao Tsung 昭宗 (A.D. 889-904) his disciples were dispersed, and as intelligent successor, he found only Ch'ing-sung 清竦" (*q.v.*).

YÜAN HUNG 遠洪.—The god of the star Ssŭ-fei 四癈. A transcendent monkey, the genie of Mei Shan 梅山, who became one of Chou Wang's 紂王 generals. Decapitated by Chiang Tzŭ-ya 姜子牙 after the battle of Mêng-ching 孟津, during the Yin-Chou 殷周 wars.

YÜAN JUNG-TSU 垣榮祖.—See *Chang Hsien* 張仙.

YÜAN-KUAN CH'AN-SHIH 綠觀禪師 (42nd generation). —A deified Buddhist monk. Ranked nineteenth in Buddhist School, VI (*q.v.*). Nothing is recorded concerning this monk, except that he taught in the Liang-shan Ssŭ 梁山寺, Liang-shan Monastery, at Lang-chou 郎州, Yünnan 雲南.

YÜAN KUANG 元光.—*See Eyebrows, The Gods of the.*

YÜAN-KUEI CH'AN-SHIH 元珪禪師.—A saintly Buddhist monk, born at I-k'ai 伊闕, of the Li 李 family. Eighth century A.D. Entering a monastery in early life, he studied the doctrine, his education being completed by the famous teacher An Kuo 安國. Later he spent some years in the Tung-yen Ssŭ 東岩寺, Tung-yen Monastery, at the foot of the sacred mountain Sung Shan 嵩山, in Honan 河南.

The principal event recorded about him is his bringing the god of this mountain to declare himself his disciple.

Meeting one day a person wearing a quaint costume, who appeared to be a high official attended by a numerous retinue, the monk asked him whence he came. The stranger then asked him how it was that he did not know him. "I make no distinction between Buddhas and men," replied Yüan-kuei 元珪, "and I make no exception with regard to you." "Do you not know that I am the god of the sacred Sung Shan 嵩山," rejoined the stranger, "and hold in my hands the destinies of human beings, both as regards life and death?" "As for myself," replied the monk, "I have never been born; how then can you shorten my days? My body is unreal. I am like you; but you cannot destroy unreality, or you would destroy yourself. Therefore you are quite unable to bring about my death."

According to the Buddhist pantheistic ontology, nothing really exists but the universal, Impersonal Spirit, with which the whole world is identified. Man's spirit, deluded into a temporary idea of separate, independent, personal existence, is an illusion of ignorance. He is identified with the great Impersonal Spirit, and will be ultimately merged into it (Monier Williams, *Buddhism,* pp. 105-6).

The god of Sung Shan 嵩山 prostrated himself respectfully before the monk and said: "I am a highly intelligent divine being, but you surpass me in wisdom." He thereupon declared himself his disciple, and accepted his teaching. Yüan-kuei 元珪 observed the Five Prohibitions of Buddhism: Do not kill—Do not steal—Do not commit adultery—Do not speak falsely—Do not take fermented drinks. On his expressing his ability to conform to these precepts, he was further instructed by the monk in the doctrine of Nirvana, and certain moral principles according to which, for him who strives for Nirvana, certain acts otherwise sinful are not sins for him: thus he may take a wife, and yet remain unmarried; may be intoxicated, and yet not be drunk; etc.

Through the good offices of this converted god, the whole country around Yüan-kuei's 元珪 temple, which lacked trees in contradistinction to the Pei Shan 北山 on the north, became thickly covered with pines and cypresses, which sprang up the morning after the god had induced a thunderstorm with heavy rain, in response to the monk's request for the beautifying of the surroundings of his temple. He died in A.D. 716.

He is one of those invited to the annual banquet of the gods (see *Hsi Wang-mu* 西王母).

YÜAN-LAI CH'AN-SHIH 元來禪師 (64th generation).—A deified Buddhist monk. Ranked fifty-fifth in Buddhist School, VI (*q.v.*). Family name Sha 沙. A native of Shu-ch'êng 舒城, Anhui 安徽. Studied under Shou Ch'ang 壽昌. Lived for some years at Po Shan 博山, Road Hill, and in A.D. 1629 settled finally at the T'ien-k'ai Ssŭ 天開寺, T'ien-k'ai Monastery, at Chin-ling 金陵 (modern Nanking 南京), where he taught for thirty years. His disciples "equalled in number the scales of several fishes" (*cf. Wên-tsai Ch'an-shih* 文載禪師). Died A.D. 1630, aged 58.

YÜAN-MÊN-CHU CH'AN-SHIH 遠門柱禪師 (66th generation).—A deified Buddhist monk. Ranked seventy-first in Buddhist School, VI (*q.v.*). Family name Ch'ên 陳. A native of Fukien 福建. His teacher was [Shih-yü] Ming-fang Ch'an-shih [石雨] 明方禪師 (*q.v.*), who taught at Chin-ming 晉明. Later, he opened his own school at Lung-t'ang 龍唐, and died there in A.D. 1654. His tomb is on Lung-t'ang Shan 龍唐山.

YÜAN-MIAO CH'AN-SHIH 原妙禪師 (55th generation). —A deified Buddhist monk. Ranked thirty-first in Buddhist

School, III (*q.v.*).   Family name Hsü 徐 .   A native of Wu-chiang 吳江.   On visiting Tsu-ch'in Ch'an-shih 祖欽禪師 (*q.v.*), the latter struck him with his staff (*cf. I-hsüan Ch'an-shih* 義玄禪師). He then devoted himself to studying the *Wu-tsu chên-tsan* 五祖 眞讚, *True Eulogies of the Five Patriarchs,* composed by the monk Wu-tsu Fa-yen 五祖法演 (*q.v.*).   Becoming suddenly illumined, he returned to the school of Tsu-ch'in Ch'an-shih 祖欽 禪師, and lived with him for five years at Lung-hsü 龍鬚.   Died at Ssŭ-kuan 死關, in the T'ien-mu Shan 天目山, Heavenly-eye Hill, where his tomb still exists.

YÜAN-SHIH T'IEN-TSUN 元始天尊.— An imaginary being.   The First Principle.   The Everlasting.   The Highest in Heaven (Yü Ch'ing 玉淸, *q.v.*).   Regarded by many authors as the first person of the Taoist Triad (San Ch'ing 三淸, *q.v.*). A Taoist god.   Without origin, without superior, he is himself the Principle of all beings.   His name is given (in the *Sui-shu ching-chi chih* 隋書經籍志) as Lo Ching-hsin 樂靜信, and he is called T'ien Pao 天寶, the Treasure of Heaven.   Some state that the name of the ruler of this first heaven is Yü Huang 玉皇 (*q.v.*), the Pearly Emperor, and in the popular mind he it is who occupies this supreme position.   The San Ch'ing 三淸 are above him in rank, but he has all the power of Heaven and earth in his hands.   He is the correlative of Heaven, or rather Heaven itself. He inhabits Yü Shan 玉山, the Jade Mountain.   The entrance to his palace is named Chin Mên 金門, the Golden Door.   He is the source of all truth.

"He was born before all beginnings; his substance is imperishable; it is formed essentially of uncreated air, invisible and without perceptible limits.   At each new *kalpa—i.e.* at each renovation of the worlds—he gives out the mysterious doctrine which confers immortality.   All who reach the knowledge attain by degrees to life eternal, become refined like the spirits, or instantly become Immortals, even while upon earth.

"Originally, Yüan-shih T'ien-tsun 元始天尊 was not a member of the Taoist triad.   He resided above the San Ch'ing 三淸, the Three Pure Ones (or Heavens), surviving the destructions and renovations of the universe, as an immovable rock in the midst of a stormy sea.   He set the stars in motion, and caused the planets to revolve.   The chief of his secret police was Tsao Chün 竈君 (*q.v.*), the Kitchen-god, who rendered to him an account of the good and evil deeds of each family.   His executive agent was Lei Tsu 雷祖 (*q.v.*), the God of Thunder, and his subordinates.   The seven stars of the North Pole were the palace of his ministers, whose offices were on the various sacred mountains. Nowadays, however, Yüan-shih T'ien-tsun 元始天尊 is generally neglected for Yü Huang 玉皇."

The legend of Yüan-shih T'ien-tsun 元始天尊 is as follows:— According to the tradition of Chin Hung 金虹, the God of T'ai

Shan 泰山 of the fifth generation from P'an Ku 盤古, this being, then called Yüan-shih T'ien-wang 元始天王, was an avatar of P'an Ku 盤古. It came about in this wise. In remote ages there lived on the mountains an old man, Yüan-shih T'ien-wang 元始天王, who used to sit on a rock and preach to the multitude. He spoke of the highest antiquity as if from personal experience. When Chin Hung 金虹 asked him where he lived, he just raised his hand toward Heaven, iridescent clouds enveloped his body, and he replied: "Whoso wishes to know where I dwell must rise to impenetrable heights." "But how," said Chin Hung 金虹, "was he to be found in this immense emptiness?" Two genii, Ch'ih Ching-tzŭ 赤精子 and Huang Lao 黃老, then descended on the summit of T'ai Shan 泰山 and said: "Let us go and visit this Yüan-shih 元始. To do so, we must cross the boundaries of the universe and pass beyond the farthest stars." Chin Hung 金虹 begged them to give him their instructions, to which he listened attentively. They then ascended the highest of the sacred peaks, and thence mounted into the heavens, calling to him from the misty heights: "If you wish to know the origin of Yüan-shih 元始, you must pass beyond the confines of Heaven and earth, because he lives beyond the limits of the worlds. You must ascend and ascend until you reach the sphere of nothingness and of being, in the plains of the luminous shadows."

Having reached these ethereal heights, the two genii saw a bright light, and Hsüan-hsüan Shang-jên 玄玄上人 appeared before them. The two genii bowed to do him homage and to express their gratitude. "You cannot better show your gratitude," he replied, "than by making my doctrine known among men. You desire," he added, "to know the history of Yüan-shih 元始. I will tell it you. When P'an Ku 盤古 had completed his work in the primitive Chaos, his spirit left its mortal envelope and found itself tossed about in space without any fixed support. 'I must,' it said, 'get reborn in visible form; until I can go through a new birth I shall remain empty and unsettled.' His soul, carried on the wings of the wind, reached Fu-yü Tai 弗于逮. There it saw a saintly lady named T'ai-yüan 太元, forty years of age, still a virgin, and living alone on Ts'o-ô Shan 嵯峨山, Mount Ts'o-ô 嵯峨. Air and variegated clouds were the sole nourishment of her vital spirits. An hermaphrodite, at once both the active and the passive principle, she daily scaled the heights of the mountain to gather there the flowery quintessence of the sun and the moon. P'an Ku 盤古, captivated by her virgin purity, took advantage of a moment when she was breathing to enter her mouth in the form of a ray of light. She was *enceinte* for twelve years, at the end of which period the fruit of her womb came out through her spinal column. From its first moment the child could walk and speak, and its body was surrounded by a five-coloured cloud. The newly-born took the name of Yüan-shih

T'ien-wang 元始天王, and his mother was generally known as T'ai-yüan Shêng-mu 太元聖母, 'the Holy Mother of the First Cause.' "—See also *San Ch'ing* 三清, *Yü Ch'ing* 玉清, *Lo Ching-hsin* 樂靜信, *T'ien Pao* 天寶, and *Shêng Jên* 聖人.

YÜAN TING-HSIANG 遠鼎相.—The god of the star Ti-chün 地俊.—See *Ti-sha* 地煞.

YÜAN TSANG 元奘.—See *Sun Hou-tzŭ* 猻猴子 and *Hsüan Tsang* 玄奘.

YÜAN-WU CH'AN-SHIH 圓悟禪師 (67th generation).—A deified Buddhist monk. Ranked forty-fifth in Buddhist Schools, III (*q.v.*). Family name Chiang 蔣. A native of I-hsing 宜興, Kiangsu 江蘇. Studied under Chêng-ch'uan Ch'an-shih 正傳禪師 (*q.v.*), and later opened a school of his own at the foot of T'ien-t'ung Shan 天童山, Heavenly-lad Mountain.

YÜEH-HSING 月刑, THE GOD OF THE STAR.—See *Ch'ên Wu* 陳梧.

YÜEH-KUANG PIEN-CHAO 月光遍照.—See *Yao-shih Fo* 藥師佛.

YÜEH-K'UEI 月魁, THE GODDESS OF THE STAR.—See *Ch'ê-ti Fu-jên* 衙地夫人.

YÜEH-P'O 月破, THE GOD OF THE STAR.—See *Wang Hu* 王虎.

YÜEH-TÊ 月德, THE GOD OF THE STAR.—See *Hsia Chao* 夏招.

YÜEH-YEN 月厭, THE GOD OF THE STAR.—See *Yao Chung* 姚忠.

YÜEH-YU 月遊, THE GODDESS OF THE STAR.—See *Shih-chi Niang-niang* 石磯娘娘.

YÜN-CHUNG TZŬ 雲中子.—Lived in the Yü-chu Tung 玉柱洞, Jade-pillar Grotto, on Chung-nan Shan 終山南. At the siege of Hsi-ch'i 西岐, Wu Wang's 武王 (1121-1114 B.C.) capital, he captured Wên Chung 閤仲 (Lei Tsu 雷祖), afterwards Minister of Thunder. Eight columns of fire issued from the earth amid loud claps of thunder, and Wên Chung 閤仲 was struck down in his prison of fire. Honoured as a demi-god.

YÜN-HSIAO 雲霄.—See *K'êng san Ku-niang* 坑三姑娘.

YÜN-KUANG 雲光.—A saintly Buddhist monk. One of those invited to the annual banquet of the gods (see *Hsi Wang-mu* 西王母).

YÜN-MÊN MO 雲門脈.—See *Buddhist Schools*, VIII.

[YÜN-MÊN] WÊN-YEN CH'AN-SHIH [雲門] 文偃禪師. —See *Buddhist Schools*, VIII.

YÜN SHAN 憚龥.—See *Pi-hsia Yüan-chün* 碧霞元君.

YÜN-SHAN TSUN-CHÊ 孕蟺尊者.—A saintly Buddhist monk. One of those invited to the annual banquet of the gods (see *Hsi Wang-mu* 西王母).

YÜN-YIN-MIAO-CH'UANG 雲音妙幢.—A dragon-king.— See *Lung Wang* 龍王.

INDEX TO MYTHS

Most of the myths included in this dictionary are traceable by the title-words of the sections in which they occur or by cross-references in the body of the work. This index includes (generally speaking) only those traceable by neither clue.

BOTTLE, ENCLOSING MAN IN A: *Chin-kang Chih.*
BOTTLE FALLS OUT OF SPACE: *Lei Kung.*
BOWL, DRAGON CAUGHT IN: *Patriarchs; Hui Nêng.*
BOX, MAGICAL: *Chiang Tzŭ-ya.*
BRAHMA HEAVEN, ORIGIN OF: *Fan T'ien.*
BREAD-BASKET CAUSES COLLAPSE OF BRIDGE: *Ta Shêng.*
BRIDGE DESTROYED THROUGH WEIGHT OF BREAD-TRAY: *Ta Shêng.*
BRIDGES RISE OUT OF SEA: *Shui Fu,* C (1) (a).
BRIGHT SPIRITS DESCEND FROM SKY: *Wu Shêng.*
BUDDHA'S TOOTH: *Hsi-yü Sêng Ch'an-shih.*
BUDDHIST RELIGION, PROTECTOR OF THE: *Wei T'o.*
BURNT TEMPLE: *Sa Chên Jên.*
BUSHEL OF CHAOTIC ORIGIN, THE GOLD: *Chiang Tzŭ-ya.*
BUTTERFLY AND THE EGO, PROBLEM OF THE: *Apotheosized Philosophers: Chuang Tzŭ.*

CARP, MAN CHANGED INTO A: *Sun Hou-tzŭ.*
CELESTIAL DOG: *Chang Hsien; Kou Ching.*
CENTIPEDE, FAN CHANGED INTO A: *Chi-kung Lao-Fo P'u-sa.*
CIURP CREADH, INSTANCES OF: *Revenge, The God of; Ts'ai Shên; Wealth, The God of.*
COCK, CROWING OF IMITATED: *Ma Ku.*
COFFINS FOUND TO BE EMPTY: *Patriarchs* (i); and *passim.*
CONVERTED GOD, A: *Yüan-kuei Ch'an-shih.*
COPE ON CORPSE: *Po I-k'ao.*
CORPSE INCORRUPT: *Pei-chi Ch'ü-hsieh Yüan;* and *passim.*
CRAB PAINTED ON FOREHEAD: *Wu-tai Yüan-shuai.*
CRANES, MONKS TRANSFORMED INTO: *Pên-ching Ch'an-shih.*
CREATION OF WORLD: *Brahma; P'an Ku.*
CREMATION OF PRIEST: *Ta-chih Ch'an-shih.*
CROSSBOW: *Chang Hsien.*
CRYING BABY COMFORTED: *Ch'ih-chiao Hsien.*

DEAD MEET LIVING: *Sa Chên-jên.*
DEMON KINGS CONQUERED: *Hsüan-t'ien Shang-ti.*
DEMONS, SLAYER OF: *Chung K'uei.*
DIAMOND KINGS: *Ssŭ ta T'ien-wang.*
DIVINE ARCHER, THE: *Shên I: Fêng Po.*
DOG, THE CELESTIAL: *Chang Hsien; Kou Ching.*
DRAGON-BOAT, ORIGIN OF: *Fêng-huo Yüan T'ien Yüan-shuai.*
DRAGON IN BOWL: *Patriarchs* (6).
DRAGON HEALED BY INJECTION OF LIQUORICE: *Ma Shih-huang.*

CHINESE DYNASTIES

	B.C.
MYTHICAL RULERS	2953–2357
T'ai Hao 太昊 (Fu Hsi Shih 伏羲氏)	2953
Yen Ti 炎帝 (Shên Nung Shih 神農氏)	2838
Huang Ti 黃帝 (Yu Hsiung Shih 有熊氏)	2698
Shao Hao 少昊 (Chin T'ien Shih 金天氏)	2598
Chuan Hsü 顓頊 (Kao Yang Shih 高陽氏)	2514
Ti K'u 帝嚳 (Kao Hsin Shih 高辛氏)	2436
Ti Chih 帝摯 (Kao Hsin Shih 高辛氏)	2366
PATRIARCHS	2357–2205
Yao 堯 (T'ao T'ang Shih 陶唐氏)	2357
Shun 舜 (Yu Yü Shih 有虞氏)	2255
HSIA 夏 DYNASTY	2205–1766
Yü 禹	2205–2197
SHANG 商 DYNASTY	1766–1121
Yin 殷 Dynasty (Change of name)	1401–1121
CHOU 周 DYNASTY	1121–255
Kingdom of Chou 周	1121–770
Ch'un Ch'iu 春秋 (Period of the Annals)	770–464
Chan Kuo 戰國 (Warring States)	464–221
CH'IN 秦 DYNASTY	255–206
HAN 漢 DYNASTY (Former Ch'ien 前 or Western Hsi 西)	260–A.D. 25
HAN 漢 DYNASTY (Later Hou 後 or Eastern Tung 東)	A.D. 25–221
THE THREE KINGDOMS (San Kuo 三國)	221–265
Wei 魏 (in North)	220–265
Minor Han 漢 or Shu 蜀 (in West)	221–265
Wu 吳 (in South)	222–280
WESTERN CHIN 晉 (Hsi Chin 西晉) Dynasty	265–317
EASTERN CHIN 晉 (Tung Chin 東晉) Dynasty	317–420

623

A.D.

PERIOD OF DIVISION BETWEEN NORTH
   AND SOUTH (Nan Pei Ch'ao 南北朝) .. 420–589
   Sung 宋 (Liu Sung 劉宋) Dynasty 420–479
   Ch'i 齊 Dynasty 479–502
   Liang 梁 Dynasty 502–557
   Ch'ên 陳 Dynasty 557–589
   N. Wei 魏 (Pei Wei 北魏) Dynasty .. 386–535
   W. Wei 魏 (Hsi Wei 西魏) Dynasty .. 535–557
   E. Wei 魏 (Tung Wei 東魏) Dynasty .. 534–550
   N. Ch'i 齊 (Pei Ch'i 北齊) Dynasty .. 550–589
   N. Chou 周 (Pei Chou 北周) Dynasty .. 557–589
SUI 隋 DYNASTY 589–618
T'ANG 唐 DYNASTY 618–907
THE FIVE DYNASTIES (Wu Tai 五代) .. 907–960
   Posterior Liang 梁 (Hou Liang 後梁) .. 907–923
     ,,   T'ang 唐 (Hou T'ang 後唐) .. 923–936
     ,,   Chin 晉 (Hou Chin 後晉) .. 936–947
     ,,   Han 漢 (Hou Han 後漢) .. 947–951
     ,,   Chou 周 (Hou Chou 後周) .. 951–960
TARTAR DYNASTIES 907–1234
   Liao 遼 (K'itan 契丹 or Iron Tunguses) .. 907–1125
   W. Liao 西遼 (Hsi Liao 西遼) 1125–1168
   Kin or Chin 金 (Nüchên 女眞 or Golden Tunguses) 1115–1234
SUNG 宋 DYNASTY (Northern Sung 宋, Pei
   Sung 北宋) 960–1127
SUNG 宋 DYNASTY (Southern Sung 宋, Nan
   Sung 南宋) 1127–1280
YÜAN 元 DYNASTY (Mongol) 1280–1368
MING 明 DYNASTY 1368–1644
CH'ING 清 DYNASTY (Manchu) 1644–1912
REPUBLIC (Min Kuo 民國) 1912–

BIBLIOGRAPHY

[CHINESE]

Chin kang ching 金綱經.
Chin kuang ming ching 金光明經.
Ch'in-ting San Kuo chih 欽定三國志.
Ching hua lu 鏡花緣.
Chung-hsi-hui shih jih-li 中西回史日歷.
Chung Kuo fêng-su shih 中國風俗史.
Fêng-shên pang 封神榜.
Fêng-shên yen-i 封神演義.
Fêng-su t'ung 風俗通.
Hsi-yu chi 西遊記.
Hsin tsêng ku shih ch'iung lin 新增故事瓊林.
Huang t'ing nei ching 黃庭內經.
I shih chi shih 壹是紀始.
Jih-chih lu 日知錄.
Ko chih ching yüan 格致鏡原.
Ku shih ch'iung lin 故事瓊林.
Kuan Ti shêng-chi t'u-chih ch'üan-chuan. 關帝聖蹟圖誌全傳.
Kuang chih p'ing lüeh 廣治平畧.
Li-tai shên-hsien t'ung-chien 歷代神仙通鑑.
Mêng-hua lu 夢華錄.
Nan-hai Kuan-yin ch'üan chuan 南海觀音全傳.
San Kuan ching 三官經.
San-kuo chih yen-i 三國志演義.
Shan-hai ching 山海經.
Shên-hsien lieh chuan 神仙列傳.
Shih wu yüan hui 事物原會.
Sou shên chi 搜神記.
T'ai-p'ing yü lan 太平御覽.
T'ai-p'ing kuang chi 太平廣記.
Wên hsien t'ung k'ao 文獻通考.
Yen Wang ching 閻王經.
Yu hsüeh ku shih ch'iung lin 幼學故事瓊林.
Yüan chien lei han 淵鑑類函.
Yün chi ch'i ch'ien 雲笈七籤.

[FOREIGN]

ALEXIEV ((B. M.), *The Gods of Wealth.*

BEAL (S.), *A Catena of Buddhist Scriptures from the Chinese.*

CHAVANNES (E.), *Le T'ai-chan.*

COULING (S.), *Encyclopaedia Sinica.*

DAVIDS (T. W. R.), *Buddhism.*

DORÉ (H.), S.J., *Recherches sur les Superstitions en Chine.*

DORÉ (H.), S.J., *Manuel des Superstions Chinoises.*

DOWSON (J.), *A Classical Dictionary of Hindu Mythology and Religion, Geography, History, and Literature.*

DU BOSE (H. C.), *The Dragon, Image, and Demon.*

EDKINS (J.), *Chinese Buddhism.*

EITEL (E. J.), *Buddhism: its Historical, Theoretical and Popular Aspects.*

EITEL (E. J.), *A Handbook of Chinese Buddhism.*

EITEL (E. J.), *A Handbook of Buddhist Scriptures.*

ELIOT (SIR C.), *Hinduism and Buddhism.*

FENELLOSA (E. F.), *Epochs of Chinese and Japanese Art.*

GEDEN (A. S.), *Studies in the Religions of the East.*

GETTY (A.), *The Gods of Northern Buddhism.*

GILES (H. A.), *A Chinese Biographical Dictionary.*

HACKMAN (H.), *Buddhism as a Religion.*

HARDY (R. S.), *The Legends and Theories of the Buddhists.*

HARDY (R. S.), *A Manual of Buddhism.*

HASTINGS (J.), *Encyclopaedia of Religion and Ethics.*

HAYES (W.), *The Book of the Cow.*

I-TSING, *A Record of the Buddhist Religion as Practised in India and the Malay Archipelago* (A.D. 671-95). Trans. by J. Takakusu.

JEVONS (F. B.), *Introduction to the Study of Comparative Religion.*

JOHNSTON (R. F.), *Buddhist China.*

KRISHNA SASTRI (H.), *South-Indian Images of Gods and Goddess.*

KERN (H.), *Saddharma-pundarika, or The Lotus of the True Law.*

KENNELLY (M.), S.J., *Researches into Chinese Superstitions.*

LAKSHNI NARASU (R.), *The Essence of Buddhism.*

LAUFER (B.), *Jade.*

LEGGE (J.), *Annals of the Bamboo Books.*

MAYERS (W. F.), *The Chinese Reader's Manual.*

PERIODICALS:—

  Chinese Recorder.

  Chinese Repository.

  Journal of the Asiatic Society of Bengal.

  Journal of the N. China Branch of the Royal Asiatic Society.

  New China Review.

RADHAKUMUD MOOKERJI, *Asoka.*

REMUSAT (A.), *Notes on Foe-koue Ki.*

SCHOTT (W.), *The Buddhism of High Asia and China.*

SIEĀCĀRA, *The Word of the Buddha.*

SMITH (A.), *Chinese Characteristics.*

SMITH (V. A.), *Asoka.*

SURENDRANATH DASGUPTA, *Yoga as Philosophy and Religion.*

TAKAKUSA (J.), *I-tsing's Records of Buddhistic Kingdoms.* See *I-tsing.*

VASILIEF (V. P.), *Le Bouddhisme.*

WADDELL (A. L.), *The Buddhism of Tibet, or Lamaism.*

WATTERS (T.), *The Eighteen Lohan of Chinese Buddhist Temples.*

WERNER (E. T. C.), *Autumn Leaves.*

WERNER (E. T. C.), *China of the Chinese.*

WERNER (E. T. C.), *The Chinese Idea of the Second Self.*

WERNER (E. T. C.), *Descriptive Sociology-Chinese.*

WERNER (E. T. C.), *Myths and Legends of China.*

WIEGER (L.), s.J., *Bouddhisme Chinois.*

WIEGER (L.), s.J., *Histoire des Croyances Religieuses et des Opinions Philosophiques en Chine.*

WILLIAMS (MONIER), *Buddhism.*

WYLIE (A), *Notes on Chinese Literature.*